D0754294

Praise for *Free Tr̶... ...eplace it and Why*

The only way to save our economy is for the U.S. to counter with trade and in-dustrial policies designed to correct the defects of free trade. Ian Fletcher's *Free Trade Doesn't Work* is the best guide to develop such policies.

—**Ernest "Fritz" Hollings,** U.S. Senator from South Carolina, 1966-2005

Fletcher has laid out a powerful critique of so-called free trade while also making the case for rethinking and reforming our current trade policies. Given the economic challenges we face in an increasingly treacherous global economy, this book provides essential tools and analysis for policy-makers and activists.

—**John J. Sweeney**, former President, AFL-CIO

Free trade is a concept that works in the classroom and in the minds of academics and others insulated from the harsh realities of global trade in the real world. In the real world, we have managed trade. This ranges from the blind free trade faith of economists, editorial boards, and politicians to the mercantilist, protectionist, predatory trade practiced by some of our major global trading "partners" like China. This book is an excellent intro-duction to these realities and what can be done about them.

—**Dan DiMicco**, Chairman and CEO, Nucor Steel Corporation

Most Americans live under the myth that sound economics says so-called free trade benefits all nations. Fletcher shows, in very readable prose, how the discipline is finally catching up with reality and common sense and changing its mind on that matter. This book will be an essential guide to the emerging debate over the wisdom of "free" trade as a sound policy for our nation.

—**Patrick A. Mulloy**, Commissioner, U.S.-China Economic and Security Review Commission; former Assistant Secretary of Commerce

Ian Fletcher has written a powerful and refreshing critique of some che-rished assumptions held by mainstream economists. It is uniformly insight-ful, often brilliant, and remarkably readable. Obama's team should read it—and soon.

—**George C. Lodge**, Professor Emeritus, Harvard Business School

In *Free Trade Doesn't Work*, Ian Fletcher makes clear that America's nearly $6 trillion trade deficit accumulated since NAFTA took effect in 1994 benefits neither workers nor the nation. The book debunks the myth of free trade and proposes a responsible alternative that would restore a measure of sanity to America's international trade policy.

—**Leo W. Gerard**, President, United Steelworkers

Ian Fletcher bravely takes on the free-trade theorists who lead cheers for the slow-motion disintegration of American prosperity and trumps them with facts and clear-eyed logic. If people will listen, Fletcher's informed voice will help turn the country toward a more promising future.

—**William Greider,** author, *One World, Ready or Not: The Manic Logic of Global Capitalism*

Fletcher knows his stuff; but he can write, too, and does a great job of explaining the proposition in his title. For sure, nearly all economic theoreticians favor absolute free trade. His book persuades me they are wrong. Check it out.

—**John Derbyshire**, conservative pundit, *National Review*

Free Trade Doesn't Work is an excellent guide to the economic realities obscured by the intellectually hollow promotion of "free" trade. It is up-to-date, comprehensive, and very readable.

—**Jeff Faux**, Distinguished Fellow, Economic Policy Institute; author, *The Global Class War: How America's Bipartisan Elite Lost Our Future*

Ian Fletcher exposes free trade arguments that have provided a cover for greed to hollow out the US economy.

—**Paul Craig Roberts,** former Assistant Secretary of the Treasury; author, *How the Economy Was Lost: The War of the Worlds*

Ian Fletcher delivers a devastating and powerful indictment of free trade economics—one that should be widely read, not the least by economists themselves. I agree with Fletcher: "We can't trust the economists." *Free Trade Doesn't Work* will spark some much-needed debate on what sort of political and economic policies we *can* trust.

—**Gavin Fridell**, Assistant Professor of Politics, Trent University; author, *Fair Trade Coffee: Prospects and Pitfalls of Market-Driven Social Justice*

If it strikes you that most of the arguments put forth for "free" trade are really just so much globaloney, you're right! Fletcher rips the mask from free trade myths, pointing out that economists increasingly reject the idea that our nation (or others) should base economic policy on such a dubious proposition. This book is a powerful tool for anyone who wants to help raise common sense to high places.

—**Jim Hightower**, bestselling author; national radio and newspaper commentator; editor, *The Hightower Lowdown*

This book is an instant classic that will be of use for many years, for it makes a major contribution to thinking on trade policy.

— **Pat Choate**, running mate of Ross Perot in 1996; author, *Dangerous Business: The Risks of Globalization for America*

Every now and then I come across a book I think it should be in the hands of every American and every member of Congress. With Fletcher's book, America now has strategic and well-reasoned answers to our economic problems.

—**Roger Simmermaker,** conservative commentator, *WorldNetDaily*

Ian Fletcher's book is of immense value in defining the parameters of the idolatry of free trade. Politicians and the general populace continue to be afraid to abandon this false god because of the kind of superstitions and inaccuracies that this book exposes very well.

—**Manuel F. Montes**, Chief, Development Strategy and Policy Analysis, United Nations Development Policy and Analysis Division.

The world needs to localize, and fast. Instead of throwing out supply lines, we need to reel them in. This book helps show why.

—**Bill McKibben**, author, *Deep Economy: The Wealth of Communities and the Durable Future*

A superb debunking of the arguments for free trade and a thoughtful examination of the alternatives. Fletcher's book is required reading for policymakers and for the general public trying to understand how the United States has fallen into a debt trap and what has to be done to escape it.

— **Richard H. Robbins**, Distinguished Professor, Plattsburgh State; author, *Global Problems and the Culture of Capitalism*

In *Free Trade Doesn't Work*, Ian Fletcher points to the ideal of "free" trade and proclaims it isn't wearing any clothes! Instead of following along with the crowd, Fletcher systematically presents the failures of an unrestrained trade system and offers up a balanced discussion of what a managed trade system could accomplish in its place.

—**Thomas S. Mullikin**, author, *Truck Stop Politics: Understanding the Emerging Force of Working Class America*

Ian Fletcher has convincingly dismantled the facade that for decades enticed U.S. cattle ranchers and their trade associations to support a free trade policy that was systematically destroying the economic integrity of their industry. A superb analysis of our nation's misdirection.

—**Bill Bullard**, CEO, Ranchers-Cattlemen Action Legal Fund, United Stockgrowers of America

Ian Fletcher's argument against free trade and in favor of tariffs is not only a courageous assault on our so-called conventional wisdom, it makes a brilliant and wildly compelling case for regulation. Economists will stand up and take notice. Wall Street will hate it.

—**David Macaray**, author, *It's Never Been Easy: Essays on Modern Labor*

This readable book dramatizes our lost history of global trade and punctures the mythology surrounding the benefits of unbridled free trade. A vital primer for anyone trying to understand the current trade debate.

—**Chuck Collins**, Institute for Policy Studies; co-author, *The Moral Measure of the Economy*

It is standard for people in policy debates to be reflexive supporters of "free" trade. This book should help people to better understand what this means, so it may change some attitudes.

—**Dean Baker**, Co-Director, Center for Economic and Policy Research; author, *False Profits: Recovering from the Bubble Economy*

Fletcher's book opens up the arcane mysteries of free trade economics for the ordinary reader and makes clear that the most up-to-date economics confirms that free trade has no justification in either history or present-day facts. It is a threat to the incomes of working people, to our environment, and to democratic sovereignty. Luckily, as he also points out, viable alternatives are available if the politicians would only wake up and take notice.

—**Maude Barlow**, Council of Canadians; co-author, *Alternatives to Economic Globalization*

You have written a bible for us. It is brilliant! You even cover issues I have been concerned about but never had time to discuss with anyone else. I started by reading it and ended by studying it. Am now going through it for the second time underlining and highlighting.

—**Brian O'Shaughnessy**, Co-Chair, Coalition for a Prosperous America; Chairman, Revere Copper Products

Ian Fletcher makes a powerful case for abandoning the simplistic mantra that markets generally maximize welfare, and tariffs or regulations reduce economic prosperity. He points to more-nuanced policies that avoid the extremes of blanket protectionism and unregulated trade.

—**Geoffrey Hodgson**, Editor-in-Chief, *Journal of Institutional Economics*, Cambridge University Press

In this sophisticated, well-informed, and comprehensive study, Ian Fletcher provides a very powerful, passionate, and convincing critique of free trade in an accessible and engaging manner. Read it.

—**Ha-Joon Chang**, University of Cambridge; author, *Bad Samaritans: The Myth of Free Trade and the Secret History of Capitalism*

A trenchant and comprehensive analysis of the gap between the theory of free trade and reality, together with a revealing description of the weaknesses of the theory itself.

—**Ralph Gomory**, Research Professor, Stern School of Business, New York University; author, *Global Trade and Conflicting National Interests*

After reading *Free Trade Doesn't Work,* I now understand why so many of the trade agreements that we negotiated never delivered the promises that were made and, if continued, never will.

—**Robert B. Cassidy**, former Assistant U.S. Trade Representative for China and for Asia and the Pacific

One of the great destructive fantasies of modern times is the idea that free-trade theory describes how the world really works—or has ever worked. None of the major world economies has risen to power or maintained its wealth by behaving the way modern textbooks say it should. Ian Fletcher's book is a sustained demonstration of this important truth.

—**James Fallows**, national correspondent, *The Atlantic;* author, *Looking at the Sun: The Rise of the New East Asian Economic and Political System*

Ian Fletcher's *Free Trade Doesn't Work* injects some urgently needed common sense and rigorous thinking into what may be the most important economic policy debate of our time.

—**Alan Tonelson**, Research Fellow, U.S. Business & Industry Council; author, *The Race to the Bottom*

Some book reviews write themselves, because the book is so clear and articulate and easily read, and the information in it so straightforward that all the reviewer needs to do is lay it out.

—**Thom Hartmann**, liberal radio talk show host

Free Trade Doesn't Work

What Should Replace It And Why

2011 Edition

Ian Fletcher

COALITION FOR A
PROSPEROUS AMERICA
2011

Second edition
Published by the Coalition for a Prosperous America
615 Boardman St.
Sheffield, MA 01257

First edition
Published 2010 by the U.S. Business & Industry Council
512 C St., NE
Washington, DC 20002

ISBN-13: 978-0-578-07967-7

Library of Congress Cataloging-in-Publication Data

Fletcher, Ian H.
    Free Trade Doesn't Work / Ian H. Fletcher;
    foreword by Edward Luttwak
        p.cm
    Includes bibliographical references and index.
    ISBN-13: 978-0-578-07967-7
    1. International economic integration. 2. Foreign trade regulation. 3. International finance. 4. Globalization—Economic Aspects—Developing Countries. 5. Globalization—Economic Aspects—Developed Countries. 6. United States—Commercial policy. 7. Free trade—United States. I. Title

Cover layout by Martin Cabral

Printed in the United States of America

10 9 8 7 6 5 4 3 2 1

For Julie

In Bangalore...I [was] standing at the gate observing this river of educated young people flowing in and out...They all looked like they had scored 1,600 on their SATs and I felt a real mind-eye split overtaking me. My mind just kept telling me, 'Ricardo* is right, Ricardo is right...' But my eye kept looking at these Indian zippies and telling me something else.

— *New York Times* columnist Thomas L. Friedman,
The World is Flat, p. 264

*David Ricardo (1772-1823), the British economist who formulated the theory of comparative advantage, cornerstone of free trade economics to this day. See Chapter Five below for why Ricardo was wrong.

CONTENTS

Foreword by Edward Luttwak xiii

Introduction: Why We Can't Trust the Economists 1

PART I: THE PROBLEM

Chapter 1: Bad Arguments for Free Trade 19
Chapter 2: Deficits, Time Horizons, and Perverse Efficiency 37
Chapter 3: Trade Solutions That Won't Work... 56
Chapter 4: Critiques of Free Trade to Avoid 78

PART II: THE REAL ECONOMICS OF TRADE

Chapter 5: Ye Olde Theory of Comparative Advantage............................... 95
Chapter 6: The Deliberately Forgotten History of Trade........................... 122
Chapter 7: The Negligible Benefits of Free Trade...................................... 149
Chapter 8: The Disingenuous Law and Diplomacy of Free Trade 165

PART III: THE SOLUTION

Chapter 9: Where Does Growth Really Come From? 183
Chapter 10: The Multiple Equilibrium Revolution...................................... 212
Chapter 11: The Natural Strategic Tariff.. 228
Chapter 12: The End of the Free Trade Coalition.. 246

Notes 270

Bibliography 300

Index 315

Foreword
by Edward Luttwak

UNTIL THE ECONOMIC DEBACLE of 2008, the power and moral authority of the United States were sustained not only by its political values, cultural magnetism, and military strength, but also by its wealth. From its investment capacity as home of the world's most sophisticated financial system to its purchasing power as the world's largest importer, the U.S. had an undoubted primacy. When the latter finally ruined the former—for huge trade deficits tolerated for decades must decapitalize as well as deindustrialize—American diplomacy suddenly had to function without much of its accustomed leverage.

Some Americans have always been displeased by the magnitude of American power, probably because they project onto the nation at large their own moral discomfort with its exercise. For them, as for assorted dictators, Islamic fanatics, and the few serious communists still breathing, the present weakening of the United States is welcome. But for others, including this writer, this weakening provokes an unwelcome question: how much power can the United States retain without this leverage? And what kind of Hobbesian world order will we face in its absence? Whatever complaints of competence or intent one may lodge against this power, the world contains alternative hegemons with far fewer scruples. A weakened American economy will embolden the enemies not only of the United

States, but of a stable world generally—especially in Latin America, the Middle East, and East Asia.

One early sign of America's weakening economic leverage was the refusal of allies like France, Germany, Italy, and the Netherlands to cooperate with the expansionary measures of the newly arrived Obama Administration in early 2009. With global economic activity sinking as declining demand dragged down production, further reducing demand, only a Keynesian jolt of public spending or tax cuts could break the downward spiral. This much was agreed by all serious players, but every major European government save Britain refused to join with the United States in implementing such measures. Instead, they tacitly proposed to let others carry the burdens of reflation—mainly increased public debt and inflation risk—knowing full well that their own exporters would nonetheless benefit from the resulting increase in global demand.

Above all, these allies could not be brought to heel with the threat of tariffs, quotas, capital controls, or other protectionist measures. This was America's natural card to play, but ruled out by an elite consensus rigidly opposed to any form of protectionism. This consensus—unshared with ordinary voters—prohibits even the milder forms of protectionism *permitted* under international agreements. Instead, it has a puritanical horror of the very concept which refuses to view protectionism as just another form of economic realpolitik, to be coldly evaluated according to its merits and costs. Instead, it is seen as a repudiation of the twin cardinal virtues of competition and openness.

This is a fact of which both America's friends and enemies are well aware, and upon which America's commercial rivals base their own neo-mercantilist trade policies. The result has been a prolonged failure to safeguard the American economy, especially manufacturing, from foreign predation. The most obvious tactic here has been currency manipulation, but this is only the tip of an iceberg whose size America's rulers still do not appear fully to comprehend. This currency manipulation, involving as it does a tidal wave of cheap foreign capital propping up the dollar by soaking up American debt and assets, has in recent years helped keep interest rates in the U.S. abnormally low. It thus helped enable the speculative property and mortgage bubbles which led to the financial collapse of 2008. Thus many of America's recent economic problems, both visibly trade-related and otherwise, are ultimately linked with an underlying trade problem.

This book, unlike many previous critiques of free trade, is no mere sulk about the harsh realities of capitalism or an extended analytical misunderstanding of what those realities are. Ian Fletcher, in fact, unequivocally favors capitalism—if perhaps more broadly shared in its prosperity, more Fordist (as in the $5 day), less dogmatic about free markets, better supported by industrial policy, and less decadently plutarchic than today. He favors free markets wherever the evidence vindicates them. These remain the sovereign cure for mediocrity and sloth, whose dynamism creates wealth and compels improvements in management, production, and distribution. Free markets stimulate innovation, the ultimate root of economic growth. All these facts this book comprehends, which should slow its dismissal by the usual suspects.

Devotees of free trade celebrate its advantages for American consumers. These are real enough. And even industry-destroying free trade can sometimes do good, by shutting down inefficient domestic production that misuses labor and capital, freeing up resources for the industries of tomorrow. But free traders celebrate these advantages and then just stop, as if Americans could be consumers and nothing but, and as if destroying obsolete industries did not beg the question of what is to replace them. The vitality of America's underlying industrial base is either ignored or papered over with questionable economic theory—if not sheer ideological hectoring.

This is where Fletcher comes into his own, for he pries open the dogmatic black box of received trade economics. Despite the myth that serious economics vindicates free trade *simpliciter*, he shows in meticulous detail how the mechanisms which supposedly vindicate unlimited free trade under all circumstances are, in fact, dubious intellectual contraptions predicated upon unrealistic assumptions. The presumption of free and unmanipulated currency markets is only the most obvious example; there are many others. Fletcher also elucidates recent theoretical breakthroughs in economics that are finally bringing realism into the doctrinaire mathematical world of academic trade economics, advances that are undermining the intellectual respectability of conventional free trade theory as now commonly understood.

These days, some of the leading practitioners of free trade, the chief executives of the largest U.S. corporations, are also quietly starting to reverse course. They, too, now proclaim that the United States must manufacture more and export more manufactured goods. Certain well-known firms are bellwethers of this change. For example, over the past 15 years,

Boeing executives made many a speech celebrating the globalization of their company's manufacturing operations. They tirelessly invoked free trade's logic of comparative advantage to explain why they dismissed American engineers and production workers while Boeing's risk-sharing partners were increasing employment overseas. They strove to impress Wall Street analysts with their periodic downsizings of thousands of workers at a time. These efforts to transfer manufacturing and design overseas were crowned in the 787 Dreamliner, whose wing box and wings were made in Japan and whose composite fuselage was mostly made in Italy—leaving little for the United States but final assembly. That overseas production might be cheaper merely because of subsidies by foreign governments seeking a foothold in this lucrative and strategic industry was irrelevant to Boeing, which is not responsible for the economy at large, but merely a business run for profit.

But Boeing's self-congratulation came to a sudden halt when the entire 787 program was crippled by devastating development delays, most caused by gross manufacturing errors overseas. The company had to change course drastically to survive, promising Wall Street analysts to bring much design and production back to the United States. With less public drama, General Electric has also changed course: after investing vast amounts in overseas manufacturing plants, America's single greatest industrial corporation is now strengthening its domestic manufacturing base and its chief executive, Jeffrey Immelt, has been publicly explaining why the country as a whole must do the same.

The reality is that manufacturing is inescapable. Few Americans can work in elite fields like corporate management or investment banking, no matter how large these loom in the consciousness of the governing class. Most service employment, such as restaurant work, pays low wages. Agriculture is a miniscule employer in all developed nations. And for all the glories of high tech, it remains a modest employer: during the auto industry wreck of 2009, Americans discovered that Ford, General Motors and Chrysler, despite of decades of decline, still employed more people than all the famous names of Silicon Valley—from Adobe to Yahoo—combined. As a result, the incomes and living standards of nonpoor Americans must largely rise and fall with manufacturing employment. Even if they do not personally work in manufacturing, a strong manufacturing sector is needed to support the labor market and the value of the dollar on which an import-dependent America now relies for its standard of living from garments to gasoline.

A new American economy is emerging, in which Americans will consume less and save more to rebuild America's capital base, and import less and export more to start retiring America's now-vast foreign indebtedness. (Indeed, America *must* do these things unless it intends to confiscate foreign dollar holdings by devaluation.) And it is hard to imagine how America can rebuild its manufacturing and rebalance its trade without repudiating free trade—to some carefully chosen extent. If nothing else, the need to neutralize foreign mercantilism demands this.

This is not just a matter of concern for Americans, because unless foreign demand increases, the global economy must shrink in proportion to falling American demand. So increased American exports are, in fact, the only way to maintain current American imports and thus global demand. It is thus that a dose of American protectionism may soon be precisely what the whole world needs.

Edward Luttwak, PhD
Chevy Chase, MD
November 2009

Dr. Luttwak is the author of *Turbo-Capitalism: Winners and Losers in the Global Economy* (1999) and *The Endangered American Dream: How to Stop the United States From Becoming a Third World Country and How to Win the Geo-Economic Struggle for Industrial Supremacy* (1993).

Introduction

Why We Can't Trust the Economists

Oh yes, I know, we have recently been told by no less than 364 academic economists that such a thing cannot be...Their confidence in the accuracy of their own predictions leaves me breathless. But having been brought up over the shop, I sometimes wonder whether they pay back their forecasts with their money.

—Margaret Thatcher, 1981[1]

AMERICA'S TRADE DEFICIT. $696 billion in 2008. $701 billion in 2007. And a world-record seven hundred and sixty billion dollars in 2006.[2] It did fall by nearly half in 2009, as in past recessions, but 2010 popped right back around the $500 billion mark, and 2011 will probably be worse.[3]

To be fair, the trade deficit is not a perfect indicator of free trade's cost. A nation can always balance its trade by crude measures like forcing down wages by political fiat. So, hypothetically, we could have a small deficit and a large trade problem. Plenty of impoverished Third World nations have balanced trade, and a single year's deficit means nothing. But with numbers this high, it's obviously a big problem if it's a problem at all.

And yet Americans remain afraid to do anything about it. The dangers of protectionism are notorious, and questioning free trade in an intellectually serious way runs into deep waters of economics very fast. So we remain paralyzed in the face of crisis.

This book aims to loosen that paralysis a little.

1

Over the last 20 years, Americans have bought over $6 trillion (that's trillion with a "t," six thousand billion, six million million) more from the world than we have sold back to it.[4] That's over $20,000 per American. Ironically, if the U.S. were a developing country, our deficits would have reached the five percent level that the International Monetary Fund takes as a benchmark of financial crisis.[5]

The U.S. economy has ceased generating *any* net new jobs in internationally traded sectors, in either manufacturing or services.[6] The comforting myth persists that America is shifting from low-tech to high-tech employment, but we are not. We are losing jobs in both and shifting to nontradable services—which are mostly low value-added, and thus ill-paid, jobs. According to the Commerce Department, *all* our net new jobs are in categories such as security guards, waitresses, and the like.

The vaunted New Economy has not contributed a single net new job to America in this century.[7] Not one.

The alchemy of international finance that lets America run a seemingly infinite overdraft against the rest of the world looks suspicious, too—because that's what it *means* to endlessly import more than we export. But where does the money come from, at the end of the day? Can we really get something for nothing forever? Or are we in for another crisis like the 2008 financial crisis? Subprime mortgages looked too good to be true, and then they blew up. The aftershocks are still hitting us. Is trade going to be the next shoe to drop?

Common sense seems to say that American workers are going to have problems when we trade with nations, such as China and India, where average pay is well under the U.S. minimum wage ($1.36 an hour for Chinese manufacturing workers, to be exact).[8] Corporate America even admits, with barely concealed glee, that competition from foreign labor has American workers pinned. As one Goodyear vice-president put it, "Until we get real wage levels down much closer to those of the Brazils and Koreas, we cannot pass along productivity gains to wages and still be competitive."[9]

Brazils? Koreas? Our wages?

These nations and others are booming as exporters to the United States. But they remain far too poor to take back enough of *our* exports to balance our trade. Their combination of dreadful wages and regulatory standards on the one hand, and winning economic strategies on the other, has so far produced nothing like the living standards needed to make them significant importers of American goods. Despite recent decades of economic growth, there are still over a billion people in Asia earning less than $2 a day.[10]

Working conditions are the flip side of low pay in developing countries. Production methods long ago abandoned in the developed world—many of them dangerous and environmentally unsound—are still widely in use. In India, for example, foundry workers often don't wear socks, shoes, protective headgear, ear plugs, or even eye protection. Often wearing no more than boxer shorts, they squat on the floor next to the roaring furnaces.[11] Charles Dickens has moved to Asia.

The environment is threatened. Thousands of foundries in China run on industrial-grade coke with no pollution control devices on their smokestacks, creating a plume of smoke that stretches across the Pacific on satellite photos. Chlorofluorocarbons (CFCs) are banned in the United States but still used in China as a blowing agent for the production of polyurethane foam cushions and the like, providing a significant cost advantage for Chinese manufacturers.[12]

None of this happens by accident. Foreign governments treat trade as war and use every trick in the book—legal and illegal under international agreements—to grab their industries a competitive advantage. And even when they don't cheat, they are often more skilled in cultivating their industries than we are. Toyota, despite its troubles, somehow didn't go bankrupt when GM did.

All these facts impinge upon America because of free trade. But economists keep telling us everything will be fine. According to them, free trade is good for us and they can prove it. Ninety-three percent of American economists surveyed support free trade.[13] This inescapably raises the question of whether they have been doing their jobs—and whether America should stick with the policy they recommend.

WHY ECONOMIC THEORY MATTERS

This is a book about real-world economic problems. Brutally real problems. But it is also a book about economic *theory* because in economics, raw facts don't mean much without a theory to interpret them. This is especially true for parts of economics that are as controversial and theoretically unsettled as trade. Wrong theories helped get America into its current trade mess, so we will need the right theories to get us out of it. Not *only* theories, of course, but we won't be able to do it without them.

Can't we just find a practical solution? That's the instinct of many Americans, who find economic theory abstruse and often baffling. Unfortunately not. To just "do what works" is only an option when what works is obvious, and in trade it isn't. Common sense tells us that airplanes shouldn't crash, but it doesn't tell us how to design a plane that will actually fly. It takes a *theory*, called aerodynamics, to do that. Luckily, the right economic theories are not all that hard to understand, if one makes the effort. And, as we shall see, all this theory has a payoff, in the form of an implied solution.

At an absolute minimum, ordinary citizens need to know enough about the economics that *supposedly* justifies free trade to hold their ground in confrontations with the experts and not get ruled out of public debate on grounds of ignorance. America can't be a democracy if one side is intimidated into silence on a question this important. So ordinary citizens need to learn how to criticize the economics of free trade in language that economists (and those who look to them for policy advice) accept as legitimate—and will have to take seriously.

But first, we're going to look at why we shouldn't just defer to what economists tell us. Because if we can, then we should just leave our trade problems to these experts, and books like this one have no place. So understanding what's wrong with economists is our first step.

FREE TRADE ISN'T JUST BOUGHT

Some people believe economists are irrelevant, and that free trade is American policy simply because big corporations and other vested interests have the political muscle to impose it. This is false. For a start, without economics, vested interests can't tell whether free trade benefits them or not, just as a company can't know whether or not it is profitable without resort to accounting principles. Vested interests can indeed see money piling up in their bank accounts under free trade. But is this more or less money than what they would have gotten *without* free trade? Without economics, they can't tell. When a policy has complex effects, it is not obvious who wins and loses from it—even to the winners and losers themselves, and especially in the long run. They have to *analyze* trade policy to know this, and one can't analyze any economic policy without theories about how the economy works. This is why the British economist John Maynard Keynes (1883-1946), arguably the greatest economist of the 20th century, wrote that:

> The ideas of economists and philosophers, both when they are right and when they are wrong, are more powerful than is commonly understood. Indeed, the world is ruled by little else. Practical men, who believe themselves to be quite exempt from any intellectual influences, are usually the slaves of some defunct economist...I am sure the power of vested interests is vastly exaggerated compared with the gradual encroachment of ideas...But, soon or late, it is ideas, not vested interests, which are dangerous for good or evil.[14]

Furthermore, vested interests are not infinitely powerful. They have to persuade the rest of the country, especially Congress, to go along with the policies they want. Despite political corruption, all the money in the world couldn't bribe Congress to pass a law requiring people to roller-skate to work; legislation always requires some non-laughable justification. Therefore lobbying successfully for free trade requires credible economic ideas that support it. This is why the famous liberal economist and *New York Times* columnist Paul Krugman, winner of the 2008 Nobel Prize for his work on trade and a thinker we will draw upon extensively in this book, wrote of his stint in government:

> What was more surprising was the way that even strong political considerations could sometimes be held at bay when a proposal seemed clearly without a good analytical foundation. I know of one corporation that had a demand widely supported by other businesses and highly placed friends in the government, yet got nowhere for more than a year, largely because the company's arguments were so easily torn apart by government economists. In the end the corporation hired some high-quality economists to help produce a well-argued report, and for that or other reasons finally got some action.[15]

So even if free trade economics *is* largely a bundle of rationalizations, these are still rationalizations the system needs in order to function. It follows that if opponents of free trade can debunk these rationalizations, these opponents can deprive free traders of camouflage, credibility, and self-confidence they can ill afford to lose. That is one purpose of this book.

ECONOMISTS KNOW MORE THAN THEY LET ON

To be completely fair, to some extent economists haven't been wrong about free trade at all. But the aforementioned seven percent who know better have allowed a mistaken impression of the disciplinary consensus to be foisted upon the public. And when the other 93 percent say they support free trade, this doesn't necessarily mean they support it *without reservation.*[16] It often just means that they know it has problems, but support it over any likely alternative—which they fear would be worse.

Above all, economists fear that admitting the known problems with free trade might provoke politicians into doing something stupid. As the 19th-century American radical economist Henry George put it, "introducing a tariff bill into a congress or parliament is like throwing a banana into a cage of monkeys."[17] The great fear is that if protectionism is conceded any legitimacy, special interests will seize control and economic logic will fall by the wayside. For example, Congress might enact a 30 percent tariff on imported steel to save Rust Belt jobs that would be disappearing soon due to technological change anyway. This could cost $300,000 per job per year, including the cost of making American manufacturers pay more for steel than their foreign competitors.[18] Then every other industry would want in and before we knew it, we would have a crazy-quilt industrial policy, set by Congressional logrolling and lobbyist bidding wars. It would be a mess: based on political pull, embodying no rational economic strategy, and costing our economy hundreds of billions of dollars per year.

Fear of such a debacle gets most (not all) economists off the hook for outright incompetence or dishonesty. But it reveals a deeper problem: this fear is not actually a part of economic science. It is just a somewhat cynical intuition about the American political system. Economists are certainly entitled to their political intuitions (which may even be true), but these intuitions are not part of their actual *knowledge* as economists. They are not something that they have PhD-level expertise in and the rest of us don't.[19] They are thus not privileged over the intuitions of ordinary informed citizens. The electorate has a right to hear both sides of the debate and make its own decision. That's democracy.

Economists' fears may also be false. Our government is sometimes corrupt and stupid, but it is also sometimes effective. The country wouldn't still be here if it wasn't. Some foreign governments certainly *seem* to have had effective protectionist policies in recent decades, using tariffs and nontariff barriers to boost their economies. Japan clearly did not become the second-richest nation in the world practicing free trade.[20] China is conceded from one end of the political spectrum to the other to thumb its nose at free trade, but it is booming.

Even Europe seems to handle these matters better than we do: Germanic and Scandinavian Europe (Germany, Switzerland, Austria, Holland, Belgium, Luxembourg, Denmark, Sweden, Norway, and Finland) usually run healthy surpluses, and the Eurozone as a whole has had its trade within pocket change of balance since the euro was created in 1999.[21] Thirteen European countries now pay their factory workers better than we do,[22] and Germany (not China!) was the world's largest exporter as late as 2008.[23] Do all these countries know something we don't?

CORRUPT POLITICIANS, VOTERS AND ECONOMISTS

Cynical comments about politicians are also an evasion. In America, we elected them, so what they do ultimately reflects what we want. If we voters are corrupt, and vote for short-term gratification, something for nothing, and sweet deals for our special interests, then the politicians we elect will be corrupt, too. But if we wise up and a sense of national crisis engenders a sense of national purpose, then we may demand (and get) a trade policy sufficiently honest and rational to work. This has happened on other issues before.

Economists can be corrupt, too. Some are simply paid shills of special interests. Economics consulting firms like Global Insight, MiCRA, and Strategic Policy Research basically retail the service of providing whatever conclusions are required, albeit with sufficient sophistication that nobody has to tell any literal lies.[24] Sometimes the corruption is more subtle, cumulative, and unconscious; indeed, it is rarely a matter of, "Say X and we'll pay you $Y." In order to win clients, economists in private practice (the author used to be one) must cultivate a reputation for saying the kinds of things clients want to hear. Certain ideas, like the problems of free trade, are just best avoided. They are not "economically correct." So they drop out of circulation and don't get the attention they deserve. A few years of that is all it takes to skew the consensus, as ignoring facts is just as effective as denying them. (Indeed, it is more so, as it avoids starting a fight that might attract unwanted attention.)

As a result, the age-old question of whether bad policy comes from corruption or bad thinking doesn't really have an answer, as these are intimately entwined. *Corruption inexorably debases the quality of thinking over time*, and a nation that insists on being told what it wants to hear will eventually lose the ability to figure out what the actual truth is.

And, of course, sometimes financial bullying and other outright coercion does occur. Economist Paul Craig Roberts, an Assistant Treasury Secretary under Reagan and today one of the most distinguished critics of free trade, reports seeing, when he was a fellow at the Center for Strategic and International Studies in Washington, memos analyzing what grants that think tank could obtain from the administration of George Bush, Sr. in exchange for firing him.[25] (He had displeased the administration by criticizing its economic policies.) Bush's science advisor, Alan Bromley, was forbidden to talk to the media for six months in 1991 after he told *The Wall Street Journal* that America needed an industrial policy.[26] In 2003, the Defense Department temporarily shut down its own Advisory Group on Electron Devices after this group released a report detailing the destruction of U.S. innovation capabilities in electronics by imports.[27] And Bruce Bartlett, one of the early figures of Reagan's supply side economics, was fired by the conservative National Center for Policy Analysis in 2005 for denouncing George Bush, Jr. as a conservative "impostor," later publishing a book by that title.[28] Who pays the piper will certainly *try* to call the tune, no government likes to hear bad news, and shooting the messenger remains one of the favored ways of making bad news go away.

Conversely, sometimes The Powers That Be simply avoid the topic of trade problems entirely. For example, in the four presidential and vice-presidential debates of the 2008 campaign, imports were never mentioned, the trade deficit was never mentioned, and exports were mentioned only once.[29] China, by contrast, was mentioned 15 times, geopolitical rivalry being much more exciting than economics.

This all raises an important question: do America's rulers secretly *know* that they're making a mess with free trade—but go on doing it for profit's sake—or do they sincerely believe in the policy? The author cannot pretend to be privy to anyone's private thoughts, but it seems to vary by individual. Most such people, especially those whose professional expertise isn't in economics, genuinely believe in the free trade consensus. They instinctively defer to the officially anointed experts, and these all tell them free trade is correct. And establishmentarians who *are* economists by training are usually among the 93 percent who believe in free trade. Even those who are among the seven percent who don't, usually keep their mouths shut for career reasons.

Change is also resisted simply because it is change; in the words of Gregory Tassey, a senior economist at the National Institute of Standards who has criticized free trade economics:[30]

> Those with a stake in the status quo and their defenders in government argue for old models of competitive strategy and economic growth. Specifically, factions with vested interests in economic assets such as physical and intellectual capital, existing labor skills, or simply a fear of the trauma and the cost of change, resist adaptation. This is the installed-base effect and it is widespread.[31]

But just as the best minds in the Kremlin never really believed in Marxism, some members of America's establishment are well aware of the harm free trade is doing. They are not stupid people, after all (especially when it comes to money), and, as we shall see, the analyses that reveal that free trade isn't working aren't that hard to do. One can sometimes see glimpses of their awareness if one pays attention. This book is littered with quotes from prominent people who have obviously grasped one aspect or another of the defects of free trade, even if they shy away from publicly conceding any recognition of the whole. Eccentric billionaires, who can afford not to care what other members of the establishment think of them, are another highly visible dissident group. Warren Buffet and Ross Perot in the U.S., and the late Sir James Goldsmith in the UK, are the best known. (We will look at some of Buffet's ideas in Chapter 11.)

ACADEMIC ECONOMISTS VS. THE REAL WORLD

Some academic economists are enervated by sheer ivory tower indifference to the real world. They are trapped in a circular system of publication and promotion procedures that tends to reinforce groupthink: they get published by impressing more-senior economists, and they get promoted based on how much they publish. Their careers are determined by their ability to impress other academics, so it is risky for them to wade into the murky waters of public debate. Nobody gets tenure for picking fights with *The Wall Street Journal.*

Academic economists often say things that people who actually deal with the realities of trade for a living—executives, diplomats, union officials—find they cannot take seriously without risking their own unemployment. Even economists employed by business schools are notorious for being out of sync with other economists on trade. This is no accident, as they have to peddle theories that actually work in practice, which economics department economists generally do not. Among other things, business school economists are much more inclined to see international trade as a *rivalry* between nations, with winners and losers, than are economics department economists, who tend to see the jungle of commerce as a beautiful rainforest (where everybody wins). If engineers and physicists did not see eye to eye, might we not start questioning physics?

For example, it has been obvious for 35 years now that America's economy needs to be internationally competitive. But many academic economists disparage the very concept of competitiveness, mainly because it has no accepted definition.[32] And indeed it hasn't, for the simple reason that all competition is defined by winning and losing, and there's no obvious standard for what it would mean for America to "win" in international economic competition.[33] But this doesn't mean America doesn't have to be competitive. Happiness doesn't have a clear definition either.

SOPHISTICATED MATH DOESN'T EQUAL SOPHISTICATED THINKING

When one scratches the editorial-page surface of economics and comes face-to-face with its intellectual core, one finds a mass of equations. This gives it the appearance of hard fact. How could anything so mathematical be a matter of opinion? (It also looks distinctly like something which people who don't understand it should keep their mouths shut about.) But in fact, sophisticated math is actually overrated as an economic tool, as hinted by the fact that hedge funds employing it fared no better than others in the financial meltdown of 2008.[34]

The overreliance of contemporary economics upon sophisticated math creates a number of problems.[35] The fundamental one is that because it is easier to mathematize some ideas than others, some ideas appear truer than

10

they really are. But the presumption physics enjoys, that mathematically elegant theories are more likely to be true, simply doesn't hold in economics, however much many economists may want it to.[36] The aggressive use of simplifying assumptions can deliver elegant math on demand, but only at the price of misrepresenting reality.

Theories which favor free trade tend to be mathematically neat— mainly because they assume markets are perfectly efficient, which makes their outcomes predictable. Theories which critique free trade, on the other hand, tend to be mathematically messy, mainly because they assume markets are *not* perfectly efficient and are thus not predictable. So economists have often favored free trade simply because the math is neater. As Paul Krugman puts it, "the theory of international trade followed the perceived line of least mathematical resistance."[37]

There is actually a serious paradox here, because intellectual rigor (which math provides in spades) certainly *sounds* like a self-evidently good thing.[38] Unfortunately, intellectual rigor can only guarantee that reasoning is internally consistent: its conclusions follow from its premises. It cannot guarantee that those premises were right in the first place, and with bad premises, even the most rigorous reasoning will produce nonsense. Premises don't even have to be *wrong* to generate false conclusions. They only have to be incomplete, and no set of premises can prove its own completeness. The more mathematically abstruse economics gets, the more basic truths get obscured behind a blizzard of symbols, making it easy to wander into falsehood unawares for lack of an obvious sanity check.

This connection between mathematical extremism and free-market extremism goes back to the dawn of contemporary economics just after WWII. For example, the prime exponent of the once-novel idea that corporations *ought* to be motivated solely by the pursuit of profit was none other than the famous University of Chicago economist and libertarian philosopher Milton Friedman (1912-2006). Revealingly, he was also the economist who argued, in a still hotly-debated 1953 scholarly article that set the tone for two generations of economists, that it doesn't matter if economic theories make unrealistic assumptions about reality, so long as they make the right predictions. As he put it:

> Truly important and significant hypotheses will be found to have 'assumptions' that are wildly inaccurate descriptive representations

of reality, and, in general, the more significant the theory, the more unrealistic the assumptions (in this sense).

The alternative? Formal mathematical modeling of the economy, where all these distortions reside, should be viewed as a tool, not as identical with economics as such, an error common in the profession since WWII.[39] Sometimes modeling can be very revealing, but sometimes it conceals realities that are hard to wrap math around.[40] Sometimes, it can even *destroy* knowledge, when it prevents important facts from being recognized simply because they are hard to mathematize. Some of the most insightful recent work in economics—by thinkers like 2009 Nobelist Oliver Williamson, Harvard Business School's Michael Porter, Tokyo-based financial journalist Eamonn Fingleton, and Norwegian economist Erik Reinert— barely uses it.[41] The economic technocrats of Beijing, Tokyo, and Seoul, who have produced amazing economic achievements in recent decades, have shown almost no interest in it at all, beyond basic statistics.[42]

VALUE JUDGEMENTS VS. ECONOMICS

Economics has some difficulties understanding the problems of free trade simply because it is a social science and therefore value-free. Many people are surprised to learn this, but there is actually nothing in economics that holds that prosperity is better than poverty, any more than neuroanatomy holds that pleasure is better than pain.[43] And yet economics uses terms, like "efficient," which certainly *sound* like value judgments. So when economists say that free trade is efficient, this actually has a narrowly technical meaning, with limited connection to economic well-being as most people would understand it.

Conversely, economics also has its true believers, for whom the infallibility of free markets, of which free trade is a part, is a "beautiful idea," a secular religion like Marxism once was. The libertarian Cato Institute in Washington is their Vatican and the old Ayn Rand cult of "objectivism" their fundamentalist sect. But these people are trying to pass off political ideology as if it were economics. It is simply not the same thing. Their favorite trick is to blame all the problems of free trade on the fact that real-world free trade isn't pure, 100 percent perfect, free trade. But nothing in the real world is 100 percent pure, so if free trade depends upon perfection to work, it's not a particularly useful ideal.

A discipline dealing in observable facts, like economics, is also not an appropriate object of *faith*, which rightly pertains to religious subjects and other nonempirical matters. If economic facts are observable, then observation should determine what we think about them. Nobody should have "faith" in free markets (or their opposites); they should have evidence either way or not hold an opinion. The Cold War gave Americans a terrible habit of turning economics into a quasi-theological clash of absolute values. Valid economics is never shrill; as Bertrand Russell once noted, no-one passionately believes two plus two make four.

ECONOMICS TAKES DECADES TO GET THINGS RIGHT

Economists have been criticizing free trade on and off since it was first advocated near the dawn of modern capitalism 400 years ago.[44] However, the current wave of academic critique is relatively young. New trade theory, the blandly named but pathbreaking critique that is the academic foundation of Part III of this book, emerged in the late 1970s. But it only achieved its breakthrough synthesis in 2000, with Ralph Gomory and William Baumol's brilliant little book *Global Trade and Conflicting National Interests* (whose ideas we will explore in Chapter 10). Because it takes time to gather data and think through objections, decades may pass before a new insight becomes the general consensus of the discipline. So it may still be a while before the economics profession as a whole digests these innovations and changes its mind about free trade.

Right now, the (slowly crumbling) consensus in economics mainly derives from work that reached acceptance in the 1980s. This was the heyday of free-market economists, Milton Friedman and others, who did brilliant work debunking the liberal Keynesian consensus under which they grew up. That consensus, which was gospel from the 1940s to the 1960s, broke down under the stagflation of the 1970s and was a product of the Great Depression. It had itself overturned an even older consensus derived from the laissez faire gold-standard world of the late nineteenth century. In the 1960s, when the political consensus was Keynesian, the profession was Keynesian. In the 1980s, when free markets resurged in political popularity under Reagan and Thatcher, economics was in eager support with so-called "efficient markets" theory. Neither of these ideas, in its orthodox form, is taken seriously by many economists today.[45] This suggests that economists are suspiciously reliable sock puppets of the political status quo, and that their reasoning is not as different from the thinking of ordinary concerned citizens as their intimidating academic facade implies.

A NONIDEOLOGICAL ECONOMIC NATIONALISM

Some economists give unhelpful answers about free trade simply because they don't think the *national* economic interest matters. Technically, they are of course correct that choosing America as the entity whose economic well-being one cares about is arbitrary, from the point of view of pure economics. There is nothing in economic science that privileges whatever nation lies between the 49th parallel and the Rio Grande.

But this is an attitude of little practical use to a nation in serious economic trouble. As economist Herman Daly of the University of Maryland, best known for his work on ecological economics, puts it, "Free trade makes it very hard to deal with these root causes at a national level, which is the only level at which effective social controls over the economy exist."[46] Because we *have* a national government, because Americans care about what happens to *their* economy, and because it is the national debate on the question that will bring changes or fail to, our trade problems will be fixed in Washington or not at all.

Globally, for good or ill, the nation-state is still where the buck of political legitimacy stops. Higher and lower political entities, from Kansas to the United Nations, enjoy legitimacy only because nation-states have given it to them. So even if other instruments for controlling the world economy can be developed over time, the nation-state will be the bottleneck for developing them. A blanket rejection of even the mildest economic nationalism—an attitude common at both extremes of the political spectrum—simply hands a blank check to multinational corporations, foreign powers, and (distorted) market forces to do as they please.

At an absolute minimum, economics should not be abused to "prove" the inappropriateness of caring about national economic well-being—which it does not do. From the point of view of pure economics, internationalist assumptions are as arbitrary as nationalist ones. People who reject the national economic interest should do so openly, not hide behind theoretical constructs that do this on the sly.

The ultimate value of nationalism vs. internationalism is a value judgment beyond the scope of this book. A nonpartisan "soft economic nationalism" is postulated herein simply to make the critique tractable, as the problems with free trade become clearest when one asks how a given nation may be helped or harmed by it. The only thing this kind of nationalism insists upon is that a nation's economy should basically be run for the benefit of its people.[47] It has no ideological commitments with regard to other usages of the term "nationalism," and leaves open to partisan debate the best way to realize its objectives. As we shall see, the trade solutions America needs could be implemented by either party and painted in a wide range of ideological colors.

Some of the analysis in this book is more relevant to other nations than to the U.S., simply because it applies to economic circumstances that obtain there more than here. We will, for example, take a long hard look at why free trade is bad for developing countries. Whether the policy implications of these analyses are also good for America depends on the analysis in question. This is *not* a univocally America First book, simply because not every valid critique of free trade implies policies that would be in America's interests. Other nations have the right to play the game for their own benefit and seek the well-being of their own people, too. Free trade is so problematic that easily half the world has something to gain by ending it. There is no point foreclosing the scope of our analysis just to avoid discovering holes in free trade that will help Costa Rica more than ourselves.

But don't worry: *America is going to get plenty out of ending free trade.*

PART I

THE PROBLEM

1

Bad Arguments for Free Trade

BEFORE WE DELVE into the defective economics of free trade, we must clear away a considerable mass of accumulated debris. The issue is bound up in the public mind with a lot of extraneous questions, from which we must disentangle it if we are ever to think straight.

For a start, we are not debating whether cosmopolitanism is a good thing. In many ways it is, but it is a cultural question with little to do with the actual hard economics of international trade. Neither are we debating the choice between, in the words of *New York Times* columnist Thomas Friedman, "the Lexus and the olive tree,"[48] that is between the efficient but soulless rationalism of the global marketplace and the rooted particularism of nations and communities. The economics *itself* of free trade is legitimately controversial, so there is no justification for bracketing it as a settled question and turning to imponderables like the relative value of prosperity vs. heritage.

We are also not debating globalization (an historical process) as such or globalism (the ideology that favors globalization).[49] Though it has ramifications that affect almost everything, free trade is, strictly speaking, a purely economic question, and globalization involves a lot more than economics. It includes cultural exchanges, population movements, global governance, the global environment, and many other things. So one can certainly oppose free trade and support globalization with respect to its noneconomic aspects—or vice-versa, for that matter.

Even a certain amount of *economic* globalization is perfectly compatible with ending free trade. If every nation on earth imposed a 10 percent tariff, this would end free trade by definition, but the world would still be globalizing economically—albeit in a slower and more controlled fashion than today. It has been estimated that the spread of air freight had the same effect as a tariff cut from 32 to 9 percent in the U.S. from 1950 to 1998.[50] But no ideological energy is expended on the problem of air freight pricing.

ECONOMIC GLOBALIZATION IS A CHOICE

Economic globalization is often debated as something that is either "good" or "bad" and will either "succeed" or "fail." But framing the alternatives as binary is too crude, and tends to force uncritical approval on both counts. It encourages the assumption that we "must" make economic globalization succeed, and as a unitary package, with no choice about its different aspects being possible. The better questions to ask are how far will it go, what shape will it take, and what measures (if any) should we take to influence either?

If economic globalization is a good thing, then it should be able to survive our getting a choice about how far it is allowed to go. Attempts to foreclose that choice betray a distinct nervousness about what people might choose on the part of those who would foreordain the outcome—usually in favor of a radically laissez faire result. The tragedy of free trade is that it gives up some of the best tools humanity has to shape what *kind* of economic globalization we get: tariffs and non-tariff trade barriers. There simply are not that many levers over the world economy that are both feasible to pull and have a large impact. If we rule out some of the best, we haven't got many left.

The fundamental message of this book is that nations, including the U.S., should seek *strategic, not unconditional* integration with the rest of the world economy.[51] Economic openness, like most things in life, is valuable up to a point—but not beyond it. Fairly open trade, most of the time, is justified. Absolutely free trade, 100 percent of the time, is an extremist position and is not. (The difference between the two is rational protectionism.) Valid economics simply doesn't support the extravagant notion that, in the words of techno-utopian *Wired* magazine:

> Open, good. Closed, bad. Tattoo it on your forehead. Apply it to technology standards, to business strategies, to philosophies of life. It's the winning concept for individuals, for nations, for the global community in the years ahead.[52]

Nations need instead a well-chosen *balance* between openness and closure towards the larger world economy.

One giveaway sign that laissez faire in foreign trade (what free trade is) is wrong is that laissez faire hasn't been taken seriously in America's domestic economy for well over 100 years—since before the era of Teddy Roosevelt's trustbusters around the turn of the 20th century. Despite perennial posturing to the contrary by free-market ideologues, we have, in fact, found reasonable levels of regulation in most parts of our economy to be best: neither outright state control nor absolute economic freedom. It is no accident that regulating international trade was well within the intention of the Founding Fathers: Article I, Section 8 of the Constitution explicitly authorizes Congress "to regulate commerce with foreign nations."

FREE TRADE IS NOT INEVITABLE

It is often said (or tacitly assumed) that in today's world, free trade is somehow inevitable. But if so, why do its supporters bother arguing for it so aggressively? The inevitability of free trade certainly does not follow from the apparent inevitability of some form of capitalism, given the long history of protectionist capitalist economies. (The U.S. itself used to be one, as we will see in Chapter Six.)

Contrary to myth, modern history has not been a one-way escalator to ever increasing global economic interconnectedness. Instead, this interconnectedness has ebbed and flowed upon larger political currents. It was pushed up by colonialism, but pushed down when former colonies, like the U.S. and India, adopted protectionist policies of their own after independence. It was pushed down by fascism on the right and socialism on the left. But it was pushed up by the Cold War. Prior to the 1970s, the peak of world trade as a percentage of world economic output was in 1914—a peak to which it did not return for two generations.[53] This flux is not an idle curiosity of history: anyone who assumes world trade can only go up in the long run should consider what Peak Oil or tightening environmental constraints may do to transport costs. Neither has increased trade always correlated with increased prosperity and its decline with the reverse: the world economy was actually *less* globalized in 1960 than in 1910, but more prosperous.[54]

Modern technology does not mandate free trade either. While technology indeed favors the expansion of trade, by reducing shipping and transaction costs, it does not mandate that this trade be *free,* rather than subject to tariffs. Indeed, if technology erodes natural trade barriers like distance, and trade barriers are sometimes beneficial (as we will shall see), then modern technology can, paradoxically, increase the justification for tariffs.

All inevitability arguments are moral evasions, anyhow, because offloading responsibility to the free market ignores the fact that we *choose* whether, and how much, to regulate markets. This is probably what the great protectionist President Teddy Roosevelt was driving at when he wrote,

> Thank God I am not a free-trader. In this country pernicious indulgence in the doctrine of free trade seems inevitably to produce fatty degeneration of the moral fiber.[55]

THE NATION-STATE IS *NOT* IRRELEVANT

It is sometimes suggested that free trade is a moot question because globalization has made the nation-state "irrelevant." As Doug Oliver of the Cessna aircraft company recently said, in response to complaints about his company outsourcing its entry-level Skycatcher plane to a firm that supplies China's air force:

> Nothing is American any more. Nothing is German any more.
> Nothing is Japanese any more. Harley-Davidson sources parts from
> all around the world. Let's face it, we're in a global economy.[56]

This is all technically true, with respect to the sourcing of parts at least, but misses the point. Even if the internationality of modern supply chains means that America's trade balance adds up at the component, rather than finished product, level, we still run a deficit or a surplus. And even if who builds which finished products isn't the key to prosperity anymore, who builds which components increasingly is.

In any case, the nation-state is a long way from being economically irrelevant. Most fundamentally, it remains relevant to *people* because most people still live in the nation where they were born, which means that their economic fortunes depend upon wage and consumption levels within that one society. Capital is a similar story. Even in the early 21st century, it hasn't been globalized nearly as much as often imagined. And it also cares very much about where it lives, frequently for the same reasons people do. (Few people wish to live *or* invest in Malawi; many people wish to live *and* invest in California.) For a start, because 70 percent of America's capital is human capital,[57] a lot of capital behaves exactly as people do, simply because it *is* people. Another 12 percent is estimated to be social capital, the value of institutions and knowledge not assignable to individuals.[58]

So although *liquid financial capital* can indeed flash around the world in the blink of an electronic eye, this is only a fraction (under 10 percent) of any developed nation's capital stock. Even most nonhuman capital resides in things like real estate, infrastructure, physical plant, and types of financial capital that don't flow overseas—or don't flow very much. (Economists call this "don't flow very much" phenomenon "home bias," and it is well documented.)[59] As a result, the output produced by all this capital is still largely tied to particular nations. So although, for reasons we will examine in detail later, capital mobility certainly causes problems, it is nowhere near big enough to literally abolish the nation-state as an economic unit.

Will it do so one day? Even this is unlikely. Even where famously dematerializing and globalizing assets like fiber optic telecom lines are added—assets that supposedly make physical location irrelevant—they are still largely being added where existing agglomerations of capital are. For example, although fiber optic backbones have gone into places like Bangalore, India, which were not global economic centers a generation ago, big increments of capacity have also gone into places like Manhattan, Tokyo, Silicon Valley, and Hong Kong, which were already important.[60] As a result, existing geographic agglomerations of capital are largely self-reinforcing and here to stay, even if new ones come into being in unexpected places. And these agglomerations have national shape because of past history; legacy effects can be *extremely* durable.[61] Previous technological revolutions, such as the worldwide spread of railroads, were at least as big as current innovations like the Internet, and they didn't abolish the nationstate.

Ironically, the enduring relevance of the national economy is clearest in some of the "poster child" countries of globalization, like Japan, Taiwan, South Korea, Singapore, and Ireland. In each of these nations, economic success was the product of policies enacted by governments that were in some sense *nationalist*. Japan industrialized after the Meiji Restoration of 1868 to avoid being colonized by some Western power. Taiwan did it out of fear of mainland China. South Korea did it out of fear of North Korea. Ireland did it to escape economic domination by England. In each case, the driving force was not simply desire for profit. This exists in every society (including resource-rich basket cases like Nigeria, where it merely produces gangsterism), but does not reliably crystallize into the policies needed for economic growth. The driving force was national *political* needs which found a solution in economic development.

There is an important related factor: as Michael Porter of Harvard Business School has observed:

> Competitive advantage is created and sustained through a highly localized process. Differences in national economic structures, values, cultures, institutions, and histories contribute profoundly to competitive success. The role of the home nation seems to be as strong as or stronger than ever. While globalization of competition might appear to make the nation less important, instead it seems to make it more so.[62]

So what we can call "economic national character" matters. One sign of this is that even multinational companies are almost always strongly tied to particular nations. Despite the myth of the stateless corporation, only a few dozen firms worldwide maintain over half their production facilities abroad.[63] According to one study, multinational companies "typically have about two-thirds of their assets in their home region/country, and sell about the same proportion in their home region/country."[64] Another meticulous 2008 study concluded that:

> Globalization as popularly understood does not exist. For example, there is no evidence that U.S. firms operate globally. Instead, they both produce and sell on a home region basis, as do MNEs [multinational enterprises] from Europe and Asia.[65]

So whatever else multinational corporations may be guilty of, vanishing into denationalized thin air isn't it.

Economic nationalism is usually held up by free traders as a dumb and reactionary force. Sometimes, of course, it is. Boneheaded economic nationalism belongs in the junkyard of history with the other ideologies rusting there. Nothing in this book is intended to defend it. But economic nationalism can also be a smart, technocratic, forward-looking force—indeed one of the key things that makes economic globalization *work*—when implemented correctly. Nations with weak or fragmented national cohesion, such as Nigeria, Afghanistan, or Iraq, haven't exactly seized the opportunities of the global economy lately.

THE MYTH OF THE BORDERLESS ECONOMY

The cliché that we live in a borderless global economy does not survive serious examination.

Because the U.S. is roughly 25 percent of the world economy, a truly borderless world would imply that imports and exports would each make up 75 percent of our economy, since our purchase and sale transactions would be distributed around the world.[66] This would entail a total trade level (imports plus exports) of 150 percent of GDP. Instead, our total trade level is 29 percent: imports are 17 percent and exports 12 percent.[67] So our economy is nowhere near borderless. And as our trade is almost certainly destined to be balanced by import contraction, rather than an export boom, in the next few years, our trade level is almost certainly poised to go down, not up.

25

A truly unified world economy would also mean that rates of interest and profit would have to be equal everywhere, or the differences would be arbitraged away. But this is nowhere near being the case. Even between adjacent and similar nations like the U.S. and Canada, national borders still count: Economist John McCallum has documented that trade between Canadian provinces is on average *20 times* as large as the corresponding trade between Canadian provinces and American states.[68] It has been estimated that the average cost of international trade (ignoring tariffs) is the equivalent of a 170 percent tariff, of which 55 percent is local distribution costs and 74 percent is international trade costs.[69] Much of international trade is interregional anyway, not global, being centered on European, North American, and East Asian blocs; this is true for just under 50 percent of both agriculture and manufactured goods.[70]

In reality, the world economy remains what it has been for a very long time: a thin crust of genuinely *global* economy (more visible than its true size due to its concentration in media, finance, technology, and luxury goods) over a network of regionally linked national economies, over vast sectors of every economy that are not internationally traded at all (70 percent of the U.S. economy, for example).[71] On present trends, it will remain this way for the rest of our lives.[72] The world economy in the early 21st century is not even remotely borderless.

FREE TRADE AS FOREIGN POLICY

Free traders since 19th-century classical liberals like the English Richard Cobden and the French Frederic Bastiat have promised that free trade would bring world peace. Even the World Trade Organization has been known to make this sunny claim,[73] which does not survive historical scrutiny. Britain, the most freely trading major nation of the 19th century, fought more wars than any other power, sometimes openly with the aim of imposing free trade on reluctant nations. (That's how Hong Kong became British.) Post-WWII Japan has been blatantly protectionist, but has had a more peaceful foreign policy than free-trading America. In reality, free trade sometimes dampens international conflict and sometimes exacerbates it. It enriches belligerent autocrats and helps them dodge democratic reforms. Today, it strengthens the Chinese military by building up China's economy and expanding its access to military technology through both trade and through purchases of American technology companies with the money earned thereby.

Attempts to link free trade to counterterrorism don't stand up, either.[74] The U.S. is the world's leading free trader, but somehow the world's biggest terrorist target anyway. Free trade's widespread global unpopularity combines with the perception that America is behind it to antagonize peoples and governments around the world as often as it rallies them to our side. Occasionally, free trade may bribe foreign governments to cooperate with the United States, but it also enriches nations, like Saudi Arabia and Venezuela, whose elites are knee-deep in funding terrorism and other international mischief. Hard-coding free trade as a legal obligation, as the WTO does, frustrates our ability to use trade concessions as leverage to win foreign cooperation against our enemies.[75]

Ironically, the Central Intelligence Agency seems to grasp many of these problems better than the supposedly economics-oriented agencies of the U.S. government. In its *Global Trends 2015* report, the agency warns that:

> The process of globalization...will be rocky, marked by chronic financial volatility and a widening economic divide...Within countries, the gap in the standard of living also will increase....Increased trade links and the integration of global financial markets will quickly transmit turmoil in one economy regionally and internationally.[76]

Neither does free trade promote human rights. If China had to rely upon domestic demand to drive its economy, locking up its population as factory slaves would not be such a viable strategy. The same goes in other nations, and free trade agreements frustrate attempts to impose sanctions on human rights violators. The sanctions imposed on South Africa in 1986 would be illegal today under World Trade Organization rules.[77]

FLASHY, EMPTY ARGUMENTS

Some arguments for free trade are sheer intellectual fluff—like the idea we should engage in it because it embodies the spirit of the age, the tide of history, or some contemporary repackaging of these dated ideas.[78] Magazines like the libertarian *Reason,* techno-utopian *Wired,* and entrepreneurship-oriented *Fast Company* reveled in such themes all through the dot-com boom years of the late 1990s.[79] The hallmark here is loose, breathless prose whose actual analytical content dissolves among vague terms and hyperbolic assertions. (See the quote on page 21.) The aim here is to make free trade *hip*: the wave of the future. But free trade's hard economics is just 19th-century laissez faire, the economics of the iron law of wages.[80] Its intellectual kernel is David Ricardo's 1817 theory of comparative advantage. Its rival, so-called new trade theory, is, by contrast, a genuinely modern—indeed 21st century—school of thought.

Skepticism about free trade is often stigmatized with *ad hominem* attacks. These mostly come down to variations on the following:

"Protectionists are dummies, losers, incompetents, hippies, rednecks, dinosaurs, closet socialists, or crypto-fascists."[81]

Here's free trader Barack Obama's version, delivered to an audience of campaign donors in the exclusive Pacific Heights neighborhood of San Francisco, a few blocks from where this book was written, while seeking the Democratic nomination in April 2008:

You go into these small towns in Pennsylvania and, like a lot of small towns in the Midwest, the jobs have been gone now for 25 years and nothing's replaced them. And it's not surprising, then, they get bitter, they cling to guns or religion or antipathy to people who aren't like them or anti-immigrant sentiment *or anti-trade sentiment* as a way to explain their frustrations.[82] (Emphasis added.)

God forbid the unemployed of an old-line industrial state should think *trade* has anything to do with their problems! How silly of them.

But economic logic isn't even really the issue here, as these arguments are really aimed at people who don't even *try* to understand economics, but do care immensely about their social status.[83] The media are saturated with this attitude. Thus magazine articles on trade problems focus on the unemployed, implying that only life's losers oppose free trade (and that their unemployment is probably their own fault, anyway). The careers of people whose jobs are being lost to offshoring? Mere "drudgery." Their lives are obviously nothing worth worrying about. *They're not like us here in Pacific Heights.*

This is largely just a chic veil thrown over class bias. Despite the documented center-left preferences of most journalists on social and cultural issues, on economic issues, including trade, they lean right.[84] A late-1990s survey by the watchdog group Fairness and Accuracy in Reporting found, for example, that only on environment-related economic issues were they to the left of the public. But on trade, they were well to the right. For example, 71 percent of editors and reporters supported Fast Track negotiating authority for the North American Free Trade Agreement, while 56 percent of the public opposed it.[85] As 95 percent of these editors and reporters had incomes over $50,000, and more than half over $100,000, this comes as no surprise.[86]

ARROGANCE AND INCOHERENCE

Free traders sometimes tell us that America's labor force is so much more skilled than other nations that free trade will cause us to cream off the best jobs in the global economy. The next minute, they tell us that our poor math skills and work ethic are the root of our economic problems and that we should only blame ourselves. These obviously can't *both* be true.

Sometimes, we are told to stop being arrogant and face up to the fact that the world isn't our oyster anymore and that Americans aren't entitled to be richer than foreigners. Fair enough: we're not *entitled* to any particular living standard. But we certainly are entitled to a government that seeks to defend our prosperity, if that's what we elected it to do.

Signs that America's trade policies are dangerously wrong are often reinterpreted as evidence that our economy is so strong that it can survive even these problems. For example, because we have survived a trade deficit which would have produced a currency collapse in any other nation, trade deficits must not matter. But that is like saying that because the strong constitution of a patient has enabled her to survive cancer, cancer isn't a disease. If free trade *is* a cancer slowly eating at our economy, we need to know now—especially if it is a problem whose solutions have long lead times, as they do.

Our present complacent attitude is the same one taken by past economic powers, such as the British, Spanish, and Chinese Empires, which postponed economic reform until it was too late. Consider the following piece of triumphalist free-trade rhetoric:

> Our capital far exceeds that which they can command. In ingenuity, in skill, in energy, we are inferior to none. Our national character, the free institutions under which we live, the liberty of thought and action, an unshackled press spreading the knowledge of every discovery and of every advance in science, combine with our natural and physical advantages to place us at the head of those nations which profit by the free interchange of their products. Is this the country to shrink from competition? Is this the country which can only flourish in the sickly atmosphere of prohibition? Is this the country to stand shivering on the brink of exposure to the healthful breezes of competition?[87]

These words could have been spoken yesterday by an American politician on either side of the aisle. In fact, they are from a speech by British Prime Minister Sir Robert Peel in 1846! His soaring confidence turned out to be misplaced, and Britain's economic decline began shortly thereafter.

America succeeded under free trade (albeit at mounting cost) during the Cold War. But that was a world that was half communist or socialist, and many other nations, as in Latin America, practiced an inward-looking economics that took them out of the game as serious competitors to us. And the Bretton Woods system of fixed exchange rates and capital controls held trade deficits to a minimum. So we didn't face true global free trade. Now we do. Like many ideals, free trade is more attractive when you don't really have to live by it.

NUMBERS THAT DON'T PAN OUT

Many popular arguments for free trade sound persuasive until real numbers intrude. For example:

> "Free trade is good for America because it means a billion Chinese are now hungry consumers of American products."

But America is running a huge deficit, not a surplus, with China. ($272 billion in 2010, about 54 percent of our total).[88] China deliberately blocks imports, mainly with non-tariff barriers, in order to decrease consumption, increase savings, and boost investment. (This high investment rate is the main reason its economy is growing so fast.) As a result, even the limited purchasing power China's mostly poor population does have rarely gets spent on American goods. The dream of selling to the Chinese functions primarily as bait to lure in American companies, which are forced by the government to hand over key technological know-how as the price of entry.[89] They then build facilities which they discover they can only pay off by producing for export. The China market remains the mythical wonderland it has been since the 19th-century era of clipper ships and opium wars (when it was hyped as aggressively as today, by the way).

A related myth is this:

"Other nations are rapidly catching up to American wage levels. India, for example, has a middle class of 250 million people."

But middle class in India means the middle of India's class system, not ours: a family income about a tenth of what it would take here. India's per capita income is only about $1,000 a year; an Indian family with $2,500 a year can afford servants.[90] For $5,000 a year, American corporations off-shoring work there can hire fresh computer-science graduates.[91]

This myth is calculated to soothe American anxieties:

"Offshoring is a tiny phenomenon."

Offshoring, of course, is just trade in services. But it's just getting started and will be big soon enough, thanks to 15 percent per year compound growth.[92] Alan Blinder, former Vice-Chairman of the Federal Reserve and now an economist at Princeton, has estimated that it will ultimately affect up to 40 million American jobs.[93]

Here is a hopeful dream some people console themselves with:

"Cheap foreign labor is not a threat to American wages because increasing prosperity will drive up wages overseas."

While this *may* be true in the long run, at currently observed rates of income growth it will take decades at best. And it may not happen at all, as

31

the past experience of nations like Japan, which rose from poverty to wages similar to the U.S., may not be replicated. Sub-Saharan Africa has a lower per capita income today than 40 years ago[94] and worldwide, the UN reported in 2003 that 54 nations were poorer than they had been in 1990.[95]

This common claim has no real quantitative basis:

"Free trade brings us enormous benefits."

But one of the dirty little secrets of free trade is that the benefits of expanding it further—as we are constantly told we must do—are actually quite small, *even according to the calculations of free traders themselves.*[96] (More on this in Chapter Seven.)

This next claim appeals to the American sense of superiority:

"We can sustain our huge trade deficit indefinitely because foreigners are so eager to invest in our wonderful business climate."

Unfortunately for this idea, most foreign investment in the U.S. goes for existing assets. For example, of the $260.4 billion invested in 2008, 93 percent went to buying up existing companies.[97] Even worse, much goes into mere government debt—which gets converted, by way of deficit spending, into consumption, not investment.

Here is a sophisticated-sounding analysis that seems to take the drawbacks of free trade seriously:

"Free trade costs America low-quality jobs but brings high-quality jobs in their place."

That would obviously be a kind of free trade we could live with. But the hard data actually show America losing *both* kinds of jobs. For example, according to the Bureau of Labor Statistics, the U.S. lost over 162,000 engineer and architect jobs between 2000 and 2009.[98]

This myth is particularly slippery:

"Savings to consumers from buying cheaper imports outweigh the wages lost by not producing these goods domestically."

But there is no data that actually proves this, particularly since the crucial data concerns the long term, which we have not yet had the opportunity to observe. And there is no principle of economics that guarantees that this will be true, *even in theory*.[99] But we do know that since George W. Bush took office, America has lost nearly five and a half million manufacturing jobs.[100]

Here is a seductive and, frankly, dangerous argument:

"America is still the world's richest country, and we're free traders, so free trade must be right."

But any case for free trade that turns on the present general prosperity of the United States ignores the fact that short-term prosperity is a *lagging* indicator of the fundamental soundness of a nation's economy. Immediate prosperity largely consists in the enjoyment of wealth, like housing stock, produced in years past, so a nation that has been rich for a long time has considerable momentum to ride on. Declining industries may even reap record profits during the years in which they liquidate their competitive positions by outsourcing production, cutting investment, and milking accumulated brand equity.

Many of the indicators used to show America economically outperforming the rest of the world are questionable, anyway. Our unemployment rate is no longer lower than other major developed nations like Germany,[101] as it long was, and looks even less impressive once prison inmates and other forms of nonemployment are factored in.[102] Our high per capita income is largely a result of Americans working longer hours than in other developed nations and of our having a higher percentage of our population in the workforce. As a result, our output per man-hour is much less impressive,[103] even less so if one assumes that our currency is unsustainably overvalued, as it is. And due to American income inequality being the highest in the developed world, less of our GDP reaches the bottom 90 percent of our population than in any other developed country.[104]

THE FREE TRADE SQUEEZE

The economic forces that cause free trade to squeeze the wages of ordinary Americans today are relentless. As Paul Krugman puts it:

It's hard to avoid the conclusion that growing U.S. trade with Third-World countries reduces the real wages of many and perhaps most workers in this country. And that reality makes the politics of trade very difficult.[105]

Free trade squeezes the wages of ordinary Americans largely because it expands the world's supply of labor, which can move from rice paddy to factory overnight, faster than its supply of capital, which takes decades to accumulate at prevailing savings rates. As a result, free trade strengthens the bargaining position of capital relative to labor. This is especially true when combined with growing global capital mobility and the entry into capitalism of large formerly socialist nations such as India and China. As a result, people who draw most of their income from returns on capital (the rich) gain, while people who get most of their income from labor (the rest) lose.

This analysis is not some Marxist canard: its underlying mechanism has long been part of mainstream economics in the form of the so-called Stolper-Samuelson theorem.[106] This theorem says that freer trade raises returns to the abundant input to production (in America, capital) and lowers returns to the scarce input (in America, labor). Because America has more capital per person, and fewer workers per dollar of capital, than the rest of the world, this tends to hurt American workers.

Free trade also affects different kinds of labor income differently. The impact of free trade on a worker in the U.S. is basically a function of how easy it is to substitute a cheaper foreign worker by importing the product the American produces.[107] For extremely skilled jobs, like investment banking, it may be easy to substitute a foreigner, but foreign labor (some yuppie in London) is just as expensive as American labor, so there is no impact on American wages. For jobs that cannot be performed remotely, like waiting tables, it is impossible to substitute a foreign worker, so again there is no direct impact. (We will look at indirect impacts later.) The occupations that suffer most are those whose products are easily tradable *and* can be produced by cheap labor abroad. This is why unskilled manufacturing jobs were the first to get hurt in the US: there is a huge pool of labor abroad capable of doing this work, and manufactured goods can be packed up and shipped around the globe.[108]

It follows from the above that free trade, even if it performs as free traders say in other respects (it doesn't), can still leave most Americans with lower incomes. And even if it expands our economy overall, it can still increase poverty. In a word: *Brazil*, where an advanced First World economy exists side-by-side with Third World squalor, the rich live behind barbed wire, and shopkeepers hire off-duty policemen to kill street children.

Latin America generally, until very recently, has not been an encouraging precedent on this score: in the words of former World Bank chief economist Joseph Stiglitz, "In Latin America, from 1981 to 1993, while GDP went up by 25 percent, the portion of the population living on under $2.15 a day increased from 26.9 percent to 29.5 percent."[109] Growth happened, but much of the population got nothing out of it. Another cautionary tale from the region is Argentina, whose per capita income was 77 percent of ours in 1910, but which underwent economic decline and whose per capita income is now only 31 percent of ours.[110] (Argentina, a ramshackle country of faded glories, foreshadows what a post-decline America might be like.)

In recent decades, trade-induced wage decay has been relentless on the bottom half of America's economic ladder, and is now starting to spread inexorably upwards. According to one summary of the data:

> For full-time U.S. workers, between 1979 and 1995 the real wages of those with 12 years of education fell by 13.4 percent and the real wages of those with less than 12 years of education fell by 20.2 percent. During the same period, the real wages of workers with 16 or more years of education rose by 3.4 percent, so that the wage gap between less-skilled and more-skilled workers increased dramatically.[111]

Taking an approximate mean of available estimates, we can attribute perhaps 25 percent of America's recent rise in income inequality to freer trade.[112] It was thus estimated in 2006 that the increase in inequality due to freer trade cost the average household earning the median income more than $2,000.[113] For many households, this was more than their entire federal tax bill—something for Republicans to bear in mind when trying to rile up such people against big government as the source of their financial woes.

The increasing availability of foreign labor to American corporations has encouraged them to view American workers not as assets, but as expensive millstones around their necks. Wages and benefits once considered perfectly acceptable pillars of First World middle-class living are now viewed by corporate America as obscenely excessive. One sign of this was the two-tier wage structure, with lower wages for new hires, agreed to by the United Auto Workers with General Motors in 2007 even *before* GM's slide into bankruptcy.[114] Under this agreement, within four years roughly a third of GM's employees would be making the new scale—about half what prior employees made. This undid America's historic achievement of an auto industry with middle class factory workers.

The U.S. government has actively abetted this process: the Big Three automakers were forced to cut wages to the levels of foreign automakers' U.S. plants as a condition for their 2008 bailout.[115] And, as shown by export superstar Caterpillar using the threat of offshoring to extract concessions from its labor force,[116] it is unlikely we can export our way out of this mess as long as free trade remains in place.

2

Deficits, Time Horizons, and Perverse Efficiency

THE TRADE DEFICIT IS the single most important statistic of America's trade problems. But because free traders are so adept at explaining why it supposedly doesn't matter, it is essential to understand, once and for all, why they are wrong.[117] It is not a mere "accounting abstraction," as one prominent free trader has called it![118] Luckily, this doesn't require any particularly sophisticated economics, only a solid grasp of some basic definitions and chains of reasoning. Time horizons work the same way. (Although not a common part of public discussion, they are a crucial part of the conceptual framework we will need to reason our way out of our trade problems.) And by putting trade deficits and time horizons together, we can make sense of exchange rates and their manipulation.

To understand trade deficits, just think through the logic below step-by-step:

> Step 1) *Nations engage in trade.* So Americans sell people in other nations goods and buy goods in return. ("Goods" in this context means not just physical objects but also services.)

> Step 2) *One cannot get goods for free.* So when Americans buy goods from foreigners, we have to give them something in return.

> Step 3) *There are only three things we can give in return*:

37

3a) Goods we produce today.

3b) Goods we produced yesterday.

3c) Goods we will produce tomorrow.

This list is exhaustive. If a fourth alternative exists, then we must be trading with Santa Claus, because we are getting goods for nothing. Here's what 3a) –3c) above mean concretely:

3a) is when we sell foreigners jet airplanes.

3b) is when we sell foreigners American office buildings.

3c) is when we go into debt to foreigners.

3b) and 3c) happen when America runs a trade deficit. Because we are not covering the value of our imports with 3a) the value of our exports, we must make up the difference by either 3b) selling assets or 3c) assuming debt. If either is happening, America is either gradually being sold off to foreigners or gradually sinking into debt to them.

Xenophobia is not necessary for this to be a bad thing, only bookkeeping: Americans are poorer simply because we own less and owe more. Our net worth is lower.

This situation is also unsustainable. We have only so many existing assets we can sell off, and we can afford to service only so much debt.[119] By contrast, we can produce goods indefinitely. So deficit trade, if it goes on year after year, must eventually be curtailed—which will mean reducing our consumption.[120]

Even worse, deficit trade also destroys jobs *right now*.[121] In 3a), when we export jets, this means we must employ people to produce them, and we can afford to because selling the jets brings in money to pay their salaries. But in 3b), those office buildings have already been built (possibly decades ago), so no jobs *today* are created by selling them.[122] And in 3c), no jobs are created today because the goods are promised for the future. While jobs will be created *then* to produce these goods, the wages of these future jobs will be paid by us, not by foreigners. Because the foreigners already gave us their goods, back when we bought from them on credit, they won't owe us anything later. So we will be required, in effect, to work without being paid.

This situation isn't only a problem for America. This sort of debt burden is something heavily indebted Third World countries, laboring under debts piled up by past (frequently dubious) regimes, often complain about. They sometimes see international debt as a new form of colonialism, designed to extract labor and natural resources without the inconvenience of running an old fashioned pith-helmet empire. This is why they hate the International Monetary Fund (IMF), which administers many of these debts after they have been junked from the private sector through bailouts.

FINANCIAL SOPHISTICATION CHANGES NOTHING

The above facts are all precisely what we should expect, simply on the basis of common sense, as there is no something-for-nothing in this world. And that is what the idea that trade deficits don't matter ultimately amounts to. There do exist, however, ways of shifting consumption forwards and backwards in time, which can certainly create the *illusion* of something for nothing for a while. This illusion is dangerous precisely because the complexities of modern finance, and the profitability of playing along with the illusion while it lasts, both tend to disguise the reality.

Most of these complexities amount to ways of claiming that the wonders of modern finance enable us either to borrow or sell assets indefinitely. But as long as one bears the above reasoning firmly in mind, it should be obvious why none of these schemes can possibly work, even without unraveling their details. These financial fairy tales usually boil down to the fact that a financial bubble, by inflating asset prices seemingly without limit, can for a period of time make it *seem* as if a nation has an infinite supply of assets appearing magically out of thin air. (Or a finite supply of assets whose value keeps going up and up.) These assets can then be sold to foreigners. And because debt can be secured against these assets, debt works the same way.

Thus a succession of financial bubbles in America since the mid-1990s (in New Economy stocks, real estate, derivatives, commodities, and the broader stock market) have helped us keep running huge trade deficits. To a significant extent, we bought imports with bubble-inflated stock, junk mortgages, bonds doomed to melt with the dollar, and other financial tinsel. Even assets that were not themselves dubious had their value propped up by a general buoyancy in the financial markets that was of dubious origin.

OUR TRADE DEFICIT, OUR CREDIT LINE

In recent years, Americans have been consuming more than they produce to the tune of up to five percent of GDP, making up the difference by borrowing and selling assets abroad. As a result of over 30 years of this, foreigners now own just under 50 percent of all publicly traded Treasury securities, 25 percent of American corporate bonds, and roughly 12 percent of American corporate stock.[123] Net foreign ownership of American assets (what they own here minus what we own there) is now $2.7 trillion—roughly a fifth of U.S. GDP.[124] (GDP is an annual figure and investments are a standing stock of wealth, so these numbers are not directly comparable, but the comparison still gives some sense of the sheer scale.)

It has been estimated that, in the past decade, the U.S. has been absorbing up to 80 percent of the world's internationally exported savings.[125] Until 1985, the U.S. was a net creditor against the rest of the world, but since then, we have slipped further into debt every year.[126] The chart below tells the story:

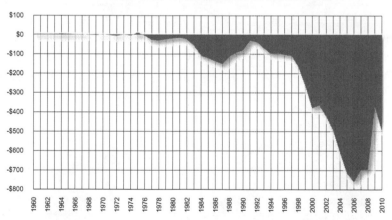

Annual U.S. Trade Balance in Billions

Source: Author's chart from "U.S. Trade in Goods and Services - Balance of Payments Basis," U.S. Census Bureau, http://www.census.gov/foreign-trade/statistics/historical/gands.txt.

It has been estimated that every billion dollars of trade deficit costs America about 9,000 jobs.[127] So it has been estimated that our deficit has cost us approximately one-fifth of all the manufacturing jobs that would otherwise exist.[128] Another way to look at it is that we lose GDP. The Economic Strategy Institute, a Washington think tank, estimated in 2001 that the trade deficit was shaving at least one percent per year off our economic growth.[129] This may not sound like much, but because GDP growth is cumulative, it compounds over time. Economist William Bahr has thus estimated that America's trade deficits since 1991 alone—they stretch back unbroken to 1976—have caused our economy to be 13 percent smaller than it otherwise would be.[130] That's an economic hole larger than the entire Canadian economy.

America's accumulated financial obligations to foreigners mean that an increasing percentage of our future output will go to their consumption, not our own. This applies to both the public and private sectors: as of 2010, 4.9 percent of the federal budget goes to interest on debt,[131] and about half the federal debt is foreign-owned.[132] In 2006, for the first time since we paid off our own 19th-century debts to Europe due to British borrowing here to pay for WWI, America paid more in interest to foreigners than we received from them.[133] Luckily for us, the average interest rate on what we own abroad (largely high-yielding corporate assets) exceeds the average interest rate on what foreigners own here (largely low-yielding government bonds), so we crossed this line long after becoming a net debtor.[134]

But we can't keep borrowing forever. Both the private sector and the government are threatened by the surging interest rates that would result from our international credit drying up. This surge could easily knock America back into recession.[135] And tens of millions of ordinary families are so indebted that they could be pushed into bankruptcy by a sustained rise in the interest rates on their credit cards and other floating-rate debt.[136]

Because wage increases have been barely outpacing inflation for 35 years,[137] consumer spending has only kept pace thanks to the ability of consumers to tap into the equity of their homes at low interest rates. Without this, the spending surge of recent years—consumer spending has gone from 63 percent of the economy in 1980 to 71 percent in 2010[138]—would have been unsustainable. Americans have, in effect, papered over their economic difficulties in recent decades by massive borrowing from abroad. Because this borrowing helped enable the deficit, and because the deficit itself has been responsible for a large part of our economic difficulties, we have been caught in a slow-motion self-reinforcing doom loop.

THE SELL-OFF OF AMERICA

America's global overdraft is not only financed by debt, of course. It is also financed by selling off existing assets. This tends to make the news only when foreigners buy some huge thing people have actually heard of, like when Japanese investors bought Rockefeller Center in 1989 or a firm controlled by the United Arab Emirates tried to buy six of our major seaports in 2006 (and withdrew upon national-security scrutiny), but it is quietly going on all the time. Sometimes the purchasers are private entities abroad, but they are sometimes actual foreign governments, by way of so-called sovereign wealth funds.

By definition, accumulated trade surpluses can only be invested a-broad. Asian sovereign funds investing such monies are expected to have $12.2 trillion by 2013, with the funds of petroleum exporting nations reaching a similar level.[139] Tiny Singapore has $380 billion.[140] Little Norway, flush with North Sea oil wealth, has $512 billion.[141] Kuwait has $203 billion[142] and China $831 billion.[143] South Korea, Brunei, Malaysia, Taiwan, and Chile also have such funds.[144] Even Canada has a huge state pension fund—which denies that it is technically a sovereign fund or would ever politicize its investment decisions, but is still a huge block of capital under foreign government control.[145]

These funds are getting more sophisticated all the time and have the ambition to become even more so. This is why China's State Investment Fund recently bought a 10 percent stake in the elite New York investment firm The Blackstone Group, which specializes in taking large private stakes in corporations and other sophisticated investment strategies. China's government not only wishes to manage its American investments more profitably, but in the long run probably also wishes to learn from this firm the fine art of corporate takeovers and other more active investing strategies.

As a result of this massive shift in wealth, the world's center of financial power is moving away from the Western nations that have held it for centuries. The Central Bank of China (Taiwan), the Bank of Japan, and the Abu Dhabi Investment Authority (ADIA) helped, in fact, bail out the crippled powerhouses of Wall Street after the 2008 financial crisis.[146] The ADIA invested $7.5 billion in Citigroup's rebuilding of its balance sheet;[147] all told, Citigroup received $17.4 billion in sovereign money.[148] The sovereign wealth funds of Kuwait and South Korea helped bail out Merrill Lynch.[149] In all, from March 2007 to June 2008, Asian sovereign wealth

42

funds contributed $36 billion to the recapitalization of Western financial institutions, with oil-based funds kicking in another $23 billion.[150] Without this money, Wall Street's bailout demands upon American taxpayers might well have been too much to stomach.

This all raises profound issues of economic security, especially as some of these governments are not reliably friendly to the U.S., especially in the long run. Unfortunately, America's mechanisms to prevent problems in this area, principally the interagency Committee on Foreign Investment in the United States (CFIUS), deliberately limit themselves to conventional national security concerns and ignore economic security. CFIUS rarely blocks transactions. Of the 404 foreign investments evaluated in the most recent reporting period (2006-2008), not one was actually blocked, although a number were withdrawn in response to scrutiny.[151] An attempt was made in 2007 to expand CFIUS's brief to include economic security, but it failed. In the words of deputy U.S. Trade Representative John Veroneau:

> Doing so would have unhinged CFIUS from its core function of assessing national security and would have left a wide and ambiguous definition of what constitutes 'economic security'...Blocking an inward investment is an extraordinarily serious exercise of governmental power and should be done in only the rarest circumstances, namely when national security interests require it.[152]

So the U.S. government, like the old Soviet Politburo, remains stuck in a narrowly military definition of national security. It has no institution explicitly dedicated to protecting America's *economic* security, and is uncertain how even to define the concept. (One can perhaps best define it on a straight analogy to conventional military security: it is the ability to prevent foreign nations from doing us harm by economic means.)

WHEN THE WELL RUNS DRY

America's massive asset sell-off must come to a halt when we run out of assets to sell. More precisely, it must end when our remaining assets promise foreign investors less return on their money than they can get elsewhere. It may taper off gradually as our government's credit rating and the attractiveness of our private assets gradually decline. Or it may grind to an abrupt halt in a financial panic due to a sudden collapse of confidence in the U.S. economy. Or it may be choked off by a political decision on the part of major buyers. They are well aware of what is going on. As Zhou Jiangong, editor of the online publication Chinastakes.com, recently asked, "Why should China help the U.S. to issue debt without end in the belief that the national credit of the U.S. can expand without limit?"[153]

Short answer: because the U.S. is importing about six percent of China's GDP.[154] China's productive capacity is mismatched with its own consumer demand, so it cannot switch overnight to supplying its domestic market. Because its own population is still far too poor to buy the fax machines and other goods its factories produce for export, China risks mass unemployment—potentially 100 million people—if it ceases to run huge trade surpluses. This pretty much requires it to keep devouring American debt and assets in return. China is in a terrible bind, and one can speculate endlessly on what sort of endgame its rulers may have in mind. Their ideal move would obviously be to segue smoothly from foreign to domestic demand, and they are clearly trying to do so, but there does not appear to be enough time to make this switch before America's capacity to absorb their trade surpluses is exhausted.[155]

In the developing world, which is not rich enough (i.e., does not have enough accumulated assets) to engage in massive asset sales, the upshot of the above problems is a bit different than for the U.S. Free trade, combined with corresponding free debt and asset flows, makes it easier for such countries to pile up huge debts. These are often worsened by the fact that these countries cannot borrow internationally in their own currency, so both their public and private sector borrowers end up owing money in a foreign currency whose local price soars when the exchange rate drops. (This is a big part of what went wrong in Thailand and other nations in the 1997 Asian Financial Crisis.)

Both the International Monetary Fund and the World Trade Organization actually understand all the above problems perfectly well, at least on paper. For example, Article XII of the worldwide General Agreement on Tariffs and Trade (annexed to the founding agreement of its World Trade Organization successor in 1994) explicitly permits nations to restrict the quantity or value of imports in order to avoid trade deficits.[156] Similarly, the IMF's frequent attempts to package free capital flows with free trade are a violation of Article VI of its own governing Articles of Agreement, which recognizes the right of nations to maintain capital controls (which limit foreign debt and asset sales).[157] Neither of these wise concessions, products of a WWII generation of policymakers more realistic about the pitfalls of free trade than those working today, are honored in practice anymore.

WHY THE FREE MARKET WON'T SAVE US

Readers with a free-market bent may wonder how all the above unpleasant outcomes are possible in a capitalist economy. They may suspect that there is some free-market comeback which proves that the above problems aren't really problems after all. After all, doesn't the free market guarantee appropriate economic decisions? Isn't that a basic axiom of capitalism?

Well, no. Not absolutely.

The root problem is simple: when free-market economics says free trade is best for our economy, it takes no position on whether this is best in the long or the short term. In fact, free-market economics takes no position on whether *any* policy it recommends is best in the long or the short term. It treats short- vs. long-term well-being as an arbitrary consumer-driven preference, like whether the economy should produce pork or beef. Some policies deliver the best short-term results, others the best long-term results, but it's an arbitrary choice which we care about more. Free-market economics certainly does *not* say that we "ought" to prefer long-term well-being, and it has no invisible hand that will push our economy toward an optimal time horizon the way it will push prices to those that match supply with demand.

The technical way of saying this is that free-market economics "treats the time discount on consumption as an exogenous preference." An "exogenous" preference is one brought to economic life from outside, like the fact that Frenchmen prefer wine and Germans prefer beer. Time discount on consumption is a reflection of the fact that economics doesn't literally deal in time *horizons*. Time horizons are the idea that outcomes matter up to some point in the future (the "horizon") and then don't matter after that. Instead, economics deals in time *discount*, which is the idea that the further into the future an economic event is, the less it means today. This is the basis of interest rates, among other things: if you lend me money today and I promise to pay you back later, the longer you have to wait, the more interest you'll demand in return. So "treating the time discount on consumption as exogenous" means that while free-market economics can give us lots of advice about the most efficient way to produce *whatever it is* we want, it cannot tell us what we ought to want (or when we ought to want it!) in the first place.

There is no way to evade this problem with minor technical adjustments, as the entire logic of free market economics is explicitly set up this way, baked into its mathematical structures from the very lowest levels. As a result, we're going to need to change that economics a bit to find a solution.

THE ART OF EFFICIENT SELF-DESTRUCTION

How does all this apply to trade? Try this small thought experiment. Imagine two neighboring nations between whom trade is forbidden. Make one a "decadent" nation which prefers short-term consumption. Make the other a "diligent" nation which prefers the long-term variety. The difference between them, of course, is time discount on consumption. In economic equations, this is usually designated with the Greek letter *rho* (ρ). A higher value of ρ means one is more short-termist, because one discounts the future more aggressively. Think of ρ as a measure of impatience.

Now lift their protectionist barriers so the two nations can trade. And let them lend each other money and sell each other assets so they can run deficits and surpluses. Then see what happens. Standard mathematical models of trade, accepted even by free traders, can then be used to run out various scenarios of what happens next.[158]

One scenario in particular is very interesting. In this scenario, the decadent nation maximizes its short-term consumption by buying all the imports it can get. So it buys all it can afford with both its exports *and* by assuming debt and selling off assets.

In the short run, both nations are happy. The decadent nation is delighted to be able to consume more *right now*. And the diligent nation is delighted that its neighbor has expanded its range of investment opportunities, which will enable it better to accumulate wealth and consume more later.

In economic language, both nations have maximized their "utility," the odd word economists use for happiness. So according to free-market economics, both are now better off. This outcome is also efficient, as free-market economics understands efficiency, and it agrees with the core libertarian intuition underlying that economics: *more freedom makes people more able to better themselves.*

So is free trade vindicated?

No, because then come the consequences. The increased well-being of both nations (as they define it, decadently or diligently) depends on the ability of the decadent nation to borrow and sell assets. And it cannot do this forever.[159] Eventually, when it exhausts its ability to sell assets and assume debt, it ends up *poorer* than it would have been if it had not had free trade with its neighbor. Because it depleted its assets and saddled itself with debt, it must now divert money from its own consumption to give to its trading partner!

This outcome should make clear the answer to the question that haunts all criticism of free trade:

How can reducing people's freedom possibly make them better off?

The answer is:

When they would use short-term freedom to hurt themselves in the long term.

The citizens of the decadent nation would have been better off if restrictions on their ability to trade had prevented them from being *quite* so decadent. Trade restraints for them would be like restrictions on an heir's squandering his inheritance. The citizens' "inheritance" is the entire accumulated wealth of their country that can be sold off to pay for imports, plus its entire debt-servicing capacity upon which debt can be floated.

The math actually reveals that under these conditions, outright Las Vegas decadence is not necessary for there to be a problem. It reveals that under free trade between nations with merely *different* time discounts, the nation with the higher discount (more impatient) will tend to maximize present consumption by having past generations (who produced the assets that can be sold off) or future generations (who will service the debt) pay for present consumption.[160] Various factors can interfere, but that's the underlying dynamic.

The fact that two separate societies are involved is key. If the "decadents" in a society can borrow only from "diligents" in the same society, then every borrower creates a lender in the same society, keeping society as a whole in balance. So no amount of decadence (whatever other problems it may cause) can reduce that society's total net worth or future consumption possibilities. But if members of a society can borrow from outside that society, then it can. Worse, things can spiral out of control, given the self-reinforcing way in which social and cultural validation of behavior creates more behavior, then more validation, and so on. So it *matters* whether people engage in economic relations with compatriots, with whom they share a social and cultural system, or with foreigners, with whom they share only arms-length economic relations. (As noted in Chapter One, nations are far from being economically irrelevant.)[161]

THE DANGERS OF PERVERSE EFFICIENCY

The profoundest fact here is actually that this entire mess is efficient, as free-market economics defines efficiency. This explains why free trade's dangers in this regard have mostly been ignored by economists.[162] Within the rigorously logical (albeit perverse) assumptions of mainstream economics, it is merely a mathematical curiosity that free trade can make a nation worse off by seducing it into decadent consumption. It wanted a short-term consumption binge; it got what it wanted; what's not to like? The problem has been defined out of existence at the level of basic premises.

Once one realizes how treacherous efficiency can be and how important preferences are, it becomes clear that economics needs to focus less on the former and more on the latter. One surprising result of all this is a renewed respect for traditional bourgeois culture, or at least that aspect of it which inculcated people to save and not consume. It seems those silly old Protestant misers had a point after all![163] (Given that they created modern capitalism, it is no surprise they were onto *something*.) Crudely put, they reinvested their money in industry, rather than spending it all on palaces as the decadent aristocrats who came before them had done.

The signs of debt addiction in the U.S. economy are not hard to see. The thrift-oriented generation that remembered the Great Depression has mostly died off, and households have become accustomed to endless consumer credit. As the interest rate on consumer debt has exceeded income growth since 1982—the classic formula for a debt trap—consumers have only remained afloat by relying on serial asset bubbles, especially in housing, to prop up their net worth.[164] Over this same time frame, the share of household income consumed by debt service has gone from 11 to 14 percent.[165] The combined debt of America's households and government is now 235 percent of GDP—more than our (understandably) high debt level at the end of borrowing to pay for WWII.[166]

Our smartest competitors, meanwhile, use every trick in the book to keep their citizens from going into debt. It is no accident that 500 million Chinese have cell phones, but only one million have credit cards.[167]

Perverse time discount has implications far beyond free trade and raises doubts about many other areas of economic policy over the last 30 years. For example, financial systems have been deregulated in many nations, especially the U.S. and UK, on the assumption that this is efficient. Efficient it may be, within a narrow definition of efficiency, but what if this just enables people to *sink into debt* more efficiently? Efficiency at the wrong things can be counterproductive. It is likely that many of the quaint old restraints on finance that have been deregulated away since about 1980 served, in theoretically unrigorous ways, to restrain the self-destructive potentials of perverse efficiency.

Perverse time discount can potentially ruin absolutely anything in the economy, given that every bad thing looks good at first (or else nobody would do it). For example, companies with short time horizons won't invest for the long term. So they will be poorly equipped to handle technological innovation, which requires costly investments that only pay off years later. (We tend to think of innovation as being about quickness and rapid response to change, but it is also about delayed financial gratification.) So this seemingly abstract problem helps explain some very concrete facts, like America's inexorably slipping lead in high technology.

Does all this mean that America must zero out its trade deficit as soon as possible? Unfortunately, the above analysis should make clear that the deficit is a chronic problem, not an acute one. It exerts a steady drag on our economic well-being, undermines our future, and we would be better off without it. But every Chicken Little who has screamed that the sky was about to fall has been embarrassed. (This has led a cynical public to conclude that no problem exists, which also is wrong.) And although failure to fix the deficit inexorably increases the ultimate risk of a financial debacle, there is no clear point predictable in advance when this will happen. We do not know exactly how much of our debt, or how many of our assets, foreign investors are prepared to hold. (They may not know either.) We only know that the one reliable way to avoid crossing that invisible line is to stop running deficits and adding to the total every year. In the meantime, our deficit inexorably depletes our future.

THE SAVINGS-GLUT EXCUSE

Based on the above realities, in which America consumes too much and saves too little, it is sometimes claimed that our trade deficit is really a savings problem in disguise. Sometimes it is admitted that America saves too little; sometimes it is claimed that the real problem is a savings glut abroad, mainly in East Asia. Either way, this implies that trade policy is irrelevant (and futile to try to change), as only changes in savings rates can alter anything. For example, the China Business Forum, an American group, claimed in a 2006 report, "The China Effect," that:

> The United States as a whole wants to borrow at a time when the rest of the world...wants to save. The result is a current account deficit in the United Sates with all countries, including China.[168]

This analysis is dubious on its face, as it implies that whether American cars and computers are junk or works of genius has no impact on our trade balance. Neither, apparently, does it matter whether foreign nations erect barriers against our exports. Nevertheless, it is stubbornly asserted in some very high places, largely because it excuses inaction.

But this analysis depends upon misunderstanding the *arithmetic* relationship between trade deficits and savings rates as a *causal* relationship. Mathematically, our savings are simply the excess of our production over our consumption—because if we don't consume what we produce, saving it is the only other thing we can do with it. (If we export it, we'll get something of equivalent value in return, which we must then also consume or save, so exporting doesn't change this equation.) And a trade deficit is simply the opposite, as if we wish to consume more than we produce, there are only two ways to get the goods: either import them, or draw down supplies saved up in the past (dissaving). As a result, trade deficits do not "cause" a low savings rate or vice-versa; they are simply the same numbers showing up on the other side of the ledger. The decision to eat one's cake does not "cause" the decision not to save one's cake; it *is* that decision. So neither our trade deficit nor our savings rate is intrinsically a lever that moves the other—or a valid excuse for the other.

Sometimes, it is even argued that foreign borrowing is good for the U.S., on the grounds that it enables us to have lower interest rates and more investment than we would otherwise have. But this argument is a baseline trick. It is indeed true that if we take our low savings rate as a given, and ask whether we would be better off with foreign-financed investment or no investment at all, then foreign-financed investment is better. But our savings rate isn't a given, it's a *choice*, which means that the real choice is between foreign- and domestically-financed investment. Once one frames the problem this way, domestically-financed investment is obviously better because then Americans, rather than foreigners, will own the investments and receive the returns they generate.

A related false analysis holds that our trade deficit is due to our trading partners' failure to run sufficiently expansive monetary policies. (This basically means their central banks haven't been printing money as fast as the Fed.) Some American officials have even verged on suggesting this is a form of unfair trade.[169] Now it is indeed true that our major trading partners have not been expanding their money supplies as fast as we have. But as we have been doing so largely in order to blow up asset bubbles, which gave us more assets to sell abroad to keep financing our deficit, it is not a policy sane rivals would imitate. We can hardly ask the diligents of the world to join us in a race of competitive decadence. If they did, the result would just be worldwide inflation.

Another dubious theory holds that America's deficit is nothing to be ashamed of because it is due to the failure of foreign nations to grow their economies as fast as ours. Thus George W. Bush's Treasury Secretary, Henry Paulson, Jr., said in 2007 that:

> We run a trade deficit because our vibrant and growing economy creates a strong demand for imports, including imports of manufac-turing inputs and capital goods as well as consumer goods—while our major trading partners do not have the same growth and/or have economies with relatively low levels of consumption.[170]

This analysis appeals to American pride because it carries the implication that we are merely victims of our own success and that our trade deficit is caused by the failure of foreign nations to be as vibrant as we are. It implies that somebody *else* ought to get his house in order. Unfortunately, it is obviously false that our deficit is caused by slow growth abroad when some of our worst deficits are with fast-growing nations like China. As for "relatively low levels of consumption" abroad causing our deficits, this is true enough, but it also implies that balancing our trade will remain impossible as long as we have major trading partners with low consumption levels, as we indeed do.

ARE FIXED EXCHANGE RATES THE SOLUTION?

The foregoing analysis gives a big clue as to why the 1945-1971 Bretton Woods system of fixed exchange rates worked so well, despite being a centrally planned system flouting the basic principle that prices (for currency, in its case) can only be efficiently set by a free market. This system generated trade deficits that were tiny by present standards, and the world economy grew faster while it was in operation, with less inequality between and within nations, than ever before or since.[171]

The key virtue of Bretton Woods, as we can now see, is that while floating exchange rates may be efficient, they are efficient at the wrong thing. They are driven by the *total* demand for a currency, that is demand to buy not only a nation's exports but also its debt and assets. As a result, demand for a nation's currency is determined not only by its export prowess, but also by its willingness to sell off assets and assume debt. But this entails treating unsustainable demand (for assets and debt) the same as sustainable demand (for exports). So floating exchange rates will *not* necessarily find the level optimal for that part of the economy devoted to present production. But this is the only part of the economy that actually *creates* wealth, as opposed to shifting it forwards and backwards in time. It is no accident that we live in an age when the financial tail often seems to be wagging the dog of the real economy! (From 1945 to 1985, the financial sector never made more than 16 percent of U.S. corporate profits, but since then, its share has steadily climbed, peaking at 41 percent in 2005.)[172]

52

Floating exchange rates famously give an economy flexibility. But this flexibility includes the ability to do the wrong things. (Nobody wants to drive over a "flexible" bridge.) Under a Bretton Woods-type system, bad economic policies that affect trade quickly run aground and produce balance-of-payments crises. Britain, for example, had such crises repeatedly during its long pre-Thatcher economic slide, in 1947, 1949, 1951, 1955, 1957, 1964, 1965, 1966, and 1967.[173] These crises force corrective action on the trade front long before serious damage, in the form of debt accumulation and asset sales, can be done. But with floating exchange rates and correspondingly free capital flows, the pressure is postponed by the cushioning effect of asset sales and debt accumulation, allowing bad policy to go on much longer. So a nation can, in effect, sell the family silver and mortgage the house to pay the gas bill, rather than be forced to ask why it is using too much gas.

Formerly, this was all well understood. As John Maynard Keynes, one of the architects of the 1944 Bretton Woods agreement, explained it, the economies of the world:

> Need a system possessed of an internal stabilizing mechanism, by which pressure is exercised on any country whose balance of payments with the rest of the world is departing from equilibrium in either direction, so as to prevent movements which must create for its neighbors an equal but opposite want of balance.[174]

The architects of Bretton Woods, traumatized by the economic chaos of the 1930s and worried about the Soviet threat, wanted a system that would avoid outright socialist central planning but still prevent financial crises. They understood that eliminating such crises entirely was utopian, so they settled for the next best thing: *to keep crises small.* Keynes himself actually wanted something even more radical: a system of fixed exchange rates mediated by an international reserve currency called the "bancor" and managed by an institution called the Clearing Union. The IMF is a vestige of this idea, but the world got the dollar as its reserve currency instead.

Unfortunately, the dollar, like all national currencies, is a sovereign political artifact, exposed to all the vagaries of American politics. The Bretton Woods system eventually broke down when Lyndon Johnson inflated the dollar to pay for the Great Society and the Vietnam War at the same time without raising taxes.[175] Initially, this "exported inflation," in the words of France's annoyed president Charles De Gaulle, as other currencies were dragged along with the dollar by their fixed parities. It eventually collapsed the system entirely as nations tried to swap their shriveling dollars for gold, by which the dollar was backed and of which we had a finite supply. The whole system ended in 1971 when President Nixon was more or less forced to abandon it.[176] Exchange rates have floated ever since.

The results have not been happy. In essence, the present system *gives nations enough rope to hang themselves with*: it lets them get into worse trouble, and then has no choice but to be more intrusive in getting them out. This doesn't produce greater economic stability (let alone more growth), but it does produce some handy opportunities for coercively imposing aggressively free-market economic policies on otherwise unwilling nations, especially in the Third World. Institutions such as the World Bank have opportunistically taken advantage of such crises to impose free market "reforms" they could not otherwise achieve.[177] For example, according to Dani Rodrik of Harvard, "no significant cases of trade reform in a developing country in the 1980s took place outside the context of a serious economic crisis."[178] Translation: *now that you're broke, privatize all those state-owned assets and stop subsidizing food for the poor, or you don't get your emergency loans.*

So perhaps the greatest advantage of fixed exchange rates is that, of all the policies available to rebalance the world's trade imbalances, they are actually among the *least* intrusive. Changing a society's time discount on consumption is very hard to do: there is no lever directly attached to this variable, and most peacetime attempts to change it in the Western world have failed. Only the authoritarian technocrats of East Asia have pulled it off, by heavy-handed measures ranging from forced savings plans (Singapore) to tight limits on consumer credit (China) to zoning that makes it hard to build large houses (Japan).[179] These are policies no Western electorate would tolerate and that most Third World governments don't have the administrative competence to pull off.

A fixed exchange rate system, on the other hand, operates at the perimeter of an economy, leaving most of its internal mechanisms untouched. It violates few economic liberties. But even though it leaves flows of goods untouched, regulating the countervailing financial flows that take place when goods are paid for imposes a balance just as effectively. If the free market won't produce the best results on its own in trade and therefore must be regulated *somewhere*, it might as well be here. And if the free market is so distorted by taxes and subsidies that these distortions need to be rectified, this would be a good place to do it. Fixed exchange rates are a complex issue, but they ought at least to be on the table as part of a solution to the United States' (and the world's) trade problems.

3

Trade Solutions That Won't Work

AMERICANS IN RECENT DECADES have not, of course, been entirely unaware that we have a trade problem. This has drawn into public debate a long list of proposed solutions. Unfortunately, many will not work, some are based on analytical confusions, and a few are outright nonsense. If we are to understand the true scope of our problem and frame solutions that will work, these false hopes must be debunked forthwith.

For example, since the early 1990s it has been repeatedly suggested that the U.S. is on the verge of an export boom that will erase our trade deficit and produce a surge of high-paying jobs. (Bill Clinton was fond of this idea[180] and Barack Obama proposed in 2010 that America double its exports in five years.) The possibility looks tantalizing when we observe that America's exports have indeed been growing rapidly—just not as rapidly as our imports. (Between 1992 and 2010, our exports more than doubled, from $892 billion to $1,834 billion.)[181] This seems to imply that we are not uncompetitive in world markets after all, and that if only our export growth would climb just a few points higher, the whole problem would go away.

Unfortunately, our deficit is now so large that our exports would have to outgrow our imports by two percent a year *for over a decade* just to eliminate the deficit—let alone run the surplus we need to start digging ourselves out from under our now-massive foreign liabilities.[182] This doesn't sound like much, but it is, in fact, a very strong export performance for a developed country, and unlikely in the present international economic environment, where every other nation is also trying to expand its exports.

Much of our recent export growth has been hollow anyway, consisting largely in raw materials and intermediate goods destined to be manufactured into articles imported back into the U.S. For example, our gross (i.e., not net of imports) exports to Mexico have been booming to feed the *maquiladora* plants of American companies along the border.[183] But this is obviously a losing race, as the value of a product's inputs can never exceed the value of a finished product sold at a profit.

Not only is America's trade deficit the world's largest, but our *ratio* between imports and exports (1.28 to 1 in 2010) is one of the world's most unbalanced.[184] Given that our imports are now 17 percent of GDP and our entire manufacturing sector only 11.5 percent,[185] we could quite literally export our entire manufacturing output and still not balance our trade. Import-driven deindustrialization has so badly warped the structure of our economy that we no longer have the productive capacity to balance our trade by exporting more goods, even if foreign nations wanted and allowed this (they don't).[186] So the solution will have to come from import contraction, one way or another.

Exporting services won't balance our trade either, as our surplus in services isn't remotely big enough, compared to our deficit in goods (in 2010, $148 billion vs. $652 billion).[187]

Neither will agricultural exports balance our trade (a *prima facie* bizarre idea for a developed nation). Our 2010 surplus in agriculture was only $28 billion—about *one eighteenth* the size of our overall deficit. 2010 was also an exceptionally good year for agricultural exports; our average annual agricultural surplus from 2000 to 2010 was a mere $15 billion.[188]

PRODUCTIVITY GROWTH WON'T SAVE US

It is sometimes suggested that America merely needs to regain export competitiveness through productivity growth. Comforting statistics, showing our productivity still comfortably above the nations we compete with, are often paraded in support of this idea. Unfortunately, those figures on the productivity of Chinese, Mexican, and Indian workers concern *average* productivity in these nations. They do not concern productivity in their export industries, the only industries which compete with our own. These nations are held to low overall productivity by the fact that hundreds of millions of their workers are still peasant farmers. But American electronics workers compete with Chinese electronics workers, not Chinese peasants.

It is narrowly true that if foreign productivity is as low as foreign wages—an easy claim to make with aggressively free-market theory and cherry-picked statistics—then low foreign wages won't threaten American workers. But a problem emerges when low foreign wages are *not* balanced by low productivity. It is the combination of Third World wages with First World productivity, thanks largely to the ability of multinational corporations to spread their technology around, that has considerably weakened the traditional correlation of low wages with low productivity.[189] For example, it takes an average of 3.3 man-hours to produce a ton of steel in the U.S. and 11.8 man-hours in China—a ratio of nearly four to one.[190] But the wage gap between the U.S. and China is considerably more than that.[191]

In any case, productivity is not in itself a guarantee of high wages. U.S. manufacturing productivity actually doubled in the two decades from 1987 to 2008,[192] but inflation-adjusted manufacturing wages rose only 11 percent.[193] From roughly 1947 to 1973, productivity and wage growth were fairly closely coupled in the U.S., but since then, American workers have been running ever faster simply to stay in place.[194] Wage-productivity decoupling has been even starker in some foreign countries: in Mexico, for example, productivity rose 40 percent from 1980 to 1994, but following the peso devaluation of 1994, real wages were *down* 40 percent.[195]

WE CAN'T JUST COMPENSATE THE LOSERS

It is sometimes argued that although free trade has some victims, its benefits exceed its costs, so it is possible for its winners to compensate its losers out of their gains, everyone thereby coming out ahead in the end. (This is, in fact, the usual fallback position of mainstream economists once they admit that free trade has drawbacks.) It is sometimes even mischievously argued that if such compensation *doesn't* happen, any problems are due to society's failure to arrange it, and are therefore not the fault of free trade per se. In theory, this might be true (if the rest of free trade economics is valid), but it also means that a bureaucratic deus ex machina is required to make free trade work *as even its supporters admit that it should.* So free trade turns out to be laissez faire on life support from big government. In any case, such compensation rarely occurs, because free trade's winners don't have to pay off its losers. They pay off their congressmen instead—to vote for more free trade agreements.

Compensating free trade's victims is the rationale for the U.S. Government's Trade Adjustment Assistance (TAA) program, which has provided supplemental unemployment benefits, training subsidies, and relocation assistance since 1974. But this program is small, compared to the damage wrought by free trade: under a billion dollars a year. Few workers have actually used it, and the concept suffers from intrinsic problems. For a start, it is often impossible to identify who has lost a job due to free trade, as changing technology and consumer tastes also cost jobs (and legitimately). Furthermore, free trade does not necessarily work its harm by reducing the *quantity* of jobs: it can reduce their quality, that is their wages and benefits, instead. And when free trade drives down wages, it can do so industry-wide, region-wide, or even nationwide, so its victims are impossible to pinpoint. TAA has tended to function simply as supplemental unemployment insurance while people wait to get their old jobs back, not as a means of helping people transition to new jobs.[196] This is its official purpose, based on the (mistaken) idea that the harm done by free trade consists entirely in transition costs.

EDUCATION WON'T SAVE US

One commonly suggested solution to America's trade problems is better education. While this would obviously make America *more* competitive, that it would be enough is unlikely, if by "enough" we mean able to maintain wage levels in the face of foreign competition. For a start, our rivals are well aware of the value of education, so it can't be a unique source of advantage for us. And unfortunately, the U.S. is simply no longer formidable from an educational point-of-view. Roughly the top third of our population enjoys the benefits of a world-class college and university system, plus other forms of training such as the military and the more serious trade schools. But the rest of our population is actually worse educated, on average, than their opposite numbers in major competing nations.

Thanks mainly to the high school movement of the early 20th century, the U.S. once led the world in high school completion, the most readily comparable international measure of education. But we have been slipping behind for decades. This is clear from the fact that while we still lead among 55-to-64-year-olds (who were schooled over 40 years ago), we rank only 11th among 25-to-34-year-olds.[197] (South Korea is first.) Not only is our college graduation rate of 34 percent behind 15 other nations, but it does not even reach the *average* for developed countries.[198] Studies designed to measure specific skill sets tell an even direr story. According to the 2006 Program for International Student Assessment, American 15-year-olds were outmatched in math and science by students from 22 other nations.[199] The very bottom of our population is more alarming still: one 2003 study reported that a third of the adults in Los Angeles County were functionally illiterate.[200]

Furthermore, it is a testable hypothesis whether education on its own can protect wages, and the evidence is to the contrary. For one thing, a college degree is no longer the ticket it once was: workers between 25 and 34 with only a BA actually saw their real earnings *drop* 11 percent between 2000 and 2008.[201] And, as David Howell of the New School for Social Research has written after looking at this problem on an industry basis, "Higher skills have simply not led to higher wages. In industry after industry, average educational attainment rose while wages fell."[202] This should be no surprise, as merely shoveling education into workers' heads obviously will not save them, or the industries they work in, if these industries are bleeding market share and revenue due to imports. Neither can people be expected to devote time and money to acquiring more education (or be able to afford it) if there are no jobs for them at the end. Who feels like pursuing advanced training in automotive engineering today? The weak education of American workers is thus a self-reinforcing problem: educated workers not only support, but require, strong industries.

Looking to education as a magic bullet can also easily slide into a de facto plan to write off the uneducated and uneducable; some remarks by Rep. Marcy Kaptur (D-OH) make this point well:

> Putting money into research is this Holy Grail for people here who are all college educated when the majority of the country is not, and who put themselves on this elevated plane thinking they know. I remember [Clinton Labor Secretary] Robert Reich saying, 'Here's what America has to do, Marcy: see this salt shaker?' 'Yeah?'

'America's going to do the design,' he said. 'It'll be made else-where, but we'll do the design.' I thought, 'Wouldn't that be an answer from a professor?' I want both! I want engineering and pro-duction because I know the people in my district who used to make goods but don't anymore, and they have a right to make what they end up buying.[203]

Not everyone is going to be able to get a master's degree in nanotech-nology.

Superior technological prowess is unlikely to save America, anyway, for the simple reason that we increasingly no longer possess it. Despite our image of ourselves as a technology leader, we no longer rank all that high by a lot of key metrics. For example, the U.S. today is 15th among nations in per capita broadband Internet penetration—which will be a serious limitation on developing the next generation of Internet applications.[204] Our share of world patents is dropping fast,[205] and federal funding for basic science is not keeping pace with rising costs, so it is declining in real terms.[206] The entire annual budget of the National Science Foundation equals less than four days of our military spending.[207]

Meanwhile, our competitors are very deliberately catching up. Accord-ing to the Organization for Economic Cooperation and Development (OECD), the umbrella group for developed economies, China was number three in the world for spending on research and development by 2005 and is still accelerating.[208] It is no accident that, according to the respected Georgia Tech Technology Index, it has now surpassed the U.S. in high-tech competitiveness, and if the 27 nations of the European Union are counted as one, the EU has, too.[209]

CREATIVITY AND FREEDOM WON'T SAVE US

Another frequently suggested solution to our trade problems is superior creativity, based on the idea that the U.S. is an exceptionally creative soci-ety. America is often contrasted with China, and we are told that China's political system prevents it from allowing its people sufficient *freedom* to be creative. This is a seductive idea because it flatters American values, everybody loves creativity, and creativity is a sufficiently vague concept that one can ascribe to it economic effects of any size one likes.

Unfortunately, many of America's serious competitors are simply not authoritarian societies in the first place. China, yes, but India? India is a democracy. So is Japan. So are our European competitors. So are many of the others.

And while it might be nice to believe that freedom is a requirement for economic success, it is simply not observably true that authoritarian societies such as China are economically foundering.[210] However disappointing to deeply held American values this fact may be, China's authoritarianism has almost certainly *helped* its growth, by enabling things like the suppressed consumption policy that gives it a 50 percent savings rate and correspondingly high investment levels.[211] Censorship of the Internet isn't strangling e-commerce there, even if it is hard to Google the Tiananmen massacre from a Chinese engineering school. Foreign businesses often like the crisp decision-making, obedient labor, and absence of democratic interference; computer chip maker Intel recently decided to build its new Asian plant in China, rather than India, for these reasons. In the words of Intel's chairman, Craig Barrett:

> India has the same issues as the United States. It is a democratic government. The decisions are slower to be made. You have to listen to all the constituencies. In China, they are much more direct... In China, it is *a central planning form of capitalism*...We were in serious discussion for chip manufacturing in India, but the government was a bit slow on semiconductor manufacturing proposals.[212] (Emphasis added.)

The results speak for themselves: India had a higher per capita GDP than China as recently as 1987 but today, China's is over three times as high and its lead is still growing.[213]

Free trade isn't going to democratize China either, a myth that has been promoted for decades to justify American trade concessions to that country. Beijing is well aware of the threat it faces and has a sophisticated and ruthless strategy combining ancient Confucian cynicism about human nature with the "global best practices" of modern authoritarianism.[214] The commercial advantages of this regime are now filling the pockets of everyone in China with the wits to turn a profit, so this authoritarianism now has a huge constituency outside the government itself.

Another version of the "freedom will save us" argument attacks cultural rather than political authoritarianism, usually taking Japan as its foil.

Now compared to the U.S., Japan's culture is indeed rather closed and insular. It may fairly be described as an ethnocentric, patriarchal, and conformist society, sometimes reminding observers of America in the 1950s. Yet its record of economic innovation has been strong. The Walkman was not created by some free spirit in a garage in Silicon Valley, but by Kozo Ohsone, manager of the tape recorder division at Sony.[215] And innovations, such as commercially viable hybrid cars and flat panel TV, have continued to flow in the decades since then. Japan's corporate conformists are today generating more high-tech initial public offerings than the U.S.[216] So whatever perfectly valid reasons one might have for objecting to that kind of culture, lack of economic creativity is not one.[217]

And if anyone wants to imagine an American advantage due to cultural diversity, Europe, with its 23 national languages and 2,500 years of high culture, has us beat hands down. (So does India, by that standard.)

Even if we forget all the above and assume that America does have a fundamental advantage in creativity, most companies, most jobs, and most people are not creative. It's easy to be dazzled by fascinating stories about entrepreneurs into forgetting that *most people are not entrepreneurs.* And most people won't ever be, simply because one can't have entrepreneurs without having a far larger number of people working for them. Even most jobs at genuinely creative companies like Apple Computer are not creative in any serious sense.

POSTINDUSTRIALISM WON'T SAVE US

Postindustrialism is sometimes suggested as a solution to our trade problems (or as a reason to believe they are not problems in the first place). Its most succinct formulation is this:

Manufacturing is old hat and America is moving on to better things.

The postindustrial economy is considerably less attractive today than it was only a few years ago, thanks largely to India's success in computer software and business process offshoring. This discredited the (rather odd) idea that our competitors were only going to compete in manufacturing. But one still hears about postindustrialism now and then, and the idea played a large role during the 1980s and 1990s in getting Americans to accept de-industrialization. It has been promoted by writers as varied as futurist Alvin Toffler, capitalist romantic George Gilder, techno-libertarian Virginia Postrel, and futurist John Naisbitt.[218] Newt Gingrich seized upon it as the supposed economic basis of his Republican Revolution of 1994.[219]

Unfortunately, the core ideas of postindustrialism don't stand up well to empirical evidence. Above all, a declining share of manufacturing in GDP is *not* an automatic correlate of economic progress. Between 1947 and 1966—a period of rapidly advancing technology and rising prosperity—manufacturing actually went *up* slightly as a share of our GDP.[220] Manufacturing's share of GDP has indeed fallen in recent years, with services expanding to fill the gap. But this merely reflects the fact that inflation has been lower in manufacturing than in services, due to higher productivity growth in manufacturing. (This is itself a clue that manufacturing might have its advantages!) If one adjusts for the inflation differential, manufacturing's share has actually been quite stable for the last 30 years or so, and only began to decline around 2000.[221] This is far too late for transition to a postindustrial economy to explain it, but entirely in line with our burgeoning trade deficit in manufactured goods. And if one looks at the trend not in America's *production* of manufactured goods, but in our *consumption*, there has been no decline at all.[222] The gap between production and consumption is (as explained in the previous chapter) just our trade deficit. So using postindustrialism to justify our trade deficit in manufactures just presupposes what it is trying to prove.

Nevertheless, postindustrialism remains popular in some very important circles. In the 2006 words of the prestigious and quasi-official Council on Competitiveness, a group of American business, labor, academic and government leaders:

> Services are where the high value is today, not in manufacturing. Manufacturing stuff per se is relatively low value. That is why it is being done in China or Thailand. It's the service functions of manufacturing that are where the high value is today, and that is what America can excel in.[223]

Unfortunately, the above paragraph is simply not true, and manufacturing is not an obsolescent sector of the economy. Low grade "screwdriver plant" final assembly manufacturing is indeed primitive, and can increasingly be done anywhere in the world, making it an intrinsically low-wage activity. But the manufacturing of sophisticated high-tech products is a different matter and remains concentrated in advanced industrial nations. The "Made in China" stamped on the outer casing of fax machines, cellular phones, and other high-tech products often just means that final "kit" assembly took place there.[224] The key internal components, which make up a large percentage of the finished product's cost, are frequently still made in high-wage nations like Japan. In the case of fax machines, this is the electro-optical read-write head. In the case of printers, it is the print engine. In the case of watches, it is the movement. Apple's iPod, for example, is assembled in China, but its display module is made in Japan, its video processor chip in Taiwan or Singapore, its memory chip in South Korea, and its central processing unit in the U.S. or Taiwan—all nations whose average incomes are multiples of China's.[225]

Even more important than the value of these components is their value per man-hour of labor required to make them, as this is the ultimate basis of high wages. For example, of the 28,556 jobs created by the iPod outside retailing and distribution, 19,190 were production jobs, of which China captured the most (11,715). But 9,366 were professional jobs, of which high-wage Japan (with 1,140) and the U.S. (with 6,101) captured the lion's share.[226] For products whose production cost mainly consists of technology and capital, not low-skilled labor, low-wage nations have no advantage, as technology and capital are not cheaper there.

The table below gives a breakdown of the cost structure of the average U.S. manufacturer:

Raw Materials	45.98 %
Labor	21.00 %
Advertising & Marketing	9.00 %
Research & Development	8.50 %
Interest	3.44 %
Transportation	2.90 %
Health & Safety	1.60 %
Energy	1.53 %
Environmental Protection	1.48 %
Land & Rent	1.46 %
Utilities	1.16 %
Software	0.80 %

Source: Peter Navarro, "Report of The China Price Project," Merage School of Business, University of California at Irvine, July 2006, p.5.

It has been estimated that direct labor is under 20 percent of production cost for half of U.S. manufacturers.[227] The average cost disadvantage of U.S. manufacturers versus their opposite numbers in low-wage nations is, in fact, estimated to be only 17 percent, a difference obviously often within the reach of smart strategies.[228] This is why manufacturing still thrives in some other high-wage nations.[229] It is why America *could* be successfully defending blue-collar wages when we are failing and why some other developed nations are succeeding at this better than we are.

About the only thing postindustrialism gets right is that selling a product with a high value per embodied man-hour almost always means selling embodied know-how. But know-how must usually be embodied in some physical package before reaching the consumer, and manufactured goods are actually a rather good package for embodying it in. Exporting disembodied know-how like design services is definitely an inferior proposition, as indicated by the fact that since 2004, America's deficit in high technology goods has exceeded our surplus in intellectual property, royalties, licenses, and fees.[230]

That some individual companies like Apple make a success out of keeping design functions at home and offshoring the manufacturing does not make this a viable strategy for the economy as a whole. Apple is a unique company; that is why it succeeds. And even fabled Apple is not quite the success story one might hope for, from a trade point-of-view. Due to its foreign components and assembly, every $300 iPod sold in the U.S. adds another $140 to our deficit with China.[231] If sophisticated American design must be embodied in imported goods in order to be sold, it will not help our trade situation.

Meanwhile, other companies are shutting their U.S. design centers and moving them closer to actual production and the know-how that accumulates where it takes place. As Douglas Bartlett, chairman of the printed circuit board manufacturer Bartlett manufacturing in Cary, Illinois, puts it:

> Anyone who knows anything about real-world manufacturing knows that the factory floor and the lab form a continuous feedback loop. Unfortunately, virtually none of our trade and economic policymakers know anything about real-world manufacturing.[232]

So the erosion continues, industry by industry. For example, in March 2007, Chrysler closed its Pacifica Advanced Product Design Center in Southern California, following the closure of nearby centers owned by Ital-design, American Specialty Cars, Porsche, Nissan, and Volvo.[233] Of GM's 11 design centers, only three are still in the U.S.[234] In the words of Eric Noble of The Car Lab, an automotive consulting company, "Advanced studios want to be where the new frontier is. So in China, studios are popping up like rabbits."[235] This trend bodes extremely ill for the future; as Stephen Cohen and John Zysman explain in their book *Manufacturing Matters*:

America must control the production of those high-tech products it invents and designs—and it must do so in a direct and hands-on way...First, production is where the lion's share of the value added is realized...This is where the returns needed to finance the next round of research and development are generated. Second and most important, unless [research and development] is tightly tied to manufacturing of the product...R&D will fall behind the cutting edge of incremental innovation...High tech gravitates to the state-of-the-art producers.[236]

Neither are individual technological or entrepreneurial genius going to save America, no matter how impressive they look on the cover of glossy magazines. Richard Florida and Martin Kenny have documented the limited (albeit real) value of stand-alone inventive genius in their book *The Breakthrough Illusion*.[237] Despite the impressive U.S. record in pure innovation, innovations actually fail to translate into mass production (and thus high employment) industries here as well as they do in Japan and elsewhere. The fragmentation of America's high-tech research into thousands of small companies in Silicon Valley and elsewhere may be optimal for innovation itself, but it is *not* optimal for mass commercialization.[238] Indeed, it has the unfortunate side effect of making it exceptionally easy for foreign companies to buy up American innovations à la carte. Among other things, this has helped make Japanese, rather than American, companies the ultimate commercial beneficiaries of much recent Pentagon-funded research.

A small American company named Ampex in Redwood City, California, encapsulates everything that is wrong with postindustrialism. This leading audio tape firm invented the video cassette recorder in 1970 but bungled the transition to mass production and ended up licensing the technology to the Japanese.[239] It collected millions in royalties all through the 1980s and 1990s and employed a few hundred people. Its licensee companies collected *tens of billions* in sales and employed *hundreds of thousands* of people.

So when someone like self-described "radical free trader" Thomas Friedman writes that "there may be a limit to the number of good factory jobs in the world, *but there is no limit to the number of good idea-generated jobs in the world*,"[240] (emphasis in original) this is simply false.[241] There is nothing about the fact that ideas are abstract and the products of factories concrete that causes there to be an infinite demand for ideas. The limit on the number of idea-generated jobs is set by the amount of money people are willing to *pay for* ideas (either in their pure form or embodied in goods) because this ultimately pays the salaries of idea-generated jobs.

The final killer of the postindustrial dream, of course, is offshoring, as this means that even if capturing primarily service industry jobs were a desirable strategy, America can't reliably capture and hold these jobs anyway. The caliber of jobs being offshored—which started with fairly mundane jobs such as call centers—is relentlessly rising. According to a 2007 study by Duke University's Fuqua School of Business and the consulting firm Booz Allen Hamilton:

> Relocating core business functions such as product design, engineering and R&D represents a new and growing trend. Although labor arbitrage strategies continue to be key drivers of offshoring, sourcing and accessing talent is the primary driver of next-generation offshoring...Until recently, offshoring was almost entirely associated with locating and setting up IT services, call centers and other business processes in lower-cost countries. But IT outsourcing is reaching maturity and now the growth is centered around product and process innovation.[242]

Among sophisticated business functions, product development, including software development, is now the second-largest corporate function being offshored. Offshoring of sophisticated white-collar tasks such as finance, accounting, sales, and personnel management is growing at 35 percent per year.[243] Meanwhile, despite a few individual companies bringing offshored call centers back home, offshoring of call centers and help desks continues to grow at a double-digit pace.[244]

It is no accident that, as noted in the Foreword, some of America's corporate elite are now starting to question postindustrialism, about which they were utterly gung-ho only a few years ago. In the February 2009 words of General Electric's chairman, Jeffrey Immelt:

> I believe that a popular, 30-year notion that the U.S. can evolve from being a technology and manufacturing leader to a service leader is just wrong. In the end, this philosophy transformed the financial services industry from one that supported commerce to a complex trading market that operated outside the economy. Real engineering was traded for financial engineering.[245]

Immelt has since argued that the U.S. should aim for manufacturing jobs to comprise at least 20 percent of all jobs—roughly double their current percentage.[246] Only a few years ago, this idea would have been dismissed as an ignorant and reactionary piece of central planning, especially if it had not been proposed by a respected Fortune 500 CEO.

MANUFACTURING AMERICA'S DECLINE

The claims of an American manufacturing revival that surface now and again are false. They are based on anecdotes, massaged figures, and airbrushing out the dependence of revived companies upon imported components. For example, the much-heralded revival of the American TV industry based on digital high-definition television (HDTV) never actually happened, and Japanese manufacturers still dominate the industry today.[247]

Even the vaunted Boeing aircraft company, the single largest U.S. manufacturing exporter, has been relentlessly hollowing itself out of real manufacturing for decades.[248] Boeing and similar companies call this "systems integration." This sounds sophisticated, but doesn't change the reality that Boeing has been morphing into a "Lego brick" assembler of European, Japanese, and increasingly Chinese components.[249] For example, the entire composite wing—master key to aircraft design because the wing determines the weight the rest of the plane can carry—for the Boeing 787 is built in Japan.[250] (By contrast, Boeing's European Airbus competitor by deliberate policy outsources no more than 35 percent of its work.)[251]

As also noted in the Foreword, Boeing has realized it got burned by this strategy[252] and is trying to bring more manufacturing back inside the company and back to the U.S. So much for inevitable globalization. But it remains to be seen whether this emerging countertrend can reach fruition on its own, or whether it is a cry of help from a corporate America that has so badly damaged its competitive position with its hollow-corporation strategy that it will need the help of tariff walls to recover. This is especially likely outside industries, like aircraft, in which America is still relatively strong.

Every few years there emerges an entire new industry, like hybrid cars, which has no strong American players—"strong" meaning not dependent on repackaging imported key components or licensing foreign technology.[253] And because America's share of world production in "sunrise" industries continues to drop, this problem is on track to get worse, not better. For example, the U.S. invented photovoltaic cells, and was number one in their production as recently as 1998, but has now dropped to fifth behind Japan, China, Germany, and Taiwan.[254] Of the world's 10 largest wind turbine makers, only one, General Electric, is American.[255] Over time, the industries of the future inexorably become the industries of the present, so this is a formula for automatic economic decline.

The U.S. has been running a deficit in high technology since 2002.[256] We even run a deficit in high technology with China,[257] a nation that is supposedly specializing in low-end manufacturing so we can specialize in the high end. But China is rapidly climbing the industrial food chain. In 2010, China sold the U.S. $127 billion in electronics, $32 billion in apparel, and less than $18 billion of that stereotypical article of "Chinese junk," toys. [258] As a result, whereas in 1989 only 30 percent of America's imports from China competed with high-wage industries in the U.S., by 1999 that percentage had reached 50 percent, and has risen further since then.[259] Chinese imports now constitute 83 percent of our non-oil trade deficit [260] and *over 100 percent* of our deficit in technology (i.e., we run a surplus against the rest of the world).[261]

America's areas of industrial advantage, measured by what we are a net exporter of, are few and shrinking: only aircraft, aircraft parts, weapons, and specialized machine tools.[262] In 2007, the nation that put a man on the moon was *a net importer of spacecraft*.[263] Given that many of these weapons and machine tools are aviation-related, this means that essentially *all* our net manufacturing exports are a legacy effect of 60 years of Pentagon industrial policy. (We are nonetheless told by free-market ideologues that industrial policy can never work; more on that in Chapter Nine.)

Even our economic rivals are beginning to worry about our health. Akio Morita, the late chairman of Sony, once accused the U.S. of "abandoning its status as an industrial power."[264] Our rivals have problems of their own, of course, but suffer far less from deindustrialization than we do. Both Japan and Germany have booming manufacturing exports. (Germany was the world's number one exporter as late as 2008.)[265] Both employ a larger percentage of their workforce in manufacturing. Both are high-wage democracies, not sweatshop dictatorships, and have less unemployment than we do. What is their secret? To some extent, simply more manufacturing-oriented business cultures. Also financial systems more oriented to the long term by their greater use of bank debt rather than stock market equity, combined with devices like cross-shareholdings to repel short-term speculators.[266] And more state investment in worker training.[267]

But also fundamental are Japan's and the EU's non-tariff trade barriers, which have helped preserve their economies against being hollowed out of manufacturing. Many of these barriers are not actual laws, and thus lurk below the surface to casual examination. For example, in the words of William Greider of the liberal magazine *The Nation*:

> In the European Union, supposedly liberalized by unifying fifteen national markets, the countries had more than seven hundred national restrictions on import quantities, many of which were converted to so-called voluntary restraints. The UK's Society of Motor Manufacturers and Traders maintained a long-standing 'gentlemen's agreement' with the Japanese Automobile Manufacturers Association that effectively limited Japanese cars to 11 percent of the British market. France and Italy had tougher restrictions. The EU periodically proclaimed its intention to eliminate such informal barriers but, meanwhile, it was tightening them. During the recessionary conditions in late 1993, Japanese auto imports to Europe were arbitrarily reduced by 18 percent.[268]

Europe has other tricks up its sleeve, such as using discretionary enforcement of antidumping laws to pressure foreign companies into locating technology-intensive functions in Europe.[269] And the EU has an institutional bias towards reciprocal market-opening agreements with foreign nations.[270] This all suggests that overt or covert protectionism is a necessary part of any solution.

CURRENCY REVALUATION WON'T SAVE US

It is sometimes suggested that our trade problems will go away on their own once currency values adjust. Bottom line? *A declining dollar will eventually solve everything.* But even if we assume currencies *will* eventually adjust, there are still serious problems with just letting the dollar slide until our trade balances.

For one thing, our trade might balance only after the dollar has declined so much that America's per capita GDP is lower, at prevailing exchange rates, than Portugal's.[271] A 50 percent decline in the dollar from early-2011 levels would bring us to this level.[272] And how big a decline would be needed to balance our trade nobody really knows, especially as we cannot predict how aggressively our trading partners will try to employ subsidies, tariffs, and nontariff barriers to protect their trade surpluses.

Dollar decline will write down the value of wealth that Americans have toiled for decades to acquire. Ordinary Americans may not care about the internationally denominated value of their money per se, but they will experience dollar decline as a wave of inflation in the price of imported goods. Everything from blue jeans to home heating oil will go up, with a ripple effect on the prices of domestically produced goods.[273]

A declining dollar may even *worsen* our trade deficit in the short run, as it will increase the dollar price of many articles we no longer have any choice but to import, foreign competition having wiped out all domestic suppliers of items as prosaic as fabric suitcases and as sophisticated as the epoxy cresol novolac resins used in computer chips.[274] (Of the billion or so cellular phones made worldwide in 2008, not one was made in the U.S.) Ominously, the specialized skills base in the U.S. has been so depleted in some industries that even when corporations do want to move production back, they cannot do so at feasible cost.

Another problem with relying on dollar decline to square our books is that this won't just make American exports more attractive. It will also make foreign purchases of American assets—everything from Miami apartments to corporate takeovers—more attractive, too. As a result, it may just stimulate asset purchases if not combined with policies designed to promote the export of actual goods.

A spate of corporate acquisitions by Japanese companies was, in fact, one of the major unintended consequences of a previous currency-rebalancing effort: the 1985 Plaza Accord to increase the value of the Japanese Yen, which carries important lessons for today. Combined with some stimulation of Japan's then-recessionary economy, it was supposed to produce a surge in Japanese demand for American exports and rectify our deficit with Japan, then the crux of our trade problems. For a few years, it appeared to work: the dollar fell by half against the yen by 1988 and after a lag, our deficit with Japan fell by roughly half, too, bottoming out in the recession year of 1991.[275] This was enough for political agitation against Japan to go off the boil, and Congress and the public seemed to lose interest in the Japanese threat. But only a few years later, things returned to business as usual, and Japan's trade surpluses reattained their former size. Japan's surplus against the U.S. in 1985 was $46.2 billion, but by 1993 it had reached $59.4 billion.[276] (It was $74.1 billion in 2008 before dipping with recession.)[277]

Relying on currency revaluation to rebalance our trade also assumes that the economies of foreign nations are not rigged to reject our exports *regardless* of their price in foreign currency.[278] Many nations play this game to some extent: the most sophisticated player is probably still Japan, about which the distinguished former trade diplomat Clyde Prestowitz has written:

> If the administration listed the structural barriers of Japan—such as *keiretsu* [conglomerates], tied distribution, relationship-based business dealings, and industrial policy—it had described in its earlier report, it would, in effect, be taking on the essence of Japanese economic organization.[279]

We cannot expect foreign nations to redesign their entire economies just to pull in more imports from the U.S.[280]

In any case, the killer argument against balancing our trade by just letting the dollar fall comes down to a single word: *oil*. If the dollar has to fall by half to do this, this means that the price of oil must double in dollar terms. Even if oil remains denominated in dollars (it is already de facto partly priced in euros) a declining dollar will drive its price up. The U.S., with its entrenched suburban land use patterns and two generations of underinvestment in mass transit, is exceptionally ill-equipped to adapt, compared to our competitors.

THERE IS NO FREE MARKET IN CURRENCIES

There is an even more fundamental problem with just waiting for the free market to fix currency values: in reality, there is no free market in currencies. The advantages to be gained by manipulating a nation's currency are simply too large for governments to resist the temptation. For example, according to the Automotive Trade Policy Council, Japan's currency manipulation gives its exporters a per-car advantage averaging $4,000 and reaching up to $10,000 on high-end vehicles like the Infiniti.[281]

China, currently the most notorious offender, manipulates the exchange rate between its yuan and the dollar mainly by preventing its exporters from using the dollars they earn as they wish.[282] Instead, they are required to swap them for domestic currency at China's central bank, which then "sterilizes" them by spending them on U.S. Treasury securities (and increasingly other, higher-yielding, investments), rather than U.S. goods. As a result, the price of dollars is propped up by a demand for dollars which does not involve buying any American exports. The amounts involved are astronomical: as of 2010, China's accumulated dollar holdings amounted to $1.6 trillion, equal to nearly a third of China's GDP.[283] The China Currency Coalition, a Washington lobby group, estimated in 2005 that the yuan was undervalued by 40 percent;[284] past scholarly estimates have ranged from 10 to 75 percent.[285]

Forcing China to stop manipulating its currency is sometimes suggested as a solution.[286] The most recent effort in this direction was the Currency Reform for Fair Trade Act, which passed the House of Representatives in September 2010 with the support of 249 Democrats (out of 255 voting) and 99 Republicans (out of 173).[287] This bill, probably doomed in the Republican Congress of 2011-2013, would have enabled U.S. companies to petition the Commerce Department for higher duties on imports from nations with manipulated currencies.

But this effort, though well-intentioned, is misguided. Above all, China's currency is manipulated relative to our own only *because we permit it*, as there is no law requiring us to sell China our bonds and other assets. We can, in fact, end this manipulation at will. All we would need to do is bar China's purchases or tax them to death. This is roughly what the Swiss did in 1972, when economic troubles elsewhere in the world generated an excessive flow of money seeking refuge in Swiss franc-denominated assets. This drove up the value of the franc and threatened to make Swiss manufacturing internationally uncompetitive. To prevent this, the Swiss government imposed a number of measures to dampen foreign investment demand for francs, including a ban on the sale of franc-denominated bonds, securities, and real estate to foreigners.[288] Problem solved.

But if China's currency manipulation is so harmful and easy to stop, why haven't we already done something about it? Mainly because if China ever did stop bingeing on American debt and assets, this would entail it ceasing to ship hundreds of billions of dollars per year of (quite cheap, as it mostly gets the low interest rate paid on government bonds) capital to the U.S. If we didn't raise our abysmal savings rate to take up the slack, this would sharply raise interest rates, simply by the operation of supply and demand for capital. So it is *our own inability to raise our savings rate* that is the binding constraint here, not anything China does or does not do. We should indeed end China's currency manipulation, but this is something we must do for ourselves, not twist China's arm to do. Ironically, China is probably doing us a favor by not giving in to our pressure until we are ready to handle the consequences.

There is an even more fundamental question here. Why treat floating exchange rates as an ideal in the first place? The tacit presumption is built into the debate over exchange-rate manipulation that the alternative is floating rates. (The idea that the underlying problem is interference with the free market appeals mightily to people ideologically committed to free markets.) But, to be quite honest, what we really want isn't floating rates at all: it's just manipulated rates more advantageous to the U.S. There's nothing wrong with this—we have as much right to play the international economic game for our own benefit as any other nation—but we shouldn't delude ourselves into thinking it's a free-market solution.

The reality? Our choice isn't fixed vs. floating, it's fixed vs. manipulated. And if exchange rates are destined to be manipulated no matter what, then going back to an explicit fixed-rate system, like the Bretton Woods agreement discussed in the previous chapter, might well be the best solution. Fixed exchange rates are, in fact, precisely the outcome when *everybody* manipulates their exchange rate, reaches a stand-off, and codifies the result.

In any case, China must eventually stop manipulating its currency at some point, because the further its manipulated rate departs from the rate that would otherwise prevail, the more expensive this gets. And the longer China keeps at it, the greater China's future loss, because the size of China's dollar-denominated holdings, and their likely future drop in value, both grow. Pegging the yuan to a declining dollar also raises inflation in China by raising the price of imports, especially oil, and encourages financial speculation.[289]

Yuan-dollar unpegging is already happening, albeit in very small steps. China first started diversifying its reserve holdings away from the dollar (which has this effect) in July 2005, and from then until July 2008 allowed the yuan to rise from 8.28 to the dollar to 6.83, where it has since been held nearly steady.[290] Does this mean the problem will solve itself automatically? No. For a start, the aforementioned appreciation, while showcased by Beijing, is nominal appreciation; after adjusting for inflation, the change was far smaller: about two percent.[291] In any case, as Bush Treasury Under Secretary for International Affairs David McCormick put it in 2007, a more expensive yuan:

> Will not provide a magic bullet for solving the problems of American industries facing overseas competition...We have already seen the resilience of China's exporters to currency appreciation.[292]

This is so because Chinese currency manipulation is, of course, only one facet of China's low-cost strategy. The China Price Project at the University of California at Irvine has estimated its various components thus:

Wages	39.4%
Subsidies	16.7%
Network Clustering[293]	16.0%
Undervalued Currency	11.4%
Counterfeiting & Piracy	8.6%
Foreign Direct Investment	3.1%
Health & Safety Neglect	2.4%
Environmental Neglect	2.3%

Source: Peter Navarro, "Report of The China Price Project," Merage School of Business, University of California at Irvine, July 2006.

And even if China did revalue its currency, it has enough other tricks up its sleeve, in the form of non-tariff barriers, that it could go on its merry way and still leave America with trade almost as unbalanced as before. Protectionism doesn't only mean obvious policies like tariffs and quotas; it also includes local content laws, import licensing requirements, and subtler measures (some of them covert, hard to detect, or infinitely disputable) such as deliberately quirky national technical standards and discriminatory tax practices. And it includes outright skullduggery such as deliberate port delays, inflated customs valuations, selective enforcement of safety standards, and systematic demands for bribes.[294] One study by the Congressional Research Service identified 751 different types of barriers to American exports worldwide.[295]

Critics who go the next logical step, and demand that China eliminate these covert trade barriers, are unrealistic. Getting foreign nations to change domestic policies for the benefit of foreigners is a tricky matter even with polite liberal democracies like Canada. Expecting this to happen with the authoritarian nationalists of Beijing is laughable. Even if China's protectionist policies actually hurt it—a repeated claim of free traders— China's government obviously doesn't think so, as *it* chooses to define its own national interest. And China is a grandmaster of evading foreign economic pressure. It has thwarted, for example, the market opening agreements it made upon joining the World Trade Organization in 2001, often honoring their letter while evading their spirit.[296]

The ongoing decline of the dollar, combined with recession, has already produced a dip in our trade deficit in 2009, so we may be fooled into thinking our problem is correcting itself. But our trade balance also temporarily improved due to recession in 1970, 1973, 1981, and 1991.[297] So we may yet again decide to let our underlying problems continue to fester. This is a false salvation to beware very carefully.

4

Critiques of Free Trade to Avoid

BECAUSE FREE TRADE has so many flaws in theory and causes so many problems in practice, it's tempting to throw at it every criticism we can think of. After all, if it is wrong, why not? But this would be a mistake. It would lead down time-wasting blind alleys, undermine attempts to ignite fruitful debate, hand free traders spurious arguments they can win, and ultimately mislead the public about alternatives. Because, like it or not, some of the most popular critiques of free trade in circulation are mistaken.

For example, it is sometimes dismissed as a policy on the grounds that it doesn't even really exist in the first place. This is not a new complaint: the great American statesman Henry Clay asserted in 1820 that free trade "has never existed, does not exist, and perhaps never will exist."[298] This is a valid point when aimed at America's major trading partners from Brussels to Beijing, who do not practice free trade towards us. But it is mere pedantry to deny that America practices free trade when U.S. tariff barriers are under one-and-one-half percent of the value of our imports and our non-tariff barriers (though by definition hard to quantify) not much more.[299]

Other criticism has alienated itself from the political mainstream by its openly anticapitalist, socialist, or even anarchist character. This invites automatic rejection by anyone who does not share its radical premises, as few voters or people in power do. Such criticism can even be counterproductive when it gives the public the impression that only its premises constitute good grounds to reject free trade, implying that anyone who does not share them should accept it. That is when the sheer *antics* of radical critics don't give opposition to free trade a freakish image that forecloses discussion with a snigger and a video clip of some teenager with green hair smashing a Starbucks window. That kind of radicalism certainly has its place in America (Boston Tea Party, anyone?) but street theatre is only effective as part of an overall strategy. The battle over free trade will be won or lost in Middle America, not Greenwich Village.

Only an appeal to *the self-interest of the average voter* will shift policy. So it is best to avoid mushy complaints like the idea that free trade is bad because it endorses a materialistic way of life or an obsession with economic efficiency. To some extent, of course, it may, and this is easy to bundle into a feel-good package that connects to a lot of other important issues.[300] But this is really a critique of consumer society as a whole, which is not something Congress can legislate out of existence. Free trade is.

Another idea to avoid is that imports as such are bad—an easy attitude to slip into tacitly even if one does not literally believe this. Imports constitute consumption, which we must define as good if we embrace broadly shared prosperity and thus a consumer society. We must, in fact, assume imports are good to enable some of the most potent arguments *against* free trade. For example, free trade can cause trade deficits, run down a nation's currency, make imports more expensive, and thus reduce living standards. So the anti-free trade position can actually be the pro-imports position in the long run! (This especially should be pointed out when free traders act like they are defending the very concept of trade, as they often do.) Nobody serious wants to turn the United States into North Korea, which seals itself off from imports entirely under its philosophy of *juché* or self reliance.[301]

GO FOR THE JUGULAR: THE HARD ECONOMICS

Only destroying the credibility of the actual hard economics of free trade will destroy the power of free traders, by destroying their reputation for technocratic competence and the moral high ground that flows from this in a technocratic society. Therefore criticism of free trade must focus on the jugular vein of economics, not side issues like culture. These issues are profoundly important in their own right and naturally emotionally vivid, but this doesn't make them effective tools for ending free trade. In public debate, what people tend to take away from side-issue critiques is that if criticism of free trade is about side issues, then the economics itself must be sound. This is fatal, as most people naturally assume that the *economics* of free trade should determine whether we continue it. Side-issue critiques are also too easy for free traders to respond to by offering non-trade-related interventions to fix any given problem, combined with continued free trade (which has been elevated to a formal ideal by economists like arch-free trader Jagdish Bhagwati of Columbia University).[302]

For example, protection of movies and magazines is a legitimate issue, but it is a cultural question that cannot be settled on economic grounds either way. It is, however, certainly illogical to demand that the world accept cultural homogenization because the protection of local cultures against Disneyfication interferes with free trade. Indeed it does, but we don't export weapons to our military enemies (even when this might be profitable) because we recognize that arms are not essentially economic in nature and therefore ought not be governed by economic logic.[303] No economic calculation can determine, for example, whether protecting a separate Canadian film industry is a boon to Canadian culture or just a subsidy for mediocre movies. That question, which is a live issue under NAFTA, can only be settled by the film critics and the audiences.

NO NEED FOR VILLAINS

If free trade is wrong, then it is coldly, factually wrong on its merits, and turning it into a drama of innocents and villains is unnecessary.

Sometimes the Third World is presented as an innocent victim of a First World trying to use free trade to keep it down. This view was expressed by the former Prime Minister of Malaysia, the bigoted but not unintelligent Mahathir bin Mohamad, thus:

> Japan was developing at a time when the Western countries did not believe that Eastern countries could actually catch up with the West, so Japan was allowed. And then, of course, later on, when Japan appeared to be doing too well all the time, the yen was revalued upwards in order to make Japan less competitive. You can see that

these are deliberate attempts to slow down the growth in Japan... and after that, of course, Southeast Asian countries, even Malaysia, began to develop fast, and there seemed to be a fear that Eastern countries might actually pose a threat to Western domination, and so something had to be done to stop them.[304]

Mahathir basically accuses the developed world of seeking to lock in its present industrial advantage, leaving the rest of the world supplying it raw materials and low-value industrial scraps. Third World nations often (understandably) perceive this as a rerun of colonialism.

But it is implausible that the First World is doing this. For a start, if it has the control over the world economy Mahathir imagines, then it should have succeeded by now. Yet Third World giants like China and India surge ahead. It is also unlikely that the First World corporations which actually conduct international trade serve the interests of the nations in which they are headquartered, as opposed to their own profits. Economic, political, and technological power are just too widely distributed in the world today for the literal fulfillment of Mahathir's scenario, even if anyone seriously wanted it (doubtful).

Sometimes the Third World is cast as the villain. But whatever harm Third World nations like China have done to America through trade, most has been due to our own foolishness in embracing free trade. The protectionist America of 1925 would have been barely scratched. Only a limited amount consists of things, like industrial espionage and brand piracy, which really are inexcusable outright theft. These are a genuine problem: two-thirds of the American computer software used in China is stolen,[305] copyright theft there is estimated to cost the U.S. $2.6 billion a year,[306] and up to 20 percent of China's growth is connected in some way with theft of intellectual property.[307]

Another villain theory is that big corporations are evil—an accusation heard at both extremes of the political spectrum, though the right tends to use words like "treasonous." But corporations don't behave as they do because they are evil (or disloyal). They behave as they do because the rules they operate under make certain behavior profitable. If free trade is legal, we should not get morally indignant when corporations fire their high-cost American workforces and move production overseas. We should change the rules that encourage this.[308] Competitive pressures force even corporations that would rather not act this way, which certainly exist, to go along.

FAIR TRADE IS NOT ENOUGH

The idea of "fair" trade is very appealing. Unfortunately, it will be only a small part of any trade solution. Fair trade in goods like coffee is a fine thing because there exists a clear idea of unfair practices in how coffee importers treat coffee farmers and how to avoid them. That sort of fair trade basically consists in First World consumers voluntarily not using the full strength of their bargaining position with Third World producers. This is admirable enough. But fair trade embraces less than one percent of trade in cocoa, tea and coffee, so it will have a small impact for the foreseeable future.[309]

Can the idea scale? Perhaps. But there is currently a huge sandbag blocking it from further acceptance: mainstream economics holds that it is largely futile, or even counter-productive. For example, it holds that the price supports implied by fair trade encourage overproduction and drive down the price for other growers. So this economics must carefully be picked apart, using its own conceptual vocabulary, before fair trade can even get a decent hearing outside those already committed to it.

The more important meaning of fair trade concerns issues like what is the fair share for U.S. firms in the Chinese airliner market? Because the greater share of America's trade problem concerns products like airliners, not coffee. These high-tech, high-value products are decisive for U.S. trade performance and will be the main objects of any future American industrial policy. This is where the battlegrounds for American jobs are.

Unfortunately, the concept of fairness is a political minefield. A political coalition strong enough to abolish free trade will need support on both sides of the aisle, and these sides disagree about what is fair every day. This problem is even worse when foreign societies are involved (as they must be in trade) because different societies define fairness differently. The Japanese, for example, consider it unfair to lay off workers in a recession.[310] Many European countries consider America's antiunion "right to work" laws unfair. As former trade diplomat Clyde Prestowitz has pointed out:

> Because the law assumes that American-style capitalism and laissez faire international trade are not only good but morally right, it implicitly defines deviations from such a system as 'unfair.' There is no provision for the possibility of a different system or for dealing with problems that arise not out of unfairness but from the grinding together of systems that simply do not mesh well.[311]

As a result, appealing to fairness to resolve trade disputes, or judging foreign actions by a standard of fairness, is unlikely to solve anything. For example, there is no particularly good reason why currency manipulation should be considered "unfair." Currency manipulation is a *tactic*, and while the U.S. should certainly fight back to restore advantageous currency values, this is about protecting the national economic interest, not ethical justice per se.

Fairness isn't even a particularly meaningful concept in much of trade economics, which turns on technicalities like capital flows and economies of scale. And fairness isn't the objective of trade policy for the most part, anyhow. Prosperity (of ourselves or others) is. Decent people naturally hope these will coincide, but one can't just a priori assume this. China's authoritarianism, for example, is morally objectionable in a dozen different ways, but it has probably raised the living standards of the Chinese. If prosperity is what we want, then we need to admit that prosperity is what we're after (subject to whatever ethical constraints we believe in).

It is similarly pointless to argue about whether America's trade mess is the "fault" of foreign nations or ourselves. Realism demands that we assume foreign nations will take advantage of any opportunities we put before them. And even if foreigners really are to blame sometimes, we don't have control over their actions; we have control over our own.

FORGET A LEVEL PLAYING FIELD

The common plaint that "all we want is a level playing field" is just another way of asking for fair trade. A true level playing field would require not just equal rules for international trade, but also that nations have the same *domestic* economic policies, as these can also confer an export advantage.

There are literally thousands of places in an economy where export subsidies can be hidden, from the depreciation schedules of the tax code to state ownership of supplier industries, land use planning, credit card laws, non-performing loans, cheap infrastructure, and tax rebates. So a true level playing field would require America to supervise the domestic policies of foreign nations, which is not feasible. Even if we reached agreements on paper to end these subsidies, we would still have to enforce these agreements on the ground.

Foreign governments often face strong domestic political pressures to keep these subsidies in place even when they want to strike a deal with the U.S. to eliminate them. China, for example, is full of effectively bankrupt state-owned companies that can't be allowed to collapse for fear of unleashing a tidal wave of unemployment. In other nations, subsidies are products of the day-to-day political bargaining that goes on in every country as governments buy political support and buy off opposition, so eliminating subsidies just to keep America happy would risk unraveling the balance of power. Our own difficulties abolishing unjustified agricultural subsidies illustrate just how hard it is to repeal entrenched subsidies.

Level playing fields tilt the other way, too: Americans tend not to realize how many subsidies our *own* economy contains. But judging by the same standards the Commerce Department applies to foreign nations, they are legion.[312] Agricultural subsidies are just the beginning, and already a flashpoint of international trade disputes. (They basically scuttled the Doha round of WTO talks in 2008.) But there are thousands of others, ranging from the Import-Export Bank (cheap loans for exporters) to the Hoover dam (cheap electricity). And that is just on the federal level; states and localities constantly bid subsidies against each other to attract businesses. Every tax credit, from R&D and worker training on down, subsidizes *something*, and if that something is exported, then it constitutes an export subsidy. So unless we are prepared to have foreign bureaucrats pass judgment on all these policies, subsidies both here and abroad are unavoidable and a true level playing field is impossible. And if a level playing field is impossible, then no free-market solution will ever balance trade, and balanced trade will have to be some kind of managed trade.

LABOR STANDARDS ARE NOT ENOUGH

Trying to solve the problems of free trade by going after low foreign labor standards is understandable. The AFL-CIO, not unreasonably, asserted in 2004 that China's repression of labor rights gives its exporters a 43 percent cost advantage.[313] Chinese workers are denied the right to form unions, are often paid less than China's own very low minimum wage, and are denied overtime pay. And if they *really* get out of line, there is always China's network of *laogai* ("reform through labor") prison camps—which conveniently supply slave labor for the manufacturing of goods for export.[314]

But if free trade is bad for labor, then we should end it, not patch it up, as its economic defects are too profound for a few labor agreements to fix. These agreements are worth having, as they will (if actually enforced) improve matters somewhat, but they are not the fundamental solution. As United Steelworkers president Leo Gerard puts it:

> The fact of the matter is you can't fix NAFTA by putting in environmental rights and labor rights and pretending that will fix it. In fact, Canada's environmental and labor standards are higher than America's. Mexico's are also higher, but they're not enforced.[315]

Another problem with using trade as leverage to raise foreign labor standards is that some nations with lower labor standards than the U.S. are democracies, so this amounts to telling them that they don't have the right to set their own labor laws. Imagine if nations like Germany and Sweden, where unions enjoy rights undreamed of in the U.S., like guaranteed board representation, were to demand that Alabama, Texas, and similar states rescind their right-to-work laws as a prerequisite for being allowed to export to the EU! And what about poor countries where unions are legal, like India? Reasonable labor rights there haven't changed the fact that wages are still desperately low.

A RACE TO THE BOTTOM?

The notorious "race to the bottom," in which free trade causes the lowest standard in the entire world for wages, working conditions, or environmental protection to become the global norm, is a slippery half-truth that needs to be carefully untangled.

The good news is that it is highly unlikely that free trade will ever *literally* cause the world's lowest standard for wages, worker rights, or environmental protection to become the world standard. While there are indeed pressures in that direction, there are also considerable countervailing pressures. If there weren't, South Korea would still be poorer than Zambia, as it was as recently as 1970.[316] And if a small and relatively powerless nation like South Korea can buck this tide, then America certainly can—*if* we play our cards correctly, which we have not been doing.[317] This is the real scandal: not that we have been caught in a hopeless situation, but that we have failed to cope with a situation we should have been able to manage reasonably well.

Free trade certainly generates downward pressure on wages for most Americans, but it is vanishingly unlikely ever to reduce American wages to present Chinese levels, which is what something like "the bottom" would really mean. Among other things, 70 percent of America's economy is in industries (from restaurants to government) that are not internationally traded.[318] So the vast majority of our economy has no direct exposure to international trade at all. Since average wages are determined by average productivity[319] and nothing low-wage foreigners do can reduce productivity in the nontraded parts of our economy,[320] there is no plausible way the entire American economy can be dragged down through trade alone.

The economic mechanism implied by the idea of a race to the bottom is real, but not infinitely powerful. Wages don't automatically hit bottom simply because one country has lower wages. That country *also* has to be a sufficiently successful competitor to push countries with higher wages out of the industry in question. So if countries with higher wages have a productivity advantage, a quality advantage, or some other factor balancing the cost of their higher wages, the lower wage won't win out.[321] It is success or failure in bringing these countervailing factors together that determines the fate of advanced economies like the U.S.; industrial policy (which we will look at in Chapter Nine) is about doing precisely that.

The industrial sectors in which a race to the bottom really does occur are generally low-value sectors where most of the cost of production is unskilled or semiskilled labor. These are intrinsically low-wage industries that are of little value to American workers, simply because they don't pay the kind of wages it takes to live in a developed country. The far bigger problem is America's eroding global position in high skill, high-wage industries—a race we are losing largely to other *developed* nations.

It is definitely a mistake to reduce all of America's trade problems to cheap foreign labor. Cheap labor would indeed explain our problems with China, India, and the rest of the developing world, but it cannot explain our huge deficits with other high-wage countries such as Japan ($57.7 billion in 2010)[322] and the EU ($79.3 billion).[323] If trade were merely about cheap labor, Bangladesh and Burundi would dominate the world economy.

Note, as a corollary to the above, that because most of our economy is nontradable, weak *domestic* productivity growth has actually done America more harm in recent decades than free trade. Turning free trade into a catch-all explanation for all our economic problems will draw attention away from needed solutions to our other economic defects. Foreign competition must not become an excuse for all of our economic failures from short-termist finance to bad secondary education and crumbling infrastructure.

FREE TRADE DOESN'T GUT GOVERNMENT

Another popular half-truth, especially on the left, is that free trade guts government by destroying its ability to tax. But the hard fact is that over the 1965-2006 period of increasingly free trade, government revenue has simply not fallen in any of the advanced economies. The table below tells the story.

Tax Revenue as a Percentage of GDP

Country	1965	1980	1990	2000	2006	Change 1965-2006
US	24.7%	27.0%	26.7%	29.6%	28.0%	+3.3%
Japan	18.3%	25.1%	30.1%	27.1%	27.9%	+9.6%
Germany	31.6%	37.5%	35.7%	37.9%	35.6%	+4.0%
France	34.5%	40.6%	43.0%	45.3%	44.2%	+9.7%
Italy	25.5%	30.4%	38.9%	42.0%	42.1%	+16.6%
UK	30.4%	35.2%	36.8%	37.4%	37.1%	+6.7%
Canada	25.6%	30.7%	35.9%	35.8%	33.3%	+7.7%
Denmark	29.9%	43.9%	47.1%	48.8%	49.1%	+19.2%
Sweden	35.0%	47.5%	53.6%	54.2%	49.1%	+14.1%
Australia	21.9%	27.4%	29.3%	31.5%	30.6%	+8.7%

Source: 1965-2000: OECD Revenue Statistics 1965-2003 (Paris: Organization for Economic Co-Operation and Development, 2004), Table 3. 2006: "OECD Tax Database," Table O.1, www.oecd.org/ctp/taxdatabase.

So whatever else increasingly free trade has been doing, withering away the state has not been it. Neither has the tax burden shifted from corporations: developed nations' average taxation of corporate income *rose* from 2.2 percent of GDP to 3.5 percent over the 1965-2004 period.[324]

But isn't it axiomatic that higher taxes render nations less competitive, something they cannot afford now that free trade enables their economic bases to pack up and flee elsewhere? Doesn't the state wear a "golden straitjacket," as they say, these days?[325] Yes and no. Above all, taxes are not *in themselves* an economic drag, as the people and corporations that pay them get something back: public services. It is the cost-benefit relationship that determines the competitiveness of a nation's tax regime, not the cost alone. Incompetent public services, misguided social programs, and military adventures unrelated to real national security needs indeed impose an economic burden. But taxes well spent do not. A weak welfare state certainly does not confer an export advantage, as comparison between the United States and the European Union makes clear: the relatively spartan U.S. is running the huge trade deficit, not the relatively generous EU.

Unwise government spending indeed makes a population poorer, by wasting its money. It undermines incentives for work and investment. High-tax countries where taxes are badly spent, like Britain, have indeed damaged their quality of life. But they remain roughly as internationally competitive as they otherwise would be. This logic breaks down at the extremes, but is valid within the range of taxation present in most major countries. It is simply not the case that high-tax countries where taxes are well spent, like Sweden, are internationally uncompetitive, according to the standard rankings.[326]

Even when taxes *are* misspent, the cost appears to come mostly out of the hide of the taxpayer and the vitality of the domestic economy, not out of the economy's international competitive position. It is easy to see why. If taxes get too high in Britain and London banks try to charge more in order to compensate, their foreign customers can take their business elsewhere far more easily than London bankers can pack up and move. So bankers will have to shave their own salaries, rather than raise their fees, to pay the tax; the cost of excessive taxation tends to get shifted to the least-mobile party.

Among advanced industrial nations, the more open economies, where trade is a higher percentage of GDP, actually have more welfare spending, not less.[327] This suggests that the welfare state is a needed buffer for people coping with an open economy and, conversely, that the welfare state may actually advance, rather than retard, trade openness. This also makes free trade, contrary to the ideological delusions of many of its promoters, an enlarger rather than reducer of big government.[328]

FREE TRADE WON'T AMERICANIZE THE WORLD

It has often been suggested—if less frequently as America has economically declined in recent years—that free trade will Americanize the rest of the world's economies. But it won't. Free trade can only cause diverse economies to converge on a single model, American or otherwise, if its underlying economics implies that one economic model is always best. But, as we shall see, the same insights that enable us to grasp why free trade isn't always best also imply that no single *domestic* economic model is always best either.[329] The world will not converge on the American variety of capitalism simply because it is unlikely to converge on any single variety. The only caveat is the basic fact that all developed nations, whatever their ideological rhetoric, are mixed capitalist-socialist economies with public sectors between a quarter and a half of GDP.[330]

This doesn't mean that all the different national varieties of capitalism are destined to be equally successful. They aren't now, and won't be in future. But it does mean that a great many of them will be sufficiently successful that foreign competitive pressures will not be strong enough to force them to change. American, Chinese, Japanese, Russian, German, Brazilian, and United Arab Emirates capitalism are meaningfully different. They will remain so. It is emphatically not the case that, in the words of Thomas Friedman, "today there is only free-market vanilla and North Korea."[331] Economic diversity—a concept poorly understood by mainstream economics—will remain a fact of life.

In fact, given the mess the U.S. is sliding into, the American version of capitalism will probably increasingly be viewed abroad as a paradigm of what *not* to do. The global economy will probably de-Americanize somewhat as our closer imitators, such as Canada, Australia and the UK, drift away from us and towards more successful models visible in Central Europe and East Asia.

HOW *NOT* TO END FREE TRADE

Any future protectionist policies must work well in practice if they are to endure. So they must avoid the mistakes of past protectionist measures, many of which have been counterproductive.

For example, the Voluntary Restraint Agreement (VRA) between the U.S. and Japan on automobiles (official from 1981 to 1994 and since continued unilaterally by Japan) is a case study in how *not* to end free trade. Despite its popularity—it cost consumers billions, ultimately failed to save the American auto industry, but attracted little opposition—this agreement was a mess.

The VRA's most obvious mistake was to limit the number of cars imported, but not their value. The result was that Japan indeed limited their number, but moved upmarket and started exporting more expensive cars. As the ability of the American auto industry to provide jobs is not a function of the number of cars it makes, but of the amount of money they bring in, this was counterproductive.

A quota is also the worst kind of protectionism from the taxpayer's point of view. Any barrier to imports—quotas, tariffs, voluntary restraints, closed distribution networks—raises the price of the imported product and its domestic substitutes. But a tariff puts much of the price increase into the taxpayer's pocket. On the other hand, a quota puts it into the hands of the foreign producer. So in effect, the VRA was legalized price-fixing for the Japanese auto industry! This price-fixing then raised that industry's profitability, enabling it to plow even more money into R&D aimed at surpassing American producers. And this effect was intensified by the fact that the VRA raised the price of Japanese cars, which were de facto rationed, more than the price of American cars, which were not.[332]

The VRA also did nothing to ensure wise use of the increased revenues it handed to the U.S. auto industry by increasing its market share and enabling it to raise prices (by an average of $659 in 1984).[333] All possible uses of revenue are not equal in their value to an industry's long-term health. The money can go to increased profits, increased investment, increased wages, or some combination of these. As it happened, most went to immediate profits and wages, not investment, the key to the industry's long-term future.[334] Twenty-five years later, the industry is paying the price, with Chrysler and General Motors having passed through bankruptcy and Ford having avoided it only by using the threat thereof to extract concessions from its unions and suppliers. In 2008, Toyota broke GM's 77-year reign as the world's largest automaker.

The intent (and effect) of the VRA was to relocate automobile production, be it by the Big Three or foreign producers, to the United States. Unfortunately, so-called transplants, the U.S. factories of German, Japanese, and Korean companies, are a problematic solution. (There are now 17 in the U.S.)[335] While they do move production jobs to the U.S., they leave most design jobs at home. Transplant-made cars also have a much heavier dependence on imported parts: the average domestic content of the Big Three is 79 percent, but transplants average only 63 percent.[336] Transplants also undermine the ability of any future tariff to revive an autonomous American auto industry, as foreign producers are now entrenched inside any future tariff wall.

POSITIVE STRATEGY VS. BAND-AIDS

It is important to avoid calling for protectionism merely to save dying industries. In recent decades, critics of free trade have reliably fretted about these industries, rarely about the harm free trade does to still healthy ones, and almost never about industries that free trade prevented America from developing in the first place. But trying to keep a primitive labor-intensive industry in the U.S. by protecting it (and perhaps stuffing it with subsidized investment) will just squander money that would have been better spent defending an industry in which America has a fighting chance. Or breaking into an entirely new sunrise industry. All over America, there are people stocking shelves at Walmart for $8 per hour who could have been HDTV manufacturing technicians at perhaps double that.[337] (This industry doesn't exist in the U.S., so we don't know what their wages would be, but we can guess by looking at other industries that require comparable skill sets.)[338] These people don't know who they are, so they don't complain about it, but they are just as big a part of our trade problem as the unemployed.

Most of the benefits of protectionism center on winning tomorrow's industries and keeping today's from falling into trouble, *not* on rescuing industries already dying. Centering protectionism on dying industries is like lecturing a heart attack victim lying in an ambulance on diet and exercise. Better than nothing, but still... Industries in trouble are often (not *always*, as free traders claim) industries in which high-wage nations like the U.S. are becoming intrinsically uncompetitive, and which we quite rightly should be shedding.

Protectionism cannot protect every job in America, even if this is the natural promise that tends to get made in the political arena. Even if we could, this would not be a rational objective, as keeping every existing job would mean that the workers in them could not be upgraded to better jobs over time, which is what we should want. And even if everyone can't upgrade to a better job, the natural progression of industry life cycles means that no job will last forever. There is no future for VCR factories, even if this was a sunrise industry in 1978. As a result, an effective defense of our industrial base will be a rolling defense, not a static one.

PART II

THE REAL
ECONOMICS
OF TRADE

5

Ye Olde Theory
of Comparative Advantage

THE THEORY EXPLAINED in this chapter is false. It is the 192-year-old theory of comparative advantage, invented by David Ricardo in 1817. Ricardo was a London stockbroker, self-made millionaire, and Member of Parliament who turned economist after reading Adam Smith's celebrated *The Wealth of Nations* on holiday. It dates from a time when most of America was wilderness, railroads were an experimental technology, doctors still used leeches, and veterans of the American Revolution walked the streets of Philadelphia. The quickest route between the United States and China was by clipper ship, which took well over two months. Trade with Japan, however, was impossible, as the country had been sealed off from the outside world by the Shogun in 1635 and would wait another 37 years for the U.S. Navy's Commodore Perry to open it up. Great Britain was the world's largest manufacturer and trading nation. World economic output was about one half of one percent of what it is today.[339] International trade was approximately three percent of that output,[340] in comparison with today's 26 percent.[341]

It is, however, absolutely necessary that we understand this quaint and unreliable theory because to this day it remains the core of the case for free trade. All the myriad things we are told about why free trade is good for us are boiled down to hard economics and weighed against the costs by this single theory and its modern ramifications. The rest is details and politics. If this theory is true, then no matter how high the costs of free trade, we can rely upon the fact that elsewhere in our economy, we are reaping benefits that exceed these costs. If it is false, we cannot. Free traders admit this, for although other theories of trade exist, their normative content is Ricardian.[342] The battle over Ricardianism is therefore decisive.

ABSOLUTE VS. COMPARATIVE ADVANTAGE

To understand comparative advantage, it is best to start with its simpler cousin: absolute advantage. The concept of absolute advantage simply says that if some foreign nation is a more efficient producer of some product than we are, then free trade will cause us to import that product from them, to the benefit of both nations. It benefits us because we get the product for less than it would have cost us to make it ourselves. It benefits the foreign nation because it gets a market for its goods. And it benefits the world economy as a whole because it causes production to come from the most efficient producer, maximizing world output.

Absolute advantage is thus a set of fairly obvious ideas. It is, in fact, the theory of international trade most people instinctively hold, without recourse to formal economics, and thus it explains a large part of public opinion on the subject. It sounds like a reassuringly direct application of basic capitalist principles. It is the theory of trade Adam Smith himself believed in.[343]

It is also false. Under free trade, America observably imports products of which *we* are the most efficient producer—which makes no sense by the standard of absolute advantage. This causes complaints like conservative commentator Patrick Buchanan's below:

> Ricardo's theory...demands that more efficient producers in advanced countries give up industries to less efficient producers in less advanced nations...Are Chinese factories more efficient than U.S. factories? Of course not.[344]

96

Buchanan is correct: this is *precisely* what Ricardo's theory demands. It not only predicts that less efficient producers will sometimes win (observably true) but argues that this is good for us (the controversy). This is why we must analyze trade in terms of not absolute but *comparative* advantage. If we don't, we will never obtain a theory that accurately describes what *does* happen in international trade, which is a prerequisite for our arguing about what *should* happen—or how to make it happen.

The theory of comparative advantage has an unfortunate reputation for being hard to understand,[345] but at bottom it simply says this:

Nations trade for the same reasons people do.

And the whole theory can be cracked open with one simple question:

Why don't pro football players mow their own lawns?

Why should this even be a question? Because the average footballer can almost certainly mow his lawn more efficiently than the average professional lawn mower. The average footballer is, after all, presumably stronger and more agile than the presumably mediocre workforce attracted to a badly paid job like mowing lawns. (If we wanted to quantify this efficiency, we could measure it in acres per hour.) Efficiency (also known as productivity) is always a matter of *how much output we get* from a given quantity of inputs, be these inputs hours of labor, pounds of flour, kilowatts of electricity, or whatever.

Because the footballer is more efficient, in economic language he has absolute advantage at mowing lawns. Yet nobody finds it strange that he would "import" lawn-mowing services from a less efficient "producer." Why? Obviously, because he has *better things to do with his time*. This is the key to the whole thing. The theory of comparative advantage says that it is advantageous for America to import some goods simply in order to free up our workforce to produce more-valuable goods instead. We, as a nation, have "better things to do with our time" than produce these less valuable goods. And, just as with the football player and the lawn mower, it doesn't matter whether *we* are more efficient at producing them, or the country we import them from is. As a result, it is sometimes advantageous for us to import goods from less efficient nations.

This logic doesn't only apply to our time, that is our man-hours of labor, either. It also applies to our land, capital, technology, and every other resource used to produce goods. So the theory of comparative advantage says that if we could produce something more valuable with the resources we currently use to produce some product, then we should import that product, free up those resources, and produce that more valuable thing instead.

Economists call the resources we use to produce products "factors of production." They call whatever we *give up* producing, in order to produce something else, our "opportunity cost." The opposite of opportunity cost is "direct" cost, so while the direct cost of mowing a lawn is the hours of labor it takes, plus the gasoline, wear-and-tear on the machine, et cetera, the opportunity cost is the value of whatever else these things could have been producing instead. Direct cost is a simple matter of efficiency, and is the same regardless of whatever else is going on in the world. Opportunity cost is a lot more complicated, because it depends on what other opportunities exist for using factors of production.

Other things being equal, direct cost and opportunity cost go up and down together, because if the time required to mow a lawn doubles, then twice as much time cannot then be spent doing something else. As a result, high efficiency tends to generate both low direct cost and low opportunity cost. If someone is such a skilled mower that they can mow the whole lawn in 15 minutes, then their opportunity cost of doing so will be low because there's not much else they can do in 15 minutes.

The opportunity cost of producing something is always the *next most valuable thing* we could have produced instead. If either bread or rolls can be made from dough, and we choose to make bread, then rolls are our opportunity cost. If we choose to make rolls, then bread is. And if rolls are worth more than bread, then we incur a larger opportunity cost by making bread. It follows that the *smaller* the opportunity cost we incur, the less opportunity we are wasting, so the better we are exploiting the opportunities we have. Therefore our best move is always to *minimize our opportunity cost*.

This is where trade comes in. Trade enables us to "import" bread (buy it in a store) so we can stop baking our own and bake rolls instead. In fact, trade enables us to do this for all the things we would otherwise have to make for ourselves. So if we have complete freedom to trade, we can systematically shrug off all our least valuable tasks and reallocate our time to our most valuable ones. Similarly, *nations* can systematically shrink their least valuable industries and expand their most valuable ones. This benefits these nations and under global free trade, with every nation doing this, it benefits the entire world. The world economy, and every nation in it, become as productive as they can possibly be.

Here's a real-world example: if America devoted millions of workers to making cheap plastic toys (we don't; China does) then these workers could not produce anything else. In America, we (hopefully) have more-productive jobs for them to do, even if American industry *could* hypothetically grind out more plastic toys per man-hour of labor and ton of plastic than the Chinese. So we're better off leaving this work to China and having our own workers do that more-productive work instead.

This all implies that under free trade, production of every product will automatically migrate to the nation that can produce it at the lowest opportunity cost—the nation that *wastes the least opportunity* by being in that line of business.

The theory of comparative advantage thus sees international trade as a vast interlocking system of tradeoffs, in which nations use the ability to import and export to shed opportunity costs and reshuffle their factors of production to their most valuable uses. And this all happens automatically, because if the owners of some factor of production find a more valuable use for it, they will find it profitable to move it to that use. The natural drive for profit will steer all factors of production to their most valuable uses, and opportunities will never be wasted.

It follows that any policy *other* than free trade just traps economies producing less-valuable output than they could have produced. It saddles them with higher opportunity costs—more opportunities thrown away— than they would otherwise incur. In fact, when imports drive a nation out of an industry, this must actually be good for that nation, as it means the nation *must* be allocating its factors of production to producing something more valuable instead. If it weren't doing this, the logic of profit would never have driven its factors out of their former uses. In the language of the theory, the nation's "revealed comparative advantage" must lie elsewhere, and it will now be better off producing according to its newly revealed comparative advantage.

QUANTIFYING COMPARATIVE ADVANTAGE

Let's quantify comparative advantage with an imaginary example. Suppose an acre of land in Canada can produce either 1 unit of wheat or 2 units of corn.[346] And suppose an acre in the U.S. can produce either 3 units of wheat or 4 units of corn. The U.S. then has absolute advantage in both wheat (3 units vs. 1) and corn (4 units vs. 2). But we are twice as productive in corn and thrice as productive in wheat, so we have *comparative* advantage in wheat.[347]

Importing Canadian corn would obviously enable us to switch some of our corn-producing land to wheat production and grow more wheat, while importing Canadian wheat would enable us to switch some of our wheat-producing land to corn production and grow more corn.

Would either of these be winning moves for us?

Every 3 units of wheat we import will free up 1 acre of our land because we will no longer need to grow those 3 units ourselves. We can then grow 4 units of corn on that acre. But selling us that wheat will force Canada to take 3 acres out of corn production to grow it, so it will cost Canada $3 \times 2 = 6$ units of corn. Canadians obviously won't want to do this unless we *pay* them at least 6 units of corn. But this means we'd have to pay 6 units to get 4. So no deal.

What about importing Canadian corn? Every 4 units of corn we import will free up 1 acre of our land, on which we can then grow 3 units of wheat. Selling us those 4 units will force Canada to take $4 \div 2 = 2$ acres out of wheat production, costing Canada $2 \times 1 = 2$ units of wheat. So we can pay the Canadians what it costs them to give us the corn (2 units of wheat) and still come out ahead, by $3 - 2 = 1$ unit of wheat. So importing Canadian corn makes economic sense. And not only do *we* come out ahead, but because the world now contains one more unit of wheat, it's a good move for the world economy as a whole, too.

The fundamental question here is whether America is better off producing corn, or wheat we can exchange for corn. Every nation faces this choice for every product, just as every individual must decide whether to bake his own bread or earn money at a job so he can buy bread in a store (and whether to mow his own lawn or earn money playing football so he can hire someone else to mow it). The entire theory of comparative advantage is just endless ramifications of this basic logic.[348]

The above scenario all works in reverse on the Canadian side, so it benefits Canada, too. Free traders generalize this into the proposition that free trade benefits every trading partner and applies to every product and factor of production.[349] As the late Paul Samuelson of MIT explains it, using China as the trading partner:

> Yes, good jobs may be lost here in the short run. But still total U.S. net national product *must, by the economic laws of comparative advantage, be raised in the long run (and in China, too)*. The gains of the winners from free trade, properly measured, work out to exceed the losses of the losers.[350] (Emphasis in original.)

LOW OPPORTUNITY COSTS EQUALS POOR NATION

Note that the opportunity cost of producing a product can vary from one nation to another even if the two nations' *direct* costs for producing the product are the same. This is because they can face different alternative uses for the factors of production involved. So having a low opportunity cost for producing a product can just as easily be a matter of having poor alternative uses for factors of production as having great efficiency at producing the product itself.

This is where underdeveloped nations come in: their opportunity costs are low because they don't have a lot of other things they can do with their workers. The visible form this takes is cheap labor, because their economies offer workers few alternatives to dollar-an-hour factory work. As Jorge Castañeda, Mexico's former Secretary of Foreign Affairs and a NAFTA critic, explains it:

> The case of the auto industry, especially the Ford-Mazda plant in Hermosillo, Mexico, illustrates a well-known paradox. The plant manufactures vehicles at a productivity rate and quality comparable or higher than the Ford plants in Dearborn or Rouge, and slightly below those of Mazda in Hiroshima. Nevertheless, the wage of the Mexican worker with equal productivity is between 20 and 25 times less than that of the U.S. worker.[351]

The plants in the U.S. and Japan are surrounded by advanced economies containing many other industries able to pay high wages. So these plants must match these wages or find no takers. The plant in Mexico, on the other hand, is surrounded by a primitive developing economy, so it only needs to compete with low-paid jobs, many of them in peasant agriculture. As a result, the productivity of any one job does not determine its wage. Economy-wide productivity does. This is why it is good to work in a developed country even if the job you yourself do, like sweeping floors, is no more productive than the jobs most people do in developing countries.

If wages, which are paid in domestic currency, don't accurately reflect differences in opportunity costs between nations, then exchange rates will (in theory) adjust until they do. So if a nation has high productivity in most of its internationally traded industries, this will push up the value of its currency, pricing it out of its lowest-productivity industries. But this is a good thing, because it can then export goods from higher-productivity industries instead. This will mean less work for the same amount of exports, which is why advanced nations rarely compete in primitive industries, or want to. In 1960, when Taiwan had a per capita income of $154, 67 percent of its exports were raw or processed agricultural goods. By 1993, when Taiwan had a per capita income of $11,000, 96 percent of its exports were manufactured goods.[352] Taiwan today is hopelessly uncompetitive in products it used to export like tea, sugar and rice. Foreign competition drove it out of these industries and destroyed hundreds of thousands of jobs. *Taiwan doesn't mind one bit.*

WHAT THE THEORY DOES *NOT* SAY

The theory of comparative advantage is sometimes misunderstood as implying that a nation's best move is to have as much comparative advantage as it can get—ideally, comparative advantage in every industry. This is actually impossible by definition. If America had superior productivity, therefore lower direct costs, and therefore absolute advantage, in every industry, we would still have a greater margin of superiority in some industries and a lesser margin in others. So we would have *comparative* advantage where our margin was greatest and comparative disadvantage where it was smallest. This pattern of comparative advantage and disadvantage would determine our imports and exports, and we would still be losing jobs to foreign nations in our *relatively* worse industries and gaining them in our *relatively* better ones, despite having absolute advantage in them all.

So what's the significance of absolute advantage, if it doesn't determine which nation makes what? It *does* determine relative wages. If the U.S. were exactly 10 percent more productive than Canada in all industries, then Americans would have real wages exactly 10 percent higher. But because there would be no *relative* differences in productivity between industries, there would be no differences in opportunity costs, neither country would have comparative advantage or disadvantage in anything, and there would be no reason for trade. There would be no corn-for-wheat swaps that were winning moves. All potential swaps would cost *exactly* as much as they were worth, so there would be no point. And under free trade, none would take place, as the free market isn't stupid and won't push goods back and forth across national borders without reason.

Conversely, the theory of comparative advantage says that whenever nations *do* have different relative productivities, mutual gains from trade *must* occur. This is why free traders believe that their theory proves free trade is always best for every nation, no matter how poor or how rich. Rich nations won't be bled dry by the cheap labor of poor nations, and poor nations won't be crushed by the industrial sophistication of rich ones. These things simply can't happen, because the fundamental logic of comparative advantage guarantees that only mutually beneficial exchanges will ever take place.[353] *Everyone* will *always* be better off.

It follows that trade conflicts between nations are always misguided and due solely to their failure to understand why free trade is always good for them. In the words of libertarian scholar James Bovard:

> Our great-grandchildren may look back at the trade wars of the twentieth century with the same contempt that many people today look at the religious wars of the seventeenth century—as a senseless conflict over issues that grown men should not fight about.[354]

Comparative advantage is thus a wonderfully optimistic construct, and one can certainly see why it would be so appealing. Not only does it appear to explain the complex web of international trade at a single stroke, but it also tells us what to do and guarantees that the result will be the best outcome we could possibly have obtained. It enables a lone economist with a blackboard to prove that free trade is best, always and everywhere, without ever getting her shoes dirty inspecting any actual factories, dockyards, or shops. She does not even need to consult any statistics on prices, production, or wages. The magnificent abstract logic alone is enough.

It is actually rather a pity the theory isn't true.

THE SEVEN DUBIOUS ASSUMPTIONS

The theory of comparative advantage tends to provoke blanket dismissal by opponents of free trade. This is unfortunate, as its flaws are easy enough to identify and it can be picked apart on its own terms quite readily. These flaws, known to economics but mostly ignored, consist of a number of dubious assumptions upon which the theory depends. To wit:[355]

Dubious Assumption #1: Trade is sustainable.

We looked at this problem before, in Chapter Two, when we analyzed why trade, if paid for by assuming debt and selling assets, is not advantageous to the importing nation in the long run. But there is a flip side to this problem. What if a nation's *exports* are unsustainable? What if an exporting nation, like the decadent importing nation we previously examined,[356] is running down an accumulated inheritance?

This usually means a nation that is exporting nonrenewable natural resources. The same long- vs. short-term dynamics we looked at before will apply, only in reverse. A nation that *exports* too much will maximize its short term living standard at the expense of its long-term prosperity. But free market economics—which means free trade—will perversely report that this is efficient.

The classic example of this problem, almost a caricature, is the tiny Pacific Island nation of Nauru, located roughly halfway between Hawaii and Australia. Thanks to millions of years of accumulated seabird droppings, the island 100 years ago was covered by a thick layer of guano, a phosphate-rich substance used for manufacturing fertilizer. From 1908 to 2002, about 100 million tons of this material was mined and exported, turning four-fifths of Nauru's land into an uninhabitable moonscape in the process. But for a few years in the late 1960s and early 1970s, Nauru had the world's highest per capita income (and tellingly acquired one of the world's worst obesity problems). But after the deposits ran out, the economy collapsed, the nation was reduced to reliance upon foreign aid, and unemployment neared 90 percent.

Nauru is obviously an extreme case, but it is hardly the only nation making its way in international trade by exporting nonrenewable resources. The oil-rich nations of the Persian Gulf are the most obvious example, and it is no accident that OPEC was the single most formidable disruptor of free trade in the entire post-WWII era. But other nations with large land masses relative to population, such as Canada, Australia, Russia, and Brazil, also depend upon natural resource exports to a degree that is unhealthy in the long run. Even the United States, whose Midwestern agricultural exports rely upon the giant Ogallala Aquifer, a depleting accumulation of water from glacial times, is not exempt from this problem.

The implied solution is to tax or otherwise restrict nonrenewable exports. And that is not free trade.

Dubious Assumption #2: There are no externalities.

An externality is a missing price tag. More precisely, it is the economists' term for when the price of a product does not reflect its true economic cost or value. The classic *negative* externality is environmental damage, which reduces the economic value of natural resources without raising the price of the product that harmed them. The classic *positive* externality is technological spillover, where one company's inventing a product enables others to copy or build upon it, generating wealth that the original company doesn't capture. The theory of comparative advantage, like all theories of free market economics, is driven by prices, so if prices are wrong due to positive or negative externalities, free trade will produce suboptimal results.

For example, goods from a nation with lax pollution standards will be too cheap. As a result, its trading partners will import too much of them. And the exporting nation will export too much of them, overconcentrating its economy in industries that are not really as profitable as they seem, due to ignoring pollution damage. For example, according to *The New York Times*:

> Pollution has made cancer China's leading cause of death...Ambient air pollution alone is blamed for hundreds of thousands of deaths each year. Nearly 500 million people lack access to safe

drinking water…Only 1% of the country's 560 million city dwellers breathe air considered safe by the European Union.[357]

Free trade not only permits problems such as these, but positively encourages them, as skimping on pollution control is an easy way to grab a cost advantage.[358]

Positive externalities are also a problem. For example, if an industry generates technological spillovers for the rest of the economy, then free trade can let that industry be wiped out by foreign competition because the economy ignored its hidden value. Some industries spawn new technologies, fertilize improvements in other industries, and drive economy-wide technological advance; losing these industries means losing all the industries that would have flowed from them in the future. (More on this in Chapter Nine.)

These problems are the tip of an even larger iceberg known as GDP-GPI divergence. Negative externalities and related problems mean that increases in GDP can easily coincide with *decreases* in the so-called Genuine Progress Indicator or GPI.[359] GPI includes things like resource depletion, environmental pollution, unpaid labor like housework, and unpaid goods like leisure time, thus providing a better metric of material well-being than raw GDP.[360] This implies that even if free trade *were* optimal from a GDP point of view, it could still be a bad idea economically.

The problem of positive and negative externalities is quite well known, even to honest free traders, because externalities are, by definition, a loophole in *all* free-market economic policies. Free traders just deny that these externalities are big enough to matter. Or they propose various schemes to internalize them and make prices right.

Dubious Assumption #3: Factors of production move easily between industries.

As noted earlier, the theory of comparative advantage is about switching factors of production from less-valuable to more-valuable uses. But this assumes that the factors of production used to produce one product can switch to producing another. Because if they can't, then imports won't push a nation's economy into industries better suited to its comparative advantage. Imports will just kill off its existing industries and leave nothing in their place.

Although this problem actually applies to all factors of production, we usually hear of it with regard to labor and real estate because people and buildings are the least *mobile* factors of production. (This is why the unemployment line and the shuttered factory are the classic visual images of trade problems.) When workers can't move between industries—usually because they don't have the right skills or don't live in the right place—shifts in an economy's comparative advantage won't move them into an industry with lower opportunity costs, but into unemployment.

This is why we so often hear of older workers being victims of free trade: they are too old to easily acquire the skills needed to move into new industries. And it explains why the big enthusiasts for free trade tend to be bright-eyed yuppies, well equipped for career mobility.

Sometimes the difficulty of reallocating workers shows up as outright unemployment. This happens in nations with rigid employment laws and high de facto minimum wages due to employer-paid taxes, as in Western Europe. But in the United States, because of our relatively low minimum wage and hire-and-fire labor laws, the problem tends to take the form of *under*employment. This is a decline in the quality rather than quantity of jobs. So $28 an hour ex-autoworkers go work at the video rental store for eight dollars an hour.[361] Or they are forced into part-time employment: it is no accident that by September 2009, the average private-sector U.S. work week had fallen to 33 hours, the lowest since records began in 1964, and has since only trivially rebounded.[362]

In the Third World, decline in the quality of jobs often takes the form of workers pushed out of the formal sector of the economy entirely and into casual labor of one kind or another, where they have few rights, pensions, or other benefits. Mexico, for example, has over 40 percent of its workers in the informal sector.[363]

This all implies that low unemployment, on its own, doesn't prove free trade has been a success. This is recognized even by the more intellectually rigorous free traders, such as former Federal Reserve Chairman Alan Greenspan, who has admitted that, "We often try to promote free trade on the mistaken ground, in my judgment, that it will create jobs."[364] Greenspan is correct: even if free trade worked completely as promised, it would not increase the *number* of jobs, only their quality.[365] And when we speak of job gains and losses from trade, these are gross, not net, numbers, as people who lose their jobs due to trade will usually end up working *somewhere*, however dismal.[366]

A recent study by the North Carolina Employment Security Commission explored the problem of workers displaced by trade. In 2005, North Carolina experienced the largest mass layoff in its history, at the bedding firm Pillowtex, costing 4,820 jobs. By the end of 2006, the workers' average wage in their new jobs was $24,488—a drop of over 10 percent from before.[367] A large number had been sidelined into temporary employment, often as health care aides.

Nationally, two-thirds of workers are working again two years after a layoff, but only 40 percent earn as much as they did previously.[368] The human cost is obvious, but what is less obvious is the purely economic cost of writing off investments in human capital when skills that cost money to acquire are never used again. This kind of cost is most visible in places such as Moscow in the 1990s, when one saw physics PhDs driving taxis and the like, but America is not exempt from this problem.

There is also a risk for the economy as a whole when free trade puts factors of production out of action. As Nobel Laureate James Tobin of Yale puts it, "It takes a heap of Harberger triangles to fill an Okun gap."[369] Harberger triangles represent the benefits of free trade on the standard graphs used to quantify them.[370] The Okun gap is the difference between the GDP our economy *would* have, if it were running at full output, and the GDP it does have, due to some of our factors of production lying idle.[371] Tobin's point is simply that the benefits of free trade are quantitatively small, compared to the cost of not running our economy at full capacity due to imports.

Dubious Assumption #4: Trade does not raise income inequality.

The gains from free trade promised by the theory of comparative advantage are only promised to the economy as a whole, not to any particular individuals or groups thereof. So it is entirely possible that even if the economy as a whole gets bigger thanks to freer trade, many (or even most) of the people in it may lose income.

We looked at this problem a bit before, at the end of Chapter One.[372] Let's take a slightly different analytical tack and look again. Suppose that opening up a nation to freer trade means that it starts exporting more airplanes and importing more clothes than before. (This is roughly the situation the U.S. has been in.) Because the nation gets to expand an industry better suited to its comparative advantage and contract one less suited, it becomes more productive and its GDP goes up, just like Ricardo says. So far, so good.

Here's the rub: suppose that a million dollars' worth of clothes production requires one white-collar worker and nine blue-collar workers, while a million dollars of airplane production requires three white-collar workers and seven blue-collar workers. (Industries often differ in this way.) This means that for every million dollars' change in what gets produced, there is a demand for two more white-collar workers and two fewer blue-collar workers. Because demand for white-collar workers goes up and demand for blue-collar workers goes down, the wages of white-collar workers will go up and those of blue-collar workers will go down. But *most* workers are blue-collar workers—so free trade has lowered wages for most workers in the economy!

This is not a trivial problem: Dani Rodrik of Harvard estimates that freeing up trade reshuffles five dollars of income between different groups of people domestically for every one dollar of net gain it brings to the economy as a whole.[373] And on top of this, we still have all the increased-inequality problems we looked at in Chapter One.[374]

Dubious Assumption #5: Capital is not internationally mobile.

Despite the wide scope of its implications, the theory of comparative advantage is at bottom a very narrow theory. It is *only* about the best uses to which nations can put their factors of production. We have certain cards in hand, so to speak, the other players have certain cards, and the theory tells us the best way to play the hand we've been dealt. Or more precisely, it tells us to let the free market play our hand *for us*, so market forces can drive all our factors to their best uses in our economy.

Unfortunately, this all relies upon the impossibility of these same market forces driving these factors right *out* of our economy. If that happens, all bets are off about driving these factors to their most productive use *in* our economy. Their most productive use may well be in another country, and if they are internationally mobile, then free trade will cause them to migrate there. This will benefit the world economy as a whole, and the nation they migrate to, but it will *not* necessarily benefit us.

This problem actually applies to all factors of production. But because land and other fixed resources can't migrate, labor is legally constrained in migrating, and people usually don't try to stop technology or raw materials from migrating, the crux of the problem is capital. Capital mobility replaces comparative advantage, which applies when capital is forced to choose between alternative uses within a single national economy, with our old friend absolute advantage. And absolute advantage contains no guarantees whatsoever about the results being good for *both* trading partners. The win-win guarantee is purely an effect of the world economy being yoked to comparative advantage, and dies with it.

Absolute advantage is really the natural order of things in capitalism, and comparative advantage is a special case caused by the existence of national borders that factors of production can't cross. Indeed, that is basically what a nation *is*, from the point of view of economics: a part of the world with political barriers to the entry and exit of factors of production.[375] This forces national economies to interact indirectly, by exchanging goods and services *made from* those factors, which places comparative advantage in control.

Without these barriers, nations would simply be *regions* of a single economy, which is why absolute advantage governs economic relations *within* nations. In 1950, Michigan had absolute advantage in automobiles and Alabama in cotton. But by 2000, automobile plants were closing in Michigan and opening in Alabama. This benefited Alabama, but it did not necessarily benefit Michigan. (It only would have if Michigan had been transitioning to a higher-value industry than automobiles. Helicopters?) The same scenario is possible for entire nations if capital is internationally mobile.

Capital immobility doesn't have to be absolute to put comparative advantage in control, but it has to be significant and as it melts away, trade shifts from a guarantee of win-win relations to a possibility of win-lose relations. David Ricardo, who was wiser than many of his own modern-day followers, actually knew this perfectly well. As he put it:

The difference in this respect, between a single country and many, is easily accounted for, by considering the difficulty with which capital moves from one country to another, to seek a more profitable employment, and the activity with which it invariably passes from one province to another of the same country.[376]

Ricardo then elaborates, using his favorite example of the trade in English cloth for Portuguese wine and cutting right to the heart of present-day concerns:

It would undoubtedly be advantageous to the capitalists of England, and to the consumers in both countries, that under such circumstances the wine and the cloth should both be made in Portugal, and therefore that the capital and labor of England employed in making cloth should be removed to Portugal for that purpose.[377]

But he does *not* say it would be advantageous to the workers of England! This is precisely the problem Americans experience today: when imports replace goods produced here, capitalists like the higher profits and consumers like the lower prices—but workers *don't* like the lost jobs. Given that consumers and workers are ultimately the same people, this means they may lose more as workers than they gain as consumers. And there is no theorem in economics which guarantees that their gains will exceed their losses.[378] Things can go either way, which means that free trade is sometimes a losing move for them.

Having observed that capital mobility would undo his theory, Ricardo then argues why capital will not, in fact, be mobile—as he knew he had to prove for his theory to hold water:

Experience, however, shows that the fancied or real insecurity of capital, when not under the immediate control of its owner, together with the natural disinclination which every man has to quit the country of his birth and connections, and entrust himself, with all his habits fixed, to a strange government and new laws, check the emigration of capital. These feelings, which I should be sorry to see weakened, induce most men of property to be satisfied with a low rate of profits in their own country, rather than seek a more advantageous employment for their wealth in foreign nations.[379]

So in the end, the inventor of the theoretical keystone of free trade had to rely upon government and instinctive economic localism in order to make his theory hold. *Something* has to anchor capital for it all to work.

Interestingly, the above paragraph hasn't just become untrue in the modern globalized era. It was *already* untrue a few years after Ricardo wrote it, when billions of pounds began flowing out of Britain to finance railways and other investments around the world. As a result, at its peak in 1914, an astounding 35 percent of Britain's net national wealth was held abroad—a figure not even remotely approached by any major nation before or since.[380] British investors' preference for building up other nations' industries, rather than their own, exacted a heavy toll on the once-dominant British economy, a story we will explore more in the next chapter.

Dubious Assumption #6: Short-term efficiency causes long-term growth.

The theory of comparative advantage is a case of what economists call static analysis. That is, it looks at the facts of a single instant in time and determines the best response to those facts at that instant. This is not an intrinsically invalid way of doing economics—balancing one's checkbook is an exercise in static analysis—but it is vulnerable to a key problem: *it says nothing about dynamic facts*. That is, it says nothing about how today's facts may change tomorrow. More importantly, it says nothing about how one might cause them to change in one's favor.

Imagine a photograph of a rock thrown up in the air. It is an accurate representation of the position of the rock at the instant it was taken. But one can't tell, from the photograph alone, whether the rock is rising or falling. The only way to know *that* is either to have a series of photographs, or add the information contained in the laws of physics to the information contained in the photograph.

The problem here is that even if the theory of comparative advantage tells us our best move today, given our productivities and opportunity costs in various industries, it *doesn't* tell us the best way to raise those productivities tomorrow. That, however, is the essence of economic growth, and in the long run much more important than squeezing every last drop of advantage from the productivities we have today. Economic growth, that is, is ultimately less about *using* one's factors of production than about *transforming* them—into more productive factors tomorrow.[381] The difference between poor nations and rich ones mainly consists in the problem of turning from Burkina Faso into South Korea; it does not consist in being the most efficient possible Burkina Faso forever. The theory of comparative advantage is not so much wrong about long-term growth as simply silent.

Analogously, it is a valid application of personal comparative advantage for someone with secretarial skills to work as a secretary and someone with banking skills to work as a banker. In the short run, it is efficient for them both, as it results in both being better paid than if they tried to swap roles. (They would both be fired for inability to do their jobs and earn zero.) But the path to personal success doesn't consist in being the best possible secretary forever; it consists in upgrading one's skills to better-paid occupations, like banker. And there is very little about being the best possible secretary that tells one how to do this.

Ricardo's own favorite example, the trade in English textiles for Portuguese wine, is very revealing here, though not in a way he would have liked. In Ricardo's day, textiles were produced in England with then-state-of-the-art technology like steam engines. The textile industry thus nurtured a sophisticated machine tool industry to make the parts for these engines, which drove forward the *general* technological capabilities of the British economy and helped it break into related industries like locomotives and steamships.[382] Wine, on the other hand, was made by methods that had not changed in centuries (and have only begun to change since about 1960, by the way). So for hundreds of years, wine production contributed no technological advances to the Portuguese economy, no drivers of growth, no opportunities to raise economy-wide productivity. And its own productivity remained static: it did the same thing over and over again, year after year, decade after decade, *century after century*, because this was where Portugal's immediate comparative advantage lay. It may have been Portugal's best move in the short run, but it was a dead end in the long run.

What happened to Portugal? It had actually been happening for over a century by the time Ricardo wrote, largely in rationalization of existing conditions. In 1703, in the Treaty of Methuen, Portugal exempted England from its prohibition on the importation of woolen cloth, while England agreed to admit Portuguese wines at a tariff one-third less than that applied to competitors. This treaty merely switched suppliers for the English, who did not produce wine, but it admitted a deluge of cheap English cloth into Portugal, which wiped out its previously promising textile industry. English capital eventually took control of Portugal's vineyards as their owners went into debt to London banks, and English influence sabotaged attempts at industrial policy that might have pushed Portugal back into textiles or other manufacturing industry. As textiles were (as they remain today) the first stepping stone to more-sophisticated industries, this all but prevented Portugal's further industrialization. Not until the 1960s, under the Salazar dictatorship, did any Portuguese government make a serious attempt to dig itself out of this trap and to this day, Portugal has not recovered its 17th-century position relative to other European economies and remains the poorest country in Western Europe.

Today, the theory of comparative advantage is similarly dangerous to poor and undeveloped nations because they tend, like Portugal, to have comparative advantage in industries that are economic dead ends. So despite being nominally free, free trade tends to lock them in place.

Dubious Assumption #7: Trade does not induce adverse productivity growth abroad.

As previously noted, our gains from free trade derive from the difference between *our* opportunity costs for producing products and the opportunity costs of our trading partners. This opens up a paradoxical but very real way for free trade to backfire.

When we trade with a foreign nation, this will generally build up that nation's industries, i.e. raise its productivity in them. Now it would be nice to assume that this productivity growth in our trading partners can only reduce their direct costs, therefore reduce their opportunity costs, and therefore increase our gains from trading with them. Our foreign suppliers will just become ever more efficient at supplying the things we want, and we will just get ever cheaper foreign goods in exchange for our own exports, right?

Wrong. As we saw in our initial discussion of absolute vs. comparative advantage, while productivity (output per unit of input) does determine direct costs, it *doesn't* determine opportunity costs. The alternative uses of factors of production do. As a result, productivity growth in some industries can actually *raise* our trading partners' opportunity costs in other industries—by increasing what they give up producing in one industry in order to produce in another. If the number of rolls they can make from a pound of dough somehow goes up (rolls get fluffier?), this will make it more expensive for them to bake bread instead. So they may cease to supply us with such cheap bread! It sounds odd, but the logic is inescapable.

Consider our present trade with China. Despite all the problems this trade causes us, we do get compensation in the form of some very cheap goods, thanks mainly to China's very cheap labor. The same goes for other poor countries we import from. But labor is cheap in poor countries because it has poor alternative employment opportunities. What if these opportunities improve? Then this labor may cease to be so cheap, and our supply of cheap goods may dry up.

This is actually what happened in Japan from the 1960s to the 1980s, as Japan's economy transitioned from primitive to sophisticated manufacturing and the cheap merchandise readers over 40 will remember (the same things stamped "Made in China" today, only less ubiquitous) disappeared from America's stores. Did this reduce the pressure of cheap Japanese labor on American workers? It did. But it also deprived us of some very cheap goods we used to get. (And it's not like Japan stopped pressing us, either, as it moved upmarket and started competing in more sophisticated industries.)

The same thing had happened with Western Europe as its economy recovered from WWII from 1945 to about 1960 and cheap European goods disappeared from our stores. Remember when BMWs were cheap little cars and Italian shoes were affordable? It's as if our football player woke up one morning and found that his lawn man had quietly saved his pennies from mowing lawns and opened a garden shop. No more cheap lawn mowings for him! (Maybe it was a bad idea to hire him so often.)

Now this is where things get slippery and non-economists tend to get lost. Because, as we saw earlier, gains from trade don't derive from absolute but comparative advantage, these gains can be killed off *without* our trading partners getting anywhere near our own productivity levels. So the above problem doesn't merely consist in our trading partners *catching up to us* in industrial sophistication. But if their *relative* tradeoffs for producing different goods cease to differ from ours, then our gains from trading with them will vanish. If Canada's wheat vs. corn tradeoff is two units per acre vs. three and ours is four vs. six, all bets are off. Because both nations now face the same tradeoff ratio between producing one grain and the other,[383] all possible trades will cost Canada *exactly* as much they benefit the US—leaving no profit, no motivation to trade, and no gain from doing so. And if free trade helped raise Canada's productivity to this point, then free trade deprived us of benefits we used to get.

It's worth retracing the logic here until it makes sense, as this really is the way the economics works. When Paul Samuelson—Nobel Laureate, dean of the profession, inventor of the mathematical foundations of modern economics while still a graduate student, and author of the best-selling economics textbook in history—reminded economists of this problem in a (quite accessible, for those readers who are curious) 2004 article, he drew scandalized gasps from one end of the discipline to the other.[384] How could anyone so distinguished criticize the sacred truth of free trade? Then he politely reminded his critics that he was merely restating a conclusion he had first published in his Nobel Lecture of 1972![385] As Samuelson noted, Ricardo himself was well aware of the problem:[386]

In Chapter 31 [of *The Principles of Political Economy and Taxation*] Ricardo discovers what he has elsewhere denied: that an improvement abroad can hurt Britain under free trade (or, as needs to be said today, that an improvement in Japan can hurt the American living standard).[387]

Most of the time, this problem has low visibility, because it consists in the unnoticed change of invisible ratios between the productivities of industries here and abroad. Few people worry about it because it has no easily understood face like cheap foreign labor. But it definitely does mean that free trade can "foul its own nest" and kill off the benefits of trade over time. Even within the most strictly orthodox Ricardian view, only the *existence* of benefits from free trade is guaranteed.[388] It is not guaranteed that changes *induced by* free trade will make these benefits grow, rather than shrink. So free trade can do billions of dollars worth of damage *even if Ricardo was right* about everything else (which he wasn't).

There are two standard rejoinders to this problem. The first is that while it proves that gains from free trade can go down as well as up, it doesn't actually prove that they can ever go below zero—which is what would have to happen for free trade to be literally bad for us. This is true. But this doesn't change the fact that if free trade *caused* our gains from trade to go down, then it reduced our economic well-being. We would have been better off under some protectionist policy that avoided stimulating so much productivity growth abroad. The second rejoinder is that productivity abroad can rise even without free trade on our part. This is also true. But if free trade sometimes causes productivity abroad to rise in a way that has the effects just described, then free trade is still sometimes bad for us.

This problem is actually even more significant than explained here because it is also the foundation of an even more radical critique of free trade we will look at later, after we have developed some needed conceptual tools. This concerns the nightmare scenario that *really* haunts Americans: the idea that free trade *can* help other nations catch up with us in industrial sophistication, driving us out of our own most valuable industries.[389]

HOW MUCH OF THE THEORY STILL STANDS?

Given that the theory of comparative advantage has all of the above-described flaws, how much validity does it retain? Some. It is a useful tool for analyzing trade in individual industries. Asking what industries a nation has comparative advantage in helps illuminate what kind of economy it has. And insofar as the theory's assumptions do hold, to some extent, some of the time, it can give us some valid policy recommendations. *Fairly open trade, most of the time, is a good thing.* But the theory was never intended to be by its own inventor, and its innate logic will not support its being, a blank check that justifies 100 percent free trade with 100 percent of the world 100 percent of the time. It only justifies free trade when its assumptions hold true,[390] and in the contemporary world, they quite clearly often do not.

One of the biggest insights remaining from the theory is that under free trade, a nation's wages will be determined, other things being equal, by its productivity in those sectors of its economy that possess comparative advantage. That is to say, wages in America aren't high because the productivity of barbers is higher here than in Ukraine. (It isn't, anyway.) Wages are higher because the productivity of aircraft manufacturing workers is higher. This is true because a nation's best industries tend to be those in which it has comparative advantage, and are thus the industries from which it exports. So under free trade, these industries expand and suck in labor, bidding up wages in other industries. This doesn't mean export industries will pay more. They will pay the same as other industries requiring the same skill level, as they draw labor from the same pool. But these industries, not other industries, will be pulling the labor market up.[391]

The converse is that it's a bad idea for a nation to lose its leading internationally traded industries. So all Americans, not just those working in these industries, have a stake in their health. Many Americans, especially those working in the 70 percent of our GDP that is in nontraded industries,[392] are indifferent to the problems of our tradable sector because they think these problems will never affect them. *Directly*, as previously noted, indeed they won't. But indirectly, they eventually will, as our wages are propped up, at the end of the day, by our ability to go work elsewhere if better money is offered. And this basically requires a strong export sector if we have free trade.[393]

MODERN DAY ELABORATIONS OF RICARDO

Free trade, of course, is not considered justified by economists today simply on the strength of Ricardo's original 1817 theory alone. His ideas have been considerably elaborated since then, and economists generally use sophisticated "computable general equilibrium" (CGE) computer models, built upon his work as the foundation, to assign actual dollar amounts to the purported benefits of free trade. These models are called "computable" because, unlike economic models that exist purely to prove theoretical points, it is possible to feed actual numbers into them and get numbers out the other end. They are called "general equilibrium" because they are based on the fundamental idea of free market economics: that the economy consists of a huge number of separate equilibria between supply and demand and that all these markets clear, or match supply with demand, at once. So it's worth looking at problems with these models a bit.

For a start, these models tend to make some rather implausible assumptions. For example, they often assume that government budget deficits and surpluses will not change due to the impact of trade, but will remain fixed at whatever they were in the starting year of the model. Worse, they assume that trade deficits or surpluses will be similarly stable, with exchange rates fluctuating to keep them constant. And they assume that a nation's investment rate will equal its savings rate: every dollar saved will flow neatly into some productive investment. These assumptions are understandable, as devices to simplify the models enough to make them workable. They are, however, both clearly untrue and serious objects of controversy in their own right.[394]

That investment will equal savings is basically a form of Say's Law, "supply creates its own demand," named after the French economist Jean-Baptiste Say (1767-1832).[395] This basically makes both underinvestment and unemployment theoretically impossible. Furthermore, these models often assume that nations enjoy magical macroeconomic stability: the business cycle has been mysteriously abolished. And their financial systems enjoy unruffled tranquility, without booms, busts, or bubbles. These assumptions are pre-Keynesian,[396] and thus at least 70 years behind mainstream domestic economics. (This is a recurring problem in free trade economics: ideas long discarded in other areas of economics recur with alarming regularity.)

These models also generally leave out transition costs. These sound temporary, but such transitions can take decades: consider the pain experienced by the Midwestern manufacturing areas of the U.S. as their industries have gradually lost comparative advantage since the mid-sixties! Given that the world economy is not static, but constantly moving into new industries, there are always new transitions being generated, which means that transition costs go on forever, as an intrinsic cost of having a global economy based on shifting patterns of comparative advantage. *Somebody* will always be the rustbelt. This does not of itself mean that economic change is a bad thing, but it does mean that these costs must be factored in to get an accurate accounting.

Trade in services (AKA offshoring) is another sticking point. The root problem here is that this trade usually isn't regulated the same way as trade in goods. Due to the fact that, prior to cheap long-distance telephony and the Internet, many services were rarely internationally traded, there are actually few outright tariffs or quotas on them. Instead, there is a crazy-quilt of hard-to-quantify barriers, ranging from licensing requirements to tacit local cartels and linguistic differences. As a result, when these barriers come down, they rarely come down in a neatly quantifiable way like reducing a tariff on cloth from 28 to 22 percent. So economists must basically guess how to quantify nonquantitative changes in order to model them. (The term for this is "tariff equivalent" numbers.) As a result, the conclusions generated by many models of trade in services are so dependent upon arbitrary guesses as to border on arbitrary themselves.

Another caveat: because all these models are predictions about the future, they are of necessity somewhat speculative under the best of circumstances and notoriously susceptible to deliberate manipulation. It is easy, for example, to generate inflated predictions of gains from trade by extrapolating calculations intended to apply only within certain limits with back-of-the-envelope calculations that go far beyond these limits. (These are known in the trade as "hockey stick" projections due to their shape when graphed.) So as Frank Ackerman of the Global Development and Environment Institute at Tufts University puts it:

> The larger estimates still being reported from some studies reflect speculative extensions of standard models, and/or very simple, separate estimates of additional benefit categories, not the core results of established modeling methodologies.[397]

Similarly, the standard way for free traders to play down the damage done to the victims of free trade is to count only workers *directly* displaced from jobs as its losers.[398] Unfortunately, these workers crowd into the labor market of everyone else with similar education and skills, dragging down wages for other people, too.

Even if all statistical gamesmanship is removed and other reforms made, there is a deeper problem with CGE models: no such model can predict what *choices of trade strategy* a nation will make. For example, none of the models used in the 1950s predicted Japan's ascent to economic superpower status. Quite probably, no model could have. Indeed, no model based upon purely free-market assumptions will ever readily predict the outcomes from such strategic choices, as free-market economics, with its insistence that it is always best to just do what the free market says, rules out a priori the possibility that most such deliberate economic strategies can even work.

IS BIG BUSINESS IN ON THE JOKE?

As we have seen, the theory of comparative advantage is considerably out of alignment with the real world. So we should, logically, expect this fact to affect the conduct of actual international businesses at some point. If the theory is wrong, that is, then surely they must deviate from it at some point simply in order to function profitably? A little investigation suffices to reveal that indeed they do: the business community is well aware of how problematic the theory is and generally avoids using it in practice. As Michael Porter, one of the stars of Harvard Business School, puts it:

> Comparative advantage based on factors of production is not sufficient to explain patterns of trade. Evidence hard to reconcile with factor comparative advantage is not difficult to find...More important, however, is that there has been a growing awareness that the assumptions underlying factor comparative advantage theories of trade are unrealistic in many industries...The theory also assumes that factors, such as skilled labor and capital, do not move among nations. All these assumptions bear little relation, in most industries, to actual competition.[399]

Nevertheless, the business community and its lobbyists in Washington use comparative advantage all the time in politics to lobby for more free trade. So to a huge extent, the American business community has been using, and broadcasting to the public through the media, economic ideas in which it does not itself believe—and refuses to live by.

6

The Deliberately
Forgotten History of Trade

WE SAW IN THE PREVIOUS CHAPTER why the theory of comparative advantage, the key justification economics offers for free trade, is a dubious construct. But if this is so, then economic history should reflect this fact. That is, successful economic powers should have prospered by defying this theory's recommendations, not by following them. This indeed turns out to be the case. But while it is widely known that economically successful nations like China and Japan have little use for free trade even today, what is less well understood is that even the nations that have historically *championed* free trade—the most important being Britain and the United States—have not actually practiced it for most of their history. Instead, they have long, successful, but *deliberately forgotten* records as protectionists.

Standard economic history taught in the United States is distorted by ideology and has key facts airbrushed out. That history, largely a product of Cold War myth-mongering about the virtues of pure free markets, attributes world economic growth to the spread of free markets to one nation after another, aided by free trade between them. Not only do free traders believe in this history, but it pretty much *has to be* true if the economics of free trade is valid. But economic history actually reveals that no major developed nation got that way by practicing free trade. Every single one did it by way of protectionism and industrial policy.

Industrial policy? That's the deliberate manipulation of the *domestic* economy to help industries grow. Although this is a book about protectionism, from this point on we will not be able to ignore industrial policy entirely. Industrial policy is inextricably bound up with protectionism because these two policies are just the domestic and foreign expressions of the same underlying fact: *100 percent pure free markets are not best.* So it is almost impossible for protectionism to be right without some kind of industrial policy being right, too. And because the mechanisms of effective protectionism are important largely for what they make happen *inside* the industries that make up an economy, understanding industrial policy helps illuminate what makes protectionism work.

One can, of course, always dismiss history as a guide to economic reality. In fact, this is precisely what contemporary economics, which is highly ahistorical, generally does.[400] It is impossible to run real controlled experiments in economics, as one can in the physical sciences, because this would require re-running history with alternative policies. Therefore one can always claim that nations which succeeded under protectionism would have succeeded without it. One can even claim that they succeeded in spite of, not because of, their protectionism, and that protectionism held them back.[401] But such criticism is empty, as it makes *any* economic claim logically immune to historical evidence. One can only let the history below speak for itself, and see what looks like the least tendentious and most plausible interpretation of the generally agreed facts.

THE GREAT BRITISH FREE-TRADE MYTH

According to the creation myth of free trade, Great Britain is the original motherland of free markets, home of Adam Smith and David Ricardo both, the first nation to break free of the misguided gold-hoarding mercantilism that came before and consequently the industrial superpower of the 19th century, erector of a global empire upon free-trade principles. As Britain was indeed a free-trading state for most of this period, this myth has surface plausibility. Among other things, the British themselves believed in it during their mid-19th-century economic zenith. Some of them still do: the British newsmagazine *The Economist* was founded in 1843 specifically to agitate for free trade, and does so today from airport newsstands on six continents.[402]

Unfortunately, this whole story depends upon tricks of historical timing and starts to fall apart once one gets a few dates right. Adam Smith published his epoch-making free-trade tract *The Wealth of Nations* in 1776. But Britain in 1776 was not a blank slate upon which free markets and free trade could work their magic. It was instead the beneficiary of several prior *centuries* of protectionism and industrial policy.[403] In the words of British economist William Cunningham:

> For a period of two hundred years [c. 1600-1800], the English nation knew very clearly what it wanted. Under all changes of dynasty and circumstances the object of building up national power was kept in view; and economics, though not yet admitted to the circle of the sciences, proved an excellent servant, and gave admirable suggestions as to the manner in which this aim might be accomplished.[404]

England in this era was, in fact, a classic authoritarian (this is long before English democracy)[405] developmentalist state: a *Renaissance South Korea*, with kings rather than the military dictators who ruled South Korea for most of the Cold War period. English industrialization must actually be traced *300 years* prior to Adam Smith, to events like Henry VII's imposition of a tariff on woolen goods in 1489.[406] King Henry's aim was to wrest the wool weaving trade, then the most technologically advanced major industry in Europe, away from Flanders (the Dutch half of present-day Belgium), where it had been thriving upon exports of English wool. Flemish producers were entrenched behind huge capital investments, which gave them economies of scale sufficient to outcompete fledgling entrants into the industry. So only government action could get England a toehold.

Even in the 15th century, there was an awareness that being an exporter of agricultural raw materials was a dead end—a problem African and Latin American nations wrestle with to this day. Henry VII created, in fact, the first *national industrial policy* of the modern era, long before the Industrial Revolution introduced artificial energy sources like steam power.[407] A whole interlocking series of now-forgotten policy moves underlay the rise of English industry; what all these measures had in common was that protectionism was essential to making them work. In the words of economist John Culbertson of the University of Wisconsin and the Federal Reserve Board of Governors:

Step after step in the cumulative economic rise of England was directly caused by government action or depended upon supportive government action: the prohibition of importation of Spanish wool by Henry I, the revision of land-tenure arrangements to permit the development of large-scale sheep raising, Edward III's attracting of Flemish weavers to England and then prohibiting of the wearing of foreign cloth, the termination of the privileges in London of the Hanseatic League under Edward VI, the near-war between England under Elizabeth I and the Hanseatic League, which supported the rise of English shipping. And then there was the prohibition of export of English wool (which damaged the Flemish textile industry and stimulated that of England), the encouragement of production of dyed and finished cloth in England, the use of England's dominance in textile manufacture to push the Hanseatic League out of foreign markets for other products, the encouragement of fishing...[408]

The aim of English policy was what would today be called "climbing the value chain": deliberately leveraging existing economic activity to break into more-sophisticated related activities. Fifteenth-century England was considerably more primitive than Bangladesh is today, so, among other things, it had not yet developed sophisticated financial markets capable of systematically identifying and exploiting business opportunities. Therefore it could not count on the free market to drive its industry into ever-more-advanced activities, but required the active intervention of the state to do so. The free market does not spring into existence fully formed and functional automatically or overnight, a lesson most recently demonstrated in the chaos of post-Communist Russia.

Henry VII's advisors got their economic ideas ultimately from the city-states of Renaissance Italy, where economics had been born as a component of Civic Humanism, their now-forgotten governing ideology.[409] The name for this forgotten developmentalist wisdom of early modern Europe that has stuck is *mercantilism*. One of the great myths of contemporary economics is that mercantilism was an analytically vacuous bundle of gold-hoarding prejudices.[410] It was, in fact, a remarkably sophisticated attempt, given the limited conceptual apparatus of the time, to advance national economic development by means that would be familiar and congenial to the technocrats of 21st-century Tokyo, Beijing, or Seoul.[411]

Mercantilists invented many economic concepts still in use today, such as the balance of payments, value added, and the embodied labor content of imports and exports. They championed the economic interests of the nation as a whole at a time when special interests (notably royal monopolies) were an even bigger problem than today. They began with obvious ideas like taxing foreign luxury goods. They progressed to the idea that exporting raw materials for foreigners to process was bad if the nation could process them itself.[412] They understood that nations rose economically by imitating the industries of already rich nations (first the more primitive industries, then the more sophisticated) and that low relative wages were the key advantage of underdeveloped nations in this game.

Even mercantilists' much-mocked obsession with the accumulation of bullion was not as irrational as it is usually depicted as being, given that under a monetary system based on gold, accumulating it is the only way to expand the money supply and drive down interest rates, a boon to investment then as now.[413] Mercantilism, in fact, created the modern European economy and thus made possible the colonial power that economically shaped much of the rest of the world. It is thus the foundation of modern capitalism itself.

Anyhow: Britain functioned on a mercantilist basis for *centuries* before its much misunderstood experiment with free trade began. Even as late as the beginning of the 19th century, Britain's average tariff on manufactured goods was roughly 50 percent—the highest of any major nation in Europe.[414] And even after Britain embraced free trade in most goods, it continued to tightly regulate trade in strategic capital goods, such as the machinery for the mass production of textiles, in order to forestall its rivals. As we saw in the previous chapter, this was rational, as the win-win logic of free trade can break down if factors of production are mobile between nations (dubious assumption #4) or if free trade induces adverse productivity growth abroad (dubious assumption #6).[415] Even Adam Smith himself was only in favor of free trade *after* Britain had consolidated its industrial power through protectionism.[416]

BRITAIN'S FREE TRADE GAMBLE

Free trade in Britain began in earnest with the repeal of the Corn Laws in 1846, which amounted to free trade in food, Britain's major import at the time. ("Corn," in the usage of the day, meant all grains.) The general election of 1852 was taken for a plebiscite on the question,[417] and free trade began inexorably to restructure the British economy from without.[418] Repealing the Corn Laws was a momentous step because this removed the last major constraint on Britain's transformation, along the lines of its then-comparative advantage in manufacturing, into the world's first industrial society, where most workers would be factory workers, not farmers: how to feed so many factory workers?

To some extent, the objective of the Corn Laws was simply to feed a bulge in population (almost a tripling in the previous 100 years) on a small island with limited agricultural potential.[419] Competition with the prairies of North America eventually devastated Britain's old rural economy and the aristocracy that had lived off its agricultural rents,[420] but so committed was Britain to free trade that this price was accepted as in no other nation. Britain's rulers expected that free trade would result in their country dominating the emerging global industrial economy due to its head start, sidelining its trading partners into agriculture and raw materials. They expected their lead in shipping, technology, scale economies, and financial infrastructure to be self-reinforcing and thus last indefinitely.[421]

If the rest of the world had been content to be played for fools, this strategy might have worked. Instead, it enjoyed a brief window of plausibility in the 1850s and 1860s, which were the zenith of classical liberalism (of which free trade was a part) in Europe generally. Then things started to sour. For one thing, this zenith of free trade coincided with a prolonged Europe-wide depression, which started to lift as protectionism began to take hold.[422] More fundamentally, the British plan for universal free trade stumbled as the U.S. and the rest of Europe declined to accept their inferior allotted roles in the global trading system. In Germany and the United States especially, people accused Britain of favoring free trade for *other* countries and only *after* having secured its own position through protectionism. The influential German economist Friedrich List (1789-1846) called this "kicking away the ladder." As one British Lord said in Parliament:

> Other nations knew, as well the noble lord opposite, and those who acted with him, that what we meant by free trade, was nothing more nor less than, by means of the great advantages we enjoyed, to get the monopoly of all their markets for our manufactures, and to prevent them, one and all, from ever becoming manufacturing nations.[423]

So despite British preaching, free trade was falling apart. Britain practiced it unilaterally in the vain hope of imitation, but the United States emerged from the Civil War even more explicitly protectionist than before, Germany under Bismarck turned in this direction in 1879, and the rest of Europe followed. During the 1880s and 1890s, tariffs went up in Sweden, Italy, France, Austria-Hungary, and Spain.[424] There was good reason for this: they worked. A study by the Irish economist Kevin O'Rourke shows a clear correlation between protection and economic growth rates in Europe in the 1875-1914 period.[425]

FOREIGN PROTECTIONISM, BRITISH DECLINE

The United States brought to global competition continental economies of scale and a more aggressively commercial culture than Britain. Germany brought industrial paternalism that delivered an efficient workforce and a prescient understanding that science-based industry was the wave of the future, quintessentially in optics, chemical engineering, and the electrical industries. Both nations forged ahead under protectionism. Britain's economy still grew, but inexorably lagged: from 1870 to 1913, industrial production rose an average of 4.7 percent per year in the U.S., 4.1 percent in Germany, but only 2.1 percent in Britain.[426] In the melancholy words of one commentator:

> The industries that formed the core of the British economy in the 19th century, textiles and steel, were developed during the period 1750-1840—before England abandoned mercantilism. Britain's lead in these fields held for roughly two decades after adopting free trade but eroded as other nations caught up. Britain then fell behind as new industries, using more advanced technology, emerged after 1870. These new industries were fostered by states that still practiced mercantilism, including protectionism.[427]

But despite the mounting failure of its great strategic gamble, Britain stuck to free trade abroad and a laissez-faire absence of industrial policy at home. Fundamentally, the country was lulled by the Indian summer of its industrial supremacy—it was surpassed economically by the U.S. only around 1880—into thinking that free trade was optimal as a permanent policy. The clarity of British thinking was not helped by the fact that certain vested interests had fattened upon free trade and established a grip upon the levers of power that was hard to break.

Britain's decline did not go unnoticed at the time, either at home or abroad. Neither did the underlying problem: in the 1906 words of Member of Parliament F.E. Smith, later famous as a friend of Winston Churchill:

> We give to our rivals a free market of 43,000,000 persons in the United Kingdom to add to their own free market. Thus the United States possess an open market of 82,000,000 persons in the United States, plus an open market of 43,000,000 persons in Great Britain, making, altogether, 125,000,000. Similarly, Germany possesses an open market of 43,000,000 in Great Britain. As against this, we possess only such residual of our open market of 43,000,000 as the unrestricted competition of foreign nations leaves unimpaired....*We call ourselves free traders, but we have never secured free trade for ourselves; we have merely succeeded in enlarging the area within which our protectionist competitors enjoy free trade.*[428] (Emphasis added.)

Some British politicians set out to do something about the problem. The great crusader to abolish free trade was the Conservative Parliamentarian Joseph Chamberlain (1836-1914), father of the more famous Neville.[429] As he put it in a major speech in 1903:

> I believe that all this is part of the old fallacy about the transfer of employment...It is your fault if you do not leave the industry which is failing and join the industry which is rising. Well—sir, it is an admirable theory; it satisfies everything but an empty stomach. Look how easy it is. Your once great trade in sugar refining is gone; all right, try jam. Your iron trade is going; never mind, you can make mouse traps. The cotton trade is threatened; well, what does that matter to you? Suppose you tried dolls' eyes...But how long is this to go on? Why on earth are you to suppose that the same process which ruined sugar refining will not in the course of time be applied to jam? And when jam is gone? Then you have to find something else. And believe me, that although the industries of this country are very various, you cannot go on forever. You cannot go on watching with indifference the disappearance of your principal industries.[430]

The British turn-of-the-last-century debate eerily echoes the free trade debate in America today. It was an era like our own, with new technologies like the steamship and the telegraph ushering in fears of what a borderless global economy might bring. The political fate of a weakening superpower with global responsibilities was bound up in fears of its economic decline. Consider these familiar-sounding agenda items from a conference of Britain's Trades Union Congress: "the need to deal with competition from the Asian colonies" and "the need to match the educational and training standards of the United States and Germany."[431]

The same accusations made in the U.S. today flew back and forth. Free traders were accused of viewing economics solely from the consumer's point of view and of favoring short-term consumption over long-term producer vitality. Protectionist concern for producer vitality was tarred as mere cover for special interests. It was debated whether protectionism stifled competition by excluding foreigners or preserved it by saving domestic competitors (New trade theory now understands it can do either).[432] It was debated whether the country was living off its past capital. It clearly was: by the late 19th century, Britain ran a chronic deficit in goods and only managed to balance its trade by exporting services as shipper and banker to the world and by collecting returns on past overseas investments. Free traders were accused of abstractionism; in the words of one book at the time:

> The free trader hardly professes to base his opinions on experience; he is content to adduce illustrations from actual life of what he believes *must* happen.[433]

Those words could have been written yesterday! The trustworthiness of British economists, ideologically mortgaged to the free-trade tradition of classical political economy, was questioned. Free traders denied the existence of a crisis on the grounds that the nation's sunrise industries were doing well (some were, but not enough to replace the sunset industries being lost). The two sides preened themselves on their cosmopolitanism and their patriotism, respectively.

In hindsight, the protectionists had the stronger case, but were outfought by the superior rhetorical and political skill of their rivals. The vested interests and experienced political tacticians were mostly on the free-trade side—which included half of Chamberlain's own Conservative party, which split on the question. Free traders were defending a status quo bound up in concepts of economic liberty believed essential to British national identity, concepts that struck at the heart of what made Britons different from statist Continental Europeans. And free trade's opponents made no attack upon the economic theory *behind* free trade, beyond blankly denying its validity. This made it impossible for them to construct a case against free trade strong enough to pull it up by its roots.

Chamberlain struggled to enact a tariff from 1903 to 1906, when his party fought a general election, largely on this very issue. The divided Conservatives lost to the free-trade Liberal party. Their next chance came in 1923 and they lost again, this time to the free trade Labour party. Thanks to the Great Depression, Britain finally abandoned free trade in 1931—but by then it was too little, too late. Although protectionism buffered Britain against the Depression somewhat, it was far too late to redeem the nation's position as a leading economic power. Today, outside the City of London's financial center, the one-time Workshop of the World, which generated a third of global industrial production in 1870,[434] is an economic asterisk.

AMERICA, SWEET LAND OF PROTECTIONISM

The idea that America's economic tradition has been economic liberty, laissez faire, and wide-open cowboy capitalism—which would naturally include free trade—resonates well with our national mythology. It fits the image of this country held by both the right (which celebrates this tradition) and the left (which bemoans it). It is believed both here and abroad. But when it comes to trade at least, it is simply not real history. The reality is that all four presidents on Mount Rushmore were protectionists. (Even Jefferson came around after the War of 1812.)[435] Protectionism is, in fact, the real American Way.

Americans were alert to the dangers inherent in trade economics even before Independence. During the colonial period, the British government tried to force its American colonies to become suppliers of raw materials to the nascent British industrial machine while denying them any manufacturing industry of their own. The colonies were, in fact, one of the major *victims* of Britain's previously-noted mercantilist policy, being under Britain's direct political control, unlike its other trading partners. As former Prime Minster William Pitt, otherwise a famous conciliator of American grievances and the namesake of Pittsburgh, said in Parliament, "If the Americans should manufacture a lock of wool or a horse shoe, I would fill their ports with ships and their towns with troops."[436]

To some extent, the American Revolution was, in fact, *a war over industrial policy*, in which the commercial elite of the Colonies revolted against being forced into an inferior role in the emerging Atlantic economy. This is one of the things that gave the American Revolution its exceptionally bourgeois character as revolutions go, with bewigged Founding Fathers rather than the usual unshaven revolutionary mobs. It is no accident that upon Independence, a tariff was the very second bill signed by President Washington.[437]

Protectionism's first American theorist was Alexander Hamilton—the man on the $10 bill, the first Treasury Secretary, and America's first *technocrat*. As aide-de-camp to General Washington during the Revolution, he had seen the U.S. nearly lose due to lack of capacity to manufacture weapons (France rescued us with 80,000 muskets and other war materiel.) He worried that Britain's lead in manufacturing would remain entrenched, condemning the United States to being a producer of agricultural products and raw materials. In modern terms, a banana republic. As he put it in 1791:

> The superiority antecedently enjoyed by nations who have preoccupied and perfected a branch of industry, constitutes a more formidable obstacle than either of those which have been mentioned, to the introduction of the same branch into a country in which it did not before exist. To maintain, between the recent establishments of one country, and the long-matured establishments of another country, a competition upon equal terms, both as to quality and price, is, in most cases, impracticable. The disparity, in the one, or in the other, or in both, must necessarily be so considerable, as to forbid a successful rivalship, without the extraordinary aid and protection of government.[438]

Hamilton's policies came down to about a dozen key measures. In his own words:[439]

1. "Protecting duties." (Tariffs.)

2. "Prohibition of rival articles or duties equivalent to prohibitions." (Outright import bans.)

3. "Prohibition of the exportation of the materials of manufactures." (Export bans on industrial inputs, like King Henry VII's ban on exporting raw wool.)

4. "Pecuniary bounties." (Export subsidies, like those provided today by the Export-Import Bank and other programs.)

5. "Premiums." (Subsidies for key innovations. Today, we would call them research and development tax credits.)

6. "The exemption of the materials of manufactures from duty." (Import liberalization for industrial inputs, so some *other* country can be the raw materials exporter.)

7. "Drawbacks of the duties which are imposed on the materials of manufactures." (Same idea, by means of tax rebates.)

8. "The encouragement of new inventions and discoveries at home, and of the introduction into the United States of such as may have been made in other countries; particularly those, which relate to machinery." (Prizes for inventions and, more importantly, patents.)

9. "Judicious regulations for the inspection of manufactured commodities." (Regulation of product standards, as the USDA and FDA do today.)

10. "The facilitating of pecuniary remittances from place to place." (A sophisticated financial system.)

11. "The facilitating of the transportation of commodities." (Good infrastructure.)

Hamilton set forth his case in his *Report on Manufactures*, submitted to Congress in 1791.[440] Due in large part to the domination of Congress by Southern planters, who favored free trade, Hamilton's policies were not all adopted right away. It took the War of 1812, which created a surge of anti-British feeling, disrupted normal trade, and drastically increased the government's need for revenue, to push America firmly into the protectionist camp. But when war broke out, Congress immediately doubled the tariff to an average of 25 percent.[441]

After the war, British manufacturers undertook one of the world's first well-documented cases of predatory dumping, whose purpose was, in the words of one Member of Parliament, to "stifle in the cradle, those rising manufactures in the United States, which the war had forced into existence."[442] In reaction, the American industrial interests that had blossomed because of the tariff lobbied to keep it, and had it raised to 35 percent in 1816. The public approved and by 1820, America's average tariff was up to 40 percent.[443]

Fast-forward a few years. Gloss over a number of important tariff-related political struggles, such as the South Carolina Nullification Crisis of 1832, one of the precursors of the Civil War, in which South Carolina tried to reject a federal tariff. There was a brief free trade episode starting in 1846, coinciding with the aforementioned zenith of classical liberalism in Europe, during which America's tariffs were lowered. But this was followed by a series of recessions, ending in the Panic of 1857, which brought demands for a higher tariff so intense that President James Buchanan—the last free-trade president for two generations—gave in and signed one two days before Abraham Lincoln took office in 1861.[444]

SLAVERY VS. THE TARIFF

The next big protectionist event in American history is the rise of the Republican party, spurred into being by the conflict over slavery but inheriting from its Whig party antecedent an agenda of aggressive government support for economic development. The new party favored a number of policies to this end, including hard money (deflation, the preference of creditors), subsidies for railroads, free land for homesteaders, and higher tariffs. In office from 1861, the Republicans lost no time raising tariffs, using the excuse of funding the Civil War and conveniently not having free-trade Southern Democrats in office. President Lincoln's economic guru was a Philadelphia economist named Henry Carey—forgotten in our day but world-famous in his own.[445]

It would be an exaggeration to say that the Civil War was "about" the tariff, as some Southern partisans claim, eager to shed the opprobrium of the South's having fought for slavery. But slavery and free trade are intimately connected as economic policies because free trade is, in fact, the ideal policy for a nation which actually *wants* to be an agricultural slave state. Because slaves are unsuitable for industrial work, slave states from Rome onward have failed to industrialize.[446] Because they have no hope of developing comparative advantage in manufacturing, their best move is to optimize the comparative advantage in slave-based agriculture they are stuck with and import most everything else. Classic Ricardian free trade fits this strategy to a "t." The antebellum South, having little manufacturing industry to protect, derived little benefit from the tariff. Economically, it was still a part of the British Empire that bought its cotton, America's leading export before 1870.[447] As the tariff was the main source of federal revenue in those pre-income tax days, the South also bore a disproportionate share of the nation's tax burden. No wonder it was in favor of free trade, which the Confederate constitution eventually mandated.[448]

There is a larger lesson here, reaching beyond American history. Almost all nations that have failed to break into modern industry have a common characteristic: in terms of U.S. history, *their equivalents of the South won their civil wars.* These were not all actual wars, of course, some being merely struggles of interest-group politics, but the pattern is consistent: agricultural or raw-materials interests won a battle with rising manufacturing interests and biased the economic policy of the state in their favor. Sometimes this outcome was imposed by a colonial overlord, but it was often self-inflicted.

This pattern goes way back, predating the industrial revolution by centuries. In Spain, for example, the key moment was arguably the *Guerra do los Comuneros* of 1520-21, in which aristocratic agricultural interests, embodied in such groups as the sheep owners' organization *La Mesta*, won control of economic policy after a failed insurrection against the Habsburg monarchy.[449] So instead of protecting its manufacturing, Spain protected agricultural products like olive oil and wine. As a result, Spanish industrialization actually went backwards and Spain gradually *de*industrialized for the remainder of the century. Then came the easy pickings of New World empire, and a flood of silver and gold caused Spain to lose interest in industrialization completely. Its economy has only converged with the level of its European peers in the last 20 years.

THE GOLDEN AGE OF AMERICAN INDUSTRY

After the Civil War, tariffs stayed high during the long Republican hegemony from 1865 to 1932. Reading the speeches of 19th-century Republican politicians today, with their expressions of concern for the wages of the American working man, one finds oneself wondering how the party slipped to its present day let-them-eat-cake position. (One can dismiss these sentiments as fraud, but the tariff was real enough.) Republicans of the robber-baron era were no angels, but they did believe that American capitalism depended upon class harmony—in contrast, as they saw it, to unstable revolutionary Europe.[450] Without a significant welfare state, America had to do *something* to smooth the rougher edges of capitalism, and the tariff was a way to unite the interests of American workers and American capitalists.

The country at large generally supported this policy, though the left- and right-wing extremists of the day naturally dissented. Extreme right wing Social Darwinists like William Graham Sumner—who published a fuming book in 1885 entitled *Protectionism, the Ism That Teaches That Waste Makes Wealth*—saw protectionism as a subsidy for the incompetent and an interference with the divine justice of the free market and the survival of the fittest.[451] Karl Marx, at the other extreme, wanted to see American capitalism break down and therefore favored free trade for its destructive potential. He wrote that:

> The protective system of our day is conservative, while the free trade system is destructive. It breaks up old nationalities and pushes the antagonism of the proletariat and bourgeoisie to the extreme point. In a word, the free trade system hastens the social revolution. It is in this revolutionary sense alone, gentlemen, that I vote in favor of free trade.[452]

The Democrats of this era, who generally supported free trade, were not Marxists, of course. But they saw the tariff as either a tax on the non-industrial regions of the country (like the South, solidly agrarian and solidly Democratic during this period) or as a racket for the benefit of big business. In the 1913 words of Democratic Congressman (later the famous House Speaker) Sam Rayburn of Texas:

> The system of protective tariffs built up under the Republican misrule has worked to make the rich richer and the poor poorer. The protective tariff has been justly called the mother of trusts [monopolies]. It takes from the pockets of those least able to pay and puts into the pockets of those most able to pay. The two great parties in the long past took distinct positions upon the tariff question—the Democratic party of the masses on the one side and the Republican party of the classes on the other side.[453]

America's tariff regime in this era was not especially sophisticated. One searches the historical record in vain for complex theories about what the tariff should be or for the elaborate technocratic institutions that managed it. There were neither. Tariff policy was mostly set by not-entirely-uncorrupt Congressional logrolling. Corruption was moderated by the fact that the dealmaking was fairly public (as tariffs were considered nothing to be ashamed of), and the tariffs themselves were moderated by the fact that one industry's output was often another's input, so lobbyists seeking higher tariffs were counterbalanced by lobbyists seeking lower ones. But that's about as subtle as things got. In Sumner's annoyed words:

> They have never had any plan or purpose in their tariff legislation. Congress has simply laid itself open to be acted upon by the interested parties, and the product of its tariff legislation has been simply the resultant of the struggles of the interested cliques with each other, and of the logrolling combinations which they have been forced to make among themselves.[454]

But it worked. This was the golden age of American industry, when America's economic performance surpassed the rest of the world by the greatest margin. It was the era in which the U.S. transformed itself from a promising mostly agricultural backwater, pupil at the knee of European industry, into the greatest economic power in the history of the world.

About the only technocratic sophistication American tariffs had was some drift towards taxing manufactured goods more than raw materials. In part, this simply reflected the fact that raw material imports were less likely to face a competing American industry lobbying for its own protection. In 1872, keeping pace with American industrialization, Congress modified the tariff from a broad-based levy on a wide range of imports to a narrower one targeted at protecting industrial wages and manufacturing industry.[455] The U.S. went from importing five percent of its imports untaxed to nearly 50 percent; tea and coffee now came in duty-free.[456]

Protectionism was the overwhelming consensus of the era. Grover Cleveland, the sole Democratic president of the 1870-1913 period, survived politically largely by keeping quiet about the tariff. Then, after his first term in office, he ran in 1888 on a platform of cutting the tariff in favor of an income tax, devoting his entire 1887 State of the Union address to this idea. He was tarred in the press as a dupe of British interests and lost to Republican Benjamin Harrison.[457] He learned his lesson and recanted. He returned to office in 1893, the only split-term president in American history.

The chart below gives the big picture. Note that this chart does not show the average tariff on *dutiable* goods (not all goods have been dutiable), and that it masks variations by product. Note also that changes in tariffs collected as a percentage of total imports can be caused not only by changes in tariff *rates*, but also by shifting proportions of what is imported. And remember that part of the significance of a tariff is that it eliminates some imports entirely, a fact that does not show up on this chart at all.

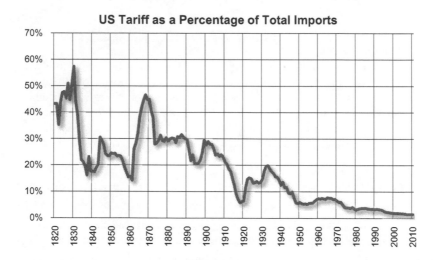

Source: author's chart from "Merchandise imports and duties, 1790-2000," Table Ee424 -430 in Historical Statistics of the United States, Earliest Times to the Present, *edited by Susan B. Carter et al. New York: Cambridge University Press, 2006, and Census Bureau and Customs & Border Protection for 2000-2010.*

AMERICA'S RETREAT FROM THE TARIFF

Contrary to what one might expect, the United States' retreat from the tariff was not caused by changes in policymakers' opinions about economics. That is, there was no point at which they decided that the economics of protectionism was false and the economics of free trade was true. Rather, this retreat was driven by essentially *political* motives, operating in a space of economic insouciance carved out by our mid-20th-century economic zenith. Fundamentally, we believed that the foundations of our economic strength were so secure that we didn't have to worry very much anymore about what they were. And for decades after we started dismantling protectionism, the legacy effects of 150 years of it shielded us from the consequences of increasingly free trade and distorted our understanding of what those consequences really were.

Woodrow Wilson was the first modern president to believe in free trade. (It was number three of his famous Fourteen Points for Peace after WWI.) He succeeded in reducing tariffs in 1913, in the course of introducing income tax for the first time since the Civil War, but Congress pushed them back up in 1921. The Roaring Twenties were a tariff era.

The "notorious" Smoot-Hawley tariff of 1930 is sometimes blamed for all or part of the Great Depression—most recently by presidential candidate John McCain, who said during the 2008 presidential campaign:

> Every time the United States has practiced protectionism we've paid a very heavy price for it. Some even claim, with some authenticity, that the Smoot-Hawley tariff act was a major contributor to the outbreak of World War II, not to mention the Great Depression.[458]

This accusation is obviously implausible, given that the Depression was already taking hold, due to the 1929 stock market crash, before Smoot-Hawley even passed Congress. And it was proved by economist Milton Friedman (at least to the satisfaction of the Nobel Prize committee) that the Depression's cause was monetary.[459] The Fed had allowed the money supply to balloon during the late 1920s, piling up in the stock market as a bubble. It then panicked, miscalculated, and let it collapse by a third by 1933, depriving the economy of the liquidity it needed to breathe. Trade policy was not involved.

As for the charge that Smoot-Hawley caused the Depression to spread worldwide? It did not affect enough trade, or raise the tariff by enough, to have plausibly so large an effect.[460] For a start, it only applied to about one-third of America's trade: about 1.3 percent of our GDP. Our average duty on dutiable goods went from 44.6 to 53.2 percent—hardly a radical change.[461] Tariffs as a percentage of total imports were higher in almost every year from 1821 to 1914.[462] America's tariffs went up in 1861, 1864, 1890, and 1922 without producing global depressions, and the recessions of 1873 and 1893 managed to spread worldwide without tariff increases.[463]

Neither does the myth of a death spiral of retaliation by foreign nations hold water.[464] According to the official State Department report on this question in 1931:

> With the exception of discriminations in France, the extent of discrimination against American commerce is very slight...By far the largest number of countries do not discriminate against the commerce of the United States in any way.[465]

World trade declined, but almost entirely due to the Depression itself, not tariffs. "Notorious" Smoot-Hawley is a deliberately fabricated myth, plain and simple.[466] *Smoot* was a moderate and routine adjustment to America's trade regime, not a major shock to the world trading system.[467]

THE TURNING POINT ON TARIFFS

America's tariffs first started to come down for good in 1934, at the instigation of FDR's Secretary of State Cordell Hull. Hull's faith in free trade had more to do with his belief it would promote world peace than any particular economic analysis. In his own words:

> I reasoned that, if we could get a freer flow of trade—freer in the sense of fewer discriminations and obstructions—so that one country would not be deadly jealous of another and the living standards of all countries might rise, thereby eliminating the economic dissatisfaction that breeds war, we might have a reasonable chance for lasting peace.[468]

This strange quasi-Marxist view that the underlying cause of war is "economic dissatisfaction" finds little support in history. But because of it, by 1937 the U.S. had reciprocally cut tariffs with Cuba, Belgium, Haiti, Sweden, Brazil, Colombia, Honduras, Canada, Switzerland, Nicaragua, Guatemala, France, Finland, Costa Rica, El Salvador, Czechoslovakia, and Ecuador.[469] This first turn towards tariff cuts was greased through Congress by being presented as "an emergency measure to deal with emergency panic conditions," and was mostly not spotted for the historic turning point it was. Because the Great Depression and World War II interfered with normal trade, it had little immediate practical effect, and the idea of tariff cutting was quietly assimilated to the New Deal consensus without much public ado, despite some fierce battles inside the administration.[470]

But a trend had taken root. As part of this change, Congress unconstitutionally (contra Article I, Section 8, which reads, "*Congress* shall have Power To lay and collect Taxes, Duties, Imposts and Excises [and] to regulate Commerce with foreign Nations") ceded control over tariffs to the President. FDR turned the task over to mid-level officials from the State Department and other government departments—men not even sufficiently highly placed to require Congressional confirmation.[471] Free traders have ever since preferred to keep tariffs out of the hands of Congress and in the hands of "experts" insulated from democratic accountability. Congress had previously managed the tariff with moderately corrupt favor trading and had had few ideological or geopolitical axes to grind. The Executive was also subject to interest-group politics, but it operated behind closed doors and had a far stronger tendency to make tariff policy the handmaiden of extraneous foreign policy agendas.[472]

FREE TRADE TO BEAT COMMUNISM

In the aftermath of World War II and in the face of British decline, the U.S. assumed Britain's mantle of global underwriter of free trade. In the 1947 negotiations that established the General Agreement on Tariffs and Trade, the world's main trading framework until establishment of the World Trade Organization in 1995, America cut its average tariff 35 percent.[473] It was easy to do at the time, with the U.S. running a substantial (4.2 percent of GDP) trade surplus from 1946 to 1947.[474]

This was a deliberate Cold War strategy aimed at strengthening the economies of the noncommunist world and binding them to the U.S.[475] It was obviously geopolitically wise, even if we know now that Communism was a less formidable economic challenger than it then seemed. "All problems of local industry pale into insignificance in relation to the world crisis," President Eisenhower told Congress in 1953.[476] Thus America became the only major market open to trade; all the others were small, poor, protected, socialist or communist.

At this stage of the game, American policymakers still had some residual awareness of the value of tariffs. (The delusion that free trade actually made economic sense only set in later.) Thus the Marshall Plan to deliberately reindustrialize Europe, and industrialize for the first time agricultural nations like Italy and semi-industrialized nations like France, employed high tariff walls and tight controls on capital mobility.[477] At the time, we believed not that free trade made economic sense for us, but that our superior productivity had bought us enough breathing room to engage in it for political reasons regardless.[478] As President Truman put it:

> Our industry dominates world markets...American labor can now produce so much more than low-priced foreign labor in a given day's work that our workingmen need no longer fear, as they were justified in fearing in the past, the competition of foreign workers.[479]

For 15 years or so, this was probably true. But our allies' economies had recovered from WWII by 1960. And by the end of the 1960s, world Communism's "We will bury you" threat to surpass us economically (which had genuinely worried rational people watching the USSR grow faster than the U.S. in the 1950s) had ceased to be credible.[480] So the original rationales for America's turn towards free trade had expired.

In retrospect, the early 1960s were the time America should have turned back from free trade. We certainly could have. Unfortunately, we instead made the exact same mistake Britain had made a century before and mistook the short-term advantages of free trade, when viewed from the perspective of the leading economy of the day, for permanent benefits. In the early 1960s, it certainly *seemed* as if imports were only penetrating low-end industries, giving us foreign goods on the cheap while leaving our high-value industrial sectors unharmed. This appeared to vindicate the Ricardian notion that free trade would always operate in our favor. So we let a policy with a temporary and political origin harden into a permanent economic dogma. We started to indulge the delusion that the underlying economics really *did* work.

FREE TRADE SOURS FOR AMERICA

In retrospect, John F. Kennedy's Trade Expansion Act of 1962 was America's decisive wrong turn on trade.[481] Quantitatively, the so-called Kennedy Round of tariff cuts was large enough to be noticed, but not earth-shaking: as this legislation was phased in, our average duty on dutiable imports fell from 14.3 percent in 1967 to 9.9 percent in 1972.[482] But this was one of history's small yet decisive turning points, occurring as it did at the same moment that America's trading partners were getting into high gear economically and the 1944-71 Bretton Woods system of fixed exchange rates was beginning to falter. And tariff cuts were exceptionally steep on high technology goods, increasing their impact.[483] Furthermore, the Trade Expansion Act should be evaluated not simply in terms of its before and after tariff levels, but contrasted with the alternative of turning back from free trade, which is what we should have done.

There were certainly warnings at the time. The famous liberal economist John Kenneth Galbraith bluntly told President Johnson in 1964 that "If we are screwed on tariffs, this will have an enduringly adverse effect on the balance of payments. It will be a serious problem for years to come."[484] And, lo and behold, the first serious trade-related cracks in the American economy began to appear in the late 1960s. Black-and-white television production left for Japan. So did cameras, transistor radios, and toys. Our trade went into deficit in 1971. We have not run a surplus since 1975.[485]

There has, of course, been a simmering revolt against free trade ever since. Organized labor, which had actually *supported* the Kennedy tariff cuts when proposed in 1962, turned against free trade by the end of the decade. In 1968, Senators Ernest Hollings (D-SC) and Norris Cotton (R-NH) managed to pass a protectionist trade bill in the Senate with 68 votes. President Johnson had it killed by House Ways and Means Committee chairman Wilbur Mills.[486] 1969 saw the first consideration, by Commerce Secretary Maurice Stans, of creating an American agency to coordinate industrial policy. Nixon abandoned the effort for lack of Congressional support.[487] In 1971, a trade deficit of one-half of one percent of GDP (about a tenth of today's level) was enough to frighten Nixon into imposing a temporary 10 percent surcharge tariff on all dutiable goods.[488] In 1972, the AFL-CIO endorsed the Burke-Hartke bill, which would have imposed quotas on imports in threatened industries and restricted the export of capital by multinational corporations.[489]

But free trade survived all these challenges. Fundamentally, protectionist forces in Congress fumbled the ball. In the words of one scholar describing the failure of the big protectionist push in the last days of the Nixon administration:

Even in Congress, protectionist industries failed to utilize their potential resources. During negotiations over general trade bills in

Congress, protectionists exerted weak influence because they lacked an umbrella association to represent them. Instead, protectionists were divided along industrial lines, each promoting its own distinct objectives....The logic of selective protectionism did not encourage industries to cooperate with each other, since the chances for congressional support increased if protectionist bills were narrowly constructed. In addition, protectionist industries did not cooperate with organized labor.[490]

The failure of this protectionist effort carries important lessons for tactical thinking about free trade today. Sen. Hollings tried again under President Carter, but Carter preferred the Cold War priority of free trade. Ronald Reagan vetoed two protectionist trade bills, in 1985 and 1988. George H.W. Bush vetoed one, in 1990.

Ronald Reagan viewed free trade as basically a good thing, but he was not a fanatic, so he was willing to deviate from it occasionally for the sake of threatened industries and to protect the technology base needed to win the Cold War. He enacted the "voluntary" automobile agreement with Japan that Carter had negotiated and imposed a tariff on motorcycles to save American icon Harley Davidson.[491] He protected steel, lumber, computer memory chips, and sundry other products.[492] Unfortunately, his trade pragmatism, while preferable to the extremism of Bill Clinton and the two Bushes, was not guided by any thoroughgoing critique of the underlying economics of free trade—beyond the idea that it sometimes didn't work in America's favor. As a result, Reagan did not go beyond relatively narrow tactical interventions.

America's last major attempt to create a full-blown industrial policy took place from 1983 to 1985 under Reagan's Commerce Secretary Malcolm Baldrige, who proposed turning the Commerce Department into a Department of Trade and Industry analogous to Japan's famed Ministry of International Trade and Industry (MITI). The proposal was killed by the ideological qualms of free-marketeers and by the efforts of the Office of the United States Trade Representative to defend its turf.[493]

JAPAN'S PROTECTIONIST HISTORY

In the 1980s, Japanese industrial policy was the object of intense American interest, which has since waned due to the deliberately cultivated misapprehension that Japan is in economic decline.[494] There was a flurry of books on the subject and for a while it seemed that America might acquire a serious industrial policy of its own (which never happened). But Japan remains much more relevant to America's situation than China—which everyone is now obsessing about—simply because Japan has wages comparable to the U.S., while China competes largely on the basis of a low-wage policy that is impossible for a developed nation to emulate. And China is following Japan's old playbook anyway, so it is well worth examining Japan's trade history.

The Japanese themselves certainly believe their economic success has been due to protectionism. No one in Japan of any standing in business, government, or academe believes that Japan's success has been due to free trade. In the words of economic historian Kozo Yamamura:

> Protection from foreign competition was probably the most important incentive to domestic development that the Japanese government provided. The stronger the home market cushion...the smaller the risk and the more likely the Japanese competitor was to increase capacity boldly in anticipation of demand growth. This can give the firm a strategic as well as a cost advantage over a foreign competitor operating in a different environment who must be more cautious.[495]

The cultural roots of Japan's repudiation of free trade are extraordinarily deep—as deep, say, as the roots that make America a capitalist culture. This was, after all, a nation which literally sealed itself off from the outside world for two centuries (1635-1853). This act is regarded by most Westerners as merely odd, but it was, in fact, profoundly consistent with the enduring character of Japanese civilization.

Japan's forcible opening to the modern world in 1853, when U.S. Commodore Matthew Perry sailed his famous "black ships" into Tokyo Bay demanding trading rights, added a new element to Japan's existing authoritarian social order: the need for economic and technological sophistication sufficient to defend its existence as an independent nation. Japan promptly set about engaging the modern world on terms congenial to its own political priorities—not those of outsiders. The key slogan of the day was *fukoku kyohei,* "rich country equals strong army." Thus private economic interests have never, except perhaps for a brief liberal moment in the 1920s, been allowed to be the primary drivers of its national economy. Instead, private interests have been subordinated to the national economic interest under a system most succinctly describable as state capitalism. And protectionism is an innate part of that system.

Japan in 1945 was economically crushed, its cities smoking ruins, its empire gone. It was poorer even than some *African* nations untouched by the B-29. It seemed so far behind the United States that there was no plausible way ever to catch up. It was widely expected that Japan would end up an economic also-ran like that neighboring island chain, the Philippines. And within the economic ideology America was promoting to Japan at the time, free trade according to comparative advantage, there seemed to be no way out, as Japan had comparative advantage only in low-value industries.

History records a fascinating exchange on this topic, which encapsulates the entire postwar free trade debate. In 1955, when the U.S. and Japan were negotiating their first post-occupation trade agreement, the head of the American delegation, C. Thayer White, told the Japanese to cut their tariff on imported cars because, in his words: [496]

1. The United States industry is the largest and most efficient in the world.

2. The industry is strongly in favor of expanding the opportunities for world trade.

3. Its access to foreign markets in recent years has been limited by import controls.

4. Although the United States Government appreciates that it is necessary for some countries to impose import restrictions for balance of payments reasons...it would be in Japan's interest to import automobiles from the United States and export items in which Japan could excel.

Upon Ricardian principles, White was, of course, 100 percent correct. But the Japanese trade negotiator, Kenichi Otabe, replied that:

1. If the theory of international trade were pursued to its ultimate conclusion, the United States would specialize in the production of automobiles and Japan in the production of tuna.

2. Such a division of labor does not take place...because each
   government encourages and protects those industries which
   it believes important for reasons of national policy.

Needless to say, Japan did not choose to become a nation of fishing villages! Instead, its rulers drew the same conclusion that Alexander
Hamilton had drawn 150 years earlier and Henry VII 300 years before that,
opting for protectionism and industrial policy. They closed Japan's markets
to foreigners in industries they wished to enter, only welcoming foreign
goods insofar as they helped build up Japan's own industries. They applied
administrative guidance to key industries and rigged Japan's banking system and stock market to provide cheap capital to industry.[497] Tokyo instead
protected its fledgling automobile industry in the 1950s, limiting imports
to $500,000 per year. (In the 1960s, prohibitive tariffs replaced this quota.)
Japan only allowed foreign investment insofar as this transferred technology to its own manufacturers. Today, it produces over two-and-a-half times
as many cars as the U.S., mostly for export.[498]

As Japan has historically been the economic leader for the whole of
Confucian Asia[499] (Japan, Korea, China, Taiwan, Vietnam, Hong Kong,
and Singapore), its protectionist policies have been shared with nearby nations to a huge extent. The ultimate basis of these policies is an attitude
towards economics that sees the economy not as an end in itself, but as an
instrument of national power. (See the quote on page 124 for a reminder of
how this attitude used to be the norm even in the Western world.) As Harvard Asia specialists Roy Hofheinz and Kent Calder have written, "For
more than a century, nationalist sentiments...have been a basic driving
force underlying East Asian economic growth."[500] Even today, Chinese industry is 30 percent owned by the state.[501] Over a dozen strategic industries
have been slated to remain under outright government ownership and control, including information technology, telecommunications, shipping, civil
aviation and steel.[502] Laissez faire this is not.

In relation to its neighbors, Japan has employed something called the
"flying geese" strategy, christened thus by the Japanese economist Akamatsu Kaname in the 1930s.[503] Japan breaks into an industry, wipes out
existing Western competitors, then successively hands the industry down
to less sophisticated neighboring economies such as Korea, Taiwan, Thail-
and, Malaysia, and Vietnam as they mature. This pattern has held for

goods from garments to televisions for five decades. Japan's withdrawal from labor-intensive goods in the 1970s opened up space for Taiwan, South Korea, Singapore, and Hong Kong, and *their* ongoing withdrawal from these goods is opening up space for China. Among other things, this nicely illustrates how rational protectionism is a dynamic, not a static, strategy, and does not consist in defending every job and every industry.

7

The Negligible Benefits of Free Trade

HAVING LOOKED at the profound theoretical and historical reasons to doubt that free trade is the best policy, let's try some quantification of what benefits America and other nations are *really* likely to get from the current agenda to relentlessly expand it. Because the surprising news here is that even the calculations of free traders themselves indicate that the benefits of expanding free trade (if they even are net benefits, which is precisely what is in dispute) are very small. Indeed, this is what Paul Krugman, a self-professed free trader despite his trenchant criticisms, has referred to as the "dirty little secret" of free trade.[504] So even if we assume that the entire dubious edifice of free trade economics is true, there's just not that much on the table for America—or anyone else, for that matter.

That the benefits of free trade are relatively modest should be intuitively comprehensible to anyone who thinks back to the economy America had as recently as 1970.[505] Then, imports were just over five percent of GDP, rather than the 17 percent they are now.[506] Yet we somehow didn't seem to *need* very many imports to have the world's highest standard of living.[507] Imports were mainly a matter of oil, natural products that don't grow here like bananas, luxury goods like Swiss watches, and a few odds and ends like Volkswagens. This rather suggests that the benefits of free trade are at best a layer of icing on our economic cake, not a fundamental basis (let alone *the* fundamental basis, a ridiculous claim that gets made all the time) of our standard of living.

The benefits of free trade are especially dubious in the long run because although we have become dependent upon many imported products and could not switch back to domestic production overnight, we could certainly do so over time. This is not some countercultural vision of the simple life or of voluntarily accepting a lower living standard: it just means going back to lower import levels. It does not mean the end of consumer society or anything like it. It does not even mean going back to the living standards of earlier decades, as our living standards without free trade (not without *trade!*) would be much higher, due to economic and technological growth in the intervening years.

Above all, the U.S. has virtually nothing to gain from pushing even further in the direction of free trade. Our government actually knows this perfectly well. The U.S. International Trade Commission periodically releases an official report, *The Economic Effects of Significant U.S. Import Restraints,* which recently put the gain from eliminating *all* remaining American trade barriers at just $3.7 billion dollars.[508] This is just over two one-hundredths of one percent of GDP—about what Americans spend on Halloween and Easter candy every year.[509] That in itself is an irony, as about a quarter of these gains consist in cheaper sugar if the U.S. ends its (admittedly pointless) sugar import quota.[510]

SMALL GAINS FOR THE REST OF THE WORLD

Expanding free trade doesn't do much for the rest of the world, either. Generally accepted estimates of the likely benefits of further trade liberalization have, in fact, been going down for years as various criticisms of free-trade economics have started to tell.[511] For example, in the run-up to the 2003 World Trade Organization negotiations in Cancun, Mexico, the most widely quoted figure for gains from further trade liberalization was $500 billion.[512] And that was for the developing world alone, with more as gravy for the industrialized nations. But only two years later, at the next round of talks in Hong Kong, with revised economic models, there were few estimates over $100 billion: a drop of 75 percent![513] Many estimates were even lower. And 85 percent of the expected benefits to developed nations were slated to go to Europe, Japan, Korea, Taiwan, Hong Kong, and Singapore.[514] The U.S. and Canada were destined for very small shares because their economies were *already* so open.

The two most important models for generating these estimates are the Global Trade Analysis Project (GTAP) model, maintained at Purdue University in Indiana, and the LINKAGE model, maintained by the World Bank in Washington.[515] The declining estimates generated by these models can be clearly seen in the table below:

Projected Benefits of Trade Liberalization

Model	Year	Benefits (in billions)	
		Developing Nations	Entire World
GTAP	2002	$108	$254
GTAP	2005	$22	$84
LINKAGE	2003	$539	$832
LINKAGE	2005	$90	$287

Source: Frank Ackerman, "The Shrinking Gains From Trade: A Critical Assessment of Doha Round Projections," Global Development and Environment Institute, Tufts University, 2005, p. 3.

The 2005 (most recent) GTAP model estimates that the total benefit, to *all* the nations in the world, of abolishing *all* remaining restrictions on trade is only $84 billion.[516] This is less than the annual sales of the CVS drugstore chain.[517] It works out to less than four cents per day per person on the planet, or less than one-half of one percent of world economic output. That's freer trade's meager payoff.

This $84 billion estimate also applies to eliminating *all* the world's remaining trade barriers, which is not realistically on the table. If one dials back liberalization to more plausible levels, the numbers go down even more. For example, for a plausible package of tariff cuts ranging from 33 to 75 percent on various goods, LINKAGE predicts gains only about a third the size 100 percent liberalization would produce.[518] This would cut them down to just over a penny a day per person in the developing world.

These gains are a one-time event, not an annual increment. They do not open any new long-term pathways to growth and once they've been exhausted, that's it. Furthermore, they will not be evenly distributed. Some people will get more than a penny a day, some will get less, and some will get nothing at all. Some people will even get less than zero: that is, they will be net losers from trade liberalization.

GTAP also gives a surprising answer regarding which industries the benefits of liberalization would occur in: mainly just agriculture. Free traders love to paint free trade as the master key to a global high-tech boom, but in fact *all* the projected net benefits of liberalization are in mundane areas. This shouldn't actually be a surprise, given that agriculture is the most (overtly) protected sector remaining in the developed world, where the big GDPs are and thus the opportunities for percentage gains to translate into large dollar amounts. Most of these gains simply consist in slightly lower consumer prices if remaining agricultural protections, from sugar in the U.S. to cheese in Europe, are eliminated. The second-largest field of prospective gains, after agriculture, is textiles—which is also the only major industry in which most of the benefits go to developing countries.[519]

FREE TRADE DOES NOT REDUCE GLOBAL POVERTY

The First World is at least rich enough to afford mistakes about trade. The Third World is not, so it matters enormously that the potential for free trade to reduce global poverty is minimal, especially compared to the hype on the subject.[520] GTAP calculates that complete global trade liberalization would be worth $57 per person per year in the developed world—but less than $5 in the developing world.[521]

Many optimistic figures on poverty reduction as a result of trade liberalization do not survive even casual scrutiny. For a start, the World Bank standard for poverty is $2 a day, so "moving a million people out of poverty" can merely consist in moving a million people from incomes of $1.99 a day to $2.01 a day. In one widely-cited study, there were only two nations in which the average beneficiary jumped from less than $1.88 to more than $2.13: Pakistan and Thailand.[522] Every other nation was making minor jumps in between. This is better than nothing, but still small stuff to set against the costs of trade liberalization. It is definitely not the qualitative jump from material misery to a decent standard of living that people imagine from the phrase "lift out of poverty."

The developing world's projected gains from trade liberalization are also concentrated in a relatively small group of nations, due to the fact that only a few developing nations have economies that are actually capable of *taking advantage of* freer trade to any meaningful extent.[523] Although it depends a bit on the model, China, India, Brazil, Mexico, Argentina, Vietnam, and Turkey generally take the lion's share.[524] This list sounds impressive, but it actually leaves out most Third World nations. Dirt-poor nations like Haiti aren't even on the radar. Even nations one notch up the scale, like Bolivia, barely figure.

Like it or not, this is perfectly logical, as increased access to the ruthlessly competitive global marketplace (which is all free trade provides) benefits only nations whose industries have something to sell *which foreign trade barriers are currently keeping out.* Their industries must both be strong enough to be globally competitive *and* have pent-up potential due to trade barriers abroad, a fairly rare combination. So the most desperately impoverished nations, which have few or no internationally competitive industries, have little to gain.

Might there perhaps be some way to share the gains from free trade more equally among nations at different levels of development? Unfortunately not, because free trade is, by definition, *not* regulated, which means that any such scheme would not be free trade at all. It would be some sort of managed trade. Any number of such share-the-wealth schemes have been proposed, but they are outside free trade entirely.[525] This also leaves open the question of whether these redistributive schemes would actually work and whether the developed nations, which have de facto veto power over all proposals to reorder the global economy, would agree to them.

FREE TRADE INCREASES GLOBAL INEQUALITY

Despite careless talk about the "global" economy, only about a third of humanity is actually integrated into modern flows of goods and capital.[526] This third consists of basically the entire population of the developed world plus varying percentages of the populations of poorer nations. But two-thirds of humanity is only peripherally involved at best. The spreading Third World affluence one sees in TV commercials only means that the thin upper crust of Western-style consumers is now more widespread than ever before. There are indeed Indians driving BMWs around Bangalore in a way that there weren't in 1970. But having more affluent people in the Third World is not the same as the Third World as a whole nearing the living standards of the First.

More importantly, what progress has occurred has *not* been due to free trade, but due to the embrace of mercantilism and industrial policy by some poor nations. According to the World Bank, the *entire* net global decline in the number of people living in poverty since 1981 has been in mercantilist China, where free trade is spurned. Elsewhere, their numbers have grown.[527] The story on global economic progress for poor nations in the last 30 years is roughly as follows:

1. China (one fifth of humanity) braked its population growth, made a quantum leap from agrarian Marxism to industrial mercantilism, and thrived—largely because the U.S. was so open to being the "designated driver" of its export-centered growth strategy during this period.

2. India (another fifth) sharply increased the capitalist share of its mixture of capitalism and Gandhian-Fabian socialism after 1991. It did reasonably well, but not as well as China and not well enough to reduce the absolute number of its people living in poverty, given unbraked population growth.[528]

3. Latin America lost its way after the oil shocks of the 1970s, experienced the 1980s as an economic "lost decade," and tried to implement the free market Washington Consensus in the 1990s. It didn't get the promised results, so some nations responded with a pragmatic retreat from free market purism, others with a lurch to the left, the former showing results in the last five years or so.

4. The collapse of Communism left some nations (Cuba, North Korea) marooned in Marxist poverty,[529] while others (Uzbekistan, Mongolia) discovered that the only thing worse than an intact communist economy is the wreckage of one. Much of Eastern Europe and the ex-USSR got burned by an overly abrupt transition to capitalism, then recovered at various speeds.

5. Sub-Saharan Africa spent much of this period in political chaos, with predictable economic results (except for South Africa and Botswana). Washington Consensus policies in the 1990s did not deliver, and the few recent bright spots have yet to deliver increased per capita income or lower unemployment.

6. Other poor countries followed patterns one through five to varying degrees, with corresponding outcomes.

China is unquestionably the star here. But even China, for all its brutal-ly efficient achievements in forcing up the living standards of its people from an extremely low base, has serious problems on this score. Most fundamentally, its growth miracle has been largely confined to the metro-politan areas of the country's coastal provinces.[530] Of the 800 million peas-ants left behind in agriculture, perhaps 400 million have seen their in-comes stagnate or even decline.[531] China has something like 200 million migrant workers—more than the entire workforce of the US—who have left their villages looking for a place to work.[532] In the words of Joshua Muldavin, a professor of Asian studies at Sarah Lawrence College who has lived in the Chinese countryside for years:

> China's rural hinterlands are in essence the engine as well as the dumping ground of China's unprecedented economic growth. These rural areas provide the country's booming cities with cheap unorga-nized labor principally drawn from extremely poor peasant com-munities in the midst of their own social and environmental crises. It's also here that the most toxic industries are located, out of sight of the world's media. Rural peasants labor in some of the world's dirtiest, most dangerous conditions in these far-flung townships and village enterprises spread across the whole country. These are industrial subcontractors not only to Chinese companies but also international companies that spew pollution into the air and water and onto the land. And when the health of rural workers is destroyed, they return to tilling decimated lands around their villages, which have become toxic waste dumps for this unregu-lated production...Rural China, its environment, and its people are on the bottom of a global commodity chain tied to China's emer-gence as global companies' industrial platform of choice.[533]

And even in urban, coastal China, most Chinese are still poor workers, who often sleep 100 to a room in cinderblock factory dormitories.

In the last 30 years of greatly expanding free trade, most of the world's poor nations have actually seen the gap between themselves and the rest of the world *increase*.[534] As Dani Rodrik reports:

> The income gap between these regions of the developing world and the industrial countries has been steadily rising. In 1980, 32 Sub-Saharan countries had an income per capita at purchasing power parity equal to 9.3 percent of the U.S. level, while 25 Latin Ameri-can and Caribbean countries had an income equal to 26.3 percent of

the U.S. average. By 2004, the numbers had dropped to 6.1 percent and 16.5 percent respectively for these two regions. This represents a drop of over 35 percent in relative per capita income.[535]

This situation is not going to improve any time soon: the United Nations Development Programme reports that if high-income countries were "to stop growing today and Latin America and Sub-Saharan Africa were to continue on their current growth trajectories, it would take Latin America until 2177 and Africa until 2236 to catch up."[536] 2236 is as far into the future as 1782 is into the past. And, of course, developed nations are unlikely to stop growing.

An even profounder problem is that this catch-up assumes it is ecologically possible for the entire world to consume at North American levels. This is impossible with current technology and therefore depends upon technological breakthroughs that may not materialize.

THE DISAPPEARANCE OF MIDDLE-INCOME NATIONS

Today, because a few formerly poor nations are succeeding economically while most have been hit with economic decline, the world is splitting into a "twin peaks" income distribution, with a hollowing out of middle-income countries.[537] (Most poor nations have high fertility, so population growth drags down their per capita income by a percentage point or two every year if economic growth does not outpace it.) And, contrary to impressions cultivated in the media, economic success is actually becoming *more* concentrated in the Western world, not less.[538] According to one summary of the data by Syed Mansoob Murshed of Erasmus University in Rotterdam, Holland:

> Between 1960 and 2000 the Western share of rich countries has been increasing; to be affluent has almost become an exclusive Western prerogative—16 out of 19 non-Western nations who were rich in 1960 traversed into less affluent categories by 2000 (for example, Algeria, Angola, and Argentina). Against that, four Asian non-rich countries moved into the first group. Most non-Western rich nations in 1960 joined the second income group by 2000, and most non-Western upper-middle-income countries in 1960 had fallen into the second and third categories by 2000. Of 22 upper-

middle-income nations in 1960, 20 had declined into the third and fourth income categories, among them the Democratic Republic of the Congo, also known recently as Zaire, and Ghana. Most nations in the third group in 1960 descended into the lowest income category by 2000. Only Botswana moved to the third group from the fourth category, while Egypt remains in the third category. *We seem to inhabit a downwardly mobile world with a vanishing middle class*; by 2000 most countries were either rich or poor, in contrast to 1960 when most nations were in the middle-income groups.[539] (Emphasis added.)

This is all no accident. Free trade tends to mean that the industrial sectors of developing nations either "make it to the big time" and become globally competitive, or else get killed off entirely by imports, leaving nothing but agriculture and raw materials extraction, dead-end sectors which tend not to grow very fast. Free trade eliminates the protected middle ground for economies, like Mongolia or Peru, which don't have globally competitive industrial sectors but were still better off *having* such sectors, albeit inefficient ones, than not having them at all.[540]

The productivity of modern industry is so much higher than peasant agriculture that it raises average income even if it is *not* globally competitive. This is why Mongolia, Peru, and similar nations actually had higher average incomes *before* free trade was introduced during the "reforms" of the 1990s.[541] Even their inefficient and protected industrial sectors set national wage floors that discouraged, among other things, overcultivation, the environmental degradation consequent upon driving the entire population into agriculture for lack of alternative job opportunities.[542]

The sudden imposition of free trade upon such nations is even worse than its gradual imposition, as sudden drops in output are especially prone to kill off industries dependent upon scale economies, which (for reasons we will explore in Chapter Nine) are the only really good industries to have. Nations which open up their economies to (somewhat) free trade relatively late in their development, and continue to support domestic firms with industrial policy, are far more likely to retain medium and high technology industry, the key to their futures, than nations which embrace full-blown free trade and a laissez faire absence of industrial policy too early in their development.[543]

There are numerous documented cases in which trade liberalization simply killed off indigenous industries without supplying anything to replace them. To take some typical examples given by the International Forum on Globalization:

> Senegal experienced large job losses following liberalization in the late 1980s; by the early 1990s, employment cuts had eliminated one-third of all manufacturing jobs. The chemical, textile, shoe, and automobile assembly industries virtually collapsed in the Ivory Coast after tariffs were abruptly lowered by 40 percent in 1986. Similar problems have plagued liberalization attempts in Nigeria. In Sierra Leone, Zambia, Zaire, Uganda, Tanzania, and the Sudan, liberalization in the 1980s brought a tremendous surge in consumer imports and sharp cutbacks in foreign exchange available for purchases of intermediate inputs and capital goods, with devastating effects on industrial output and employment. In Ghana, liberalization caused industrial sector employment to plunge from 78,700 in 1987 to 28,000 in 1993.[544]

One unhappy corollary of this is the so-called Vanek-Reinert effect, in which the most advanced sectors of a primitive economy are the ones destroyed by a sudden transition to free trade.[545] Once these sectors are gone, a nation can be locked in poverty indefinitely.

NAFTA, CASE STUDY IN FAILURE

The North American Free Trade Agreement, America's biggest free trade controversy of the last 20 years, is a veritable case study in failure. This is all the more damning because this treaty was created, and is administered, by the very Washington elite that is loudest in proclaiming free trade's virtues. So there is no room for excuses about incompetent implementation, the standard alibi for free trade's failures in the developing world. This is all the more true given that, with the heavy penetration of American industry into Mexico, the American elite hasn't just been running the American side, but much of the Mexican side as well. And when it hasn't been, the Mexican economy has been under the control of American-trained technocrats such as President Ernesto Zedillo (PhD, economics, Yale) and President Carlos Salinas (PhD, economics, Harvard). So if free trade was going to work anywhere, it should have been here.

Instead, what happened? NAFTA was sold as a policy that would reduce America's trade deficit. But our trade balance actually worsened against both Canada and Mexico. For the four years prior to NAFTA's implementation in 1994, America's annual deficit with Canada averaged a modest $8.1 billion.[546] Twelve years later, it was up to $71 billion.[547] Our trade with Mexico showed a $1.6 billion *surplus* in 1993[548] but by 2010, our deficit had reached $61.6 billion.[549]

Eccentric billionaire and 1992 presidential candidate H. Ross Perot was roundly mocked for predicting a "giant sucking sound" of jobs going to Mexico if NAFTA passed. But he has been vindicated. The Department of Labor has estimated that NAFTA cost America 525,000 jobs between 1994 and 2002.[550] According to the more aggressive Economic Policy Institute:

> NAFTA has eliminated some 766,000 job opportunities—primarily for non-college-educated workers in manufacturing. Contrary to what the American promoters of NAFTA promised U.S. workers, the agreement did not result in an increased trade surplus with Mexico, but the reverse. As manufacturing jobs disappeared, workers were down-scaled to lower-paying, less-secure services jobs. Within manufacturing, the threat of employers to move production to Mexico proved a powerful weapon for undercutting workers' bargaining power.[551]

The idea of Mexico as a vast export market for American products is a sad joke; Mexicans are simply too poor. In the 1997 words of *Business Mexico*, a *pro*-NAFTA publication of the American Chamber of Commerce of Mexico:

> The reality is that only between 10 and 20 percent of the population are really considered consumers. The extreme unequal distribution of wealth has created a distorted market, the economy is hamstrung by a work force with a poor level of education, and a sizable chunk of the gross domestic product in devoted to exports rather than production for home consumption.[552]

According to official figures that year, fewer than 18 million Mexicans made more than 5,000 pesos a month.[553] And even that was only about $625: roughly half the U.S. *poverty line* for a family of four. This has not improved much since, so, as Paul Krugman has pointed out, "Mexico's economy is so small—its GDP is less than four percent that of the United States—that for the foreseeable future it will be neither a major supplier nor a major market."[554]

But if NAFTA wasn't a plausible economic bonanza for the U.S. and America's establishment knew it, then what was going on? Krugman again supplies an answer, writing in *Foreign Affairs* that, "For the United States, NAFTA is essentially a foreign policy rather than an economic issue."[555] The real agenda was to keep people like President Carlos Salinas, friendly with powerful interests in the U.S., in power in Mexico City. Free trade was pushed not because of any sincerely anticipated economic benefits, but to serve an extraneous foreign policy agenda. To his credit, Krugman later admitted the utter chicanery of it all, writing in *The New Democrat* in 1996 that:

> The agreement was sold under false pretences. Over the protests of most economists, the Clinton Administration chose to promote NAFTA as a jobs-creation program. Based on little more than guesswork, a few economists argued that NAFTA would boost our trade surplus with Mexico, and thus produce a net gain in jobs. With utterly spurious precision, the administration settled on a figure of 200,000 jobs created—and this became the core of the NAFTA sales pitch.[556]

NAFTA was sold in Mexico as Mexico's ticket to the big time. Mexicans were told they were choosing between gradually converging with America's advanced economy and regressing to the status of a backwater like neighboring Guatemala. But the income gap between the United States and Mexico actually *grew* (by over 10 percent) in the first decade of the agreement.[557] (This doesn't mean America boomed; we didn't. But Mexico slumped terribly.) In NAFTA's first decade, the Mexican economy averaged 1.8 percent real growth per capita.[558] By contrast, under the protectionist economic policies of 1948-73, Mexico had averaged 3.2 percent growth.[559]

Because Mexico's labor force grows by a million people a year, job creation must get ahead of this curve in order to raise wages; this is simply not happening. Mexican workers can often be hired for less than the *taxes* on American workers; the average *maquiladora* wage is $1.82/hr.[560] The *maquiladora* sector is deliberately isolated from the rest of the Mexican economy and contributes little to it. Workers' rights, wages, and benefits are deliberately suppressed. Environmental laws are frequently just ignored.

Mexican agriculture hasn't benefitted either: NAFTA turned Mexico from a food exporter to a food importer overnight and over a million farm jobs were wiped out by cheap American food exports,[561] massively subsidized by our various farm programs.[562] Contrary to Ricardian assumptions (dubious assumption #3), jobs did not magically appear for these people.

Promoters of NAFTA have tried to cover up its problems by using inappropriate yardsticks of success. For example, they have claimed that the expansion of total trade among the three nations vindicates the pact. But this expansion has been due to a growing American deficit.[563] Because a growing deficit means, by definition, that our imports have been growing faster than our exports, there is no way that economic growth per se will ever solve the problem. Congress was right to reject NAFTA initially, which never enjoyed sincere majority support in either the House or the Senate and was bought with sheer patronage by Bill Clinton.[564]

To be fair, NAFTA is not the only thing that has been wrong with the Mexican economy in recent decades. But NAFTA was the capstone to a *series* of dubious free-market economic experiments carried out there since the early 1980s. Between 1990 and 1999, Mexican manufacturing wages fell 21 percent.[565] Nevertheless, Mexico is now losing manufacturing jobs to China in such areas as computer parts, electrical components, toys, textiles, sporting goods, and shoes: 200,000 in the first two years of the millennium alone.[566] Mexico's trade deficit against the rest of the world has actually worsened since NAFTA was signed. In the words of commentator William Greider, "The Mexican *maquiladora* cities thought they were going to become the next South Korea, but instead they may be the next Detroit."[567]

NAFTA is not America's only free trade agreement, of course. But our other agreements tell similar tales. We have signed 11 since 2000: with Australia, Bahrain, Chile, Colombia, Jordan, Korea, Oman, Morocco, Singapore, Panama, and Peru. (El Salvador, Nicaragua, Honduras, Guatemala, and the Dominican Republic were lumped together in the Central America Free Trade Agreement or CAFTA.) Every agreement but one has coincided with greater American deficits. The only exception is Singapore, where our existing surplus increased somewhat. But Singapore is tiny, a mere city-state.[568] Nevertheless, our government pushes for more. As of 2011, country agreements with Colombia, South Korea, Oman and Panama were pending ratification, and the U.S. was in stalled negotiations with Malaysia, Thailand and the United Arab Emirates.[569] Next on the list are reportedly Algeria, Egypt, Tunisia, Saudi Arabia and Qatar.[570] In December 2009, the Obama administration announced its intention to eventually join the existing Trans-Pacific Partnership and elevate it into a full-blown free trade area comprising the U.S. plus Singapore, Chile, New Zealand, Brunei, Australia, Peru, and Vietnam. In December 2010, the Obama administration reached a slightly-improved deal with South Korea and announced it would push for Congressional ratification.

THE PHONY SUCCESSES OF FREE TRADE

It is possible to explain away these problems with NAFTA and our other trade agreements by using cherry-picked data and other forms of statistical opportunism. Conversely, it is also possible to unjustly *credit* free trade for economic successes in foreign countries that it did not really cause. This is usually done by interpreting paper trade liberalizations (the legal forms of which were not reflected in facts on the ground) as substantive in order to claim that these liberalizations triggered economic takeoffs in nations that actually took off under earlier protectionist policies.

China and India, for example, both opened up their economies to the world about a decade after their growth rates took off, so free trade cannot be the cause of their growth. Trade liberalization is, in fact, far more likely to be an effect than a cause of economic growth: once an economy is primed by protectionism and industrial policy and starts growing, it starts to have something to gain from somewhat freer trade (not free trade per se) and its political masters act upon this fact—with moderation and selectivity if they are wise.

For example, from its first post-communist reforms in 1978 to 2001—a period of over two decades—China did not allow unconstrained imports. (It does not really do so even today.) If it had, it could easily have ended up like Mongolia or the African nations which unwisely opened their markets too soon: its (meager at the time) domestic industries could have been wiped out by imports and it might never have become the economic powerhouse it is now. Instead, it only joined the WTO (and opened up its markets on paper) in 2001, *after* mastering the fine art of non-tariff barriers, largely with Japanese help. Thereafter, it has only opened its markets very selectively and under tight, often covert, controls. It has defied the spirit of WTO rules, and sometimes their letter, ever since.

Case in point: China did not open its financial markets to foreign players until very recently (this is an incremental process, so no single date can be given) and even then has kept them on a tight leash of regulations. This is wise, as an uncontrolled financial system is intrinsically liable to profound mischief (as Americans presumably realize by now). Interestingly, China was unscathed by either the 1997 Asian Crisis or the 2008 financial meltdown. Neither has China allowed full convertibility of its currency. It has not even allowed foreign investors genuine property rights: it allows them plenty of profits by producing for export, but no real ownership of corporations, land, or real estate.[571] India has been similarly sluggish and cagey about opening completely to foreign goods and capital, albeit in different ways corresponding to its socialist rather than communist past, democratic government, and British-derived legal system.[572]

Advocates of free trade trumpet a supposed correlation between a nation's openness to the world economy and its observed growth rate. But a more careful review of the data reveals that it is actually *growth in exports* that correlates with economic growth, not openness as such.[573] And even high exports do not in themselves bring growth: Sub-Saharan Africa has a higher ratio of exports to GDP than Latin America, but is still poorer and slower growing.[574] *Economic openness per se simply does not produce growth.*[575] (See the quote on page 21 for contrast.) Empirically, a rational amount of closure, combined with good domestic industrial policies, does far better.

Many nations trumpeted as evidence of the wonders of free trade have, in fact, succeeded for other reasons. Many of the star performers with respect to tariff reduction, such as Ukraine, Moldova, and Mongolia, have done badly, and some of the most tariff-protected nations, such as Lebanon and Lesotho, have actually done quite well.[576] In fact, for the decade of the 1990s, one major study found that there was no clear statistical relationship *at all* between tariffs and growth rates; if anything, the data had an inconclusive drift towards the conclusion that higher tariffs actually correlate with more growth, not less.[577] So a simplistic take on the data (to be fair, insufficient to settle the question) actually favors protectionism.[578]

Some commentators argue that free trade isn't what is hurting the Third World, but the lack of it. Ironically, this view tends to find its support among both right-wing free market types and left-wing antipoverty activists like the British-based charity Oxfam International.[579] They point out that developed nations impose much higher tariffs on developing nations (by a factor of four, on average) than they do on other developed nations. Thus Angola pays as much in tariffs to the U.S. as Belgium, Guatemala as much as New Zealand,[580] Bangladesh as much as France, and Cambodia more than Singapore.[581] This is not due to intentional discrimination, but to the fact that developed nations protect their agriculture. Unfortunately, the implied gains of abolishing these discrepancies are very small: between three-tenths and six-tenths of one percent of the GDPs of the exporting nations.[582] Furthermore, free trade in food and the end of First World agricultural subsidies could easily raise global food prices by 10 percent. (That's what eliminating a subsidy *does*.)[583] So Third World nations could easily slip down the path of the old Ireland: exporting food while their own people starve.

Free trade would, however, give them somewhat more-efficient poverty.

8

The Disingenuous Law
and Diplomacy of Free Trade

FREE TRADE AND FREE trade *agreements* are not the same thing. Nations
certainly do not need free trade agreements to have free trade. They just
need to drop their tariffs, quotas, and other overt and covert barriers to the
flows of goods and services. So (contrary to what one might imagine from
the mainstream media) NAFTA, our other country trade agreements, and
the WTO treaties are not really free trade agreements at all. Although they
contain free trade agreements, and their sponsors would certainly like the
public to debate them as if they were nothing else, 90 percent of their legal
substance concerns other things.

Foremost among these is protection for foreign investors. The American oil industry, for example, is haunted by the memory of Mexico's president Lázaro Cárdenas nationalizing its holdings there in 1938.[584] So these
agreements seek to tie governments into legal straitjackets that will prevent such expropriations in future. Unfortunately, these agreements go
beyond securing honest foreign investors against theft by opportunistic
politicians (which is perfectly reasonable) and embrace the dangerously e-
lastic principle that any action which reduces the future *profitability* of
investments constitutes expropriation.[585]

Taken to its logical conclusion, this ultimately amounts to the idea that
the profitability of investments must be the supreme priority of state poli-

cy—overriding health, safety, human rights, labor law, fiscal policy, macroeconomic stability, industrial policy, national security, cultural autonomy, the environment, and everything else. While there is no justification for going to the opposite extreme and allowing governments to ride roughshod over legitimate property rights, these agreements thus rigidly mandate market-based, property-first solutions to questions where societies must strike a reasonable balance between public and private interests. They assume a model of economics where externalities (see p. 105) and public goods (goods not reducible to private property) do not exist.[586]

A similar ideological bias is evident in other aspects of these agreements, like their attempts to force the privatization of public services. Supposedly, this is to create a level playing field between foreign and domestic producers of these services. Reserving the provision of these services to the state, the reasoning goes, is a form of protectionism because the state is a domestic producer. But this reaches beyond free trade to the far more radical proposition that *everything should be traded*, which not even the strictest Ricardianism implies. So, in the words of the International Forum on Globalization, a left-leaning group:

> Those negotiations involve changes in many services that were until recently reserved for governments, like public broadcasting, public education, public health, water delivery and treatment, sewage and sanitation services, hospitals, welfare systems, police, fire, social security, railroads and prisons....We could end up with Mitsubishi running Social Security, Bechtel controlling the world's water, Deutschebank running the jails (and maybe the parks), Disney running the British Broadcasting Corporation, Merck running the Canadian health care system.[587]

But the privatization of natural monopolies just substitutes private monopolies for public ones, frequently shrugging off layers of democratic accountability in the process. And in the resulting absence of competition, profit seeking finds its natural outlet in higher prices, not higher efficiency. Private producers can often skim off the profitable parts of the market and saddle the taxpayer with the dregs. Privatization is frequently no more than a one-time sell-off of future profits by the current government—with a cut of the proceeds going, of course, to its friends. In fact, privatization of physical and social infrastructure usually lacks justification, unlike the privatization of goods-producing companies, which have often been successfully privatized around the world over the last 30 years.

OVERRULING DEMOCRACY

All these free trade agreements are profoundly antidemocratic. For a start, they take precedence over national, state, and local laws whenever a trade angle can be found. What kind of laws have been struck down? *A laundry list*. In the 1993 words of Lori Wallach of Global Trade Watch (referring to the WTO's predecessor, the General Agreement on Tariffs and Trade or GATT):

> Successfully challenged under GATT as trade barriers have been the U.S. Marine Mammal Protection Act of 1972, several laws conserving fish resources, and Thai cigarette limitations. Currently under challenge at GATT are the U.S. fuel economy standards, the U.S. gas guzzler tax, and the EU ban on the use of growth hormones in beef. Challenges have been threatened under GATT against restrictions on drift net fishing by the U.S., export bans on raw logs in Indonesia, the Philippines and the U.S., the U.S. 1990 Consumer Education and Nutrition Food Labeling Act, California's Proposition 65, which requires labeling of carcinogens, German packaging recycling laws, and the recycling laws of several U.S. states, the Pelly Amendment, which enforces a ban on commercial whaling, state procurement laws requiring a certain content of recycled paper, and more. As a result of past pressure of such challenge threats, meat inspection along the U.S.-Canadian border was all but eliminated for a period of years and now remains very limited, a bill banning import of wild-caught birds into the U.S. was delayed and then watered down in Congress as contrary to GATT, Danish bottle recycling requirements were weakened, Canada is now required to accept U.S. food imports that contain 30 percent more pesticide residues than were allowed under their national laws before the 1988 U.S.-Canada Free Trade Agreement, a Canadian plan for provincial auto insurance was scrapped when attacked by U.S. insurers as a subsidy, as was a British Columbia reforestation program challenged as an unfair subsidy to the timber industry.[588]

The U.S. was forced in 1996 to weaken Clean Air Act rules on gasoline contaminants in response to a challenge by Venezuela and Brazil. In 1998, we were forced to weaken Endangered Species Act protections for sea turtles thanks to a challenge by India, Malaysia, Pakistan and Thailand concerning the shrimp industry. The EU today endures trade sanctions by the U.S. for not relaxing its ban on hormone-treated beef.[589] In 1996, the WTO ruled against the EU's Lome Convention, a preferential trading scheme for 71 former European colonies in the Third World.[590] In 2003, the Bush administration sued the EU over its moratorium on genetically modified foods.

The WTO not only strikes down laws, but prevents good laws from being made in the first place. For example, the State of Maryland was intimidated against passing sanctions on the Nigerian dictatorship for fear of WTO complications.[591]

RIGGED NEGOTIATIONS

In adopting these agreements, democratic debate is sabotaged at every turn. Because their details are ill-equipped to stand the light of day, most contain both public and secret (so-called side letter) provisions, to which only the governments signing them are privy. American trade negotiators have even been known to withhold details of these treaties from other U.S. government departments whose laws they would overturn.[592] When George H.W. Bush announced finalization of the NAFTA text in 1992, he trumpeted this "achievement," but was so afraid of public reaction to the details that he would not release the text until after he had left office. The House of Representatives has exacerbated this erosion of democracy by agreeing to so-called Fast Track provisions (effective 1974-1994 and 2002-2007), which forfeit its right to debate details, restrict it to a mere 20 hours of debate, and require a straight yes-or-no vote with no amendments. The Senate has given up its right to filibuster.[593]

These agreements are administered by distant (in the WTO's case, Geneva, Switzerland) and unaccountable bureaucrats. They are susceptible to deliberate manipulation by corporations whose interests, by their own blithe admission, do not align with those of the United States—or any other country, for that matter.[594] These bureaucrats operate largely in secret and even when they do not, they employ a deliberate technical abstruseness calculated to frustrate review of their actions by outsiders. Corporate lobbyists are welcomed and have the funding to intervene seriously. Corporations "rent" their own governments, which then cloak their agendas in the name of their respective nations. Most developing nations simply cannot afford the hordes of expensive staffers needed to negotiate effectively, even assuming they had leverage to negotiate with in the first place. Only a token presence from citizen groups is allowed.

When WTO agreements are negotiated, the organization's one-nation, one-vote principle goes by the board and the real deals are struck in so-called "green rooms" by the big players, who then present the results to the others on a take-it-or-leave-it basis.[595] (The term of art for this tacit abrogation of one-nation, one-vote is "invisible weighting.") Liberal commentator William Greider has thus described the WTO as:

> A private club for deal-making among the most powerful interests, portrayed as a public institution searching for international "consensus"...The WTO aspires, in effect, to create a Bill of Rights for capital...The system defends property rights but dismisses human rights and common social concerns as irrelevant to trade.[596]

The de facto internal politics of the WTO usually consists in aggressive U.S. pushes for freer trade, restrained somewhat by the EU, with the larger developing nations like Brazil and India representing the interests of the developing world.

REVERSING EXISTING PROGRESS

These trade agreements threaten legislative progress already made. For example, only three major environmental treaties enjoy protection from potentially being overruled by NAFTA as trade restrictions: the Convention on International Trade in Endangered Species, the Montreal Protocol on Substances that Deplete the Ozone Layer, and the Basel Convention on the Control of Transboundary Movements of Hazardous Wastes.[597] All the rest are fair game. And the world has 200 or so other environmental agreements vulnerable to being overruled as trade restrictions by the WTO.[598] In the words of Carl Pope, head of the Sierra Club environmental group:

> The treaties that we have negotiated do not permit the enforcement of international environmental obligations. These are basically get-out-of-jail-free cards for the governments of these countries that say they don't have to abide by these international treaty obligations. These are not treaties to enforce environmental laws. These are treaties designed to shield all of the countries, including the United States, from our international environmental obligations under treaty law.[599]

While (as its supporters endlessly point out) the WTO cannot *literally* strike down American laws as the Supreme Court can, it can still demand that the U.S. change its laws or suffer a penalty. This has the same effect, especially when our government is already looking for an excuse to ditch an existing law. WTO tribunals do not observe elementary principles of justice, such as requiring the burden of proof to be on the challenger to existing laws,[600] and they require unduly stringent standards of proof before allowing trade restrictions to prevent harm to human health or the environment.[601] Nevertheless, their rulings are deemed to be treaty law, which American courts are required to enforce (and place above domestic laws) under Article VI, Clause 2 of the U.S. Constitution.[602] Nations can theoretically leave the WTO, but in practice this is difficult after their economies have adjusted to the trade concessions involved in joining.

Even when the WTO does not overturn laws, it still refuses to place its enforcement powers, like authorizing trade sanctions, at the service of anything except free trade. Not environmental violations, not labor standards, not human rights, not even invading one's neighbors.[603] Except it does have a nasty little device called cross-conditionality, which means trade sanctions *can* be used to enforce the dictates of the IMF and the World Bank.[604] (Conversely, refusal of loans by these institutions has been used to enforce trade openings, as has withdrawal of foreign aid.)[605] So although free trade advocates would prefer to separate discussion of free trade from the rest of the free-market so-called Washington Consensus, these policies are tied together in practice.

Like many clubs, the WTO has a sneaky tendency to impose higher standards on those who want to get in than it asks of existing members. Even desperately poor nations have been subjected to this: Cambodia was forced to comply with intellectual property standards on a schedule even faster than that required of other developing nations like India.[606] And, thanks to the WTO's so-called "single undertaking," nations must agree to its entire package of requirements in order to join. No consideration of the diverse needs of economies at different stages of development, or with different strengths and weaknesses, is allowed.

The WTO also implements a number of problematic ancillary legal structures, like Trade-Related Intellectual Property Measures (TRIPs). These basically require foreign nations to adopt American-style patent law. This has encouraged, even if it has not literally caused, chicanery such as patenting medicines and seed varieties "discovered" by commercializing the botanical knowledge found in the traditional cultures of nations like India. Genetically modified seeds, 99 percent of whose design is the work of millennia of breeding by ordinary farmers, have received one percent modifications and then been denominated entirely new creations, protected by patent.[607] Even more brazenly, specific *properties* of plants already known to traditional medicine have been patented.[608]

Trade agreements between the U.S. and individual countries are rife with all sorts of mischief, tucked away in various clauses. For example, strict requirements on the protection of intellectual property have been incorporated into trade agreements with nations such as Jordan and Chile. Within reason, this is a good thing, but these agreements have thereby narrowly restricted poor nations' use of compulsory licensing of patented drugs to force prices down.[609] With perverse evenhandedness, these agreements have imposed the same restrictions back upon the U.S.—which may permanently block use of this policy to control drug prices and thus the taxpayer's costs for medical programs. The WTO reached an agreement on paper in 2001 to allow public health to take priority over patent rights, but the U.S. has used individual trade agreements to evade it. The EU, while not actively pursuing this strategy itself, has nonetheless benefited from foreign nations tailoring their patent laws to this American pressure; such "piggybacking" is a common strategy of this sly bloc.[610]

THE GATT: LESS RIGIDITY, BETTER RESULTS

The WTO promotes itself as a universal, consistent, and objective "rules-based" system, fairer than its 1947-1994 predecessor the GATT or General Agreement on Tariffs and Trade, which was a loose framework of country-by-country agreements. The WTO's universal rules supposedly let even the weakest players in the global economy, with insufficient leverage to force open foreign markets on their own, enjoy the same benefits of free trade that the strongest enjoy. But the price of this universality is twofold: first, it makes no sense *at all* unless its underlying premise (free trade is best) is correct, and second, it entails rigidity and authoritarianism.

The resulting lack of room for compromise has actually made the WTO *more* unstable, crisis-prone, and contentious than the GATT ever was.[611]

The GATT was a free-trade system, too, so it was far from innocent, but it did allow, for example, "special and differential treatment" exceptions to free trade for such purposes as controlling trade deficits and promoting infant industries.[612] As a result, developing nations could carve out solutions to their own particular circumstances and levels of development. And the GATT was more counterbalanced by regional trading blocs, such as the Southern Common Market (in Latin America), the South Asian Association for Regional Cooperation, the Southern African Development Community, and the Association of Southeast Asian Nations, which often sided with the interests of developing countries.[613]

The WTO's Trade-Related Investment Measures (TRIMs) also ban many policies developing nations can use to obtain a modicum of leverage over multinational corporations, such as local employment requirements and export quotas.[614] TRIMs also rule out help for local corporations like subsidized loans and export subsidies. And the WTO has tried to prohibit limiting foreign ownership of corporations to under 50 percent—an understandable way for developing nations to bring in foreign capital and expertise without completely surrendering control of their economies.

The WTO now prohibits many of the trade and industrial policies with the best records of success in the developing world. For example, it bans domestic content requirements, export performance requirements, import quotas, and foreign exchange rationing. While it still *technically* allows some of these policies, they are only permitted as exceptional and temporary provisions, or require agreement between the two trading partners. The latter, especially, tends to make them mere bargaining chips to induce developing nations to submit to demands in other areas, not fundamental commitments of the system, built into it because the policies are understood to work.

THE POWER POLITICS OF TRADE

It was only after about 1980, as the GATT's ideological arteries began to harden prior to its morphing into the WTO in 1995, that its former flexibility began to disappear. Cynically, one might blame the decline of the Soviet Union and world socialism generally. The GATT's 1950-1980 heyday seems to have coincided with global capitalism's Cold War need to coax the rest of the world out of the Communist camp.[615] It is quite possibly no accident that the Third World made its greatest economic strides from about 1950 to 1980: more Third World nations experienced periods of solid growth and fewer went through economic crises. According to one group of scholars at the UN's Department of Economic and Social Affairs:

> In the 1960s and 1970s, nearly 50 out of a sample of 106 developing countries experienced one or more prolonged episodes of sustained and high per capita income growth of more than 2 percent per year. Since 1980, however, only 20 developing countries have enjoyed periods of sustained growth. In contrast, no less than 40 developing countries have suffered growth collapses, or periods of five years or longer during which there was no growth, or a decline, in per capita income.[616]

The WTO has not been particularly kind to the United States, either— which should give pause to those who regard the whole thing as a vast American plot. Under the GATT, the U.S. lost only 61 percent of the disputes it submitted for adjudication. But under the WTO, it has lost 74 percent of the time.[617] The WTO has also engaged in judicial activism aimed at systematically rewriting American trade law to American disadvantage. As Robert Lighthizer, a former Deputy U.S. Trade Representative, told a hearing of the House Trade Subcommittee in 2007:

> Rogue WTO panel and Appellate Body decisions have consistently undermined U.S. interests by inventing new legal requirements that were never agreed to by the United States....Our trading partners have been able to obtain through litigation what they could never achieve through negotiation. The result has been a loss of sovereignty for the United States in its ability to enact and enforce laws for the benefit of the American people and American businesses. The WTO has increasingly seen fit to sit in judgment of almost every kind of sovereign act, including U.S. tax policy, foreign policy, environmental measures, and public morals, to name a few.[618]

For example, the WTO ruled in 2007 that the Unlawful Internet Gambling Enforcement Act interfered with free trade in "recreational services." More importantly, it has made a string of rulings too technically abstruse to inflame public sentiment but nonetheless important for their behind-the-scenes effects.[619] Perhaps the most flagrant was forcing repeal of the Byrd Amendment, a 2000-2006 American law that caused penalty tariffs in dumping[620] cases to be paid to the victimized industries themselves, rather than to the U.S. Treasury. In response to protests by the EU and seven other nations, the WTO ruled the amendment illegal in 2002 despite the fact that there is nothing in any WTO treaty even *mentioning* what governments may do with penalty money. In 2005, backed by WTO permission, the EU thus imposed a 15 percent retaliatory tariff on American paper, farm goods, textiles, and machinery.[621] (This is standard procedure: the WTO has no enforcement powers of its own, but works by authorizing retaliation by the injured party against goods chosen to maximize political pressure.) In 2006, Congress folded and repealed the amendment.

POWER-HUNGRY BUT BIDING ITS TIME

All these problems with the WTO are no secret. They are the major reason its drive for ever tighter global economic integration has stalled in recent years. The 1990s were, in retrospect, the gung-ho era for free trade, but a visible turning point occurred in 1999, when the famous Battle in Seattle protestors disrupted the WTO's meeting there. Unfortunately, the main lesson the WTO seems to have learned was, "Don't hold meetings where protests are legal," so in 2001, the next round of talks was held in Doha, capital of authoritarian Qatar. Protests were simply banned.[622] This did nothing, of course, to restore the rapidly eroding credibility of free trade or the WTO's authoritarian implementation of it, so the talks collapsed after only four days. The next round of meetings in 2005, in similarly well-policed Hong Kong, was held in an atmosphere of deliberately lowered expectations. These were fulfilled, and the WTO's agenda has slowed to a crawl in the years since.

But despite its currently slow progress, the WTO retains an inexorable bureaucratic will to power. It is clearly waiting out a tide that it expects will eventually turn. The desires of the multinational corporations and relentlessly power-accreting bureaucrats that are its driving force have not changed, even if both are pragmatic enough to draw back occasionally.

The WTO's tendency is to expand over time on two separate tracks. Track one, for those powerless to resist its dictates (or foolish enough to actually believe in them), consists in ever-more-rigid rules, of ever greater scope, designed to usher in a borderless world economy, at least on paper. Its ultimate ambition has been described as "writing the constitution of a single global economy."[623] Track two, for nations shrewd enough to practice mercantilism while preaching free trade, is a puppet show designed to square these nations' policies with the legal framework that props open their foreign markets. Since this puppet show furthers both the power of the bureaucrats and the profits of the corporations, neither has any reason to announce publicly what both know perfectly well: *free trade is largely a charade*, the real meaning of which is well understood by those in the know but differs markedly from the literal meaning of the phrase.

Thanks to the many ways in which trade is manipulated, it is, in fact, estimated that only about 15 percent of world trade is genuinely free.[624] So perhaps the saddest defect of the WTO is that despite its undemocratic and authoritarian implementation of an economic ideal that makes no sense even in theory, it actually has *failed* to deliver where free trade might do some good. Rational protectionism is the best policy, followed by a genuinely level playing field; the WTO has delivered neither.

The WTO is rife with posturing of all kinds. The big news at Hong Kong, for example, was the U.S. government's announcement that it would lower its tariff on imported cotton. But the U.S. is a cotton *exporter*. Such empty stunts are not confined to the U.S., of course: in 2001, the EU's "Everything But Arms" initiative unilaterally opened its markets duty-free to the 49 poorest nations in the world—*which have almost no commercially viable exports* (or they wouldn't be the 49 poorest nations in the first place). The EU also imposes very restrictive rules of product origin, so only about half the products eligible for this program in principle are eligible in practice; tricks like this riddle the system.[625] Japan long ago perfected the art of combining nominally open borders with a closed distribution system inside the country, and its pupils China, Korea, and Taiwan have followed right behind. Offset requirements—buy $X of our exports and we'll buy $Y of yours—are illegal but common.[626] The Articles of Agreement of the IMF prohibit members from manipulating their exchange rates.[627]

Is this situation likely to improve? Unfortunately, it is almost certainly on track to get even *worse* in the next few years because the U.S., the great global underwriter of free trade, is now being forced by economic crisis into the same sorts of illegal subsidies that other nations have long employed. The 2008-2009 bailout of the U.S. auto industry, for example, was full of subsidies brazenly illegal under WTO rules.[628] As a result, America is losing whatever standing it ever had to complain about such practices abroad. (Ironically, foreign subsidies were, of course, one of the things that got the U.S. auto industry into trouble in the first place.)

The WTO-endorsed free trade loophole most harmful to the U.S. is probably Value-Added Tax or VAT. Every other major nation levies VAT, which resembles a state sales tax except that it is levied *every* time goods change hands on their journey from raw materials to consumer, not only when they are sold by the retailer. (Because governments let businesses deduct VAT paid earlier in the supply chain from their tax liability, its cost is ultimately borne by the consumer.) Governments rebate VAT on exported goods because their consumers are abroad and thus not the intended objects of taxation. Conversely, they levy VAT on imports because these goods have not already paid their share of the nation's tax burden by passing through a domestic supply chain. This all makes sense, according to the logic of VAT, but it also means that when a country with VAT trades with a country without it, exports enjoy a subsidy and imports suffer a tariff. The average VAT worldwide is 15.7 percent (in the EU it averages 19.4 percent),[629] so America's trade balance faces a total pressure around 30 percent. U.S. negotiators agreed to this system in 1955, when VAT was fairly rare and in the two to four percent range anyway.

UNCLE SAM, GLOBAL SUCKER?

If the trade agreements our government signs are so disadvantageous, why does it sign them in the first place? In large part, simply because it does not take their dangers seriously. Given its underlying assumptions about the universal benevolence of free trade, there is, of course, no reason for it to.

Surprisingly, these assumptions rarely consist in outright intellectual fanaticism about the economics of free trade. That is easy enough to find in academia and the strange wonderland of the editorial pages, but quite rare in our trade negotiators and diplomatic service generally. Instead, there is usually a hazy, almost undergraduate, sense that "economics says free trade is best" which renders our trade negotiators helpless in the face of corporate pressures for more trade agreements. This helplessness is worsened by inexperience and a lack of institutional memory about past negotiations.[630] Indeed, our diplomats often have remarkably shallow knowledge of trade subjects: as Jeffrey Garten, Undersecretary of Commerce under Bill Clinton, noted in 1997, "The executive branch depends almost entirely on business for technical information regarding trade negotiations."[631]

Can business handle this role? It cannot, because its interests do not align well with the interests of the U.S. economy as a whole. The interests of individual powerful corporations do not even align well with the interests of the U.S. *business community* as a whole, a fact exacerbated by the "every man for himself" mentality of American businesses abroad. (Contrast this with the notorious solidarity of, say, Japan, Inc., which plays as a team due to government pressure and financial ties between its corporations.) American companies frequently bid against each other overseas, even over sensitive long-term issues such as technology transfer. Among other things, this makes them exceptionally easy for foreigners to manipulate. When, for example, Japanese companies form alliances with them, this tends to neutralize them as opponents of Japanese trade practices. In the words of distinguished former trade diplomat Clyde Prestowitz, "Once a company has got a deal with Hitachi, they become silent on those issues. Why attack your partner?"[632] Similarly, American aircraft producers have been silenced about Airbus by complaints from their European customers.[633]

Many of the largest American companies are now so dependent on their overseas operations, and thus so vulnerable to pressures by foreign governments, that they have become outright Trojan horses with respect to American trade policy. As former congressman Duncan Hunter (R-CA), for years one of the outstanding critics of trade giveaways in Congress, has put it, "For practical purposes, many of the multinational corporations have become Chinese corporations."[634]

When our trade negotiators work to open foreign markets, they usually do so willy-nilly, with no sense that some industries are more strategic than others. This assumption, too, is profoundly wrong, for reasons we will explore in the next chapter. Superficial attempts at hard bargaining occasionally reflect some well-organized industry that has managed to flag the attention of Congress, but are mainly just posturing. America's trade bureaucrats have little sense of loyalty to American industry or understanding that their efforts must ultimately be judged by quantifiable success in America's trade balances.[635] One metric of our government's sheer *unseriousness* about trade diplomacy is that between 1972 and 1990, fully half the American trade diplomats who left government service went to work for foreign nations.[636] Imagine if this were happening with our military officers!

America's trade diplomacy thus leaves America naked in a world where other nations pursue the most sophisticated mercantilist policies their bureaucrats can devise, backed up by disciplined diplomacy that puts economic objectives first. Our nakedness has, ironically, made us even more desperate in pushing for free trade: having disarmed ourselves by throwing open our markets, we desperately need to disarm everyone else by forcing their markets open, too. But—we try to do this *after* having thrown away our principal leverage: access to our own market. We rationalize this implausible approach with the fantasy that the rest of the world "must" inevitably embrace our own laissez faire economic ideals, including free trade, due to their innate superiority, one day soon.

Our main method of getting the rest of the world to fold its cards has, of course, been bribing foreign nations to join our vision of a rules-based global trading system under the WTO, which enjoys fanatical American support despite its anti-American actions. Unfortunately, this bribe has mainly consisted in letting foreign nations run surpluses against us. We have thus become the global buyer of last resort and the subsidizer of a system that in theory needs no subsidy because it supposedly benefits everyone.[637] One irony of this is that the U.S. has been diligently working to pry open foreign markets for Japan, China, and the other mercantilist states. (As noted in Chapter Six, Britain had precisely this problem 100 years ago.)[638]

We have not even applied the above misguided strategy with systematic discipline, as we have usually treated trade as a political issue first and an economic one second, the reverse of most foreign nations. China, for example, uses the prospect of large import orders as a wedge to break up solidarity between the U.S. and Europe regarding its human rights record, which might bring trade sanctions.[639] By contrast, the first Bush administration bought, to take only one example, Turkey's support in the Gulf War with, among other things, increases in that nation's import quotas for apparel, fabric and yarn.[640] Even in peacetime, American military bases abroad have given foreign nations leverage over U.S. trade policy. This has been quintessentially true of Japan, but has also been true of Spain, Portugal, and several other nations.[641] As a report by the Senate Finance Committee once put it:

> Throughout most of the postwar era, U.S. trade policy has been the orphan of U.S. foreign policy. Too often the Executive has granted trade concessions to accomplish political objectives. Rather than conducting U.S. international economic relations on sound economic and commercial principles, the executive has set trade and monetary policy in a foreign aid context. An example has been the Executive's unwillingness to enforce U.S. trade statutes in response to foreign unfair trade practices.[642]

Supremely confident in its own brilliant trade performance, the U.S. government spends billions trying to help other nations improve theirs. In 2008, the United States spent $2.3 billion on its various Aid for Trade programs, and it remains official U.S. policy to be "the largest single-country provider of trade-related assistance, including development of trade-related physical infrastructure."[643] The 9/11 attacks intensified this effort; apparently what Osama *really* wants is to export.

American efforts to negotiate reasonable trade agreements are handicapped by the fact that some American politicians have an unrealistic idea of international law. International law is not like ordinary civil or criminal law because there exists no sovereign to compel the obedience of nations. Instead, it is analogous to the rules of a game of stickball being played by children on a vacant lot: its rules only mean anything insofar as they are enforced *by the players upon themselves*. Obviously, as in the case of stickball, the players will enforce certain rules, because that is the only way they can have a game. So international law is not a completely vacuous concept, as some cynics suggest. But the players also *won't* enforce any rule grossly to the disadvantage of any particularly powerful player.

This means that the Anglo-American legal framework Americans tend to take for granted simply does not exist internationally, and therefore that a trading model based upon neutral and consistent enforcement of legal obligations is not feasible. There is no way to take power politics out of trade, which means that there is no way to leave everything in the hands of a neutral and rational free market once we but construct the right international legal machinery.

Foreign nations sometimes seem genuinely puzzled why the U.S. does not grasp the game being played. So they occasionally make the U.S. offers which we logically would accept if we did understand, offers they expect would quiet down Uncle Sam and make his politicians stop uttering bizarre complaints about "unfair" trade.[644] For example, Japan in 1990 offered a deal to limit its trade surpluses to two percent of its GDP if we would stop trying to reorder Japan's economy to solve our trade difficulties.[645] We showed no interest. Japan's 1990 surplus with the U.S. of $41 billion almost doubled over the next 10 years. It has remained at comparable levels ever since, dipping only with recession in 2009.[646]

PART III

THE SOLUTION

9

Where Does Growth Really Come From?

IF WE ARE SERIOUS about finding and justifying an alternative to free trade, we are ultimately going to need more than the long list of negative criticisms examined so far in this book. We are ultimately going to need an alternative *positive* explanation of economic growth, one that doesn't turn on pure free markets and thus free trade.[647] We need an explanation not just of how free trade does economies harm, but of how protectionism does them good.

In the free trade view, growth comes from nations integrating themselves ever more tightly with the wider world economy through unconstrained imports, exports, and capital flows, enabling them to ever-better exploit their comparative advantage.[648] But even free traders admit, in unguarded moments, that they actually have little idea *where* growth really comes from. This is a fatal flaw. As the aggressively pro-free-trade magazine *The Economist* has written:

> Economists are interested in growth. The trouble is that, even by their standards, they have been terribly ignorant about it. The depth of the ignorance has long been their best-kept secret.[649]

But if free-trade economics is bad at explaining growth and knows it, then we really shouldn't be taking its recommendations on how to *get* growth so seriously—starting with free trade.

Economic history contradicts free-trade economics at a number of points. For example, the all-important theory of comparative advantage promotes specialization as the path to growth. Supposedly, a nation's best move is to concentrate its factors of production on the products in which it has comparative advantage and import most everything else. (Hewing to this, the World Bank has repeatedly advised heavily indebted Third World nations to specialize in one or two crops or raw materials for export.)

But if this theory is true, it would imply that economies should concentrate on fewer industries as they become richer. Instead, the reverse is observed. In reality, economies starting out from a primitive state tend to *expand* the range of products they produce as they grow.[650] They only start reconcentrating when they are well past the middle-income stage and start building entrenched positions in a few sophisticated high value-added industries.[651] Narrow specialization is actually a hallmark of impoverished one-crop states, colonies managed for the benefit of distant rulers, and accidental raw materials-based economies like the Gulf oil producers.

Successful nations diversify. This is an important clue that economic growth may actually be less about comparative advantage and more about something else. Economic history, in fact, suggests that development doesn't come from increasing specialization, that is, from focusing ever more on what one already produces well, but from learning to produce entirely *new* things. But something new that a nation learns to produce is, by definition, not something in which it already *had* comparative advantage. So Ricardian thinking is not useful here. Even if comparative advantage applies after the fact, when a nation has mastered a new industry, it cannot tell a nation today what new industries it should try to break into tomorrow or how. Ireland didn't have any comparative advantage in IT in 1970, but this industry has been a big driver of its later growth. Same for India. There is no way this industry made sense for either nation in advance based on Ricardo.

There is an even larger lesson here: economic growth is, by definition, a *dis*equilibrium event, in which an old equilibrium level of output is replaced by a new and higher level.[652] So the economics of equilibrium, which means most of free-market economics (whose supply and demand curves intersect *in equilibrium*), is of little use for understanding it. That is why the quote at the beginning of this chapter cuts so extremely deep. Among other things, equilibrium economics cannot explain entrepreneurship, whose profits represent the value of creatively *upsetting* the existing equilibrium in an industry. Equilibrium is a useful concept for examining how things stand once the dust has settled and the economy has reached a new stable state, but it is intrinsically weak at analyzing change. This is why, when confronted with entrepreneurship and innovation, mainstream economics tends to quietly give up and reach for concepts, such as the Austrian economist Joseph Schumpeter's (1883-1950) idea of creative destruction, that are genuinely illuminating but lie outside the mathematical structures of mainstream economics. And as the logic of classic equilibrium-based economics still inescapably leads to Ricardo, this ad hoc patching doesn't lead mainstream economics to the right conclusions about trade.

COMPARATIVE ADVANTAGE VS. LADDER EXTERNALITIES

But if specialization and, more generally, following one's comparative advantage *aren't* the key to growth, what is? What is that "something else" mentioned above?

Let's start with the common observation that real-world economic growth often seems to involve a virtuous cycle, in which the upgrading of one industry causes others to upgrade and so on. This has been seen time and again in nation after nation, industry after industry.[653] For example, as one industry becomes a more sophisticated consumer of inputs, it may demand that its supplier industries become more sophisticated.[654] Conversely, it may enable its downstream industries to increase the sophistication of their outputs. This process then ripples through the economy and repeats.

Crucially, some industries are better at starting this process (or keeping it going if it has already started) than others. And the free market, *and thus free trade*, won't optimize this process automatically. Why? Because the value of an industry for the *next* step in industrial growth is often an externality, from the point-of-view of today.

We met externalities before, in dubious assumption #2 (there are no externalities) of Chapter Five. They occur when the profits of an industry do not reflect its full economic value. In this case, this means that the industry's present owners will not see profits that reflect its long-term ability to help the economy upgrade or break into other industries. As a result, the industry will remain underdeveloped, relative to its long-term value to the economy, and the free market will *not* give the optimal answer for how much of this industry the economy should contain.

When focusing on the technological aspects of this problem, economists have called these effects "location-specific technological externalities."[655] More generically and colloquially, they have been called "ladder"
externalities. That such externalities exist is taken as obvious by governments from Utah to Uttar Pradesh. That is why they compete to attract industries—mainly high technology—which they believe will further their
economic development in a way that they *don't* get excited about somebody opening a chain of convenience stores employing just as many
people.

The existence of these externalities is also taken as a given by businesses in newly industrializing nations, which is why conglomerate-like
structures like the Japanese *keiretsus*, the Korean *chaebols*, and the family
networks of Taiwan and Italy have played such large roles there. These
structures *capture* ladder externalities by taking positions in related and
newly emerging industries, so their profits don't end up in the hands of
someone else.[656]

Even American managers are well aware of how one industry catalyzes
another, though the short-termism imposed on them by the American financial system undermines their ability to exploit this fact strategically.[657]
In the words of former tech CEO Richard Elkus, who has been on the
boards of over a dozen companies:

> Some markets are considered more strategic than others. By target-
> ing strategic markets, an infrastructure can be built that ensures a
> solid basis for economic expansion. However, the leverage is not
> based simply on the importance of one market over another, but ra-
> ther on the assumption that, as they develop, strategic markets will
> become interrelated and interdependent, with the whole becoming
> substantially larger than the sum of its parts...Every product be-
> comes the basis for another, and every technology becomes the
> stepping-stone for the next.[658]

One consequence of this is that *economic growth is path-dependent*. To
grow, an economy must continually break into new industries. But to do
this, it needs strong *existing* positions in the right industries. So a national
economy that doesn't get onto the right path (and stay on it) risks being
sidelined into industries which lead nowhere in the long run. We noted this
problem before in Chapter Five: 18th-century Portugal derived no other industries from winemaking, while Britain derived many from textiles be-

cause the construction of textile machinery spawned a machine-tool industry that could produce innovative machinery for other industries. Similarly, electric cars may be the wave of the future today, but without a strong position in conventional cars, a nation is unlikely to have the know-how or supplier industries to build them.

Path dependence applies to economies at all levels of development, not just those starting to industrialize. Infant-industry protection is, of course, one of the best-known cases for protectionism and industrial policy. (It is often the one case grudgingly conceded even by free traders.) But it is, in fact, only the most obvious case of the more general phenomenon of the path dependence of economic growth. Infant industries are merely the first rungs of the ladder.

A key concept here is the "driver" technology, which enables progress in multiple other technologies. As former Commerce Department advisor Clyde Prestowitz, now with the Economic Strategy Institute, writes of Japan's makers of industrial policy:

> They knew that the RAM [random-access memory chip] is the lynchpin of the semiconductor industry because, as the best-selling device, it generates not only revenue but also the long production runs plant managers use to test, stabilize, and refine the production and quality-control processes. Compared with many other chips, it is a relatively simple product, which makes it a more attractive vehicle for developing new techniques. The latest technology has always been incorporated first in RAMs, which have always been the first product to appear as a new generation. Once RAMs are refined, new generations of other products follow...The Japanese knew that if they could grow faster than the Americans in the RAM segment of the market, they could become the low-cost producer of RAMs. And if they controlled RAMs, they would have taken a long step toward dominance in other semiconductors. And if they had semiconductors, semiconductor equipment, materials, and everything that semiconductors went into, such as computers, would be next.[659]

Free market, free-trade economics systematically maintains the opposite of all this. It maintains that *any* industry can drive an economy upwards, just so long as it enjoys comparative advantage *right now*. And because free trade economics holds that free trade automatically steers an economy into those industries where it enjoys comparative advantage, it holds that free trade will therefore maximize economic growth.[660] For free-trade economics, there is, in fact, no important distinction between the long and the short term: comparative advantage is always right, period. Free-trade economics holds, in fact, that it is profoundly impossible for one industry to be "better" than another. This is the cause of an infamous (and subsequently denied) comment by Michael J. Boskin, George H.W. Bush's chairman of the Council of Economic Advisers:

> It doesn't matter whether America exports computer chips, potato chips, or poker chips! They're all just chips![661]

Why would Boskin make a statement so brazenly contrary to common sense with such confidence? Because free-trade economics holds that markets are so efficient that no industry *can* be special. In its view, there can be no ladder externalities because there can be no industry externalities at all—certainly none that are big enough and visible enough to understand and manipulate. Every industry's profits today *must* accurately reflect its value in both the short and the long term. Why? Because if any industry *did* have superior value for future growth, its expected profitability today would reflect this, that expected profitability would draw new firms into the industry, and the superior profits would be competed away.

If every industry's short-term profitability were indeed a correct measure of its long-term value, this would indeed be the case. But when long-term returns may well accrue to another company, even another industry, and someone else may capture them, short-term profitability is not a reliable metric of long-term value. So any strategy that relies on short-term profitability alone to steer an economy will necessarily underperform. (As noted in Chapter Two, short-termism is a crucial hidden part of America's trade and industrial problems.)

"Just chips" economics is wrong because industries are very much *not* alike in their long term consequences. In the words of Laura D'Andrea Tyson, Bill Clinton's chairperson of the Council of Economic Advisors:

> The composition of our production and trade does influence our economic well-being. Technology-intensive industries, in particular, make special contributions to the long-term health of the American economy. A dollar's worth of shoes may have the same effect on the trade balance as a dollar's worth of computers. But...the two do not have the same effect on employment, wages, labor skills, productivity, and research—all major determinants of our economic health.[662]

(Bill Clinton, who flirted with serious industrial policy during the 1992 campaign, never took his own advisor's advice on this subject, preferring the free-trade extremism of NAFTA. The political moment was lost, and America's much-anticipated turn to serious industrial policy never happened.)

NOT ALL COMPARATIVE ADVANTAGE IS CREATED EQUAL

Free market, free-trade thinking can't comprehend the above realities. But it still has a contribution to make to our understanding here. In light of these realities, comparative advantage doesn't disappear from the picture entirely. But a crucial insight is added: *not all comparative advantage is created equal.*[663] It is better to have comparative advantage in some industries than others, and *what* a nation has comparative advantage in determines its standing in the global economic pecking order. In the words of Paul Krugman:

> Each country has a "niche" in the scale of goods; the higher a country is on the technological ladder, the further upscale is the range of goods in which it has comparative advantage.[664]

This may sound obvious, but this reality is relentlessly obscured by free-trade thinking, which defines away the possibility of some kinds of comparative advantage being better than others by its insistence that it is always best to act according to the comparative advantage that one has *today.*[665] As the Norwegian economist Eric Reinert puts it:

> The very idea of a nation lifting itself to higher levels of living standards through competitiveness—being engaged in activities that raise the national living standard more than other activities—goes directly against the assumptions and beliefs which form the foundations of the neoclassical economic edifice. This is not the way economic growth is supposed to take place in the neoclassical model.[666]

One implication of all this is that national economies tend to rise (or decline! Read "Argentina") over time to the level of income embodied in their exports. Economist Dani Rodrik has summarized this fact as "you become what you export."[667] This is a fact with vast significance for industrial policy—especially for developing countries, which are desperately trying to *become* something other than what they already are. And this fact profoundly contradicts Ricardian economics. As Rodrik observes:

> Under received theory, a country with an export package that is significantly more sophisticated than that indicated by its current income level is one that has misallocated resources (by pushing them into areas where the country does not have a comparative advantage). Such a country should perform badly relative to countries whose export packages are more in line with current capabilities.[668]

That climbing a ladder of industry externalities can lift an economy upward shows up in the data in the fact that economies with more-sophisticated exports are not only richer today (which one would expect) but also grow faster over time.[669] The latter fact, although not terribly shocking to common sense, is not obvious at all to free-trade economics. But in reality, having a foothold in industries which *intrinsically lead somewhere* is a big part of what makes economies grow.

All of the above was, of course, well known to mercantilist governments for centuries. In the words of economist John Culbertson:

> This view...had been well understood by governments and writers on economic subjects centuries before Adam Smith, that industries are not homogenous. Some lead to cumulative advances in knowledge and technology, some bring new skills and capabilities to people and firms, some permit high incomes to be earned in foreign markets because of the absence of competing producers—especially of competing low-wage producers. Other lines of production have none of these favorable characteristics, and are dead ends. The nation that specializes in them will be economically second rate, at best.[670]

This is why it matters so much that America not get pushed out of the industries of the future, regardless of what our immediate comparative advantage says.

WHAT ARE GOOD INDUSTRIES?

If the industries a nation needs in order to grow economically are those whose intrinsic nature it is to lead onward and upward, and free trade *won't* automatically nourish them, which lucky industries might these be?

190

Let's start with the fact that sustained economic growth only really occurs in industries which exhibit increasing returns. This means that for a given increase in inputs, output goes up by *more than* the size of that increase. For example, because the cost of baking bread consists in a one-time investment in an oven plus a per-loaf cost for ingredients, the cost per loaf will go down with each additional loaf baked, as the cost of the oven is spread out over more loaves. So 10 percent more money will deliver 11 percent more bread and so on. The opposite of increasing returns is diminishing returns: after a certain point, 10 percent more money delivers nine percent more output, then eight percent and so on.

Increasing returns is a simple concept, but it ramifies endlessly, forming the ultimate basis of a long list of the opposite characteristics of "good" (increasing returns) and "bad" (diminishing returns) industries.[671] Historically, manufacturing is the quintessential increasing-returns industry and agriculture the quintessential diminishing-returns one. But some types of each behave like the other and since the mid-1970s, the line between manufacturing and services has blurred, with a *small* segment of high-end services acquiring some of the desirable characteristics traditionally associated with manufacturing. And low-end manufacturing has increasingly come to resemble agriculture. But the underlying characteristics of increasing and diminishing returns industries have remained stable, even as which industries exhibit these characteristics has changed.

Having a lot of increasing returns industries is really the only way to be a developed economy. This is, in fact, the fundamental purely economic difference between the First and Third Worlds: the former is full of such industries, the latter is not. As a result, examining why some industries exhibit increasing returns and some do not can tell us a lot about why some economies grow and some do not. And how free trade can easily lead an economy astray.

WHY DO SOME INDUSTRIES HAVE INCREASING RETURNS?

Industries which exhibit increasing returns do so mainly because they can absorb endlessly rising capital investment. Not all industries can: buying another $1,000,000 worth of tractors for a coffee plantation that already has tractors won't increase the plantation's productivity very much.[672] Neither will buying every lawyer at a law firm another desk. But putting another $1,000,000 into production machinery in an automobile or semi-conductor plant will do a lot. And capital doesn't just mean factory floor machinery. It also means human capital or skills accumulation, and research and development.

Why are some industries so good at absorbing capital? One big reason is that they are susceptible to innovation, and R&D is a big capital absorber. This activates a virtuous cycle in which innovation absorbs capital and repays it by raising profitability, generating more capital and repeating the cycle. It is no accident that manufacturing and related fields generate over 70 percent of research & development in the U.S.[673] And within manufacturing, high technology accounts for roughly 20 percent of output, but 60 percent of R&D.[674]

This susceptibility to innovation derives largely from the fact that good industries tend to produce goods capable of infinite improvement, like laptops or airplanes, while bad industries produce goods whose character is fixed, like fruit or t-shirts. The products of good industries are also susceptible to meaningful *variety*, so firms don't end up selling the exact same product in pure head-to-head competition. This spares firms the raw price competition that drives down profits, wages, and funds available for further investment. Instead, they compete on quality, reliability, reputation, marketing, service, product differentiation, special understanding of buyer needs, rapid innovation, and managerial sophistication. This enables them to accumulate strongly entrenched competitive positions where vulnerability to pure price competition—crucially by cheap foreign labor—is not a big issue.

This lack of perfect competition in good industries activates something free-market economics despises: *market power*, also known as monopoly or quasi-monopoly power. From the point of view of free markets, this is inefficient on first principles, because companies and industries with monopoly power earn higher profits than the free market would allow. They are parasitic. The confusing term economists use for this excess profit is "rent" (which has nothing to do with rent in the normal sense)[675] so, in the words of Eric Reinert:

> In the static system of neoclassical economics, rent-seeking is seen as a negative term. In a world where increasing returns to scale, imperfect information, and huge barriers to entry dominate all industries of any importance, *dynamic rent-seeking* seems to be a key factor for economic growth and competitiveness.[676] (Emphasis added.)

This dynamic rent-seeking generates a number of virtuous spirals. One is that rising worker incomes provide the purchasing power to sustain industrial growth. And as incomes rise, what economists call "quality of demand" also rises: people demand not just more but *better* products, driving the industries of their home nation to upgrade and reinforcing the ladder externalities discussed earlier.[677]

Good industries also readily absorb rising human capital or skill. That capital accumulates in the workers themselves tends to encourage well-cared-for labor for the same reason factory owners do not let valuable machinery rust away. It generates corporate and state paternalism and the Galbraithian "countervailing powers," like bargaining leverage by workers, that spread the profits of industry beyond its owners.[678] This broad sharing of profits is reinforced by the fact that good industries tend to produce products for which income elasticity is high, i.e., people buy more as their incomes go up. As a result, productivity gains don't just drive down the price of the product, and output can rise along with productivity, enabling wages to stay steady despite productivity gains which require fewer and fewer workers per unit of output.

BAD INDUSTRIES AND DEAD-END ECONOMIES

The opposite of good industries is, of course, bad ones. These are *dead-end jobs writ large*. For centuries, this has meant agriculture and raw materials extraction, but since the mid-1970s, unskilled manufacturing has been inexorably joining this category. In these industries, diminishing rather than increasing returns apply, so all the previously discussed benevolent dynamics are absent—or run in reverse.

These industries are hobbled by their very nature. For a start, demand for agricultural products is intrinsically less elastic than demand for manufactured goods, simply because of the finite size of the human stomach.[679] As a result, productivity growth in agriculture tends to translate into lower prices for consumers, not higher wages for farmers. Because productivity growth in agriculture tends to go into lower prices, while productivity growth in manufacturing does not, agricultural prices generally decline over time relative to the price of manufactured goods.[680] This problem has been around for a very long time: according to one British estimate of

1938, the same quantity of primary products bought only 63 percent as many manufactured goods as it had in 1860.[681] Thus nations whose main exports are agricultural or raw material products have slipped further behind the industrial nations, decade by decade.[682]

Agriculture and raw materials also tend to be bad industries simply because they are too easy for competitors to break into and thus attract too many rivals. When Vietnam, on the advice of the World Bank, started exporting coffee and rapidly became the number two producer after Brazil, this flooded the market and drove the price down from 70 cents a pound to around 40 cents.[683] Economies dominated by bad industries are subject to volatile income swings due to distant commodities markets, swings exacerbated by undiversified exports and impossible to hedge against. The dependence of agriculture on the weather only makes this worse.

Most agriculture simply can't absorb technological innovations that upgrade productivity and wages on anything like the scale manufacturing can. For example, as Eric Reinert notes:

> Mexico specializes in unmechanizable production (harvesting strawberries, citrus fruit, cucumbers and tomatoes), which reduces Mexico's opportunities for innovation, locking the country into technological dead-ends and/or activities that retain labor-intensive processes.[684]

Because agriculture can't absorb technology, it can't absorb capital, either, as there's nothing to spend the money on that will pay back a return. In any case, without a strong manufacturing sector, it's hard to raise even *agricultural* productivity, because increased productivity means fewer workers are needed, and there's nowhere for the workers released from agriculture to go. So fear of mass unemployment locks society in place.[685] For most of the people they employ, agriculture and other bad industries also tend to hit a fairly low ceiling in the amount of skill they can usefully absorb, so human capital doesn't accumulate any more than capital invested in technology. As a result, these industries remain undercapitalized and the societies that host them do not accumulate wealth in these industries. Whatever money is made is siphoned off elsewhere: into castles in Medieval Europe, into Europe in colonial Africa.

Agriculture and other bad industries occasionally do exhibit innovation. But this is generally only in the production process, not the product itself. And innovations, when they come, tend to come from *outside* bad industries. Agriculture, for example, has benefited from genetic engineering and improved tractors, but created neither of these innovations itself. As a result, innovations do not establish virtuous cycles of innovation → more profit → more innovation *inside* bad industries.

One telltale sign that a formerly good industry is turning bad is that product innovation exhausts itself and the industry turns to process innovation. And when a bad industry turns downright terrible, even process innovation exhausts itself and the industry just seeks cheaper labor. One can trace this process in individual industries over time. The shoe business, for example, began as a First World handicrafts industry, was mechanized over the second half of the 19th century, and began moving to the Third World in the 1950s—just as its productivity growth flattened out.

Which industries are good and bad changes over time as the technological frontier of the world economy moves forward. The textile industry was good for a rising economy like Britain in the early 19th century, but is not good for developed nations today. These "has been" industries either migrate to developing nations or gently stagnate in place. As an economy accumulates more and more of them (as Britain did in the early 20th century) this is a clear sign that economic decline is around the corner.

No nation can plausibly hope to have its entire economy consist only of good industries, as some bad industries are sectors one can't live without. One cannot go without haircuts, even if the productivity of barbers is no greater than 200 years ago. And even stagnant sectors contribute some output and employ some people. But the more of a nation's economy is in good industries, the stronger its economy will be today and the better its growth prospects tomorrow.

ENTIRE ECONOMIES STUCK IN BAD INDUSTRIES

The poor and slow-growing economies of the Third World are that way because they are predominantly composed of bad industries and the path-dependence of industry entry traps them there. They are stuck in industries that have no increasing returns, no technological advances, and no ladder externalities. These problems mutually reinforce each other, ramify over time, and are the ultimate basis in hard economics for the well-known phenomenon that the rich get richer. (Marx correctly observed that this happens, but he mistakenly thought that it was because the rich were *exploiting* the poor. Sometimes they do, but that's not the fundamental problem.) The United Nations Development Programme has thus estimated that the income gap between the top fifth of the world's nations and the bottom fifth was 3:1 in 1820, 7:1 in 1870, 11:1 in 1913, 30:1 in 1960, and 74:1 in 1997.[686]

Ironically, the gap between poor nations and rich ones was actually much smaller in the 19th-century heyday of colonialism than it is today. But this makes perfect sense: 150 years ago, there was *relatively* more to grab in colonies; there's no point in an advanced nation conquering Rwanda today, when its own per capita output is 75 times greater. Insofar as colonialism, traditional or modern, overt or covert, is a deliberate economic strategy, it is about *locking subject nations into bad industries*.[687] For example, the English government stifled Ireland's nascent industrialization in 1699 by banning its exportation of woolen cloth outside the British Isles.[688] Ireland obediently specialized in agriculture and even became a successful exporter. But it continued to export food even when its own people were starving. It had the capacity to produce nothing else.

Colonialism per se isn't the problem here, as the economic mechanisms that do the damage are perfectly capable of operating in nations that are politically independent. (We noted Spain as an example in Chapter Six.)[689] And not all colonies have been subjected to this treatment. The danger of being trapped in bad industries was, in fact, well understood by a number of small, raw materials-rich colonial nations which managed to avoid this fate. Australia, Canada, New Zealand, and (oddly enough) South Africa are the classic examples. All these nations were beneficiaries of the British Empire getting burned trying to make the U.S. a banana republic, as the imperial authorities allowed these colonies to raise tariffs against British goods in order to pursue their own industrialization.[690]

THE PATHOLOGIES OF BAD INDUSTRIES

Free trade does not automatically assign nations good industries. This is the fundamental problem. Acting according to their immediate comparative advantage, it can just as easily assign them bad ones. This may be optimal in the short term, but if a nation's comparative advantage today is in producing bananas, then it will be stuck with roughly the same productivity 30 years from now.[691] That isn't true in industries like computers or automobiles. And in the presence of a large wage gap between nations, low-wage nations will automatically tend to attract bad industries under free trade, as here will lie their immediate comparative advantage.

The interaction of free trade with bad industries is toxic in a wide variety of ways, not all of them obviously trade-related. For example, free trade tends to exacerbate all the "bad habits" of modern agriculture, as the attempt to extract more returns from a diminishing-returns industry to keep up with declining terms of trade generates a relentless squeeze. This tends to increase the amount of land under cultivation and undermine conservation programs. It tends to force intensive use of pesticides and fertilizers. It tends to replace diversified operations with large-scale feed lots and mono-crop agriculture. It tends to reduce specialty crops to commodities. And it tends to place absentee owners in control, undermining family farming and rural communities.

The First World palliates (not the same thing as solving) these problems with agricultural subsidies because it can afford to. This has the unfortunate spillover effect in the Third World of generating a tidal wave of cheap exported food that destroys farm jobs the same way manufactured imports destroy factory jobs in industrial countries. Given that the combined agricultural subsidies (including hidden ones such as cheap water) of the U.S., EU, and Japan equal almost 75 percent of the *entire income* of Sub-Saharan Africa, it is no accident that African farmers, for example, cannot compete.[692] Once they can no longer support themselves on the land, they have no choice but to seek urban, mainly slum, life. When a Third World nation converts its food production to export and becomes dependent on imported food, it becomes vulnerable to volatility in its export markets. Bubbles in commodities such as biofuels make this worse, as when the bubble ends, it is impossible to convert back to food production in time to avoid food riots.

Raw materials extraction is the other sector notorious for bad industries. It tends to harbor many of the same pathologies as agriculture, plus a few nasty quirks of its own. Raw materials like oil notoriously breed parasitic elites composed of whomever manages to establish political control of the spot where the oil comes out of the ground. Unlike the elites of manufacturing-oriented economies, they contribute little in managerial or technical skill to the economies they dominate. They can get away with misgoverning their countries in ways that would ruin the productivity of a manufacturing-oriented economy. They have no need to share widely the wealth derived from the raw materials they extract (except with local war-lords and security forces), and little incentive to reinvest more than a fraction of that wealth in the industry itself.

During the Cold War, much opposition to capitalism was motivated not so much by literal hatred of private property (let alone actual love of communism) as by the deep-seated fear that advanced industrial modernity was a closed club of the United States and Western Europe.[693] Other nations, it was feared, could never break in, but would remain eternally trapped in bad industries—which would then guarantee their poverty and political subordination. So socialism was the only way out, with the USSR as its ultimate geopolitical anchor, even if obviously extreme as a literal economic model to imitate. But once a nation understands the above *mechanisms* of underdevelopment—better yet, how to manipulate them through protectionism and industrial policy—abandoning capitalism entirely shows itself to be an unnecessarily extreme solution. Japan and its followers in East Asia understood this, which is a big part of why they were so staunchly anticommunist during this period. Other parts of the world did not, and thus found socialism considerably more interesting.

GOOD AND BAD INDUSTRIAL POLICY

If free markets and free trade aren't always best, this *necessarily* opens up the possibility that some other policy might be better, if properly designed and implemented. This, at bottom, is what makes successful protectionism and industrial policy possible.

It is no accident that when reviewing purported free-trade success stories around the world, one often finds protectionism and industrial policy right under the surface. In Brazil, for example, the steel and aircraft industries are legacies of past import-substitution policies;[694] in Mexico, motor vehicles are; in Chile, grapes, forest products, and salmon. In fact, of the top 20 exporting corporations in Chile in 1993, at least 13 were creations of a single government agency, the *Corporación de Fomento de la Producción* (CORFO).[695]

Over the last 40 years, there have been two key laboratories of protectionism and industrial policy: East Asia and Latin America. As recently as the early 1970s, both regions were at similar levels economically, and

Latin America was actually much richer at the end of WWII.[696] And yet East Asia has succeeded economically, while Latin America stagnated from about 1975 until very recently. (The above examples are happy exceptions.) Protectionism and industrial policy clearly come in both effective and ineffective varieties, and neither concept deserves an uncritical endorsement.

We are now in a position to understand why some kinds of each work and some don't.[697] In the words of Harvard economist Dani Rodrik, both regions employed the "carrot," that is, tariffs, industrial subsidies, et cetera, to help their industries. But only East Asian governments were politically disciplined enough to employ some needed "stick" as well, i.e., measures to prevent their industries from merely converting this help into immediate profits, not long-term upgrading of their capabilities.

An export requirement is one example of a "stick." This improves the nation's balance of payments and forces domestic producers to meet global standards for quality and cost. This policy can be implemented in a wide variety of ways, some not immediately obvious as such, like giving companies import quotas for raw materials based on their export performance. Another method is a so-called "rolling" local content requirement, where a company importing goods is required to produce a gradually increasing percentage of the final value of the product domestically. This creates a pressure to produce locally *without* getting so far ahead of market outcomes as to be hopelessly inefficient.

Other patterns of successful industrial policy emerge. It has tended to maintain domestic rivalry within industries, rather than concentrating resources on a single superficially-strong national champion.[698] It has tended to involve local ownership *and* understanding of core technologies, rather than the "Lego brick" manipulation of sophisticated inputs in an unsophisticated way. It has tended to combine investment in education with investment in industries that can actually absorb educated workers. It has tended to use access to the national market as leverage to get foreign corporations to locate a share of production there, not merely as a shield for domestic producers or as a source of tariff revenue to be wasted on political pork. (Pulling in state-of-the-art foreign producers also keeps domestic producers on their competitive toes *without* subjecting the economy to an uncontrolled flood of imports.)

What did Latin America do wrong? It allowed domestic competition to wane. It permanently protected mature industries that should have been able to survive on their own by that point. It lacked an interest in exporting, so its industries were not disciplined to reach world standards. Lack of exports then caused a lack of the foreign currency needed to import state-of-the-art production technology. Its industrial know-how therefore lagged behind the rest of the world, as it never developed comparable domestic sources of technology either. And Latin American nations either failed to emphasize education, or failed to create industries that could absorb educated workers, the latter causing investments in education to dissipate in brain drain abroad rather than accumulate as human capital at home.

THE WORST AND BEST INDUSTRIAL POLICY

In the developing world, the very worst industrial policy has tried to break into new industries merely on the basis of having cheaper factors of production, which mostly comes down to cheap labor. (Number two is probably cheap raw materials, followed by cheap land.) Unfortunately, industries based on cheap labor continually attract new entrants because cheap labor is an undifferentiated commodity, available all over the world. But incumbents are blocked from exit by costs they have already incurred, trapping them in these industries. Today's cheapest labor source is always vulnerable to being undercut by an even cheaper one tomorrow, and rival governments will subsidize even where there is no preexisting cost advantage.[699] This is where the sad scramble for immediate comparative advantage ends up.

A nearby example of this misguided strategy is Mexico's string of *maquiladora* plants along the U.S. border. These 3,000 American-owned factories employ over a million workers. Though they often contain the latest production technology and have the highest productivity of any industry in Mexico, they have spawned no industrial revolution there. Although these plants often consume fairly sophisticated technology, in the form of imported capital equipment, what they *do with* this technology is not especially sophisticated. So the Mexican economy accumulates neither human nor any other kind of capital; the products produced there have no all-important scale economies *at the assembly stage*.[700] For example, according to Rick Goings, CEO of Tupperware, which has a major plant in Toluca, Mexico failed to grasp the opportunity handed to it by NAFTA:

> When all of a sudden the borders opened and all these [jobs] were created for assembly and sending [products] back to the United States, they didn't invest what they needed to in building the skill base of Mexican workers. So you go down there now and what are they complaining about? Losing their jobs to China. All you have to do is follow Nike's pattern over the last 25 years: Korea, China, Vietnam. You just keep following that low labor cost—you just keep following that dragon. Unless you build in these countries an infrastructure and a skill base, they may have a short-term advantage, but it won't last.[701]

Such industry is a technological and economic dead end. For all that anybody will ever learn or develop by working in it or even owning it, they might as well be picking coffee beans by hand—or owning a plantation. The question a nation should always be asking about its industries is, "Is there anything left to learn here?" If there isn't, it's time to let another nation further down the ladder of industrial development take over that industry and move on. And if it isn't feasible to move on, then something is wrong with the nation's industrial strategy, because it has gotten stuck, and growth requires that it continually be able to upgrade.

What does the most successful industrial policy look like? As economies try to make the jump from the Third World to Newly Industrialized Country status and finally to the First World, the real key to growth turns out to be proactively *anti*-Ricardian, namely getting *away from* their immediate comparative advantage. They try to *shape* it, rather than just submitting to it.

Above all, good policy means getting away from advantage based merely on given factors of production and transitioning towards advantage based on *created* factors of production. Ultimately, it means transitioning from so-called lower-order sources of advantage to higher-order sources. As Harvard Business School's Michael Porter explains it:

> Lower-order advantages, such as low-cost labor or cheap raw materials, are relatively easy to imitate. Competitors can often readily duplicate such advantages by finding another low-cost location or source of supply, or nullify them by producing or sourcing in the same place...Also at the lower end of the hierarchy of advantage

are cost advantages due solely to economies of scale using technology, equipment, or methods sourced from or also available to competitors....

Higher-order advantages, such as proprietary process technology, product differentiation based on cumulative marketing efforts, and customer relationships protected by high customer costs of switching vendors, are more durable. Higher-order advantages are marked by a number of characteristics. The first is that achieving them requires more advanced skills and capabilities such as specialized and highly trained personnel, internal technical capability, and, often, close relationships with leading customers. Second, higher-order advantages usually depend on a history of *sustained and cumulative investment* in physical facilities and specialized and often risky learning, research and development, or marketing.[702] (Emphasis in the original.)

INDUSTRIAL POLICY, AMERICAN-STYLE

For contemporary Americans, one common roadblock to understanding industrial policy and protectionism is the myth that our most successful industries have made it on their own, without government help. We tend to see industrial policy (if we accept it at all) as perhaps suitable for up-and-coming nations, but not for nations like ourselves that have already arrived. But in reality, the fingerprints of industrial policy are easy to find in our own economy, even in the post-WWII era of increasingly free trade (and increasingly strident laissez faire rhetoric after about 1980).[703] Let's look at two of America's most touted industries, semiconductors and aircraft, to see how they *really* became so strong—and therefore why the free market-free trade model of economic growth is so wrong.

Silicon Valley is a famous success story of free enterprise, and to a large extent it deserves this reputation. Nevertheless, its rise was shot through with government support, without which it would probably never have existed. In fact, everywhere in the world where a semiconductor industry has developed, it has been a target of state industrial policy.[704]

The entire semiconductor industry is based upon the transistor, which was invented by Bell Laboratories in 1947. Bell Labs, however, was no product of free-market capitalism, but was the research wing of the old American Telephone and Telegraph (AT&T), a government-sanctioned monopoly. This company could only afford to support an expensive laboratory full of Nobel-caliber scientists precisely *because* it was a monopoly: protected from competitive pricing pressures, assured that no competitor would capture the commercial value of what it invented, and dedicated to the long term. It is Exhibit "A" against the canard that large, bureaucratic, government-subsidized companies protected from foreign competition can't innovate. (This is not to say that these characteristics are positive goods in their own right, but it does rather suggest that the true determinants of industrial dynamism often lie outside laissez faire clichés.)[705]

The semiconductor industry was a massive beneficiary of infant-industry subsidies from the start. As it hatched and grew in the late 1950s and early 1960s, close to 100 percent of its output was bought by the military,[706] which needed expensive high-performance semiconductors for uses like missile guidance systems at a time when most consumer electronics still ran on vacuum tubes. Even as late as 1968, the Pentagon bought nearly 40 percent of the semiconductors produced in the U.S.[707] Military demand enabled companies to stake their risky investments at a time when nobody else would buy their expensive cutting-edge technology.[708] It enabled them to build the expertise that was later applied to civilian markets and achieve the scale economies needed to bring costs down into the range affordable for mass consumption.

Aviation is another example of the dependence of America's most successful industries on industrial policy. The entire 7x7 series of Boeing planes derives from the 707 launched in the late 1950s, which was the civilian twin of the KC-135 aerial-refueling plane built for the Air Force. Boeing actually *lost* money on its commercial aircraft operations for the first 20 years.[709] To give further examples of the military lineage that made U.S. civil aviation possible:

> Lockheed sold commercial versions of its C-130, C-141, and C-5A. [The Lockheed L-1011, McDonnell-Douglas DC-10] and Boeing 747 were all spawned by technical advances on the engines used for the C5-A. In short, every generation of the new civilian air transport has relied heavily on technology developed for the military.[710]

Other industries have been born from U.S. government industrial policy. The latest, of course, is the Internet, which derives from the military ARPANET built to enable communications between computers used for defense research. Even Google, the ultimate better-mousetrap free-market success story, was based on research done by founders Larry Page and Sergey Brin at Stanford while supported by a National Science Foundation grant to research digital libraries.[711] And the biotech industry has been incubated by, and has depended upon basic research funded by, the National Science Foundation and the National Institutes of Health.

Unfortunately, if present trends continue, America's harvest from federally funded industrial policy will inexorably diminish. Even the military itself is now lagging. According to John Young, former head of the Pentagon's Advanced Technology and Logistics division:

> The [Defense] Department is coasting on the basic science investments of the last century and is losing the force multiplier advantage conferred by harvesting those investments. The last 15 years (since the demise of the Soviet Union) have seen the Department pull back substantially from many science areas. Yet, scientific knowledge is the underpinning of the current U.S. capability overmatch in most areas.[712]

It seems Sputnik did us a bigger favor than we knew! The need to beat the Soviet Union appears to have been *the* decisive factor in disciplining the U.S. government to pursue an effective industrial policy, and when the Cold War ended, serious industrial policy seems to have ended with it.

During the final push of the Cold War under President Reagan, the Defense Intelligence Agency and CIA created Project Socrates, whose purpose was to understand America's declining economic and technological competitiveness and develop industrial policies in response. But just as this project was nearing fruition, the Berlin Wall came tumbling down. President Bush was ideologically hostile to industrial policy and systematically destroyed the project.[713] He had Defense Advanced Research Projects Agency (DARPA) director Craig Fields reassigned and ordered all records of the project destroyed to frustrate Freedom of Information Act requests.[714] Thus died what should have been the crowning achievement of Cold War industrial policy: a systematic codification of its economic insights. Ironically, some of the key staff of this project have since worked on economic strategy for foreign nations like Poland and Malaysia, which have diligently used this knowledge to compete with the U.S.

With the end of the Cold War, even the most basic elements of purely military industrial policy began to get short shrift. For one thing, the Pentagon ceased to care very much about buying American. In the words of then-Secretary of Defense Dick Cheney, a key figure in this shift, policies favoring American defense producers "raise questions about my spending money on things I could get cheaper elsewhere, and it raises the specter of having to rely upon less than first-rate technology in certain areas."[715] Thanks to nearly two decades of such policies, the U.S. is now unable to put a single military aircraft into the sky without using components made by potential adversaries. As a 2005 Defense Department report put it:

> The potential effects of this restructuring are so perverse and far reaching and have such opportunities for mischief that, had the United States not significantly contributed to this migration, it would have been considered a major triumph of an adversary nation's strategy to undermine U.S. military capabilities.[716]

The Pentagon is now facing a rash of counterfeit electronic components in military systems, which lays the U.S. open to the kind of deliberate sabotage we have ourselves employed against adversaries such as Saddam Hussein.[717] We also now face politically motivated refusal of foreign suppliers to provide needed components. The best known case is a Swiss company, Micro Crystal AG, which refused to supply piezoelectric timing crystals for the guidance system of the Joint Direct Attack Munition (JDAM) smart bomb at the time of the Iraq war.[718] (One surviving American company was found.) The military is not unaware of this problem, but is hamstrung by the political power of defense contractors, who find outsourcing parts very profitable.[719]

INDUSTRIAL POLICY IN REVERSE: DEINDUSTRIALIZATION

Deindustrialization is a more complex process than is usually realized. It is not just layoffs and crumbling buildings. It is, in fact, *industrial policy in reverse*. As a result, understanding industrial policy helps illuminate the complex way in which industries die.

When American producers are pushed out of foreign and domestic markets, it is not just immediate profits that are lost. Declining sales undermine their scale economies, driving up their costs and making them even less competitive. Less profit means less money to plow into future technology development. Less access to sophisticated foreign markets means less exposure to sophisticated foreign technology and diverse foreign buyer needs.[720] When an industry shrinks, it ceases to support the complex web of skills, many of them outside the industry itself, upon which it depends. These skills often take years to master, so they only survive if the industry (and its supporting industries, several tiers deep into the supply chain) remain in continuous operation. The same goes for specialized suppliers. Thus, for example, in the words of the *Financial Times's* James Kynge:

> The more Boeing outsourced, the quicker the machine-tool companies that supplied it went bust, providing opportunities for Chinese competitors to buy the technology they needed, better to supply companies like Boeing.[721]

Similarly, America starts being invisibly shut out of future industries which struggling or dying industries would have spawned. For example, in the words of tech CEO Richard Elkus:

> Just as the loss of the VCR wiped out America's ability to participate in the design and manufacture of broadcast video-recording equipment, the loss of the design and manufacturing of consumer electronic cameras in the United States virtually guaranteed the demise of its professional camera market....Thus, as the United States lost its position in consumer electronics, it began to lose its competitive base in commercial electronics as well. The losses in these related infrastructures would begin to negatively affect other downstream industries, not the least of which was the automobile....*Like an ecosystem, a competitive economy is a holistic entity, far greater than the sum of its parts.*[722] (Emphasis added.)

Free market economics systematically denies this greater-than-the-sum-of-its-parts aspect of the economy, as it assumes on principle that every *part* of the economy is always correctly priced by the market, rendering impossible any holistic effects in which the whole is worth more than their sum. The fruits of this reductionist way of thinking are visible all over the U.S. economy today.

For example, the U.S. is today inexorably losing the position in semiconductors it built up with past industrial policy. This is visible in declining plant investment relative to the rest of the world. In 2009, the whole of North America received only 21 percent of the world's investment in semiconductor capital equipment, compared to 64 percent going to China, Japan, South Korea, and Taiwan.[723] The U.S. now has virtually no position in photolithographic steppers, the ultra-expensive machines, among the most sophisticated technological devices in existence, that "print" the microscopic circuits of computer chips on silicon wafers. America's lack of a position in steppers means that close collaboration between the makers of these machines and the companies that use them is no longer easy in the U.S. This collaboration traditionally drove both the chip and the stepper industries to new heights of performance. American companies had 90 percent of the world market in 1980, but have less than 10 percent today.[724]

The decay of the related printed circuit board (PCB) industry tells a similar tale. An extended 2008 excerpt from *Manufacturing & Technology News* is worth reading on this score:

> The state of this industry has gone further downhill from what seems to be eons ago in 2005. The bare printed circuit industry is extremely sick in North America. Many equipment manufacturers have disappeared or are a shallow shell of their former selves. Many have opted to follow their customers to Asia, building machines there. Many raw material vendors have also gone.

> What is basically left in the United States are very fragile manufacturers, weak in capital, struggling to supply [Original Equipment Manufacturers] at prices that do not contribute to profit. The majority of the remaining manufacturers should be called 'shops.' They are owner operated and employ themselves. They are small. They barely survive. They cannot invest. Most offer only small lot, quick-turn delivery. There is very little R&D, if any at all. They can't afford equipment. They are stale. The larger companies simply get into deeper debt loads. The profits aren't there to reinvest. Talent is no longer attracted to a dying industry and the remaining manufacturers have cut all incentives.

> PCB manufacturers need raw materials with which to produce their wares. There is hardly a copper clad lamination industry. Drill bits are coming from offshore. Imaging materials, specialty chemicals, metal finishing chemistry, film and capital equipment have disappeared from the United States. Saving a PCB shop isn't saving anything if its raw materials must come from offshore. As the mass exodus of PCB manufacturers heads east, so is their supply chain.

> It's the big picture that needs to be looked into. There isn't one single vertically integrated North American shop that could independently supply a circuit board. Almost every shop stays in business supported solely by revenues from 'brokering' Asian boards.[725]

All over America, other industries are quietly falling apart in similar ways. Losing positions in key technologies means that whatever brilliant innovations Americans may dream up in small start-up companies in future, large-scale commercialization of those innovations will increasingly take place abroad. A similar fate befell Great Britain, which invented such staples of the postwar era as radar, the jet passenger plane, and the CAT scanner, only to see huge industries based on each end up in the U.S.

America's increasingly patchy technological base also renders it vulnerable to foreign suppliers of "key" or "chokepoint" technologies. These, though obscure and of small dollar value in themselves, are technologies without which major other technologies cannot function.[726] For example, China recently restricted export of the "rare earth" minerals required to make advanced magnets for everything from headphones to electric cars. Another form this problem takes is the refusal of oligopoly suppliers to sell their best technology to American companies as quickly as they make it available to their own corporate partners.[727] It doesn't take much imagination to see how foreign industrial policy could turn this into a potent competitive weapon against American industry. For example, Japan now supplies over 70 percent of the world's nickel-metal hydride batteries[728] and 60-70 percent of the world's lithium-ion batteries.[729] This will give Japan a key advantage in electric cars.

IMPOSSIBLE *NOT* TO HAVE AN INDUSTRIAL POLICY

Because of the myriad impacts that government decisions have upon industries, there is no option of "not having" an industrial policy. There is only good and bad industrial policy. In the words of James C. Miller III, chairman of the Federal Trade Commission under Reagan, "Any discussion of industrial policy should begin with recognition that we have one. The issue is what type."[730] A nation that refuses to have a conscious industrial policy will still have a de facto industrial policy because the sum of its short-term tactical choices will amount to a long-term strategic choice whether intended or not.

If nothing else, the brute fact of foreign mercantilism means that the option of genuinely free trade has long since been taken away from us. In the words of Laura D'Andrea Tyson:

> We must not be hoodwinked by the soothing notion that, in the absence of U.S. intervention, the fate of America's high-technology industries will be determined by market forces. Instead, they will be manipulated by the trade, regulatory, and industrial policies of our trading partners.[731]

Free trade and the absence of deliberate industrial policy are not neutral choices, free of government interference; they are *positive strategic bets in their own right*, which will only pay off if their key underlying economic assumption is true: pure free markets, at home and abroad, are always best. Taking an ideological stand against "central planning" misses the point, because the central planning that has rightly disgraced itself is *socialist* central planning, something entirely different. Similarly, ideological fulmination against "government picking winners" misunderstands the role that federal support plays. As Michael Borrus, founding general partner of the Silicon Valley venture capital firm X/Seed Capital, explains, referring to the National Institute of Science and Technology's Advanced Technology Program:

> ATP is sometimes labeled with the profoundly misleading and profoundly misinformed characterization of 'picking winners and losers.' That is, frankly, flat wrong. No investor, private or public, picks winners and losers in technology innovation. Rather, it is the market (customers) that does the picking. By contrast, with ATP and other federal technology programs, the government is really helping to plant long-term technology seeds in areas of private market failure or acute public need. Some of those technology seeds will sprout, others will not. But the planting, the activity as a whole, must go forward if long-term economic gains are to be effectively harvested.[732]

Opponents of industrial policy claim to oppose all industrial policy, but actually only oppose varieties they disapprove of. Despite the laissez faire myth that industrial policy was discredited with the end of the Cold War, worldwide, as Dani Rodrik explains:

> The reality is that industrial policies have run rampant during the last two decades—and nowhere more than in those economies that have steadfastly adopted the agenda of orthodox [free market] reform. If this fact has escaped attention, it is only because the preferential policies in question have privileged exports and foreign investment—the two fetishes of the Washington Consensus era—and because their advocates have called them strategies of 'outward orientation' and other similar sounding names instead of industrial policies.[733]

Export processing zones are one example of this industrial-policy-by-another-name. These receive duty-free access to raw material and component inputs, tax holidays on corporate, personal, and property taxes, exemption from usual regulations (including labor laws), and subsidized infrastructure. Another example is the wide array of subsidies, ranging from tax advantages to one-stop-shop help navigating local bureaucracy, given to encourage foreign direct investment (FDI).

Meanwhile, the federal government continues to stick its head in the sand. For example, it allowed the SEMATECH semiconductor research consortium to be effectively dismantled in 1996 by opening it up to foreign manufacturers.[734] The competitive difficulties of the American semiconductor industry in the late 1980s were treated as a one-off anomaly requiring merely tactical intervention, rather than as a symptom, destined to be repeated, of the difficulties experienced by an American industry trying to compete on its own against foreign industries backed by effective state industrial policy. America's tax credit for research and development, once the world's most generous, is now surpassed by 17 other nations.[735] This is despite the fact that, according to one rigorous 1988 study:

> A substantial gap exists between the private and social returns [to R&D] despite the availability of patents. The social rate of return is between 50 and 100 percent, so to be conservative we will say that the excess return to R&D is 35 to 60 percent above the return to ordinary capital.[736]

The George W. Bush administration abolished the only program specifically designed to increase the competitiveness of American industry by funding development of technologies that the private sector would not fund on its own: the aforementioned Advanced Technology Program. Free market ideologues repeatedly tarred this program as corporate welfare despite the fact that an audit by the respected National Academy of Sciences vindicated its claim to generate economic benefits far exceeding its cost.[737] One single $5.5 million grant, for example, seeded development of the small disk drive industry, which enabled creation of the iPod, the iPhone, TiVo and the Xbox.[738] It was replaced by an alternative carefully trimmed to avoid such accusations: the Technology Innovation Program. This program is well run, but pitifully underfunded at a mere $65 million per year.[739]

The Obama administration has proved only slightly better than the Bush administration. Although not blinded by an ideological fetish for free markets, its priorities for allocating serious money are decidedly elsewhere. Thus the giant stimulus package it passed in 2009 included money for every Congressional pork barrel under the sun, but nothing for one of the industrial-policy programs with the best track record of saving and creating jobs, the Manufacturing Extension Partnership,[740] despite a campaign promise to double the program's funding.[741] This program maintains a network of centers in every state designed to help American manufacturers adopt innovative technologies. One evaluation found that it generated $1.3 billion a year in cost savings for manufacturers and $6.25 billion in increased or retained sales, all for an annual federal outlay of only $89 million.[742]

As a result of America's neglect of industrial policy, there is a starvation of basic and applied research in areas such as biocomputing, computer architecture, software, optoelectronics, aeronautics, advanced materials, factory automation, sensors, energy conversion and storage, nanomanufacturing, and robotics. The U.S. will pay a serious price for this in the decades ahead. By following, rather than shaping, our comparative advantage, we are heading for industrial decline.

10

The Multiple Equilibrium Revolution

WE SAW IN THE PREVIOUS CHAPTER how profoundly the real origins of economic growth contradict free-market, free-trade economics. Real-world growth in less about obeying comparative advantage than shaping it. Real-world growth is path dependent, reliant upon scale economies and "good" industries, and inefficient by the standards of pure free markets. This last point is the most important, because it means that a purely free-market approach to economic policy, which rejects protectionism abroad and industrial policy at home, will *necessarily* underperform a competent embrace of these policies. But although this has been known and successfully applied by governments (including our own) for centuries, its underlying economics has never been properly mathematized. This has been the Achilles' heel of this knowledge in post-WWII America, because academic economists have therefore not taken it seriously. Until now. Finally, someone has found a way to translate this eminently practical wisdom into the abstruse mathematics economists are prepared to consider "serious" economics. This is, in fact, the intellectual innovation that well may eventually end economists' faith in free trade for good.[743]

The theoretical breakthrough in question was made by economists Ralph Gomory and William Baumol, starting around 1991 and reaching its crowning synthesis in their 2000 book *Global Trade and Conflicting National Interests*.[744] Ralph Gomory, currently Research Professor at the Stern School of Business at New York University in New York City, holds a PhD in mathematics from Princeton, spent 30 years with IBM, managed its world-famous Research Division, and was its senior vice-president for science and technology. (Two Nobels were won under his direction.) William Baumol, currently Professor of Entrepreneurship at the Stern School, is Professor Emeritus of economics at Princeton and a former president of the American Economic Association. Prior to his work in trade economics, he was best known for having carved out a place in economic theory for entrepreneurs.

So this is serious economics, albeit cutting-edge and thus controversial. It is not some crank theory, an ideological shibboleth, special-interest pleading, or an academic fad. It is, above all, not going to go away any time soon, but will almost certainly challenge the existing free trade consensus until one or the other gives way or a new synthesis emerges.[745]

MATHEMATIZING SCALE ECONOMIES

The easiest way to understand Gomory and Baumol's work is to add another assumption to the list in Chapter Five of the dubious assumptions of the theory of comparative advantage:

Dubious Assumption #8: There are no scale economies.

Gomory and Baumol assume instead that there are. This is both true and, as we saw in the previous chapter, a fact with vast implications. Scale-economy industries are where the action is when it comes to economic growth, and they are the key trade battlegrounds for advanced economies. And because they are the highly capitalized and knowledge intensive industries that most strongly *defy* Ricardian economics, Gomory and Baumol's analysis is thus highly appropriate for understanding those industries where free trade *isn't* America's best move. This makes theirs an excellent analysis for anyone who wants to criticize free trade—and figure out what the rational alternative might be.

213

WHAT ARE RETAINABLE INDUSTRIES?

Gomory and Baumol's analysis is founded on the implications they draw from a key fact about scale-economy industries. Because, by definition, their cost per unit goes down as their output goes up, which nation is the world's low-cost producer is, other things being equal, a function of which nation is producing *more*. So whichever nation reaches large production volume *first* in a scale-economy industry thereby becomes the world's low-cost producer in that industry. The winner's cost advantage then locks other nations out.

Under these circumstances, the only way a challenger can succeed is to start on day one at a production volume equal to the incumbent's. This is rarely feasible. Not only would the challenger have to match the investments that incumbent had already made to reach high-volume production, but the payoff would be a Pyrrhic victory: head-to-head competition with an entrenched incumbent. As this sort of competition tends to drive profits toward zero, it is rarely financially viable to challenge an incumbent under these circumstances. Gomory and Baumol call industries that behave this way "retainable" industries and if a nation can acquire them, it can generally hang onto them.

The important thing here is the lockout phenomenon. Even if another nation hypothetically *might* have been an even lower-cost producer, the first arrival is so entrenched that the latecomer never gets a chance. This is the opposite of what happens in Ricardo's model. In his model, historical accidents of which nation reaches high-volume production first certainly happen, but they don't *matter* because they get washed away afterwards by competitive forces. Potentially superior latecomers realize their potential superiority and win, so if one nation reaches high-volume production before another, this has no particular significance. Ricardo didn't allow for scale economies and in their absence, a head start doesn't permanently lower a nation's costs below its rivals. So without entrenched scale economies, there can be no lockouts.

This is, of course, how the world ended up with half its large passenger aircraft being built in Seattle and two-thirds of its fine watches being made in Switzerland. Ricardian comparative advantage is useless for explaining why Bangladesh exports many t-shirts and few soccer balls, while Pakistan exports the reverse. Why does South Korea export so many microwave ovens, and almost no bicycles, while Taiwan is the other way around?

There is nothing intrinsic about South Korea that makes it a good place to build microwave ovens. Entrenched scale economies are the reason.

GOOD-BYE PERFECT COMPETITION

As noted in the previous chapter, scale economies are incompatible with perfect competition. Instead, firms that possess them will be (at least partly) sheltered from competition and will therefore realize quasi-monopoly profits. When two or three firms in an industry all have scale economies, this will tend to make that industry an oligopoly. Imperfect competition is thus generally a happy thing for those who own and work in such industries, as these industries can reap and pay higher-than-normal profits and wages. Of particular interest to residents of advanced industrial nations, these industries are sheltered against cheap foreign labor if their scale economies are large enough.

From the general public's point of view, the best thing about these industries is that they pay higher wages to their employees. Hypothetically, they could just return greater profits to their owners, but the empirical data actually suggests that workers receive a greater benefit. The most authoritative study on this question is by Harvard economists Lawrence Katz and Lawrence Summers (former president of Harvard and Secretary of the Treasury, then chief economic advisor to President Obama). They found that "variations in labor rents [extra wages] across industries are at least two to three times as important as variations in the rents accruing to shareholders [extra profits]."[746] Among other things, their analysis changes the evaluation of industrial policy; as they note with respect to the European aircraft industry:

> Once labor rent considerations are recognized, the overall assessment of the Airbus program for European welfare turns from marginally negative to strongly positive. Even in the less favorable case, the subsidy generates a welfare gain representing about half its cost....Policies promoting domestic production that appear undesirable without taking account of labor market imperfections yield large gains once the existence of these imperfections is acknowledged.[747]

Imperfect competition has other benefits. As previously noted, it supports innovation, as the only way innovation can be profitable is if firms which finance it get at least *quasi*-exclusive rights to sell its application. And because knowledge *itself* leads to scale economies as the cost of an innovation is amortized over a rising number of units of product sold, this is a self-reinforcing process. More innovation leads to more scale economies, which lead to more profits and more money to finance innovation. Therefore scale economies, in the presence of a healthy financial system with long time horizons, tend to drive an economy to endlessly seek out innovation.

So, despite myths about high technology being the ultimate arena of pure competition and free markets being the master key to innovation, high technology actually tends to be an area in which pure free market principles do *not* operate. In the words of one OECD study:

> Oligopolistic competition and strategic interaction among firms and governments, rather than the invisible hand of market forces, condition today's competitive advantage and international division of labor in high-technology industries.[748]

Ralph Gomory got a good look at this fact during his time at IBM, which once held 70 percent of the market for mainframe computers and faced a Department of Justice antitrust investigation.[749]

GOOD-BYE RICARDO'S EFFICIENCIES

In a Ricardian world, as noted when we first examined the theory of comparative advantage in Chapter Five, every industry automatically migrates to the lowest-possible-cost producer.[750] But in a Gomory-Baumol world, it may or it may not—because historical accidents can interfere. In fact, in a Gomory-Baumol world there isn't even *just one* answer to the question of which nation *is* the lowest-possible-cost producer. Instead, there are an infinite number of possible answers, depending on which nation reaches large production volume first.

This has profound implications. For one thing, it means that some possible outcomes are "bad" outcomes, in which the winning nation locks out potentially more-efficient rivals. Would the world enjoy cheaper fine watches if Japan had captured this industry, rather than Switzerland? We'll never know, because the accidental equilibrium that placed this industry in Switzerland is now entrenched. Would the world have better small cars if Brazil had captured this industry, rather than Japan? Same problem. If the "wrong" nations win the race in various industries, the world economy may get stuck incurring opportunity costs it could have avoided if other nations had won.[751] Thus it will waste opportunities and be less productive than it could have been. So all bets are off about free trade necessarily producing the best possible outcome for the world economy as a whole.[752]

The same goes for individual nations. Would Germany be a richer country if it had a commanding position in airplanes, rather than cars? Maybe, but maybe not. The fact that the free market steered Germany's factors of production into the car industry does *not* guarantee that this was the best possible use for them.[753] Because lockout can interfere, free trade won't necessarily allocate every nation its most appropriate industries, and mere bad luck can deprive a nation of the industries that would actually have been best for it.

One more point: the Ricardian assumption that departing industries will automatically be replaced by better ones becomes even more problematic than already noted with Chapter Five's dubious assumption #2 (factors of production move easily between industries) because lockout can interfere with breaking into the right replacement industries. Michigan is not going to neatly segue into the helicopter industry after all.

WEIGHING THE POSSIBLE OUTCOMES

If the Ricardian contention that free trade outcomes are always the best possible is no longer tenable, the obvious next question is just how good *are* the various outcomes that can occur, and for which nations? Is there an intelligible pattern to the quasi-arbitrary outcomes Gomory and Baumol seem to imply, with historical accidents tripping up nice predictable efficiency as often as not? We need some kind of *map* of the possible distributions of retainable industries among nations, showing who gets which industries when—and how big are the economic benefits when they do.

These possible distributions of retainable industries among nations are the subject of a computer model constructed by Gomory and Baumol on the basis of their theory. This model runs out different possible scenarios of industry assignment between two imaginary nations A and B. In some scenarios, A wins the automobile, aircraft, and semiconductor industries, plus two others, while B wins the rest. In other scenarios, B wins those industries, three others, and A wins the rest. With a model containing just two nations (the UN recognizes 194) and 10 industries (the Commerce Department recognizes about 1,800),[754] there are over 1,000 possible distributions of industries between nations. So this model is highly simplified, compared to the real world. But it still suffices to draw out the key implications of Gomory and Baumol's ideas.

GREEDY, BUT NOT TOO GREEDY

Whenever a nation captures an industry, that industry's output will become part of its GDP, so the nation will be richer for it. Thus one might, at first sight, conclude that a nation's best move is simply to capture as many retainable industries as it can, by winning the race to high-volume production in each. But if one looks closely at the graph on the next page generated by the computer model, there is clearly more to the story.[755]

Each dot on the graph on the next page represents one *scenario*, that is one possible distribution of retainable industries between A and B. Nonretainable industries will be distributed Ricardo-fashion, and nontraded industries will not be (directly) affected by trade at all, but will form a base of unchanging economic activity at the bottom of the graph. The horizontal axis shows what percentage of the world's retainable industries A has captured (B gets the rest); the vertical axis shows A's GDP. So the further to the right a dot is, the more retainable industries A has captured, and the higher a dot is, the richer A is in that scenario.

The graph opposite shows that, in general, the more retainable industries A captures, the higher its GDP. No surprise there. But there's also a surprise: it is *not* nation A's best move to capture all the retainable industries in the world! If it does, it actually ends up poorer than if it captures, say, 70 percent. Thus the cluster of dots is actually lower at the far right side of the graph than if we move a little to the left. A's best move is apparently to *be greedy, but not too greedy.*

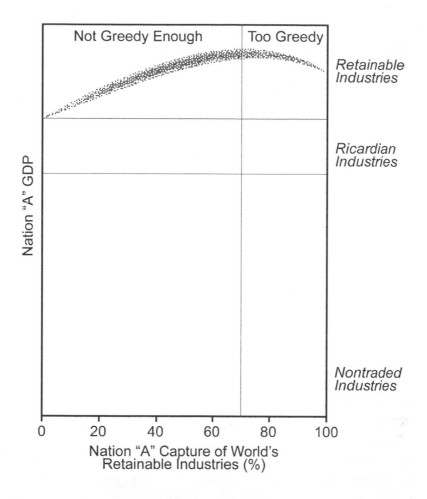

There are a number of reasons for this. For a start, A taking 100 percent of the world's retainable industries would mean A taking industries for which it is fundamentally ill-suited, despite its luck in winning them. (As noted, a nation can sometimes be a "bad" winner.) When an industry would have been significantly more efficient in B, A would be better off allocating its factors of production to other industries and importing those goods from B instead. Why? Because A has to balance the monopoly profits from winning a retainable industry against the Ricardian cost of producing for itself goods that B could have produced more cheaply.

We already know about Ricardian costs: these are the costs a nation incurs when it defies free trade and makes for itself things it should import. Nothing in Gomory and Baumol's theory makes these costs go away. But their theory introduces quasi-monopoly profits that sometimes outweigh them. Would America be better off if we produced for ourselves the fine watches we currently import from Switzerland? Maybe, because this would mean hosting a sophisticated high-paying industry. But maybe not, if we turned out to be a grossly inferior producer and the extra wages and profits were outweighed by the cost of ending up with inferior and more expensive watches.

Ricardo understood the Ricardian cost side of this perfectly, but not the monopoly profits side. In his world, there *are* no monopoly profits because all industries operate under perfect competition all the time—and without scale economies and lockout, it is basically impossible to have an international monopoly or quasi-monopoly.

There is another problem with A capturing every retainable industry: this would mean dividing up A's finite labor force and capital among them. This would spread A's labor and capital too thin to realize the maximum possible scale economies in each. America has such a large economy that we tend not to take this issue seriously, but for most nations this is a serious issue. Finland, for example, has a world-class position in cellular phones (Nokia). But Finland is probably too small to support both that *and* world-class positions in avionics, nanotechnology, fiber optics, and genetic engineering. So nation A has to balance its monopoly profits against a scale-economies loss, too.

The final problem is that capturing every retainable industry will mean depriving B of retainable industries of its own. As a result, B won't have enough high-value exports to afford very many imports from A, which would have enabled A to increase its exports from its own *best* industries even more. So A has to balance its monopoly profits against a trading loss as well.

A good analogy to A's bundle of tradeoffs would be to an exceptionally lucky jack-of-all-trades who manages to monopolize all the most lucrative jobs in an isolated small town. He is the town's lawyer, its doctor, its banker, et cetera. Obviously, up to a point, this might be very lucrative. But if he takes it too far, he will make less profit than if he relinquished a few jobs to other people. His best move? Pick some desirable occupation, whether or not someone else would be better at it, but a) he shouldn't grab any job he's terrible at, b) he shouldn't spread himself too thin, and c) he shouldn't lock everyone else out of good careers entirely. Point a) means there's no point imposing meritocracy on yourself if this just means somebody else taking your dream job. But equally, you shouldn't try to be your own doctor if you're no good at medicine. Point b) means that working several jobs means several paychecks, but you probably can't make a success out of a profession you practice for only a few hours a day. Point c) means that it's nice to have the best job in town, but unless other people have good jobs too, you won't have many customers.

Clearly, the old Ricardian logic has its place in a Gomory-Baumol world. It just isn't the whole story anymore. The successful pursuit of economic self-interest, for both nations and people, is a *tradeoff* between simply grabbing what one wants and submitting to various demands of efficiency. Nations, like people, benefit from importing and exporting in order to allocate their finite productive abilities to their most productive activities. But nations, like people, *also* benefit by capturing monopoly positions (nations capture good industries, people hold good jobs) *whether or not* this is efficient. As noted in Chapter Five, nations trade for the same reasons people do.

Gomory and Baumol's analysis also warns us that when someone *else* holds a lucrative job, they will use it to extract monopoly profits from us. And they may not be the best person for the job, anyway, merely someone who managed to entrench themselves in it. This reasoning extends to nations: not only is it advantageous to win good industries, but it is *dis*advantageous to end up at the mercy of other nations that have—because this entails paying them tribute in the form of their monopoly profit margins. (You feel exploited, and they may not be the best possible suppliers anyway.) Americans are only really conscious of this problem in the case of OPEC, which is a natural oligopoly. But if we end up 30 years from now with a solar-powered economy dependent on Japanese-made solar cells, we will be in the exact same position, especially because American-made solar cells might have been cheaper and better, if we had gotten our act together and developed this industry.

WIN-WIN VS. WIN-LOSE TRADE

There is a twin to nation A in the above analysis: its trading partner nation B. When A has 100 percent of the world's retainable industries, B has 0 percent; when A has 90 percent, B has 10 percent, and so on. What does B's experience of the above scenarios look like? Let's plot both nations on the same graph and see.[756]

The interesting thing about this graph is that in the two side regions (labeled Zone of Mutual Gain), any change in A's industry capture that benefits A, benefits B also. Whenever A captures more industries and its GDP goes up, B's GDP goes up, too. And whenever A captures fewer industries and its GDP goes down, B's GDP goes down, too. So anything either nation does to benefit itself *also* benefits its trading partner. This means a world in which economic rivalry does not exist because all outcomes are win-win. (This is how Ricardians believe the world works all the time.) However, as one can also see, in the region at the center, things work very differently. There, gain for one nation coincides with loss for the other. In this region, economic rivalry is a fact of life.

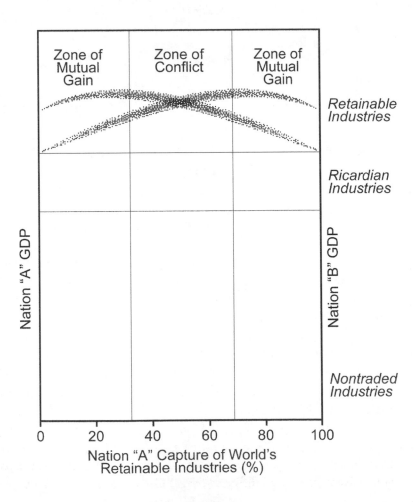

Gomory and Baumol are definitely onto something here, because they have managed to bridge the gap between the Pollyannaish "international trade is always win-win" Ricardian view and the overly pessimistic "international trade is war" view. The former view is naïve and, due to Chapter Five's dubious assumptions #5 (capital is not internationally mobile) and #7 (trade does not induce adverse productivity growth abroad), untenable even *without* their insights. The latter view ignores the fact that economics precisely *isn't* war because it is a positive-sum game in which goods are produced, not just divided, making mutual gains possible.

So here, at long last, we have a theoretical framework that can accommodate economic reality as we actually experience it, not just lecture us on what "must" happen as Ricardianism does. It's both a dog-eat-dog *and* a scratch-my-back-and-I'll-scratch-yours world. *Economics has finally given common sense permission to be true.* Gomory and Baumol's analysis is obviously just the beginning of a whole new way of looking at international trade, which will require decades of elaboration before it becomes a complete new theory of the world economy. But the importance of their work should be obvious already. It will have enormous repercussions for economics (and the real-world policy decisions that depend on it) in the years to come.

COMPARATIVE ADVANTAGE IN THE RIGHT INDUSTRIES

What are the policy implications of Gomory and Baumol's work? Basically that a wise nation will willingly let other nations have their share of the world's industrial base, but will try to grab the *best* industries for itself, by means of shrewd protectionism and the industrial policies discussed in the previous chapter. Then it will sit back (here's where laissez faire plays its legitimate role) and let the rest of the world compete—head to head, driving the price down through the perfect competition in free markets it seeks to avoid for itself—to produce for it the things it doesn't want to produce itself. Free markets are best for *other* people.

Here Ricardo's ghost rears its head yet again: comparative advantage remains a valid principle, but a nation's best move is not simply to trade according to the comparative advantage it already has. It is to *seek* comparative advantage in the best industries. Ricardianism is about finding the best use for the comparative advantage one already has (mistaking this for the entire question); Gomory and Baumol are about what kind of comparative advantage it is best *to have*. (Chapter Nine was about how to get it.)

The top retainable industries will be the best ones to have comparative advantage in, followed by the lesser retainable industries. What makes one retainable industry better than another? It ideally should be large, strongly retainable, and with a long future potential for innovation, and many spin-off industries, ahead of it. As Michael Porter explains, referring to such industries as "structurally attractive" ones:

> Structurally attractive industries, with sustainable entry barriers in such areas as technology, specialized skills, channel access, and brand reputation, often involve high labor productivity and will earn more attractive returns to capital. Standard of living will depend importantly on the capacity of a nation's firms to successfully penetrate structurally attractive industries. The attractiveness of an industry is not reliably indicated by size, rapid growth, or newness of technology, attributes often stressed by executives and by government planners.[757]

The industries it is *worst* to have are the nonretainable, no-scale-economies industries. These behave according to the old Ricardian model: head-to-head free-market competition that drives down prices, profits, and wages. Cynically speaking, these are what a wise nation wants its trading partners to specialize in.

But this doesn't mean a wise nation wants its trading partners to be destitute. Then they would have few tradable industries of any kind and low productivity in those they did have. This would make it impossible to realize significant gains by trading with them. (Nobody gets rich trading with Eskimos, no matter how shrewd, efficient, or even downright exploitive they are, because Eskimos just don't have that much *stuff* in the first place.)[758] Instead, the ideal trading partner is one that perfectly *complements* a nation's own more sophisticated economy. The ideal trading partner is less like a slave (the colonial exploitation model) than like the perfect employee. He skillfully performs all the tasks his employer *doesn't* want to perform, freeing that employer to perform more-valuable tasks. But he *isn't* so skillful that he threatens his employer's entrenched position doing the tasks he wishes to reserve to himself. Every lawyer wants an efficient paralegal; no lawyer wants one so skilled that she sets up a competing legal practice next door!

The ideal trading partner thus has the highest possible productivity in the industries that a nation *doesn't* want to compete in, but low productivity in those it does want to compete in.[759] For example, because Japan is a net importer of oil, Japan should want all oil exporting nations to be the most efficient possible oil producers, as this will provide Japan the cheapest possible oil. But Japan should not want Kuwait to become an efficient producer of cars.

There is a fundamental asymmetry here: a productivity increase in Japan's car industry will always benefit Kuwait, by enabling Kuwait to buy cheaper cars. But a productivity increase in Kuwait's car industry (from zero, as it does not currently have one) will *not* necessarily benefit Japan. The only time it might is if Kuwait started building car parts that enabled Japan to build *better* cars, or if Kuwait started building cheap cars, enabling Japan to stop producing these for itself and produce more-expensive ones instead. Productivity gains by the leader (Japan) are always win-win, but gains by followers (Kuwait) can sometimes be win-lose.[760] This is why the most visible pressures for protectionism appear in threatened leading nations, while the most successful protectionism and industrial policy are visible in catching-up nations. Once one views these phenomena under Gomory-Baumol assumptions, they make perfect sense, while Ricardian thinking sees only misguided complaining driven by special-interest politics and unnecessary protectionism of industries that would have succeeded anyway.

DEFENDING RETAINABLE INDUSTRIES

We have just scratched at a serious issue. Retainability is real, but it is not absolute and it does have to be defended over time as old industries decay into obsolescence and new ones emerge, rendering yesterday's entrenched positions irrelevant. As noted earlier, retainability exists in the first place because scale economies entrench productivity differences among nations, which entrench industry assignments among nations. But what if productivity differences are not due to entrenched scale economies, but are just *there*, unentrenched? Then, as long as they last, the same implications will flow from them that flow from entrenched productivity differences—only *these* implications will be unstable. So the same Gomory-Baumol analyses will apply. Unfortunately, this also means that the win-lose implications of the Gomory-Baumol analysis will apply, too. So there will be a Zone of Conflict and a Zone of Mutual Gain. There will be harmony and rivalry. There will be winners and losers. Productivity gains by one nation will either help or hurt the other, depending on where on the graph they both are.

This is extremely important. Because it finally gives us a sound theoretical basis for saying what ordinary Americans (and highly sophisticated international businesspeople) tend to regard as obvious, even if most American economists do not:

> *Foreign productivity growth can take entire industries away from us without conferring any compensating benefits.*[761]

This is neither an illusion promoted by special interests nor a myth invented by demagogic politicians. Here, Ricardianism is completely out of touch with reality and catastrophically wrong.

The illusion of permanent advantage that transient productivity differences create explains a fact noted in Chapter Six:[762] nations at the peak of their economic power, like Britain in 1860 or the U.S. in 1960, can garner the mistaken impression that free trade is universally beneficial to them. But this illusion depends upon productivity differences between them and their rivals that will not endure forever. We encountered this problem before, in milder form, with dubious assumption #7 (free trade does not induce adverse productivity growth abroad). By previously analyzing the problem without using multiple-equilibrium ideas, we merely noted that foreign productivity growth can roll back *existing* gains from trade. This is much worse.

ARE INDUSTRIES NATIONAL?

There is one final, and very important, caveat to the whole Gomory-Baumol analysis. When we noted that half the world's large passenger aircraft are built in Seattle and two-thirds of its fine watches in Switzerland, the reason this is true is that the American aircraft and Swiss watch industries are relatively *localized*. That is, the companies that make up these industries, though they have international operations, are still significantly tied to their national home bases. (As noted in Chapter One, this is still largely true even for most multinational corporations.)[763] As a result, it is meaningful to talk about the national location of these corporations and thus about national industries.

This is critical, because scale economies mostly reside in companies, not industries as such. As a result, if companies are truly internationalized, the Gomory-Baumol analysis will get no traction on them, and the more internationalized they are, the less traction it will get. As a result, the less any solution based on this analysis will succeed. Luckily, it is, of course, free trade *itself* that tends to denationalize companies, so protectionism can push back at denationalization. Successful protectionism based on Gomory and Baumol's ideas will therefore be a two-pronged policy: first, to maintain in corporations a sufficiently national character for policies imposed at the national level to work, and second, to impose the right national policies.

Strictly speaking, matters are even more complicated than this. What really matters actually isn't how national a company's production is, but how national the *scale-economy stages* of its production are. The supply chain of a product from raw materials to the consumer can have widely differing scale economies at different stages. The classic example is consumer electronics, where the manufacture of silicon chips, liquid crystal displays, and other key components enjoys huge scale economies, but the final assembly of these components into a finished device enjoys comparatively few. The former activities depend upon massive R&D, require expensive and sophisticated machinery for physical fabrication, and employ highly trained engineers and scientists. The latter activities often require almost no R&D and are done by hand (perhaps on a 1920s-style assembly line) by semiskilled labor, often in developing countries. One possible strategy this implies is to be fairly agnostic about where companies locate overall, but seek to capture the segments of their production that enjoy scale economies. This is, in fact, roughly the strategy pursued by Singapore, which (unlike Japan) has no internationally recognizable brand-name companies but has managed, through aggressive industrial policy, to systematically capture the high-value segments of foreign corporations' supply chains.

11

The Natural Strategic Tariff

AS WE HAVE SEEN, free trade depends upon a long list of assumptions that are often false. So there is no justification for assuming that it will be the best policy. But while this necessarily opens up the possibility that some kind of protectionism could be better, it doesn't give us an obvious formula for what form that protectionism should take. Which imports, that is, should we tax, how much, and when? If we impose a tariff incorrectly, we will merely force Americans to buy more-expensive domestically produced goods without a gain in wages big enough to compensate. To tell us what to do, we have only scraps of insight here and there based on the various flaws in free trade we have examined, with no synthesis uniting them into a coherent policy implication. Even Gomory and Baumol's breakthrough insights, while they do tell us what a better outcome than free trade would *look like* (more good, i.e. scale economy or retainable industries), do not tell us how to attain that outcome. Merely stapling together the tariff wish lists of every complaining industry in America will do no good, as this embodies no particular rational economic strategy.

We do, however, have one obvious starting point for reasoning out a tariff policy. If free trade is wrong because of the list of its flaws we have compiled, might the right policy consist in systematically *fixing* these flaws? There is, in fact, an entire school of thought that aims to "restore the lost innocence" of free trade in this way.[764] Because many (not all) of these flaws consist in failures of the free market to work properly, the great attraction of this approach is that it satisfies people who are ideologically attached to free trade as a broken ideal that can be achieved after all, once repaired.

Can this approach work? Let's look at the list of dubious assumptions underlying free trade to see if we can fix free trade by imposing policies that will make these assumptions hold true after all. To wit:

Dubious Assumption #1: Trade is sustainable. (Original discussion on pages 47 and 104.)

Environmental sustainability is a problem intrinsic to the entire modern industrial economy. In the context of trade, the obvious solution is to tax trade that depletes nonrenewable resources.

Financial sustainability is, as analyzed at length in Chapter Two, achievable by controlling either trade or the countervailing financial flows that must take place when trade is paid for.[765]

Problem fixable? Yes.
Problem fixable without ending free trade? No.

Dubious Assumption #2: There are no externalities. (Original discussion on page 105.)

For negative externalities like environmental damage, the obvious solution is to tax imports produced in environmentally harmful ways.

Positive externalities like technological spillovers can be addressed by tax credits for research and development. This is already U.S. policy to some extent, though without protectionism, it can just end up subsidizing research whose value is harvested by production abroad—yet another connection between protectionism and industrial policy.[766]

Problem fixable? Yes.
Problem fixable without ending free trade? No.

Dubious Assumption #3: Factors of production move easily between industries. (Original discussion on page 106.)

This problem mostly comes down to labor. We can do little about it because the U.S. already has one of the most flexible labor markets in the developed world. We could expand palliative adjustment programs and worker retraining, but they have limited ability to solve this problem, for reasons analyzed in Chapter Three.[767]

Problem fixable? No.
Problem fixable without ending free trade? No.

Dubious Assumption #4: Free Trade does not raise income inequality. (Original discussion on pages 34 and 109.)

Free trade raises income inequality in the U.S. because it lowers returns to the scarce factor of production (labor) and raises returns to the abundant factor (capital).[768] It also hits low-skill workers harder than high-skill workers.[769] Although other nations have mitigated these problems somewhat with various nontrade policies, such egalitarian interventions are unlikely in the U.S.

Problem fixable? Yes.
Problem fixable without ending free trade? No.

Dubious Assumption #5: Capital is not internationally mobile. (Original discussion on page 109.)

The controls on international capital flows associated with a new Bretton Woods-style system of fixed exchange rates would help here,[770] but this is not a free-trade solution unless we consider it free trade when we lack freedom in the financial flows that pay for that trade.[771]

Problem fixable? Yes.
Problem fixable without ending free trade? No.

Dubious Assumption #6: Short-term efficiency causes long-term growth. (Original discussion on page 112.)

As analyzed in Chapter Two,[772] short-term efficiency can be downright destructive if people have short time horizons, something only authoritarian governments have been able to correct.

As analyzed in Chapter Nine,[773] even with long time horizons, economic growth is largely about ladder externalities and related dynamics; most effective strategies for exploiting these are contrary to free trade because Ricardianism (and thus free trade) is about best exploiting *immediate* comparative advantage.[774]

Problem fixable? Yes.
Problem fixable without ending free trade? No.

Dubious Assumption #7: Trade does not induce adverse productivity growth abroad. (Original discussion on page 114.)

This problem is almost impossible to solve without abandoning free trade, as it concerns events in foreign nations not under our control. Ceasing to import so many goods, especially at the frontier of our trading partners' technological capabilities, would obviously slow them down, but only somewhat.

Problem fixable? No.
Problem fixable without ending free trade? No.

Dubious Assumption #8: There are no scale economies. (Original discussion on page 213.)

The existence of scale economies is a fundamental fact of modern industry. They are not the product of any particular policy decision, so nothing can be done to make them go away, short of a return to premodern technology.

Problem fixable? No.
Problem fixable without ending free trade? No.

So it appears that we can't plausibly hope to fix these eight problems without giving up free trade to some meaningful extent. The above list implies some policies to mitigate free trade's harmful effects, but no fundamental solution that will redeem free trade as such.

IS THERE A NATURAL STRATEGIC TARIFF?

Here's the nightmare that haunts all criticisms of free trade in this country: what if these criticisms imply that America needs a complicated technocratic tariff policy? This seems to be suggested by the complexity of the defects in free trade and by the fact that the nations which have most successfully repudiated free trade actually *have* complicated technocratic tariff policies. That would spell trouble, as the political difficulties of achieving such a solution in America are no secret. In the words of Alan Blinder, a member of Bill Clinton's Council of Economic Advisors and former Vice Chairman of the Federal Reserve Board,

> In Japan, industrial policy was and is run by a cadre of intelligent, respected, and powerful technocrats largely insulated from political interference and acting in the national interest. The United States, I am afraid, is too democratic for that. Political considerations would quickly overwhelm economic merits; industrial policy would more closely resemble life support for dying industries than incubation of emerging ones.[775]

It is, in fact, sorely tempting to take these political difficulties as an excuse to do nothing at all. The dangers of a special-interest takeover are not imaginary. But we can't afford to quail at the challenge of making the politics work, as we are competing with rivals who have already done so. Like it or not, they have raised the bar for us. For the U.S. to concede that there exists an area of national policy this important that our rivals can master and we can't is a decision in favor of voluntary national decline.

Billionaire investor Warren Buffett says that one of his criteria for investing in a company is that it must have a business that even a fool can run—because sooner or later a fool will. A similar philosophy should guide our construction of a tariff policy. We need a broad-based policy that can survive imperfect implementation and political meddling, a certain amount of which will be inevitable. We do *not* need an intricate, brittle, difficult policy that will only create work for bureaucrats, lawyers, and lobbyists. Among other things, a policy too complex for the public to understand will be beyond the reach of democratic accountability, the only ultimate guarantee that any tariff policy will remain aimed at the public good.

As noted in Chapter Six,[776] one of the great puzzles of American economic history is how the U.S. once succeeded so well under tariff regimes that were not particularly sophisticated. This is where the idea of a so-called natural strategic tariff comes in. This idea says that there may be some simple *rule* for imposing a tariff which will produce the complex *policy* we need. The simple rule will produce a complex policy by interacting with the existing complexity of the economy. All the complexity will be on the "economy" side, not the "policy" side, so all *specific* decisions about which industries get protection, how much, and when will be made by the free market. No intricate theory, difficult technocratic expertise, or corruptible political decision-making will be required.

There are obviously any number of possible natural strategic tariffs. The one we will look at here (probably the best) is actually the simplest:

A flat tax on all imported goods and services.

Prima facie, this is strategically meaningless because it protects, and thus promotes, domestic production in all industries equally. And if a tariff is going to win the U.S. better jobs, it will do so by winning us more positions in good industries (as defined in Chapters Nine and Ten). While a flat tariff would help with the deficit, which is good, it would provide the same incentive for domestic production of computer and potato chips alike, so it would not push our economy towards good industries.

Or would it? The natural strategic tariff is a bet that it would. The key reason is this:

Industries differ in their sensitivity and response to import competition.

Although this is a complex issue, the fundamental dynamic is clear from the fairly obvious fact that a flat tariff would trigger the relocation back to the U.S. of some industries but not others. For example, a flat 30 percent tariff (to pluck a not-unreasonable number out of thin air) would not cause the relocation of the apparel industry back to the U.S. from abroad. The difference between domestic and foreign labor costs is simply too large for a 30 percent premium to tip the balance in America's favor in an industry based on semi-skilled labor. But a 30 percent tariff quite likely *would* cause the relocation of high-tech manufacturing like semiconductors. This is key, as these industries are precisely the ones we *should* want to relocate. They have the scale economies that cause retainability, high returns, high wages, and all the other effects of good industries. *Therefore a flat tariff would, in fact, be strategic.*

TARIFF EFFECTS ON SCALE-ECONOMY INDUSTRIES

A natural strategic tariff would interact with different industries in surprisingly sophisticated ways. There is not the space here to discuss all of them, but one key example is the fact that it would have different effects on

industries that were at different points on their curves of cost per unit produced. The key here is that the cost curves of scale-economy industries are
concave. That is, they go down like this ⌣ , not like this ⟍ . This is not
the place to go into the details, but a concave cost curve is actually *guaranteed* whenever production cost consists of an investment in capital
(physical, human, or intellectual) plus an incremental cost for each additional unit of output.[777] As a result, these curves have steeper slopes in their
earlier than later stages. That is, they look something like the graph below,
though their exact shape will vary:

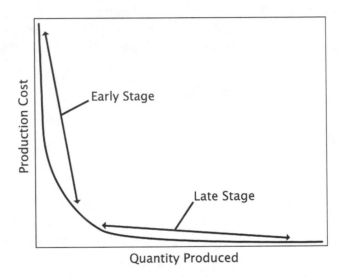

The difference in slope between the early and late stages is the key.
When a tariff is imposed upon an industry that is in the early stages of its
cost curve, costs fall rapidly with relatively small increases in output. So if
we start at the far left on the graph above and move to the right a little, the
curve goes down a long way. (See the graph on the next page.) Therefore,
when a scale-economy industry in its early stages is given tariff protection
and its sales increase as a result, it will enjoy a large cost decline. This
induced cost decline will then improve its cost advantage over its foreign
competitors by even more than the size of the tariff itself. This will result
in further sales increases, further cost declines, and so on until its cost
curve bottoms out. Therefore a flat tariff will, under these circumstances,
trigger a virtuous cycle, and a fairly small tariff will produce a much larger
ultimate cost advantage for the domestic producer. This advantage will
outlast tariff protection and lock in retainability. (In the extreme case, this

virtuous cycle will end only when the domestic industry has wiped out all its foreign competitors and become globally dominant.)

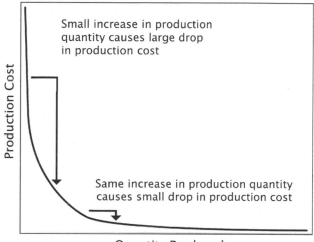

Quantity Produced

On the other hand, when a tariff is imposed on a mature industry (which, by definition, will be in the *late* stage of its cost curve), the slope of its cost curve will be relatively flat, so even fairly large increases in sales will not shift its costs very much. Therefore tariff protection will not trigger a virtuous cycle, and the domestic industry's cost advantage will not greatly exceed the tariff itself.

The net effect of strong impacts on some industries and weak impacts on others will be a bias towards stimulating industries that a) have concave cost curves and b) are on the early part of those curves. These will necessarily be *nascent scale-economy industries*: nascent because of b) and having scale economies because of a). In other words, a flat tariff will be *self-targeting on precisely those industries we should want to target.*

This mechanism is not perfect, and in the real world it would suffer a thousand quibbles, complications, and exceptions. Sometimes it would even backfire. But it is real enough to be worthwhile, as it is the effect on average that will matter.

This all resembles, of course, a classic infant industries tariff, but without the contentious problem of deciding which industries should be targeted or for how long. Strictly speaking, a true infant industries tariff would have the same effect as the natural strategic tariff, only more efficiently, as it would not waste any tariff incentive on mature industries, or on industries without concave cost curves. But, as noted earlier,[778] infant industries are only the first rungs of the larger phenomenon of the path-dependence of economic growth, so even a perfect infant-industries tariff would not be ideal.

TOO GOOD TO BE TRUE?

One is justifiably suspicious of cure-alls. So it is worth understanding why the natural strategic tariff is neither a gimmick nor too good to be true. It is neither a magic trick to make economic vitality appear out of nowhere nor a hammock to enable lazy and uncompetitive American industries to survive, and anyone supporting it for these reasons will be disappointed.

Fundamentally, the natural strategic tariff only works because it interacts with the *existing* competitive strengths of the U.S. economy. Specifically, it works because:

1. The U.S. is closer to being cost-competitive in good industries than in bad ones.

2. The U.S. domestic market is big enough to support scale economy industries.

3. A tariff has different effects on industries at different points on their cost curves.

It follows that if we do not cultivate the existing strengths of our economy, a natural strategic tariff will not do us much good. If implemented, such a tariff would be the cornerstone of trade reform, without which other measures will not work very well. But we would still need to fix our substandard education system, our crumbling infrastructure, and our short-termist financial system. We would still need to return to America's Hamilton-to-Reagan tradition of industrial policy to some extent.[779]

THE REST OF THE WORLD

What about other nations? What should they do? The solution for most of them will not be the natural strategic tariff described above. If a Third

World nation like Costa Rica, for example, imposed it, it would not push the Costa Rican economy towards good industries. The reason is that Costa Rica, unlike the U.S., is not closer to being cost competitive in good industries than in bad ones, as it is not richer than other nations in skilled labor, capital, or technological know-how. And because Costa Rica's domestic market (smaller than Jacksonville, Florida)[780] is too small to support, say, a complete aircraft industry, its domestic market is not a viable launch pad for significant scale-economy industries.

The right policy for a nation in Costa Rica's position will be one centered on:

1. Avoiding trade deficits, asset sell-offs, and foreign debt, as discussed in Chapter Two.[781]

2. Avoiding free trade's tendency to wipe out the most advanced sectors of developing nations, as discussed in Chapter Seven.[782]

3. Avoiding the authoritarianism associated with the WTO and related institutions discussed in Chapter Eight.[783]

4. Implementing the good newly-industrializing-country industrial policies discussed in Chapter Nine.[784]

The biggest choice developing nations must make is whether they are aiming to build up globally competitive industries and ultimately make the jump to the First World, or merely aiming to achieve comfortable (and by no means impoverished) mediocrity. Economist Erik Reinert refers to the latter as the lost art of creating middle-income countries;[785] it is a concept basically nonexistent in mainstream economics. Such nations are inefficient by the standards of the global free market, but they are better off succeeding at the lower standard that they aim for as protected economies than tacitly aiming at world standards through free trade and failing. As analyzed in Chapter Seven, these nations aim to build up industrial sectors that, while inefficient, are still higher value-added sectors than the peasant agriculture to which their populations would otherwise be confined.[786]

This all raises an important question: is there a fundamental us vs. them dynamic in America's trade with the developing world? Is a sound trade policy for ourselves ultimately about nothing better than grabbing an economic advantage at the expense of other nations, especially poorer ones? No. The serious economic rivals of the U.S. and other developed nations are "big boys" whom nobody needs to cry over. We need not have ethical qualms about taking industries away from Japan. This is true even of the advanced sectors of nations that are still poor overall, such as India and China, as it is not the Third World peasant sectors of these nations that meaningfully compete with us; it is the developed sectors of these nations, which are like islands of First World industry in the Third World. The yuppies of Bangalore are legitimate objects of our rivalry.

The real conflict in international trade isn't so much rich nations vs. poor as mercantilist nations vs. non-mercantilist ones. Exposing the underlying economics that makes mercantilism work will tend to level the playing field between the former and the latter. What Third World nations really need is things like, in the words of the International Forum on Globalization:

> The right to control financial flows across their borders, set the terms of foreign investment, give preference to domestic finance and ownership, place limits on resource extraction, and favor local value-added processing of export commodities.[787]

None of this is a particularly meaningful threat to American prosperity, so there is no reason for us to object. These policies would bring significant benefits to poorer nations, but impose trivial or zero costs on us. Corporate interests in the U.S. will certainly complain—and doubtless dress up their complaints as the interests of the U.S. economy as a whole—but there is no reason to expect these policies to impose meaningful harm on America at large. In fact, any U.S. strategy based on exploiting poor nations will be a waste of time for us. Like colonialism as analyzed in Chapters Nine and Ten,[788] it is a low-quality economic strategy that will be outperformed by better strategies. We should be battling it out with Japan, Europe and the emerging technological powers in high technology, not fighting to keep cocoa processing from migrating to Ghana.

A POLITICS-PROOF SOLUTION

The natural strategic tariff is imperfect, but infinitely better than free trade and relatively politics-proof. Above all, it is a policy people are unlikely to support for the wrong reasons (like producer special interests) because it does not single out any specific industries for protection. It thus maximizes the incentive for voters and Congress to evaluate protectionism in terms of whether it would benefit the country as a whole—which is precisely the question they *should* be asking. It would also create the right balance of special-interest pressures: some interests would favor a higher tariff, others a lower one. This is a prerequisite for fruitful debate, as it means both views will find institutional homes and political patrons.

The exact level at which to set the tariff remains an open question. Thirty percent was given as an example because it is in the historic range of U.S. tariffs[789] and is close to the net pressure on America's trade balance due to our lack of a VAT.[790] The right level will not be something trivial, like two percent, or prohibitive, like 150 percent. But there is absolutely no reason it shouldn't be 25 or 35 percent, and this flexibility will provide wiggle room for the compromises needed to get the tariff through Congress.

A natural strategic tariff has other benefits. For one thing, it avoids the danger of getting stuck with a tariff policy that made sense when it was adopted but gradually became an outdated captive of special interests over time, always a risk with tariffs. Although it is a fixed policy, it would not be fixed in its effects, but would automatically adapt to the evolution of industries over time. In 1900, for example, it would have protected the American garment industry from foreign (then mostly European) competition. It wouldn't do that today. As which industries are good industries changes over time, which industries it protects will change accordingly.

The tariff's uniformity across industries also avoids the problems that occur when upstream but not downstream industries get tariff protection. For example, if steel-consuming industries do not get a tariff when steel gets one, they will become disadvantaged relative to their foreign competitors by the higher cost of American-made steel. And why should steelworkers be protected from foreign competition at the price of forcing everyone else to pay more for goods containing steel? The only reasonable solution is that steelworkers should pay a tariff-protected price for the goods *they* buy, too. This logic ultimately means that all goods should be subject to the same tariff.

The political bickering that a tariff varying by industry would cause also militates in favor of a flat tariff: as we saw in Chapter Six, the inability of different industries to coalesce around a common tariff proposal sabotaged efforts to achieve a tariff in 1972-74.[791] But this is a policy around which the greatest possible number of industries can unite.

The natural strategic tariff is also more ideologically palatable than most other tariff solutions. Above all, it respects the free market by leaving all specific decisions about which industries a tariff will favor up to the marketplace. It will thus be considerably easier for ideological devotees of free markets to swallow than some scheme in which tariffs are set by a federal agency, leading to that nightmare of free-marketeers: *government picking winners*. In the real world, zero government intervention in the economy is impossible, so the issue for believers in economic freedom and small government is to design policies that work through the *smallest possible, carefully chosen* interventions. This is precisely what the natural strategic tariff offers because it operates at the periphery of our economy, leaving most of its internal mechanisms untouched. In fact, the more wisely we control our economic border, the less we will probably need to control the inside of our economy.[792]

REASONABLE OBJECTIONS TO A TARIFF PART I: DOMESTIC

One obvious objection is simply that a tariff is a tax increase. So it is. But it does not have to be a *net* tax increase if the revenue it generates is used to fund cuts in other taxes. In order to obtain a "clean" policy debate, in which the tariff is debated purely on its merits as a trade policy, unmuddied by differing opinions about the total level of taxation, any tariff proposal should be packaged with precisely compensating cuts in other taxes.

A related concern is that a tariff is a tax on consumption. This is generally better than a tax on income because it rewards saving and avoids penalizing work. Unfortunately, consumption taxes also reduce the progressivity of the tax system because the poor consume, rather than save, a higher percentage of their incomes. So any tax rebate financed by the tariff should also be designed to leave the overall progressivity of the tax system unchanged.[793]

Another objection to a tariff is that if American industry is granted tariff protection, it will just slumber behind it. Many industries indeed long to shut out foreign competition, reach a lazy detente with domestic rivals, then coast along with high profitability and low innovation. But the natural strategic tariff resists this danger because it does not hand out a blank check of protection: it gives a certain percentage and no more. Any industry that cannot get its costs within striking distance of its foreign competitors will not be saved by it. This discipline, although unpleasant for the losers, is the price we must pay for having a tariff that actually *works*, rather than one which eliminates the discipline of foreign competition entirely and protects all industries, whether or not their protection is useful to the economy as a whole.

It is sometimes objected that protectionism stifles competition. This, too, is a real threat. As a result, antitrust policy will become even more important than it already is. Luckily, there is a compensating benefit: rivalry between domestic firms actually appears to be a *more* potent competitive force than rivalry with foreign ones. As Michael Porter of Harvard Business School observes:

> Domestic rivals fight not only for market share but for people, technical breakthroughs, and, more generally, 'bragging rights.' Foreign rivals, in contrast, tend to be viewed more analytically. Their role in signaling or prodding domestic firms is less effective, because their success is more distant and is often attributed to 'unfair' advantages. With domestic rivals, there are no excuses.

> Domestic rivalry not only creates pressures to innovate but to innovate in ways that *upgrade* the competitive advantages of a nation's firms. The presence of domestic rivals nullifies the types of advantage that come simply from being in the nation, such as factor costs, access to or preference in the home market, a local supplier base, and costs of importing that must be borne by foreign firms...This forces a nation's firms to seek *higher-order* and ultimately more sustainable sources of competitive advantage.[794] (Emphasis in the original.)

So replacing foreign rivalry with strong domestic rivalry is probably a net plus. Japan's ferociously competitive (and protected) automobile and consumer electronics industries illustrate this well.[795]

If a tariff gives companies back market share and lets them raise prices, they may just harvest profits, rather than reinvesting them in long-term growth. As noted previously, this was a problem with one of America's largest recent protectionist undertakings: the Voluntary Restraint Agreement with Japan on automobiles.[796] As also noted, one major difference between effective and ineffective industrial policy is that effective industrial policy involves not only the "carrot" of tariffs and subsidies, but also the "stick" of measures to prevent companies from merely taking out added revenues as profit, rather than investing them in long-term upgrading of their capabilities.[797] Does this mean that a tariff should be accompanied by agreements on investment levels? No; the needed investment may be in another industry anyway. The solution probably lies in creating *generalized* incentives for investment. Since increased investment is a good thing even if we leave trade out of the picture, and already the object of tax incentives supported across the ideological spectrum, this should not be too hard to swallow politically.

REASONABLE OBJECTIONS TO A TARIFF PART II: FOREIGN

Another common objection to a tariff is that our trading partners would just shrug it off by increasing subsidies to their exporters.[798] This would force us into an endless game of matching these moves on a country-by-country, industry-by-industry, and even product-by-product basis. However, such subsidies by our trading partners would be restrained by the fact that they would be very expensive *in the face of an American tariff*. Right now, these subsidies are relatively affordable only because they don't have to climb an American tariff wall. But if they did, their cost would increase dramatically. Currency manipulation is probably the only subsidy that is affordable over prolonged periods of time (and even then problematic in the end), as it involves buying foreign assets and debt, thus accumulating wealth rather than just expenditures. But other subsidies amount to a give-away from the exporting to the importing nation. While this doesn't pre-vent them absolutely, it does tend to set a limit. This is all we need, es-pecially as we have no hope of eliminating or countervailing *all* foreign subsidies no matter what we do, tariff or no tariff.

The same goes for the objection that our trading partners would just devalue their currencies. As previously noted, we can end foreign currency manipulation at any time simply by restricting or taxing foreigners' ability to lend us debt and buy our assets.[799] We would need to raise our own sav-ings rate if we did this (or face rising interest rates), but we need to do this anyway.

Another objection is that any tariff large enough to mean anything would impose a sudden shock on the U.S. and world economies, which would tip them into recession as other shocks, notably the 1973-4 oil shock, have done. This is a legitimate concern, as economies do not adapt well when the rules governing them change faster than the economy itself can keep up with. If a 25 percent tariff suddenly makes it economically rational to manufacture disk drives in Colorado rather than Kyushu, this doesn't make plants sprout in Colorado overnight. So until the U.S. and Japanese economies adapt to the newly implied distribution of industries between them, they will be out of balance and thus underperform. Phasing in a tariff over five years or so would mitigate this.

Another objection is that a tariff would trigger a downward spiral of retaliation and counter-retaliation with our trading partners, resulting in an uncontrolled collapse of global trade. But this oft-bandied doomsday scenario is unlikely. Above all, our trading partners know that *they* are the ones with the huge trade surpluses to lose, not us. Foreign nations would probably raise their tariffs somewhat, but there is no reason to expect the process to get out of control. After all, the world has survived their trade barriers long enough.

Indeed, there is an opposite possibility. Suppose we tell foreign nations that our tariff increase is in retaliation for their own various trade barriers. (This is, of course, largely true.) And suppose we then threaten to raise our tariff even higher if they don't open up, but offer to drop it back down somewhat if they do. Then our trading partners may even *reduce* their barriers in response to our imposing a tariff. So our imposing a tariff could, paradoxically, further the cause of global trade openness, not retard it.

We can call this alternative "managed open trade." It is not the same thing as free trade. Fully elaborated, it would be based on the internationally shared twin goals of zero tariffs and zero deficits. These goals would be shared, despite the reality of international rivalry and the absence of a sovereign to enforce them, because every nation would know that a) other nations would retaliate in response to excessive surpluses inflicted upon them, and b) the alternative is the system breaking down for everyone, including themselves.[800] This substitute for free trade would spare a lot of ideological sacred cows, as it would come fairly close to free trade if it worked. (Many people who think they are defending free trade are actually defending covertly managed trade with zero tariffs, anyway.) But it would depend upon our ability to credibly threaten a tariff if our bluff were called. It would therefore depend upon our having viable contingency plans to function with a tariff. Therefore even free traders thinking through how to save as much of free trade as they can should take the option of a natural strategic tariff seriously.

ALTERNATIVES TO A NATURAL STRATEGIC TARIFF

There are a number of alternative proposals on the table for solving America's trade problems. Perhaps the most famous is billionaire investor Warren Buffet's proposal for import certificates. He proposes that exporters be given a $1 certificate for every dollar of their exports, and that importers would then have to buy a certificate from them for every dollar of goods they imported. This would, of course, force America's trade into balance automatically.

It is not a bad idea, but contains less than meets the eye. If the certificates traded on the open market (as proposed) then an equilibrium price would be set, which price would then be the de facto tariff on imports. Since the revenue from selling the certificates would go to exporters, the scheme would thus amount to an import tariff plus an export subsidy. Because the tariff would be flat, it would have the same natural strategic effects as a natural strategic tariff.

The main differences between Buffet's idea and the natural strategic tariff are that Buffet's proposal would operate on both imports and exports, and it would not raise money for the government. Because it would not raise money, it could not finance progressivity-preserving cuts in other taxes, and would therefore make the tax code more regressive. (It would also be a giant transfer of wealth to our export industries.) The main advantage of Buffett's scheme is automatic tariff setting at a level that would zero out the deficit. But a flat tariff (or a U.S. VAT) could be calibrated over time to do this, too.

Another possibility is simply to institute a VAT in the U.S.[801] Although this is a well tried system of taxation, used in every other developed country, it is generally regarded in this country as a strange European affectation, which probably dooms its rational consideration.[802] Although mentioned recently as a possibility by Senate Budget Committee chairman Kent Conrad (D-ND) and others, it has attracted vehement opposition.[803] As with a natural strategic tariff, it would not have to be a *net* tax increase, and would not have to change the overall progressivity of the tax code. The great advantage of a VAT is that, while a natural strategic tariff and import certificates would abrogate America's NAFTA, WTO, and other treaty obligations, a VAT would not. This is an attractive option for legalistic minds in the State Department, for those who fear the consequences of unraveling the international legal infrastructure, and for those who wish to withdraw from free trade while obfuscating this fact for ideological reasons. (Perversely, the obvious alternative of a so-called Border Adjustable Tax or BAT, which resembles a VAT but without its domestic aspects, would be illegal.) Another big advantage of a VAT is that, like a tariff, it is a consumption tax. Its biggest disadvantage is simply that it would mean having a domestic VAT, a giant change in domestic tax policy simply to address a foreign trade issue.

Another alternative to the natural strategic tariff is a tariff on manufactured goods that exempts raw materials and agricultural products. This is roughly what traditional mercantilism has done for 400 years, is what Alexander Hamilton proposed in 1791, and is commensurate with U.S. policy in our tariff era after 1872.[804] It is based on the idea that we are not trying to capture raw material or agricultural industries. The main problems are that if unprocessed goods are admitted duty-free and processed goods are subject to a tariff, then a) we lose the apolitical simplicity of a flat tariff, b) we have to deal with borderline cases and successive stages of processing, and c) we avoid dealing with America's dependence on foreign raw materials. Furthermore, our only really big raw material import is oil, and there are energy conservation and national security reasons to tax imported oil anyway. And members of Congress from agricultural and raw materials-producing states will object if the industries of other states are protected and theirs are left to fend for themselves.

One final point: a natural strategic tariff would need to include a rebate on reexported goods in order to avoid handicapping American exporters. This would include both goods that are transshipped without modification and goods that are exported after value-added processing. The latter includes everything from chocolate made from imported cocoa to computers made from imported chips. This is not an add-on to the policy, but implied by its intrinsic logic as a tax on domestic consumption. As noted earlier,[805] other nations follow the same logic in rebating VAT to their exporters.

12

The End of the
Free Trade Coalition

DOES AMERICA HAVE A SERIOUS chance of getting the trade policy it needs? The best way to hazard a guess at the issue's political future is to look at its underlying social dynamic.[806] The key is to grasp the way free trade is experienced by ordinary voters:

Free trade is cheap labor embodied in goods.

Although, as we have seen, our trade problems cannot all *literally* be reduced to cheap foreign labor, this is still the aspect that dominates public consciousness and thus mass political opinion.

The first rift this implies is between people who obtain most of their income from work and those who obtain most of their income from returns on capital. People in the latter category obviously want all labor to be as cheap as possible. People in the former category want the labor they consume (directly or embodied in goods) to be as cheap as possible, but the labor that they produce and sell, namely their own wages, to be expensive.

This implies the possibility of an electoral coalition in which one part of society treats itself to cheap foreign labor at the expense of another.

As long as the self-perceived enjoyers of cheap labor exceed the self-perceived victims in number, this coalition is politically viable. For example, there can be a coalition of everyone who is *not* a manufacturing worker (91 percent of the labor force today, up from 66 percent in 1950)[807] against everyone who is. While manufacturing workers suffer competition from cheap foreign labor, everyone else enjoys cheap foreign manufactured goods, so a majority is happy. The indirect effects of a decline in manufacturing are either not noticed—partly because they are not understood—or they are postponed for years by America's ability to accumulate debt and sell assets.

This doesn't mean, however, that these indirect effects aren't real. As we have seen, they are inexorable.[808] But what if we go from 10 percent of the population harmed and 90 percent benefited to 20/80? Or 30/70? Or 50/50? Or 70/30 the other way? Our coalition will start to fall apart. Where are we now on this scale? It is impossible to quantify precisely, but commentator Kevin Phillips estimated in 1995 that free trade was "obviously beneficial to perhaps 10 to 15 percent of the population, detrimental to some 30 to 50 percent," and things have clearly shifted considerably since then.[809]

Free traders will respond by claiming that even if we reach 90 or even 100 percent of the population being harmed by competition with cheap foreign labor, Americans will still be better off because goods will be cheaper. The problem, as is obvious to any laid-off worker who has ever contemplated the cheap goods on sale at Walmart, is that a drop in the cost of merchandise never means as much as a lost job. How many people have voted against incumbents because they were unemployed or underemployed? Compare this to how many have done so because they couldn't buy a pair of scissors for $.99. Has there ever been a demonstration in the streets about the latter? And (as noted several times in this book) there is no law of economics that guarantees that free trade's benefits in the form of lower prices will exceed its cost in job loss and lower wages for most people.[810]

There is not much left of the American economy that is invulnerable to pressures from trade. Even large parts of the 70 percent of our economy that is in nontraded sectors are inexorably becoming tradable due to offshoring, and workers displaced from tradable sectors are driving down wages in nontradable sectors. The remaining sheltered occupations are these:

1. Jobs that must be performed in person, such as policing, cooking, bagging groceries, teaching school, being a criminal, etc.

2. Jobs, like construction, performed on physical objects too large or heavy to be shipped from abroad.

3. Jobs performed on or relative to objects fixed in place: agriculture, mining, and transportation.

4. Jobs where America enjoys significant technological superiority tied to oligopoly industries or specialized local labor pools, a shrinking category.

5. Jobs, like law or advertising, which depend on uniquely American knowledge. But even this is breaking down as law firms, for example, start to offshore work.

6. Jobs dependent upon sovereign power, such as the military. But given our use of "civilian security contractors" in our wars, this can be nibbled away at in surprising ways. And, as noted in Chapter Eight,[811] the WTO would like to privatize even more public services, opening them up to offshoring.

The trouble is, these categories are not enough. In particular, they don't add up to enough *high-wage* jobs because most (not all) of these jobs are relatively low paid. So our beggar-my-neighbor coalition starts to fall apart. What happens next?

LEFT AND RIGHT, WRONG ON TRADE

The bad news for Republicans is that what we can call the *psychological bourgeoisie* starts to shrink. This term refers to everyone who identifies emotionally and politically with the ownership of capital, whether or not a majority of their income is investment income. Wall Street financial analysts whose jobs may get offshored are the clearest example, but there are people in this category all over the U.S. The key psychological bargain such people have had with the system until now is that economic forces are things that happen to *other* people. (One can take an amazingly dispassionate view of economic efficiency when this is the case.)

The bad news for Democrats is that, at the level of the presidency and party leadership, they sold out so completely to free trade under Bill Clinton (and never came back) that they threw away their natural position, earned over 70 years, as the party that protects Americans from the rougher edges of capitalism. They should be capitalizing on the economic mess following eight years of Republican rule right now but on trade, as on most other economic issues, Barack Obama hasn't even tried.

Both right and left are playing a double game on trade in America today.

Right-of-center Americans generally want to hear that America's trade problems are caused by unfair distortions of free markets by our trading partners. To some extent, of course, they are, but, as we have also seen, even 100 percent genuine free trade would not solve America's problems. And our trading partners are mostly just ruthless players of the game, as we used to be. The multinational corporate right (other factions exist, but have no power over Republican economic policy) claims, on ultimately Ricardian grounds, that free trade is in the national interest. But when pressed by contrary evidence, its corporate chieftains fall back on the position that their companies owe no loyalty to the U.S., so internationalized are their operations and diverse the nationalities of their shareholders and employees.

Left-of-center Americans generally want to hear that America's trade problems are caused by greedy corporations and exploitative capitalism. But the problem is not that corporations are greedy per se, it is that corporate pursuit of profit has been decoupled, by means of free trade, from the success of the American economy as a whole. And although economics certainly shows that exploitation in trade is possible, it doesn't show that exploitation must occur for free trade to do harm. The American left is also as conflicted as the right: at some point, it must choose between opposing free trade in the interests of ordinary Americans, and opposing it in the interests of the world as a whole. Intellectually and emotionally, the latter is its obvious choice, but this is unlikely to play in Peoria.

The ideal political position from which to oppose free trade would be a kind of nationalist liberalism, but this Trumanesque or Jacksonian position does not exist in American politics today.[812]

It is often disputed whether protectionism is a left- or a right-wing policy. It puzzles people in this regard because it has deep ideological and historical roots on both sides. The truth is that while protectionism obviously contradicts the *free-market* right, the dominant strand in the U.S. since the collapse of the old protectionist Taft wing of the Republican party in 1952, it is perfectly in tune with old-school "paleo" conservatism, the nationalist right, and bourgeois paternalism. And while protectionism contradicts the modern, Clintonite, Blairite (as in Tony) globalist left, it is perfectly in tune with any left that genuinely cares about American workers, the global environment, democratic control over the economy, or the depredations of free trade upon poor nations abroad. If one accepts the basic contention of this book that correctly implemented protectionism is beneficial, then it is probably most accurate to think of protectionism as leftist if its benefits are captured primarily by labor, rightist if they are captured primarily by capital, and centrist if they are evenly divided.

The fact that wildly different partisan figures ranging from Patrick Buchanan on the right to Ralph Nader on the left oppose free trade is a strength for protectionism, not a sign of ideological incoherence, as it means that protectionism can be credibly sold to voters from one end of the political spectrum to the other. Protectionism can plausibly be packaged as anything from a right-wing tub-thumping America First appeal to a left-wing tie-dyed hippie sob story. Even better, it can be packaged as a moderate and reasonable "commitment to a middle class society" that will appeal to voters in the center. Believe it or not, the following quote is from the *Republican* platform of 1972:

> We deplore the practice of locating plants in foreign countries solely to take advantage of low wage rates in order to produce goods primarily for sale in the United States. We will take action to discourage such unfair and disruptive practices that result in the loss of American jobs.[813]

How far we have fallen! If Barack Obama had said this in 2008, he'd have been accused of being an economic ignoramus, if not a closet socialist. (If John McCain had said it, he'd have been considered a candidate for the psychiatric ward.) However, what is reasonable can be redefined overnight—mainly by the media—when the underlying constellations of perceived self-interest shift among the elite. A single cover story in *Time* magazine or *The New York Times Magazine* could make protectionism a respectable conversation topic again. A single speech by a cabinet-level official, if openly supported by the President, could do it.

HOW FREE TRADE WILL FALL APART

Support for free trade will probably fall apart over the next few years. As of early 2011, there are four missing prerequisites for free trade to explode as an issue:

1. Everyone is still preoccupied with the financial crisis, its aftermath, and recovery from recession, especially job recovery.

2. There remains a residual sense in the minds of the public and the lawmakers that somehow free trade, despite all its problems, is still sound economics, and that perhaps we should just keep on eating our spinach because it will be good for us in the end.

3. There is no obvious alternative policy on the table. There is instead a grab bag of issues, ranging from Chinese currency manipulation to the proposed Korea, Colombia, and Panama free trade agreements. This paucity of credible alternatives feeds the attitude that nothing fundamental can be done.

4. A specific crisis has not happened to *force* the system out of its old way of doing things as the debacle in subprime mortgages upended our financial system in 2008 and made continuation of prior policy impossible whether anyone wanted it or not.

For the first prerequisite above to be supplied, all it will take is time, as recessions, even double-dip recessions (?), always eventually end, and the financial crisis of 2008 was successfully patched (albeit at astronomical cost and without fixing its underlying causes, risking a repeat).

For the second prerequisite to be supplied, all it will take is sufficient public debate, between persons perceived as credible, for free trade to become established in the public mind as an issue with *two* legitimate sides to it. As the reader has hopefully gathered by now, once one seriously scrutinizes the underlying economics of free trade, even if one is not disabused of the policy outright it becomes hard to deny that it is a legitimately controversial issue. The pure "100 percent free trade with 100 percent of the world 100 percent of the time" position is simply not intellectually serious.[814] So when public debate finally cracks open, free trade will lose its innocence very fast.

Once protectionism is perceived as a *legitimate* choice, it will become the *actual* choice of large numbers of people whose protectionist instincts have been held back by the belief that it is somehow an ignorant position to take. They will not need to master the details of *why* it is legitimate; they will only need to know that it *is* legitimate. Sen. Sherrod Brown (D-OH), one of the leading opponents of free trade in the Senate, records that ever since he came to Congress in 1993, every free trade vote has been accompanied by predictions by the White House of economic disaster if it was not passed.[815] Trade wars, stock market decline, and recession were predicted every time. The power of this rhetoric to intimidate is going to end. Protectionism will cease to be a canard and become just another policy option.

The third prerequisite above (no obvious alternative) can emerge overnight if some major political figure launches a tariff proposal that captures the public's imagination. Or the myriad individual issues that currently comprise the opposition to free trade could force the soldering together of an omnibus proposal on the floor of Congress.

The fourth prerequisite (a sudden crisis) is difficult to predict as to time, but we can rely securely upon the fact that unsustainable trends are always, in the end, not sustained. At some point, America's giant overdraft against the rest of the world must come to an end. Although our government is trying to postpone the day of reckoning as long as possible, this day will come. Secretary of State Hillary Clinton flying to China to beg its government to keep buying our bonds (as she did in February 2009) won't make much difference in the end.

Once protectionism is conceded to be a valid political position, it will eventually win the public debate, if free trade's unpopularity continues to mount at the pace it has been mounting over the last 10 years. (This pace is, if anything, likely to accelerate.) When this happens, the status quo will be sustained only by the tacit bargain of the American political duopoly, in which the two parties agree not to make trade a serious issue, whatever tactical feints they may deploy. This bargain will hold as long as the benefits of keeping it, which mainly consist in keeping the corporate backers of both parties happy, exceed the benefits of defecting from it, which consist in winning votes. Once one party defects, protectionism will, if rationally designed and competently implemented, almost certainly be sufficiently successful in practice (and therefore popular) that the other party will have no choice but to follow. The alternative, if one party insists on handicapping itself by clinging to an unpopular position on such a major issue, is an era of one-party political dominance like 1860-1932 or 1932-80.

FREE TRADE'S POPULARITY IS WANING

Free trade's popularity has been declining for years. Polls show that even affluent voters have been inexorably losing their dotcom-era enthusiasm for it for some time. A 2004 poll by the University of Maryland revealed nearly three-fourths of Americans earning over $100,000 per year opposing additional free trade agreements.[816] (As late as 1999, a similar percentage had been in support.)[817] These people are disproportionately influential and they, if anyone, should be beneficiaries and thus supporters of free trade. In a September 2007 NBC-*Wall Street Journal* poll of likely Republican primary voters, respondents favored the proposition "foreign trade has been bad for the U.S. economy because imports from abroad have reduced demand for American-made goods, cost jobs here at home, and produced potentially unsafe products" over a free-trade alternative by 59 to 32 percent.[818] So free trade's natural constituency has been falling into doubts. And if it can't hold these people, it won't be able to hold anyone.

Nevertheless, the public remains quite conflicted on trade.[819] Another 2007 survey revealed a plurality of Democrats, Republicans, and independents saying free trade is good for the country even though they *also* said that it costs jobs and lowers American wages.[820] But this incoherent position is obviously not particularly stable, is going to have to break one way or the other eventually, and is highly unlikely to break in favor of free trade. For now, the public mainly just has a profound sense that *something* is deeply wrong with U.S. trade policy, to the extent that one 2006 poll found that protecting American jobs against foreign competition was the single foreign policy issue on which the public was most dissatisfied with government performance.[821] But the public doesn't really know what to think or do about it. According to the same poll:

The public also seems frustrated about where to place responsibility. Close to eight in 10 (78 percent) say the government could do something about protecting American jobs. But a majority (52 percent) do not think it's realistic for the government to control corporate outsourcing. However, those surveyed don't hold American companies responsible either. Close to three-quarters (74 percent) think it's unrealistic to expect that companies will keep jobs in the United States when labor is cheaper elsewhere.[822]

So voters register their protests when given the chance, but otherwise remain stymied in their attempts to crystallize an opinion of what solution they want. A lot of voters, egged on by the rhetoric of certain well-intentioned politicians, favor solutions like "trade that is free *and* fair"—a bromide that neatly reconciles both sides of the debate, is completely contradictory, and impossible as policy.

The most puzzling thing about recent public opinion polls is that while the economy consistently ranks high on voters' priority lists, trade per se does not, suggesting that voters have yet to connect all the dots about why trade is the root cause of so many of America's economic ills. But if trade *is* the cause, then presumably this will eventually tell upon public opinion and trade will move up voters' priority lists.

Let us now take a look at the last few election cycles for signs of how the above dynamics are slowly starting to play out in the voting booth. Because although the trade issue has yet to solidify enough to start proactively driving politics on its own, electoral evidence shows an issue bubbling right under the surface of American politics, waiting to explode.

2004: BUSH VS. KERRY

Offshoring first flared as a political controversy in 2004. The thing about it that differed from previous trade-induced job losses was, of course, that it threatened the white-collar middle class. But in the end, the controversy didn't really go anywhere, in the sense of producing serious political realignments or policy changes. Offshoring was adjudged by the two parties to be a political flashpoint but fundamentally just another political issue, which changed nothing important and should be handled the way most political issues usually are: by jockeying for advantage within the established policy consensus.

So politicians set out to win votes on the issue *without* taking the risks inherent in doing anything substantial. The Democrats, quintessentially Sen. John Kerry in his 2004 presidential campaign, sought to make the smallest policy proposals sufficient to position themselves as "the good guys" on the issue for voters who cared about it, while signaling to everyone else that they weren't about to go too far. The Republicans, meanwhile, defended a status quo that they were no more or less responsible for than the Democrats using the same old (basically Ricardian) arguments that have always been used on free trade. Both responses were standard procedure for day-to-day Washington politics—which is precisely why they occurred.

Kerry, handicapped by his vote for NAFTA in 1993, did tack left a bit in the 2004 primaries. Facing vocal NAFTA opponents in the sincere Rep. Dick Gephardt (D-MO) and the opportunistic Sen. John Edwards (D-NC), he began railing against what he called "Benedict Arnold" corporations which were moving jobs overseas. This rhetoric effectively blunted Edwards' and Gephardt's attacks on his NAFTA vote, enabling his wins in Ohio, Wisconsin, Michigan, and other industrial states especially hurt by free trade. Then, in May, with his nomination secure, Kerry tacked right again. In an interview with *The Wall Street Journal,* he claimed his Benedict Arnold reference had been misconstrued:

'Benedict Arnold' does not refer to somebody who in the normal course of business is going to go overseas and take jobs overseas. That happens. I support that. I understand that. I was referring to the people who take advantage of non-economic transactions purely for tax purposes—sham transactions—and give up American citizenship.[823]

Offshore tax domiciling is, of course, an entirely different issue than offshoring. Kerry had folded his cards.

From that point on, the issue virtually disappeared from the campaign. Kerry's refusal to engage George W. Bush on trade reached its nadir during the third presidential debate, when moderator Bob Schieffer of CBS asked Bush what he would say to "someone in this country who has lost his job to someone overseas who's being paid a fraction of what that job paid here in the United States."[824] Bush offered the stock Republican responses: he talked about creating the new jobs of the 21st century, improving primary and secondary education, expanding Trade Adjustment Assistance, increasing Pell Grants to college students, and helping displaced workers attend community college. (We examined in Chapter Three why these solutions are insufficient.)

Bush's position gave Kerry a clear opportunity to define himself politically with his response at a critical juncture in the campaign. But instead of taking on Bush over trade, Kerry accepted Bush's basic premise that free trade is best and that his proposed solutions could work, and attacked him for cutting job training funds, Pell Grants and Perkins loans.[825] *Bunt.* Amazingly, Schieffer gave Kerry another chance to exploit the issue minutes later. Kerry squandered it again, with a self-consciously defeatist answer dressed up as political courage:

> Outsourcing is going to happen. I've acknowledged that in union halls across the country. I've had shop stewards stand up and say, 'Will you promise me you're going to stop all this outsourcing?' And I've looked them in the eye and I've said, 'No, I can't do that.'[826]

In other words, trade *isn't really a political issue at all*, because there's nothing the government can do about it. Not only is there no meaningful difference between Republicans and Democrats on the issue, there cannot be one. Kerry went on to talk about tangential issues—corporate tax loopholes, violations of international trade rules, subsidies by Airbus, Chinese currency manipulation, and fiscal discipline.[827] Bush had won by forfeit.

In retrospect, it is entirely plausible that Kerry's decision to bunt on trade cost him Ohio and thus the entire 2004 election.[828] This problem extended far beyond the narrow confines of trade as such. By refusing to separate himself from Bush on economics on the single best issue for doing so—where Bush was furthest away from the opinions of swing voters—Kerry allowed social issues summed up as "God, guns and gays" to determine the election for the lower-middle and working-class voters who were his natural constituency. This problem continues to fester: a 2008 study of the electorate in Ohio by the Center for Working-Class Studies at Youngstown State University suggests that thanks to Bill Clinton's support for NAFTA in 1993, working-class voters "still do not trust Democrats and they haven't come back to the Democrats."[829] As a result, these voters have tended to view Republicans and Democrats as equally unlikely to protect their economic interests and have therefore voted on noneconomic issues. (At the national level, this trend has been analyzed by Thomas Frank, who took Kansas as his case study in his book *What's The Matter With Kansas?*)[830]

2002-2006: FREE TRADE OPPONENTS START WINNING

No Republican has ever won the presidency without carrying national bell-wether Ohio. The trade issue's ability to tip Congressional races was first noticed in a 2002 race for the 17th District (around Youngstown) of that state. In the Democratic primary, Tom Sawyer, an eight-term incumbent who had voted for NAFTA in 1993, faced Tim Ryan, a 28-year-old former high school quarterback and first-term state senator. Writing in the liberal magazine *The Nation,* John Nichols described the dynamics of this race:

> Sawyer and his Democratic challengers agreed on most issues. But trade was the dividing line. And trade mattered—especially in Youngstown and other hard-hit steel-mill communities up and down the Mahoning Valley. Though Sawyer had voted with labor on some trade issues—including the December Fast Track test—he is known in Ohio as the Democrat who backed NAFTA, and for un-employed steelworkers and their families NAFTA invokes the bit-terest of memories.[831]

Sawyer lost by *13 points*. In the wry post-mortem words of Howard Wolf-son, executive director of the Democratic Congressional Campaign Com-mittee (DCCC) in Washington, "[In] some districts in this country, a free trade position is not helpful."[832]

The 2006 midterm elections proved Wolfson prescient. In these con-tests, a number of Republicans were taught the same lesson Rep. Sawyer had learned: opposition to free trade could push challengers over the top in competitive races. According to a post-election analysis by the left-leaning Naderite group Global Trade Watch, no fewer than seven Senate and 30 House seats flipped from pro- to anti-free trade in this election.[833] Seventy-three percent of *winning* Democratic candidates emphasized trade as an issue in their campaigns, while 72 percent of losing Democratic candidates did not. [834] Not a single candidate of either party ran on free trade as a pos-itive agenda, and not a single opponent of free trade was ousted by a free trader in either the House or the Senate.[835]

Certain individual races epitomized the trade aspects of this election. In Pennsylvania's 8th District, north of Philadelphia, Democrat Patrick Mur-phy challenged Republican incumbent (and CAFTA supporter) Mike Fitzpatrick. Because Murphy was not expected to win, he did not receive significant support from the DCCC and was therefore unaffected by its decision not to use free trade as an issue. Murphy attacked Fitzpatrick for "crippling" the local economy by supplying the deciding vote for CAF-TA.[836] This assault, plus a trade oriented get-out-the-vote program, enabled him to upset Fitzpatrick by 1,521 votes. In central Florida's 16th district, Tim Mahoney also made CAFTA a centerpiece of *his* successful campaign to capture the seat vacated by scandal-disgraced Republican Mark Foley.[837] And in southeast Iowa's 2nd District, Democrat Dave Loebsack exploited trade themes to dislodge 30-year GOP incumbent—and staunch free trader—Jim Leach.[838]

The trade wave crashed over the Senate as well in 2006. Six anti-free-trade Democrats—Sherrod Brown of Ohio, Claire McCaskill of Missouri, Jon Tester of Montana, Bob Casey of Pennsylvania, Sheldon Whitehouse of Rhode Island, and Jim Webb of Virginia, plus Independent Bernie Sanders of Vermont—captured seats formerly held by free traders.

In addition to the above victories, it has been estimated that another 10 to 20 failed Democratic challengers *could* have won, had they attacked free trade.[839] Unfortunately, the DCCC was headed by Rahm Emanuel, the former suburban Chicago congressman who later became President Obama's chief of staff, then mayor of Chicago. Emanuel, who had played a leading role in securing Democratic votes to pass NAFTA while serving as a White House staffer under Bill Clinton in 1993, decided not to use the issue.[840] But for this decision, Democrat Lois Murphy, for example, might have beaten Republican Jim Gerlach, rated by nonpartisan observers as one of the most vulnerable GOP incumbents in the nation, in Pennsylvania's 6th district northwest of Philadelphia.[841] Instead, Gerlach squeaked back in with 1.2 percent of the vote after the DCCC effectively vetoed a trade-oriented get-out-the-vote program.[842]

2008: OBAMA, HILLARY AND MCCAIN

Like John Kerry four years earlier, Barack Obama was a vocal critic of free trade during the Democratic primaries. In debates with Hillary Clinton and responses to questionnaires from groups like the Pennsylvania Fair Trade Coalition, he denounced Chinese currency manipulation, promised to take a tough stance against dumping, opposed extension of Fast Track negotiating authority, and criticized NAFTA.[843] His denunciations of free trade sharpened as he approached the crucial March 4 Ohio primary. Trailing badly in the state after winning 11 primaries and caucuses in a row, he unleashed a direct mail piece which charged that "Hillary Clinton thought NAFTA was a 'boon' to the economy," asserted that she "was not with O-hio when our jobs were on the line," and claimed that "only Barack Obama consistently opposed NAFTA."[844] Clinton fired back with a mailer of her own documenting Obama's own past support for free trade and had phone bank calls made in which she claimed Obama had distorted her record.[845]

The rhetorical battle between the two candidates reached its climax in their debate at Cleveland State University on February 26, 2008. Responding to a question from moderator Tim Russert, both said they would pull out of NAFTA if Canada and Mexico refused to renegotiate:

> *Clinton*: I have said that I will renegotiate NAFTA, so obviously, you'd have to say to Canada and Mexico that that's exactly what we're going to do...Yes, I am serious...I will say we will opt out of NAFTA unless we renegotiate it, and we renegotiate on terms that are favorable to all of America.

> *Obama*: I will make sure that we renegotiate, in the same way that Senator Clinton talked about. And I actually think Senator Clinton's answer on this one is right. I think we should use the hammer of a potential opt-out as leverage to ensure that we actually get labor and environmental standards that are enforced.[846]

Broadly speaking, it was a draw between the two candidates on trade. Both were making loud gestures of opposition, though neither was especially convincing to anyone familiar with the candidates' records.

Voters' suspicions were quickly confirmed. Four years earlier, Sen. Kerry had at least waited until securing his party's nomination before backtracking on trade. Obama, on the other hand, began sending signals that his opposition to free trade was mere posturing even *before* he stopped bashing NAFTA on the campaign trail. He sent one of his top economic advisers, Prof. Austan Goolsbee of the University of Chicago, to meet with Canadian diplomats in Chicago on February 8, 2008 to allay that nation's concerns about his stand on free trade. Joseph De Mora, a Canadian official, later summarized the meeting in an official memorandum that was leaked to the Associated Press:

> He was frank in saying that the primary campaign has been necessarily domestically focused, particularly in the Midwest, and that

much of the rhetoric that may be perceived as protectionist is more reflective of political maneuvering than policy. He cautioned that this messaging should not be taken out of context and should be viewed as more about political positioning than a clear articulation of policy plans.[847]

After some denials by the Obama camp, news of this meeting leaked on February 27, six days before the Ohio primary.[848] This all but doomed Obama's chances in that contest, which he lost 45 to 53 percent. He nevertheless won seven of the eight primaries over the next six weeks, his single and telling defeat occurring in Pennsylvania. This was a state that had lost 208,000 manufacturing jobs, and suffered a two percent decline in real median wages, between 2001 and 2007.[849] Clinton scored a nine-point victory there, fueled in large part by white male blue-collar workers—whom she won by 30 points. [850]

After securing the nomination, Obama went into full retreat on trade. He retracted the pledge he had made in Cleveland to opt out of NAFTA unilaterally if Canada and Mexico refused to renegotiate and attributed his remarks to "overheated" campaign rhetoric, modestly explaining that, "Politicians are always guilty of that, and I don't exempt myself."[851] His capitulation on free trade, combined with John McCain's lifelong support for it, meant that the 2008 general election was the *fourth* consecutive presidential contest devoid of any real national debate on the issue, the last being Ross Perot's third-party candidacy in 1992.

John McCain, of course, took a classic triumphalist line on trade. Speaking to the National Association of Latino Appointed and Elected Officials on June 28, 2008, he said:

> The global economy is here to stay. We cannot build walls to foreign competition, and why should we want to? When have Americans ever been afraid of competition? America is the biggest exporter, importer, producer, saver, investor, manufacturer, and innovator in the world. Americans don't run from the challenge of a global economy. We are the world's leaders, and leaders don't fear change, hide from challenges, pine for the past and dread the future. That's why I reject the false virtues of economic isolationism. Any confident, competent government should embrace competition—it makes us stronger—not hide from our competitors and cheat our consumers and workers. We can compete and win, as we always

have, or we can be left behind. Lowering barriers to trade creates more and better jobs, and higher wages.[852]

For a glimpse of how old this rhetoric is (and what record of predicting economic success it has), take a look at the 1846 British speech on page 30.

Such thinking is, of course, no surprise from a Republican. But Barack Obama, who had more of a choice, took a very similar line in a speech to workers in depressed Flint, Michigan, subject of Michael Moore's withering 1989 comic documentary on deindustrialization, *Roger and Me*:

> There are some who believe that we must try to turn back the clock on this new world; that the only chance to maintain our living standards is to build a fortress around America; to stop trading with other countries, shut down immigration, and rely on old industries. I disagree. Not only is it impossible to turn back the tide of globalization, but efforts to do so can make us worse off. Rather than fear the future, we must embrace it. I have no doubt that America can compete and succeed in the 21st century. And I know as well that more than anything else, success will depend not on our government, but on the dynamism, determination, and innovation of the American people.[853]

We looked at why economic globalization is *not* an uncontrollable force in Chapter One.[854] We looked at why dynamism, determination, and innovation won't save America in Chapter Three.[855]

THE 2008 CONGRESSIONAL ELECTIONS

Despite the lack of motion on the trade front in the 2008 presidential race, progress continued in the House and Senate. After declining to run ads attacking free trade in 2006, the DCCC, startled by the issue's potency in 2006 even when neglected, relented and aired spots on the topic in 2008. In the words of the nonpartisan *Congress Daily,* which detected this shift in strategy one week before the election:

> References to "job-killing trade deals," outsourcing and anti-China sentiment abound, with more than 100 trade-related advertisements and counting…Aiding the effort are the Senate and House Demo-

cratic Campaign Committees, which have spent heavily on ads criticizing Republicans on trade.[856]

By the end of the election cycle, the DCCC, the Democratic Senatorial Campaign Committee, and individual candidates had run more than 160 different anti-free-trade ads across the country.[857]

When the dust had settled, 36 new free-trade opponents had been elected to the House: 13 in contests against incumbents, 20 in battles for open seats, and three in special elections. (Eight free-trade opponents lost, so the net gain was 28.)[858] And seven new free-trade opponents were elected to the Senate: Mark Begich of Alaska, Mark Udall of Colorado, Jeanne Shaheen of New Hampshire, Tom Udall of New Mexico, Kay Hagan of North Carolina, Jeff Merkley of Oregon, and Al Franken of Minnesota.[859] The hallmark trade race of this cycle was in northwest Pennsylvania's 3rd District, where Democrat Kathy Dahlkemper ousted GOP incumbent Phil English, who had provided one of the final two votes needed to pass CAFTA.[860] Winners also included 10 *Republican* opponents of free trade who either held or won seats while campaigning against free trade.[861]

THE OBAMA PRESIDENCY

In office, President Obama's free trade convictions have not changed. Ironically, this is probably the correct position for him to take for the time being, as he appears to know nothing about trade beyond the received Ricardian wisdom and therefore has no rational alternative. This was demonstrated by his appointment of free trader Ron Kirk, the former mayor of Dallas, to be United States Trade Representative. In his first policy address, at Georgetown University, Kirk assured the audience of Obama's allegiance to conventional analyses of the problems of free trade and his consequent determination to push forward with existing policy:

> While the pain of trade can be concentrated at times, its benefits are lasting and widespread. One in six American manufacturing jobs is already supported by trade. Agricultural exports support nearly a million more...And jobs supported by exports of goods pay 13 to 18 percent more than the national average...So we will seek ways to sharpen U.S. trade policy, and to shore up the foundations of global

trade today...by rejecting protectionism and supporting the global rules-based trading system.[862]

Consistent with this position, Obama's appointees to the important Economic Recovery Advisory Board have been, with the sole exception of Richard Trumpka of the AFL-CIO (since elected head of that organization), free traders.[863]

Obama announced in April of 2009 that he would not, contrary to his campaign promise, be renegotiating NAFTA.[864] He continues to press for passage of more free trade agreements, such as the proposed Trans-Pacific Partnership (Singapore, Chile, New Zealand, Brunei, Australia, Peru, and Vietnam). He fought the Buy American provisions included by Congress in the giant stimulus package of 2009 as that old bogeyman Protectionism.[865] In March 2009, reversing his earlier position, he agreed to allow Mexican trucks on U.S. highways despite safety concerns, exposing American truckers to foreign competition.[866] He spoke out against the carbon tariff included in the Cap and Trade legislation passed by the House of Representatives in June 2009,[867] only consenting in the end to very watered-down provisions—despite the fact that Energy Secretary Stephen Chu backed serious carbon tariffs[868] and the WTO has recently announced its cautious acquiescence.[869]

Like his predecessors, President Obama has tactically bunted and talked out of both sides of his mouth to keep minor trade flashpoints from blowing up into something bigger. For example, he imposed a tariff on Chinese tire imports in September 2009 in retaliation for dumping. While this brought forth howls of ideological anguish from the usual suspects, it was actually a very small move. He did not even impose the full 55 percent tariff permitted by the rules China agreed to when it joined the WTO and recommended by the U.S. International Trade Commission. Instead, he only imposed 35 percent, a clear piece of "I'm not serious" signaling to nervous free traders.[870] In December 2010, he announced he would push for Congressional ratification of the Korea-U.S. Free Trade Agreement originally negotiated by Bush in 2007.

THE END GAME ON TRADE

President Obama is not going to be able to support free trade forever. Crisis will eventually come, probably when the dollar finally melts, which will force the public to ask why this happened and thus force the question of whether America's trade policy has been wise. A sharp decline in the dollar would generate an inflationary shock—and a shock in interest rates—that would capture public attention and quite likely knock the economy back into recession.[871]

Ironically, an outright crisis would probably benefit Obama politically, as it would give him room to maneuver out of his earlier free-trade position without looking foolish. It would also help break up the logjam of special interests that currently locks free trade in place. These interests seem impregnable even today in early 2011, but the ground is shifting under their feet for two reasons: first, the present trading order depends financially upon America's inexorably doomed international credit and second, it depends politically upon the public continuing to believe that free trade is sound economics.

Other events could trigger the final collapse of free trade. For example, the U.S. government has slipped into a tacit commitment to bail out key industries, starting with banking and automobiles. It has thus far been able to do this by means of the bankruptcy code plus massive infusions of public money. But in the case of automobiles, it resisted doing the one thing that would have done the most to help this industry: giving it back the market share it has lost to imports. A tariff was half-heartedly considered in the early stages of the crisis, but vetoed by "Toyota Republicans" led by Alabama Senator Richard Shelby, whose state is the site of auto plants owned by Hyundai, Honda, Mercedes, and Toyota.[872] If the cost of providing further industry bailouts without tariff protection becomes intolerable, tariffs may eventually prove irresistible, especially if the U.S. government's ability to pay for bailouts with borrowed cash instead declines.

Another possible trigger for the final breakdown of free trade is global warming.[873] Even free trader economists such as Paul Krugman have recently conceded that the economic rationale for imposing tariffs on nations which fail to control pollution adequately is impeccable, even within the most utterly conventional economic assumptions.[874] In terms of this book, it does not require any of the controversial analyses of Chapters Nine or Ten, only dubious assumption #2 (there are no externalities) of Chapter Five. Americans usually imagine this would involve the U.S. imposing a tariff on polluting nations like China.[875] However, it could quite easily involve nations with higher environmental standards than our own, like the

Europeans together with Japan, imposing a tariff on the U.S! As French president Nicholas Sarkozy said in September 2009:

> I will not accept a system...that imports products from countries that don't respect the rules [on carbon emission reductions]. We need to impose a carbon tax at [Europe's] borders. I will lead that battle.

This is managed trade, not free trade.

DEEPER POLITICAL REALITIES OF THE TRADE ISSUE

Perhaps the greatest benefit of protectionism is ultimately not directly economic but political. If capital must turn a profit mainly by selling goods made *by* Americans *to* Americans, then this *forces capital to care* about Americans' capacity to produce and consume, a combination practically identical with prosperity.

But until capital does thus care, both political parties are feeling the heat of an intensifying global economic challenge to the U.S. and are looking for ways to take the pressure off their voters.

Withdrawing from free trade (to an as yet undefined extent) is emerging as the consensus Democratic response, even if the party's leadership doesn't yet realize how deep are the forces driving this or how far it is likely to go.

The emerging Republican response seems to be keeping free trade while opposing immigration—which does not enlarge America's shrinking economic pie, but does cut it into fewer slices per voter and is therefore politically salable.[876]

The clearest sign of this emerging twin consensus was a pair of Congressional votes: on CAFTA on July 27, 2005 and on immigration amnesty on June 28, 2007. Prior to these votes, American politics was aligned on roughly nationalist vs. internationalist lines, with pro-free-trade and pro-immigration views tending to coincide on one side and anti-free-trade and anti-immigration views on the other. Because the pro side dominated both parties, the anti side was effectively deprived of influence over public policy despite representing a majority or near-majority of public opinion.[877] But these two votes revealed a majority of Congressional Democrats embracing a pro-immigration, anti-free-trade position that may fairly be described as leftist, while a majority of Congressional Republicans embraced an anti-immigration, pro-free-trade position that may fairly be described as rightist.[878] The nationalist and internationalist positions had few remaining supporters in either party.[879]

Both parties thus seemed at that point in time to be reverting to their natural partisan positions of offering competing left- and right-wing solutions to the same underlying problem. (As previously noted, protectionism is *intrinsically* neither rightist nor leftist, but as long as Republicans remain free-market oriented, it is a left-of-center position in contemporary American politics.)

This firming of the ideological battle lines hinted that the trade issue might be resolved in a classic left vs. right firefight. This kind of transparent and accountable partisan choice is, of course, precisely the way democracy is supposed to work.

2011 EDITION UPDATE

Thus matters stood in early 2010 when this book initially went to press. Since then, some aspects of the trade issue have evolved as expected, while others have diverged.

As expected, public opinion has continued to sour on free trade. An NBC-*Wall Street Journal* poll in September 2010 found 53 percent of Americans believing free trade agreements hurt the U.S., with only 17 percent believing them beneficial; the split had been 30 vs. 39 percent in 1999.[880] Eighty-six percent named outsourcing to low-wage nations the key cause of America's failure to emerge fully from recession and create jobs, significantly outranking choices like the federal deficit.[881] This turn against free trade was sharpest among the affluent and cut across boundaries of class, region, and political affiliation.

2010's biggest legislative move on trade was the Currency Reform for Fair Trade Act, which passed the House in September with the support of 249 Democrats (out of 255 voting) and 99 Republicans (out of 173).[882] This bill, had it passed the Senate and been signed by the President, would have enabled companies to petition the Commerce Department for higher duties on products from nations with manipulated currencies. While this measure, originally devised by Kevin Kearns of the U.S. Business and Industry Council, was definitely a positive move, its limitations were noted on pages 74-76. And unfortunately, because a new Congress has since convened, the bill would need to be re-passed, and the new Republican House leadership opposes it.

The midterm election of 2010 became a recession referendum on the overpromised Obama presidency, resulting in a Republican tidal wave that overshadowed trade and many other specific issues. As a result, this election did not increase the number of free-trade opponents sitting in Congress. But shifting public opinion still had a discernable effect: Democrats who ran against free trade were three times as likely to survive as those who ran for it.[883] And a record 75 Republicans campaigned opposing free trade, of whom 43 won.[884]

The big unexpected event of this election cycle was the sharpening turn of mass *conservative* opinion against free trade. For example, though given to libertarianism on many domestic issues and heavily funded by pro-free-trade economic interests, 61 percent of Tea Party members surveyed said free trade agreements have hurt the U.S.[885] This right-wing populist movement is thus now more opposed to free trade than the average voter. Unfortunately, its grass roots disagree on the issue with the national organizations, like Tea Party Nation, which claim to lead this loose insurgency.

Obviously, this sets up a battle inside the Republican Party. The Republican establishment has already lost battles in Republican primaries to the Tea Party, so if a fight breaks out, it well may lose. This establishment's best hope is to fob off opponents of free trade with paper concessions which leave its substance intact, but they will be constrained by the risk that the Democrats will outbid them in general elections with authentic opposition.

CONCLUSION

The trade debate has thus not yet fully crystallized, depriving the democratic process of a firm grip on the question. It may yet do so. Or it may crystallize along partisan lines but get bogged down in secondary issues, making other issues decisive for the electoral fortunes of the two parties. This could easily place a party in power whose trade position opposes what a majority of voters want.

Luckily, even a broken and incoherent debate could produce an acceptable policy outcome. For example, the U.S. could adopt emergency measures under the pressure of immediate crisis without any fundamental ideological shift—and these measures could prove effective and be followed up later by ideological rationalizations. The clearest precedent for such an emergency move is the 10 percent tariff adopted (and unfortunately abandoned) by President Nixon in 1971.[886] This kind of ad hoc solution is also roughly what happened during the Great Depression, when de facto welfare-state Keynesianism was adopted with the ideological infrastructure solidifying later. It may not be the cleanest or most intellectually satisfying way to produce policy, but it does have a history of working.

NOTES

1 Margaret Thatcher, speech to Scottish Conservative Conference, Perth, Scotland, May 8, 1981.

2 "U.S. Trade in Goods and Services - Balance of Payments (BOP) Basis," U.S. Census Bureau, June 10, 2009, http://www.census.gov/foreign-trade/statistics/historical/gands.pdf.

3 2006-2009 data from "U.S. International Trade in Goods and Services," U.S. Census Bureau; 2010 extrapolated from January-September data available at press time. America's trade deficit may even be 10-15% larger than this, due to a 1988 lawsuit that forces the U.S. government to calculate the value of imports based on their value when they left their foreign factory, as opposed to their value when they enter the U.S. See Richard McCormack, "The Plight of American Manufacturing" in Richard McCormack, ed., *Manufacturing a Better Future for America* (Washington: Alliance for American Manufacturing, 2009), p. 61.

4 Author's calculation from "U.S. International Transactions Accounts Data," Bureau of Economic Analysis, http://www.bea.gov/international/xls/table1.xls, accessed November 28, 2009.

5 Five percent.

6 "Employees on nonfarm payrolls by industry sector and selected industry detail," Bureau of Labor Statistics, http://www.bls.gov/webapps/legacy/cesbtab1.htm.

7 Paul Craig Roberts, "The New Face of Class Warfare," *Counterpunch*, July 2006.

8 "International Comparisons of Hourly Compensation Costs in Manufacturing, 2008," Bureau of Labor Statistics, August 26, 2010, p. 4.

9 Louis Uchitelle, "As Output Gains, Wages Lag," *The New York Times*, June 4, 1987.

10 "ADB's Poverty Reduction Strategy," Asian Development Bank, April 18, 2008, p. 1.

11 "Bush Decision on Chinese Imports Leads to Loss of 500 Very Good Jobs," *Manufacturing & Technology News*, March 29, 2007, p. 6.

12 Polyurethane Foam Association, written testimony submitted to hearing on "Aiding American Businesses Abroad: Government Action to Help Beleaguered American Firms and Investors," Committee on Foreign Affairs, U.S. House of Representatives, July 17, 2008.

13 Dan Fuller and Doris Geide-Stevenson, "Consensus Among Economists: Revisited," *Journal of Economic Education*, Fall 2003, p. 372.

14 John Maynard Keynes, *The General Theory of Employment, Interest and Money* (Hamburg: Management Laboratory Press, 2009), p. 395.

15 Paul Krugman, *Strategic Trade Policy and the New International Economics* (Cambridge, MA: MIT Press, 1986), p. 3.

16 About 20% of economists surveyed support free trade "with provisos," according to Dan Fuller and Doris Geide-Stevenson, "Consensus Among Economists: Revisited," *Journal of Economic Education*, Fall 2003, p. 372.

17 Henry George, *Free Trade or Protectionism: An Examination of the Tariff Question With Especial Regard to the Interests of Labor* (New York: Doubleday, 1905), p. 169.

18 One exact figure, for example, is $326,000 for the steel industry, reported by Pete DuPont in "Bush's Steel Crucible: Will He Help Big Industry at Consumers' Expense?" *The Wall Street Journal*, January 2, 2002.

19 There is a branch of economics, public choice theory, which attempts to model these problems, but it has not vindicated its aspiration to objective expertise, tending to generate conclusions that are merely cynical and right wing.

20 Contrary to myth, Japan has been doing quite well lately; see the website unsustainble.org for details. Although China's aggregate GDP recently surpassed Japan's, China's per-capita GDP is still a fraction of Japan's, and Japan has much greater accumulated wealth because it has been a developed nation for decades now.

21 "Balance of Payments (MEI): Current Account Balance," Organization for Economic Cooperation and Development, 2009, http://stats.oecd.org.

22 "International Comparisons of Hourly Compensation Costs in Manufacturing, 2007," Bureau of Labor Statistics, March 26, 2009, Table 1, http://www.bls.gov/news.release/pdf/ichcc.pdf.

23 "International Trade (MEI): International Trade Exports," Organization for Economic Cooperation and Development, 2009, http://stats.oecd.org.

24 These firms are named simply as examples of the industry; they are neither exceptionally bad nor good in this regard.

25 Paul Craig Roberts, "How the Economic News is Spun," *Manufacturing & Technology News*, March 17, 2006, p. 10.

26 Richard McCormack, "U.S. Military Fails to Learn An Ancient Military Lesson: No Industrial Economy Equals No Army," *Manufacturing & Technology News*, October 17, 2008, p. 1.

27 Joseph I. Lieberman, White Paper, "National Security Aspects of the Global Migration of the U.S. Semiconductor Industry," Office of Senator Lieberman, June 2003.

28 Among other things. See Bruce Bartlett, *Impostor: How George W. Bush Bankrupted America and Betrayed the Reagan Legacy* (New York: Doubleday, 2006).

[29] "Presidential Debates: Not Much Stuff Amidst the Fluff," *Manufacturing & Technology News*, October 17, 2008, p. 4. There were also a few comments that could be interpreted as obliquely touching on the trade deficit. The debate transcripts are at http://www.debates.org/pages/debtrans.html.

[30] Gregory Tassey, *The Technology Imperative* (Northampton, MA: Edward Elgar, 2009), p. 36.

[31] Ibid., p. 303.

[32] Both of Paul Krugman's books *Pop Internationalism* (Cambridge, MA: MIT Press, 1996) and *Peddling Prosperity* (New York: W.W. Norton & Co., 1994) contain extended attacks on the concept of competitiveness. Also see the Cato Institute's Daniel T. Griswold, "The U.S. Trade Deficit: A Sign of Good Times," testimony before U.S. Trade Deficit Review Commission, August 19, 1999.

[33] There are, of course, any number of formal definitions available, even if economists do not accept them.

[34] Matthew Craft, "Crash of the Rocket Scientists," *Forbes*, 11 May 2009.

[35] This is not to say mathematics has no place in economics, only that it is fraught with opportunities for bias masked by its objectivity. As long as production, consumption, and wealth are quantifiable, mathematics will have a place.

[36] In technical terms, there is an excessive premium on closed-form solutions. Obviously, such solutions are desirable if they can be obtained, due to their great explanatory power, but their value does not justify ignoring other solutions or twisting facts to achieve closed form.

[37] He was primarily referring to trade models ignoring scale economies. See Paul Krugman, *Rethinking International Trade* (Cambridge, MA: MIT Press, 1994), p. 5.

[38] The desirability of reducing the *conceptual foundations* of economics to a mathematical system, as Paul Samuelson did in his era-defining 1947 book, *Foundations of Economic Analysis*, does not logically entail the desirability of mathematizing economics as a whole.

[39] Warnings about the dangers of over-mathematizing economics go way back: in 1752 the Italian mathematician, Ignazio Radicati, wrote to some economists headed in this direction that, "You will do with political economy what the scholastics did with philosophy. In making things more and more subtle, you do not know where to stop." Quoted in Erik S. Reinert, *How Rich Countries Got Rich and Why Poor Countries Stay Poor* (New York: Carroll and Graf, 2007), p. 45

[40] The main problem is that some mathematical models of the economy produce equations with closed-form solutions and some don't. Economists strongly prefer the former, and will sacrifice the accuracy of models by making simplifying assumptions in order to get them. For example, in trade models, they ignore the effects of scale economies. As discussed in Chapter 10, these are crucial.

[41] For example, neither Michael Porter's *The Competitive Advantage of Nations* (New York: The Free Press, 1990), nor Eamonn Fingleton's *Blindside* (New York: Simon & Schuster, 1995), nor Eric Reinert's *How Rich Countries Got Rich and Why Poor Countries Stay Poor* (New York: Carroll & Graf, 2007) use any math beyond basic statistics. This is not a new phenomenon: going back a few decades, some extremely important economists, like John Kenneth Galbraith and Joseph Schumpeter, were notoriously unmathematical.

[42] Their views of economics do not lend themselves well to mathematical formalism. See Eamonn Fingleton, *Blindside: Why Japan is Still on Track to Overtake the U.S. by the Year 2000* (New York: Houghton Mifflin, 1995) for details.

[43] If this idea has any place in the discipline today, it is as a premise brought to it from outside, not as something that economics actually proves. Furthermore, the idea of prosperity tends to be reduced to satisfaction of "preferences," which can lead, as we shall see in Chapter 2, to vindicating short-term preferences with negative long-term economic consequences.

[44] Consider, for example, free traders Hugo Grotius (1612), Francisco Suarez (1612), and Alberico Gentili (1612), or protectionists Antonio Serra (1613), Edward Misselden (1623), and Charles King (1721).

[45] Though Keynes has enjoyed something of a revival in real world policy decisions dealing with the financial crisis of 2008, and many of his ideas have been absorbed into the disciplinary consensus.

[46] Herman E. Daly and John B. Cobb, Jr., *For the Common Good* (Boston: Beacon Press, 1989) p. 235.

[47] A good discussion of what this means, and what issues it raises in regard to corporate America especially, appears in the first five chapters of Clinton Labor Secretary Robert Reich's book *The Work of Nations* (New York: Alfred A. Knopf, 1991).

[48] This phrase is the title of a book by self-described "radical free trader" Thomas Friedman, *The Lexus and the Olive Tree: Understanding Globalization* (New York: Farrar, Straus & Giroux, 1999).

[49] Vincent Cable, a British Liberal Democrat MP, lists five kinds of antiglobalizers: nationalists (in the full sense), mercantilists (economic nationalists), regionalists (as in the EU or other blocs), dependency theorists (updated Leninism), and deep greens. See Vincent Cable, *Globalization and Global Governance* (London: Royal Institute of International Affairs, 1999), pp. 121-3.

[50] David Hummels, "Time as a Trade Barrier," Center for Global Trade Analysis, Purdue University, July 2001, p. 25.

[51] This phrase is from Dr. Ha-Joon Chang of Cambridge University.

[52] Peter Schwartz and Peter Leyden, "The Long Boom: A History of the Future, 1980—2020," *Wired*, July 1997.

[53] Michael Bordo, "Globalization in Historical Perspective," *Business Economics*, January 2002, p. 22.

[54] Prosperity measured by per capita economic output. For measures of relative globalization over time, see Michael Bordo, "Globalization in Historical Perspective," *Business Economics*, January 2002.

[55] Letter to Henry Cabot Lodge, 1895, quoted in Jacob Viner and Douglas A. Irwin, ed., *Essays on the Intellectual History of Economics* (Princeton, NJ: Princeton University Press, 1991), p. 246.

[56] "Why Cessna Outsourced Manufacture of Its Skycatcher to Chinese Fighter Jet Company," *Manufacturing & Technology News*, December 21, 2007, p. 2.

[57] Estimate of Nobelist Gary Becker of the University of Chicago. See Gary S. Becker, "The Age of Human Capital," in Hugh Lauder, ed., *Education, Globalization & Social Change* (Oxford, UK: Oxford University Press, 2006), p. 292.

[58] Based on Gary Becker's estimate above subtracted from intangible capital estimate in Kirk Hamilton et al., "Where is the Wealth of Nations? Measuring Capital for the 21st Century," World Bank, 2006, p. 20.

[59] This was first rigorously documented in Kenneth French and James Poterba, "Investor Diversification and International Equity Markets," *American Economic Review*, January 1991. Although it has declined since then, it remains substantial, as reported in Amir A. Amadi, "Equity Home Bias: A Disappearing Phenomenon?" Department of Economics, University of California at Davis, 2004.

[60] Mitchell L. Moss, "Why Cities Will Thrive in The Information Age," *Urban Land*, October 2000, p. 2.

[61] See, for example, Richard Florida, "The World is Spiky," *The Atlantic Monthly*, October 2005, p. 48.

[62] Michael Porter, *The Competitive Advantage of Nations* (New York: Free Press, 1990), p.19.

[63] Winfried Ruigrok and Rob van Tulder, *The Logic of International Restructuring: The Management of Dependencies in Rival Industrial Complexes* (New York: Routledge, 1996) p. 159. Although this study and the one cited immediately below are from the mid-1990s, matters do not appear to have shifted significantly since then. According to one 2003 study, "Therefore, in the overall set of 20 highly internationalized MNEs, the case of a global strategy and structure can be made for only six firms, with the additional observation that even these firms exhibit regional elements. The others are either strongly home triad-based or are from small countries peripheral to the triad and are focused in one of the other triad markets. Most of the other 80 of the top 100 MNEs are even less global and are either domestic or home-based MNEs. Location and region matter even to MNEs." Alan M. Rugman and Alain Verbeke, "Regional Multinationals and Triad Strategy," *Research in Global Strategic Management*, vol. 8 (Greenwich, CT: JAI Press, 2003). According to a 2008 study, "There is no evidence of a trend towards the globalization of international business activity." Alan Rugman and Chang H. Oh, "Friedman's Follies: Insights on the Globalization/Regionalization Debate," *Business and Politics*, August 2008, p. 12.

[64] Paul Hirst and Grahame Thompson, "Globalization," *Soundings*, Autumn 1996, p. 56.

[65] Alan Rugman and Chang H. Oh, "Friedman's Follies: Insights on the Globalization/Regionalization Debate," *Business and Politics*, August 2008, p. 13.

[66] Remember distance counts as an incremental barrier to trade, even if it is not a discrete one.

[67] 2008 figure, from "U.S. International Trade in Goods and Services: Exports, Imports, and Balances," Bureau of Economic Analysis, 2009, http://www.bea.gov/newsreleases/international/trade/trad_time _series.xls.

[68] John McCallum, "National Borders Matter: Canada–U.S. Regional Trade Patterns," *The American Economic Review*, June 1995, p. 616.

[69] James E. Anderson & Eric van Wincoop, "Trade Costs," *Journal of Economic Literature*, September 2004, p. 694.

[70] Graham Dunkley, *Free Trade: Myth, Reality, and Alternatives* (New York: Zed Books, 2004), p. 88. With respect to multinationals, see Alan M. Rugman and Alain Verbeke, "Regional Multinationals and Triad Strategy," in *Research in Global Strategic Management* (Stamford, CT: JAI Press, 2003), p.1.

[71] Stephen Tokarick, "Quantifying the Impact of Trade on Wages: The Role of Nontraded Goods," International Monetary Fund, 2002, p. 14.

[72] Paul Krugman, "A Global Economy is not the Wave of the Future," *Financial Executive*, March 1, 1992.

[73] *World Trade Organization Annual Report, 1998* (Geneva: WTO Publications, 1998), pp. 37-38.

[74] Just over a week after 9/11, U.S. Trade Representative Robert Zoellick used counter-terrorism as an argument for expanding presidential fast-track authority to negotiate trade agreements, in an editorial in the *Washington Post*: "Countering Terror With Trade," September 20, 2001. See also, for example, Brink Lindsey, "The Trade Front: Combating Terrorism with Open Markets," Cato Institute, August 5, 2003.

[75] Not that trade policy should always be used as a political tool (a problem discussed in Chapter 8), but the WTO is giving us the worst of both worlds: trade concessions without political good behavior in exchange for them.

[76] "Global Trends 2015: A Dialogue About the Future With Nongovernment Experts," Central Intelligence Agency, December 2000, pp. 10, 38.

[77] John Cavanagh, Jerry Mander et al, *Alternatives to Economic Globalization: A Better World is Possible* (San Francisco: Berrett-Koehler, 2002), p. 118. To be fair, the WTO has not yet formally ruled on this question, though the language of its agreements appears to prohibit treating different nations differently in trade for political reasons. Brussels certainly thinks so: in 1998, the European Union brought a case before the WTO against the U.S. over a Massachusetts law prohibiting that state from doing business with companies that operated in Burma due to Burma's human rights record. The U.S. Supreme Court struck down the Massachusetts law before the WTO heard the case, so no WTO ruling was made. It can, of course, be argued that such sanctions are WTO-compliant, but the best arguments turn on such weak reeds as the WTO's "protecting public morals" clause. See "Are EU Trade Sanctions on Burma Compat-

ible With WTO Law?" Robert L. Howse and Jared M. Genser, *Michigan Journal of International Law*, Winter 2008, pp. 184-188.

[78] Free traders have employed this sort of fuzzy logic for centuries. Free trader economist Arthur Latham Perry wrote around 1883 that ,"to relax commercial systems and not to restrict them is alone in accord with the spirit of the age and the leading commercial nations, the United States alone excepted, have been relaxing their commercial systems." Giles Badger Stebbins, *The American Protectionist's Manual* (Detroit: Thorndike Nourse,1883), p. 19.

[79] See, for example, Peter Schwartz and Peter Leyden, "The Long Boom: A History of the Future, 1980 - 2020," *Wired*, July 1997, or John Nye, "No Pain, No Gain: Opposing Free Trade Means Opposing Innovation," *Reason*, May 1996.

[80] This law claims that the masses will always be paid subsistence wages because whenever they are paid more, they simply have more children until they are living at the subsistence level again.

[81] Thomas Friedman's version runs thus: "Let's face it: Republican cultural conservatives have much more in common with the steelworkers of Youngstown, Ohio, the farmers of rural China, and the mullahs of central Saudi Arabia, who would also like more walls, than they do with investment bankers on Wall Street or service workers linked to the global economy in Palo Alto, who have been enriched by the flattening of the world." Thomas Friedman, *The World is Flat* (New York: Picador, 2005), p. 258. Friedman also wrote in his column: "These anti-WTO protesters... are a Noah's ark of flat-earth advocates, protectionist trade unions and yuppies looking for their 1960s fix." Thomas Friedman, "Senseless in Seattle," *The New York Times*, December 1, 1999.

[82] Tim Reid, "Barack Obama's 'Guns and Religion' Blunder Gives Hillary Clinton a Chance," *The Times*, April 8, 2008.

[83] Free traders have been playing this game for a very long time. One protectionist complained in 1883: "It is the fashion in many of our colleges to assume that free trade is the ideal of the noblest persons and the best minds in the Old World, while protection is a vulgar and selfish matter advocated by those of lesser note and narrower culture." Giles Badger Stebbins, *The American Protectionist's Manual* (Detroit: Thorndike Nourse, 1883), p.19.

[84] Whether free trade and protectionism are leftist or rightist positions is genuinely controversial, and is addressed in the last chapter of this book. Here, the conventional acceptation of these issues in contemporary American politics is taken as a given.

[85] David Croteau, "Challenging the 'Liberal Media' Claim: On Economics, Journalists' Private Views Are to Right of Public," *Extra!*, July/August 1998, p. 8.

[86] Ibid., p. 5.

[87] Speech of January 27, 1846, quoted in Augustus Mongredien, *History of the Free Trade Movement in England* (New York: G.P. Putnam's Sons, 1881), p.155.

[88] Author's calculation based on first 10 months of 2010 from "U.S. International Trade in Goods and Services," Exhibit 1, U.S. Census Bureau, http://www.census.gov/foreign-trade/statistics/historical/exhibit_history.xls and "Trade in Goods (Imports, Exports, and Trade Balance) with China," http://www.census.gov/foreign-trade/balance/c5700.html#2010.

[89] Eamonn Fingleton, *In the Jaws of the Dragon: America's Fate Under Chinese Hegemony* (New York: St. Martin's Press, 2008), p. 66.

[90] Income: "Gross national income per capita 2008, Atlas method and PPP," World Bank, 2008.
Servants: Aakar Patel, "The Servant in the Indian Family," *The International News*, May 31, 2009.

[91] Ron Hira, "The Globalization of Research, Development and Innovation" in Richard McCormack, ed., *Manufacturing a Better Future for America* (Washington: Alliance for American Manufacturing, 2009), p. 171.

[92] "Worldwide and U.S. Business Process Outsourcing 2006-2010," IDC, November 14, 2006.

[93] Alan S. Blinder, "Free Trade's Great, but Offshoring Rattles Me," *The Washington Post*, May 6, 2007, p. B4.

[94] Benno Ndulu, "Challenges of African Growth: Opportunities, Constraints, and Strategic Directions," World Bank, 2007, p. 33.

[95] United Nations Development Programme, "Human Development Report 2003," UNDP, 2003, p. 34.

[96] See p. 151 for details.

[97] Most recent data available; author's calculation based on Thomas Anderson, "Foreign Direct Investment in the United States," Bureau of Economic Analysis, June 2009, p. 55. It can be argued that investment in existing companies enables American capital to be invested in creating new ones, and the situation is considerably more complex than this one statistic can measure, but this fact is strongly suggestive of problems in this area.

[98] Author's calculation from:
2000 data: "2000 National Occupational Employment and Wage Estimates, Architecture and Engineering Occupations," Bureau of Labor Statistics, http://www.bls.gov/oes/2000/oes_17Ar.htm.
2009 data: "May 2009 National Occupational Employment and Wage Estimates, United States," Bureau of Labor Statistics, http://www.bls.gov/oes/2009/may/oes_nat.htm#17-0000.

[99] As phrased by Dani Rodrik of Harvard, "There is no theorem that guarantees that the partial-equilibrium losses to import-competing producers are more than offset by gains to consumers from lower prices." Blog entry of April 28, 2007, http://rodrik.typepad.com/dani_rodriks_weblog/2007/04/can_the_

wrong_a.html, accessed November 29, 2009.

[100] "Employment, Hours, and Earnings from the Current Employment Statistics survey (National)," Bureau of Labor Statistics, http://data.bls.gov/cgi-bin/surveymost, accessed January 2, 2011.

[101] "International Unemployment Rates and Employment Indexes, Seasonally Adjusted, 2007-2010," Bureau of Labor Statistics, January 6, 2011.

[102] Counting prison inmates as unemployed would raise the male unemployment rate by well over a percentage point, and more for certain ethnic groups. America also has a higher proportion of "McJobs" than many other developed nations.

[103] "While per capita income in the United States [in 2006] was 25% higher than the peer average, only 12 of those percentage points can be attributed to higher productivity, whereas 10 percentage points are due to the fact that U.S. workers work more annual hours on average, and 3 percentage points are due to the fact that the United States employs a larger portion of its population." Lawrence Mishel, Jared Bernstein, and Heidi Shierholz. *The State of Working America 2008-2009* (Ithaca, NY: Cornell University Press, 2009), p. 366.

[104] Ibid. p. 380.

[105] Paul Krugman, "Trouble With Trade," *The New York Times*, December 30, 2007.

[106] Wolfgang Stolper and Paul Samuelson, "Protection and Real Wages," *Review of Economic Studies*, November 1941, p. 58.

[107] This is not, of course, the entire story, but close enough for purposes of the present analysis.

[108] Dani Rodrik, *Has Globalization Gone Too Far?* (Washington: Institute for International Economics, 1997), p. 12. Increased inequality is also the result predicted by Edward Leamer in a three-factor model (unskilled labor, skilled labor, and capital), as reported in "Wage Effects of a U.S.-Mexican Free Trade Agreement," in *The Mexico-U.S. Free Trade Agreement*, P.M. Garber, ed. (Cambridge, MA: MIT Press, 1993), pp. 57-125.

[109] Joseph Stiglitz, *Making Globalization Work* (New York: W.W. Norton & Co, 2006), p.45.

[110] Angus Maddison, "Historical Statistics of the World Economy: 1-2006 AD," University of Groningen, March 2009, http://www.ggdc.net/maddison/Historical_Statistics/horizontal-file_03-2009.xls.

[111] Robert C. Feenstra, *Advanced International Trade: Theory and Evidence* (Princeton, NJ: Princeton University Press, 2004), p. 101.

[112] See Peter H. Lindert and Jeffrey G. Williamson, "Does Globalization Make the World More Unequal?" National Bureau of Economic Research, April 2001, p. 33. This is also the upper end of the estimate in "The U.S. Trade Deficit: Causes, Consequences and Recommendations for Action," U.S. Trade Deficit Review Commission, 2000, pp.110-18. According to William Cline in *Trade and Income Distribution* (Washington: Institute for International Economics, 1997), 37 percent of the recent increase in inequality is due to trade. Also see Thomas Palley, "Accounting for income inequality in the U.S.," AFL-CIO Technical Papers, 1999, in which 34 percent of increased inequality is attributed to increased trade, taking into account trade's negative impact on unionization rates.

[113] Josh Bivens, "Globalization and American Wages: Today and Tomorrow," Economic Policy Institute, October 10, 2007, p. 2. Technically, this paper quantifies the impact of larger trade flows as such, not free trade per se.

[114] "New Wage and Benefit Structure for Entry-Level Employees," United Auto Workers, http://www.uaw.org/contracts/07/gm/gm03.php.

[115] Peter Whoriskey, "UAW's Sacrifices Look to Some Like Surrender," *The Washington Post*, December 20, 2008.

[116] Louis Uchitelle, "Two Tiers, Slipping Into One," *The New York Times*, February 26, 2006.

[117] For an example of free traders depicting trade deficits as a positive good, see the Cato Institute's Daniel T. Griswold, "The U.S. Trade Deficit: A Sign of Good Times," testimony before U.S. Trade Deficit Review Commission, August 19, 1999.

[118] Dan Griswold, *Mad About Trade* (Washington, DC: Cato Institute, 2009), p. 73.

[119] Obviously, this limit can change over time, but that is not the same as its being infinitely elastic at any given time. Bond rating agencies exist for a reason.

[120] There is an exception to this fact if we are running a deficit to import capital goods rather than consumption goods. But this just means we are importing goods that make more goods, so we are back to 3a.

[121] Gross, not net.

[122] These are gross, not net, jobs. The workers who would have been employed building aircraft will presumably (*pace* cyclical and frictional unemployment) find jobs doing *something*.

[123] James K. Jackson, "Foreign Ownership of U.S. Financial Assets: Implications of a Withdrawal," Congressional Research Service, January 14, 2008, p. 1.

[124] "U.S. Net International Investment Position at Yearend 2009," Bureau of Economic Analysis, June 25, 2010.

[125] Greg Jensen and Jason Rotenberg, "Bridgewater Daily Observations," Bridgewater Associates, March 25, 2003, p. 1.

[126] "International Investment Position of the United States at Yearend, 1976-2008," Bureau of Economic Analysis, 2009, http://www.bea.gov/international/xls/intinv08_t2.xls.

[127] 2004 data; author's calculation from David Ratner's appendix to Robert Scott's paper, "Revisiting NAFTA," Economic Policy Institute, 2006, Tables 1-1a, 1-1b. Note that these are *gross* jobs, not net

jobs (jobs gained minus jobs lost), as workers who lose their jobs due to imports will presumably eventually find *some* other jobs, however ill paid. The unemployment rate is primarily a function of the economic cycle and the de facto minimum wage, not gains and losses due to trade.

[128] Raymond L. Richman et al., *Trading Away Our Future: How to Fix Our Government-Driven Trade Deficits and Faulty Tax System Before It's Too Late* (Pittsburgh: Ideal Taxes Association, 2008), p. 2.

[129] "China's Financial System and Monetary Policies: The Impact on U.S. Exchange Rates, Capital Markets, and Interest Rates," hearing of U.S.-China Economic and Security Review Commission, August 22, 2006, p. 93.

[130] William Bahr, *The Economic Consequences of Blind Faith in Free Trade* (Draft), Ch. 5. William A. Lovett in 2004 estimated that, "With stronger, reciprocity-based trade policy, U.S. GDP could have been 10 to 20 percent higher," in William Anthony Lovett, Alfred E. Eckes & Richard L. Brinkman, *U.S. Trade Policy: History, Theory and the WTO* (Armonk, NY: M.E. Sharpe & Co., 1999), p. 130. Another estimate of the size of the problem, by economist Charles McMillion of MBG Information Services, notes that in the 25 years up to 1980, our real GDP grew at an average of 3.8 per year. But in the 25 years afterwards, as our trade deficit ballooned, it grew at only 3.1 percent. Charles McMillion, "Guest Editorial: Forever in Their Debt," *Manufacturing & Technology News*, October 25, 2006, p. 5.

[131] "Fiscal Year 2010 Budget Overview Document," Office of Management and Budget, 2009, Table S-3.

[132] James K. Jackson, "Foreign Ownership of U.S. Financial Assets: Implications of a Withdrawal," Congressional Research Service, January 14, 2008, p. 1.

[133] Net international obligations, per Mark Whitehouse, "U.S. Foreign Debt Shows Its Teeth As Rates Climb: Net Payments Remain Small But Pose Long-Term Threat to Nation's Living Standards," *The Wall Street Journal*, September 25, 2006, p. A1.

[134] Matthew Higgins, Thomas Klitgaard, and Cédric Tille, "Borrowing Without Debt? Understanding the U.S. International Investment Position," Federal Reserve Bank of New York, 2006, p. 7.

[135] As stated in a recent report by BRUEGEL, a think tank in Brussels, the Korea Institute for International Economic Policy in Seoul and the Peterson Institute for International Economics in Washington: "A market-led adjustment might involve global recession, abrupt and excessive changes in key exchange rates and assets prices, and, as a consequence, aggravated trade friction. The recent volatility in global financial markets is a reminder of the dangers of failing to act promptly." Alan Ahearne, William R. Cline, Kyung Tae Lee, Yung Chul Park, Jean Pisani-Ferry, and John Williamson, "Global Imbalances: Time for Action," Peterson Institute for International Economics, March 2007, p. 3.

[136] Robert A. Blecker, "The Ticking Debt Bomb: Why the U.S. International Financial Position is Not Sustainable," Economic Policy Institute, June 1, 1999, p. 11.

[137] Lawrence Mishel and Jared Bernstein, "Economy's Gains Fail to Reach Most Workers' Paychecks," Economic Policy Institute, August 30, 2007, Figure A.

[138] Strictly speaking, personal consumption spending; author's estimate based on first three quarters of 2010. "National Income and Product Accounts Table, Last Revised December 22, 2010," Bureau of Economic Analysis, http://www.bea.gov/national/nipaweb/TableView.asp?SelectedTable=5& FirstYear=1980&LastYear=2010&Freq=Qtr.

[139] Diana Farrell, Susan Lund, Eva Gerlemann, and Peter Seeburger, "The New Power Brokers: Gaining Clout in Turbulent Markets," McKinsey Global Institute, June 2008, p. 20.

[140] Sovereign Wealth Fund Institute, 2011, http://www.swfinstitute.org/swfs/government-of-singapore-investment-corporation and http://www.swfinstitute.org/swfs/temasek-holdings.

[141] Ibid., http://www.swfinstitute.org/swfs/norway-government-pension-fund-global.

[142] Ibid., http://www.swfinstitute.org/swfs/kuwait-investment-authority.

[143] Ibid., http://www.swfinstitute.org/swfs/china-africa-development-fund, http://www.swfinstitute.org/swfs/china-investment-corporation, http://www.swfinstitute.org/swfs/national-social-security-fund, and http://www.swfinstitute.org/swfs/safe-investment-company.

[144] Testimony of David Marchick Before U.S.-China Economic & Security Review Commission on "The Extent of the Government's Control of China's Economy, and its Impact on the United States," May 24, 2007.

[145] "The CPP Fund and CPP Investment Board are not Sovereign Wealth Funds," Canada Pension Plan Investment Board, December 10, 2007, http://www.cppib.ca/files/PDF/SWFBkgr_Dec10_2007.pdf.

[146] Diana Farrell, Susan Lund, Eva Gerlemann, and Peter Seeburger, "The New Power Brokers: Gaining Clout in Turbulent Markets," McKinsey Global Institute, June 2008, p. 6.

[147] Ibid., p. 6.

[148] Ibid., Exhibit 2.

[149] Ibid., p. 6.

[150] Ibid., p. 9.

[151] "CFIUS Annual Report to Congress: November 2009: Public/Unclassified Version," U.S. Treasury, November 2009, p. 3. 15 transactions were withdrawn during investigation, a fact open to interpretation.

[152] Ambassador John Veroneau, "The Challenges of Foreign Investment," speech to United States Council for International Business, February 26, 2008.

[153] Zhou Jiangong, "China on Wall Street: Buy? Yes. Lend? No," ChinaStakes.com, October 2, 2008.

[154] China GDP: "China," *CIA World Factbook*, Central Intelligence Agency, https://www.cia.gov/library/publications/the-world-factbook/geos/ch.html.

U.S. imports from China: "Trade With China: 2010," U.S. Census Bureau, http://www.census.gov/foreign-trade/balance/c5700.html#2010.

[155] "China Says Domestic Demand Can't Fill Export Hole," Reuters, May 14, 2009.

[156] "General Agreement on Tariffs and Trade," World Trade Organization, 1947, http://www.wto.org/english/docs_e/legal_e/gatt47_01_e.htm.

[157] "Articles of Agreement," International Monetary Fund, 1945, http://www.imf.org/external/pubs/ft/aa/aa06.htm#3.

[158] One good example for the present analysis is Joseph Stiglitz, "Factor Price Equalization in a Dynamic Economy," *Journal of Political Economy,* May-June 1970, especially p. 466.

[159] Assuming, as *ex hypothesi* in this thought experiment, that the decadent nation is importing consumption goods. If it is importing capital goods, that is, goods which increase its future capacity to produce goods, it may do fine. America has not been doing this.

[160] For a detailed working-out of reasoning similar to this, see Joseph E. Stiglitz, "Factor Price Equalization in a Dynamic Economy," *Journal of Political Economy*, May/June 1970, especially p. 466.

[161] See p. 22.

[162] Though not by billionaire Warren Buffett, who calls the two nations Thriftville and Squanderville and does not examine how deep the theoretical problem goes.

[163] Max Weber's famous point in his 1905 book, *The Protestant Ethic and the Spirit of Capitalism.*

[164] Robert W. Parenteau, "U.S. Household Deficit Spending," Levy Economics Institute, November 2006, p. 8.

[165] "Household Debt Service and Financial Obligations Ratios," Federal Reserve Board, http://federalreserve.gov/releases/housedebt/default.htm.

[166] Author's calculation based on:
Debt ($34.6 trillion): "Flow of Funds Accounts of the United States: Flows and Outstandings Third Quarter 2010," Federal Reserve Bank, December 9, 2010, p. 2.
GDP ($14.75 trillion): "Gross Domestic Product," news release, Bureau of Economic Analysis, December 22, 2010.

[167] Don Evans, Hearing before Committee on Financial Services, "U.S. Interests in the Reform of China's Financial Sector," U.S. House of Representatives, June 6, 2007, http://ftp.resource.org/gpo.gov/hearings/110h/37551.txt.

[168] "The China Effect: Assessing the Impact on the U.S. Economy of Trade and Investment with China," China Business Forum, 2008.

[169] During the Clinton administration, U.S. Trade Representative Charlene Barshefsky and Commerce Secretary William M. Daley made this argument.

[170] Henry M. Paulson, Jr., Speech before the Economic Club of Washington, March 1, 2007.

[171] Gavin Cameron and Christopher Wallace, "Macroeconomic Performance in the Bretton Woods Era, And After," University of Oxford, October 2002, pp. 4-5.

[172] Former IMF chief economist Simon Johnson, "The Quiet Coup," *The Atlantic*, May 2009.

[173] Kathleen Burke and Alec Cairncross. *Goodbye, Great Britain: The 1976 IMF Crisis* (New Haven, CT: Yale University Press, 1992), p. 5. Whatever economic problems Britain had in this period, excessive debt accumulation and asset sales were not among them.

[174] John Maynard Keynes, "Proposal for an International Clearing Union," in John Maynard Keynes, *The Collected Writings of John Maynard Keynes*, vol. 25 (Cambridge, UK: Cambridge University Press, 1980) p. 170.

[175] Jeffrey W. Helsing, *Johnson's War/Johnson's Great Society: The Guns and Butter Trap* (Westport, CT: Praeger Publishers, 2000), p. 230.

[176] Nixon tried to defend it in 1970 by raising interest rates, but the domestic political fallout proved too great in the face of the 1972 election and he asked the Fed to reverse course.

[177] Naomi Klein, *The Shock Doctrine: The Rise of Disaster Capitalism.* (New York: Metropolitan Press, 2007).

[178] Dani Rodrik, "The Rush to Free Trade in the Developing World: Why So Late? Why Now? Will It Last?" in Stephan Haggard and Steven B. Webb, eds., *Voting for Reform: Democracy, Political Liberalization and Economic Adjustment* (New York: Oxford University Press, 1994) p. 81.

[179] Eamonn Fingleton, *In the Jaws of the Dragon: America's Fate Under Chinese Hegemony* (New York: St. Martin's Press, 2008), p. 128.

[180] For example, he said upon concluding a round of GATT negotiations in 1993, "This new agreement will foster more jobs and more incomes in America by fostering an export boom." President Bill Clinton speech, December 15, 1993, quoted in U.S. Department of State Dispatch, December 20, 1993.

[181] "U.S. International Trade in Goods and Services, 1992 - Present," U.S. Census Bureau, http://www.census.gov/foreign-trade/statistics/historical/exhibit_history.xls, 1992 figure adjusted to 2010 dollars using "Gross Domestic Product: Implicit Price Deflator," Bureau of Economic Analysis, http://research.stlouisfed.org/fred2/data/GDPDEF.txt.

[182] Author's calculation based on 2008 imports and exports.

[183] In 1992, exports to Mexico were $40.6 billion; in 2008, they were $151.2 billion. "Trade With Mexico," U.S. Census Bureau, http://www.census.gov/foreign-trade/balance/c2010.html#2009. Mexico supplies only 3% of primary materials and packaging, according to, "How Much Maquiladora Output is Made in Mexico," *Cross-Border Economic Bulletin*, June 2001.

[184] Author's calculation based on first 9 months of 2010. "U.S. International Trade in Goods and Services," U.S. Census Bureau, http://www.census.gov/foreign-trade/statistics/historical/exhibit_history.xls.

[185] Manufacturing: "Value Added by Industry as a Percentage of Gross Domestic Product," Bureau of Economic Analysis, 2009, http://www.bea.gov/industry/gpotables/gpo_action.cfm?anon=108681&table_id=24753&format_type=0.
Imports: "U.S. International Trade in Goods and Services: Exports, Imports, and Balances," Bureau of Economic Analysis, 2009, http://www.bea.gov/newsreleases/international/trade/trad_time_series.xls.

[186] See also David Hale, "Don't Rely on the Dollar to Reduce the Deficit," *Financial Times*, January 25, 2005.

[187] Author's estimate based on first 10 months of 2010. "U.S. International Trade in Goods and Services, 1992-Present," U.S. Census Bureau, accessed January 4, 2011, http://www.census.gov/foreign-trade/statistics/historical/exhibit_history.xls.

[188] Author's calculation based on "Total Value of U.S. Agricultural Trade and Trade Balance, Monthly: updated 12/10/2010," U.S. Dept. of Agriculture, http://www.ers.usda.gov/Data/Fatus/DATA/moUStrade.xls.

[189] In any case, this correlation is only true, even in theory, in equilibrium. Given gigantic exogenous shocks like the sudden entry of billions of new workers into the global trading system due to the decline of socialism, the world can potentially be out of equilibrium for decades.

[190] Data from "World Cost Curve for Steel Sheet Plants," World Steel Dynamics, quoted in "Steel Industry Trends," International Steel Group, 2004, p. 37.

[191] This is not to imply, of course, that direct labor is the only production cost. If it were, American steel makers could obviously never be competitive with these numbers.

[192] "Major Sector Productivity and Costs Index," Bureau of Labor Statistics, http://data.bls.gov/PDQ/outside.jsp?survey=pr.

[193] 10.7%, to be precise. Author's calculation from "Major Sector Productivity and Costs Index," Bureau of Labor Statistics, http://data.bls.gov/cgi-bin/surveymost.

[194] Madeline Zavodny, "Unions and the Wage-Productivity Gap," *Federal Reserve Bank of Atlanta Economic Review*, Q2 1999, Chart 2. See also Lawrence Mishel, Jared Bernstein, and Heidi Shierholz, *The State of Working America 2008/2009* (Ithaca, NY: Cornell University Press, 2009), Chapter 3, Figure 30.

[195] William Greider, *One World, Ready or Not* (New York: Touchstone Press, 1997), p. 75.

[196] For one fairly negative evaluation of TAA's effectiveness, see General Accounting Office, "Trade Adjustment Assistance: Trends, Outcomes, and Management Issues in Dislocated Worker Programs," GAO-01-59, October 2000. TAA is also a deeply dysfunctional program. According to a recent ruling by the U.S. Court of Inter-national Trade (*Former Employees of BMC Software Inc. v. the United States Secretary of Labor*), it routinely denies legitimate assistance requests by workers.

[197] Organization for Economic Cooperation and Development, "Education at a Glance 2009: OECD Indicators," OECD, 2009, Tables A1, 2a.

[198] Ibid., Chart A3.1.

[199] Stéphane Baldi, Ying Jin, Melanie Skemer, Patricia J. Green & Deborah Herget, "Highlights from PISA 2006: Performance of U.S. 15-Year-Old Students in Science and Mathematics Literacy in an International Context," National Center for Education Statistics, December 2007, p. iii.

[200] "State & County Estimates of Low Literacy," National Assessment of Adult Literacy, http://nces.ed.gov/naal/estimates/StateEstimates.aspx.

[201] Census Bureau figure, reported in Michael Mandel, "College: Rising Costs, Diminishing Returns," *BusinessWeek*, September 28, 2009, p. 20. The raw data is at (for 2000) "Educational Attainment–People 25 Years Old and Over, by Total Money Earnings in 2000, Work Experience in 2000, Age, Race, Hispanic Origin, and Sex," http://pubdb3.census.gov/macro/032001/perinc/new03_021.htm and (for 2008) "Educational Attainment–People 25 Years Old and Over, by Total Money Earnings in 2008, Work Experience in 2008, Age, Race, Hispanic Origin, and Sex," http://www.census.gov/hhes/www/cpstables/032009/perinc/new03_021.htm.

[202] David R. Howell, "The Skills Myth," *The American Prospect*, June 23, 1994.

[203] Interview, "Why should Democrats be for more trade deficits?" *Manufacturing & Technology News*, January 5, 2007, p. 9.

[204] "OECD Broadband Statistics," Organization for Economic Cooperation and Development, December 2008, Table 1d.

[205] Michael Arndt, "The U.S. is Losing its Lead in Patents," *BusinessWeek*, April 22, 2009.

[206] Richard McCormack, "A Big Lump of Coal: President & Congress Give A Christmas Present to the Federal Science Agencies," *Manufacturing & Technology News*, December 21, 2007.

[207] "Budget of the United States Government: Fiscal Year 2009," U.S. Government Printing Office, http://www.gpoaccess.gov/usbudget/fy09/browse.html.

[208] Organization for Economic Cooperation and Development, "OECD Science, Technology and Industry Scoreboard 2007," 2007, Graph A-2, http://oberon.sourceoecd.org/vl=9612937/cl=27/nw=1/rpsv/sti2007/ga2-4.htm.

[209] "Technology Indicators: Move Over U.S.–China to be New Driver of World's Economy and Innovation," *Georgia Tech Research News*, January 24, 2008, http://www.gtresearchnews.gatech.edu/newsrelease/high-tech-indicators.htm. The study itself is at http://www.tpac.gatech.edu/hti.php.

[210] Thomas Friedman writes that China "will soon be reaching a point where its ambitions for economic growth will require more political reform. China will never root out corruption without a free press and active civil society institutions. It can never really become efficient without a more codified rule of law. It will never be able to deal with the inevitable downturns in its economy without a more open political system that allows people to vent their grievances." *The World is Flat* (New York: Picador, 2005), p. 149.

[211] "Article IV Consultation with the People's Republic of China" International Monetary Fund, July 22, 2009, https://www.imf.org/external/np/sec/pn/2009/pn0987.htm.

[212] "Intel CEO Barrett: India and U.S. Are A Lot Alike," *Manufacturing & Technology News*, September 17, 2007, p. 9.

[213] International Monetary Fund, "Report for Selected Countries and Subjects," http://www.imf.org/external /pubs/ft/weo/2009/01/weodata/weorept.aspx?pr.x=25&pr.y=15&sy=1987&ey=2008&ssd=1&sort=coun try&ds=.&br=1&c=924%2C534&s=NGDPDPC&grp=0&a=.

[214] Tokyo-based financial journalist Eamonn Fingleton has documented this at length in *In the Jaws of the Dragon: America's Fate Under Chinese Hegemony* (New York: St. Martin's Press, 2008).

[215] "The History of the Sony Walkman," http://inventors.about.com/od/wstartinventions/a/Walkman.htm.

[216] Ernst & Young, "Q1'09 Global IPO Update," April 2009, p. 9.

[217] Japan has a lot more countercultural creativity than it is usually given credit for, anyway.

[218] Alvin Toffler, *Future Shock* (New York: Bantam, 1970); George Gilder, *Telecosm: How Infinite Bandwidth Will Revolutionize Our World* (New York: Free Press, 2000); Virginia Postrel, *The Future and Its Enemies* (New York: Pocket Books, 1999); John Naisbitt, *Megatrends: Ten New Directions Transforming Our Lives* (New York: Warner Books, 1982).

[219] Newt Gingrich, *To Renew America* (New York: Harper Paperbacks, 1995), pp. 56-68.

[220] "Value Added by Industry as a Percentage of Gross Domestic Product," Bureau of Economic Analysis, http://www.bea.gov/industry/gpotables/gpo_action.cfm.

[221] Josh Bivens, "Shifting Blame for Manufacturing Job Loss: Effect of Rising Trade Deficit Shouldn't Be Ignored," Economic Policy Institute, April 8, 2004.

[222] Ibid.

[223] "Innovation Index: Where America Stands," Council on Competitiveness, 2006.

[224] The imported content of China's exports is estimated to be 50%. Robert Koopman, Zhi Wang, and Shang-Jin Wei, "How Much of Chinese Exports is Really Made In China? Assessing Domestic Value-Added When Processing Trade is Pervasive," National Bureau of Economic Research, June 2008, p. 4.

[225] 2005 data. Greg Linden, Kenneth L. Kraemer and Jason Dedrick, "Who Captures Value in a Global Innovation System? The Case of Apple's iPod," Personal Computing Industry Center, University of California at Irvine, June 2007, p. 6.

[226] 2006 data. Greg Linden, Jason Dedrick and Kenneth L. Kraemer, "Innovation and Job Creation in a Global Economy: The Case of Apple's iPod," Personal Computing Industry Center, University of California at Irvine, January 2009, p. 7.

[227] Ross Perot and Pat Choate, *Save Your Job, Save Our Country* (New York: Hyperion, 1993) p. 69. See also Susan Helper, "The High Road for U.S. Manufacturing," *Issues in Science and Technology*, National Academy of Sciences, Winter 2009.

[228] Michigan Manufacturing Technology Center, "The National Context: Is Manufacturing in the U.S. Toast?" *ManufactLINE*, September 2007, p. 12.

[229] National Research Council, *Dispelling the Manufacturing Myth: American Factories Can Compete in the Global Marketplace* (Washington: National Academies Press, 1992), Chapter 2.

[230] Charles McMillion, "The Economic State of the Union, 2008," *Manufacturing & Technology News*, January 24, 2008.

[231] Author calculation based on Greg Linden, Kenneth L. Kraemer, and Jason Dedrick, "Who Captures Value in a Global Innovation System? The case of Apple's iPod," Personal Computing Industry Center, University of California at Irvine, p. 6. Note that the $140 figure includes reexport from China of components imported into China from other countries, including the U.S.

[232] "Small Manufacturers Make The Case For An Across-the-Board 'Surcharge' On Imports," *Manufacturing & Technology News*, July 24, 2006, p.11.

[233] Paul Craig Roberts, "A Workforce Betrayed: Watching Greed Murder the Economy," *Manufacturing & Technology News*, July 31, 2008.

[234] Ibid.

[235] Ibid.

[236] Stephen S. Cohen and John Zysman, *Manufacturing Matters: The Myth of the Post-Industrial Economy* (New York: Basic Books, 1988) p. 8. Obviously, this should not be interpreted as implying that it is impossible to separate research and production functions, especially for routine production of products based on past innovation. But the fact remains that the arms-length approach is out-competed by a more integrated approach to research and production.

[237] Richard Florida and Martin Kenney, *The Breakthrough Illusion* (New York: Basic Books, 1990), p. 8.

[238] "SAIC scientist says U.S. needs a broad new system to commercialize technology," *Manufacturing & Technology News*, March 17, 2006, p. 11.

[239] Richard J. Elkus, *Winner Take All* (New York: Basic Books, 2008), p. 46.

[240] Thomas Friedman, *The World is Flat* (New York: Picador, 2005), p. 269.

[241] One rigorous scholarly critique of Thomas Friedman's economic ideas, which do not stand up well to hard data, is Alan Rugman and Chang H. Oh, "Friedman's Follies: Insights on the Globalization Debate," *Business and Politics*, August 2008.

[242] Arie Y. Lewin and Vinay Couto, *Next Generation Offshoring: the Globalization of Innovation* (Durham, NC: Fuqua School of Business, Duke University, 2007), p. 7.

[243] Ibid. p. 19.

[244] Ibid.

[245] Jeffrey Immelt, "Letter to Shareholders," General Electric, February 6, 2009.

[246] Jim Irwin, "General Electric's Immelt says manufacturing jobs should comprise 20 percent of U.S. employment," Associated Press, June 26, 2009.

[247] "HDTV Manufacturers," *HDTV Review Lab*, http://www.hdtvreviewlab.com/hdtv-manufacturers.

[248] Eamonn Fingleton, "Boeing, Boeing, Gone," *The American Conservative*, January 31, 2005.

[249] David Pritchard and Alan MacPherson, "Strategic Destruction of the North American and European Aircraft Industry: Implications of the System Integration Business Model," Canada-United States Trade Center, State University of New York at Buffalo, January 2007.

[250] Ibid., p. 6.

[251] Speech by Noël Forgeard, CEO of Airbus, to the International Metalworkers Federation World Aerospace Conference in Toulouse, France, June 19, 2002.

[252] Dominic Gates, "Boeing 787 Wing Flaw Extends Inside Plane," *The Seattle Times*, July 30, 2009.

[253] Every mass-produced American-made hybrid car uses technology under license (or some other agreement, like patent-sharing) in all or in part from either Toyota or Honda. There is some dispute as to how much of Ford's cross-licensed technology originated at Ford; GM has an indigenous hybrid technology for buses only.

[254] Jonathan G. Dorn, "Solar Cell Production Jumps 50 Percent in 2007," Earth Policy Institute, December 27, 2007, http://www.earth-policy.org/datacenter/xls/indicator12_2007_3.xls.

[255] Per Krogsgaard and Birger T. Madsen, "International Wind Energy Development: World Market Update 2009," BTM Consult ApS, March 25, 2009.

[256] Christian E. Weller and Holly Wheeler, "Our Nation's Surprising Technology Trade Deficit," Center for American Progress, March 2008, p. 3.

[257] "U.S. Trade with China in Advanced Technology Products," Census Bureau, http://www.census.gov/foreign-trade/statistics/product/atp/2008/12/ctryatp/atp5700.html, accessed November 30, 2009.

[258] "Value of Exports, General Imports, and Imports by Country by 3-digit NAICS: China (5700)," U.S. Census Bureau, http://censtats.census.gov/cgi-bin/naic3_6/naicCty.pl. Electronics includes computers and excludes items classified as electrical goods; apparel includes accessories; toys includes games and children's vehicles.

[259] James Burke, "U.S. Investment in China Worsens Trade Deficit," Economic Policy Institute, May 1, 2000, p. 2.

[260] Robert E. Scott, "China Dominates U.S. Non-Oil Trade Deficit in 2009," Economic Policy Institute, July 23, 2009. Data from U.S. International Trade Commission.

[261] 2009 figure through Q3. "Exports, Imports, and Balance of Advanced Technology Products by Technology Group and Selected Countries and Areas," U.S. Census Bureau, http://www.census.gov/foreign-trade/Press-Release/current_press_release/exh16a.pdf

[262] "Global Patterns of U.S. Merchandise Trade," U.S. International Trade Administration, http://tse.export.gov/NTDChart.aspx?.

[263] "2007 U.S. Exports of Aerospace Vehicles and Equipment," U.S. Department of Commerce, http://www.trade.gov/wcm/groups/internet/@trade/@mas/@man/@aai/documents/web_content/aero_stat_expqtr.pdf and "2007 U.S. Imports of Aerospace Vehicles and Equipment," http://www.trade.gov/wcm/groups/public/@trade/@mas/@man/@aai/documents/web_content/aero_stat_impqtr.pdf.

[264] "Akio Morita, Co-Founder of Sony and Japanese Business Leader, Dies at 78," *The New York Times*, October 4, 1999.

[265] "International Trade (MEI): International Trade Exports," Organization for Economic Cooperation and Development, 2009, http://stats.oecd.org.

[266] Laura D'Andrea Tyson, *Who's Bashing Whom? Trade Conflict in High Technology Industries* (Washington: Institute for International Economics, 1993), p. 100. See also William Greider, *One World, Ready or Not* (New York: Touchstone Press, 1997), p. 367. One good analysis of the way in which takeover pressure can drive management to sacrifice long-term interests in order to increase short-term profits is Jeremy Stein's "Takeover Threats and Managerial Myopia," *Journal of Political Economy*, February 1988.

[267] James Jacobs, "The Diminished Role of Training and Education in Manufacturing and the Imperative for Change," in Richard McCormack, ed., *Manufacturing a Better Future for America* (Washington: Alliance for American Manufacturing, 2009), p. 235.

[268] William Greider, *One World, Ready or Not* (New York: Touchstone Press, 1997), p. 136.

[269] David C. Mowery and Joanne Oxley, "Inward Technology Transfer and Competitiveness: the Role of National Innovation Systems," p. 159.

[270] Laura D'Andrea Tyson, *Who's Bashing Whom*? (Washington: Institute for International Economics, 1993), p. 7.

[271] "Nominal per capita GDP Tables," World Economic Outlook Database, International Monetary Fund, http://imf.org/external/pubs/ft/weo/2008/02/weodata/weoselgr.aspx.

[272] One detailed estimate, 43% (with slightly different objectives) of how far the dollar needs to fall is that of Goldman Sachs's Jim O'Neill: "Features of a Dollar Decline," in C. Fred Bergsten and John Williamson *Dollar Overvaluation and the World Economy*, (Washington: Institute for International Economics, 2003), p. 15.

[273] Given that 82% of our consumption is produced domestically (2008 data), most of our consumption is unaffected by the value of the dollar. But if our international purchasing power falls by half, that would mean a 9% decline in American consumption, other things being equal.

[274] Fabric suitcases: "Another U.S. Industry Gone," *Manufacturing & Technology News*, November 16, 2007, p. 1.
Epoxy cresol novolac resin: Eamonn Fingleton, "Statement Before the U.S.-China Economic and Security Review Commission," April 21, 2005.

[275] "U.S. International Transactions, by Area - Japan," Bureau of Economic Analysis, http://www.bea.gov /international/bp_web/simple.cfm?anon=71&table_id=10&area_id=11.

[276] "Trade in Goods (Imports, Exports and Trade Balance) with Japan," U.S. Census Bureau, http:// www.census.gov/foreign-trade/balance/c5880.html. 2008 was the latest year for which complete data were available at press time; Japan's surplus with the U.S. in the recession year of 2009 is projected to be $44 billion.

[277] Ibid.

[278] In the 1971 words of Treasury Secretary George Shultz, "We can change exchange rates until hell freezes over, and we still won't get anything in return." Gabor Steingart, *The War for Wealth: The True Story of Globalization, or Why the Flat World is Broken* (New York: McGraw-Hill, 2008), p. 71.

[279] Clyde V. Prestowitz, Jr., *Trading Places: How We Are Giving Our Future to Japan and How to Reclaim It* (New York: Basic Books, 1993), p. 61.

[280] One good analysis of the import-excluding effects of the Japanese *keiretsu* is that of Robert Z. Lawrence, "Efficient or Exclusionist? The Import Behavior of Japanese Corporate Groups," Brookings Institution, 1991.

[281] "U.S. Automakers Endorse Japan Currency Manipulation Act, Applaud Stabenow Legislation to Force Action Against Japanese Currency Misalignment," *Auto Channel*, March 28, 2007.

[282] Although China's currency has technically been floating since June 2005, it is managed by China's government in order not to appreciate too much against the currencies of China's export markets.

[283] "Heavy in Dollars, China Warns of Depreciation," Reuters, September 3, 2010.

[284] "Chinese Currency Manipulation Fact Sheet April 2005," China Currency Coalition, http://www. chinacurrencycoalition.org/pdfs/0405_factsheet.pdf.

[285] For a list of various estimates, see Peter Navarro, "Benchmarking the Advantages Foreign Nations Provide Their Manufacturers" in Richard McCormack, ed., *Manufacturing a Better Future for America* (Washington: Alliance for American Manufacturing), p. 127. Also see "Chinese Currency Manipulation Fact Sheet April 2005," China Currency Coalition, http://www.chinacurrencycoalition.org/pdfs/ 0405_factsheet.pdf, p. 1.

[286] For an analysis of the various bills, see Vivian Jones, "Trade Remedy Legislation: Applying Countervailing Action to Nonmarket Economy Countries," Congressional Research Service, January 31, 2008.

[287] Bunning-Stabenow: HR 2378, S 1027.

[288] Benedicte Vibe Christensen, "Switzerland's Role as an International Financial Center," International Monetary Fund, 1986, p. 21.

[289] The yuan peg also generates other problems, such as negative real interest rates and the resulting stock-market speculation caused by capital avoiding the low real returns on deposit accounts.

[290] With some token gains starting in June 2010.

[291] About two percent, per oral statement of David A. Hartquist on behalf of the China Currency Coalition, Senate Task Force on Manufacturing, October 26, 2007, http://www.chinacurrencycoalition.org/pdfs/STF_Manf/STF_Manf_oral_report.pdf, slide 2.

[292] "Treasury Official Says China Currency Change Won't Impact Imports," *Manufacturing & Technology News*, October 31, 2007, p. 10.

[293] This means the state-organized centralizing of specific industries in specific regions, as Detroit is a center for automobiles.

[294] Peter Navarro, "Benchmarking the Advantages Foreign Nations Provide Their Manufacturers" in Richard McCormack, ed., *Manufacturing a Better Future for America* (Washington: Alliance for American Manufacturing), p. 109.

[295] U.S. House of Representatives, Committee on Energy and Commerce, Subcommittee on Oversight and Investigations, *Unfair Foreign Trade Practices: Barriers to U.S. Exports*, 99th Cong., 2nd sess., May 1986, Committee Print 99-BB, p. 2.

[296] "China's economic policies violate the spirit and letter of World Trade Organization membership requirements," according to "2007 Report to Congress," U.S.-China Economic and Security Review Commission (Washington: U.S. Government Printing Office, 2007), p. 3.

[297] Trade balance: "U.S. Trade in Goods and Services - Balance of Payments (BOP) Basis," U.S. Census Bureau, http://www.census.gov/foreign-trade/statistics/historical/gands.pdf.

Recessions: "U.S. Business Cycle Expansions and Contractions," National Bureau of Economic Research, December 2008, http://www.nber.org/cycles.html.

[298] Calvin Colton, *The Speeches of Henry Clay* (New York: Barnes & Co., 1857), vol. 5, p. 221.

[299] Customs revenue: "Import Trade Trends, Fiscal Year 2010 Year-End Report," U.S. Customs & Border Protection, p. 4.
Import volume: "U.S. Trade in Goods and Services - Balance of Payments (BOP) Basis," U.S. Census Bureau, http://www.census.gov/foreign-trade/statistics/historical/gands.txt

[300] See, for example, Bill McKibben, *Deep Economy: The Wealth of Communities and the Durable Future* (New York: Henry Holt and Co., 2007), p. 12.

[301] This doesn't mean that a reasonable bias in favor of things like locally-produced food is wrong.

[302] Jagdish Bhagwati, "Optimal Intervention to Achieve Non-Economic Objectives," *The Review of Economic Studies*, January 1969.

[303] The term for making cultural choices on non-cultural grounds is "philistinism."

[304] Gail Billington, "Malaysian Prime Minister: 'We Had to Decide Things For Ourselves'," *Executive Intelligence Review*, February 19, 1999.

[305] Estimate by Prof. Michael Porter of Harvard Business School, as reported in "Porter: Unfair Trade Plays a role in Declining U.S. Competitiveness," *Manufacturing & Technology News*, June 30, 2008, p. 7.

[306] "Competitiveness Index: Where America Stands," Council on Competitiveness, 2007, p. 77.

[307] Peter Navarro, *The Coming China Wars: Where They Will be Fought and How They Can be Won.* (Upper Saddle River: Pearson Education, 2008) p. 25.

[308] For an extended discussion of this issue, see Robert Reich, *Supercapitalism* (New York, Alfred A. Knopf, 2007), p. 213.

[309] The 2007 figure is 0.8%; author calculation from "Annual Report 2007," Fairtrade Labeling Organizations International, p. 11 and World Food and Agriculture Organization, http://faostat.fao.org/site/567/DesktopDefault.aspx?PageID=567#ancor. There are a few encouraging signs, like Nestlé's recent announcement that it will henceforth make Kit-Kat bars sold in Europe out of fairly traded chocolate.

[310] For core employees at major corporations that have the financial wherewithal to avoid doing so. Different rules apply elsewhere, e.g., in small businesses and low-tier supplier companies.

[311] Clyde V. Prestowitz, Jr., *Trading Places: How We Are Giving Our Future to Japan and How to Reclaim It* (New York: Basic Books, 1993), p. 61.

[312] James Bovard, *The Fair Trade Fraud* (New York: Palgrave Macmillan, 1992), p. 172.

[313] "Key Elements of the AFL-CIO's 301 Petition Regarding Violation of Workers' Rights in China," AFL-CIO, http://www.aflcio.org/issues/jobseconomy/globaleconomy/upload/china_keyelements.pdf.

[314] Testimony of Harry Wu, Executive Director, Laogai Research Foundation, before U.S.-China Economic and Security Review Commission, June 19, 2008.

[315] James O'Toole, "State Looks Like Prime Territory for Clinton," *Pittsburgh Post-Gazette*, March 9, 2008.

[316] "GDP (per capita) (1970) by country," Economy Statistics, http://www.nationmaster.com/red/graph/eco_gdp_percap-economy-gdp-per capita&date=1970.

[317] This is also true of such problems as increasing income inequality in the U.S. The nations of Western Europe, for example, have experienced far less economic polarization in the last 30 years than we have.

[318] Stephen Tokarick, "Quantifying the Impact of Trade on Wages: the Role of Nontraded Goods," International Monetary Fund, 2002, p. 14.

[319] If, of course, we count returns on capital paid to individuals as "wages," and make appropriate adjustment for returns paid outside the country and other conflating factors.

[320] This is true to a first approximation if we ignore various complicated effects involving linkages between traded and nontraded industries.

[321] A good summary of other factors countervailing cheap foreign labor appears in Phillip Blackerby, "We're Moving Overseas! Are We Making a Big Mistake?" Blackerby Associates, 2003, http://www.blackerbyassoc.com/Overseas.html.

[322] Author's extrapolation from first 10 months of 2010; "Trade with Japan," U.S. Bureau of the Census, http://www.census.gov/foreign-trade/balance/c5880.html#2010.

[323] Author's extrapolation from first 10 months of 2010; "Trade with European Union," U.S. Bureau of the Census, http://www.census.gov/foreign-trade/balance/c0003.html#2010.

[324] 1965-2000: *OECD Revenue Statistics 1965-2003* (Paris: Organization for Economic Co-Operation and Development, 2004), Table 12.
2004: "Fundamental Reform of Corporate Income Tax," OECD, 2007, Table 1.12.

[325] The phrase is the title of Chapter 6 of Thomas Friedman's *The Lexus and the Olive Tree: Understanding Globalization* (New York: Farrar, Straus and Giroux, 1999).

[326] "The Global Competitiveness Report 2009-2010," World Economic Forum, 2009, Table 4, http://www.weforum.org/en/initiatives/gcp/Global Competitiveness Report/index.htm.

[327] Dani Rodrik, "Sense and Nonsense in the Globalization Debate," *Foreign Policy*, Summer 1997, p. 26.

[328] This is corroborated by the failure of either Reagan or Thatcher to actually reduce government as a percentage of GDP. It is no accident that America's own welfare state has grown in parallel with freer trade, and that back when the U.S. was a high-tariff economy, the American welfare state was very small.

[329] The reason for this is that if we use the multiple-equilibrium model of international trade explained in Chapter 10, it is obvious that multiple equilibria also apply to economies domestically, so there is no

one ideal economy toward which all developed nations should be expected to converge—even leaving aside issues of different factor endowments, etc.

330 Philip A. Klein, *Economics Confronts the Economy* (Northampton, MA: Edward Elgar, 2006), p. 228.

331 Thomas Friedman, *The Lexus and the Olive Tree* (New York, Anchor Books, 1999), p. 104.

332 According to one estimate, the price difference between a Toyota Corolla or Nissan Sentra sold in Japan, and the same cars sold in the U.S., jumped from about $500 to $3000 after the VRA. See Robert W. Crandall, "Detroit Rode Quotas to Prosperity," *The Wall Street Journal*, January 29, 1986. See also Daniel P. Kaplan, "Has Trade Protection Revitalized Domestic Industries?" Congressional Budget Office, November 1986, p. 86.

333 U.S. International Trade Commission estimate, reported in Daniel P. Kaplan, "Has Trade Protection Revitalized Domestic Industries?" Congressional Budget Office, November 1986, p. 86.

334 Rachel Dardis and Jia-Yeong Lin, "Automobile Quotas Revisited: The Costs of Continued Protection," *Journal of Consumer Affairs,* Winter 1985, p. 19. Also Joshua Yount, "The Voluntary Export Restraint: Bad Medicine for a Sick Patient," *The Park Place Economist*, 1996, p. 24.

335 Blog entry, Bill Testa, "Regional Distribution of Assembly Lines," Federal Reserve Bank of Chicago, http://midwest.chicagofedblogs.org/archives/Auto-Assembly-Table.html.

336 2006 model year, from Thomas H. Klier and James M. Rubinstein, "Whose Part is it? Measuring Domestic Content of Vehicles," Federal Reserve Bank of Chicago, October 2007, p. 1.

337 Wal-Mart pays an average wage of $8.23/hr. "Wal-Martization of Workers' Wages and Overtime Pay," United Food and Commercial Workers, http://www.ufcw.org/press_room/fact_sheets_and_backgrounder/walmart/wages.cfm.

338 Hourly wages for different manufacturing jobs are recorded by the Bureau of Labor Statistics: http://www.bls.gov/oes/2008/may/oes_nat.htm#b51-0000.

339 Author's calculation based on J. Bradford DeLong, "Estimating World GDP, One Million BC – Present," University of California at Berkeley, May 24, 1998, http://econ161.berkeley.edu/TCEH/1998_Draft/World_GDP/Estimating_World_GDP.html.

340 A.G. Kenwood and A.L. Lougheed, *The Growth of the International Economy 1820-1900: An Introductory Text* (New York, Routledge, 1999), p. 79.

341 World GDP (exchange-rate basis) 2008: $61.07 trillion, exports $15.97 trillion, from *CIA World Factbook*, https://www.cia.gov/library/publications/the-world-factbook/geos/xx.html.

342 In the sense that Ricardian tradeoffs define the standard for free trade to be beneficial, so other theories must project outcomes meeting or exceeding this standard if they are to vindicate free trade.

343 "If a foreign country can supply us with a commodity cheaper than we ourselves can make it, better buy it of them with some part of the produce of our own industry, employed in a way in which we have some advantage." Adam Smith, *The Wealth of Nations*, Book IV, Chapter 2.

344 Patrick J. Buchanan, *The Great Betrayal: How American Sovereignty and Social Justice Are Being Sacrificed to the Gods of the Global Economy* (New York: Little, Brown and Co., 1998), p. 67.

345 Paul Krugman wrote an entire essay in 1994, "Ricardo's Difficult Idea," complaining about how hard it is for people to understand it: http://web.mit.edu/krugman/www/ricardo.htm.

346 These are not necessarily the same size units, and prices are left out to keep things simple. The example would work the same way with these complexities added.

347 Absolute advantage is the *difference* in cost for the same product; comparative advantage is the *ratio* of costs for different products.

348 Comparative advantage is so fundamental an economic principle that it applies even outside capitalism; it applied to trade between communist Poland and communist Bulgaria in 1970. The difference is that under communism, there is no free market to make it work automatically thanks to the price system. So central planners must (somehow!) *calculate* the comparative advantages of the trading partners.

349 Ricardo's own example is this: "Two men can both make shoes and hats, and one is superior to the other in both employments; but in making hats he can only exceed his competitor by one-fifth or 20 per cent; and in making shoes he can excel him by one-third or 33 per cent: will it not be in the interest of both that the superior man should employ himself exclusively in making shoes, and the inferior man in making hats?" David Ricardo, *The Principles of Political Economy and Taxation* (Mineola, NY: Dover Publications, 2004), p. 136.

350 Paul A. Samuelson, "Where Ricardo and Mill Rebut and Confirm Arguments of Mainstream Economists Supporting Globalization," *Journal of Economic Perspectives*, Summer 2004, p. 135.

351 Jorge G. Castañeda and Carlos Heredia et al., *The Case Against Free Trade: GATT, NAFTA, and the Globalization of Corporate Power* (San Francisco: Earth Island Press, 1993), p. 87.

352 Danny M. Leipziger, *Lessons From East Asia* (Ann Arbor, MI: University of Michigan Press, 2001), p. 85.

353 The idea that all voluntary exchanges must be mutually beneficial is misleading anyway, because it says nothing about the context of relative bargaining power in which exchanges take place. It may be mutually beneficial for a starving man to sell his shoes!

354 James Bovard, *The Fair Trade Fraud: How Congress Pillages the Consumer and Decimates American Competitiveness.* (New York: Palgrave Macmillan, 1992), p. 5.

355 *Pace,* for now, other criticisms we will examine later.

356 See pp. 46-48.

357 Joseph Kahn & Jim Yardley, "As China Roars, Pollution Reaches Deadly Extremes," *The New York Times*, August 25, 2007, p. A1.

358 There are, of course, countervailing pressures due to pollution costs that cannot be externalized, especially at the level of the national economy as a whole, as opposed to the individual firm. This is why China, for example, appears to be now making some efforts to control pollution. And there are also empirical questions on how strong the pro-pollution incentive is. Nevertheless, the underlying dynamic described here is obviously real, regardless of its size.

359 "Genuine Progress Indicator," Redefining Progress, http://www.rprogress.org/sustainability_indicators/genuine_progress_indicator.htm.

360 John Cavanagh, Jerry Mander et al, *Alternatives to Economic Globalization: A Better World is Possible* (San Francisco: Berrett-Koehler, 2002), p. 204.

361 The commonly quoted figure of $70-$73 per hour for autoworkers includes health benefits and legacy costs. Their cash wages were about $28/hr, plus $2.25 for payroll taxes and $7 for a health insurance package. Source: United Auto Workers.

362 To 33.6 hours by October 2010. "Employment & Earnings, November 2010," Bureau of Labor Statistics, p. 71, http://www.bls.gov/opub/ee/empearn201011.pdf. This does not contradict the fact, noted earlier, that Americans generally work longer hours than workers in other Western developed nations because these other nations have workweeks that are even *shorter* than ours. See "Annual Hours Worked: Per Capita and Per Worker, 2008," Organization for Economic Cooperation and Development, 2009, http://stats.oecd.org/Index.aspx?DataSetCode=ANHRS.

363 World Bank figure, quoted in John MacArthur, *The Selling of Free Trade: NAFTA, Washington, and the Subversion of American Democracy* (New York: Hill & Wang, 2000) p. 81.

364 Sherrod Brown, *Myths of Free Trade: Why America's Trade Policies Have Failed* (New York: The New Press, 2004), p. 137.

365 Lower consumer prices are equivalent to a higher real (inflation-adjusted) wage.

366 When we noted in Chapter 2 that deficit trade costs jobs in the present, these are gross, not net, jobs.

367 Betty McGrath, Employment Security Commission of North Carolina, statement before U.S.-China Economic and Security Review Commission, September 6, 2007, p. 3.

368 Bureau of Labor Statistics, quoted in Louis Uchitelle, "Retraining Laid-Off Workers, But for What?" *The New York Times*, March 26, 2006.

369 Quoted in Robert Kuttner, *Everything for Sale: the Virtues and Limits of Markets* (New York: Knopf, 1997), p. 25.

370 See http://upload.wikimedia.org/wikipedia/en/4/4d/EffectOfTariff.svg.

371 See http://upload.wikimedia.org/wikipedia/commons/0/0a/Actual_potential_GDP_output_gap_CBO_Jan_09_outlook.png

372 See p. 34.

373 Dani Rodrik, *Has Globalization Gone Too Far?* (Washington: Institute for International Economics, 1997), p. 30.

374 See p. 34.

375 It is also the reason why economics recognizes such a subject as international trade, with facts and principles different from domestic economics.

376 David Ricardo, *The Principles of Political Economy and Taxation* (Mineola, NY: Dover Publications, 2004), p. 83.

377 Ibid.

378 In technical terms, there is no theorem guaranteeing that partial-equilibrium losses to import-competing producers are more than offset by gains to consumers due to reduced prices. This problem has been formally modeled in Masao Oda and Robert Stapp, "Factor Mobility, Trade, and Wage Inequality," in Takashi Kamihigashi and Laixun Zhao, eds., *International Trade and Economic Dynamics* (Berlin: Springer, 2008). See also Robert C. Feenstra, *Advanced International Trade* (Princeton, NJ: Princeton University Press, 2004), p. 117.

379 David Ricardo, *The Principles of Political Economy and Taxation* (Mineola, NY: Dover Publications, 2004), p. 83.

380 Lance E. Davis, Robert E. Gallman, *Evolving Financial Markets and International Capital Flows: Britain, the Americas, and Australia, 1865-1914* (Cambridge, UK: Cambridge University Press, 2001), p. 58.

381 Michael Porter, *The Competitive Advantage of Nations* (New York: The Free Press, 1990), p. 21.

382 Nathan Rosenberg, *Inside the Black Box: Technology and Economics.* (New York: Cambridge University Press, 1982), p. 73.

383 Remember that this toy example only works if all trade between Canada and the U.S. is barter of corn and wheat. For a fully computed analysis of this whole problem, see Paul A. Samuelson, "Where Ricardo and Mill Rebut and Confirm Arguments of Mainstream Economists Supporting Globalization," *Journal of Economic Perspectives*, Summer 2004, p. 141.

384 Paul A. Samuelson, "Where Ricardo and Mill Rebut and Confirm Arguments of Mainstream Economists Supporting Globalization," *Journal of Economic Perspectives*, Summer 2004.

385 "International Trade for a Rich Country," lecture before the Swedish-American Chamber of Commerce, New York City, May 10, 1972 (Stockholm: Federation of Swedish Industries pamphlet, 1972). Samuelson won the Nobel Prize in 1970.

386 Ricardo also noted this problem in Chapter 7 of the *Principles* (the main chapter on foreign trade): "England exported cloth in exchange for wine because, by so doing, her industry was rendered more productive to her; she had more cloth and wine than if she had manufactured both for herself; and Portugal imported cloth and exported wine because the industry of Portugal could be more beneficially employed for both countries in producing wine. But let there be more difficulty in England in producing cloth, or in Portugal in producing wine, or let there be more facility in England in producing wine, or in Portugal in producing cloth, and the trade must immediately cease." David Ricardo, *The Principles of Political Economy and Taxation* (Mineola, NY: Dover Publications, 2004), p. 86.

387 Paul Samuelson, "Mathematical Vindication of Ricardo on Machinery," *Journal of Political Economy*, April 1988, p. 21. The actual passages to which Samuelson refers are not quoted here because they are drawn out and abstruse, but may be found in David Ricardo, *The Principles of Political Economy and Taxation* (Mineola, NY: Dover Publications, 2004), pp. 263-271.

388 Assuming nations have different opportunity cost ratios.

389 See p. 230.

390 *Pace,* for now, other problems we will look at later.

391 This is not true *by definition*; it is empirically true most of the time, other things being equal.

392 Stephen Tokarick, "Quantifying the Impact of Trade on Wages: the Role of Nontraded Goods," International Monetary Fund, 2002, p. 14.

393 This phenomenon is familiar domestically, too. The high wage auto industry famously propped up wages in the industrial Midwest for decades during its heyday.

394 See Frank Ackerman, "The Shrinking Gains From Trade: A Critical Assessment of Doha Round Projections," Global Development and Environment Institute, Tufts University, 2005.

395 Ibid., p. 19.

396 That is, prior to the thinking of John Maynard Keynes (1883-1946), the British economist who revolutionized economic theory and practice by understanding how economies do *not* naturally reach an equilibrium of full employment, and how deficit spending can help economies climb out of recessions.

397 Frank Ackerman, "The Shrinking Gains From Trade: A Critical Assessment of Doha Round Projections," Global Development and Environment Institute, Tufts University, 2005.

398 See, for example, Scott Bradford, Paul Grieco, and Gary Clyde Hufbauer, "The Payoff to America from Global Integration," in C. Fred Bergsten, ed., *The United States and the World Economy: Foreign Economic Policy for the Next Decade* (Washington: Institute for International Economics, 2005).

399 Michael Porter, *The Competitive Advantage of Nations* (New York: The Free Press, 1990), p. 12.

400 Most economics PhD programs no longer even require economic history.

401 See, for example, Douglas Irwin on Ha Joon Chang's *Kicking Away the Ladder—Development Strategy in Historical Perspective* (London: Anthem Press, 2002), http://eh.net/bookreviews/library/0777.

402 "About Us," *The Economist*, http://www.economist.com/about/about_economist.cfm.

403 Ha-Joon Chang, *Kicking Away the Ladder: Development Strategy in Historical Perspective* (London: Anthem Press, 2003), pp. 20-22.

404 William Cunningham, *The Rise and Decline of the Free Trade Movement* (London: Cambridge University Press,1914), p. 133.

405 The term England is used to refer to England prior to union with Scotland in 1707.

406 Erik S. Reinert and Arno M. Daastøl, "The Other Canon: The History of Renaissance Economics," p. 34, in Erik S. Reinert, ed., *Globalization, Economic Development and Inequality: An Alternative Perspective* (Cheltenham, UK: Edward Elgar, 2004).

407 Eric Reinert, *How Rich Countries Got Rich and Why Poor Countries Stay Poor* (New York: Carroll & Graf, 2007), p. 79.

408 John M. Culbertson, *The Trade Threat and U.S. Trade Policy* (Madison, WI: 21st Century Press,1989) p. 52.

409 Modern economics, that is, as distinct from the *oikonomia* (literally, household management) of the ancient world and the economic theology of the Middle Ages with its just-price theory, etc.

410 See, for example, the pro-free trade but otherwise fairly wise William Bernstein, *A Splendid Exchange: How Trade Shaped the World* (New York: Atlantic Monthly Press, 2008), p. 257.

411 A good analytical summary of its policies appears in Eric Reinert, *How Rich Countries Got Rich and Why Poor Countries Stay Poor* (New York: Carroll & Graf, 2007), p. 82.

412 Eric Reinert, *How Rich Countries Got Rich and Why Poor Countries Stay Poor* (New York: Carroll & Graf, 2007), p. 87.

413 John Maynard Keynes, *The General Theory of Employment, Interest and Money* (Cambridge, UK: Cambridge University Press, 1936), Chapter 23.

414 Mehdi Shafaeddin, "How Did Developed Countries Industrialize? The History of Trade and Industrial Policy: The Cases of Great Britain and the U.S.A," United Nations Conference on Trade and Development, December 1998, Table 2.

415 This is not to say that this is the only way of dealing with the problem. Export of capital goods can be a good thing if a nation is successfully following a strategy of exporting capital goods.

416 Peter Schweitzer, "On the Other Invisible Hand...Was Adam Smith, Fabled Free Trader, A Crypto-Protectionist?" *The Washington Post*, July 22, 1990. See also Eric Reinert, *How Rich Countries Got Rich and Why Poor Countries Stay Poor* (New York: Carroll & Graf, 2007), p. 133.

[417] Donald Grove Barnes, *A History of the English Corn Laws: From 1660-1846* (Abingdon, UK: Routledge, 2006), p. 291.

[418] Imposing free trade in Britain was an incremental process, with true free trade arguably being attained not before 1860.

[419] Ronald Findlay and Kevin O'Rourke, *Power and Plenty: Trade, War, and the World Economy in the Second Millennium* (Princeton, NJ: Princeton University Press, 2007), p. 330.

[420] See David Cannadine's *The Decline and Fall of the British Aristocracy* (New Haven, CT: Yale University Press, 1990).

[421] William Anthony Lovett, Alfred E. Eckes & Richard L. Brinkman, *U.S. Trade Policy: History, Theory and the WTO* (Armonk, NY: M.E. Sharpe & Co., 1999), p. 3.

[422] Paul Bairoch, *Economics and World History: Myths and Paradoxes* (Chicago: University of Chicago Press, 1993), p. 46.

[423] Lord Goderich during a debate on abrogation of the Treaty of Methuen, as quoted in Giles Badger Stebbins, *The American Protectionist's Manual* (Detroit: Thorndike Nourse, 1883), p. 26.

[424] Peter Matthias et al, *Cambridge Economic History of Europe* (Cambridge, UK: Cambridge University Press, 1989), p. 62.

[425] Kevin O'Rourke, "Tariffs and Growth in the Late 19th Century," *The Economic Journal*, April 2000. O'Rourke calculates that a 10% increase in average tariffs was associated with increased growth of nearly 0.2% a year.

[426] B.R. Mitchell and Phyllis Deane, *Abstract of British Historical Statistics* (Cambridge, UK: Cambridge University Press, 1971), pp. 520-21.

[427] John P. Creegan, *America Asleep: The Free Trade Syndrome and the Global Economic Challenge* (Washington: U.S. Industrial Council Educational Foundation, 1992), p. 59.

[428] John Campbell, *F.E. Smith, First Earl of Birkenhead* (London: J. Cape, 1983), p. 192.

[429] Technically, Chamberlain was a Liberal Unionist, a breakaway faction of the Liberal party that functioned as Conservatives, ultimately merging with them in 1912.

[430] C.W. Boyd, ed., *Mr. Chamberlain's Speeches*, vol. 2 (London: Houghton Mifflin, 1914), p. 428.

[431] Thomas Friedman, *The Lexus and the Olive Tree: Understanding Globalization* (New York: Anchor Books, 1999), p. xvii.

[432] Sonali Deraniyagala and Ben Fine, "New Trade Theory Versus Old Trade Policy: A Continuing Enigma," *Cambridge Journal of Economics*, November 2001, p. 3.

[433] William Cunningham, *The Case Against Free Trade* (London: John Murray, 1911), p. 142.

[434] Walt Whitman Rostow, *The World Economy: History & Prospect* (Austin, TX: University of Texas Press, 1978), Table II-2.

[435] Merrill D. Peterson, *The Jefferson Image in the American Mind* (Charlottesville, VA: University Press of Virginia, 1998), p. 24.

[436] Claude Halstead Van Tyne, *The Causes of the War of Independence* (New York: Houghton Mifflin, 1922), p. 65.

[437] The Tariff Act of 1789 (1 Stat. 24), July 4, 1789.

[438] Alexander Hamilton, *Report on the Subject of Manufactures: Made in His Capacity of Secretary of the Treasury* (Philadelphia: William Brown, 1827), p. 5.

[439] Ibid., pp. 50-61. Explanations adapted from Ha-Joon Chang, *Bad Samaritans: the Myth of Free Trade and the Secret History of Capitalism* (New York: Bloomsbury Press, 2008), p. 232.

[440] Alexander Hamilton, *Report on the Subject of Manufactures: Made in His Capacity of Secretary of the Treasury* (Philadelphia: William Brown, 1827).

[441] Cynthia Clark Northrup, *The American Economy: A Historical Encyclopedia* (Santa Barbara, CA: ABC-CLIO, 2003), p. 233.

[442] Emory R. Johnson et al., *History of the Domestic and Foreign Commerce of the United States* (Washington: Carnegie Institute, 1915), vol. 2, p. 35.

[443] Ha-Joon Chang, *Bad Samaritans: the Myth of Free Trade and the Secret History of Capitalism* (New York: Bloomsbury Press, 2008), p. 51.

[444] President James Buchanan supported tariffs for revenue-raising purposes only, not as a spur to industrial development, which put him on the low-tariff or anti-tariff side of the issue as framed in his day.

[445] Alfred E. Eckes, Jr., *Opening America's Market: U.S. Foreign Trade Since 1776* (Chapel Hill, NC: University of North Carolina Press, 1995), p. 57. Carey was described by Karl Marx as the only important American economist; Marx understood perfectly how tariff-based paternalism threatened his communist alternative.

[446] For a discussion of why a slave-based society has difficulty industrializing in the American context, see Fred Bateman and Thomas Weiss, *A Deplorable Scarcity: The Failure of Industrialization in the Slave Economy* (Chapel Hill, NC: University of North Carolina Press, 2002), p. 29 and following. Not only do slaves adapt poorly to jobs requiring technical skill and self-supervision, but slave-holding elites see new industries (which they cannot themselves enter) as threats to their power and as requiring undesirable social policies such as mass literacy.

[447] Alfred E. Eckes, Jr., *Opening America's Market: U.S. Foreign Trade Since 1776* (Chapel Hill, NC: University of North Carolina Press, 1995), p. 59.

[448] Article I, Section 8, Clause 1.

[449] Eric Reinert, *How Rich Countries Got Rich and Why Poor Countries Stay Poor* (New York: Carroll & Graf, 2007), p. 85.

[450] William Anthony Lovett, Alfred E. Eckes & Richard L. Brinkman, *U.S. Trade Policy: History, Theory and the WTO* (Armonk, NY: M.E. Sharpe & Co., 1999), p. 48.

[451] William Graham Sumner, *Protectionism, the Ism That Teaches That Waste Makes Wealth* (New York: Henry Holt and Co., 1885).

[452] Karl Marx, "Speech to the Democratic Association of Brussels at its Public Meeting of January 9, 1848" in *Marx & Engels Collected Works, Volume 6* (London: International Publishers, 1975), p. 450.

[453] *Congressional Record*, May 6, 1913.

[454] William Graham Sumner, *Protectionism, the Ism That Teaches That Waste Makes Wealth* (New York: Henry Holt and Co., 1885), p. 28.

[455] Alfred E. Eckes, Jr., *Opening America's Market: U.S. Foreign Trade Since 1776* (Chapel Hill, NC: University of North Carolina Press, 1995), p. 46.

[456] Ibid.

[457] William Anthony Lovett, Alfred E. Eckes & Richard L. Brinkman, *U.S. Trade Policy: History, Theory and the WTO* (Armonk, NY: M.E. Sharpe & Co., 1999), p. 49.

[458] Ramesh Ponnuru, "The Full McCain: an Interview," *National Review*, March 5, 2007.

[459] See Chapter 7 of his book with Anna Jacobson Schwartz, *A Monetary History of the United States, 1867-1960*, which was cited in the Nobel presentation speech as part of the reason for his award.

[460] William J. Bernstein, *A Splendid Exchange: How Trade Shaped the World* (New York: Atlantic Monthly Press, 2008), p. 354.

[461] Comparison between trade under the Fordney-McCumber tariff in 1930 and to trade under the Smoot-Hawley tariff in 1931. From Alfred E. Eckes, Jr., *Opening America's Market: U.S. Foreign Trade Since 1776* (Chapel Hill, NC: University of North Carolina Press, 1995), p. 107. The effects of Smoot-Hawley were also blunted by currency depreciation in America's major trading partners.

[462] Alfred Eckes, Jr., *Opening America's Market: U.S. Foreign Trade Policy Since 1776* (Chapel Hill, NC: University of North Carolina Press, 1995), p. 106.

[463] In fact, America cut its tariff just before the recessions of 1857 and 1872. Alfred E. Eckes, Jr., *Opening America's Market: U.S. Foreign Trade Since 1776* (Chapel Hill, NC: University of North Carolina Press, 1995), p. 112.

[464] Peter Temin, *Lessons From the Great Depression* (Cambridge, MA: MIT Press, 1989), p. 46.

[465] Alfred Eckes Jr., quoted in Sherrod Brown, *Myths of Free Trade: Why America's Trade Policies Have Failed* (New York: New Press, 2004), p. 180.

[466] This myth has its origin in the need of supply-side crank economists for an alternative explanation of the Great Depression. Paul Krugman, *Peddling Prosperity: Economic Sense and Nonsense in an Age of Diminished Expectations* (New York: W.W. Norton & Co., 1994), p. 93.

[467] Gertrud Fremling, "Did the United States Transmit the Great Depression to the Rest of the World?" *American Economic Review*, December 1985.

[468] Cordell Hull, *The Memoirs of Cordell Hull* (New York: Macmillan Company, 1948), p. 81.

[469] Cynthia Clark Northrup and Elaine C. Prange Turney, *Encyclopedia of Tariffs and Trade in U.S. History* (Westport, CT: Greenwood Press, 2003) p. 172.

[470] Michael A. Butler, *Cautious Visionary: Cordell Hull and Trade Reform, 1933-1937* (Kent, OH: Kent State University Press, 1998), Chapters 2, 3, 4.

[471] Alfred E. Eckes, Jr., *Opening America's Market: U.S. Foreign Trade Since 1776* (Chapel Hill, NC: University of North Carolina Press, 1995), p. 143.

[472] Nitsan Chorev, *Remaking U.S. Trade Policy: From Protection to Globalization* (Ithaca, NY: Cornell University Press, 2007), p. 57.

[473] Douglas A. Irwin, "The GATT's Contribution to Economic Recovery in Post-War Western Europe," Board of Governors of the Federal Reserve System, March 1993, p. 10.

[474] Trade surplus: E.A. Brett, *The World Economy Since the War*, (Santa Barbara, CA: Praeger Publishers, 1985), p. 106.
GDP: "Gross Domestic Product," Bureau of Economic Analysis, http://www.bea.gov/national/nipaweb/TableView.asp?SelectedTable=5.

[475] Alfred E. Eckes, Jr., *Opening America's Market: U.S. Foreign Trade Since 1776* (Chapel Hill, NC: University of North Carolina Press, 1995), p. xix.

[476] Stephen D. Cohen, Robert A. Blecker, and Peter D. Whitney, *Fundamentals of U.S. Foreign Trade Policy: Economics, Politics, Laws, and Issues* (Boulder, CO: Westview Press, 2003), p. 36.

[477] Eric Reinert, *How Rich Countries Got Rich and Why Poor Countries Stay Poor* (New York: Carroll & Graf, 2007), p. 180.

[478] Alfred Eckes, Jr., *Opening America's Market: U.S. Foreign Trade Policy Since 1776* (Chapel Hill, NC: University of North Carolina Press, 1995), p. 158

[479] Unpublished pages from "memoirs," Truman Library, Independence, Missouri, quoted in Alfred E. Eckes, Jr., *U.S. Trade Policy: History, Theory, and the WTO* (Armonk, NY: M.E. Sharpe, 2004), p. 62.

[480] The phrase is from a famous speech by Soviet Premier Nikita Khrushchev in 1956.

[481] In the words of historian and former chairman of the U.S. International Trade Commission Alfred Eckes, "Viewed from a historical perspective, the Kennedy Round was a watershed. In each of the se-

venty-four years from 1893 to 1967 the United States ran a merchandise trade surplus (exports of goods exceeded imports). During the 1967-72 implementation period for Kennedy Round concessions, the U.S. trade surplus vanished and a sizable deficit emerged." From Alfred E. Eckes, Jr., *Opening America's Market: U.S. Foreign Trade Policy Since 1776*. (Chapel Hill, NC: University of North Carolina Press, 1995), p.202.

[482] Alfred E. Eckes, Jr., *U.S. Trade Policy: History, Theory, and the WTO* (Armonk, NY: M.E. Sharpe, 2004), p. 204.

[483] Ibid., p. 197.

[484] Galbraith to Johnson, March 11, 1964, White House Central File, Lyndon B. Johnson Library, Austin, TX, quoted in Alfred E. Eckes, Jr., *Opening America's Market: U.S. Foreign Trade Policy Since 1776*. (Chapel Hill, NC: University of North Carolina Press, 1995), p. 202.

[485] "U.S. International Transactions Accounts Data," Bureau of Economic Analysis, http://www.bea.gov/international/xls/table1.xls.

[486] Interview, "Fritz Hollings on How to Make Government Work for American Manufacturers," *Manufacturing & Technology News*, August 29, 2008, p. 8.

[487] Lewis Branscomb, ed., *Empowering Technology: Implementing a U.S. Strategy* (Cambridge, MA: MIT Press, 1993), p. 64.

[488] The aim was to force other nations to revalue their currencies to save the Bretton Woods system of fixed exchange rates. This happened, resulting in the Smithsonian Agreement of 1971—which collapsed shortly thereafter due to domestic economic problems in the U.S. Cynthia Northrup, *The American Economy: A Historical Encyclopedia*, (Santa Barbara, CA: ABC-CLIO, 2003), p. 260.

[489] John B. Judis, *The Paradox of American Democracy* (New York: Routledge, 2001), p. 114.

[490] Nitsan Chorev, *Remaking U.S. Trade Policy: From Protection to Globalization*. (Ithaca, NY: Cornell University Press, 2007), p. 89.

[491] The VRA was instigated at the end of the Carter administration, but Reagan chose to go through with it.

[492] For a list of Reagan's protectionist acts, see Sheldon L. Richman, "Ronald Reagan: Protectionist," *The Free Market*, May 1988.

[493] William Anthony Lovett, Alfred E. Eckes and Richard L. Brinkman, *U.S. Trade Policy: History, Theory and the WTO* (Armonk, NY: M.E. Sharpe & Co., 1999), p. 149.

[494] See Eamonn Fingleton, *Blindside: Why Japan is Still on Track to Overtake the U.S. by the Year 2000* (New York: Houghton Mifflin, 1995) or Robert Locke, "Japan, Refutation of Neoliberalism," *Post-Autistic Economics Review*, January 2004.

[495] Kozo Yamamura, "Caveat Emptor: the Industrial Policy of Japan" in Paul Krugman, ed., *Strategic Trade Policy and the New International Economics* (Cambridge, MA: MIT Press, 1987), p. 177.

[496] Transcription from Meeting, March 26, 1955, International Trade Files, RG 43, National Archives; quoted in William A. Lovett, Alfred E. Eckes, Jr. and Richard L. Brinkman, *U.S. Trade Policy: History, Theory, and the WTO* (Armonk, NY: M.E. Sharpe, 2004), p. 64.

[497] UBS and Goldman Sachs' internal estimates are that the average cost of capital in Japan is about 4%, vs. 8% in the U.S. See Robertson Morrow, "The Bull Market in Politics," Clarium Capital Management, February 2008, p. 10.

[498] "2008 Production Statistics," International Organization of Motor Vehicle Manufacturers, http://oica.net/2008-production-statistics.

[499] This is used as a not-unjustified term of convenience, not as a detailed cultural analysis.

[500] Roy Hofheinz, Jr. and Kent E. Calder, *The Eastasia Edge* (New York: Basic Books, 1982) p. 46.

[501] 2007 figure, excluding enterprises with annual sales below 5 million renminbi. Ligang Song and Wing Thye Woo, eds., *China's Dilemma: Economic Growth, the Environment and Climate Change* (Washington: Brookings Institution Press, 2008), p. 164. For an analysis of the enduring significance of state-owned enterprises in China, see Xiao Geng, Xiuke Yang, and Anna Janus, "State-owned Enterprises in China: Reform Dynamics and Impacts," *in China's New Place in a World in Crisis: Economic, Geopolitical and Environmental Dimensions* (Canberra: Australian National University Press, 2009).

[502] Mikael Mattlin, "Chinese Strategic State-owned Enterprises and Ownership Control," Brussels Institute of Contemporary China Studies, p. 13.

[503] Kaname Akamatsu, "A Historical Pattern of Economic Growth in Developing Countries," *Journal of Developing Economies*, March-August 1962. Also see http://www.bookrags.com/wiki/Flying_Geese_Paradigm for a summary of different forms of this concept.

[504] The exact quote is: "Yet there is a dirty little secret in international trade analysis. The measurable costs of protectionist policies—the reductions in real income that can be attributed to tariffs and import quotas—are not all that large." Paul Krugman, "Dutch Tulips and Emerging Markets: Another Bubble Bursts," *Foreign Affairs*, July/August 1995. Krugman has identified some exceptions to free trade that he accepts, such as environmental externalities; see his blog entry of June 26, 2009, http://krugman.blogs.nytimes.com/2009/06/26/the-wto-is-making-sense/. See also arch-free trader Jagdish Bhagwati: "Ever since the Harberger-Johnson estimates of the cost of protection, measured as the deadweight losses (the so-called Harberger triangles) that typically ran at 2-3 percent of GDP, there has been a sense that, even if free trade is the best policy, protection is not anything you need to worry about too much since the cost of it is rather small," in Jagdish Bhagwati, *Free Trade Today* (Princeton, NJ: Princeton University Press, 2002), p. 33.

[505] This is not intended to be a literal demonstrative economic argument, only an illustration to establish intuitive plausibility.

[506] "Gross Domestic Product," Bureau of Economic Analysis, http://www.bea.gov/newsreleases/international/trade/trad_time_series.xls.

[507] Excepting microstates Aruba, Bermuda, and Monaco. "GDP, Per Capita GDP - US Dollars," National Accounts Main Aggregates Database, United Nations Statistics Division, http://unstats.un.org/unsd/snaama/selbasicFast.asp, accessed January 15, 2010.

[508] "The Economic Effects of Significant U.S Import Restraints: Fifth Update 2007," United States International Trade Commission, February 2007, p. xvii.

[509] "2008 Industry Review," National Confectioners Association, p. 23, http://www.candyusa.com/files/2008_Annual_%20Review.ppt.

[510] $811 million, from "The Economic Effects of Significant U.S Import Restraints: Fifth Update 2007," United States International Trade Commission, February 2007, p. xxiii.

[511] See, for example, Kym Anderson, Will Martin, and Dominique van der Mensbrughe, "Doha Policies: Where are the Pay-offs?" in Richard Newfarmer, ed., *Trade, Doha, and Development: A Window into the Issues* (Washington: World Bank Publications, 2005).

[512] Frank Ackerman, "The Shrinking Gains From Trade: A Critical Assessment of Doha Round Projections," Global Development and Environment Institute, Tufts University, 2005, p. 2.

[513] Ibid.

[514] Ibid., p. 8.

[515] Both models use the same raw data from GTAP.

[516] Frank Ackerman, "The Shrinking Gains From Trade: A Critical Assessment of Doha Round Projections," Global Development and Environment Institute, Tufts University, 2005, p. 3. There is a 2008 GTAP database, but no model has yet been generated from it.

[517] "Fortune 500 2009," *Fortune*, May 4, 2009.

[518] Frank Ackerman, "The Shrinking Gains From Trade: A Critical Assessment of Doha Round Projections," Global Development and Environment Institute, Tufts University, 2005, p. 8.

[519] Ibid., p. 5.

[520] Ibid., p. 9.

[521] Ibid., p. 5.

[522] Mark Weisbrot, David Rosnick and Dean Baker, "Poor Numbers: The Impact of Trade Liberalization on World Poverty," Center for Economic and Policy Research, 2004, p. 6.

[523] The logic we examined in Chapter 5, according to which any nation, no matter how rich or poor, can realize gains from trade runs afoul of the various flaws in the theory of comparative advantage noted in that chapter. This logic also does not guarantee that gains from trade will clear the hurdle imposed by transaction costs, which include everything from transportation to political corruption. Therefore it is entirely possible for some nations to derive no benefit from trade in practice.

[524] Frank Ackerman, "The Shrinking Gains From Trade: A Critical Assessment of Doha Round Projections," Global Development and Environment Institute, Tufts University, 2005, p. 7.

[525] See, for example, Rajesh Makwana, "Reforming International Trade," Share the World's Resources, February 2006.

[526] Robin Broad and John Cavanagh, "Global Economic Apartheid," in John Cavanagh, Jerry Mander et al., *Alternatives to Economic Globalization: A Better World is Possible* (San Francisco: Berrett-Koehler, 2002), p. 34.

[527] "2008 World Development Indicators: Poverty Data Supplement," The World Bank, 2008, p. 10.

[528] Ibid., p. 11.

[529] There is some evidence that Cuba, though not North Korea, has actually performed better than conventional GDP measures suggest.

[530] "The human poverty index is just under 20% in coastal provinces, but more than 50% in inland Guizhou," per "Human Development Report 1999," United Nations Development Programme, p. 3.

[531] Statement of Joshua Muldavin, Hearing on "Major Internal Challenges Facing the Chinese Leadership" before the U.S.–China Economic and Security Review Commission, U.S. House of Representatives, February 2-3, 2006, p. 95.

[532] Theo Sommer, "Is the 21st Century Going to be the Asian Century," *Asien*, July 2006, p. 74.

[533] Statement of Joshua Muldavin, Hearing on "Major Internal Challenges Facing the Chinese Leadership" before the U.S.–China Economic and Security Review Commission, U.S. House of Representatives, February 2-3, 2006, p. 95.

[534] Branko Milanovic, *Worlds Apart: Measuring International and Global Inequality* (Princeton, NJ: Princeton University Press, 2005), p. 78.

[535] Ricardo Hausmann and Dani Rodrik, "Doomed to Choose: Industrial Policy as Predicament," John F. Kennedy School of Government, Harvard University, 2006, p. 3.

[536] Kevin Watkins, ed., "Human Development Report 2005," United Nations Development Programme, 2005, p. 37.

[537] Branko Milanovic, *Worlds Apart: Measuring International and Global Inequality* (Princeton, NJ: Princeton University Press, 2007), p. 47.

[538] Ibid., p. 61.

[539] Syed Mansoob Murshed, "The Conflict–Growth Nexus and the Poverty of Nations," Institute of Social Studies, 2007, p. 2.

[540] Eric S. Reinert, *How Rich Countries Got Rich and Why Poor Countries Stay Poor* (New York: Carroll & Graf, 2007), pp. 161-4.

[541] Ibid.

[542] Ibid., pp. 161-4, 183.

[543] Jose Antonio Ocampo, Jomo K.S. and Rob Vos, *Explaining Growth Divergences* (New York: Zed Books, 2007), p. 161.

[544] John Cavanagh, Jerry Mander et al., *Alternatives to Economic Globalization: A Better World is Possible* (San Francisco: Berrett-Koehler, 2002), p. 214.

[545] Eric Reinert, "International Trade and the Economic Mechanisms of Underdevelopment," PhD diss., Cornell University, 1980.

[546] Years 1990-3. "Trade with Canada: 1990, 1991, 1992, 1993," U.S. Census Bureau, http://www.census.gov/foreign-trade/balance/c1220.html#1990.

[547] "Trade with Canada: 2006," Census Bureau, www.census.gov/foreign-trade/balance/c1220.html#2006.

[548] "Trade with Mexico: 1993," Census Bureau, www.census.gov/foreign-trade/balance/c2010.html#1993.

[549] "Trade with Mexico: 2010," Census Bureau, www.census.gov/foreign-trade/balance/c2010.html#2010.

[550] Based on the number of workers certified as displaced by imports by the NAFTA Transitional Adjustment Assistance (NAFTA-TAA) program. See Gary Clyde Hufbauer and Jeffrey Schott, *NAFTA Revisited: Achievements and Challenges* (Washington: Institute for International Economics, 2005) p. 41.

[551] Bruce Campbell, Carlos Salas, and Robert E. Scott, Economic Policy Institute, "NAFTA at Seven: Its Impact on the Workers in all Three Nations," Economic Policy Institute, April 2001.

[552] *Business Mexico*, April 1997.

[553] John R. MacArthur, *The Selling of "Free Trade": NAFTA, Washington, and the Subversion of American Democracy* (New York: Hill and Wang, 2000), p. 81.

[554] Paul Krugman, "The Uncomfortable Truth about NAFTA: It's Foreign Policy, Stupid," *Foreign Affairs*, November 1993.

[555] Ibid.

[556] Paul Krugman, "How is NAFTA Doing? It's Been Hugely Successful—As a Foreign Policy," *The New Democrat*, May/June 1996.

[557] Joseph Stiglitz, *Making Globalization Work* (New York: W.W. Norton & Co., 2006), p. 64.

[558] Ibid.

[559] Stiglitz, Joseph, "The Broken Promise of NAFTA," *The New York Times,* Jan 6, 2004.

[560] John H. Christman, "Mexico's Maquiladora Industry Outlook: 2004-2009 And Its Future Impact on the Border Economy," Global Insight, Inc., December 3, 2004, p. 5.

[561] Demetrios Papademetriou, John Audley, Sandra Polaski, and Scott Vaughan, "NAFTA's Promise and Reality: Lessons from Mexico for the Hemisphere," Carnegie Endowment for International Peace, November 2003, p. 20.

[562] Mexican farmers produce maize at 4 cents/lb, vs. 6 cents/lb for American farmers. But American maize is subsidized down to 3 cents/lb. Craig Sams, "Subsidized Theft," *Resurgence*, May/June 2006, p. 14.

[563] Examples include Richard Mills of the U.S. Trade Representative's office (*Washington Post*, Letters, July 28, 2001) and Robert Zoellick, currently president of the World Bank and then U.S. Trade Representative in "Countering Terror With Trade," *Washington Post*, September 20, 2001, p. A35.

[564] John MacArthur, *The Selling of Free Trade: NAFTA, Washington, and the Subversion of American Democracy* (New York: Hill & Wang, 2000), pp. 257, 264, 275.

[565] Bruce Campbell, Carlos Salas, Robert E. Scott, "NAFTA at Seven," Economic Policy Institute, p. 19.

[566] Joseph Stiglitz, *Making Globalization Work* (New York: W.W. Norton & Co., 2006), p. 65.

[567] Ralph Nader, William Greider et al., *The Case Against Free Trade: GATT, NAFTA and the Globalization of Corporate Power* (San Francisco: Earth Island Press,1993), p. 211.

[568] "Trade in Goods (Imports, Exports and Trade Balance) with Singapore," Census Bureau, 2009, http://www.census.gov/foreign-trade/balance/c5590.html.

[569] "U.S. FTAs," Bilaterals.org, http://www.bilaterals.org/rubrique.php3?id_rubrique=55.

[570] Ibid.

[571] Peter Ping Li and Steven Tung-Lung Chang, "The Effect of Property Rights on International Joint Ventures in China," in Ilan Alon, ed., *Chinese Culture, Organizational Behavior, and International Business Management* (Westport, CT: Praeger, 2003).

[572] India's global trade is still disproportionately small relative to India's size, and it still maintains relatively high tariffs. For its tariffs, see *2009 National Trade Estimate Report on Foreign Trade Barriers* (Washington: Office of the United States Trade Representative, 2009), p. 235.

[573] Dani Rodrik & Francisco Rodriguez and Dani Rodrik, "Trade Policy and Economic Growth: A Skeptic's Guide to the Cross-National Evidence," in Ben Bernanke and Kenneth S. Rogoff, eds., *Macroeconomics Annual 2000* (Cambridge, MA: MIT Press, 2001), pp. 261-325.

[574] "World Development Indicators Database," World Bank, April 2009, http://ddp-ext.worldbank.org/ext/ddpreports/ViewSharedReport?REPORT_ID=9147&REQUEST_TYPE=VIEWADVANCED.

[575] Edsel Beja, "Things are Different When You Open Up: Economic Openness, Domestic Economy, and Income," Manila University, January 2009.

[576] Jose Antonio Ocampo, Jomo K.S. and Rob Vos, *Explaining Growth Divergences* (New York: Zed Books, 2007) p. 174.

[577] Dani Rodrik, *One Economics, Many Recipes* (Princeton, NJ: Princeton University Press, 2008) p. 217, based on Dollar and Kraay 2000 dataset.

[578] David N. DeJong and Marl Ripoli also report that "we find no evidence globally of a negative relationship between growth and the trade barrier we measure directly," in "Tariffs and Growth: An Empirical Exploration of Contingent Relationships," *The Review of Economics and Statistics*, October 2006.

[579] Kevin Watkins and Penny Fowler, *Rigged Rules and Double Standards* (Oxford, UK: Oxfam International, 2002) p.5.

[580] Joseph Stiglitz, *Making Globalization Work* (New York: W.W. Norton & Co., 2006), p. 78.

[581] Martin Wolf, *Why Globalization Works* (New Haven, CT: Yale University Press, 2004), p. 213.

[582] Calculated on a purchasing-power parity basis to remove distortions due to exchange rates, figures from Graham Dunkley, *Free Trade: Myth, Reality, and Alternatives.* (New York: Zed Books, 2004), p. 195.

[583] Ibid.

[584] John MacArthur, *The Selling of Free Trade: NAFTA, Washington, and the Subversion of American Democracy* (New York: Hill & Wang, 2000), p. 135.

[585] See Chapter 11 of NAFTA, for example.

[586] Public goods are goods, like national security, that cannot be provided on an individual basis.

[587] John Cavanagh, Jerry Mander et al., *Alternatives to Economic Globalization: A Better World is Possible* (San Francisco: Berrett-Koehler, 2002), p. 23.

[588] Jorge G. Castaneda and Carlos Heredia et al., *The Case Against Free Trade: GATT, NAFTA, and the Globalization of Corporate Power* (San Francisco: Earth Island Press, 1993), p. 25.

[589] The U.S. maintains retaliatory tariffs on Dijon mustard, Roquefort cheese, and truffles worth more than $125 million per year.

[590] The Lome Convention was replaced by the Cononou Agreement in 2000. This imposed more conditions on recipient nations and was organized as a set of trade and cooperation pacts with individual countries.

[591] "The WTO Erodes Human Rights Protections: Three Case Studies," Global Exchange, November 15, 1999.

[592] Ross Perot and Pat Choate, *Save Your Job, Save Our Country* (New York: Hyperion, 1993), p. 20.

[593] Despite the fact that since 1960 it has ratified over 25 treaties on subjects as sensitive as nuclear arms without doing so.

[594] As Cyrill Siewert, CFO of Colgate-Palmolive, put it, "The United States does not have an automatic call on our resources. There is no mindset that puts this country first." Louis Uchitelle, "U.S. Businesses Loosen Link to Mother Country," *The New York Times*, May 21, 1989.

[595] Ha-Joon Chang, *Bad Samaritans: the Myth of Free Trade and the Secret History of Capitalism* (New York: Bloomsbury Press, 2008), p. 36.

[596] William Greider, "The Battle Beyond Seattle," *The Nation*, December 9, 1999.

[597] U.S. Department of State, "North American Free Trade Agreement," December 17, 1992, Article 104, Section 1. Two less important American agreements, one with Mexico and one with Canada, also enjoy protection.

[598] Peter Dauvergne and Jennifer Clapp, *Paths to a Green World: The Political Economy of the Global Environment* (Cambridge, MA: MIT Press, 2005), p. 146.

[599] "Ardent Foes of Trade Promotion Authority Begin to Make Their Case With Congress," *Manufacturing & Technology News*, February 23, 2007, p.1.

[600] Gary Clyde Hufbauer and Diana Orejas, "NAFTA and the Environment: Lessons for Trade Policy," Speech delivered at The Bildner Center, New York, February 28, 2001.

[601] John Cavanagh, Jerry Mander et al., *Alternatives to Economic Globalization: A Better World is Possible* (San Francisco: Berrett-Koehler, 2002), p. 76.

[602] Which reads, "This Constitution, and the Laws of the United States which shall be made in Pursuance thereof; and all Treaties made, or which shall be made, under the Authority of the United States, shall be the supreme Law of the Land; and the Judges in every State shall be bound thereby, any Thing in the Constitution or Laws of any State to the Contrary notwithstanding." State laws are overruled no matter when they were made; Federal laws are only overruled if made before the treaty.

[603] Tibet.

[604] Ennio Rodriguez and Stephany Griffith-Jones, *Cross-Conditionality, Banking Regulation and Third World Debt* (Basingstoke, UK: Palgrave MacMilllan, 1992).

[605] Refusal of loans: Ennio Rodriguez and Stephany Griffith-Jones, *Cross-Conditionality, Banking Regulation and Third World Debt* (Basingstoke, UK: Palgrave MacMilllan, 1992).
Withdrawal of aid: Kanaga Raja, "North Tactics to Split Developing Country Alliances Exposed," *Third World Network*, July 26, 2004.

[606] Joseph Stiglitz, *Making Globalization Work* (New York: W.W. Norton & Co., 2006), p. 321.

[607] Vandana Shiva, *Stolen Harvest* (New York: Zed Books, 2001), pp. 85, 89.

[608] Randeep Ramesh, "India Moves to Protect Traditional Medicines From Foreign Patents," *The Guardian*, February 22, 2009.

[609] Robert Weissman and James Love, "U.S.-Chile Free Trade Agreement," Press Release, Health Gap Global Access Project, January 29, 2001, http://www.healthgap.org/press_releases/01/012901_EA

_CPT_TRADE_CHILE.html.

[610] Rohit Malpani and Mohga Kamal-Yanni, "Patents Versus Patients: Five Years After the Doha Declaration," Oxfam International, November 14, 2006.

[611] William Anthony Lovett, Alfred E. Eckes & Richard L. Brinkman, *U.S. Trade Policy: History, Theory and the WTO* (Armonk, NY: M.E. Sharpe & Co., 1999), p. 178.

[612] Ibid., p. 141.

[613] This includes not only the groups named, but various institutional predecessors. John Cavanagh, Jerry Mander et al., *Alternatives to Economic Globalization: A Better World is Possible* (San Francisco: Berrett-Koehler, 2002), p. 226.

[614] Edward F. Buffie, *Trade Policy in Developing Countries* (Cambridge, UK: Cambridge University Press, 2001), Ch. 9.

[615] William Greider, *One World, Ready or Not* (New York: Touchstone Press, 1997) p. 362.

[616] Jose Antonio Ocampo, Jomo K.S. and Rob Vos, *Explaining Growth Divergences* (New York: Zed Books, 2007), p. 3.

[617] Nitsan Chorev, *Remaking U.S. Trade Policy: From Protection to Globalization* (Ithaca, NY: Cornell University Press, 2007), p. 163.

[618] Testimony of Robert E. Lighthizer, hearing on "Trade Enforcement for a 21st Century Economy," Finance Committee, U.S Senate, June 12, 2007.

[619] For example, it ruled against zeroing in antidumping cases; deemed America's "foreign sales corporation" provision an export subsidy; and repudiated the Uruguay Round understanding that it would generally defer to national authorities in dumping cases.

[620] Dumping is when foreign producers sell products in the U.S. at below production cost, or below their home-market price, in order to drive American producers out of the U.S. market.

[621] "EU Commission Puts Forward Proposal for Sanctions Against U.S. Byrd Amendment," Delegation of the European Commission to the U.S.A, March 31, 2005.

[622] A few token protests were allowed.

[623] Though these words are actually a misquotation when attributed to former WTO Director General Renato Ruggerio. Bernard M. Hoekman, *The Political Economy of the World Trading System*, 2nd ed. (New York: Oxford University Press, 2001), p. 3.

[624] Estimate of Lawrence B. Krause, University of California at San Diego, quoted in William Greider, *One World, Ready or Not* (New York: Touchstone Press, 1997), p. 137.

[625] Jan Orbie, *Europe's Global Role* (London: Ashgate Publishing, 2008), p. 58.

[626] Offset deals can also include coproduction, licensed production, subcontracting deals, technology transfers, directed investment, and export promotion.

[627] Article IV, revised, which went into effect in 1978.

[628] "Auto bailouts in the United States and elsewhere largely fall within the purview of the WTO definition of actionable subsidies." This is the conclusion, with much obfuscation, of Claire Brunel and Gary Clyde Hufbauer, "Money for the Auto Industry: Consistent With WTO Rules?" Peterson Institute for International Economics, February 2009, p. 10.

[629] Worldwide average: "Border Tax Equity Act: Legislative Overview," Coalition for VAT Fairness, http://www.bordertaxequity.org/.
EU average: "The Border Tax Equity Act: VAT - The Problem," National Textile Association, http://www.nationaltextile.org/VAT/problem.htm.

[630] Alfred E. Eckes, Jr., *Opening America's Market: U.S. Foreign Trade Since 1776* (Chapel Hill, NC: University of North Carolina Press, 1995), p. xvi.

[631] Jeff Garten, "Business and Foreign Policy," *Foreign Affairs,* May/June 1997, pp. 70-71.

[632] William Greider, *One World, Ready or Not* (New York: Touchstone Press, 1997), p. 188.

[633] Ibid. p. 139.

[634] Interview "Behind the Sound Bites of Republican Presidential Hopeful Rep. Duncan Hunter: U.S. Multinationals Have Become Chinese Corporations," *Manufacturing & Technology News,* March 13, 2007, p. 1.

[635] William Anthony Lovett, Alfred E. Eckes and Richard L. Brinkman, *U.S. Trade Policy: History, Theory and the WTO* (Armonk, NY: M.E. Sharpe and Co., 1999), p. 139.

[636] Sherrod Brown, *Myths of Free Trade: Why America's Trade Policies Have Failed* (New York: The New Press, 2004), p. 19.

[637] William Greider, *One World, Ready or Not* (New York: Touchstone Press, 1997), p. 192.

[638] See p. 131.

[639] William Greider, *One World, Ready or Not* (New York: Touchstone Press, 1997), p. 132.

[640] Ross Perot and Pat Choate, *Save Your Job, Save Our Country* (New York: Hyperion, 1993), p. 19.

[641] Nitsan Chorev, *Remaking U.S. Trade Policy: From Protection to Globalization* (Ithaca, NY: Cornell University Press, 2007), pp. 112, 137.

[642] U.S. Senate, Committee on Finance, *Trade Reform Act of 1974*, pp.94-95; Public Law 93-618.

[643] "United States Promotes Development Through Aid for Trade," Press Release, United States Trade Representative, December 16, 2008.

[644] William Greider, *One World, Ready or Not* (New York: Touchstone Press, 1997), p. 189.

[645] Eamonn Fingleton, *Blindside: Why Japan is Still on Track to Overtake the U.S. by the Year 2000* (New York: Houghton Mifflin, 1995), p. 47.

[646] "Trade with Japan: 2000," U.S. Census Bureau, http://www.census.gov/foreign-trade/balance/c5880. html#2000 and "Trade with Japan: 2009," U.S. Census Bureau, http://www.census.gov/foreign-trade/balance/c5880.html#2009.

[647] Even if the reality is only 99% or 98% free trade, the underlying logic turns upon the idea of 100% free trade.

[648] One can, of course, argue that free trade in goods and free movement of capital are different issues, as does Jagdish Bhagwati in *Free Trade Today* (Princeton, NJ: Princeton University Press, 2002), p. 10. But free movement of goods, without free movement of the money to pay for them, is only "free" trade in a pedantic sense: it is like freedom to shop without freedom to pay.

[649] "Explaining the Mystery," *The Economist*, January 4, 1992.

[650] Jean Imbs & Romain Wacziarg, "Stages of Diversification," *American Economic Review*, March 2003. Also see Bailey Klinger & Daniel Lederman, "Diversification, Innovation, and Imitation Inside the Global Technological Frontier," World Bank, 2006.

[651] Dani Rodrik, *One Economics, Many Recipes* (Princeton, NJ: Princeton University Press, 2008), p. 103.

[652] "Precisely because economic theory is concerned with static equilibrium, not with the dynamics of development, it is hard to find within traditional theory a basis on which a systematic and positive policy for competitiveness or development can be built." Stephen S. Cohen and John Zysman, *Manufacturing Matters: The Myth of the Post-Industrial Economy* (New York: Basic Books, 1988), p. 214.

[653] Michael Porter, *The Competitive Advantage of Nations* (New York: The Free Press, 1990), p. 103.

[654] Ibid., p. 139.

[655] These externalities extend far beyond technology per se. See Porter, *The Competitive Advantage of Nations* (New York: The Free Press, 1990), p. 144. Further evidence that location-specific externalities exist is the fact that industries often cluster in specific cities or regions, a strategy deliberately employed by China today in the form of the "network clustering" mentioned in the table on p. 76.

[656] See Michael Porter, *The Competitive Advantage of Nations* (New York: The Free Press, 1990) p. 153 concerning *keiretsus*, p. 446 concerning Italy, and p. 472 concerning *chaebols*. Conglomerates have suffered a poor reputation in the U.S. in recent years. This is mainly due to the fact that the U.S. conglomerates such as ITT and Gulf+Western were not deliberately run to exploit these externalities. Those that have been, such as GE and 3M, have actually been very successful: note as one case GE's use of digital imaging technology from one of its military divisions, to take the CAT scanner market from EMI.

[657] American venture capital firms have an extremely hard time functioning beyond a five-year time horizon.

[658] Richard J. Elkus, *Winner Take All: How Competitiveness Shapes the Fate of Nations* (New York: Basic Books, 2008), p. 67.

[659] Clyde Prestowitz, *Trading Places: How We Are Giving Our Future to Japan and How to Reclaim It* (New York: Basic Books, 1993), pp. 139-141.

[660] Technically, of course, Ricardian comparative advantage is not a growth model at all like, say, the Solow growth model. But if it doesn't advise on how to obtain growth, it lacks policy relevance.

[661] Lester Thurow, "Microchips, Not Potato Chips," *Foreign Affairs*, July/August 1994.

[662] Laura D'Andrea Tyson, *Who's Bashing Whom? Trade Conflict in High-Technology Industries* (Washington: Institute for International Economics, 1993), p. 12.

[663] Stephen S. Cohen and John Zysman, *Manufacturing Matters: The Myth of the Post-Industrial Economy* (New York: Basic Books, 1988), p. 216.

[664] Paul Krugman, *Rethinking International Trade* (Cambridge, MA: MIT Press, 1994), p. 157.

[665] Strictly speaking, the theory of comparative advantage finesses this problem by treating comparative advantage as exogenous, i.e., as a given. This is logically coherent but renders the theory useless for determining how to *obtain* the best comparative advantage.

[666] Eric S. Reinert, *How Rich Countries Got Rich and Why Poor Countries Stay Poor* (New York: Carroll & Graf, 2007).

[667] Ricardo Hausmann, Jason Hwang, and Dani Rodrik, "What You Export Matters" Center for International Development, Harvard University, March 2006. The caveat, of course, is that the exporting industries have to be genuine viable industries, not hothouse flowers permanently dependent upon subsidies.

[668] Ricardo Hausmann and Dani Rodrik, "Doomed to Choose: Industrial Policy as Predicament," John F. Kennedy School of Government, Harvard University, p. 6.

[669] Hausmann, Ricardo, Jason Hwang, and Dani Rodrik, "What You Export Matters," *Journal of Economic Growth*, March 2007.

[670] John M. Culbertson, *The Trade Threat and U.S. Trade Policy* (Madison, WI: 21st Century Press,1989), p. 72.

[671] Eric S. Reinert, *How Rich Countries Got Rich and Why Poor Countries Stay Poor* (New York: Carroll & Graf, 2007), p. 262.

[672] For details, see William Easterly, *The Elusive Quest for Growth: Economists' Adventures and Misadventures in the Tropics* (Cambridge, MA: MIT Press, 2002), p. 49.

[673] "The Facts About Modern Manufacturing," 2002 data, per National Association of Manufacturers, 7th ed., October 2, 2006, Section 2, p. 24.

[674] Laura D'Andrea Tyson, *Who's Bashing Whom? Trade Conflict in High-Technology Industries,* (Washington: Institute for International Economics, 1992), p. 32.

[675] Strictly speaking, rent is any return to a factor of production above the amount required to cause that factor to participate in that production. As returns in a pure free market will be competed down to that minimum, anything above that is rent.

[676] Erik S. Reinert, "Competitiveness and its Predecessors—a 500-year Cross-National Perspective," STEP Centre for Innovation Research, p. 5.

[677] Michael Porter, *The Competitive Advantage of Nations* (New York: The Free Press, 1990), p. 89.

[678] This now unfashionable term derives from economist John Kenneth Galbraith in his 1952 book, *American Capitalism: the Concept of Countervailing Power* (Boston: Houghton Mifflin, 1952).

[679] The importance of this fact was noted by Adam Smith (and quoted by Ricardo): "The desire for food is limited in every man by the narrow capacity of the human stomach, but the desire of the conveniences and ornaments of building, dress, equipage, and household furniture, seems to have no limit or boundary." Adam Smith, *The Wealth of Nations*, Book. I, Chapter XI, Part II, quoted in David Ricardo, *On the Principles of Political Economy and Taxation*, Chapter 21.

[680] See Hans Singer, "The Distribution of Gains Between Investing and Borrowing Countries," *American Economic Review*, May 1950; Raúl Prebisch, *The Economic Development of Latin America and its Principal Problems* (Lake Success, NY: United Nations Department of Economic Affairs, 1950).

[681] *Board of Trade Journal*, August 4, 1951, reprinted in B.R. Mitchell and Phyllis Deane, *Abstract of British Historical Statistics* (Cambridge, UK: Cambridge University Press, 1962), p. 332. This fact had actually been known for a very long time; it is discussed at length in Alexander Hamilton's 1791 *Report on the Subject of Manufactures* (Philadelphia: William Brown, 1827), pp. 44-45.

[682] In the last ten years, the industrialization of China has driven up the prices of raw materials, but this trend has still held true on a larger historical time scale.

[683] The World Bank disputes this, pointing out that it only directly financed a small part of the Vietnamese coffee industry.

[684] Eric Reinert, *How Rich Countries Got Rich and Why Poor Countries Stay Poor* (New York: Carroll & Graf, 2007), p. 112.

[685] It has been estimated that modernizing Indian agriculture would put 600 million people in need of new employment. Colin Tudge, "Time for a Peasant Revolution," *Resurgence*, May-June 2005, p.14.

[686] "Human Development Report 1999," United Nations Development Programme, p. 3. Note that economic growth in India and China mean that on a population-weighted basis, global inequality peaked in 1992, and has dropped slightly since then.

[687] Of course, some colonial powers lack the understanding of economic mechanisms to do this, and some colonies, such Canada, weren't true colonies in the economic sense or, as in the case of Manchukuo, were operated according to entirely different economic strategies. And some colonialism doesn't even get this far, but operates by mere plunder or mere territorial conquest without economic content.

[688] Lawrence A. Peskin, *Manufacturing Revolution: The Intellectual Origins of Early American Industry* (Baltimore: Johns Hopkins University Press, 2003), p. 20.

[689] See p. 135.

[690] Paul Bairoch, *Economics and World History: Myths and Paradoxes* (Chicago: University of Chicago Press, 1993), p. 38.

[691] For a precise Ricardian analysis of this problem, framed in terms of changing productivity over time, see Frank D. Graham, "Some Aspects of Protection Further Considered," *The Quarterly Journal of Economics*, February 1923.

[692] Joseph Stiglitz, *Making Globalization Work* (New York: W.W. Norton & Co, 2006), p. 85. Total OECD subsidies from OECD, *Agricultural Policies in OECD Countries: Monitoring and Evaluation* (Paris: OECD, 2005), p. 7.

[693] The success of Japan was a hidden factor in persuading the Soviet elite to abandon Marxism. The success of China left them no choice, as the U.S.SR would have declined to irrelevancy within a visible time frame. Because it was America's need to keep Japan anticommunist that allowed Japan the breathing space to rebuild its economic machine after catastrophic losses in 1945, it is arguable that the Cold War was won in Tokyo.

[694] Marcelo de P. Abreu, Afonso S. Bevilaqua, and Demosthenes M. Pinho, "Import Substitution and Growth in Brazil, 1890s-1970s," Department of Economics, Pontifical Catholic University of Rio de Janiero, p. 21.

[695] Betsy Rakocy, Alejandro Reuss, Chris Sturr et al., *Real World Globalization* (Boston: Economic Affairs Bureau, 2007), p. 210. One of the hidden stories of Chile is the conflict within the Pinochet regime between the notorious free market "Chicago boys" and their *right*-wing opponents in the military government who leaned, like militarist regimes from General Park's Korea to General Franco's Spain, towards authoritarian developmentalism and disliked free markets.

[696] Anthony Elson, "What Happened? Why East Asia Surged Ahead of Latin America and Some Lessons for Economic Policy," *Finance & Development*, June 1, 2006.

[697] This section largely based on Eric Reinert, *How Rich Countries Got Rich and Why Poor Countries Stay Poor* (New York: Carroll & Graf, 2007), pp. 311-2.

[698] Michael Porter, *The Competitive Advantage of Nations* (New York: The Free Press, 1990) p. 117.

[699] This paragraph: see Michael Porter, *The Competitive Advantage of Nations* (New York: The Free Press, 1990), p. 15.

[700] Eric Reinert, *How Rich Countries Got Rich and Why Poor Countries Stay Poor* (New York: Carroll & Graf, 2007), p. 182.

[701] "Americans Are Misinformed: Caterpillar, Deere and NAM Say Multinationals Are Saving the U.S. Economy," *Manufacturing & Technology News*, June 30, 2008, p. 6.

[702] Michael Porter, *The Competitive Advantage of Nations* (New York: The Free Press, 1990), p. 50. Porter is actually referring to competitive, not comparative, advantage in this passage, but the import of the two concepts is the same in this context.

[703] Martha Caldwell Harris and Gordon E. Moore, eds., *Linking Trade and Technology Policies: An International Comparison of the Policies of Industrialized Nations* (Washington: National Academies Press, 1992), p. 125.

[704] Laura D'Andrea Tyson, *Who's Bashing Whom? Trade Conflict in High-Technology Industries* (Washington: Institute for International Economics, 1993), p. 85.

[705] Alert readers will have noticed that the case of ATT (and IBM and other quasi-monopoly companies) contradicts earlier assertions about the value of rivalry. It does: the truth here is complicated, different in different industries, and beyond the scope of this book.

[706] Ibid., p. 88.

[707] Michael Borrus, "Responses to the Japanese Challenge in High Technology: Innovation, Maturity, and U.S.–Japanese Competition in Microelectronics," Berkeley Roundtable on the International Economy, University of California at Berkeley, 1983.

[708] Dieter Ernst and David O'Connor, *Competing in the Electronics Industry: The Experience of Newly Industrialising Economies* (Paris: Development Centre Studies, OECD, 1992).

[709] Office of Technology Assessment, *Competing Economies: America, Europe, and the Pacific Rim*, (Washington: U.S. Government Printing Office, 1991), p. 346.

[710] Sydney Carroll, "The Market for Commercial Airliners," in R. Caves and M. Roberts, eds., *Regulating the Product: Quality and Variety*, (Cambridge, MA: Ballinger Publishing Co., 1975), p. 148.

[711] "Method for Scoring Documents in a Linked Database," U.S. Patent Office, Patent ID U.S.6799176, http://www.patents.com/Method-scoring-documents-a-linked-database/U.S.6799176/en-U.S./

[712] John Young, "Department of Defense Science and Technology (S&T) Program," Memorandum to Robert Gates, Secretary of Defense, August 24, 2007, p. 5.

[713] Author's telephone conversation with Project Socrates Director, Michael C. Sekora, May 22, 2009.

[714] Ibid., July 2, 2009.

[715] "Cheney: Don't Expect Pentagon to Bail Out Industrial Base," *Aerospace Daily,* January 23, 1992, p. 115.

[716] "Report of the Defense Science Board Task Force on High Performance Microchip Supply," Office of the Under Secretary of Defense For Acquisition, Technology, and Logistics, February 2005, p. 15.

[717] "Defense Industrial Base Assessment: U.S. Integrated Circuit Design and Fabrication Capability," Bureau of Industry and Security, March 2009, p. 96.

[718] "Swiss Delay of Military Parts Sparks 'Buy American' Push," *The Washington Times*, July 24, 2003.

[719] In the (unheeded) words of a 2003 memo by then Deputy Defense Secretary Paul Wolfowitz, "The health of the defense IC supplier community depends on the health of the larger commercial IC base…Therefore the DOD will support policies that provide a level playing field internationally for the procurement of commercial products." See Richard McCormack, "DOD Broadens Trusted Foundry Program to Include Microelectronics Supply Chain," *Manufacturing & Technology News*, February 28, 2008, p.1.

[720] A good discussion of the complexities of how industries fall apart on the inside and lose the dynamics that push them to excel is in Michael Porter, *The Competitive Advantage of Nations* (New York: The Free Press, 1990), p. 166.

[721] James Kynge, *China Shakes the World* (New York: Houghton Mifflin, 2006), p. 112.

[722] Richard J. Elkus, *Winner Take All: How Competitiveness Shapes the Fate of Nations* (New York: Basic Books, 2008), p. 75.

[723] "SEMI Reports 2009 Global Semiconductor Equipment Sales of $15.92 Billion," Semiconductor Equipment and Materials International, March 10, 2010.

[724] Richard J. Elkus, *Winner Take All: How Competitiveness Shapes the Fate of Nations* (New York: Basic Books, 2008), p. 149.

[725] "Commentary: Manufacturers Know All About Economic Collapse," *Manufacturing & Technology News*, September 30, 2008, p. 4.

[726] Laura D'Andrea Tyson, *Who's Bashing Whom?* (Washington: Institute for International Economics, 1993), p. 146.

[727] See, for example, Christine Tierney, "Ford Slams Toyota on Hybrids," *Detroit News*, August 8, 2005.

[728] "U.S. Trades Dependence on Foreign Oil for Dependence on Foreign Batteries," *Manufacturing & Technology News*, February 28, 2008, p. 8.

[729] "Overview of Global Li-ion Battery Industry," Market Avenue, Inc., March 14, 2008.

[730] Anthony H. Harrigan et al., *Putting America First: A Conservative Alternative* (Washington: United States Industrial Council Educational Foundation, 1987), p. 21.

[731] Laura D'Andrea Tyson, *Who's Bashing Whom?* (Washington: Institute for International Economics, 1993), p. 14.

[732] Testimony of Michael Borrus before the Committee on Science and Technology, Subcommittee on Technology and Innovation, U.S. House of Representatives, February 15, 2007.

[733] Dani Rodrik, *One Economics, Many Recipes* (Princeton, NJ: Princeton University Press, 2008), p. 119.

[734] "Sematech History," SEMATECH, 2009, http://www.sematech.org/corporate/history.htm.

[735] "The Research & Development Credit: Creating Jobs, Growing America's Economy," R&D Credit Coalition, October 21, 2009, p. 1, http://www.investinamericasfuture.org/PDFs/TalkingPoints10212009.pdf

[736] Martin Neil Baily and Alok K. Chakrabarti, *Innovation and the Productivity Crisis* (Washington: Brookings Institution Press, 1988), p. 39.

[737] Charles W. Wessner, *The Advanced Technology Program: Assessing Outcomes* (Washington: National Academies Press, 2001), p. 5.

[738] Richard McCormack, "The Plight of American Manufacturing" in Richard McCormack, ed., *Manufacturing a Better Future for America* (Washington: Alliance for American Manufacturing, 2009), p. 45.

[739] Wendy H. Schacht, "The Technology Innovation Program," Congressional Research Service, August 20, 2008.

[740] "A Stimulus for Everyone Save Domestic Manufacturers," *Manufacturing & Technology News*, February 20, 2009, p. 1.

[741] "Barack Obama Campaign Promise No. 7: Double Funding for the Manufacturing Extension Partnership, A Program That Encourages Manufacturing Efficiency," St. Petersburg Times, http://www.politifact.com/truth-o-meter/promises/promise/7/double-funding-for-the-manufacturing-extension-par/. The program did get a 13.4% increase in the regular 2010 budget.

[742] "What the Data Show," Manufacturing Extension Partnership, http://www.mep.nist.gov/manufacturers/services/business-operations/results.htm, accessed December 31, 2009.

[743] Gomory and Baumol themselves largely disavow the protectionist policy implications of their work, for various reasons.

[744] Their first published work of multiple-equilibrium trade theory was Ralph E. Gomory, "A Ricardo Model With Economies of Scale," *Proceedings of the National Academy of Sciences*, September 1991. Their book is Ralph Gomory and William Baumol, *Global Trade and Conflicting National Interests.* (Cambridge, MA: MIT Press, 2000).

[745] Gomory and Baumol were not the first economists to identify the value of winning retainable industries or establish firm theoretical grounds for the possibility that government intervention might help a nation win them. Credit for rediscovering this ancient truth and putting it into the theoretical framework of modern economics must go to James Brander and Barbara Spencer of the University of British Columbia, who developed a theory of so-called strategic trade around 1983. Their point, elaborated without Gomory and Baumol's multiple-equilibrium approach, was that in monopoly industries a well-timed government subsidy could potentially hand a "winner take all" industry to one nation or another by getting a national industry to high volume production first.

[746] Lawrence F. Katz and Lawrence H. Summers, "Can Interindustry Wage Differentials Justify Strategic Trade Policy?" in Robert C. Feenstra, ed., *Trade Policies for International Competitiveness* (Chicago: University of Chicago Press, 1989), p. 86.

[747] Ibid., p. 103.

[748] Dieter Ernst and David O'Connor, *Competing in the Electronics Industry: The Experience of Newly Industrialising Economies* (Paris: Development Centre Studies, Organization for Economic Cooperation and Development, 1992) p. 27.

[749] Paul E. Ceruzzi, *A History of Modern Computing* (Cambridge, MA: MIT Press, 1998), p. 248.

[750] See p. 100.

[751] See p. 99 for the original explanation of opportunity costs.

[752] Technically speaking, each such distribution will be "locally" optimal (more efficient than any *similar* distribution) but may or may not be "globally" optimal (more efficient than any *possible* distribution). Therefore, any actually existing distribution may be suboptimal both for maximizing world output and for maximizing the output of any given nation.

[753] *Pace*, of course, the fact that the German auto industry is in significant part a product of deliberate non-free-market industrial-policy decisions, starting with the Marshall Plan.

[754] Based on the number of North American Industry Classification System (NAICS) codes.

[755] Chart adapted from Ralph Gomory and William Baumol, *Global Trade and Conflicting National Interests* (Cambridge, MA: MIT Press, 2000), p. 31.

[756] Ibid, p. 37.

[757] Michael Porter, *The Competitive Advantage of Nations* (New York: The Free Press, 1990), p. 36.

[758] Of course, if they *do* have something valuable, such as knowledge of medicinal plants, this changes.

[759] Among other things, this means that old-fashioned colonialism, in which colonies are pushed into bad industries, is not the most profitable international economic strategy. If it had been, England would not have been outperformed economically by Germany in the late 19th century heyday of the colonial era.

[760] This result is actually true independently of Gomory & Baumol's insights and is known to economics as the Hicks Theorem. See Hicks, John, "An Inaugural Lecture," *Oxford Economic Papers*, June 1953.

[761] A similar result has also been confirmed, using a comparison between hypothetical technologically advanced and undeveloped nations, in Paul R. Krugman & Anthony Venables, "Globalization and the Inequality of Nations," *The Quarterly Journal of Economics*, November 1995.

[762] UK: see p. 130; U.S.: see p. 142.

[763] See p. 25.

[764] See Jagdish Bhagwati, *Free Trade Today* (Princeton, NJ: Princeton University Press, 2002), p. 27.

[765] See p. 54.

[766] There do exist, of course, circumstances when this is exactly what we *want* to happen, as when overseas production effectively complements domestic research and development, but generally, the point is to capture jobs based on R&D, not shed them.

[767] See p. 59.

[768] See p. 34.

[769] See p. 109.

[770] See pp. 52-55.

[771] One can, of course, argue that free trade in goods and free movement of capital are different issues, as does Jagdish Bhagwati in *Free Trade Today* (Princeton, NJ: Princeton University Press, 2002), p. 10. But free movement of goods, without free movement of the money to pay for them, is only "free" trade in a pedantic sense: it is like freedom to shop without freedom to pay.

[772] See pp. 45-49, 54.

[773] See p. 186.

[774] See p. 113.

[775] Quoted in Ralph E. Gomory and William J. Baumol, "Toward a Theory of Industrial Policy–Retainable Industries," C.V. Starr Center for Applied Economics, New York University, December 1992, p. 25.

[776] See p. 137.

[777] We are talking about *average* cost, not marginal cost. The reader can try this out in Excel or another spreadsheet program without difficulty.

[778] See p. 187.

[779] As noted in Chapter 9, Reagan's industrial policy was purely military, but was as such very serious, and subsequent presidents have not even employed military industrial policy.

[780] Costa Rica: *CIA World Fact Book 2008*, https://www.cia.gov/library/publications/the-world-factbook/geos/cs.html.
Jacksonville: Bureau of Economic Analysis, "Gross Domestic Product by Metropolitan Area," http://www.bea.gov/regional/gdpmetro/action.cfm.

[781] See pp. 46-48.

[782] See pp. 156-158.

[783] See pp. 171-172.

[784] See pp. 198-202.

[785] Eric S. Reinert, *How Rich Countries Got Rich and Why Poor Countries Stay Poor* (New York: Carroll & Graf, 2007), p. 271.

[786] See p. 158.

[787] John Cavanagh, Jerry Mander et al., *Alternatives to Economic Globalization: A Better World is Possible* (San Francisco: Berrett-Koehler, 2002), p. 230.

[788] Ch. 9: see p. 198; Ch. 10: see p. 227.

[789] See p. 138.

[790] See p. 176 for the original discussion of VAT.

[791] See p. 144.

[792] For example, there is something of an inverse relationship between protectionism and industrial policy, as is visible in nations such as Singapore which have fairly free trade but very aggressive industrial policy.

[793] It is no accident that most nations with VAT have larger welfare states than the U.S., as this is an obvious way to mitigate the progressivity issues of a VAT.

[794] Michael Porter, *The Competitive Advantage of Nations* (New York: The Free Press, 1990), p. 119.

[795] This holds in many other Japanese industries as well. See Michael Porter, *The Competitive Advantage of Nations* (New York: The Free Press, 1990), p. 118.

[796] See p. 90.

[797] See p. 199.

[798] They are constantly alert to threats against their trading position: China, for example, was recently reported in *China Daily* as increasing export rebates on 3,800 items "to maintain growth." See "China Raises Export Rebate to Spur Growth," *China Daily*, March 28, 2009.

[799] See p. 74.

[800] In other words, it is plausible to expect an approximate Nash Equilibrium to emerge, though of course some turbulence would occur.

[801] See p. 176 for the original discussion of VAT.

[802] In particular, American conservatives now vehemently oppose it, despite the fact that in the early 1980s, most conservative economists supported it. See Bruce Bartlett, "Support the VAT," Forbes.com, October 23, 2009.

[803] Lori Montgomery, "Value-Added Tax, Once Taboo, is Getting Attention in Washington," *Los Angeles Times*, May 28, 2009.

[804] Victor Selden Clark, *History of Manufactures in the United States: 1607-1860* (Washington: Carnegie Institution, 1916), p. 288.

[805] See p. 176.

[806] This analysis was originally published in modified form in as "Things Fall Apart: the Coming End of the Free Trade Coalition," *The American Conservative*, September 2004.

[807] 2009: 91%, to be exact. "Employment Situation Summary," Bureau of Labor Statistics, August 7, 2009. 1950: Ronald E. Kutscher, "The American Work Force, 1992-2005: Historical Trends, 1950-92, and Current Uncertainties," *Monthly Labor Review*, November 1993, p. 6.

[808] This section is adapted from the article, "Things Fall Apart," originally published in *The American Conservative*, September 27, 2004.

[809] Kevin Phillips, *Arrogant Capital* (New York: Little, Brown & Co, 1995), p. 89.

[810] In technical terms, there is no theorem guaranteeing that partial-equilibrium losses to import-competing producers are more than offset by their gains as consumers due to reduced prices. See Chapters 1 and 5.

[811] See p. 166.

[812] Michael Lind gave an interesting description of what such a position might look like in *The Next American Nation* (New York: Free Press, 1995).

[813] "Republican party Platform of 1972," The American Presidency Project, University of California at Santa Barbara, http://www.presidency.ucsb.edu/ws/index.php?pid=25842.

[814] Free traders will, of course, respond that none of them actually believe in literal 100% free trade. The reader may judge whether the various kinds of 99% free trade they believe in are significantly different.

[815] Sherrod Brown, *Myths of Free Trade: Why American Trade Policy Has Failed* (New York: The New Press, 2004), p. 11.

[816] Peronet Despeignes, "Poll: Enthusiasm for Free Trade Fades Dip Sharpest for $100K Set; Loss of Jobs Cited," *U.S.A Today*, February 24, 2004.

[817] Ibid.

[818] "NBC/Wall Street Journal GOP Primary Voters Survey," Hart/Newhouse, September 2007, p. 5.

[819] "Support for Free Trade Recovers Despite Recession," Pew Center for the People and the Press, April 28, 2009, http://people-press.org/reports/pdf/511.pdf.

[820] Scott Keeter and Richard Morin, "The Complicated Politics of Free Trade," Pew Center for the People and the Press, January 4, 2007.

[821] Ana Maria Arumi and Scott Bittle, "Confidence in U.S. Foreign Policy Index," *Public Agenda*, Winter 2006, p. 17.

[822] Ibid., p. 11.

[823] "Excerpts From An Interview With John Kerry," *The Wall Street Journal*, May 3, 2004.

[824] "Debate Transcript: The Third Bush–Kerry Presidential Debate," Commission on Presidential Debates, 13 October 2004.

[825] Ibid.

[826] Ibid.

[827] Ibid.

[828] Bush won by 286 electoral votes to 251; Kerry lost Ohio, which has 20.

[829] "Ohio Voters Don't Trust Democrats on Economic Issues," *Manufacturing & Technology News*, March 14, 2008, p. 1.

[830] Thomas Frank, *What's The Matter With Kansas?* (New York: Metropolitan Books, 2004).

[831] John Nichols, "A Congressman's Defeat Spells Trouble for Business Democrats," *The Nation*, May 10, 2002.

[832] Ibid.

[833] Todd Tucker, "Election 2006: No to Staying the Course on Trade," Public Citizen, November 8, 2006, p. 4., http://www.citizen.org/documents/Election2006.pdf.

[834] Chris Slevin and Todd Tucker, "The Fair Trade Sweep," *The Democratic Strategist*, January 7, 2007.

[835] Ibid.

[836] Greta Wodele, "Fitzpatrick Touts Record, Murphy National Issues In Debate," *Congress Daily PM*, October 26, 2006.

[837] Jeremy Wallace, "Democrats Say Venus Man Can Beat Foley," *Sarasota Herald-Tribune*, December 12, 2005.

[838] Todd Tucker, "Election 2006: No to Staying the Course on Trade," Public Citizen, November 8, 2006, p. 18, http://www.citizen.org/documents/Election2006.pdf.

[839] Chris Slevin and Todd Tucker, "The Fair Trade Sweep," *The Democratic Strategist*, January 7, 2007, p. 6.

[840] Ibid., p. 5.

[841] Ibid., p. 5.

[842] Stuart Rothenberg, "Rothenberg's Ten Most Endangered House Incumbents," *The Rothenberg Report*, February 21, 2006.

[843] "2008 Presidential Candidate Questionnaire," Ohio Conference on Fair Trade, http://www.citizen.org/documents/OhioCFTQuestionnaireObama.pdf.

[844] "NAFTA Takes Center Stage in Ohio Primary Battle," *The Wall Street Journal*, February 25, 2008.

[845] Susan Davis and Nick Timiraos, "Washington Wire," *The Wall Street Journal*, February 25, 2008.

[846] "The Democratic Debate in Cleveland," *The New York Times*, February 26, 2008.

[847] "Report on U.S. Elections–CHCGO Meeting with Obama Advisor Austan Goolsbee," memorandum, Consulate General of Canada, Chicago, February 2008, http://www.nytimes.com/images/promos/politics/blog/20070303canmemo.pdf.

[848] "Obama Staffer Gave Warning of NAFTA Rhetoric," CTV, February 27, 2008, http://www.ctv.ca/servlet/ArticleNews/story/CTVNews/20080227/dems_nafta_080227/20080227.

[849] Robert Scott, "Pennsylvania Stagnation: Is NAFTA the Culprit?" *The New York Times,* April 15, 2008.

[850] Real Clear Politics, "Pennsylvania Democratic Primary," http://www.realclearpolitics.com/epolls/2008/president/pa/pennsylvania_democratic_primary-240.html.

[851] Nina Easton, "Obama: NAFTA Not So Bad After All," *Fortune,* June 18, 2008.

[852] John McCain, speech to National Association of Latino Appointed and Elected Officials, June 28, 2008.

[853] Barack Obama, "Renewing American Competitiveness," speech in Flint, MI, June 16, 2008.

[854] See pp. 20-26.

[855] See pp. 59-63.

[856] Paul Cohn, "Dems Ads In Tight Races Tap Into Anti-Trade Sentiment," *Congress Daily*, Wednesday, October 29, 2008.

[857] Figure derived by combining the number of trade ads run by individual candidates and those run by the Democratic Congressional Campaign Committee and Democratic Senatorial Campaign Committee in the general election cycle. "Election 2008: Fair Trade Gets an Upgrade," Global Trade Watch, November 5, 2008, pp. 4-5.

[858] "Election 2008: Fair Trade Gets an Upgrade," Global Trade Watch, November 5, 2008, p. 2.

[859] Ibid.

[860] Ibid., p. 3.

[861] Ibid., p. 5.

[862] Ron Kirk, "Trade and the Economic Agenda: Serving America's Families and the Global Recovery," speech at Georgetown University Law Center, April 23, 2009.

[863] Prof. Laura D'Andrea Tyson, University of California at Berkeley, has done great work as a theorist of protectionism, but has retreated from this position in her public statements in recent years.

[864] Doug Palmer, "No Need to Renegotiate NAFTA to Improve It–USTR," Reuters, April 20, 2009.

[865] David Sanger, "Senate Agrees to Dilute 'Buy American' Provisions," *The New York Times*, February 4, 2009.

[866] "Mexican Truck Program Revival Clears First Hurdles," *Today's Trucking*, July 28, 2009.

[867] John M. Broder, "Obama Opposes Trade Sanctions in Climate Bill," *The New York Times*, June 28, 2009.

[868] Ian Talley and Tom Barkley, "Energy Chief Says U.S. Is Open to Carbon Tariff," *The Wall Street Journal*, March 18, 2009.

[869] Fiona Harvey, "WTO Signals Backing for Border Taxes," *Financial Times*, June 26, 2009.

[870] Alan Tonelson, "Obama's Tire Tariff Decision: False Promise From a Free-Trade Administration," *American Economic Alert*, September 18, 2009.

[871] Peter Morici, "Trade Deficit Threatens a Double-Dip Recession, Economic Armageddon," *Online Journal*, November 13, 2009, http://onlinejournal.com/artman/publish/article_5260.shtml.

[872] Senator Richard Shelby, *NBC Meet the Press,* Nov 16, 2008.

[873] As of this writing, the ultimate outcome of the global warming controversy remains to be seen.

[874] Paul Krugman, blog entry of June 26, 2009, http://krugman.blogs.nytimes.com/2009/06/26/the-wto-is-making-sense/.

[875] This could have significant protectionist effects given that China's carbon emissions per unit of GDP are roughly eight times those of the U.S. According to Jeff Rubin of CIBC, "With OECD's carbon tolerance diminishing with every tonne of CO2 spread into the atmosphere by non-OECD countries, environmentalism will soon become a significant barrier to trade. A carbon tariff imposed by the U.S. on emissions embodied in Chinese exports would not only abolish the implicit subsidies on the carbon content currently enjoyed by Chinese exports, but it would be large enough to start reversing current trade and off-shoring patterns." See http://research.cibcwm.com/economic_public/download/smar08.pdf.

[876] This section is based on Robertson Morrow, "The Bull Market in Politics," Clarium Capital Management, February 2008, p. 14.

[877] Trade polls 1992-2008: "Polls on NAFTA and Free Trade," American Enterprise Institute, June 26, 2008, p. 3, http://www.aei.org/docLib/20031203_nafta2.pdf.
Immigration Polls: Tim Bolin, "Public Opinion on Immigration in America," Mirage Foundation for the American Dream, p. 8, http://www.meragefoundations.com/MFAD%20Occasional%20Papers/Immigration%20Occasional%20Paper.Final.10.27.05.pdf.

[878] The final CAFTA vote in the House had almost every Democrat against and almost every Republican in favor. In the Senate, 78 percent of Republicans were in favor while 76 percent of Democrats were opposed. On amnesty, the Senate vote was 12 Republicans and 34 Democrats in favor, 37 Republicans and 15 Democrats against. (There was no House vote on this bill or an equivalent.) See Robertson Morrow, "The Bull Market in Politics," Clarium Capital Management, February 2008, p. 15.

[879] Robertson Morrow, "The Bull Market in Politics," Clarium Capital Management, February 2008, p. 16.

[880] NBC News and *The Wall Street Journal*, "Survey: Study #101061," September 28, 2010, p. 19, http://online.wsj.com/public/resources/documents/WSJNBCPoll09282010.pdf.

[881] Ibid., p. 20.

[882] Bunning-Stabenow: HR 2378, S 1027.

[883] In open-seat and competitive races. Todd Tucker, "Election 2010: The Best Defense Was a Good Fair Trade Offense," Public Citizen, November 3, 2010, p. 6.

884 Ibid., p. 3.
885 Ibid., p. 14.
886 See p. 143.

SELECT BILIOGRAPHY

BOOKS

Ackerman, Frank and A. Nadal. *The Flawed Foundations of General Equilibrium: Critical Essays on Economic Theory*. New York: Routledge, 2004.

Akyüz, Yilmaz. ed. *Developing Countries and World Trade. Performance and Prospects*. London: Zed Books, 2003.

Alam, Shawakat. *Sustainable Development and Free Trade: Institutional Approaches*. New York: Routledge, 2007.

American Free Trade League. *Proceedings of the National Conference of Free Traders and Revenue Reformers*. New York: New York Free Trade Club, 1885.

Archibugi, Daniele and Jonathan Michie. *Technology, Globalization and Economic Performance*. Cambridge, UK: Cambridge University Press, 1997.

Ariffin, Anuar. *The Free Trade Doctrine: Evolution, Economic Effects, and Influences on Trade Policy*. Saarbrücken, Germany: VDM Verlag, 2008.

Amsden, Alice H. *Asia's Next Giant: South Korea and Late Industrialization*. New York: Oxford University Press, 1989.

Amsden, Alice H. *The Rise of "The Rest": Challenges to the West from Late Industrializing Economies*. New York: Oxford University press, 2001.

Anderson, Sarah, ed. *Views from the South: The Effect of Globalization and the WTO on Third World Countries*. San Francisco: International Forum on Globalization, 2000.

Arthur, W. Brian. *Increasing Returns and Path Dependency in the Economy*. Ann Arbor, MI: University of Michigan Press, 1994.

Ashley, J.W. *The Tariff Problem*. London: P.S. King & Son, 1904.

Audley, John J., Demetrious G. Papademetriou, Sandra Polaski, and Scott Vaughan. *NAFTA's Promise and Reality: Lessons from Mexico for the Hemisphere*. Washington: Carnegie Endowment for International Peace, 2003.

Bairoch, Paul. *Economics and World History*. Chicago: University of Chicago Press, 1993.

Barker, Debi and Jerry Mander. *Invisible Government: The World Trade Organization, Global Government for the Millennium*? San Francisco: International Forum on Globalization, 1999.

Barry, Christian and Sanjay G. Reddy. *International Trade and Labor Standards: A Proposal for Linkage*. New York: Columbia University Press, 2008.

Barton, John H. et al. *The Evolution of the Trade Regime: Politics, Law and Economics of the GATT and WTO*. Princeton, NJ: Princeton University Press, 2006.

Batra, Ravi. *The Myth of Free Trade: The Pooring of America*. New York: Touchstone Books, 1993.

Baumol, William and Ralph Gomory. *Global Trade and Conflicting National Interests*. Cambridge, MA: MIT Press, 2000.

Beaudreau, Bernard C. *Making Sense of Smoot-Hawley: Technology and Tariffs*. Bloomington, IN: iUniverse, 2005.

Beinhocker, Eric D. *The Origin of Wealth: Evolution, Complexity, and the Radical Remaking of Economics*. Boston: Harvard Business School Press, 2007.

Belderbos, René A. *Japanese Electronics Multinationals and Strategic Trade Policies*. Oxford, UK: Clarendon Press, 1997.

Beltz, Cynthia. *High-Tech Maneuvers: Industrial Policy Lessons of HDTV*. Washington: American Enterprise Institute Press, 1991.

Bernstein, William J. *A Splendid Exchange: How Trade Shaped the World*. Boston: Atlantic Monthly Press, 2008.

Beveridge, Sir William. *Tariffs: The Case Examined*. London: Longmans, Green and Company, 1931.

Bhagwati, Jagdish N. *Free Trade Today*. Princeton, NJ: Princeton University Press, 2002.

Bhagwati, Jagdish N. *In Defense of Globalization*. New York: Oxford University Press, 2007.

Bhagwati, Jagdish and Robert E. Hudec, eds., *Fair Trade and Harmonization: Prerequisites for Free Trade*? Cambridge, MA: MIT Press, 1996.

Bhagwati, Jagdish N. *Protectionism*. Cambridge, MA: MIT Press, 1988.

Bhalla, Surjit S. *Imagine There's No Country: Poverty, Inequality, and Growth in the Era of Globalization*. Washington: Peterson Institute, 2002.

Bluestone, Barry and Bennett Harrison. *The Deindustrialization of America: Plant Closings, Community Abandonment, and the Dismantling of Basic Industry*. New York: Basic Books, 1982.

Bovard, James. *The Fair Trade Fraud: How Congress Pillages the Consumer and Decimates American Competitiveness*. New York: St. Martin's Press, 1991.

Bourgin, F. *The Great Challenge: The Myth of Laissez-faire in the Early Republic*. New York: George Braziller, 1989.

Bradford, Scott C. and Robert Z. Lawrence. *Has Globalization Gone Far Enough? The Costs of Fragmented Markets*. Washington: Peterson Institute for International Economics, 2004.

Brown, Sherrod. *Myths of Free Trade: Why American Trade Policy Has Failed.* New York: The New Press, 2004.

Buchanan, Patrick J. *The Great Betrayal: How American Sovereignty and Social Justice Are Being Sacrificed to the Gods of the Global Economy.* Boston: Little, Brown & Co., 1998.

Buffie, Edward. *Trade Policy in Developing Countries.* Cambridge, UK: Cambridge University Press, 2001.

Burnett, Patrick and Firoze Manji, eds. *From the Slave Trade to 'Free' Trade: How Trade Undermines Democracy and Justice in Africa.* Oxford, UK: Fahamu, 2007.

Cain, P.J. and A.G. Hopkins. *British Imperialism: Crisis and Deconstruction 1914-1990.* London: Longman, 1993.

Cameron, Maxwell A. and Brian W. Tomlin. *The Making of NAFTA: How the Deal Was Done.* Ithaca, NY: Cornell University Press, 2002.

Carey, Matthew. *Displaying the Rise and Progress of the Tariff System of the United States: the Various Efforts Made from the Year 1819, to Establish the Protecting System; Its Final Triumph in the Tariff of 1824.* Philadelphia: Thomas B. Town, 1833.

Carrapatoso, Astrid Fritz. *The Greening of Free Trade.* Saarbrücken, Germany: VDM Verlag, 2007.

Castañeda, Jorge G. and Carlos Heredia et al. *The Case Against Free Trade: GATT, NAFTA, and the Globalization of Corporate Power.* San Francisco: Earth Island Press, 1993.

Cavanagh, John et al. *Alternatives to Economic Globalization: A Better World Is Possible.* San Francisco: Berrett-Koehler, 2002.

Central Intelligence Agency, *Global Trends 2015: A Dialogue About the Future With Nongovernment Experts.* Langley, VA: CIA, 2000.

Chang, Ha-Joon. *Bad Samaritans: The Myth of Free Trade and the Secret History of Capitalism.* New York: Bloomsbury Press, 2008.

Chang, Ha-Joon. *Globalization, Economic Development and the Role of the State.* New York: Zed Books, 2002.

Chang, Ha-Joon. *Kicking Away the Ladder: Development Strategy in Historical Perspective.* New York: Anthem Press, 2003.

Chang, Ha-Joon. *Reclaiming Development: An Economic Policy Handbook for Activists and Policymakers.* New York: Zed Books, 2004.

Chang, Ha-Joon. *The East Asian Development Experience: The Miracle, the Crisis, and the Future.* New York: Zed Books, 2007.

Chang, Ha Joon, ed. *Rethinking Development Economics.* London: Anthem Press, 2003.

Cho, Dong-Sung and Hwy-Chang Moon. *From Adam Smith to Michael Porter: The Evolution of Competitiveness Theory.* Hackensack, NJ: World Scientific Publishing, 2000.

Choate, Pat. *Dangerous Business: The Risks of Globalization for America.* New York: Alfred A. Knopf, 2008.

Chorev, Nitsan. *Remaking U.S. Trade Policy: From Protectionism to Globalization.* Ithaca, NY: Cornell University Press, 2007.

Cline, William R. *International Economic Policy in the 1990s.* Cambridge, MA: MIT Press, 1995.

Cline, William R. *Trade and Income Distribution.* Washington: Institute for International Economics, 1997.

Cline, William R. *Trade Policy and Global Poverty.* Washington: Peterson Institute, 2004.

Cohen, Stephen, Joel R. Paul, and Robert A. Blecker. *Fundamentals of U.S. Foreign Trade Policy: Economics, Politics, Laws and Issues.* Boulder, CO: Westview Press, 1996.

Cohen, Stephen and John Zysman. *Manufacturing Matters: The Myth of the Post-Industrial Economy.* New York: Basic Books, 1987.

Collier, Paul. *The Bottom Billion: Why the Poorest Countries Are Failing and What Can Be Done About It.* Oxford, UK: Oxford University Press, 2007.

Collins, Susan M. and Carol Graham. Brookings Trade Forum 2004: *Globalization, Poverty and Inequality.* Washington: Brookings Institution Press, 2004.

Copeland, Brian R. and M. Scott Taylor. *Trade and the Environment: Theory and Evidence.* Princeton, NJ: Princeton University Press, 2005.

Corden, Max, *The Theory of Protection.* Oxford, UK: Oxford University Press, 1971.

Creegan, John P. *America Asleep: The Free Trade Syndrome and the Global Economic Challenge.* Washington: U.S. Industrial Council Educational Foundation, 1991.

Culbertson, John M. *The Dangers of "Free Trade."* Madison, WI: 21st Century Press, 1985.

Culbertson, John M. *The Trade Threat and U.S. Trade Policy.* Madison, WI: 21st Century Press, 1989.

Cunningham, William. *The Case Against Free Trade.* London: John Murray, 1914.

Cunningham, William. *The Rise and Decline of the Free Trade Movement.* Cambridge, UK: Cambridge University Press, 1905.

Daly, Herman E. and John B. Cobb, Jr. *For the Common Good.* Boston: Beacon Press, 1989.

DeCarlo, Jacqueline. *Fair Trade: A Beginner's Guide.* Oxford, UK: Oneworld Publications, 2007.

Dervis, Kemal and Ceren Ozer. *A Better Globalization: Legitimacy, Governance, and Reform.* Washington: Center for Global Development, 2005.

Destler, I.M. *American Trade Politics.* Washington: Institute for International Economics, 1995.

Development Prospects Group, *Global Economic Prospects and the Developing Countries (2000-2009).* Washington: World Bank, 1999-2008.

DiMicco, Dan. *Steeling America's Future: A CEO's Call to Arms: Saving Manufacturing Through Free Trade.* Charlotte, NC: Vox Populi Publishers, 2006.

Dobbs, Lou. *Exporting America: Why Corporate Greed Is Shipping American Jobs Overseas.* New York: Business Plus, 2006.

Dorgan, Byron. *Take This Job and Ship it: How Corporate Greed and Brain-Dead Politics Are Selling Out America.* New York: Thomas Dunne Books, 2006.

Dunkley, Graham. *Free Trade: Myth, Reality and Alternatives.* New York: Palgrave Macmillan, 2004.

Easterly, William. *The Elusive Quest for Growth: Economists' Adventures and Misadventures in the Tropics.* Cambridge, MA: MIT Press, 2002.

Eckes, Alfred E., Jr. *Opening America's Market: U.S. Foreign Trade Policy Since 1776.* Chapel Hill, NC: University of North Carolina Press, 1995.

Eckes, Alfred E., Jr., William A. Lovett and Richard L. Brinkman. *U.S. Trade Policy: History, Theory, and the WTO.* Armonk, NY: M.E. Sharpe, 1999.

Eichengreen, Barry. *Globalizing Capital: A History of the International Monetary System.* Princeton, NJ: Princeton University Press, 2008.

Elkus, Richard J. *Winner Take All: How Competitiveness Shapes the Fate of Nations.* New York: Basic Books, 2008.

Ernst, Dieter and David O'Connor, *Competing in the Electronics Industry: The Experience of Newly Industrializing Economies.* Paris: Organization for Economic Cooperation and Development, 1992.

Farina, Francesco and Ernesto Savaglio. *Inequality and Economic Integration.* New York: Routledge, 2006.

Faux, Jeff. *The Global Class War: How America's Bipartisan Elite Lost Our Future–And What It Will Take to Win It Back.* New York: John Wiley & Sons, 2006.

Fawcett, Henry. *Free Trade and Protection.* London: Macmillan & Co., 1878.

Feenstra, Robert C. *Trade Policies for International Competitiveness.* Chicago: University of Chicago Press, 1989.

Feenstra, Robert C. *Advanced International Trade: Theory and Evidence.* Princeton, NJ: Princeton University Press, 2004.

Findlay, Ronald and Kevin H. O'Rourke. *Power and Plenty: Trade, War and the World Economy in the Second Millennium.* Princeton, NJ: Princeton University Press, 2007.

Fingleton, Eamonn. *Blindside: Why Japan is Still On Track to Overtake the U.S. by the Year 2000.* New York: Houghton Mifflin, 1995.

Fingleton, Eamonn. *In Praise of Hard Industries: Why Manufacturing, not the Information Economy, is the Key to Future Prosperity.* New York: Buttonwood Press, 1999.

Fingleton, Eamonn. *In the Jaws of the Dragon: America's Fate Under Chinese Hegemony.* New York: St. Martin's Press, 2008.

Firebaugh, Glenn. *The New Geography of Global Income Inequality.* Cambridge, MA: Harvard University Press, 2003.

Florida, Richard and Martin Kenney. *The Breakthrough Illusion: Corporate America's Failure to Move from Innovation to Mass Production.* New York: Basic Books, 1990.

Folsom, Burton W., ed. *The Industrial Revolution and Free Trade.* Irvington, NY: Foundation for Economic Education, 1997.

Folsom, Ralph H. *NAFTA and Free Trade in the Americas in a Nutshell.* St. Paul, MN: West Group, 2008.

Frank, Thomas. *What's the Matter With Kansas?* New York: Metropolitan Books, 2004.

Friedman, Thomas L. *The Lexus and the Olive Tree: Understanding Globalization.* New York: Farrar Straus Giroux, 1999.

Friedman, Thomas L. *The World Is Flat: a Brief History of the Twenty-First Century.* New York: Picador, 2005.

Galbraith, John Kenneth. *American Capitalism—The Concept of Countervailing Power.* New York: Houghton Mifflin, 1952.

Gallagher, Kevin P. *Free Trade and the Environment: Mexico, NAFTA, and Beyond.* Palo Alto, CA: Stanford University Press, 2004.

George, Henry. *Protection or Free Trade: an Examination of the Tariff Question, With Especial Regard to the Interests of Labor.* New York: Robert Schalkenbach Foundation, 1935.

Gerschenkron, Alexander. *Economic Backwardness in Historical Perspective.* Cambridge, MA: Harvard University Press, 1962.

Gereffi, Gary, David Spener, and Jennifer Bair, eds. *Free Trade and Uneven Development: The North American Apparel Industry After NAFTA.* Philadelphia: Temple University Press, 2002.

Giddens, Anthony. *Runaway World: How Globalization is Reshaping Our Lives.* New York: Routledge, 2000.

Goldsmith, Sir James. *The Response: GATT and Global Free Trade.* New York: Macmillan, 1995.

Goldstein, Natalie and Frank W. Musgrave. *Globalization and Free Trade.* New York: Checkmark Books, 2008.

Gordon, Bernard K. *America's Trade Follies: Turning Economic Leadership Into Strategic Weakness.* New York: Routledge, 2001.

Goss, John Dean. *History of Tariff Administration in the United States: From Colonial Times to the McKinley Administration Bill.* New York: Columbia University Press, 1891.

Gray, John. *False Dawn: The Delusions of Global Capitalism.* New York: The New Press, 1998.

Greider, William. *One World, Ready or Not: The Manic Logic of Global Capitalism*. New York: Touchstone, 1997.

Greenwald, Bruce C.N. and Judd Kahn. *Globalization: n. The irrational fear that someone in China will take your job*. New York: Wiley, 2008.

Grimwade, Nigel. *International Trade Policy: A Contemporary Analysis*. New York: Routledge, 1996.

Grossman, G. M., ed. *Imperfect Competition and International Trade*. Cambridge, MA: MIT Press, 1992.

Grossman, G. M. and E. Helpman. *Innovation and Growth in the Global Economy*. Cambridge, MA: MIT Press, 1991.

Hamilton, Alexander. *Alexander Hamilton's Report on the Subject of Manufactures, Made in His Capacity as Secretary of the Treasury*. Philadelphia: William Brown, 1827.

Harney, Alexandra. *The China Price: The True Cost of Chinese Competitive Advantage*. New York: Penguin, 2009.

Harrigan, Anthony H. et al. *Putting America First: A Conservative Alternative*. Washington: United States Industrial Council Educational Foundation, 1987.

Harriman, Daniel G. *American Tariffs From Plymouth Rock to McKinley*. New York: The American Protective Tariff League, 1892.

Harrison, Ann E., ed. *Globalization and Poverty*. Chicago: University of Chicago Press, 2007.

Hartmann, Thom. *Screwed. The Undeclared War Against the Middle Class—And What We Can Do about It*. San Francisco: Berrett-Koehler, 2007.

Harvey, David. *A Brief History of Neoliberalism*. New York: Oxford University Press, 2007.

Heckscher, Eli. *Mercantilism*, London: Allan and Unwin, 1935.

Held, David and Ayse Kaya. *Global Inequality*. London: Polity Press, 2007.

Helpman, Elhanan and Paul Krugman. *Trade Policy and Market Structure*. Cambridge, MA: MIT Press, 1989.

Helpman, Elhanan and Assaf Razin, eds. *International Trade and Trade Policy*. Cambridge, MA: MIT Press, 1991.

Hertz, Noreena. *The Silent Takeover: Global Capitalism and the Death of Democracy*. New York: Free Press, 2001.

Hira, Ron and Anil Hira. *Outsourcing America: The True Cost of Shipping Jobs Overseas and What Can Be Done About It*. New York: American Management Association, 2008.

Hirst, Paul and Grahame Thompson. *Globalization in Question: The International Economy and the Possibilities of Governance*. Cambridge, UK: Blackwell Publishers, 1996.

Hobson, J.A. *Imperialism: A Study*. London: Nisbet and Co., 1902.

Hufbauer, Gary Clyde and Jeffrey J. Schott. *North American Free Trade: Issues and Recommendations*. New York: New York University Press, 1992.

Hufbauer, G. and K. Elliot. *Measuring the Costs of Protection in the United States*. Washington: Institute for International Economics, 1994.

Hufbauer, Gary C., Diane T. Berliner and Kimberly A. Elliot. *Trade Protection in the United States: 31 Case Studies*. Washington: Institute for International Economics, 1986.

Hufbauer, Gary Clyde and Jeffrey J. Schott. *NAFTA Revisited: Achievements and Challenges*. Washington: Institute for International Economics, 2005.

Hugill, Peter J. *World Trade Since 1431: Geography, Technology and Capitalism*. Baltimore: Johns Hopkins University Press, 1993.

Irwin, Douglas A. *Against the Tide: An Intellectual History of Free Trade*. Princeton, NJ: Princeton University Press, 1996.

Irwin, Douglas A. *Free Trade Under Fire*. Princeton, NJ: Princeton University Press, 2002.

Johnson, Emory R. et al. *History of the Domestic and Foreign Commerce of the United States*. Washington: Carnegie Institute, 1915.

Kaldor, Nicholas. *Causes of Slow Rate of Economic Growth of the United Kingdom*. Cambridge, UK: Cambridge University Press, 1966.

Kaplinsky, Raphael. *Globalization, Poverty and Inequality*, London: Polity Press, 2005.

Kelly, Charles et al. *High-Technology Manufacturing and U.S. Competitiveness*. Santa Monica, CA: RAND Corporation, 2004.

Klein, Naomi. *The Shock Doctrine: The Rise of Disaster Capitalism*. New York: Picador, 2008.

Klein, Philip A. *Economics Confronts the Economy*. Northampton, MA: Edward Elgar, 2006.

Kletzer, Lori. *Job Loss from Imports: Measuring the Costs*. Washington: Institute for International Economics, 2001.

Kozul-Wright, Richard and Paul Rayment. *The Resistible Rise of Market Fundamentalism: Rethinking Development Policy in an Unbalanced World*. New York: Zed Books, 2007.

Krauss, Melvyn. *How Nations Grow Rich: The Case for Free Trade*. New York: Oxford University Press, 1997.

Krugman, Paul R. *Market Structure and Foreign Trade*. Cambridge, MA: MIT Press, 1985.

Krugman, Paul R. *Peddling Prosperity: Economic Sense and Nonsense in an Age of Diminished Expectations*. New York: W.W. Norton & Company, 1994.

Krugman, Paul R. *Pop Internationalism*. Cambridge, MA: MIT Press, 1996.

Krugman, Paul R. *Rethinking International Trade*. Cambridge, MA: MIT Press, 1994.

Krugman, Paul R, ed. *Strategic Trade Policy and the New International Economics*. Cambridge, MA: MIT Press, 1986.

Krugman, Paul R. and Alasdair Smith, eds. *Empirical Studies of Strategic Trade Policy*. Chicago: University of Chicago Press, 1994.

Kuttner, Robert. *Everything for Sale: The Virtues and Limits of Markets*. New York: Alfred A. Knopf, 1997.

Kynge, James. *China Shakes the World*. New York: Houghton Mifflin, 2006.

Landes, David. *The Wealth and Poverty of Nations: Why Some Are So Rich and Some So Poor*. New York: W.W. Norton & Co., 1998.

Lawrence, Robert Z. and Robert E. Litan. *Saving Free Trade: A Pragmatic Approach*. Washington: Brookings Institution, 1986.

Leamer, Edward E. *Sources of Comparative Advantage: Theory and Evidence*. Cambridge, MA: MIT Press. 1984

Legrain, Philippe. *Open World: The Truth About Globalization*. Chicago: Ivan R. Dee, 2004.

Leipziger, Danny M. *Lessons From East Asia*. Ann Arbor, MI: University of Michigan Press, 2001.

Lieb, Hermann. *The Protective Tariff: What It Does For Us!* Chicago: Belford, Clarke & Co., 1888.

Lippoldt, Douglas, ed. *Trading Up: Economic Perspectives on Development Issues in the Multilateral Trading System*. Paris: Organization for Economic Cooperation and Development, 2006.

List, Friedrich. *The National System of Political Economy*, trans. S. S. Lloyd. London: Longmans, Green, and Co, 1885.

Longworth, Richard C. *Caught in the Middle: America's Heartland in the Age of Globalism*. New York: Bloomsbury USA, 2009.

Lovett, William A. et al. *U.S. Trade Policy: History, Theory and the WTO*. Armonk, NY: M.E. Sharpe, 2004.

Luttwak, Edward N. *The Endangered American Dream: How to Stop the United States From Becoming a Third-World Country and How to Win the Geo-Economic Struggle for Industrial Supremacy*. New York: Touchstone, 1993.

Luttwak, Edward N. *Turbo-Capitalism: Winners and Losers in the Global Economy*. New York: Harper Perennial, 2000.

Lynn, Barry C. *End of the Line: The Rise and Coming Fall of the Global Corporation*. New York: Doubleday, 2005.

MacArthur, John R. *The Selling of "Free Trade:" NAFTA, Washington, and the Subversion of American Democracy*. New York: Hill and Wang, 2000.

Maddison, Angus. *The World Economy: A Millennial Perspective*, Paris: OECD, 2001.

Madeley, John. *Hungry for Trade: How the Poor Pay for Free Trade*. New York: Zed Books, 2001.

Magaziner, Ira and Mark Patinkin. *The Silent War: Inside the Global Business Battles Shaping America's Future*. New York: Random House, 1989.

Magnusson, Lars. *The Tradition of Free Trade*. New York: Routledge, 2004.

Maneschi, A. *Comparative Advantage in International Trade: A Historical Perspective*. Cheltenham, UK: Edward Elgar, 1998.

Markell, David L. and John H. Knox, eds. *Greening NAFTA: The North American Commission for Environmental Cooperation*. Palo Alto: Stanford Law and Politics, 2003.

Martinez, Mark A. *The Myth of the Free Market: The Role of the State in a Capitalist Economy*. Sterling, VA: Kumarian Press, 2009.

Matthias, Peter et al. *Cambridge Economic History of Europe*. Cambridge, UK: Cambridge University Press, 1989.

McKinley, William. *The Tariff: A Review of the Tariff Legislation of the United States From 1812 to 1896*. New York: G.P. Putnam's Sons, 1904.

Merrett, Christopher D. *Free Trade: Neither Free Nor About Trade*. Cheektowaga, NY: Black Rose Books, 1996.

Milanovic, Branko. *Worlds Apart: Measuring International and Global Inequality*. Princeton, NJ: Princeton University Press, 2005.

Mishel, Lawrence, Jared Bernstein, and Heidi Shierholz. *The State of Working America, 2008/2009*. Ithaca, NY: Cornell University Press, 2009.

Mongredien, Augustus. *History of the Free Trade Movement in England*. New York: G.P. Putnam's Sons, 1881.

Morris, Jane Anne. *Gaveling Down the Rabble: How "Free Trade" Is Stealing Our Democracy*. New York: Apex Press, 2008.

Mullikin, Tom. *Truck Stop Politics: Understanding the Emerging Force of Working Class America*. Charlotte, NC: Vox Populi Publishers, 2006.

Nader, Ralph et al. *The Case Against Free Trade: GATT, NAFTA and the Globalization of Corporate Power*. San Francisco: Earth Island Press, 1993.

Nafziger, Wayne. *Economic Development*, 4th ed. Cambridge, UK: Cambridge University Press, 2006.

Nelson, Richard, ed. *National Innovation Systems*. New York: Oxford University Press, 1993.

Newfarmer, Richard, ed. *Trade, Doha, and Development: A Window into the Issues*. Washington: World Bank Publications, 2005.

Northrup, Cynthia Clark. *The American Economy: A Historical Encyclopedia*. Santa Barbara, CA: ABC-CLIO, 2003.

Ocampo, José Antonio, K.S. Jomo and Rob Vos. *Growth Divergences: Explaining Differences in Economic Performance*. New York: Zed Books, 2007.

Office of Technology Assessment, *Competing Economies: America, Europe, and the Pacific Rim*. Washington: U.S. Government Printing Office, 1991.

304

Orme, William A. Jr. *Understanding NAFTA: Mexico, Free Trade, and the New North America.* Austin, TX: University of Texas Press, 1996.

O'Rourke, Kevin H. and Jeffrey G. Williamson. *Globalization and History: The Evolution of a Nineteenth-Century Atlantic Economy.* Cambridge, MA: MIT Press, 1999.

Overbeek, Johannes. *Free Trade Versus Protectionism: A Source Book of Essays and Readings.* Northampton, MA: Edward Elgar Publishing, 1999.

Palley, Thomas I. *Plenty of Nothing: The Downsizing of the American Dream and the Case for Structural Keynesianism.* Princeton, NJ: Princeton University Press, 1998.

Pages, Erik R. *Responding to Defense Dependence: Policy Ideas And The American Defense Industrial Base.* Westport, CT: Prager, 1996.

Peach, Terry. *Interpreting Ricardo.* Cambridge, UK: Cambridge University Press, 2009.

Perez, Carlota. *Technological Revolutions and Financial Capital: The Dynamics of Bubbles and Golden Ages.* Northampton: Edward Elgar, 2002.

Perkins, John. *Confessions of an Economic Hit Man.* New York: Plume, 2004.

Perot, Ross and Pat Choate. *Save Your Job, Save Our Country: Why NAFTA Must Be Stopped—Now!* New York: Hyperion, 1993.

Phillips, Kevin. *Arrogant Capital: Washington, Wall Street, and the Frustration of American Politics.* New York: Little, Brown & Co., 1995.

Phillips, Kevin. *Staying On Top: The Business Case for a National Industrial Strategy.* New York: Random House, 1984.

Pincus, Jonathan. *Pressure Groups and Politics in Antebellum Tariffs.* New York: Columbia University Press, 1977.

Polak, Paul. *Out of Poverty: What Works When Traditional Approaches Fail.* San Francisco: Berrett-Koehler, 2008.

Porter, Michael. *The Competitive Advantage of Nations.* New York: The Free Press, 1990.

Postrel, Virginia. *The Future and Its Enemies.* New York: Simon & Schuster, 1998.

Prestowitz, Clyde V. Jr. *Three Billion New Capitalists: The Great Shift of Wealth and Power to the East.* New York: Basic Books, 2006.

Prestowitz, Clyde V. Jr. *Trading Places: How We Are Giving Our Future to Japan and How to Reclaim It.* New York: Basic Books, 1988.

Rakocy, Betsy, Alejandro Reuss, Chris Sturr et al. *Real World Globalization.* Boston: Economic Affairs Bureau, 2007.

Reich, Robert. *Supercapitalism: The Transformation of Business, Democracy, and Everyday Life.* New York: Vintage, 2007.

Reich, Robert. *The Work of Nations: Preparing Ourselves for 21st Century Capitalism.* New York: Vintage, 1992.

Reinert, Erik S. *How Rich Countries Got Rich and Why Poor Countries Stay Poor.* New York: Caroll & Graf, 2007.

Ricardo, David. *The Principles of Political Economy and Taxation.* Mineola, NY: Dover Publications, 2004.

Rivera, Juan, Manuel Chavez, and Scott Whiteford, eds. *NAFTA and the Campesinos: The Impact of NAFTA on Small-Scale Agricultural Producers in Mexico and the Prospects for Change.* Scranton, PA: University of Scranton Press, 2009.

Rivera-Batiz, Luis A. *International Trade: Theory, Strategies, and Evidence.* New York: Oxford University Press, 2004.

Roberts, Russell. *The Choice: A Fable of Free Trade and Protectionism.* Upper Saddle River, NJ: Pearson, 2001.

Rodrik, Dani. *Has Globalization Gone Too Far?* Washington: Institute for International Economics, 1997.

Rodrik, Dani. *One Economics, Many Recipes: Globalization, Institutions, and Economic Growth.* Princeton, NJ: Princeton University Press, 2007.

Rosen, Ellen Israel. *Making Sweatshops: the Globalization of the U.S. Apparel Industry.* Berkeley, CA: University of California Press, 2002.

Rosenberg, Jerry M. *Encyclopedia of the North American Free Trade Agreement, the New American Community, and Latin American Trade.* Westport, CT: Greenwood Press, 1994.

Ross, Andrew. *Fast Boat to China: High-Tech Outsourcing and the Consequences of Free Trade—Lessons from Shanghai.* New York: Vintage Books, 2007.

Ruigrok, Winfried and Rob van Tulder. *The Logic of International Restructuring.* New York: Routledge, 1995.

Sachs, Jeffrey. *The End of Poverty: Economic Possibilities For Our Time.* New York: Penguin Books, 2005.

Sally, Razeen. *New Frontiers in Free Trade: Globalization's Future and Asia's Rising Role.* Washington: Cato Institute, 2008.

Sassen, Saskia. *Globalization and Its Discontents: Essays on the New Mobility of People and Money.* New York: New Press, 1998.

Schattschneider, Eric. *Politics, Pressures and the Tariff.* New York: Arno Press, 1974.

Semmel, Bernard. *The Rise of Free Trade Imperialism.* Cambridge, UK: Cambridge University Press, 1970.

Shorrocks, Anthony and Rolph van der Hoeven, eds. *Growth, Inequality, and Poverty: Prospects for Pro-Poor Economic Development.* New York: Oxford University Press, 2004.

Shutt, Harry, D. *The Myth of Free Trade.* Oxford, UK: Basil Blackwell, 1985.

Singer, Peter. *One World: The Ethics of Globalization.* New Haven, CT: Yale University Press, 2002.

Smick, David M. *The World is Curved: Hidden Dangers to the Global Economy*. New York: Portfolio Group, 2008.

Smith, Adam. *The Wealth of Nations*. Chicago: University of Chicago Press, 1976.

Soludo, Charles, Osita Ogbu, and Ha-Joon Chang, eds. *The Politics of Trade and Industrial Policy in Africa: Forced Consensus*. Trenton, NJ: Africa World Press, 2004.

Soros, George. *George Soros on Globalization*. New York: Public Affairs, 2002.

Stebbins, Giles. *American Protectionist's Manual*. Detroit: Thorndike Nourse, 1883.

Steingart, Gabor, *The War for Wealth: The True Story of Globalization, or Why The Flat World is Broken*. New York: McGraw-Hill, 2008.

Stiglitz, Joseph. *Globalization and Its Discontents*. New York: W.W. Norton & Co., 2002

Stiglitz, Joseph. *Making Globalization Work*. New York: W.W. Norton & Co., 2006.

Stiglitz, Joseph and Andrew Charlton. *Fair Trade for All: How Trade Can Promote Development*. New York: Oxford University Press, 2005.

Streek, Wolfgang and Kozo Yanamura, eds. *The Origins of Nonliberal Capitalism: Germany and Japan in Comparison*. Ithaca, NY: Cornell University Press, 2001.

Sumner, William Graham. *Protectionism: The -Ism That Teaches That Waste Makes Wealth*. New York: Henry Holt and Company, 1888.

Tassey, Gregory. *The Technology Imperative*. Northampton, MA: Edward Elgar, 2007.

Tausig, F.W. *The Tariff History of the United States*. New York: Capricorn Books, 1964.

Thurow, Lester. *Head to Head: The Coming Economic Battle Among Japan, Europe, and America*. New York: William Morrow & Co., 1992.

Thurow, Lester. *Fortune Favors the Bold: What We Must Do to Build a New and Lasting Global Prosperity*. New York: Harper Collins, 2003.

Tonelson, Alan. *The Race to the Bottom: Why a Worldwide Worker Surplus and Uncontrolled Free Trade Are Sinking American Living Standards*. Cambridge, MA: Westview Press, 2002.

Trentmann, Frank. *Free Trade Nation: Commerce, Consumption and Civil Society in Modern Britain*. Oxford, UK: Oxford University Press, 2009.

Turney, Elaine C. Prange and Cynthia Clark Northrup, eds. *Tariffs and Trade in U.S. History: An Encyclopedia*. Westport, CT: Greenwood Press, 2003.

Tyson, Laura D'Andrea. *Who's Bashing Whom? Trade Conflict in High-Technology Industries*. Washington: Institute for International Economics, 1992.

Unger, Roberto Mangabeira. *Free Trade Reimagined: The World Division of Labor and the Method of Economics*. Princeton, NJ: Princeton University Press, 2007.

Urmetzer, Peter. *From Free Trade to Forced Trade: Canada in the Global Economy*. Toronto: Penguin Canada, 2003.

Villard, Oswald Garrison. *Free Trade Free World*. New York: Robert Schalkenbach Foundation, 1947.

Wallach, Lori, Patrick Woodall, and Ralph Nader. *Whose Trade Organization? A Comprehensive Guide to the World Trade Organization*. New York: New Press, 2004.

Walter, Andrew and Gautam Sen. *Analyzing the Global Political Economy*. Princeton, NJ: Princeton University Press, 2008.

Watkins, Kevin and Penny Fowler. *Rigged Rules and Double Standards: Trade, Globalization, and the Fight Against Poverty*. Oxford, UK: Oxfam International, 2002.

Watkins, Kevin, ed. *Human Development Report 2005*. New York: United Nations Development Programme, 2005.

Weintraub, Sidney. *NAFTA's Impact on North America*. Washington: Center for Strategic and International Studies, 2004.

Wolman, Paul. *Most Favored Nation: The Republican Revisionists and U.S. Tariff Policy, 1897-1912*. Chapel Hill, NC: University of North Carolina Press, 1992.

Wolf, Martin. *Why Globalization Works*. New Haven, CT: Yale Nota Bene, 2004.

Wood, Adrian. *North-South Trade, Employment, and Inequality: Changing Fortunes in a Skill-Driven World*. Oxford, UK: Clarendon Press, 1994.

World Bank. *Globalization, Growth and Poverty: Building an Inclusive World Economy*. Washington: World Bank, 2002.

Yamamura, Kozo. *The Economic Emergence of Modern Japan*. Cambridge, UK: Cambridge University Press, 1997.

Yanamura, Kozo, ed. *Japan's Economic Structure: Should It Change?* Seattle: Society for Japanese Studies, 1990.

Yergin, Daniel and Joseph Stanislaw. *The Commanding Heights: The Battle for the World Economy*. New York: Touchstone, 1998.

Zeiler, Thomas W. *Free Trade, Free World: The Advent of GATT*. Chapel Hill, NC: University of North Carolina Press, 1999.

ARTICLES

Abdelal, Rawi and Adam Segal, "Has Globalization Passed its Peak?" *Foreign Affairs*, January/February 2007.

Acemoglu, Daron, Simon Johnson and James A. Robinson, "The Colonial Origins of Comparative Development: An Empirical Investigation," *American Economic Review*, December 2001.

Ackerman, Frank, "The Shrinking Gains From Trade: A Critical Assessment of Doha Round Projections," Global Development and Environment Institute, Tufts University, October 2005.

Ackerman, Frank, "Still Dead After All These Years: Interpreting the Failure of General Equilibrium Theory," *Journal of Economic Methodology*, June 2002.

Ackerman, Frank, "An Offer You Can't Refuse: Free Trade, Globalization, and the Search for Alternatives," in Frank Ackerman and Alejandro Nadal. *The Flawed Foundations of General Equilibrium: Critical Essays on Economic Theory*. London: Routledge, 2004.

Akamatsu, Kaname, "A Theory of Unbalanced Growth in the World Economy," *Review of World Economics*, June 1961.

Alderson, Arthur S., "Explaining Deindustrialization: Globalization, Failure or Success?" *American Sociological Review*, October 1999.

Amiti, Mary, "Are Uniform Tariffs Optimal?" International Monetary Fund, April 2004.

Amiti, Mary, and Shang-Jin Wei, "Fear of Service Outsourcing: Is it Justified?" *Economic Policy*, April 2005.

Aykūz, Yilmaz, "The WTO Negotiations on Industrial Tariffs: What is at Stake for Developing Countries?" Third World Network, May 2005.

Akyūz, Yilmaz, Richard Kozul-Wright, and Joerg Mayer, "Trade and Industrial Upgrading: Catching Up and Falling Behind," in Will Milberg, ed. *Labour and the Globalisation of Production: Causes and Consequences of Industrial Upgrading*. New York: Palgrave Macmillan, 2004.

Akyūz, Yilmaz. "Trade, Growth and Industrialization: Issues, Experience and Policy Challenges," Third World Network, 2005.

Alderson, A. S. and Nielsen, F., "Globalization and the Great U-turn. Income Inequality Trends in 16 OECD Countries." *American Journal of Sociology*, March 2002.

Anderson, James E. and Eric Van Wincoop, "Trade Costs," National Bureau of Economic Research, May 2004.

Anderson, Kym, "Subsidies and Trade Barriers," Centre for International Economic Studies, University of Adelaide, May 2004.

Anderson, Kym W. Martin and D. Van Der Mensbrugghe, "Doha Policies: Where Are the Pay-offs?" in Richard Newfarmer, ed. *Trade, Doha, and Development: A Window into the Issues*. Washington: World Bank, 2005.

Auty, Richard M. and Alan G Gelb, "Political Economy of Resource Abundant States," in Richard M. Auty, ed. *Resource Abundance and Economic Development*. Oxford, UK: Oxford University Press, 2001.

Bahmani-Oskooee, Mohsen, and Avik Chakrabarti, "Import Competition, Employment and Wages in U.S. Manufacturing," *Journal of Policy Modeling*, December 2003.

Baily, Martin N., and Diana Farrell, "Exploding the Myths of Offshoring," *McKinsey Quarterly*, June 2004.

Baily, Martin N., and Robert Z. Lawrence, "What Happened to the Great U.S. Job Machine? The Role of Trade and Electronic Offshoring." *Brookings Papers on Economic Activity*, September 2004.

Bairoch, Paul, "Free Trade and European Economic Development in the 19th Century," *European Economic Review*, November 1972.

Bairoch, Paul and Richard Kozul-Wright, "Globalization Myths: Some Historical Reflections on Integration, Industrialization, and Growth in the World Economy," United Nations Conference on Trade and Development, 1996.

Baker, Dean and Mark Weisbrot, "Will New Trade Gains Make Us Rich? An Assessment of the Prospective Gains From New Trade Agreements," Center for Economic and Policy Research, October, 2001.

Baker, Dean and Mark Weisbrot, "The Relative Impact of Trade Liberalization on Developing Countries," in Eric Hershberg et al., eds. *The Development Imperative*. New York: Social Science Research Council, 2005.

Baldwin, Richard E., "World Trade Facts," Graduate Institute of International Studies, Geneva, 2006.

Baldwin, Richard E., "Market Access and International Competition: A Simulation Study of 16K Random Access Memories," in Robert Feenstra, ed. *Empirical Studies of International Trade*. Cambridge, MA: MIT Press, 1988.

Baldwin, Richard E., and Philippe Martin. "Two Waves of Globalization: Superficial Similarities, Fundamental Differences," National Bureau of Economic Research, 1999.

Baumol, William, "Productivity Growth, Convergence, and Welfare: What the Long-Run Data Show," *American Economic Review*, December 1986.

Bergoeing, Raphael, "Trade Theory and Trade Facts," Federal Reserve Bank of Minneapolis, October 2003.

Berman, Eli, John Bound, and Zvi Griliches, "Changes in the Demand for Skilled Labor within U.S. Manufacturing Industries: Evidence from the Annual Survey of Manufacturing," *Quarterly Journal of Economics*, August 1994.

Berry, Albert, Francois Bourguignon and Christian Morrison, "Changes in the World Distribution of Income Between 1950 and 1977," *Economic Journal*, June 1983.

Blecker, Robert A, "Is America's Large and Growing Trade Deficit Economically Sustainable? A Symposium of Views," *International Economy*, May/June 1999.

Brander, James A. and Spencer, Barbara J., "International R&D Rivalry and Industrial Strategy," *The Review of Economic Studies*, October 1983.

Becker, Gary S. "The Age of Human Capital," in E. P. Lazear. *Education in the Twenty-First Century*. Palo Alto, CA: Hoover Institution Press, 2002.

Bhagwati, Jagdish, "Trade Liberalization and 'Fair Trade' Demands: Addressing the Environmental and Labour Standards Issues," *The World Economy*, November 1995.

Bhagwati, Jagdish, "Optimal Intervention to Achieve Non-Economic Objectives," *The Review of Economic Studies*, January 1969.

Bhagwati, Jagdish, Arvind Panagariya and T.N. Srinivasan, "The Muddles Over Outsourcing," *Journal of Economic Perspectives*, Fall 2004.

Bhagwati, Jagdish, "Is Free Trade Passé after All?" *Review of World Economics*, March 1989.

Bhagwati, Jagdish, "Free Trade: Old and New Challenges," *Economic Journal*, March 1994.

Bhalla, Surjit, and Lawrence J. Lau, "Openness, Technological Progress, and Economic Growth in Developing Countries," World Bank, 1992.

Bivens, L. Josh, "Globalization and American Wages: Today and Tomorrow," Economic Policy Institute, October 10, 2007.

Bivens, L. Josh, "Marketing the Gains From Trade," Economic Policy Institute, June 19, 2007.

Bivens, L. Josh, "Shifting Blame for Manufacturing Jobs Loss: Effect of Rising Trade Deficit Shouldn't be Ignored," Economic Policy Institute, April 2004.

Bivens, L. Josh, "EPI Issue Guide: Offshoring," Economic Policy Institute, May 2006.

Bivens, L. Josh, "Truth and Consequences of Offshoring: Recent Studies Overstate the Benefits and Ignore the Costs to American Workers," Economic Policy Institute, August 2005.

Blattman, Christopher, Michael A. Clemens, and Jeffrey G. Williamson "Who Protected and Why? Tariffs Around the World 1870-1938," Conference on the Political Economy of Globalization, Trinity College, Dublin, August 2002.

Blecker, Robert A., "The Ticking Debt Bomb: Why the U.S. International Financial Position is Not Sustainable," Economic Policy Institute, June 1999.

Blecker, Robert A., "NAFTA and The Peso Collapse: Not Just a Coincidence," Economic Policy Institute, May 1997.

Blecker, Robert A., "NAFTA, the Peso Crisis, and the Contradictions of the Mexican Economic Growth Strategy," Center for Economic Policy Analysis, New School for Social Research, 1996.

Blecker, Robert A., "The Political Economy of the North American Free Trade Agreement," in Robert A. Blecker, ed. *U.S. Trade Policy and Global Growth*. Armonk, NY: M.E. Sharpe, 1996.

Blecker, Robert A., "The North American Economies After NAFTA: A Critical appraisal." *International Journal of Political Economy*, Fall 2005.

Blinder, Alan S., "Offshoring: The Next Industrial Revolution?" *Foreign Affairs*, March/April 2006.

Booz, Allen, Hamilton and The Fuqua School of Business, "Next Generation Offshoring: The Globalization of Innovation," Booz, Allen, Hamilton and The Fuqua School of Business, Duke University, March 2007.

Bradford, Scott, Paul Grieco, and Gary Hufbauer, "The Payoff to America from Global Integration," in Fred Bergsten, ed. *The United States and the World Economy: Foreign Economic Policy for the Next Decade*. Washington: Peterson Institute for International Economics, 2005.

Brander, J. and Spencer, B., "Tariffs and the Extraction of Foreign Monopoly Rents Under Potential Entry," *Canadian Journal of Economics*, August 1981.

Brander, J. and Spencer, B., "Tariff Protection and Imperfect Competition," in Henry K. Kierzkowski, ed. *Monopolistic Competition and International Trade*. Oxford, UK: Clarendon Press, 1984.

Bronfenbrenner, Kate, "We'll close! Plant Closings, Plant-Closing Threats, Union Organizing, and NAFTA," *Multinational Monitor*, March 1997.

Bronfenbrenner, Kate, "Uneasy Terrain: The Impact of Capital Mobility on Workers, Wages, and Union Organizing," U.S. Trade Deficit Review Commission, September 2000.

Brunel, Claire and Gary Clyde Hufbauer, "Money for the Auto Industry: Consistent with WTO Rules?" Petersen Institute for International Economics, February 2009.

Burbach, Roger and William I. Robinson, "The Fin de Siècle Debate: Globalization as Global Shift," *Science and Society,* Spring 1999.

Bureau of Economic Analysis, "U.S. Net International Investment Position at Yearend 2008," Bureau of Economic Analysis, June 26, 2009.

Burke, James, "U.S. Investment in China Worsens Trade Deficit: U.S. Firms Build Export-Oriented Production Base in China's Low-Wage Low Labor-Protection Economy," Economic Policy Institute, May 2000.

Campbell, Bruce, Carlos Salas, and Robert E. Scott, "NAFTA at Seven: Its Impact on the Workers in All Three Nations," Economic Policy Institute, April 2001.

Cashell, Brian W., "The Economics of the Federal Budget," Congressional Research Service, October 6, 2006.

Chambers, R.G., "Tariff Reform and the Uniform Tariff," *Economic Studies Quarterly*, Fall 1994.

Champion, Karven Vossler, "Who Pays for Free Trade? The Dilemma of Free Trade and International Labor Standards," *North Carolina Journal of International Law and Commercial Regulation*, Fall 1996.

Charlton, Andrew H. and Joseph E. Stiglitz, "A Development-Friendly Prioritization of Doha Round Proposals," *The World Economy*, March 2005.

Charnovitz, Steve, "Addressing the Environmental and Labor Issues in the World Trade Organization," Progressive Policy Institute, November 1999.

Champion, Karven Vossler, "Who Pays for Free Trade? The Dilemma of Free Trade and International Labor Standards," *North Carolina Journal of International Law and Commercial Regulation*, Fall 1996.

Chase-Dunn, Christopher, "Globalization: A World-Systems Perspective," *Journal of World-Systems Research,* Summer 1999.

Chase-Dunn, Christopher K., Yukio Kawano, and Benjamin D. Brewer, "Trade Globalization since 1795: Waves of Integration in the World-System," *American Sociological Review,* February 2000.

Clemens, M.A. and J. G. Williamson, "A Tariff-Growth Paradox? Protection's Impact the World Around 1875-1997," National Bureau of Economic Research, September 2001.

Congressional Budget Office, "How Changes in the Value of the Chinese Currency Affect U.S. Imports," Washington: CBO, July 2008.

Congressional Budget Office, "The Benefits and Risks of Federal Funding for SEMATECH," Washington: CBO, September 1987.

Congressional Budget Office, "What accounts for the Decline in Manufacturing Employment?" Washington: CBO, February 2004.

Corbo, V., "Development Strategies and Policies in Latin America: A Historical Perspective," International Center for Economic Growth, April 1992.

Corden, W.M., "Booming Sector and Deindustrialization in a Small Open Economy," *The Economic Journal,* December 1982.

Croteau, David, "Challenging the 'Liberal Media' Claim: On Economics, Journalists' Private Views Are to Right of Public," Fairness and Accuracy in Reporting, July/August 1998.

Crucini, M.J., "Sources of Variation in Real Tariff Rates: The United States 1900-1940," *American Economic Review,* June 1994.

Cummings, Bruce, "The Origins and Development of the Northeast Asian Political Economy: Industrial Sectors, Product Cycles, and Political Consequences," *International Organization,* December 1984.

Dardis, Rachel and Jia-Yeoung Lin, "Automobile Quotas Revisited: The Costs of Continued Protection," *Journal of Consumer Affairs*, Winter 1985.

Davis, Donald, and Weinstein, David, "Does Economic Geography Matter for International Specialization?" National Bureau of Economic Research, 1996.

DeJong, David N. and Marla Ripoll, "Tariffs and Growth: An Empirical Exploration of Contingent Relationships," University of Pittsburgh, 2005.

DeLong, Bradford and Steve Dowrick, "Globalization and Convergence," in M. Bordo, A.M. Taylor and J. Williamson, eds. *Globalization in Historical Perspective*. Chicago: University of Chicago Press, 2003.

Dempsey, Jack, "Semiconductors and SEMATECH: Rebirth of a Strategic Industry," Industrial College of the Armed Forces, 1993.

Dixit, A. "Strategic Aspects of Trade Policy," in T. F. Bewley, ed. *Advances in Economic Theory. Fifth World Congress*. New York: Cambridge University Press, 1987.

Dorman, Peter, "The Free Trade Magic Act: In a Dubious Study, First You See the Benefits of Globalization, Then You Don't," Economic Policy Institute, October 2001.

Dorman, Peter, "Low Savings or a High Trade Deficit? Which Tail is Wagging Which?" *Challenge*, July-August 2007.

Dorman, Peter, "Policies to Promote International Labor Standards: An Analytical Review," U.S. Department of Labor, 1995.

Dowrick, Steve and Jane Golley, "Trade Openness and Growth: Who Benefits?" *Oxford Review of Economic Policy*, 2004.

Easterly, William, N. Loayza and P. Montiel, "Has Latin America's Post-Reform Growth Been Disappointing?" *Journal of International Economics*, November 1997.

Edwards, Sebastian, "Trade Orientation, Distortions, and Growth in Developing Countries," *Journal of Development Economics*, July 1992.

Edwards, Sebastian, "Openness, Trade Liberalization, and Growth in Developing Countries," *Journal of Economic Literature*, September 1993.

Engel, Charles and John H. Rogers, "How Wide is the Border?" *American Economic Review*, December 1996.

Esfahani, Hadi S., "Exports, Imports, and Growth in Semi-Industrialized Countries," *Journal of Development Economics*, January 1991.

European Commission Research Directorate-General, "The Seventh Framework Programme," European Commission, 2007.

Farber, Henry S, "Job Loss in the United States, 1981-2001," National Bureau of Economic Research, May 2003.

Farrell, Diana, Susan Lund, and Koby Sadan, "The New Power Brokers: Gaining Clout in Turbulent Markets," McKinsey Global Institute, July 2008.

Faux, Jeff, "Fast Track to Trade Deficits: Mushrooming Foreign Debt Begs for Strategic Pause Before Approving New Agreements," Economic Policy Institute, November 2001.

Faux, Jeff, "NAFTA at Seven: Its Impact on Workers in All Three Nations," Economic Policy Institute, 2001.

Feenstra, Robert C., "New Evidence on the Gains From Trade," *Review of World Economics*, December 2006.

309

Feenstra, Robert C., "Trade and Uneven Growth," *Journal of Development Economics*, 1996.

Florida, Richard, "The World Is Spiky," *The Atlantic Monthly*, October 2005.

Fox, Alan K., "The Economic Effects of Significant U.S. Import Restraints," United States International Trade Commission, February 2007.

Frankel, Jeffrey and David Romer, "Does Trade Cause Growth?" *American Economic Review*, June 1999.

Frankel, Jeffrey, "Assessing the Efficiency Gains from Further Trade Liberalization," John F. Kennedy School of Government, Harvard University, 2000.

Freeman, Richard B., "Are Your Wages Set in Beijing?" *Journal of Economic Perspectives*, Summer 1995.

Freeman, Richard B., "A Hard Headed Look at Labor Standards," in *International Labor Standards and Global Economic Integration: Proceedings of a Symposium.* Washington: U.S. Department of Labor, 1994.

Fuller, Dan and Doris Geide-Stevenson, "Consensus Among Economists: Revisited," *Journal of Economic Education*, Fall 2003.

Gloub, Stephen, "International Labor Standards: Are They an Appropriate Response to Global Competitiveness?" *U.S. Information Agency Electronic Journal*, February 1998.

Godley, W., "Seven Unsustainable Processes: Medium-term Prospects and Policies for the United States and the World," Levy Economics Institute, January 1999.

Godley, Wynne, Dimitri B. Papadimitriou, and Gennaro Zezza, "Prospects for the United States and the World: A Crisis That Conventional Remedies Cannot Resolve," Levy Economics Institute, December 2008.

Gomory, Ralph, "Shipping American Jobs Overseas: A Hearing on the Bush Administration's Claim That Outsourcing is Good for the U.S. Economy," Senate Democratic Policy Committee Hearing, March 5, 2004.

Graham, Frank D., "Some Aspects of Protection Further Considered," *The Quarterly Journal of Economics*, February 1923.

Grossman, G. M., "The Employment and Wage Effects of Import Competition," *Journal of International Economic Integration,* Spring 1987.

Grossman, G. M. and E. Helpman, "Protection for Sale," *American Economic Review*, September 1994.

Guillén, M., "Is Globalization Civilizing, Destructive or Feeble? A Critique of Five Key Debates in the Social Science Literature," *Annual Review of Sociology*, August 2001.

Gustafson, Bjorn, and Mats Johansson, "In Search of Smoking Guns: What Makes Income Inequality Vary Over Time in Different Countries?" *American Sociological Review*, August 1999.

Hamilton, Kirk et al, "Where is the Wealth of Nations? Measuring Capital for the 21st Century," World Bank, 2006.

Hausmann, Ricardo, Jason Hwang, and Dani Rodrik, "What You Export Matters," *Journal of Economic Growth*, March 2007.

Haveman, Jon, Nair, Usha, and Jerry Thursby, "The Effects of Protection on the Pattern of Trade: A Disaggregated Analysis" in Demetri Kantarelis, ed. *Business and Economics for the 21st Century.* Worcester, MA: Business & Economics Society International, 1998.

Hertel, Thomas, David Hummels, Maros Ivanic and Roman Keeney, "How Confident Can We Be in CGE-Based Assessments of Free Trade Agreements?" Center for Global Trade Analysis, Purdue University, May 2003.

Hirst, Paul and Grahame Thompson, "Globalization," *Soundings*, Autumn 1996.

Hummels, David, "Time as a Trade Barrier," Krannert School of Management, Purdue University, 2001.

Hummels, David, "Toward a Geography of Trade Costs," Krannert School of Management, Purdue University, 1999.

Irwin, Douglas A., "Tariffs and Growth in Late Nineteenth Century America," National Bureau of Economic Research, 2000.

Irwin, Douglas A., "Interpreting the Tariff-Growth Correlation of the Late Nineteenth Century," National Bureau of Economic Research, 2002.

Irwin, Douglas A., "Did Import Substitution Policies Promote Growth in the Late Nineteenth Century?" National Bureau of Economic Research, 2002.

Irwin, Douglas A., "New Estimates of the Average Tariff of the United States, 1790-1820," National Bureau of Economic Research, 2003.

Irwin, Douglas A., "U.S. Trade Policy Controversies: A Historical Perspective," Federal Reserve Bank of Dallas, November 2004.

Irwin, Douglas, A., "Tariffs and Growth in Late Nineteenth Century America," National Bureau of Economic Research, 2000.

Irwin, Douglas A., "The United States in a New Global Economy? A Century's Perspective," *American Economic Review, Papers and Proceedings 86*, May 1996.

Jackson, James K., "Foreign Ownership of U.S. Financial Assets: Implications of a Withdrawal," Congressional Research Service, January 14, 2008.

Jackson, James K., "The United States as a Net Debtor Nation: Overview of the International Investment Position," Congressional Research Service, October 29, 2007.

Jensen, J. Bradford, and Lori G. Kletzer, "Tradable Services: Understanding the Scope and Impact of Services Offshoring," Institute for International Economics, September 2005.

Johnson, Simon, "The Quiet Coup," *The Atlantic*, May 2009.

Klinger, Bailey and Daniel Lederman, "Diversification, Innovation, and Imitation Inside the Global Technological Frontier," World Bank, 2006.

Krueger, Anne O., "Supporting Globalization," Remarks at the 2002 Eisenhower National Security Conference, September 26, 2002.

Krueger, Anne O., "The Effects of Trade Strategies on Growth," *Finance and Development*, June 1983.

Krueger, Anne O., "Why Trade Liberalisation is Good for Growth," *The Economic Journal*, September 1998.

Krugman, Paul R., "A Model of Innovation, Technology Transfer, and the World Distribution of Income," *Journal of Political Economy*, 1979.

Krugman, Paul R., "A 'Technology Gap' Model of International Trade," in K. Jungenfelt and D. Hague. *Structural Adjustment in Advanced Open Economies*. New York: St. Martin's, 1987.

Krugman, Paul R., "Does the New Trade Theory Require a New Trade Policy?" *World Economy*, 1992.

Krugman, Paul R., "Endogenous Innovation, International Trade, and Growth," in Paul Krugman. *Rethinking International Trade*. Cambridge, MA: MIT Press, 1994.

Krugman, Paul R., "Import Protection as Export Promotion: International Competition in the Presence of Oligopoly and Economies of Scale," in Henryk Kierzkowski, ed. *Monopolistic Competition and International Trade*. Oxford, UK: Clarendon Press, 1984.

Krugman, Paul R., "The Increasing Returns Revolution in Trade and Geography," *American Economic Review*, June 2009.

Krugman, Paul R., "Ricardo's Difficult Idea," 1994, http://web.mit.edu/krugman/www/ricardo.htm.

Krugman, Paul R., "Increasing Returns and the Theory of International Trade," in Truman F. Bewley. *Advances in Economic Theory, Fifth World Congress*. Cambridge, UK: Cambridge University Press, 1987.

Krugman, Paul R., "Increasing Returns, Monopolistic Competition and International Trade," *Journal of International* Economics, 1979.

Krugman, Paul R., "Industrial Organization and International Trade," in Paul Krugman. *Rethinking International Trade*. Cambridge, MA: MIT Press, 1994.

Krugman, Paul R., "Scale Economies, Product Differentiation, and the Pattern of Trade," *American Economic Review*, December 1970.

Krugman, Paul R., "Intraindustry Specialization and the Gains from Trade," *Journal of Political Economy*, October 1981.

Krugman, Paul R., "Does the New Trade Theory Require a New Trade Policy?" *World Economy*, July 1992.

Krugman, Paul R., "The Narrow Moving Band, the Dutch Disease, and the Competitive Consequences of Mrs. Thatcher: Notes on Trade in the Presence of Dynamic Scale Economies," *Journal of Development Economics*, October 1987.

Krugman, Paul R., "Trade, Accumulation, and Uneven Development," *Journal of Development Economics*, April 1981.

Lai, Huiwen and Daniel Trefler, "On Estimating the Welfare Gains From Trade Liberalization," May 2004.

Lall, Sanjaya, "Reinventing Industrial Strategy: The Role of Government Policy in Building Industrial Competitiveness," United Nations Conference on Trade and Development, April 2004.

Lall, Sanjaya, "Technological Change and Industrialization in the Asian Newly Industrializing Economies: Achievements and Challenges," in L. Kim and R.R. Nelson, eds. *Technology, Learning and Innovation*. New York: Cambridge University Press, 2000.

Lawrence, Robert Z. and Matthew Slaughter, "International Trade and American Wages in the 1980s: Giant Sucking Sound or Small Hiccup?" Brookings Institution, 1993.

Lawrence, Robert Z., "Offshoring White Collar Work: Exploring the Empirics," in Susan M. Collins and Lael Brainard, eds. *Offshoring White Collar Work*. Washington: Brookings Institution, 2005.

Levinsohn, Jim and Wendy Petropoulos, "Creative Destruction or Just Plain Destruction? The U.S. Textile and Apparel Industries since 1972," National Bureau of Economic Research, June 2001.

Linden, Greg, Kenneth L. Kraemer, and Jason Dedrick, "Who Captures Value in a Global Innovation System? The Case of Apple's iPod," Personal Computing Industry Center, University of California at Irvine, June 2007.

Lindert, P.H. and J. G. Williamson, "Does Globalization Make the World More Unequal?" National Bureau of Economic Research, April 2001.

Magee, S.P. and L. Young, "Endogenous Protection in the United States, 1900-1984," in Kevin O'Rourke and J. G. Williamson. *Globalization and History*. Cambridge, MA: MIT Press, 1999.

Maneschi, Andrea, "How New is the 'New Trade Theory' of the Past Two Decades?" Vanderbilt University, July 2000.

Mankiw, N. Gregory and Phillip Swagel, "The Politics and Economics of Offshore Outsourcing," Harvard University and American Enterprise Institute, April 2006.

Markusen, James, "Modeling the Offshoring of White collar Services: From Comparative Advantage to the New Theories of Trade and FDI," in Susan M. Collins and Lael Brainard, eds. *Offshoring White Collar Work*. Washington: Brookings Institution, 2005.

Mastel, Greg, Andrew Szamosszegi, John Magnus and Lawrence Chimerine, "Enforcing the Rules: Strong Trade Laws as the Foundation of a Sound American Trade Policy," Alliance for American Manufacturing, May 2007.

Mataloni, Raymond J., "U.S. Multinational Companies Operations in 2003," *Survey of Current Business*, July 2005.

McCallum, John, "National Borders Matter: Canada—U.S. Regional Trade Patterns," *The American Economic Review*, June 1995.

311

McCarthy, John, "3.3 Million U.S. Jobs to Go Offshore," Forrester Research, November 11, 2002.

McKinsey Global Institute, "Offshoring: Is it a Win-Win Game?" August 2003.

Meardon, Stephen. "A Tale of Two Tariff Commissions and One Dubious 'Globalization Backlash'," Inter-American Development Bank, November 2002.

Melitz, M.J., "When and How Should Infant Industries be Protected?" *Journal of International Economics*, May 2005.

Melo, Alberto, "Industrial Policy in Latin America at the Turn of the Century," Inter-American Development Bank, August 2001.

Milanovic, Branko, "Global Income Inequality: What it is and Why it Matters?" World Bank, August 2006.

Morici, Peter and Evan Schultz, "Labor Standards in the Global Trading System," Economic Strategy Institute, 2001.

Morin, Richard and Scott Keeter, "The Complicated Politics of Free Trade," Pew Center for the People and the Press, January 4, 2007.

Morici, Peter, "The Trade Deficit: Where Does it Come From and What Does it Do?" Economic Strategy Institute, October 1997.

Morrow, Robertson, "The Bull Market in Politics," Clarium Capital Management, February 2008.

Nemeth, Roger, and David A. Smith, "International Trade and World-System Structure: A Multiple Network Analysis," *Review: A Journal of the Fernand Braudel Center*, Spring 1985.

Murshed, S. Mansoob, "When Does Natural Resource Abundance Lead to a Resource Curse," International Institute for Environment and Development, 2004.

Nordas, Hildegunn, Sébastien Miroudot and Przemyslaw Kowalski, "Dynamic Gains From Trade," Organization for Economic Cooperation and Development, November 2006.

Nye, John, "No Pain, No Gain: Opposing Free Trade Means Opposing Innovation," *Reason*, May 1996.

Odagiri, Hiroyuki, and Akira Goto, "The Japanese System of Innovation: Past, Present, and Future," in Richard R. Nelson, ed. *National Innovation Systems: A Comparative Analysis*. New York: Oxford University Press, 1993.

Organization for Economic Cooperation and Development, "Science, Technology and Industry Outlook 2006," OECD, December 2006.

O'Rourke, Kevin H., "Tariffs and Growth in the Late 19th Century," *The Economic Journal*, April 2000.

O'Rourke, Kevin H., "Globalization and Inequality: Historical Trends." National Bureau of Economic Research, 2001.

Palley, Thomas I., "Rethinking Trade and Trade Policy: Gomory, Baumol, and Samuelson on Comparative Advantage," Woodrow Wilson Center, June 13, 2006.

Panagariya, A., "The Economics and Politics of Uniform Tariffs," Department of Economics, University of Maryland, November 1996.

Panagariya, A. and Dani Rodrik, "Political-Economy Arguments for a Uniform Tariff," *International Economic Review*, August 1993.

Parenteau, Robert W., "U.S. Household Deficit Spending: A Rendezvous With Reality," Levy Economics Institute, 2006.

Prasch, Robert E. "Reassessing the Theory of Comparative Advantage," *Review of Political Economy*, January 1996.

Reich, Robert, "But Now We're Global," *The Times Literary Supplement*, August 31, 1990.

Reinert, Erik S., "Catching Up From Way Behind: A Third World View Perspective on First World History," in Fagerberg, Jan et al. *The Dynamics of Technology, Trade, and Growth*. London: Edward Elgar, 1994.

Reinert, Erik S., "Competitiveness and its Predecessors: a 500-Year Cross-National Perspective," STEP Group, May 1994.

Reinert, Erik S., "The Other Canon: The History of Renaissance Economics," in Erik S. Reinert, ed. *Globalization, Economic Development and Inequality: An Alternative Perspective.* London: Edward Elgar Publishers, 2004.

Reinert, Eric S., "International Trade and the Economic Mechanisms of Underdevelopment," PhD diss., Cornell University, 1980.

Reinert, Erik S., "Raw Materials in the History of Economic Policy," in Gary Cook, ed. *The Economics and Politics of International Trade*. New York: Routledge, 1998.

Richardson, J. David, "'New' Trade Theory and Policy a Decade Old: Assessment in a Pacific Context," National Bureau of Economic Research, September 1993.

Rodriguez-Clare, Andres, "Clusters and Comparative Advantage: Implications for Industrial Policy," Inter-American Development Bank, June 2004.

Rodrik, Dani, "Industrial Policy for the Twenty-First Century," John F. Kennedy School of Government, Harvard University, September 2004.

Rodrik, Dani, "The Global Governance of Trade as if Development Really Mattered," United Nations Development Programme, July 2001.

Rodrik, Dani and Ricardo Hausmann, "Doomed to Choose: Industrial Policy as Predicament," John F. Kennedy School of Government, Harvard University, September 2006.

Rodrik, Dani and Ricardo Hausmann, "Economic Development as Self-Discovery," John F. Kennedy School of Government, Harvard University, April 2003.

Rodrik, Dani and Arvind Panagariya, "Political Economy Arguments for a Uniform Tariff," *International Economic Review*, August 1993.

Rodrik, Dani and Francisco Rodriguez, "Trade Policy and Economic Growth: a Skeptic's Guide to the Cross-National Evidence," John F. Kennedy School of Government, Harvard University, May 2000.

Rodrik, Dani, "Taking Trade Policy Seriously: Export Subsidization as a Case Study in Policy Effectiveness," in A. Deardorff, J. Levinson, and R. Stern, eds. *New Directions in Trade Theory.* Ann Arbor, MI: University of Michigan Press, 1995.

Rodrik, Dani & Francisco Rodriguez, "Trade Policy and Economic Growth: A Skeptic's Guide to the Cross-National Evidence," in Ben Bernanke and Kenneth S. Rogoff, eds. *Macroeconomics Annual 2000*, Cambridge, MA: MIT Press, 2001.

Rowthorn, Robert and Ramana Ramaswamy, "Growth, Trade, and Deindustrialization," International Monetary Fund, April 1998.

Ruggie, John G., "Trade, Protectionism, and the Future of Welfare Capitalism," *Journal of International Affairs*, Summer 1994.

Rugman, Alan M. and Alain Verbeke, "Regional Multinationals and Triad Strategy," in *Research in Global Strategic Management.* Oxford, UK: Elsevier, 2003.

Sachs, Jeffrey and Andrew Warner, "The Curse of Natural Resources," *European Economic Review*, May 2001.

Sachs, Jeffrey and David Warner, "Fundamental Sources of Long-Run Growth," *American Economic Review*, May 1997.

Sachs, Jeffrey and Howard Shatz, "Trade and Jobs in U.S. Manufacturing," Brookings Institution, 1994.

Samuel, Howard D., "The Turning Point for Labor and Trade," Economic Strategy Institute, 2000.

Samuelson, Paul A., "International Trade and the Equalization of Factor Prices," *Economic Journal*, June 1948.

Samuelson, Paul A., "Mathematical Vindication of Ricardo on Machinery," *Journal of Political Economy*, April 1988.

Samuelson, Paul A., "Where Ricardo and Mill Rebut and Confirm Arguments of Mainstream Economists Supporting Globalization," *Journal of Economic Perspectives*, Summer 2004.

Samuelson, Paul A. and Wolfgang Stolper, "Protection and Real Wages," *Review of Economic Studies*, November 1941.

Schwartz, Peter and Peter Leyden, "The Long Boom: A History of the Future, 1980—2020," *Wired*, July 1997.

Scott, Robert E., "The China Wage Toll: Widespread Wage Suppression, 2 Million Jobs Lost in the U.S.," Economic Policy Institute, July 30, 2008.

Scott, Robert E., "The Hidden Costs of Insourcing: Higher Trade Deficits and Job Losses for U.S. Workers," Economic Policy Institute, August 23, 2007.

Scott, Robert E., "The Facts About Trade and Job Creation," Economic Policy Institute, August 24, 2000.

Scott, Robert E., "Distorting the Record: NAFTA's Promoters Play Fast and Loose With Facts," Economic Policy Institute, July 13, 2001

Scott, Robert E., Carlos Salas, Bruce Campbell, and Jeff Faux, "Revisiting NAFTA: Still not Working for North America's Workers," Economic Policy Institute, September 28, 2006.

Schmitt, J. and L. Mishel, "Did International Trade Lower Less-Skilled Wages During the 1980s? Standard Trade Theory and Evidence," Economic Policy Institute,1996.

Slaughter, Matthew, "Globalization and Wages: a Tale of Two Perspectives," *World Economy*, July 1999.

Smith, David A. and Douglas R. White, "Structure and Dynamics of the Global Economy: Network Analysis of International Trade 1965-1980," *Social Forces*, June 1992.

Stanford, James, "CGE Models of North American Free Trade: A Critique of Methods and Assumptions," testimony before public hearing on "Economy-Wide Modeling of the Economic Implications of Free Trade," U.S. International Trade Commission, 1992.

Stiglitz, Joseph E. "Factor Price Equalization in a Dynamic Economy," *Journal of Political Economy*, May/June 1970.

Subramanian, Arvind, Ali Ibrahim, and Luis A. Torres-Castro, "Optimal Tariffs: Theory and Practice," International Monetary Fund, June 1993.

Summers, Lawrence H. and Lawrence F. Katz, "Can Interindustry Wage Differentials Justify Strategic Trade Policy?" in Robert C. Feenstra, ed. *Trade Policies for International Competitiveness.* Chicago: University of Chicago Press, 1989.

Tarr, David G., "Arguments For and Against Uniform Tariffs" in Bernard Hoekman, Aaditya Mattoo and Philip English, eds. *Development, Trade, and the WTO.* Washington: World Bank, 2002.

Taylor, Lance, and Codrina Rada, "Can the Poor Countries Catch Up? Extended Sources of Growth Projections Give Weak Convergence for the Early 21st Century," Schwartz Center for Economic Policy Analysis, New School for Social Research, June 2003.

Thurow, Lester, "Microchips, Not Potato Chips," *Foreign Affairs*, July/August 1994.

Trefler, Daniel, "Offshoring: Threats and Opportunities," in Susan M. Collins and Lael Brainard, eds. *Offshoring White collar Work.* Washington: Brookings Institution, 2005.

Tucker, Todd, "Election 2008: Fair Trade Gets an Upgrade," Public Citizen, November 5, 2008.

United States International Trade Commission, "The Economic Effects of Significant U.S Import Restraints: Fifth Update 2007," USITC, 2007.

Vamvakidis, A., "How Robust is the Growth-Openness Connection? Historical Evidence," *Journal of Economic Growth*, July 2002.

Van Der Mensbrugghe, D., "Estimating the Benefits of Trade Reform: Why Numbers Change," in Richard New-farmer, ed. *Trade, Doha, and Development: A Window into the Issues*. Washington: World Bank, 2006.

Wei, Shang-Jin, "Intranational Versus International Trade: How Stubborn are Nations in Global Integration?" National Bureau of Economic Research, April 1996.

Weisbrot, M., D. Rosnick and D. Baker, "Poor Numbers: the Impact of Trade Liberalization on World Poverty," Center for Economic and Policy Research, November 2005.

Weller, Christian E., Robert E. Scott, and Adam S. Hersh, "The Unremarkable Record of Liberalized Trade," Economic Policy Institute, October 2001.

Westphal, Larry E., "Empirical Justification for Infant Industry Promotion," World Bank, March 1981.

Westphal, L.E., "Industrial Policy in an Export-Propelled Economy: Lessons from South Korea's Experience," *Journal of Economic Perspectives*, Summer 1990.

Williamson, Jeffrey G., "Globalization and Inequality Then and Now: The Late 19th and Late 20th Centuries Compared," National Bureau of Economic Research, 1996.

Williamson, Jeffrey G., "Two Centuries of Globalization: Backlash and Bribes for the Losers," World Institute for Development Economics Research, September 2002.

Winters, Alan, Neil McCulloch and Andrew McKay, "Trade Liberalization and Poverty: Evidence so Far," *Journal of Economic Literature*, March 2004.

Wise, Timothy A. and Kevin P. Gallagher, "No Fast Track to Global Poverty Reduction," Global Development and Environment Institute, Tufts University, April 2007.

Wolf, Holger, "Trade Orientation: Measurement and Consequences," *Estudios de Economia,* June 1993.

Wood, Adrian, "How Trade Hurt Unskilled Workers," *Journal of Economic Perspectives*, Summer 1994.

World Bank, "2005 International Comparison Program Preliminary Results," 17 December 2007.

Wright, G., "The Origins of American Industrial Success, 1879-1940," *American Economic Review*, September 1990.

Yamamura, Kozo, "Caveat Emptor: the Industrial Policy of Japan" in Paul Krugman, ed. *Strategic Trade Policy and the New International Economics*. Cambridge, MA: MIT Press, 1987.

Yenikkaya, Halit, "Trade Openness and Economic Growth: A Cross-Country Empirical Investigation," *Journal of Development Economics*, October 2003.

314

INDEX

A

absolute advantage, 96, 102, 110
abstractionism, 130
Abu Dhabi Investment Authority, 42
ad hominem attacks, 28
Adobe, xvi
Advanced Technology and Logistics division, 204
Advanced Technology Program, 209, 211
adverse productivity growth, 223
Advisory Group on Electron Devices, 8
aerodynamics, 4, 211
Afghanistan, 25
AFL-CIO, 84
Africa, 32, 124, 156, 162, 163, 172, 194, 197
agricultural subsidies, 197
agriculture, 26, 57, 102, 127, 134, 135, 152, 157, 161, 164, 191, 197, 245, 248
Aid for Trade, 179
air freight, 20
Airbus, 69, 177, 256
aircraft, 4, 22, 69, 70, 117, 177, 192, 198, 202, 203, 205, 214, 215, 218, 226, 237, 274
Alabama, 85, 110
Alaska, 262
Algeria, 162
America First, 15, 250
American Chamber of Commerce of Mexico, 159
American Economics Association, 213
American Revolution, 95, 132
American Telephone and Telegraph, 202
Ampex, 67
anarchism, 78
Angola, 164
antitrust, 216, 241
apparel, 178
Apple Computer, 63, 66
architects, 32
Argentina, 35, 153, 156
aristocracy, 48, 127, 134
Arnold, Benedict, 255
Articles of Agreement (WTO), 44
American Speciality Cars, 67
Asian Crisis, 44
assets, 39, 40, 104, 247
Associated Press, 259
Association of Southeast Asian Nations, 172
Australia, 87, 89, 105, 162, 196, 263
Austria, 7, 128
authoritarianism, 62, 83, 171, 174, 237, 293
auto insurance, 167
autocrats, 26
automobiles, xvi, 50, 70, 71, 74, 90, 91, 110, 146, 147, 158, 192, 197, 218, 225, 241
Automotive Trade Policy Council, 74

B

B-29, 146
Bahr, William, 41

Bahrain, 161
bailouts, 264
balance of payments, 44, 53, 125, 146, 199
Baldrige, Malcolm, 144
banana republics, 132, 196
bancor, 53
Bangalore, xiii, 24, 153, 238
Bangladesh, 87, 125, 164, 214
bank debt, 71
Bank of Japan, 42
banks, 88
barbers, 117, 195
Barrett, Craig, 62
Bartlett, Bruce, 8
Bartlett, Douglas, 66
Basel Convention, 169
batteries, 208
Battle in Seattle, 174
Baumol, William, 213, 228
Begich, Mark, 262
Beijing, 125
Belgium, 7, 124, 140, 164
Bell Laboratories, 202
Berlin Wall, 204
Bhagwati, Jagdish, 80
bicycles, 214
billionaires, 9
bin Laden, Osama, 179
bin Mohamad, Mahathir, 80, 81
biocomputing, 211
biofuel, 197
birds, 167
Blackstone Capital, 42
Blair, Tony, 250
Blinder, Alan, 31, 232
blue-collar workers, 109
BMW, 115
Boeing, xvi, 69, 203, 206
Bolivia, 153
bonds, 74
bookkeeping, 38
Booz Allen Hamilton, 68
Border-Adjustable Tax, 245
borderless world, 26, 175
borrowing, 40, 41, 252
Boston Tea Party, 79
Botswana, 154, 157
bottle recycling, 167
bourgeoisie, 48, 136, 248, 250
Bovard, James, 103
brand equity, 33
brand piracy, 81
Brander, James, 295
Brin, Sergey, 204
Brazil, 2, 35, 89, 105, 140, 153, 167, 169, 194, 198, 217, 293
bread, 98, 100, 115, 191
Bretton Woods, 52, 53, 75, 143
Bright, John, 26
Britain, xiv, 26, 30, 53, 71, 88, 95, 112, 116, 122-124, 126-132, 142, 186, 195, 208, 226
British Broadcasting Corporation, 166
British Empire, 123, 135, 196
broadband, 61
Bromley, Alan, 8
Brown, Sherrod, 252, 258

Brunei, 42, 162, 263
bubbles, 39, 119, 139
Buchanan, James, 134
Buchanan, Patrick, 96, 250
Buffett, Warren, 232, 244
buildings, 107
bureaucrats, 84, 168
Bush, George H.W., 8, 144, 168, 188, 204
Bush, George W., 33, 255
business climate, 32
Business Mexico, 159
business schools, 10
BusinessWeek, 10
buy American, 263
Byrd Amendment, 174

C

CAFTA, 161, 257, 265
Calder, Kent, 147
California, 23, 167
call centers, 68
Cambodia, 164, 170
cameras, 143
camouflage, 5
Canada, 26, 41, 42, 77, 80, 85, 87, 89, 100, 101,
    103, 105, 116, 140, 150, 159, 167, 196, 259,
    260, 272, 275, 279, 283, 289, 290, 293, 297,
    306, 311
cancer, 29, 105
Cancun, 150
candy, 150
Cap and Trade, 263
capital, 23, 24, 34, 65, 111, 113, 124, 142, 147,
    158, 200, 242, 248
capitalism, 13, 82, 136
capitalists, 111, 136
carbon tariff, 263, 265
carcinogens, 167
Cardenas, Lázaro, 165
cartels, 120
Carter, Jimmy 144
Casey, Bob, 258
Castañeda, Jorge, 101
castles, 194
CAT scanners, 208
Caterpillar, 36
Cato Institute, 12
cellular phones, 65
Center for Strategic and International Studies, 8
Center for Working-Class Studies, 256
Central Bank of China, 42
central planning, 209
CFCs, 3
CFIUS, 43
chaebols, 186
Chamberlain, Joseph, 129
chemical engineering, 128
chemicals, 158
Cheney, Dick, 205
chief executives, 249
Chile, 42, 162, 198, 263
China, xiii, 2, 3, 7, 8, 22, 24, 26, 27, 30, 31, 34,
    42, 44, 50, 52, 54, 58, 61, 62, 64-66, 67, 70,
    74-77, 81, 83, 84, 86, 95, 99, 101, 105, 115,
    122, 145, 147, 148, 153-155, 161-163, 175,
    178, 201, 205, 207, 238, 252, 261, 263, 264,
    273, 275-281, 283, 287-289, 293, 294, 296,
    298, 303-305, 308, 313
China Business Forum, 50

China Currency Coalition, 74
Chinastakes.com, 44
chokepoint technologies, 208
Chrysler, xvi, 66, 90
Chu, Stephen, 263
Citigroup, 42
City of London, 131
civic humanism, 125
Civil War (American), 135
civilian security contractors, 248
class, 29, 136
classical liberalism, 127, 130, 134
Clean Air Act, 167
Clearing Union, 53
Cleveland, Grover, 137
Cleveland State University, 259
Clinton, Bill, 144, 160, 161, 177, 249, 258
Clinton, Hillary, 252, 259
clipper ships, 95
cloth, 111
Cobden, Richard, 26
cocoa, 238, 245
coffee, 82, 137, 191, 194, 201, 293
Cohen, Stephen, 67
Cold War, 13, 30, 122, 141, 144, 173, 198, 210
colleges, 59
Colombia, 140, 161, 162
colonialism, 22, 24, 39, 81, 135, 196, 238
Colorado, 243, 262
Commerce Department, 2, 70, 74, 84, 144, 187,
    218, 266
commodity bubble, 39, 197
communism, xiii, 141
comparative advantage, 95, 96, 98, 99, 100, 102,
    104, 105, 107, 109, 112, 113, 114, 117, 121,
    122, 127, 134, 146, 183-185, 187, 189, 196,
    213, 214, 223, 228
comparative disadvantage, 102
competition, 30, 199, 214, 224, 241
competitive advantage, 241
competitiveness, 10, 57, 59, 88, 189, 192, 211
components, 23, 65, 161
compulsory licensing, 171
computer chips, 72, 207
computers, 245, 161
Confucianism, 62
Congo, 157
Congress, xx, 5, 6, 21, 73, 79, 133, 137, 139-
    141, 143, 161, 167, 174, 177, 178, 239, 245,
    248, 252, 261, 263, 265, 275, 277, 280, 282,
    290, 297, 298, 300, 309, 311
Congress Daily, 261
Conrad, Kent, 244
Conservative party, 130
Constitution, U.S., 21, 170
construction, 248
consulting firms, 7
consumer electronics, 203, 227, 241
consumer tastes, 59
consumers, 111, 130
consumption, 39, 41, 47, 52, 62, 240, 245
Continental Europe, 130
convenience stores, 186
cooking, 248
copper, 207
copyright, 81
CORFO, 198
corn, 100, 103
Corn Laws, 126, 127
corporations, 4, 24, 177, 249, 250
corruption, 5, 6, 7, 8

cosmopolitanism, 19, 130
cost curves, 234, 235
Costa Rica, 15, 140, 237, 296
cotton, 120, 129, 135
Cotton, Norris, 143
Council of Economic Advisors, 232
Council on Competitiveness, 64
countervailing powers, 193
courts, 170
Crash of 1929, 52
creativity, 61, 63
credit cards, 83
crime, 248
crisis, 53, 54, 268
crops, 184
cross-conditionality, 170
cross-shareholdings, 71
Cuba, 140, 154, 288
Culbertson, John, 190
cultural differences, 120
cultural diversity, 63
cultural exchange, 20
culture, 79, 80
Cunningham, William, 124
currencies, 29, 73, 74, 79, 163; manipulation,
     xiv, 75, 242, 251, 256, 258
customers, 221
customs valuations, 77
CVS, 151
Czechoslovakia, 140

D

Dahlkemper, Kathy, 262
Dallas, 262
De Mora, Joseph, 259
De Gaulle, Charles, 54
Dearborn, MI, 101
debates, presidential, 8
debt, xvii, 32, 44, 47-49, 104, 247
decadence, 46, 47, 48
defense, 92, 203, 205
Defense Advanced Research Projects Agency,
     204
defense contractors, 205
Defense Department, 205, 294
Defense Intelligence Agency, 204
deficit (trade), xiii, 1, 8, 23, 31, 32, 38, 40, 41,
     49-52, 56, 57, 64, 66, 70, 73, 118, 130, 143,
     159, 161, 233, 244, 270, 271, 274, 275, 283,
     287
deflation, 134
deindustrialization, 64, 107, 135, 261
democracy, 4, 266
Democratic Congressional Campaign
     Committee, 257, 258, 261, 262
Democratic Senatorial Campaign Committee,
     262
democratization, 62
Democrats, 74, 134, 136, 249, 253, 255, 256,
     258, 265-267, 277, 297, 298
demonstrations, 247
Denmark, 7, 87, 88
Department of Justice, 216
Department of Labor, 159
derivatives, 39
Detroit, 161
deus ex machina, 58
Deutschebank, 166

diligence, 46, 47
disk drives, 243
Disney, 166
diversification, economic, 184
diversity, 249
Doha, 174
dolls, 129
domestic-content requirements, 172
dormitories, 155
dough, 115
downstream industries, 185, 206, 239
drill bits, 207
drudgery, 28
drugs, 171
Dublin, 196
Duke University, 68
dumping, 71, 133
dying industries, 91, 232
dynamism, 261

E

ear plugs, 3
East Asia, 50, 198, 198, 199
economic growth, 7, 24, 35, 62, 112, 122, 128,
     147, 161, 162, 163, 184, 186, 187, 189, 192,
     212, 236
economic history, 122, 232
economic liberty, 54, 130, 240
economic nationalism, 14, 15, 25
Economic Policy Institute, 159
Economic Strategy Institute, 41, 187
economics, 3, 14, 19 14, 237, 189
economists, 1, 3-7, 9, 10, 11, 13, 14, 48, 112,
     130, 160, 192, 193, 215, 295
Ecuador, 140
editors, 29
education, 35, 59, 60, 87, 130, 255;
Edward III, 125
Edward VI, 125
Edwards, John, 255
efficiency, 48, 49, 248
Egypt, 157, 162
Eisenhower, Dwight 141
El Salvador, 140, 161
Elkus, Richard, 186, 206
election cycles, 254
electric cars, 187, 208
electrical industries, 128
Emanuel, Rahm, 258
employees, 249
endangered species, 169
energy, 65
engineers, 10, 32
England, 24, 111
English, Phil, 262
entrepreneurship, 63, 184, 185, 213
environment, 20, 22, 105, 156, 157, 161, 166,
     264
epoxy resins, 72
equilibria, 53, 118, 184, 185, 226, 244, 295
Eskimos, 224
ethics, 22, 83
Europe, 7, 63, 71, 82, 89, 152, 244, 265
European Union, 61, 71, 88
Eurozone, 7
evil, 81
exchange rates, 52, 53, 75, 175; fixed, 52, 53, 54,
     143

experiments, 123
experts, 4, 9, 141
exploitation, 249
export bounties, 244
export industries, 118
export processing zones, 210
Export-Import Bank, 133
export-performance requirements, 172
externalities, 105, 106, 185, 186, 188, 190, 193, 229, 230, 264, 287, 292
eye protection, 3

F

Fabian socialism, 154
fabric, 178
fabrication, 227
factor costs, 241
factories, 103
factors of production, 98, 99, 101, 106, 107, 109, 110, 121, 126, 200, 201, 217, 219
fair trade, 82, 254
Fairness and Accuracy in Reporting, 29
faith, 13
family networks, 186
fanaticism, 176
farmers, 82, 127, 171, 193, 197
fascism, 22
Fast Track, 29, 168, 257, 258
fax machines, 44, 65
Federal budget, 41
Federal Reserve, 31, 107, 139
fees, 66
fertilizer, 104, 197
fiber optics, 23
Fields, Craig, 204
film, 80, 207
finance, 2, 26, 39
financial analysts, 248
financial engineering, 69
financial panic, 44
financial services, 69
Fingleton, Eamonn, 12
Finland, 7, 140, 220
First World, 35, 36, 58, 82, 152, 164, 197, 201, 237
fishing, 147
Fitzpatrick, Mike, 257
Flanders, 124
flat tariff, 233, 235, 242, 244
flat panel displays, 233
Flint, MI, 261
Florida, 237
Florida, Richard, 67
"flying geese" strategy, 147
food riots, 197
Ford Motors, xvi, 91
foreign exchange, 158
foreign investment, 32, 51, 75, 147, 210, 238
foreign investors, 165
foreign policy, 26, 141, 173, 253
Founding Fathers, 21, 132
foundries, 3
Fourteen Points for Peace, 139
France, xiv, 45, 54, 71, 87, 128, 132, 140, 142, 164, 265, 279
Franco, Francisco, 293
Frank, Thomas, 256
Franken, Al, 262

free markets, 12, 13, 45, 75, 122, 123, 124, 192, 212, 216, 240; ideology, 21; limitations of, 185; offloading responsibility to, 22
free press, 30
free trade agreements, 27, 165, 167, 253, 263
freedom, 21, 47, 61, 62
Friedman, Milton, 11, 13, 139
Friedman, Thomas, xiii, 19, 68, 89
fruit, 192
fukoku kyohei, 145
Fuqua School of Business, 68

G

gains from trade, 103, 115-117, 120, 152, 226, 288
Gandhi, 154
garments, 109, 239
Garten, Jeffrey, 177
gas, 53
GATT, 167, 171-173, 276, 282, 286, 289, 290, 300-302, 304, 306
gays, 256
General Agreement on Tariffs and Trade, 44, 141, 167, 171, 172, 276
General Electric, xvi, 69
General Motors, xvi, 3, 36, 90, 91
genetic engineering, 168, 171, 195
Geneva, 168
Genuine Progress Indicator, 106
Georgetown University, 262
Georgia Tech, 61
Gephardt, Dick, 255
Gerard, Leo, 85
Gerlach, Jim, 258
Germany, xiv, 7, 23, 45, 70, 71, 85, 87, 89, 127, 128, 129, 130
Ghana, 157, 158, 238
Gilder, George, 64
Gingrich, Newt, 64
Global Insight, 7
Global Trade Analysis Project, 151
Global Trade Watch, 167, 257, 298
globalism, 15, 19, 250
globalization, 20, 22, 24, 25
God, 256
Goings, Rick, 200
gold, 123, 126, 135
"golden straitjacket," 88
Goldsmith, James, 9
Gomory, Ralph, xvi, 13, 213, 214, 216-219, 221, 223-228, 295, 296, 300, 310, 312
good industries, 157, 192, 193, 195, 196, 221, 233, 236, 237, 239
Goodyear, 2
Goolsbee, Austan, 259
GPI, 106
graduation rates, 60
Great Depression, 13, 48, 131, 139, 140, 268
Great Society, 53
greed, 249
green rooms, 169
Greenspan, Alan, 107
Greider, William, 71, 161, 169
groupthink, 9
guano, 104
Guatemala, 140, 160, 161, 164
Guerra do los Comuneros, 135
Gulf oil producers, 184

guns, 256

H

Hagan, Kay, 262
Haiti, 140, 153
Halloween, 150
Hamilton, Alexander, 132, 133, 147, 236, 245
Hanseatic League, 125
happiness, 10, 47
Harberger triangles, 108
hard money, 134
Harley Davidson, 144
Harrison, Benjamin, 137
Harvard Business School, 24, 121, 241
hazardous waste, 169
health, 166
health care aides, 108
heart attack, 92
hedge funds, 10
helicopters, 110
help desks, 68
Henry Carey, 134
Henry George, 6
Henry VII, 124, 132, 147
heritage, 19
Herman Daly, 14
hidden assumptions, 264
high school movement, 60
high technology, xvi, 49, 70, 82, 238
hippies, 250
Hiroshima, 101
historical accidents, 214, 217
Hitachi, 177
hockey-stick projections, 120
Hofheinz, Roy, 147
Holland, 7, 156
Hollings, Ernest, 143, 144
home bias, 23
home market, 241
Honda, 264
Honduras, 140, 161
Hong Kong, 26, 147, 148, 150, 174, 175
Hoover dam, 84
hormone-treated beef, 167
horse shoes, 131
House of Lords, 127
House of Representatives, 257, 261
House Trade Subcommittee, 173
Howell, David R., 60
Hull, Cordell, 140
human capital, 192
human nature, 62
human rights, 27, 166, 178, 169
Hunter, Duncan 177
Hussein, Saddam, 205
hybrid cars, 63
Hyundai, 264

I

IBM, 213, 216
ideology, 15, 82, 243, 244, 250, 268
IMF, 44, 53
Immelt, Jeffrey, 69
Immelt, Jeffrey R., xvi
immigration, 261, 265
imperfect competition, 215, 216

imperialism, 39
import certificates, 244
import dependence, 245
import quotas, 172
Import-Export Bank, 84
Imposts, 141
income, 156, 193, 246
increasing returns, 191, 193, 195
incumbents, 247
Independence, American, 131
independents, 253
India, 2, 3, 22, 24, 31, 34, 62, 63, 81, 85, 86,
    153, 154, 162, 163, 167, 169-171, 184, 238,
    278, 289, 290, 293
Indonesia, 167
industrial espionage, 81
industrial policy, xv, 6, 71, 73, 82, 83, 114, 122-
    124, 131, 132, 143, 144, 147, 187, 198, 200,
    202-204, 208, 215, 225, 232, 239, 241
industrial revolution, 135
industrialization, 135, 187
industries: advantageous, 223; capital-
    intensive, 233; declining, 33; diminishing-
    returns, 196; dying, 92; high-wage, 86;
    high-technology, 157; infant, 172, 187, 235;
    internationally-traded, 102; life cycles, 92;
    mature, 199, 235; medium-technology, 157;
    non-tradable, 2; non-traded, 118; retainable,
    214, 224; science-based, 128, 204; service,
    57; state-owned, 83; sunrise, 91
inequality, 33
inflation, 41, 53, 64, 264
information technology, 184
infrastructure, 23, 83, 87, 166, 179, 201, 210
initial public offerings, 63
innovation, xv, 8, 13, 24, 49, 63, 67, 68, 133,
    185, 192, 194, 195, 208, 209, 212, 216, 224,
    240, 261, 278
inputs, 185
installed-base effect, 9
integrated circuits, 294
integration, economic, 21
Intel, 62
intellectual capital, 9
intellectual property, 66, 170
intellectual rigor, 11
interest rates, 41, 46, 51, 75, 126, 264
International Forum on Globalization, 158, 166,
    238
international law, 179, 244
International Monetary Fund, 2, 39, 170
internationalism, 14, 15, 265, 266
Internet, 61, 62
investment, 51, 90, 234, 242
investment banking, 34
investment income, 248
investment rate, 31, 119
investors, foreign, 165
Iowa, 258
iPod, 65
Iraq war, 205
Ireland, 24, 164, 184, 196
Italdesign, 67
Italy, xiv, xvi, 71, 115, 142, 271
Ivory Coast, 158
ivory towers, 9

J

jack-of-all-trades, 220
Jackson, Andrew, 249
Jacksonville, FL, 237
jam, 129
Japan, 23, 24, 32, 62, 65, 67, 70, 71, 73, 74, 80,
    81, 86, 87, 89, 90, 95, 115, 116, 122, 143-
    147, 150, 178, 180, 187, 197, 207, 208, 216,
    225, 232, 238, 241, 265
Japanese Automobile Manufacturers
    Association, 71
Jefferson, Thomas, 131
Jiangong, Zhou, 44
jobs, 38; dead-end, 193; high wage, 248; low-
    wage, 2
Joint Direct Attack Munition, 205
judicial activism, 173
junkyard of history, 25
justice, 83

K

Kansas, 14, 256
Kaptur, Rep. Marcy, 60
Katz, Lawrence, 215
Kearns, Kevin, 266
keiretsus, 73, 186
Kennedy, John F., 142
Kennedy Round, 142
Kenny, Martin, 67
Kerry, John, 255, 256, 258, 259, 297
Keynes, John Maynard, 5, 13, 53, 268
"kicking away the ladder", 127
Kirk, Ron, 262
kit assembly, 65
Korea, 2
Krugman, Paul, 5, 11, 149, 160, 189, 264
Kuwait, 42, 225
Kyushu, 243

L

La Mesta, 135
labor, 2, 29, 34, 36, 39, 59, 65, 86, 91, 98, 103,
    107, 110, 111, 118, 121, 125, 142, 143, 144,
    147, 148, 160, 170, 193, 194, 195, 200, 215,
    216, 220, 230, 233, 237, 246, 247, 248;
    cheap, 115, 192, 246
labor laws, 107, 210
labor standards, 85
Labour party, 131
ladder externalities, 185
laissez faire, 28, 82, 131, 178, 202, 210
land tenure, 125
laogai, 85
laptops, 192
Latin America, xiv, 30, 35, 124, 156, 163, 198,
    199
law, 248; Anglo-American, 179; international,
    170
law firms, 248
lawn mowers, 97
lawyers, 225
LCD displays, 227
Leach, Jim, 258
Lebanon, 163

leeches, 95
left, 22, 29, 131, 164, 249, 250
legacy effects, 24
Lego, 69, 199
Lesotho, 163
level playing field, 83, 84, 166
Lexus, 19
liberal democracy, 77
Liberal party, 131
liberalism, 249
libertarianism, 103
liberty, economic, 131
licensing, 67, 70, 119
life forms, 171
Lighthizer, Robert, 173
Lincoln, Abraham, 134
List, Friedrich, 127
lithium-ion batteries, 208
lobbyists, 6, 168
local-content requirement, 199
localities, 84
location-specific technological
    externalities, 186
Lockheed, 203
lockout, 214, 217, 220
locomotives, 113
Loebsack, Dave, 258
logrolling, 6
Lome Convention, 167
London, 88, 114
Los Angeles, 60
lumber, 144
Luttwak, Edward, xvii
luxury goods, 26, 126

M

machine tools, 70, 113
macroeconomic stability, 119
magazines, 28
Mahoney, Tim, 258
Mahoning Valley, 257
Malaysia, 42, 80, 147, 162, 167
managed trade, 243, 265
Manhattan, 24
manufactured goods, 102, 194, 245
manufacturers, 211
manufacturing, xvi, 2, 33, 34, 41, 57, 58, 63, 64-
    66, 67, 69-71, 91, 114, 117, 127, 131, 132,
    134, 135, 158, 159, 161, 191, 193, 197, 206,
    233, 247
manufacturing regions, 119
Manufacturing Extension Partnership, 211
maquiladoras, 57, 160, 161, 200
market power, 192
market share, 60
Marshall Plan, 141
Marx, Karl, 9, 136, 140, 195
Maryland, 168
mass production, 67
mathematics, 10-12, 29, 11
Mazda, 101
McCain, John, 139, 250, 260
McCallum, John, 26
McCaskill, Claire, 258
McDonnell-Douglas, 203
meat, 167
media, 8, 26, 28, 121, 155, 156, 250
Medicaid, 171

Medieval Europe, 194
Meiji Restoration, 24
memory chips, 144
mercantilism, 123, 125, 128, 178, 209
Mercedes, 264
Merck, 166
Merkley, Jeff, 262
Merrill Lynch, 42
metal finishing, 207
Mexico, 57, 58, 101, 107, 150, 153, 159-161,
     165, 194, 198, 200, 259
Mexico City, 160
Miami, 72
Michigan, 110, 255, 273, 278, 282, 300, 304,
     313
MiCRA, 7
Micro Crystal AG, 205
microwave ovens, 214
Middle America, 79
middle class, 36, 254
middle income countries, 156, 237
Midwest, 119, 259
military, xiii, 27, 43, 59, 61, 80, 88, 124, 178,
     203-205, 292, 293
military bases, 178
military industrial policy, 203
military officers, 178
Miller, James C. III, 208
mining, 248
missiles, 203
Mitsubishi, 166
Moldova, 163
Mongolia, 157, 163
monkeys, 6
monopoly, 166, 192
Montana, 258
moon, 70
Moore, Michael, 261
moral fiber, 22
Morita, Akio 71
mortgages, xiv
Moscow, 108
motorcycles, 144
Mount Rushmore, 131
mouse traps, 129
movies, 80
Muldavin, Joshua, 155
multinational corporations, 14, 25, 58, 172
Murphy, Lois, 258
Murphy, Patrick, 257
Murshed, Syed Mansoob, 156

N

Nader, Ralph, 250
NAFTA, xiii, 29, 80, 85, 101, 159-162, 165,
     168, 169, 201, 244, 251, 255-260, 274, 282,
     283, 289, 290, 297, 298, 300-306, 308, 309,
     313
nanomanufacturing, 211
National Association of Latino Appointed and
     Elected Officials, 260
National Center for Policy Analysis, 8
national economies, 24
national income accounting, 50
National Institute of Science and Technology,
     209
National Institute of Standards, 9
National Institutes of Health, 204

national power, 147
National Science Foundation, 204
national security, 245
nationalism, 15, 23-25, 147, 249, 265, 266;
natural strategic tariff, 232, 233, 235, 236, 238-
     240, 242-245
Nauru, 104
NBC, 253
Netherlands, the, xiv
neuroanatomy, 12
new economy, 2
New Hampshire, 262
New School for Social Research, 60
New Trade Theory, 13
New Zealand, 162, 263
Nicaragua, 140, 161
Nichols, John, 257
nickel-metal hydride, 208
Nigeria, 24, 25, 158, 168
Nissan, 67
Nixon, Richard, 268
Nobel Prize, 5, 116, 139
Noble, Eric, 67
noneconomic issues, 256
non-performing loans, 83
non-quantitative changes, 120
non-renewable resources, 104, 229
non-tariff barriers, 7, 20, 31, 76, 77
non-tradable sectors, 247
North American Free Trade Agreement, 158,
     290, 305, 308
North Carolina, 108, 262
North Carolina Employment Security
     Commission, 108
North Korea, 24, 89

O

O'Rourke, Kevin, 128
Obama, Barack, xiii, xiv, 28, 56, 162, 211, 215,
     249, 250, 258-264, 267, 273, 295, 297, 298
obesity, 105
objectivism, 12
OECD, 61, 87, 216, 277, 281, 293, 294, 298,
     304, 307, 312
office buildings, 38
Office of Management and Budget, 208
offsets, 175
offshoring, 28, 31, 36, 63, 66, 68, 116, 119, 248,
     254
Ogallala Aquifer, 105
Ohio, 255-257, 258, 260, 273, 297
Ohsone, Kozo, 63
oil, 73, 165, 197, 225, 242, 245
Okun Gap, 108
oligopoly, 215, 248
olive oil, 135
olive trees, 19
Oman, 162
OPEC, 105
openness, 89, 163, 243
opportunity costs, 98, 114, 217
optics, 128
optoelectronics, 211
Otabe, Kenichi, 146
outsourcing, 22, 33, 205, 256, 261, 266
overdraft, 42
overseas investments, 130
overtime, 84

ownership, 163
Oxfam, 164
ozone layer, 169

P

Pacific, 3
Pacific Heights, 28, 29
Pacifica Advanced Product Design Center, 66
Page, Larry, 204
Pakistan, 152, 167, 214
palaces, 48
Panama, 162
Panic of 1857, 134
paper, 174
Park, Gen., 293
Parliament, 133
patents, 61, 133, 171
path dependence, 212
patriotism, 130
Paulson, Henry Jr., 51
Peak Oil, 22
peasants, 58, 155, 237
Pell Grants, 255, 256
Pelly Amendment, 167
Pennsylvania, 257, 258, 260, 262
Pentagon, 67
Peoria, IL, 249
perfect competition, 215
Perkins loans, 256
Perot, Ross, 9, 159, 260
Perry, Matthew, 95, 145
Persian Gulf, 105, 184
personnel management, 68
Peru, 157, 162, 263
perverse efficiency, 49
pesticides, 167, 197
Philadelphia, 95, 257, 258
Philippines, 146
Phillips, Kevin, 247
photolithographic steppers, 207
photovoltaics, 70
physical sciences, 123
physics, 10, 11
picking winners, 209, 240
piezoelectric crystals, 205
Pillowtex, 108
Pinochet, Augusto, 293
pith helmets, 39
Pitt, William, 131
plantations, 191
plasma TV, 63
Plaza Accord, 73
plebiscite, 126
policing, 248
Politburo, 43
politicians, 7
polls, 253, 254
pollution, 105, 155, 264
polyurethane foam, 3
Pope, Carl, 169
population growth, 127
Porsche, 67
port delays, 77
Porter, Michael, 12, 121, 241
Portugal, 111, 113, 114, 186
post-Communism, 125
post-industrialism, 63, 64, 66
Postrel, Virginia, 64

poverty, 12, 152
premises, 11
Prestowitz, Clyde, 73, 82, 177, 187
price competition, 192
prices, 104, 247
primary products, 194
printed circuit boards, 66, 207
printers, 65
prison inmates, 33
private equity, 42
privatization, 166
prizes, 133
pro football, 97
product development, 68
product standards, 133
production cost, 65, 234
production volume, 216
productivity, 2, 57, 58, 86, 102, 115, 142, 193,
    194; growth, 193; adverse
    growth, 114, 226, 231
profit, 99, 214, 240
Program for International Student Assessment,
    60
progressivity, 244
Project Socrates, 204
proletariat, 136
prosperity, 12, 19, 33
protectionism, xvi, xiv, xvii, 1, 6, 21, 71, 90, 91,
    92, 123, 124, 126, 127, 128, 130, 131, 136,
    138, 139, 144-148, 152, 162, 164, 166, 175,
    183, 187, 198, 202, 212, 223, 225, 227-239,
    241, 249, 250, 252, 263, 265, 266, 273, 296,
    298
protective headgear, 3
Protestants, 48
psychological bargain, 248
public services, 88, 166, 248
puritanism, xiv

Q

Qatar, 162, 174
quality, 86, 192
quality of life, 88
quotas, 90, 165

R

R&D, 67, 68, 84, 90, 192, 207, 210, 227, 229,
    295, 296, 308; tax credit, 133
"race to the bottom," 85
radar, 208
radicalism, 79
railroads, 24, 95, 112
Rand, Ayn, 12
Random-Access Memory, 187
rationalism, 19
rationalizations, 5
raw materials, 57, 127, 131, 135, 176, 184, 196-
    198, 245
Rayburn, Sam, 136
Reagan, Ronald, 8, 144
real estate, 23, 39, 75, 107, 163
realism, 83
Reason, 28
recession, 1
recessions, 77, 251, 252
reciprocity, 71

Redwood City, CA, 67
reforestation, 167
regional trade blocs, 26
regulation, 2, 163
Reich, Robert, 60
Reinert, Eric, 12, 189, 192, 194
reliability, 192
Renaissance, 124, 125
rent, 192, 215
reporters, 29
Republicans, 35, 134, 136, 248, 250, 253, 255-257, 262, 265
restaurants, xvi, 86
retainable industries, 218, 219, 221, 225, 228, 295
retaliation, 140, 243
revolution, 132, 136
rhetoric, 252, 254
rho, 46
Rhode Island, 258
Ricardo, David, xiii, 28, 95, 96, 109-113, 116, 118, 123, 135, 142, 146, 184, 185, 214, 217, 220, 223-225, 262
Richard Nixon, 54, 143
right, 22, 131, 249
Rio Grande, 14
Roberts, Paul Craig, 8
robotics, 211
rock, 112
Rockefeller Center, 42
Rodrik, Dani, 54, 109, 155, 189, 199, 210, 273, 274, 276, 281, 283, 288-290, 292, 295, 310, 312
Roger and Me, 261
roller skates, 5
rolls, 98, 115
Rome, 134
Roosevelt, Franklin Delano, 141
Roosevelt, Theodore, 21, 22
Rotterdam, 156
royalties, 66, 68
Russert, Tim, 259
Russia, 89, 105, 125
Rust Belt, 6
rustbelt, 119
Rwanda, 23
Ryan, Tim, 257

S

safety, 166
Salazar, Antonio, 114
Salinas, Carlos, 158
Samuelson, Paul, 101, 116
sanctions, 170
Sanders, Bernie, 258
Santa Claus, 38
Sarah Lawrence College, 155
Sarkozy, Nicholas, 265
Saudi Arabia, 27, 162
savings rate, 31, 34, 50, 51, 62, 75, 76, 242
Sawyer, Tom, 257
Say, Jean-Baptiste, 119
scale economies, 127, 157, 205, 212-216, 200, 220, 225, 227;
Scandinavia, 7
Schieffer, Bob, 255
Schumpeter, Joseph, 185
scientists, 203

scissors, 247
sea turtles, 167
seaports, 42
Seattle, 226
secrecy, 168
secretary, 113
security guards, 2
SEMATECH, 210
semiconductors, 192, 202, 203, 206, 210, 218
Senate, 168, 257, 261
Senegal, 158
sensors, 211
Seoul, 12, 125
servants, 31
Shaheen, Jeanne, 262
sham transactions, 255
shareholders, 249
sheep, 125, 135
Shelby, Richard, 264
shipping, 22, 127
shoes, 3, 115, 158, 195
Shogun, 95
short-termism, 7, 45, 87, 188
shrimp, 167
Sierra Club, 169
Sierra Leone, 158
Silicon Valley, xvi, 24, 63, 67, 202, 209
silicon wafers, 207
silver, 135
Singapore, 24, 42, 54, 65, 147, 148, 150, 161, 162, 164, 227, 263, 289, 296
skills base, 201
slavery, 134
Slovenia, 72
slums, 197
Smith, Adam, 96, 124, 126, 190
Smoot-Hawley, 139
soccer balls, 214
social capital, 23
Social Darwinism, 136
social issues, 256
social programs, 88
socialism, 22, 28, 34, 78, 89, 172, 198, 277; Indian, 163
Society of Motor Manufacturers and Traders, 71
socks, 3
software, 65, 68, 81, 211
Sony Walkman, 63
South (Confederacy), 135
South Africa, 27, 154, 196
South Asian Association for Regional Cooperation,, 172
South Carolina, 134
South Korea, 2, 24, 42, 60, 65, 85, 86, 113, 124, 148, 161, 162, 201, 207, 214
South, antebellum, 135
Southeast Asia, 81
Southern African Development Community, 172
Southern California, 67
Southern Common Market, 172
sovereign wealth funds, 42
sovereignty, 248
Soviet Union, 43, 53, 172, 198
spacecraft, 70
Smith, F.E., 129
Spain, 30, 128, 135
special interests, 4, 5, 7, 126, 130, 177, 225, 232, 239, 264

specialization, 184, 185
specialty chemicals, 207
specialty crops, 197
speculators, 71
Spencer, Barbara, 295
Sputnik, 204
standard of living, 150, 189
Stans, Maurice, 143
Starbucks, 79
State Department, 140, 244
state ownership, 83
states, 84
static analysis, 112
status quo, 9, 14
steamship, 129
steamships, 113
steel, 6, 58, 128, 144
steel industry, 239, 257
Stern School of Business, 213
sticks, 199
stickball, 179
Stiglitz, Joseph, 35
stimulus package, 211, 263
stock market, 39, 71, 252
stockholders, 90
Stolper-Samuelson theorem, 34
strategic markets, 186
Strategic Policy Research, 7
street children, 35
subcontractors, 155
subprime mortgages, 2, 251
subsidies, xvi, 55, 59, 72, 83, 84, 133, 134, 164,
    172, 176, 197, 199, 203, 210, 241, 242, 256,
    291-293, 298
suburbia, 248
Sudan, 158
sugar, 129, 150, 152
Summers, Lawrence, 215
Sumner, William Graham, 136, 137
sunrise industry, 92
supplier industries, 185, 241
supply chain, 227
suppressed consumption, 31
Supreme Court, 170
sweatshops, 71
Sweden, 7, 85, 87, 128, 140, 149
Switzerland, 7, 74, 75, 140, 149, 168, 205, 214,
    216, 217, 220, 226, 280, 294
synergy, 195
systems integration, 69

T

Taft, Robert, 250
Taiwan, 24, 42, 65, 70, 102, 147, 150, 186, 207,
    214
Tanzania, 158
tariffs, 6, 20, 22, 26, 31, 70, 71, 76, 78, 90, 91,
    113, 120, 124, 126, 131-134, 136-144, 146,
    151, 163, 174-176, 199, 228, 231-236, 239-
    245, 252, 263, 264, 268, 281, 285, 286, 298
Tariff Nullification Crisis (1832), 134
Tassey, Gregory, 9
taxes, 35, 88, 90, 74, 87, 141, 173, 210, 240,
    242, 245, 275, 298
taxis, 108
taxpayers, 88
tea, 137
Tea Party, 267

technocrats, 12, 54, 132
technological spillovers, 105, 106
technology, 22, 26, 59, 61, 65, 68, 110, 200
Technology Innovation Program, 211
techno-utopianism, 21
telegraph, 129
television, 69, 91, 143
terms of trade, 194
terrorism, 27
Tester, Jon, 258
Texas, 85
textiles, 111, 126, 128, 152, 158, 174, 195
Thailand, 44, 64, 147, 152, 162, 167
Thatcher, Margaret, 1
The Car Lab, 67
The China Effect, 50
The Economist, 123, 183
The Wealth of Nations, 95
theft, 81
theology, 13
Third World, 1, 35, 39, 54, 58, 81, 82, 107, 152,
    153, 164, 173, 184, 191, 201
Tiananmen massacre, 62
timber, 167
time discount, 45
time horizons, 37, 45
tires, 263
Tobin, James, 108
Toffler, Alvin, 64
Tokyo, 12, 125
Toluca, Mexico, 201
Toyota, 3, 91, 264
toys, 99, 143, 161
tradable sectors, 2, 86
Trade Adjustment Assistance, 59
trade agreements, 3, 179
trade barriers, 22, 119, 243
Trade Expansion Act, 143
trade liberalization, 150
trade negotiators, 177
trade surpluses, 7, 42, 44, 73, 143, 180, 243
trade wars, 103
tradeoffs, 99, 115, 221
Trade-Related Investment Measures, 172
Trades Union Congress, 130
trading partners, 52, 173, 224, 243
traditional medicine, 171
training, 130
transaction costs, 22
transistors, 202
transistor radios, 143
transition costs, 59, 119
Trans-Pacific Partnership, 162
trans-plants, 91
transportation, 248
Treasury securities, 74
Treaty of Methuen, 113
trucks, 263
Truman, Harry, 142, 249
Trumpka, Richard, 263
trustbusters, 21
t-shirts, 192
tuna, 146, 147
Tunisia, 162
Tupperware, 200
Turkey, 153, 178
two-party system, 252
two-tier wages, 36
Tyson, Laura D'Andrea, 188, 209

U

U.S. International Trade Commission, 150, 263
U.S. Trade Representative, 144
Udall, Mark, 262
Udall, Tom, 262
Uganda, 158
UK, 89
Ukraine, 117, 163
UN Department of Economic and Social Affairs, 173
Uncle Sam, 180
underemployment, 107, 247
unemployment, 10, 33, 44, 59, 84, 107
unfair trade, 51, 180
unions, 85
United Arab Emirates, 42, 89, 162
United Auto Workers, 36
United Nations, 14
United Nations Development Programme, 196
United Steelworkers, 85
universities, 59
Unlawful Internet Gambling Enforcement Act, 173
unsafe products, 253
USBIC, 266
USSR, 204
USTR, 262
utilities, 65
utility, 47

V

value judgements, 12
Vanek-Reinert effect, 158
Value-Added Tax, 176, 239, 244, 243, 291, 296
VCR, 92, 206
Venezuela, 27, 167
venture capital, 209
Vermont, 258
Veroneau, John, 43
vested interests, 4, 5, 128, 130
video, 107
Vietnam, 53, 147, 153, 162, 194, 201, 263
villains, 80
Virginia, 258
virtuous cycles, 192, 195, 235
volatility, 197
Volkswagens, 149
Voluntary Restraint Agreement, 90, 91, 241
Volvo, 67
voters, 256

W

wages, 2, 41, 58, 65, 86, 90, 101, 102-104, 115, 194, 215, 233, 246

waitresses, 2
Wall Street Journal, 253
Wallach, Lori, 167
Walmart, 91, 247
War of 1812, 133
wars, 248
Washington Consensus, 154, 170, 210
watches, 65, 149, 214, 226
weapons, 70, 80
Webb, Jim, 258
welfare state, 88, 136
whaling, 167
What's The Matter With Kansas?, 256
wheat, 100, 103
White, C. Thayer, 146
white-collar workers, 109
Whitehouse, Sheldon, 258
Wilson, Woodrow, 139
Williamson, Oliver, 12
wine, 45, 111, 113, 135
wings, 69
Wired, 21, 28
Wisconsin, 124, 255
Wolfson, Howard, 257, 294
wool, 113, 124, 125, 131
work ethic, 29
work hours, 33
workers, 35, 111, 136, 199, 239
World Bank, 35, 39, 54, 151, 152, 154, 170, 184, 194, 272, 273, 283, 288, 289, 292, 293, 301, 304, 306-308, 310, 312-314
World Trade Organization, 26, 27, 44, 150, 163, 165, 169, 178, 244, 248, 263, 280
World War II, 115, 139

X

X/Seed Capital, 209
xenophobia, 38

Y

Yahoo, xvi
Yale, 158
Yamamura, Kozo, 145
yarn, 178
Yen, 73
Youngstown State University, 256
yuppies, 107, 238, 273

Z

Zaire, 157, 158
Zambia, 85, 158
Zedillo, Ernesto, 158
Zysman, John, 67

Ian Fletcher is Senior Economist of the
Coalition for a Prosperous America, a
nationwide grass-roots organization dedicated to fixing America's trade policies and comprising representatives
from business, agriculture, and labor.
He was previously Research Fellow at
the U.S. Business and Industry Council,
a Washington think tank, and before
that, an economist in private practice
serving mainly hedge funds and private
equity firms. Educated at Columbia
University and the University of Chicago, he lives in San Francisco.

Part I

Living with Schizophrenia

Chapter One

A Disease Unlike Any Other

EVERYTHING BAD IS GOOD AGAIN

Spring 1999

On the day my twenty-one-year-old son was admitted to the psychiatric unit at University of North Carolina (UNC) hospital, my overwhelming emotion was relief. At least I knew where he was: He was safe; and he was with people who understood what was wrong. I was too numb, then, to appreciate how irrevocably our lives would change after that day.

I had noticed something wrong with my son's behavior for months, maybe even years. During a weekend visit home in the fall of his sophomore year, he talked nonstop. The words fit together in sentences, but the sentences didn't fit together into coherent thoughts. When he finally finished rambling, I was not sure what he had said, if anything at all. Parents, however, have an uncanny ability to explain away unusual behavior in their children, and I am no exception. I told myself that David was just excited about all the new ideas he was being exposed to at the university.

When the incessant talking gave way to angry emotional outbursts and verbal abuse, it was no longer possible to find an innocent explanation. I recalled all the warnings about behavioral changes associated with illicit drug use, all the signs indicating that your teenager is using drugs. I assumed David was experimenting with marijuana, cocaine, or something worse. I confronted him about the dangers of drugs and lectured him about the permanent effects that drug use could have on his brain. I encouraged him to seek help, to just say "no." I expect that most parents would come to the same conclusion I did. The possibility of mental illness never crossed my mind.

3

Given the warning signs, I cannot say that I was surprised when the break occurred. David's college friends called to say that he was in the emergency room; they had notified the police because he was talking about killing himself. Nonetheless, I was stunned at the diagnosis of *schizophrenia*, and shocked to find David almost completely delusional when I finally could talk with him. What do you say when your son tells you, in all seriousness, that he thinks he is God? I asked if he had enough clean underwear for the hospital.

Schizophrenia turns your world upside-down. David was admitted as an inpatient and remained hospitalized for nearly three weeks, a lengthy and expensive stay that would have been impossible without health insurance. As I visited him over those weeks I discovered that my naïve perceptions of psychiatric units, shaped by popular films such as *One Flew over the Cuckoo's Nest* and *Girl, Interrupted*, were not at all representative of current reality. Clinical staff on the psychiatric unit at UNC hospital were some of the most caring, compassionate, and patient people I have ever met. On one afternoon a patient passed the time walking in circles round and round the room. An aide walked beside him, round and round. Why he needed to be accompanied on these circuits I do not know, but he needed to walk, so she walked with him. Round and round and round.

A modern psychiatric unit is, in fact, a relatively safe place for the parent of a young adult with mental illness. The bizarre behavior, intermittent outbursts, and incoherent talk that are so confusing and embarrassing in the "real" world are completely acceptable here. I can recall one afternoon when David put a pencil between his toes and began writing on the wall. I was embarrassed and asked him to stop, but he just continued to write, and no one seemed to care. In a psychiatric unit, the abnormal is normal. In schizophrenia, some things you thought were bad, like psychiatric hospitalization, turn out to be very good indeed.

Drug use is an example of a bad that appears good (or at least *relatively* not so bad) through the lens of schizophrenia. When David was first hospitalized, one of the clinical staff commented that it would be useful to know what kinds of drugs, if any, he had been taking before he became ill. Eager to help in any way I could, I grilled David's college friends to get the information, and relayed it back to a nurse. She said, "Dear, I know you wish this could be drugs, but it is not." When would a parent *hope for* a diagnosis of drug abuse? If the alternative is schizophrenia, you wish the problem was "only" drugs.

Smoking is another example. The psychiatric unit had a balcony set aside for patients who wanted to smoke. Given the health hazards associated with smoking, I was surprised that a hospital would allow patients to smoke on site. I later learned that the prevalence of tobacco smoking is higher among persons with schizophrenia than among the general population; and some

research suggests that nicotine improves measures of cognitive functioning among this population. I do not mean to suggest that smoking is good for persons with serious mental illness, but when David was acutely ill, smoking appeared to be the lesser evil.

Schizophrenia also makes some good things appear bad, or at least not so good. On my daily visits to the psychiatric unit David often spent the entire time talking about Jesus and the path to salvation. Throughout his illness, religion was a principal theme of his delusions. One day another visitor commented on how nice it was that my son had such a strong faith. I told her no, the religious talk was a symptom of his illness; I would know he was getting better when he talked about religion less.

I should not imply that the psychiatric unit insulated me from the horror of mental illness; there is no such escape. On various occasions when I visited David he would tell me that the television commercials were sending messages to him, or that a former friend of his was stalking the halls, or that he had watched his roommate "shrink and grow" all night. Sometimes he was angry at the doctors, or suspicious of other patients. Sometimes he called me at work, telling me nothing was wrong with him and begging me to get him released. When he asked me to take him out for Easter dinner on a "day pass," I panicked, wondering how I would get him back to the hospital.

I should not have worried. Midway through dinner, he said we had to be sure to be back by 7:00, because they were going to color Easter eggs. Schizophrenia turns your world upside-down.

THE INCIDENCE AND IMPACT OF SCHIZOPHRENIA

Schizophrenia is not a rare disease. The lifetime risk of developing schizophrenia is approximately 0.7 percent; its prevalence at any point in time is approximately 4.5 per one thousand persons.[1] Schizophrenia appears among all populations, in all regions of the world, with pockets of relatively high or low prevalence. Prevalence is higher within developed versus less-developed countries; and among lower versus higher socioeconomic classes.[2] Schizophrenia has been reported in the medical literature only since the mid-nineteenth century, but there is evidence that the illness appeared long before then.

History and Speculation

Historical records of illnesses that resemble schizophrenia are worthwhile for consideration not only because the accounts are interesting, but also as a reminder that so much about the disease remains unknown. At least since the medieval period, there are case records of individuals with schizophrenia-like illnesses.

Opicinus de Canistrus (1296–1350) was an illustrator and scribe employed in the papal offices in Avignon, France. At age thirty-eight he developed a sudden illness that left him unconscious for several days. By his own account, when he awoke his "right hand [was] weak in worldly work, but strong in spiritual endeavors."[3] The physical symptoms suggest that Opicinus suffered a stroke, from which he gradually recovered. Nonetheless, over the seven years that followed the "event," he produced more than fifty large drawings and maps on parchment, a manuscript with nearly two dozen additional maps, and an accompanying commentary. The maps are examples of what could be called "interpretive geography," in which Canistrus depicts various European countries as parts of his body; the commentary associates aches and pains he is feeling with current or impending events in the corresponding regions of Europe.[4] Eventually, Canistrus withdrew from papal employment to devote his time fully to these endeavors.

The thought patterns revealed in Canistrus's writings suggest that his illness is a "historical case of possible schizophrenia."[5] Persons who have read the commentary say the language is often incoherent and the reasoning illogical, at times becoming mere verbiage. Many of the features of Canistrus's illness (disorganized thinking, grandiose delusions, incoherent writing, and prolonged duration of symptoms) are typical features of schizophrenia, although no such disease had been identified at the time.

Franz Xaver Messerschmidt (1736–1783) was a talented sculptor and artist who was appointed to the Academy of Fine Arts in Vienna in 1769. When he was denied academic promotion in 1774, the responsible minister noted (emphasis added) that:

> The most important objection . . . is the fact that for three years he has shown signs of some *confusion*. . . . Although [the confusion has] subsided . . . it occasionally is still evident . . . in that he believes all other professors and directors to be *his enemies*.[6]

Despite his considerable artistic talent, Messerschmidt's career came to a near screeching halt. He was no longer entrusted with students and soon moved on to Munich. He spent the last three years of his life in near-total isolation in Bratislava because "it seems that all Germany feels obliged to persecute me."[7] Messerschmidt claimed, during this period, that demons made nocturnal visits to his rooms to torture him. One demon, in particular, envied the perfect proportions Messerschmidt achieved in his sculptures.

At the time of his death, more than sixty sculpted heads were found in his studio. Their expressions ranged from blank faces to contorted screams; some have been interpreted as self-portraits captured during his attempts to ward off the demons. Speculation aside, Messerschmidt unquestionably ex-

perienced hallucinations, along with delusions of grandeur and persecution. Whatever afflicted him seriously hampered his quality of life.

Recent History

The disease concept that we now call schizophrenia first appeared in the medical literature in the mid-nineteenth century. At the end of the century, Emil Kraeplin labeled the disease, "dementia praecox," and described its characteristic features to be onset in late adolescence, with a course of chronic and permanent deterioration of mental functioning.[8] Kraeplin distinguished dementia praecox from "folie circulaire," an illness characterized by acute and episodic dementia, no chronic deterioration of mental functioning, and a more favorable prognosis, which he labeled "manic depressive insanity."[9] Thus, Kraeplin's early distinction between the two disorders laid the groundwork for our current classification of schizophrenia and manic-depressive (bipolar) disorder. Recent genetic research, however, has identified genes that appear to be implicated in both schizophrenia and bipolar disorder, as well as evidence of shared genetic susceptibility to the two disorders. These findings have called into question the sharp dichotomy of two identifiably distinct mental disorders.[10]

It is currently believed that, around 1911, Eugen Bleuler conceived the name "schizophrenia" for the illness Kraeplin had called dementia praecox. In describing the disease, Bleuler placed particular emphasis on the *loss of association* or *splitting* of various psychic functions that patients exhibited, hence the name schizophrenia ("split mind").[11] According to Bleuler, the fundamental symptoms of the disease, crucial for a diagnosis, were inappropriate affect, loss of attention, lack of motivation, ambivalence, and autism; delusions and hallucinations were considered accessory symptoms, secondary for a diagnosis.[12] Bleuler viewed schizophrenia, not as a single disease entity, but as a heterogeneous group of mental disorders. The disorders had common clinical features, but different etiology, development, and clinical outcomes. For some patients, the clinical course might be more favorable than that which was postulated by Kraeplin, but complete remission of symptoms was unlikely.

Today, in contrast to Bleuler's characterization of fundamental and accessory symptoms, delusions or hallucinations are considered characteristic features of schizophrenia, and among the most useful clinical factors in arriving at a diagnosis. Current research does, however, support Bleuler's view that schizophrenia is not a single disorder but a syndrome with "multiple disease entities, multiple etiological factors, multiple relevant pathophysiological processes, multiple symptom dimensions, multiple protective and pathoplastic factors."[13] The different clinical manifestations of the syndrome, in combination with currently available treatments, yield different courses of illness and wide variance in patient outcomes.

Symptoms

Schizophrenia is generally diagnosed based on the presence of *positive* and *negative symptoms*, when other factors, such as substance use or another neurological illness, cannot account for the psychotic (positive) symptoms of the disease.[14] Positive symptoms may involve delusions, hallucinations, or other distortions of reality.[15] *Delusions* are implausible beliefs that are unfounded in reality (such as David's belief that he was the risen Christ, or Canistrus's belief that his aches and pains were signals of events occurring in Europe). The most frequent are delusions of persecution, and delusions that seemingly innocuous events have special meaning or significance (such as David's belief that the television was talking directly to him). *Hallucinations* are abnormal sensory or perceptual experiences that are unrelated to real stimuli (such as David seeing his roommate "shrink and grow," or Messerschmidt feeling demons torturing him). Hallucinations can be related to any of the five senses, but auditory hallucinations (hearing voices) are most common. When an individual is experiencing positive symptoms, they may also exhibit increased emotional arousal or emotional reactivity.[16]

The negative symptoms of schizophrenia create the opposite affect—a lack of emotion or impulse. Negative symptoms may manifest as a *lack of drive* to perform activities or pursue goals; a *lack of will* or ability to act decisively; a *lack of interest* or enthusiasm; or, a *lack of ability to experience pleasure*. Other characteristic negative symptoms include *poverty of speech*, a *flattened affect*, and *difficulty focusing attention*. In the first few months after David was released from the hospital, I came home every day to have lunch with him. I was worried and anxious, he was indifferent. Our conversation was strained. He was mostly silent and expressionless, I chattered on about anything to fill the void.

Other symptoms associated with schizophrenia include: cognitive impairments, such as disorganized thinking and behavior; a slowing, or acceleration, of psychomotor activity; mood symptoms, such as anxiety or depression; and a lack of insight into the illness. A "significant majority of patients with schizophrenia either believe that they do not have any disorder, or acknowledge symptoms but misattribute them to other causes, or deny any need for treatment."[17] This denial or disbelief is critical, because insight is strongly correlated with functional outcomes in schizophrenia. Indeed, lack of insight may be one of the most frustrating aspects of the illness for family members. How can one convince an individual to seek treatment, when they do not believe they have an illness at all?

Yet schizophrenia is most definitely an illness. It is not an assortment of odd behaviors that an individual could control if they made an effort to do so. Recent studies, using new imaging and neurophysiological techniques, as well as postmortem examinations, have revealed that schizophrenia is associated with alterations in brain functioning, abnormalities in brain structure and brain chemistry; and changes in the electrical activity of the brain.[18] Through these studies, we have made amazing progress in identifying the ways the brain is affected in schizophrenia, but the exact causes of the disease remain more elusive.

Causation

Manfred Bleuler (son of Eugen Bleuler and also a psychiatrist) discussed the causes of schizophrenia in a 1968 address to physicians at the University of Zurich. Describing his findings from a twenty-three-year longitudinal study of 208 patients with chronic schizophrenia, Bleuler concluded that,

> Neither heredity alone nor environment alone is sufficient to explain the morbid development into a schizophrenic psychosis. We must assume a collective activity, an interplay of both.[19]

Half a century later, we have amassed mountains of evidence on the genetic and environmental correlates of the disease, but the exact physiological process whereby genes and environment interact to bring on acute symptoms of schizophrenia is still unknown.

Genetic factors, by themselves and through interactions with environmental factors, contribute about 80 percent of liability for developing the disease.[20] The lifetime risk of schizophrenia increases, from an average of 0.7 percent in the general population, to 10–15 percent if a sibling has the illness, and to 40–50 percent if an identical twin has the illness. Several specific chromosomal abnormalities have been linked to schizophrenia, but none have been identified as a necessary or sufficient indicator for the illness. At most, the presence of an individual genetic abnormality increases the lifetime risk of developing schizophrenia to only 1.5 percent.[21]

A number of environmental factors have been linked to increased liability for developing schizophrenia. Some of these occur before or immediately after birth, including: maternal infection or malnutrition, older age of father at conception, complications during pregnancy or delivery, and birth during late winter or early spring (especially in regions where winters are severe). Other environmental risk factors occur during childhood, adolescence, or young adulthood. Migration, residence in an urban area, and the use of marijuana or stimulants are each associated with a higher risk for schizophrenia, but the exact relevance remains unknown. A number of other environmental factors have been linked to liability for developing the disease, so many that one expert cautions, "our field at large runs the risk of being buried under a plethora of unrelated and undigested findings."[22]

One popular model that attempts to make sense of the disparate findings is the stress-vulnerability, or diathesis-stress model. The model posits that development of schizophrenia is a function of interactions between three categories of factors, namely: *genetic vulnerabilities, environmental stressors,* and *protective factors.*[23] According to the model, genetic abnormalities determine the vulnerability (diathesis) of individuals to developing psychosis; environmental stress precipitates the onset of illness (or relapse) in vulnerable individuals; and protective factors mitigate symptoms or reduce the probability of relapse. Thus, individuals with equal vulnerability to schizophrenia may or may not develop the disease, depending on their exposure to risk or protective factors. Similarly, individuals experiencing equal levels of environmental stress may or may not develop the disease (or experience relapse) depending on their underlying genetic vulnerability and the presence or absence of protective factors.

Two psychologists propose a version of the diathesis-stress model in which a hormone, cortisol, is the mechanism whereby genetic vulnerability and environmental stress interact.[24] According to this model, environmental stress causes the release of cortisol to the brain. The elevated cortisol levels exacerbate brain abnormalities in individuals who are genetically liable to schizophrenia. In this way, stress triggers the onset of psychotic symptoms. If the stress is chronic, the response is cumulative, causing permanent changes in brain structure that enhance responses to future stress.

Another version of the diathesis-stress model is the "two-hit" model. This model posits that genetic risk, together with abnormalities in early development, constitute a "first hit" that increases the vulnerability of individuals to environmental risk factors occurring in later development. When those risk factors occur, the "second hit" leads to onset of the disease.[25]

In concluding this section, it is important to emphasize the positives over the negatives. The positive view is that, since Manfred Bleuler gave his lecture, research into the causes of schizophrenia has made enormous progress. The progress is multidimensional in terms of both understanding possible genetic abnormalities associated with schizophrenia and identifying a host of environmental risk factors for the disease. Genetic and neurological research continues to investigate hypotheses suggested by the diathesis-stress model, as well as models of schizophrenia focused on developmental abnormalities, mechanisms of the brain, or clinical expressions of the illness.[26] The negative view is that Bleuler's blanket reference to the interplay of heredity and environment still characterizes the vastness of what we do not know about schizophrenia. We do not yet have a definitive explanation of the cause of the disease, or know how to prevent it. And no cure is on the horizon. It is even unclear if schizophrenia is a single, complex disease that manifests in different ways, or a continuum of diseases with overlapping symptoms. However, one reason for emphasizing the positives is that, despite our limited understanding of the etiology of schizophrenia, the disease has become more and more treatable over the last fifty years.

Treatment

At present, the only treatment for schizophrenia with proven effectiveness in clinical trials, is a regimen of one or more antipsychotic drugs, all of which chemically alter dopamine activity in the brain.[27] The first generation of these drugs, the most powerful and most successful of which was haloperidol, were developed in the 1950s.

Haloperidol was synthesized by Janssen Pharmaceutica in 1958.[28] Clinical evidence on the efficacy of the drug, as well as its adverse side effects, was published in the medical literature the following year. Those results are still valid today: haloperidol can control the positive symptoms of schizophrenia (hallucinations, delusions, agitation) in many patients, at dosages far lower than the dosages required of other first-generation antipsychotics. However, the drug's side effects, predominantly motor disorders, can be severe. These include restlessness, Parkinsonism (tremors, rigidity, and instability), involuntary muscle contractions, and tardive dyskinesia (involuntary movements, usually of the lower face).[29] Haloperidol is still in use for the treatment of schizophrenia, but today it has largely been replaced by a second generation of "atypical" antipsychotics with less severe side effects.

The first of the atypical antipsychotics, clozapine, was introduced for treatment of schizophrenia in the late 1960s. Clozapine represents a significant improvement over first-generation antipsychotics with regard to both efficacy and the absence of motor side effects. In particular, clozapine is effective in treating the positive symptoms of schizophrenia among some patients who are not responsive to first-generation drugs. The elimination of motor side effects is another important plus, but clozapine is associated with other negative side effects that limit its usefulness in clinical practice. Most importantly, patients who take clozapine over long periods have an increased risk of developing agranulocytosis, a potentially fatal blood disorder characterized by a dangerous reduction in white blood cells.[30]

Since the early 1990s, more than a dozen other "second-generation" antipsychotics (e.g., olanzapine, quetiapine, risperidone) have been approved for treatment of schizophrenia. The drugs have proven efficacy in treating the positive symptoms of the disease, but are less consistently effective in treating its negative symptoms. Moreover, large-scale clinical trials indicate that the second-generation drugs are no more effective than first-generation drugs in treating either positive or negative symptoms (except that clozapine is superior for treating patients who are not responsive to other drugs).[31] The primary benefit of the newer drugs is a more tolerable side-effect profile.

That is not to say the side effects of the atypical antipsychotics are negligible. Patients taking second-generation drugs have an increased risk of developing metabolic syndrome (weight gain, high-blood pressure, excess body fat around the waist, high blood sugar levels, abnormal blood cholesterol levels) and its related conditions (diabetes, heart disease).[32] Individual antipsychotics differ in their specific side-effect profiles, but other common side effects include sedation, low-blood pressure, cardiac arrhythmias, sexual dysfunction, and anticholinergic side effects (e.g., dry mouth, drowsiness, blurred vision, confusion).[33] Collectively, the side effects amount to more than a nuisance; they are the reason why many patients stop taking the drugs that provide their only bridge to a normal life.

Despite the potential for adverse side effects, the discovery of effective drug therapies for schizophrenia was one of the factors that enabled the movement of patients out of mental hospitals and into the community. Prior to the 1950s, there were no effective treatments for schizophrenia, and the most severely ill patients had little hope of life outside an institution. Since the advent of haloperidol, clozapine, and the other antipsychotic drugs, physicians are able to alleviate the most bizarre symptoms of the disease for many patients, offering them a realistic hope of leading a productive and meaningful life. The curious fact is that the tremendous advances in treatment of schizophrenia over the last fifty years have done little to reduce the economic and social burdens of the disease.

Postscript

A recent study estimates the total costs of schizophrenia in the United States in 2002 to be $62.7 billion.[34] The costs include direct expenditures associated with inpatient and outpatient medical care, housing and other social services, and involvement with the criminal justice system; as well as indirect costs associated with disability and premature mortality. Of these cost factors, the single largest component is the loss of productive output attributed to unemployment of individuals with the disease.

The large employment losses associated with schizophrenia are not surprising, given that onset of the disease typically occurs around the time a young adult is ready to enter the labor force full time. What *is* surprising is that improved treatments for the disease have had so little impact on employment outcomes for patients. Persons with schizophrenia fare poorer than almost any other disadvantaged group in the labor market. Employment rates and wages are lower for persons with disabilities than for nondisabled persons; lower for persons with mental disorders than for persons with other types of disabilities; and lower for persons with schizophrenia than for persons with other types of mental disorders.[35] Patients, providers, and families have a right to ask why, with improved treatments that are effective in controlling the symptoms of the disease for many patients, there has not been a parallel improvement in employment outcomes.

Chapter Two

The Mark of Schizophrenia

THAT COULD BE MY SON

In *The Scarlet Letter*, Nathaniel Hawthorne tells the story of Hester Prynne, a Puritan woman sentenced to wear a scarlet letter A upon her breast as punishment for adultery. The letter was symbolic of the sin that purportedly set Hester Prynne apart from others in the town. The townspeople cooperated in her punishment by shunning her:

> It had the effect of a spell, taking her out of the ordinary relations with humanity, and enclosing her in a sphere by herself. [1]

This is what it feels like to be the object of stigma—to be set apart, to be alone, to be different. Until you experience it, stigma is only a word. Once you encounter it, you become a different person; stigma changes you; you begin to view the world as less kind, less friendly, less safe.

Spring 1999

Shortly after David was released from the psychiatric unit, we were scheduled to attend the wedding of my husband's niece. The most conspicuous positive symptoms of David's illness were controlled by olanzapine, but the negative symptoms were perhaps heightened by its side effects. I was skeptical about his ability to cope with a large social event, when he could barely carry on a short conversation with me. But David wanted to attend, and both his doctor and social worker encouraged us to take the trip, believing it would be good for his recovery. It was not so good for me.

During the wedding ceremony, which required little social interaction, everything appeared normal with my in-laws. At the reception, we were seated at a large table with extended family. David was quiet and withdrawn, but no one seemed to notice. Soon after dinner, however, I became aware that everyone had drifted away from the table, and no one was coming back. We sat there alone, David and I and one perceptive sister-in-law (to whom I will be forever grateful), while groups of relatives mingled a "safe" distance away. Fifteen years later, I still feel the anger, hurt, and humiliation of sitting there with my son, hoping he wouldn't notice that everyone was avoiding us.

Since that early experience of being shunned, I have become more sensitive to the nature of stigma against mental illness. It is pervasive, enduring, and so *acceptable*! Even in a world of hypersensitivity, in which derogatory terms once used to describe women, racial or ethnic groups, and persons with physical disabilities have been eradicated from politically correct speech, the term "schizo" remains acceptable. The word stings me, like Hester's scarlet A burned through her clothes.

Summer 2005

The pervasive stigma against serious mental illness causes many patients and family members to conceal diagnoses of schizophrenia or other psychotic disorders. An example caught me unawares while visiting Amsterdam's Van Gogh museum several years ago. I enjoy art history and pay close attention to the artist notes that appear next to each painting. According to the notes, Van Gogh's behavior exhibited classic symptoms of psychosis, but the captions bore no mention of any diagnosis of schizophrenia or bipolar disorder. Upon reflection, I realized that I had never seen such a diagnosis mentioned in my readings on the artist's work. A close friend and art history teacher unraveled the puzzle. After Van Gogh's death (from a self-inflicted gunshot wound), his family vigorously promoted his legacy, but insisted that no mention of mental illness should ever appear in art catalogs or museums displaying his work.

For many years, I too avoided telling people about David's illness. Although I was researching the subject, lecturing to community groups, and teaching about mental illness in my classes, I avoided discussing my personal connection. I do not know why my attitude changed, but I remember exactly when I first told my story in public. In October 2006, I delivered a keynote presentation on job accommodations for mental illness for the Mental Health Association of Arizona. At the beginning of my talk, without any advance preparation, I briefly told my son's story. The talk was well received, but I was apprehensive about how *I* would be received afterward. It was a revelation to me how many people came forward to tell *their* stories of loved ones with mental illness.

Fall 2013

Today, I lecture on mental illness in many of my classes, and I usually weave David's story throughout the presentation. It is a vulnerable position, opening up to students about such a personal trauma. However, I have been rewarded by hearing my students' stories of friends and relatives with mental illness, and by their comments on the lectures. One student remarked, "I will never look at a homeless person the same way again."

I do not always have the courage to speak out when I should. One morning, several years ago, I was walking with a colleague to a meeting in Washington, D.C. As we waited to cross the street, I found myself standing next to a man, dressed in disheveled clothing and carrying a large plastic bag over his shoulder. He was having an animated conversation with himself. His words were incoherent and rambling, but I recognized the disorganized speech pattern of the monologue. I suppose my colleague thought I was uncomfortable or uneasy, because he suddenly moved to stand between us and quietly said, "You don't want to be next to *that*." I was not uncomfortable or uneasy. I thought, *that could be my son*. I wish I had said it.

STIGMA

The word "stigma" comes into English from a Greek word meaning a mark or brand made by a pointed stick or other sharp instrument. By the seventeenth century, it had acquired negative associations of evil or subjugation, and by the mid-nineteenth century it was being used in medical texts in reference to drug addiction and mental illness. Today, *stigma* has evolved to mean "a mark of disgrace or infamy; a sign of severe censure or condemnation."[2] Many physical disorders are stigmatized, epilepsy and cerebral palsy being good examples, but serious mental illness is different. The intensity, pervasiveness, and acceptability of stigma directed toward schizophrenia makes it a disease unlike any other.

Social Distance

Numerous studies have documented the intensity of stigma against mental illness relative to physical illness, and against schizophrenia relative to other mental illnesses. The typical study measures intensity of stigma by the degree to which average people prefer to maintain *social distance* from individuals with a particular "mark," or stigma. The concept of desire for social distance as a measure of intensity of stigma originated in the work of Emory Bogardus in the 1930s. Bogardus developed a *social distance scale*, using brief descriptions of social relationships that connote increasing degrees of familiarity. For example, regarding a particular stigmatized group, is the average person willing to "marry" a member of the group, to "work beside them in an office," or "to have them merely as a speaking acquaintance"?[3]

Thirty years later, Erving Goffman provided a theoretical explanation for the link between stigma and social distance. Goffman suggests that stigma is evoked by negative stereotypes which devalue an individual "from a whole and usual person to a tainted and discounted one."[4] Goffman identifies three potential sources of negative stereotypes that generate stigma: physical disability or deformity (e.g., blindness, paraplegia); deviant behavior (e.g., mental illness, crime); and tribal identity (e.g., race, nationality). He theorizes that discomfort involved in social interactions with a stigmatized person generates a desire to minimize such interactions, in other words, to maintain social distance.[5]

When social distance is used to measure the intensity of stigma directed toward alternative health conditions, mental illness *always* ranks among the most stigmatized. A good example of these types of studies is one conducted with a multiethnic sample of health practitioners in Australia. Participants were asked to rate the acceptability of twenty chronic conditions, within their community, on a scale from 1, representing no acceptance ("people would prefer a person with this disability be kept in an institution or out of sight") to 5, representing full acceptance ("people would accept a person with this disability marrying into their immediate family").[6] Psychiatric illness received an average ranking of 2, representing low acceptance ("people would try and avoid a person with this disability").[7] Only AIDS elicited stronger stigma.

Similar studies indicate that the stigma directed toward persons with mental illness is equivalent to that directed toward ex-convicts, alcoholics, or drug addicts.[8] The hierarchical rankings of health conditions are remarkably stable across populations (racial or ethnic groups, employers, health care providers, etc.), age groups (children, university students, adults) and over time (1970–1993).

More recent research compares the intensity of stigma directed toward persons with different types of mental disorders. One study team compared alcohol dependence, cocaine dependence, major depression, schizophrenia, and a "troubled" person (described as nervous, sad, and worried).[9] Subjects were presented with vignettes describing the symptoms of each disorder and asked to rank their willingness to interact socially with the individual described in the vignette. Subjects were least willing to interact when the vignette described symptoms of alcohol or cocaine dependence. Among the three types of mental disorders, schizophrenia elicited far greater stigma (63 percent unwilling to interact) than major depression (47 percent) or the "troubled" person (29 percent). Other studies, investigating social distance responses to vignettes describing schizophrenia or depression, consistently find that schizophrenia elicits more intense stigma.[10]

Some of the most intriguing social distance studies of mental illness have been conducted by psychologist Marc Weiss, among Chicago schoolchildren. In 1986, Weiss reported the results of a study in which he assessed the attitudes of 577 children, grades kindergarten through eight, toward persons with various types of mental disorders.[11] Weiss later conducted a follow-up study with thirty-four of the original kindergarteners, then in grade eight.[12]

In both studies, students were given a series of abstract drawings that were said to represent a person who was: "normal," "mentally retarded," "mentally ill," "crazy," "emotionally disturbed," "physically handicapped," or a "convict." Students were asked to draw stick figures representing themselves at a distance where they would feel comfortable being around the other person. The outcome measure, social distance, was literally a measure of the linear distance between the two figures.

Weiss's results suggest that negative attitudes toward persons with mental illness are well established by the time a child enters kindergarten, and fairly stable through eighth grade.[13] Eighth graders distinguished five groups with significantly different social distance rankings: (1) normal (most accepted); (2) physically handicapped; (3) emotionally disturbed, mentally ill, or mentally retarded; (4) convict; (5) crazy (least accepted).[14] Thus, by grade eight, the attitudes expressed by children mirror the attitudes expressed in social distance studies with adult subjects. The intensity of stigma directed toward a "crazy" person is on par, or greater than, the intensity of stigma associated with criminal behavior.

Stereotypes of Mental Illness

The remarkable cross-cultural and intertemporal consistency of societal attitudes toward mental illness begs for a rational explanation. To be sure, the negative associations are partly the vestiges of superstition, wherein mental illness was once associated with demonic possession. Stories are passed from one generation to the next and children adopt negative attitudes toward mental illness at an early age. Social scientists, however, have devoted considerable effort to move beyond folklore and superstition in our understanding of the genesis of stigma.

Two prominent social theories of mental illness stigma, labeling theory and attribution theory, proceed from Goffman's idea that stigma is evoked by negative stereotypes associated with a disfavored group. Labeling theory identifies the specific stereotypes (or labels) that generate feelings of fear and uneasiness around persons with serious mental illness (SMI). Three of the most prominent stereotypes label persons with mental illness as *dangerous*, *incompetent*, and *unpredictable*.[15] Attribution theory investigates the circumstances under which the negative stereotypes associated with a "marked" group elicit more intense stigma. In particular, the theory suggests that stigma increases with the degree to which others attribute *responsibility* for a mark to members of a stigmatized group, and the degree to which others perceive the mark to be *stable* (i.e., impossible to escape).[16]

My purpose here is not to assess the relative merits of the two theories, but to focus on the inferences that can be drawn from the vast array of empirical work they have spawned. Accordingly, I shall consider all five characteristics as factors that help to explain the intense and pervasive stigma against persons with SMI.

Responsibility

The degree to which an individual is perceived to be responsible for a stigmatizing mark, or any negative outcome, is a key factor in determining how others respond to that individual. Consider, for example, a college student who fails a calculus exam. If the student has attended class and completed all assignments, the failure is ascribed to a lack of mathematical ability (for which the student *is not* responsible). A visit to the professor's office is likely to elicit sympathy and help. If, on the other hand, the student is obviously bright but has skipped classes and ignored homework assignments, the poor exam performance will be ascribed to lack of effort (for which the student *is* responsible). In this case, the professor is likely to respond with blame and disapproval.

Bernard Weiner applied the responsibility attribution to conceptualize differences between "disease" and "illness."[17] According to Weiner's paradigm, a disease (e.g., pneumonia, meningitis) occurs because the body is invaded by a bacteria or virus, for which the unfortunate individual cannot be held responsible. Such conditions elicit little stigma and often considerable help (e.g., neighbors prepare meals, others assist with child care, the mother-in-law arrives). In contrast, an illness occurs because of behaviors an individual can control (e.g., chronic liver disease caused by alcohol abuse). Such conditions elicit stigma and condemnation, rather than sympathy and help.

Stability

The degree to which negative outcomes are perceived to be *stable* over time also affects the way others respond to a marked individual. If a negative outcome is perceived to be unstable (i.e., if it can change or be reversed), others are likely to offer help toward recovery. If it is perceived to be stable, and the outlook for the future appears to be hopeless, helping responses are perceived to be a waste of time.[18]

When David was first diagnosed with schizophrenia, I remember being struck by the cynicism of some of the people whom I encountered in family support groups. They told stories of evicting children from home, of siblings estranged from their brother, of fathers who simply walked away from their family. I expressed surprise that someone could abandon a loved one who was seriously ill. One mother responded, "You're new to this dear, wait until you've been dealing with it for years." Over the years I have come to understand why family members may distance themselves from a relative with SMI, when the prognosis appears hopelessly stable and the only reprieve is avoidance.

Incompetence

One of the most common stereotypes associated with mental illness is *incompetence* or helplessness: the perception that persons with mental disorders are incapable of making rational decisions, of handling responsibility, of managing a career or family.[19] The stereotype of incompetence is so pervasive that some type of discrimination against the mentally ill is codified into law in nearly every state.[20] As of 1999, forty-four states restricted the right of persons with mental illness to serve on a jury; thirty-seven states restricted their right to vote; twenty-four states restricted their right to hold elective office; twenty-seven states allowed parental rights to be restricted solely on the basis of mental illness. Between 1989 and 1999, as pharmaceutical treatments for mental illness were *improving*, fourteen states *expanded* legal discrimination against persons with mental illness, while none removed restrictions already in place.

There is a sinister irony in associating incompetence with mental illness: Persons with mental illness are perceived to be incapable of making responsible decisions as parents or citizens, at the same time they are perceived to be *responsible* for their behavior and symptoms.

Unpredictability

Another common stereotype of SMI is unpredictability. Although mental *illness* is perceived to be stable, with predictably negative long-run outcomes, the *behavior* of persons with mental illness is perceived to be erratic from day to day or moment to moment. In other words, persons with SMI are perceived as unable or unwilling to follow predictable social norms. The perceived unpredictability generates apprehension that a person with SMI will say or do something unexpected or inappropriate (like writing on the wall with a pencil between his toes). The emotional response is insecurity and uncertainty, which translates to anger, avoidance, and stigma.

Dangerousness

If perceived unpredictability evokes feelings of uneasiness, the perception of danger magnifies the uneasiness into fear. Numerous studies show that persons with mental illness are perceived to be dangerous and prone to violence.[21] Persons with schizophrenia or psychotic disorders are perceived to be even more dangerous than persons with other types of mental disorders, with the possible exception of persons who abuse alcohol.[22] In the presence of perceived danger, fear provokes instinctive avoidance, in other words, stigma.

Empirical Studies of Mental Illness Stigma

To what extent do the various stereotypes of mental illness explain the patterns of stigma reported in social distance studies? Have recent advances in our understanding of mental illness altered the stereotypes of persons with SMI? A number of studies have investigated these questions.

Correlations with Social Distance Measures

Two recent studies investigated the relationship between perceptions that persons with schizophrenia are unpredictable, and preferences for social distance from such persons. In one study involving two hundred undergraduate students at a London university, the researchers found strong and significant correlations between the perception that persons with schizophrenia were often socially inappropriate (i.e., rude, upsetting, or embarrassing when interacting with others), and the desire for social distance.[23] Another research team found the same result with data from a representative survey of more than five thousand German citizens.[24]

A number of studies have directly addressed the question, "What drives the *intensity* of the stigma toward mental illness?" using sophisticated statistical models to parse out the main effects. One such study involved two hundred undergraduate students at a Canadian university. The results showed that mental illnesses which were perceived to be dangerous or unpredictable elicited the strongest stigma.[25] In the study of German citizens, stereotypes of dangerousness, unpredictability, and stability (of a negative outcome) were found to be significant predictors of social distance.[26] Other studies produce slightly different lists of the most stigmatizing characteristics attributed to persons with mental illness, but the characteristics that appear on *every* list are unpredictability and dangerousness.[27]

Thus, the stigma directed toward mental illness in general, appears to be driven by a number of negative stereotypes, with perceptions of danger, unpredictability, and a stable and bleak prognosis being particularly important. The more intense stigma directed toward schizophrenia appears to be driven primarily by perceptions that persons with schizophrenia are more unpredictable, and more dangerous, than persons with other types of mental illness.

Changing Perceptions over Time

In general, the public is more likely to impute responsibility for an illness to persons with mental versus physical disorders.[28] Accordingly, strategies to reduce stigma toward persons with mental illness have often focused on educating the public about the biological origins of the disease, in an effort to combat the tendency to blame individuals for SMI. The campaigns emphasize that, "mental illness is a disease, just like any other."[29]

The efforts to educate the public about SMI appear to be having an effect. Recent research, using data from large population-based surveys, shows that people increasingly endorse genetic and biological factors as the source of mental illness. One U.S. study, for example, reported that the proportion of respondents endorsing a "chemical imbalance in the brain" as a potential cause of schizophrenia increased from 78 to 87 percent between 1996 and 2006. Over the same period, the proportion endorsing chemical imbalance as a potential cause of major depression increased from 67 to 80 percent. Less than one-third of respondents endorsed "his or her own bad character" as a source of mental illness.[30]

Another study, from the United Kingdom, investigated how attributions of responsibility for various mental disorders changed between 1998 and 2008. The results indicated that, by 2008, only a small minority of the public endorsed the responsibility attribution with respect to mental illness. When asked about depression or anxiety disorders, fewer than 15 percent of respondents agreed with the statement, "people with [this disorder] have only themselves to blame for their condition."[31] When asked about schizophrenia, only 9 percent ascribed blame.

Today, the vast majority of people do not hold persons with mental illness responsible for their conditions. However, the increased understanding that serious mental illness has biological origins has done little to change public perceptions that the outlook for patients is anything but stable and grim. While the proportion of the public endorsing medical treatment for persons with mental illness has increased with the increased acceptance of biological origins, the proportion who believe that medical treatment *will be effective* has not.[32] A stable 15–18 percent of respondents in the U.K. study believe that persons with mental illness "will not improve even if given treatment." One-fourth of respondents believe that persons with anxiety or depression "will never recover fully"; more than 40 percent believe that persons with schizophrenia "will never recover fully."[33]

Psychologist John Read at the University of Auckland argues that efforts to educate the public about the biological origins of mental illness have actually *increased* the stigma against schizophrenia. He posits that biological and genetic explanations of SMI reinforce the perception that persons with SMI are *fundamentally and irrevocably* different from "normal" people. According to Read, mental illness is perceived to be even more immutable than it was before, and the result is even greater stigma.[34] A study using population-based data from France supports Read's hypothesis. Researchers found that endorsing brain disease or chemical imbalance as causes of schizophrenia was associated with greater fear (but also greater sympathy).[35]

Other negative stereotypes of persons with SMI continue to be widely endorsed. Results from the U.K. study indicate that perceptions of unpredictability have declined only slightly over time.[36] Other research indicates that perceptions of dangerousness, associated with schizophrenia in particular, have *increased* in recent years.[37] Participants in one U.S. study, for example, were asked how likely it is that a person with mental illness will "do something violent toward other people." In 2006, 60 percent of respondents believed a person with schizophrenia was "somewhat" or "very" likely to be dangerous (up from 54 percent in 1996).[38]

Media Stereotypes

Some experts contend that news reports reinforce the negative stereotypes of mental illness that generate stigma. Patrick Corrigan and others have conducted surveys to document the way persons with mental illness are portrayed in the news. Corrigan is a psychology professor at the Illinois Institute of Technology, and an internationally recognized expert on mental illness stigma. He and his colleagues collected an exhaustive sample of stories on mental illness, from seventy U.S. newspapers with the largest daily circulations, over six one-week periods in 2002.[39] The study team searched for stories using the key words, "mental," "psych," or "schizo." More than 3,300 stories were retrieved.

The study team coded the content of each story into four broad themes (blame, dangerousness, treatment/recovery, advocacy actions/concerns) and a number of more specific sub-themes. Overall, stories related to dangerousness were most common, representing 39 percent of the sample. That proportion represents a favorable trend over time, down from 50 to 75 percent of stories related to dangerousness in studies from the late 1980s. However, within the dangerousness theme, two-thirds of stories dealt with violent crimes in which a person with mental illness was the perpetrator; these stories, together with stories dealing with suicide or self-injury, dominated front-page news coverage of mental illness. The authors concluded that, "the public is still being influenced with messages about mental illness and dangerousness" out of proportion to the number of violent crimes actually perpetrated by persons with SMI.[40]

Several recent episodes of horrific violence (e.g., the attack on Representative Gabrielle Giffords in Tucson, the theater shootings in Colorado, and the murders of children and teachers at Sandy Hook Elementary School) have been committed by persons whose behavior suggests untreated mental illness. News coverage of these events has reinforced the negative stereotype that persons with SMI are dangerous, even though far more acts of violence are committed by persons who do not have a diagnosis or symptoms of SMI (e.g., the Oklahoma City bombing, 9/11 attacks on the World Trade Center, bombings at the 2013 Boston Marathon, and recent attacks on police officers). The facts are:

- The risk of violence is increased by *acute* psychosis, but the vast majority of violent crimes (95–99 percent) are *not* committed by persons with psychotic disorders.[41]
- Males between ages fifteen and twenty-four are *more likely* to commit acts of violence than are persons with psychotic disorders (17 percent versus 12 percent).[42]
- Persons with mental illness are more likely to be the *victims* of violent crime than the perpetrators. Victimization rates among persons with schizophrenia are twelve times higher than among the general population.[43]

In short, public perceptions far overestimate the actual probability of danger associated with an individual who has schizophrenia.

The entertainment media also contribute to the distorted image that persons with SMI are prone to violence. Consider how often persons with mental illness are portrayed as the perpetrators of violent crimes in movies or on television. From my many years as a devoted fan of *Law and Order*, I remember only one episode in which a person with schizophrenia was depicted as a sympathetic character suffering from a serious illness. Before David became ill, I hardly noticed the one-sided portrayal of the mentally ill. Now the word "schizo" has a bite.

Workplace Stigma

One of the most damaging effects of stigma is that it restricts the opportunities of the stigmatized group across multiple facets of their everyday life. Stigma infects schools, communities, social groups, and the workplace, which is the particular focus of this book. Gary Becker, a Nobel prize-winning economist from the University of Chicago, was a pioneer in applying the concepts of social distance (which he called "tastes for discrimination") to study the impact of stigma in the workplace. In so doing, he created an entirely new field of study, the economics of discrimination.

According to Becker, there are three potential sources of discrimination in the labor market, all motivated by tastes for discrimination.[44] These include: (1) Discriminatory *employers*, who prefer not to hire members of a stigmatized group and will do so only at less than the usual wage; (2) discriminatory *coworkers*, who prefer not to work with members of a stigmatized group and will accept a lower wage to avoid them; (3) discriminatory *customers*, who prefer not to interact with members of a stigmatized group and will pay a higher price to avoid them. In all three cases, the desire for social distance devalues the labor of the stigmatized. In turn, discrimination *lowers the probability that members of a stigmatized group will be hired, and reduces their wages if they are.*

One of Becker's most useful insights is that the size of the wage (employment) differential between stigmatized and nonstigmatized groups can be interpreted as a measure of the intensity of stigma. In other words, *given that two groups are equally productive, on average,* the difference in their wages (or employment rates) will vary directly with the strength of preferences for social distance from the disadvantaged group. Becker's insight suggests that:

1. Discriminatory wage (employment) differentials will be larger for workers with mental disorders than for workers with physical disorders (because mental disorders elicit more intense stigma).
2. Discriminatory wage (employment) differentials will be larger for workers with psychotic disorders than for workers with other mental disorders (because psychotic disorders elicit more intense stigma).

In fact, we observe large wage and employment differentials between workers with and without disabilities, between workers with mental versus physical disorders, and between workers with psychotic disorders versus other types of mental disorders. Economists have developed statistical methods to identify what part of an observed differential is *explained* by differences in average productivity (Becker's theory applies to groups of equally productive workers) and what part is *unexplained*, and potentially attributable to discrimination. When the methods are applied to data for workers with disabilities, the estimates of discrimination effects are strongly consistent with the stigma rankings in the social distance studies.[45] Estimates of the potential effects of discrimination are larger for workers with mental versus physical disorders, and larger for workers with psychotic disorders versus other mental disorders.[46]

In one study, we used data from the 1999 Medical Expenditure Panel Survey to estimate the impact of stigma on employment rates for persons with mental disorders, relative to a no-disorder comparison group. We considered four types of mental disorders, namely: mood, anxiety, adjustment, and psychotic disorders. Here, I describe results for psychotic versus mood disorders, the two most disadvantaged groups.

The difference in estimated employment rates between persons with psychotic disorders versus the "no-disorder" control group was thirty-eight percentage points (51 percent versus 89 percent employed), compared to a sixteen percentage point differential (73 percent versus 89 percent) for mood disorders.[47] The majority of the employment differentials could be explained by differences in productivity measures (e.g., the groups with mental illness had less education, on average, than the nondisabled group). However, the unexplained differential (potentially attributed to discrimination) was larger for the group with psychotic disorders in both absolute (11 percentage points versus 3.5 for mood disorders) and relative (28 percent of the total differential versus 21 percent) terms. Hence, the results are consistent with results of the social distance studies suggesting that persons with psychotic disorders are subject to greater stigma and discrimination than persons with other types of mental disorders.

In another study, using data from the National Health Interview Survey, we compared workers' self-reports of work-related discrimination to our econometric measures.[48] Nearly one-third (29 percent) of workers with psychotic disorders reported experiences of discrimination at work, compared to only 21 percent of workers with mood or anxiety disorders. The experiences ranged from being refused employment or promotion, to being fired, laid off, or told to resign. Workers' self-reports of stigma and discrimination corresponded to our econometric measures, suggesting that the workers knew when they were being discriminated against.

Other evidence of workplace stigma directed toward persons with mental illness comes from interview studies with individual workers. Two researchers, an anthropologist and a psychiatrist, conducted one-on-one interviews with ninety persons who had diagnoses of schizophrenia or schizoaffective disorder. They aimed to learn about the participants' experiences of stigma in various social settings. The sample was relatively high-functioning and asymptomatic: all participants were clinically stable and being treated with atypical antipsychotics in the community. Nevertheless, 96 percent of participants reported experiences of stigma across a variety of social settings.[49]

More than half of participants who were currently working reported experiences of stigma in the workplace. They mentioned hostile, fearful, and insensitive attitudes on the part of coworkers or supervisors. They also reported experiences involving teasing, negative stereotyping, unfair treatment, and violations of confidentiality. Often, participants responded to stigma with feelings of shame, and efforts to conceal their illness. For example:

> When I was working in the hospital, I stopped taking the medication a couple of weeks or so after I got hired because I felt bad about having to take medication and having an illness and being diagnosed as schizophrenic. Instead of educating myself or educating other people about it, I chose to just stop taking it. That was bad.[50]

The comments of this individual describe one of the most insidious effects of stigma directed toward mental illness, namely, its power to invade the minds of victims, who then direct stigma toward themselves.

Self-Stigma

It is quite common for members of a stigmatized group to adopt the negative stereotypes associated with that group into their own self-image. I grew up, for example, in an era when male and female roles were sharply delineated. While my brother learned to work with tools and repair automobiles, I learned to cook and clean and sew. Until I was divorced, it never occurred to me that I was capable of a simple home repair, and to this day the automobile engine is a thing of mystery to me. How much more damaging is the self-stigma of persons with schizophrenia, who adopt the negative stereotypes of themselves as incompetent, volatile, and hopelessly ill!

Among persons with schizophrenia, self-stigma is associated with loss of self-esteem and self-efficacy, and with feelings of incompetence, inferiority, and guilt.[51] Such feelings cause shame and embarrassment, often inducing efforts to conceal the illness from others.[52] One woman likens her efforts to conceal her mental illness to putting on a mask:

> The mask is what we wear to conceal who we really are because of stigma. We can't be the real patient that we are like the person with cancer or diabetes or a broken leg can be. We have to be something other than who we are.[53]

The end result of self-stigma is loss of personhood. One either hides behind a mask of concealment or loses all other aspects of their personality to the stereotype of mental illness.

Certainly, there are many persons with SMI who do not become victims of self-stigma. Some react to the negative stereotypes of mental illness with anger, and become energized to advocate against stigma directed toward the mentally ill. Others react with indifference, as if the stigma were irrelevant or unimportant to them. In another of his many studies on mental illness stigma, Corrigan (working with coauthor, Amy Watson) proposed a situational model to explain the different individual reactions to stigma, where the key mediating factors are: (1) the extent to which an individual views negative stereotypes as a *legitimate description of themselves*, and (2) the extent to which an individual *identifies with the stigmatized group*.[54]

According to the model, when an individual with SMI encounters the negative stereotypes associated with the "mark" of mental illness, they must decide if the stereotypes apply to them. Those who accept the stereotypes as legitimate tend to assimilate the negative attitudes (stigma) into their self-image. Goffman describes the self-stigmatizing process as follows: Individuals who experience stigma eventually realize they are not being accorded the respect that other persons in their social position receive, and that the stigmatized person would normally expect. The object of stigma comes to understand that they are viewed as "tainted," as undeserving of the attention, friendship, employment, or other rewards reserved for "normal" people. They may reconcile the stigma directed toward them by identifying attributes *within themselves* that justify such treatment. In this way, the individual begins to adopt the negative stereotypes of mental illness as a legitimate description of themselves. [55]

The inclination to view a stereotype as legitimate or illegitimate depends partly on whether the realization (of membership in a stigmatized group) is gradual or abrupt. Persons who are born into a "marked" group (such as African Americans or Jews) learn about their stigma gradually, knowing they are a member of the group. As part of the group, they realize that the stereotypes do not apply to all members of the group, perhaps not even to a majority of the group, and need not apply to them.

In contrast, persons who develop a serious mental illness, typically as a teenager or young adult, find themselves abruptly included in a stigmatized group they have been taught to shun. All the negative stereotypes they have learned to associate with mental illness suddenly apply to *them*. Self-stigma would seem to be almost inevitable. Indeed, in a study of Chicago high school students, researchers found evidence of self-stigma related to a diagnosis of mental illness, as early as adolescence. [56] Students with and without mental illness were equally likely to perceive persons with mental illness as "threatening" or "out of control."

If a person with mental illness does not accept the negative stereotypes of the disease as a legitimate description of themselves, their response to stigma is likely to depend upon how they identify with others who have a mental illness. Strong group identification helps an individual maintain their self-esteem, even in the face of stigma. With a strong sense of group identity and intact self-esteem, individuals who reject the stereotypes of mental illness "may become righteously indignant about the negative social identity and discrimination bestowed on them." [57] One angry young man, for example, likens mental illness stigma to an "invisible cage":

> What bothers me is that my ambition is being restrained. They are trying to force me into some sort of a cliché and they don't leave me any possibility for development. The doctors said that I shouldn't bother studying, I mean, continuing my studies. I would really like to work as a programmer, but they tell me that isn't possible, because with that illness [schizophrenia], I wouldn't be capable for that. That's what bothers me, you know! [58]

Anger is empowering, so it is not surprising that many of these individuals become vocal advocates against stigma toward mental illness.

On the other hand, there are persons with SMI who reject the negative stereotypes associated with mental illness, but do not identify strongly with others who are mentally ill. These individuals appear to be relatively unaffected by stigma, either oblivious or indifferent to it. Their self-esteem is not injured by stigma, and they do not seek the protection of others like them. [59] It is unclear what factors protect this group from self-stigma: intrinsic personality traits, support and encouragement from significant others, quality of mental health care, nature of illness? I suspect one of the most important factors is their determination not to be defined by their illness—that is, to break out of the invisible cage:

> What is schizophrenia? It's an eighteen year old whose time is spent as if she only lives in the present. She begins to see that one doctor is right. "No expectations," he told her, "just pay attention." Time passes and the anxiety and anger and noise persist, but she begins to see that she has a chance to break the spell of the master oppressor. She sees where she failed before and forges ahead of where the counselors ever thought she would be able to go. She can look down and see that they were just border markers of her domain. [60]

Postscript

Unlike his mother, David has always been one of those individuals who appear to be indifferent to the stigma associated with mental illness. The two of us responded quite differently to that first experience of stigma at the wedding reception. David, only recently discharged from the hospital, was unaware of, and untouched by, the stigma that we experienced. I, on the other hand, was very much aware. I was mortified when I realized that family members were avoiding us, and I responded with anger to the perceived insult to my son. At the first opportunity, I told my husband, "We are leaving."

I am not sure what has protected David from stigma and kept his self-esteem intact. He tells me he held on to five words that his psychiatrist said to him as he was about to be discharged from that first hospital stay: "You can recover from this."

I do know that David is determined not to be defined by his illness. When he first came home from the hospital, schizophrenia was my chief concern and my constant preoccupation. I watched for any change of mood, outburst of anger, or unusual behavior that might signal a relapse. My response is not unusual. Mental illness can alter the way an individual is perceived such that in some sense the patient *becomes* the illness. [61] One day, David said to me, "Mom, when I look at you all I see is the worry in your eyes." I could not see past the illness to find my son.

The extent to which persons with schizophrenia (and their relatives and friends) succumb to self-stigma has a direct impact on a patient's capacity to achieve a fulfilling life. Accepting the stigma of schizophrenia as applicable to oneself is an impediment to recovery, because self-stigma is demoralizing and fosters feelings of shame, unworthiness, and incompetency.[62] Accepting the stigma as applied to one's child (or brother, or spouse) is also an impediment to recovery, because it is an implicit agreement to conform to the limitations society places on those who suffer from the disease. Accepting the diagnosis of schizophrenia, but rejecting its negative stereotypes, is the first important step to escaping the invisible cage.

Chapter Three

Life Interrupted

HELL NO!

They say there's something special in the air at Chapel Hill such that every freshman who inhales it never wants to leave. In fact, there is something almost mystical about the campus, the oldest public university in the United States, with its centerpiece an old well dating back to 1897. To anyone standing there in springtime, when the azaleas and dogwoods are in bloom, there truly seems to be a "little bit of heaven in North Carolina."

Graduates of UNC are Tarheel fans for life. The school has a proud history of championship athletic teams, and the basketball team, in particular, is legendary. David attended school when Antawn Jamison, Vince Carter, and Brendan Haywood were stars of the team. He lived in the same building as the basketball players and knew many of them on a first-name basis. He was an avid fan of both the football and basketball teams, but still managed to attend classes often enough to make the dean's list. In short, David reveled in college life until, in the spring semester of his junior year, he got sick.

When I arrived at the emergency room, the first person to meet me was a university staff member with papers to be signed to officially withdraw David from classes. She reassured me that her office would take care of all the paperwork necessary to withdraw David from school without penalty. At the time I was grateful for her help; I did not know how much more difficult it would be for David to be *readmitted* to school in the fall.

Summer 1999

During those first months at home David was lethargic, quiet, and withdrawn. He rarely went outside and no friends came to visit. I struggled to entertain him as best I could: We played Scrabble in the evenings; we took his dog for long walks; and I bought furniture for him to refinish, in anticipation of his return to school. Overall, an aura of sadness surrounded him. One afternoon I found him lying on his bed, staring at the ceiling, with tears running down his face. When I asked what was wrong he said, "My mind's playing tricks on me again, Mom." I suppose it was a good sign—he knew the delusions were not real—but his despair broke my heart.

One day I made a suggestion that roused him briefly from his lethargy. With fall semester approaching, I was apprehensive about David returning to school. I wanted to keep him close by, so I could monitor his meds and know that he was safe. I suggested that he stay home for a semester, take some classes at the local university, and then return to UNC in the spring. David simply stared at me as I talked. When I finished, he responded with more emotion than I had heard in months, "*Hell, no!*" And with that response, his determination to return to UNC became mine as well.

David's physician approved his return to school on a part-time basis, so we began the process of getting him reinstated for the fall semester. The Student Disability Services Office seemed to be a logical place to begin. The staff person there asked why David was only returning as a part-time student. I explained that we were complying with his physician's orders. "If he's not ready to return full-time, he shouldn't come back at all," I was told. I explained that David's physician believed it would help his recovery for him to return to school, but taking a full-time load would be too stressful. The staff person said, "Well, when your son got in trouble . . ." I stopped him in midsentence. "My son did *not* get in trouble," I said, "My son *got sick*."

In anger and frustration, I appealed to the social worker assigned to David's research study. She connected us with the Student Services Offices at UNC, helped us complete the paperwork required for readmission, and obtained a statement from David's psychiatrist certifying that David was asymptomatic and capable of returning to school. Nevertheless, the dean decided that the Emergency Action and Evaluation Committee must approve David's readmission.

The committee, composed of UNC faculty and administrators, is convened whenever someone in authority believes that a student's behavior poses a threat to campus safety. In particular, the committee has jurisdiction over admission and readmission decisions involving students with a history of violence or criminal behavior, or of violating university drug policies. It exists to protect the campus community from anyone whose behavior makes them a potential threat to themselves or others. David had no history of violence or criminal behavior, or of violating university policies; and his psychiatrist said he was not a danger to himself or others. Why was it necessary to convene the committee at all? Would there have been a hearing if the diagnosis had been "adjustment disorder," instead of schizophrenia? I was offended by such a thinly veiled attempt at discrimination.

The committee hearing lasted for several hours. David testified, as well as his doctor, his social worker, and his father and me. When it was my turn, I walked into the hearing room where the dean, the board members, and my son were seated. I said:

> I am an economist who studies disability-related discrimination. If you would like to discuss my son's rights to an education under the Americans with Disabilities Act, I would be happy to do so. In fact, I have brought a sample of my published research on the topic. [I arrayed an assortment of reprints of journal articles on the table.] However, I would rather not talk about the ADA. I would prefer to talk about why my son deserves to be reinstated as a student in good standing at this university.

I continued on with my reasons: David had no record of any disciplinary action at the university. He had consistently maintained an academic record as a "student in good standing." His physician believed his return to school was important to his recovery. Finally, *it is illegal for an academic institution to discriminate against an otherwise-qualified student solely on the basis of disability.* The board was silent.

Within thirty minutes we received word from the dean that David could return to school. I like to think my legal arguments were the persuasive factor, but that is probably taking too much credit. More likely it was David's demeanor, as he sat there for three hours, calmly making his case and answering questions, which convinced the committee it was safe to allow him to come back to school.

David enrolled in three classes for fall semester and we settled him, and the newly refinished furniture, into an apartment near the UNC campus. I made excuses to travel to the Triangle area (Raleigh–Durham–Chapel Hill) on a frequent basis, so I could visit David without saying I was "checking up" on him. I frequently stayed overnight, cleaned the apartment, and stocked the refrigerator with food. That fall he successfully completed the two classes. After he completed four more in the spring, we began to think that he might graduate only one semester behind schedule. We did not realize that he had stopped taking his medication.

In July 2000, sixteen months after his first episode of psychosis, David suffered a serious relapse and was hospitalized again. This time his symptoms receded quickly once he was back on the medication, and he was released within a few days. The timing was good. Fall semester was scheduled to begin in only a few weeks; David was in and out of the hospital without ever having to withdraw from school.

Spring 2001

David graduated from UNC–Chapel Hill in May 2001, with a bachelor's degree in management and society. We had a small party with a few close friends and relatives. It was a joyful celebration—one I thought I might never see—and a huge credit to the strength and willpower of my son. I will never forget what he said to me as we were leaving, "Mom, no matter what happens, they can never take this away from me."

INVESTMENTS IN HUMAN CAPITAL

The fact that David developed schizophrenia while he was in college is not unusual. Measles, mumps, and chicken pox are, or used to be, diseases of childhood. Arthritis, heart disease, Alzheimer's disease, and other forms of dementia are diseases of the aged. Schizophrenia is a disease of young adulthood. It typically strikes around the time that a young person completes their formal education and is about to enter the labor force. The disease has no known cure and can be severely disabling, sometimes resulting in a lifetime of lost productivity. Economists call this a loss of *human capital*.

The term "human capital" refers to the productive potential embedded in human beings. Like investment capital, or capital equipment, human capital is an input into the production process. At any given age, each individual has a stock of human capital. That stock is determined, in part, by an initial endowment of health, intelligence, and basic personality characteristics acquired in early childhood; and, in part, by investments in human capital the individual makes over their lifetime. These investments can take the form of education, vocational training, work experience, or efforts to preserve or enhance one's health status.

For healthy persons, human capital accumulation typically peaks somewhere in middle age. The stock of human capital rises rapidly at younger ages, when an individual is making full-time investments in education or vocational training. Human capital continues to accumulate into middle age, as the individual gains work experience and on-the-job training. At some point, however, the stock of human capital begins to diminish with the effects of aging. The point at which the decline begins varies considerably, in part reflecting one's occupation and lifestyle choices. My brother-in-law worked in heavy construction all his life and retired at age fifty. Although he was the youngest of six siblings, he looked much older. He always said, "I may be younger than the others, but I have more mileage on me."

A typical profile of human capital accumulation and deterioration over the life cycle slopes steeply upward until approximately age twenty-five, rises more slowly until around age fifty, and then begins a slow decline that continues with age. Accordingly, a diagnosis of schizophrenia at age twenty can have a tremendous impact on productive potential. In Canistrus's time, and until the middle of the twentieth century, the onset of schizophrenia was typically accompanied by an almost total loss of human capital. Persons with the disease spent their lives writing treatises on interpretive geography, or living in an institution, or cared for by family and friends. If the symptoms of the disease were acute and unremitting, the entire productive capacity of a lifetime could be lost.

Modern pharmacology has miraculously produced effective treatments for schizophrenia. The drugs have the potential for restoring many persons with the disease to a more normal trajectory of human capital. Yet the second-generation antipsychotics have been on the market for more than twenty years and have scarcely made a dent in the expected earnings of persons with SMI. Why have these discoveries not had a greater impact on employment outcomes for this population? Part of the explanation may be the tremendous stigma that still surrounds mental illness; but the poor outcomes also reflect the disruptive impact a mental illness has on the process of accumulating human capital.

The Nature of Human Capital

Two broad types of human capital are valued in the labor market. *General human capital* encompasses the knowledge, skills, and abilities that increase a worker's productivity at many different firms or worksites. *Job-specific human capital* encompasses the sort of "insider information" that is valuable with only one employer, or at only one worksite.

General human capital may be acquired either before or after a worker is hired, because it is applicable in many different jobs. Health is an example of general human capital. Other examples are the knowledge that one acquires through formal education, and the technical skills (e.g., carpentry, drafting, electrical repair) derived from vocational training programs. Investments in general human capital are typically financed by workers, because employers have no incentive to pay for human capital that a worker may transfer elsewhere.

Job-specific human capital, on the other hand, is only valuable at a specific firm and must, therefore, be acquired after a worker is hired. The relationship between a worker and their supervisor is a form of job-specific human capital—so is understanding things like the layout of the workplace, where to find supplies, whom to call for help, and how to access the computer systems. None of these skills are transferable to another job. Employers typically pay for investments in job-specific human capital, because workers have no incentive to pay for skills that they cannot transfer elsewhere.

Which type of human capital is most valuable to workers with SMI? *General human capital* is most important for any worker, because general skills are transferable if a worker should need to change jobs. General human capital is even more important to workers with SMI, because of the cyclic nature of mental illness. If a worker with SMI is forced to leave their job because acute symptoms recur, the *transferable skills* associated with general human capital will facilitate a return to work once their symptoms are in remission.

One aspect of human capital that transcends the general/job-specific dichotomy is *social capital*. Social capital encompasses the person-to-person connections and interpersonal relationship skills that both enhance the quality of life and increase the likelihood of success in the labor market. Specifically, social capital refers to "the social characteristics . . . which enable [a person] to reap market and non-market returns from interactions with others."[1] Not surprisingly, research shows that the quality, strength, and diversity of an individual's social networks is a significant predictor of positive employment outcomes.[2]

Social capital may be job-specific (e.g., relationships with supervisors, clients, and coworkers) or general (e.g., relationships with friends, mentors, and others outside the workplace). Many top MBA programs require students to work in teams, attend training sessions in job interviewing, and even practice formal dining, to build the general social capital essential for a leadership position. After graduates are hired, they begin to accumulate the job-specific social capital that will be essential to their success with a particular employer.

SMI is often associated with deficits in social capital. The negative symptoms of schizophrenia, for example, make it difficult to communicate and to establish interpersonal relationships. The lack of social skills may impact both the ability to obtain a job (how is the individual perceived in a job interview?) and workplace relationships if they are hired (how is the individual perceived by coworkers and supervisors?).[3]

The destruction of social capital associated with schizophrenia is perhaps greater than with any other disease. This fact may help to explain why schizophrenia is perceived to be a "disease unlike any other" in terms of its negative impact on health.

Health Capital

Epidemiologists use the concept of *disease burden* to measure the overall loss of health capital associated with an illness or injury. The most current information on the disease burden associated with serious mental illness comes from the 2010 Global Burden of Diseases, Injuries, and Risk Factors (GBD) project. The project recently published estimates of the disease burden associated with 220 illness/injury categories for 2010, with comparison data for 1990 and 2005. The first results fill almost the entire December 2012 issue of *Lancet.*

Measures of Disease Burden

The summary unit of disease burden for the 2010 GBD is disability-adjusted life-years (DALYs), which incorporates both mortality losses (a measure of *years of life lost*) and morbidity losses (a measure of *years lived in a less than healthy state*) associated with a particular illness/injury.[4] Estimating the years of life lost to an illness/injury is a simple statistical exercise that accounts for the number of deaths associated with the illness/injury in a given year, the age at which those people died, and their life expectancy in good health. For example, when a forty-year-old with a life expectancy of seventy-five years dies of lung cancer, thirty-five years of life lost are attributed to lung cancer.

Estimating years lived in a less than healthy state is much trickier because it requires subjective assessments of the relative reduction in quality of life associated with an illness/injury. For example, a year spent in permanent confinement to a wheelchair is valued as less than a full year of healthy life, but exactly how much less? The GBD 2010 project assigns each of the 220 illness/injury categories a discount factor, or "disability weight," reflecting the reduction in quality of life associated with that illness/injury. In an effort to obtain disability weights that reflect a global consensus, investigators surveyed more than thirty thousand persons from five countries.[5] Respondents were presented with paired descriptions of illness/injury categories, written in lay language, and asked to select, for each pair, which category represents a higher level of health. Without dwelling on details, it is instructive to note that acute schizophrenia was assigned a discount factor of 0.756 (about 25 percent of perfect health), the highest disability weight of all 220 categories.[6]

Once the disability weights have been assigned, years lived with disability are computed by multiplying the number of persons living with a disabling illness/injury in a particular year by the disability weight assigned to that illness/injury category. Thus, if two hundred people in a given population suffer from migraine headaches, the years lost to disability associated with migraine headaches are 86.6 (200 times 0.433, the disability weight assigned to migraines).

Disease Burden of Mental Illness

It turns out that *mental disorders are not among the leading causes of disease burden* worldwide. The main reason is that mental disorders do not involve nearly as much loss of life as the leading causes. According to the GBD, cardiovascular/circulatory diseases, and infectious diseases (such as pneumonia and meningitis), were the leading causes of disease burden in 2010.

These killer diseases accounted for more than 30 percent of years of life lost; whereas mental and substance use disorders accounted for less than 1 percent.[7]

Schizophrenia is not a disease that kills. Although suicide rates are above average among persons with schizophrenia and other mental disorders, these deaths are attributed to self-harm, not to mental illness, in the GBD. Because schizophrenia is not an important cause of lives lost, it ranked only forty-third in importance as a cause of global disease burden in 2010.[8]

The story is different with regard to morbidity. When the focus shifts to nonfatal illnesses, *mental and substance use disorders are the number one cause of global disease burden.* Together, they accounted for 23 percent of the disease burden attributed to morbidity (years lived with disability) in 2010. Musculoskeletal disorders, the number two cause of morbidity losses, accounted for 21 percent.[9]

Across all 220 illness/injury categories, schizophrenia itself ranked sixteenth in importance as a global cause of years lived with disability.[10] Recall that schizophrenia has the highest disability weight of any illness/category, but it drops to sixteenth as a cause of years lived with disability, because its prevalence is far lower than the leading causes of morbidity (low back pain and major depression). Moreover, when a person with schizophrenia commits suicide, the years of life lost are attributed to self-harm, and the morbidity losses associated with schizophrenia are actually reduced!

Changes in Disease Burden over Time

The GBD study is an ongoing project, so it is possible to trace how the disease burden associated with various illnesses/injury categories has changed over time. Comparing results from GBD 1990 and 2010, we find the overall burden of disease declined over the twenty-year period. If we measure disease burden in terms of DALYs per one hundred thousand persons, to control for population growth, the decrease was an amazing 23 percent. This huge decrease in the population-adjusted burden of disease is explained foremost by a tremendous decrease in the burden associated with communicable diseases (–44 percent).[11]

Contrary to the overall trend, the population-adjusted disease burden associated with mental and behavioral disorders *increased by 6 percent* during this period.[12] Among the mental disorders, drug use and schizophrenia had the highest percentage increases in DALYs per 100,000 persons (17 percent and 11 percent, respectively). The 17 percent increase in disability burden associated with drug use disorders was primarily driven by a tremendous increase in the prevalence of opioid use over the twenty-year period.[13] In contrast, the prevalence of schizophrenia has remained stable over time. The 11 percent increase in disease burden associated with schizophrenia is primarily explained by differences in the disability weights assigned to the disease in GBD 1990 and 2010.

Perception versus Reality

Both GBD 1990 and GBD 2010 estimate morbidity losses for two categories of schizophrenia, but the titles and lay descriptions of the two schizophrenia states are different in the two studies. In GBD 1990, the disability weight for "untreated schizophrenia" was 0.627, and for "treated schizophrenia" was 0.351.[14] In GBD 2010, the disability weight for "acute schizophrenia" was 0.756, and for "residual schizophrenia" was 0.576.[15] Notably, neither lay description of schizophrenia in 1990 mentioned violence or self-harm as characteristic of the disorder, whereas both descriptions did so in 2010. Hence, we cannot know if the changes in disability weights (and morbidity losses) associated with schizophrenia in the two surveys reflect changes in public attitudes toward the *disease*, or toward its *description*.

In 1988, when the world's attention was focused on the AIDS epidemic, the editor of the journal *Nature* wrote, "Schizophrenia is arguably the worst disease known to mankind, even AIDS not excepted."[16] Apparently the editor would agree with the harsh assessments of disability accorded to schizophrenia in GBD 2010. Nonetheless, it is hard to believe that having schizophrenia in 2010 was worse than having the disease in 1990. That said, poverty is still commonplace among the population with schizophrenia, and the prognosis for a productive work life remains poor.[17]

Education

Education is crucial to success in the modern labor market. The U.S. economy is increasingly reliant on industries that demand a highly educated, highly skilled labor force. Education provides the human capital necessary to meet those demands, and a signal to employers that a worker has acquired the necessary skills. Better-educated workers typically have higher employment rates, and more stable jobs, than less-educated workers. Better-educated workers can also expect jobs with higher wages and lifetime earnings, more generous benefit packages, and greater intrinsic rewards (autonomy, creativity, novelty, opportunity for advancement) than their less educated counterparts.

Among persons with serious mental illness, education is consistently shown to be one of the strongest and most significant predictors of positive employment outcomes.[18] A meta-analysis of sixty-two studies analyzing predictors of employment for persons with schizophrenia, for example, shows that education and cognitive skills are more consistently related to positive outcomes than diagnosis, current symptoms, or history of hospitalizations.[19] When mental illness strikes at an early age, therefore, an individual is disadvantaged not only by the loss of health capital associated with the illness, but also by the *loss of potential human capital* associated with a disrupted education.

A recent study shows that persons with early-onset disabilities also earn *lower returns to education* than persons with late-onset disabilities. The study uses data from the 1993 Survey of Income and Program Participation (SIPP) to estimate the impact of additional years of education on the wages of men with early versus late-onset disability (onset of disability before/after age twenty-five), relative to a control group of nondisabled men. Holding severity of disability constant, men with early-onset disability have *lower* returns to education than nondisabled men, whereas men with late-onset disability have *higher* returns. Estimated returns for an additional year of secondary education, for example, are less than 1 percent for men with early-onset disability, compared to 9.4 percent for nondisabled men and 23.4 percent for men with late-onset disability.[20]

The authors speculate that education acts as an "insurance policy" against the possibility of becoming disabled later in life. That is, the higher returns to education experienced by adults with late-onset disability "protect" these workers from some of the human capital losses associated with a health shock. How might such an insurance policy work? One possible explanation relates to the role of education as a *signal* of productivity; another explanation relates to the role education plays in *job matching*.

Education as a Signal

Education not only functions as a means to acquire human capital for the labor market, but also as a "signal" of worker quality. The most visible quality signal is a diploma, indicating that an individual has completed a required course of study at an acceptable level. Thus, a diploma is more valuable than the equivalent years of schooling as a signal of productivity to employers. Someone with a bachelor's degree has better prospects in the labor market, on average, than someone with four years of college but no degree.

In a classic article, Michael Spence (an economist at New York University and winner of the 2001 Nobel Prize in Economics) outlines a conceptual model of the role of signals in the labor market.[21] Spence views the hiring decision as an investment that involves risk, because employers cannot observe the productivity of job applicants at the time of hiring (and perhaps even for some time after). When an employer decides to hire, the wage they offer is no greater than the applicant's expected *marginal value product* (that is, the value of the additional output the worker is expected to contribute to the firm). Otherwise, it is not profitable to hire the worker at all. But how is expected value determined, if productivity cannot be observed in advance of hiring?

According to Spence, the employer observes a host of other characteristics that provide indications of the productivity to be expected from a job applicant. Employers evaluate expected productivity based on their experience with workers exhibiting similar characteristics, whose productivity has been observed. Suppose, for example, a financial firm hires an MBA from Anywhere University who turns out to be an outstanding performer. The firm is likely to look favorably on other applicants from Anywhere U, may even recruit graduates from Anywhere U, given the performance of the graduate they have observed.

Some observable characteristics are fixed by nature (e.g., age, gender) but others, like education, are alterable. Spence calls these alterable characteristics "signals," because individuals can acquire these characteristics in hopes of increasing their wage offers. So, why do we not observe everyone investing in a PhD? Clearly because there are costs associated with education, so individuals acquire education only to the point where the expected returns on the investment (higher wages) exceed the costs. A key assumption in the Spence model is that *the costs of investment in a productivity signal are inversely correlated with expected productivity.* More intelligent workers, for example, have lower costs of acquiring an advanced degree than less intelligent workers, who may have to study harder, pay for tutoring, and take longer to graduate. Hence, the education signal acquires value because workers with higher expected productivity (more intelligence) have lower investment costs and are more likely to invest in advanced degrees.

The education signal is potentially even more valuable for workers with mental disorders than for nondisabled persons. Why might this be so? Goffman provides a clue in his discussion of mechanisms for combating stigma: "The stigmatized individual can also attempt to correct his condition indirectly by devoting much private effort to the mastery of areas of activity ordinarily felt to be closed . . . to one with his shortcoming."[22]

One of the negative stereotypes attributed to persons with mental illness is incompetence; they are thought to be incapable of rational decision making. Persons who are incompetent are expected to be high school dropouts, not to earn advanced degrees. What better way to confound the stereotype of incompetence than to earn a diploma? Based on the signaling model, education is exceptionally valuable for persons with mental disorders because it suggests productivity *far beyond what is expected* of them.

Education and Job Matching

Another way that education may "insure" against the human capital losses associated with disability is by enabling better matches between a worker's functional capacities and the demands of their job. The match is important because the impact of functional limitations on a worker's productivity depends upon the nature of their job. A person confined to a wheelchair, for example, may be equally as productive as their nondisabled coworkers in a sedentary job. The same worker employed in a job that requires movement around the workplace would tend to be slower at accomplishing tasks (less productive) than their nondisabled counterparts.

A colleague and I have examined the importance of job matching for workers with physical disabilities (i.e., health impairments that affect mobility, strength, or endurance). Workers are said to be "mismatched" in a job, if their physical limitations affect their ability to perform important job functions. Using data from the SIPP (1996–2008), we find that workers who are mismatched in their jobs earn lower wages than their counterparts whose physical limitations do not impact important job functions. By itself, this result is not surprising. The more important finding is that *education is a highly significant determinant* of the probability of finding a good match.[23] In other words, better-educated workers are more likely than less-educated workers to be in jobs where their functional limitations have little impact on important job functions. Some persons with mental disorders, for example, are easily distracted by extraneous noises. Such a person is more likely to be successful working in their own office (with good soundproofing), than working in a cubicle or open space. Education increases the value of this person in the labor market, making it more likely they can find, or bargain for, a job that accommodates their functional limitations.

Supported Education

For all these reasons (acquisition of human capital, signaling to counteract stigma, opportunity to find a good job match), education is a valuable investment for persons with serious mental illness. There are a few programs, primarily in the United States, Canada, and Australia, which aim to support persons with SMI who want to pursue a college education. The supported education programs fall into three categories:

- The *self-contained classroom*, in which students with SMI take classes in segregated settings, with instructors and teaching methods that accommodate their needs.
- *Mobile support*, in which students are enrolled in regular classes at a postsecondary institution, but receive support from mental health professionals in the community (e.g., staff at community mental health centers or clubhouses).

- *On-site support*, in which students are enrolled in regular classes at a postsecondary institution, and receive support from specially trained staff at the institution. [24]

These programs are a good beginning, but they are not designed to meet the needs of students who aspire to a four-year university degree. One problem is that most current supported education programs do not focus on graduation as a specifically defined objective. The authors of an article describing one of the Australian programs, for example, say that the purpose of supported education is, "to increase the ability of people with psychiatric disabilities to access and participate in post-secondary education, by providing necessary supports." [25] Access and participation are good first steps, but graduation is the signal that creates opportunities in the labor market.

Another problem is that existing supported education programs are not, for the most part, located on college or university campuses. To be specific, there were about one hundred supported education programs operating in the United States and Canada in 2005. [26] The majority of these programs follow the mobile support model. Suppose that the total number of programs had doubled in the last ten years. Even so, given that there are more than 4,250 postsecondary degree granting institutions in the United States, the likelihood that a student with SMI finds a supported education program *on their campus* is almost nil.

Training

Most jobs in a developed economy require a combination of general and job-specific human capital. The formal educational system focuses on developing general human capital, but vocational training can be either general or job-specific. Automobile mechanics, bartenders, electricians, hair stylists, home health aides, plumbers, all have *general training* for their jobs, that increases their value in many firms. By way of contrast, within a large hospital: Admissions clerks are trained to use the computer software that processes a patient into the hospital. Cleaning staff are trained to know where supplies are kept and how to dispose of different types of waste. Nurses are trained to know the color-coding scheme for medical supplies, and how to use the computer software that tracks patient medications. None of these job-specific skills can be readily transferred to another hospital system.

The litany of examples of general and job-specific skills may be getting tedious, but the distinction is probably the most important in all of human capital theory. It should be clear by now that general human capital (and therefore general training) is more valuable to workers than job-specific human capital (and job-specific training), because general human capital is *transferable*. It is unfortunate, therefore, that mainstream models of vocational training for persons with SMI have evolved in a way that places far greater (almost exclusive) emphasis on job-specific skills.

Mainstream Models

Historically, vocational training for persons with mental illness has been provided by free-standing psychiatric rehabilitation centers.[27] Perhaps the best-known model is the clubhouse, which provides a place where persons with mental illness can work and socialize in a supportive environment. The original clubhouse, Fountain House, was founded in Manhattan in 1948 by a group of former patients of a nearby mental hospital.[28] As the name indicates, the program operates as a club. Participants are called "members," and are expected to operate the clubhouse themselves, with support from paid staff. The model clubhouse program offers vocational training in three modes: the work-ordered day (volunteer work at the clubhouse), transitional employment (jobs at local firms set aside for clubhouse members), and supported employment (mainstream jobs with appropriate employment supports, such as on-site job training).[29]

Beginning in the 1990s, other approaches to vocational training for persons with mental illness began to emerge. One model, the Diversified Placement Approach (DPA), was initiated at Thresholds, a psychiatric rehabilitation agency in Chicago. Founded in 1959, Thresholds originally followed the clubhouse model of vocational training, until studies in the 1970s raised questions about its effectiveness. Thresholds eventually phased out the transitional employment program in favor of diversified placement, which offers "members" an array of job options, ranging from employment in businesses that are run by the agency, to independent employment in competitive jobs. Upon entry into the DPA program, clients are assigned to unpaid jobs in the agency's day program, where their "work readiness" is assessed. Members receive prevocational job training, and are eventually placed in jobs consistent with their readiness. DPA is characterized by a gradual entry to employment, in a paid job that may or may not be competitive, often with placement in local businesses that have established partnerships with the agency.[30]

Today, the gold standard in vocational training for persons with mental illness is the Individual Placement and Support (IPS) model. Unlike DPA, the focus of IPS is competitive employment, defined as "regular community jobs, alongside nondisabled coworkers, that pay at least minimum wage."[31] The core philosophy of IPS is to achieve rapid job placement consistent with consumer preferences, accompanied by benefits counseling and personalized job supports.[32] Vocational services are integrated with other services provided to patients, so most IPS programs are operated by agencies within, or aligned with, the mental health system. The distinguishing feature of the program is its emphasis on immediate placement in a competitive job ("place, then train") as opposed to the pre-vocational training emphasized in the DPA ("train, then place").

Studies comparing IPS to other models of vocational training consistently show that IPS achieves superior employment outcomes.[33] A recent meta-analysis pooled results from four such studies. All the studies were randomized trials comparing outcomes of IPS to outcomes of another model of vocational training (DPA, group skills training, psychosocial rehabilitation, and training in a sheltered workshop), among persons with mental illness who expressed a desire to work. The results indicate that IPS produces better competitive employment outcomes—that is, higher rates of job placement and longer job tenure, than other models, regardless of patients' demographic or clinical characteristics.[34]

Nevertheless, research shows that the IPS model does not achieve high rates of stable competitive employment for its target population.[35] One study, for example, evaluated employment outcomes among participants in an IPS training program funded by the Massachusetts Department of Mental Health. The program maintained high fidelity with the core principles of IPS, and produced employment outcomes as good as, or better than, other IPS programs described in the literature. Still, the average participant earned less than $200 per month over the four-and-one-half-year observation period.[36] Two-thirds of job placements were in low-paid service or sales jobs. More than 80 percent of jobs involved working less than twenty hours per week, and less than 5 percent of jobs paid benefits. More than 90 percent of participants continued to receive federal disability benefits and, in fact, were counseled on how to maximize earnings while maintaining benefit eligibility.

Another study, involving clients of a mental health agency serving inner-city Baltimore, compared employment outcomes of patients randomly assigned to IPS or to a psychosocial rehabilitation program. Clients participating in IPS were more likely to obtain jobs, worked more hours, and had higher earnings over the study period than the comparison group. However, the jobs obtained by IPS patients were "short-term, entry-level, part-time jobs."[37] Job retention was also a problem. The average job duration among clients assigned to either program was less than four months.

The sad fact is that most participants in vocational training programs for persons with SMI do not attain regular earnings above the poverty level. A fundamental problem is that mainstream supported employment programs do not help participants acquire the general human capital that enhances their value in the labor market. The "place, then train" principle underlying IPS implies that the program is almost exclusively focused on job-specific training. To achieve rapid employment, participants must be placed in unskilled jobs that require no general training or certification. To be sure, some of the clientele participating in supported employment programs may have residual symptoms or functional limitations that make sustained competitive employment impossible. For those who are capable, however, the focus on job-specific as opposed to general training is counterproductive to long-term, stable employment outcomes.

Alternative Models

Some experimental programs are underway which augment supported employment with general skills training. One model combines a supported employment program with neurocognitive enhancement therapy (NET). NET is a remediation program specifically designed to address the cognitive and social limitations associated with schizophrenia. In one trial of a NET intervention, seventy-two patients with schizophrenia were randomized to receive either vocational services plus NET, or vocational services only.[38] The vocational services program was a hybrid transitional/supported employment model, consistent with the core philosophy of IPS. The NET intervention included computer-based cognitive training and twice-weekly participation in small-group meetings. At the meetings, one participant presented a talk on an issue encountered in their job, following which other participants offered feedback and constructive criticism. Participation in group meetings required good oral communication skills, as well as the ability to recognize and relate to another person's feelings, all of which are essential aspects of social capital.

The employment experiences of study participants were followed over a two-year period. Compared to the control group (vocational services only), persons in the experimental group achieved higher rates of employment, worked more hours, and were more likely to sustain employment in the second year of follow-up, after NET training had ceased.[39] One particularly important finding was that persons with the poorest social functioning at intake benefitted most from the NET intervention, reinforcing the idea that investments in training can compensate, somewhat, for the losses of social capital associated with schizophrenia.

Other pilot projects combining supported employment with supported education (SE/SE) are underway in Ra'anana, Israel, and Ontario, Canada.[40] The training program in Israel consists of three stages: Stage I (three months or less) provides general training in cognitive, computer, and social skills. Stage II (up to one year) is a supported education program that prepares participants for a skilled occupation, such as accounting, computer programming, electrical repair, graphics design, etc. Stage III is on-the-job training in the individual's chosen field, with employment supports if necessary.

The number of participants in the pilot project was small (ninety-six), and only preliminary data have been published to date, but early results were promising. Two years into the project, 40 percent of participants had completed Stage I; four-fifths of those were in Stage II training. Sixteen percent of participants had completed Stages I and II. Among the graduates of stage II: 40 percent were competitively employed in their vocation of choice, 47 percent were in transitional/supported employment or further training, and the remainder (two persons) were looking for work. [41]

The alternative models of vocational training for persons with serious mental illness represent a clear departure from mainstream supported employment services. The new models place a strong emphasis on acquisition of general human capital. An implicit assumption underlying the models is that many persons with SMI are capable of working independently in competitive jobs that demand higher-level cognitive and social skills. These types of jobs are seldom an outcome of mainstream vocational training for this population. The preliminary evidence on SE/SE and NET is promising, but it remains to be seen if the newer models can demonstrate significantly better outcomes than IPS when applied to larger and more diverse populations.

Postscript

The first episode of acute positive symptoms of schizophrenia usually occurs in the late teens or early twenties, exactly the time when a young person is making the investments in human capital that will determine their future earnings potential. One of the great tragedies of the disease is the loss of self-reliance and self-esteem associated with being denied a productive work life. Although medical science has made tremendous progress in restoring the health capital of persons afflicted with schizophrenia, this progress has not been translated into significant gains in employment.

I have argued that investments in human capital can significantly improve employment outcomes for persons with schizophrenia, and other serious mental illness. Completing a two- or four-year college degree increases their value in the labor market, acts as a signal of achievement to employers, and facilitates a good job match. Vocational training programs that match patients' aptitudes and interests with transferable skills that are valued in the labor market can have a similar impact. A premise of this book, to which I shall return in later chapters, is that employment outcomes for persons with SMI can improve if: (1) educational supports are in place to ensure that young adults can return to school, after onset of SMI, and complete their formal education; and (2) vocational training programs focus on general human capital, as opposed to job-specific skills that are valuable to only one employer.

Over the last twenty-five years we have learned that advances in pharmacology are not sufficient, by themselves, to restore persons with serious mental illness to productive and fulfilling lives. Investments in human capital are important. So is the mental health services system, but that system has not evolved in ways that encourage stable competitive employment and financial independence for persons with SMI. The next chapter tells that story.

Chapter Four

The Supply of Mental Health Services

WE CAN'T DO ANYTHING

A diagnosis of schizophrenia thrusts you abruptly into a strange new world—the U.S. mental health services system. With all its varied parts: medical professionals (psychiatrists, psychologists, psychiatric nurses, etc.), community care centers, state social service systems, general and specialty hospitals, case managers, vocational counselors, and nonprofit support organizations, one would expect a plethora of services available for patients and their families. In fact, the refrain I heard repeatedly was, "*I can't do anything for you.*" Overall, my experiences with the mental health system remind me of the nursery rhyme about the little girl who had a curl right in the middle of her forehead: "When it was good, it was very, very good; but when it was bad, it was horrid."

Spring 1999

The very best was the care David received at the University Hospital in Chapel Hill, after he was first diagnosed with schizophrenia. The hospital was a study site for clinical trials comparing two antipsychotic medications: halopenidol, a first-generation drug, and olanzapine, one of the new atypical antipsychotics. David agreed to participate in the study and was randomly assigned to one of the drugs. In theory, the study was double-blind: *Neither* patients nor providers were told which drug a particular patient was receiving. In reality, the side-effect profiles of the two drugs are distinctly different, so the nurses knew within days that David had been assigned to olanzapine.

At Chapel Hill, the study was directed by Diana Perkins, a psychiatrist with a national reputation for her research on the treatment of psychiatric illness. The study staff included a social worker, who served as case manager for patients and liaison to their families. In exchange for regular neurological and psychiatric testing, David received his medical care at no charge. After he was discharged from the hospital and living at home, the study provided a private car and driver to transport him back to Chapel Hill for weekly follow-up visits and testing.

The study sought to compare how the two drugs performed under nearly ideal conditions, so the protocols included education and support for family members, who were the patients' informal caregivers. The social worker was our contact to answer questions, resolve problems, or simply listen to our frustrations. She also conducted a monthly support group for families. Each spring, the research team held a one-day conference on treatment options for schizophrenia, to which patients' families were invited. In short, we were surrounded by a community of experts who were committed to helping us provide the best possible care for our sons, daughters, or spouses.

I met with Dr. Perkins several times in those first months, but I particularly remember one meeting between the three of us immediately before David was discharged. The point she emphasized repeatedly was, "Stay on your medication." We were lucky, she said, that David was so responsive to the drug, but if he stopped taking the meds his psychotic symptoms would recur. He could function normally for a while because the drug levels recede gradually from the brain, but eventually he would relapse. Dr. Perkins told David that, after each successive relapse, it would become more difficult to bring him back, and his recovery level of functioning would be lower. By the end of the meeting I was sufficiently frightened, David not so much. One year later and back at school, David stopped taking his meds; within a few months, he experienced a second psychotic break.

Summer 2000

Police found David wandering the streets of Durham in the middle of the night and immediately took him to the state psychiatric hospital. I was out of state when I received a phone call from my husband telling me what had happened. I immediately called the hospital, in a panic to know about David's condition. "Have you contacted his psychiatrist? Have you given him any medication?" I asked. The response was maddening; beyond confirming that my son was a patient, the nurses could not provide any information. "*I can't tell you anything.* Your son refused to give permission for us to release any information." I was furious: at the nurse who wouldn't talk to me; at my son who refused permission to release information to me; at a system designed to protect a patient's privacy before his well-being. "But can you just tell me if you know what medication he's supposed to be on?" I pressed the nurse. "*I can't say anything,*" she said, "but I can listen to whatever information you'd like to give me." I was beyond furious. I told the woman, "If you won't talk to me, I'm certainly not going to talk to you."

I took the redeye home and met with David the following morning. He said "Mom, they gave me a bunch of papers to sign, but I didn't think I was in any shape to sign anything." I had to agree. That day we transferred David back to the UNC Hospital. In less than a week he had responded to the meds, the positive symptoms of illness disappeared, and he returned to school. I thought he had learned his lesson, but I was wrong. Twice more David stopped taking the meds.

Spring 2005

By 2005, David was living in Charlotte and had landed a job as sales representative for a commercial security systems company. We had moved to Arizona three years earlier. David seemed stable on his meds, although a Christmas visit in December 2004 should have been an early warning sign. He was more than usually talkative—but the talk made sense. He was somewhat irritable—but irritations often arise when families gather for the holidays. Such are the rationalizations of parents who do not want to see what they are seeing. In January, back in Charlotte, David suffered another psychotic break.

This time the phone call came from David's uncle in Wake Forest. David's roommates had contacted him because they had not seen or heard from David for several days. They told my brother that David's employer was also looking for him. I made plans to fly to Charlotte; my older son offered to drive to North Carolina and accompany me. We agreed to meet at my brother's home. When I arrived, my sister-in-law was at the doorway with a stricken face. "Aaron's been in an accident—a head-on collision a few miles from here. His car is totaled." It was the worst day of my life.

Thankfully, no one was hurt in the crash. Aaron insisted on traveling to Charlotte with me as planned. When we arrived, we found David's life in a shambles. He had thrown most of his belongings in the trash; he had parked his car on the street, locked it, and thrown away the keys; he had "quit" his job without notifying his employer; he was staying in a hotel, running up credit card bills. But he was bright and cheerful. He thought he had met his future wife. He was not troubled about quitting his job, because he had a great idea for a career as the "date doctor." (Are you having trouble meeting women? I can cure your problem.) He had even printed and passed out advertising flyers. Life was great and he was sure glad to see us!

We took David to the psychiatrist who was treating him in Charlotte. He gave David his meds and watched him swallow them in his office. Then he gave David an ultimatum—stay with your mother for the following week and take your meds as prescribed, or I will put you in the hospital. So we spent the following week together: David angry and sullen as he came down from his mania; I frightened and uncomfortable in my role as Nurse Ratched. When we returned to the psychiatrist the following week, I was certain there would be another ultimatum—go to Arizona with your parents or go into the hospital.

But no. David had been on his meds for a full week. He was no longer psychotic. There was no need for him to be hospitalized. I pleaded with the doctor, "You know he won't take his meds after I leave. He'll just get sick all over again. He can't stay here." The psychiatrist agreed David should return home with us but said, *"There's nothing I can do."* And so I left my son there, with no job and no money, and returned to Arizona to await the inevitable disaster.

Back home, I called Adult Protective Services in Charlotte and told them about David's situation. They picked him up and took him to the Mental Health Center, where he was evaluated. The psychiatrist on call determined that David was not a danger to himself or others, and he was released. Adult Services called back to tell me, *"There's nothing we can do."* I called the local police, warned them that my son had schizophrenia, was not taking his meds, and I was worried about what might happen. Until someone gets hurt, they told me, *"There's nothing we can do."* A former girlfriend called to say she had convinced David to admit himself voluntarily to the psychiatric hospital, but the hospital had refused to admit him. "He's not sick enough," they said. *"There's nothing we can do."*

There was nothing left for me to do but wait, and take care of myself. My physician recommended two psychologists to help me deal with the stress. I called the first, told him that my son had schizophrenia and I needed help dealing with it. "Schizophrenia," he said, *"I don't handle anything as serious as that."* "I wish I didn't have to either," I replied.

And when it was bad, it was horrid.

PLANNERS VERSUS SEARCHERS

The history of mental health services in the United States is a chronicle of unfulfilled promises. Repeated efforts to reform the system have been accompanied by promises that serious mental illness can be cured and prevented. Each reform movement has failed. To the present day, we have been unable to construct a mental health system that consistently provides compassionate and effective treatment to persons with the most serious mental illnesses. The evidence is on the streets (an estimated 216,000 persons with SMI were homeless in 2010);[1] and in the jails (2.1 million persons with SMI were booked into jail in 2007).[2] Part of the problem is money, although billions of dollars are spent on state and federal programs that provide health care and other assistance to persons with mental illness. Part of the problem is an ill-placed faith in the plans of "experts" (bureaucrats, social scientists, public health officials) to solve a problem from which they are far removed.

We can draw parallels between failed attempts to solve the problem of mental illness, and failed attempts of Western nations to solve the problem of poverty in developing countries. Economist William Easterly makes the case that too much foreign aid is allocated to the grandiose ideas of "Planners," and not enough to grass roots efforts of "Searchers." According to Easterly, Searchers succeed where Planners fail because:

> Planners announce good intentions but don't motivate anyone to carry them out; Searchers find things that work and get some reward. Planners determine what to supply; Searchers find out what is in demand. Planners never hear whether the planned got what it needed; Searchers find out if the customer is satisfied.[3]

Free markets abound with Searchers hunting for solutions that generate profits. Consider John Freund, Frederic Moll, and Rob Younge, who developed the da Vinci robotic surgical system;[4] Paul Janssen, who discovered Haloperidol;[5] and Wilson Greatbatch, who invented the implantable cardiac pacemaker and manufactured fifty prototypes in a backyard workshop.[6] Profit-making in health care is sometimes branded as immoral, but to economists the search for profits is a sign of a healthy marketplace. Profits give Searchers the incentive to solve problems and deliver solutions to consumers; losses hold Searchers accountable when they fail.

Alas, we cannot leave either foreign aid or mental health care entirely up to free markets! In theory, government planners can intervene in these markets in ways that will enhance social welfare; but in practice, public officials often respond to economic incentives, social attitudes, and political ideologies in ways that undermine their lofty goals. As we trace the evolution of the U.S. mental health system from its colonial beginnings until today, we observe the collective effect of these forces. The system that has emerged has the *capability* to deliver high-quality, compassionate care, but usually *fails* to meet the needs of patients and their families in crisis. That situation will not change until we pay more attention to the Searchers who deal with the reality of mental illness every day.

The Case for Government Intervention

In many ways, mental health services are analogous to ordinary goods and services like food, shelter, clothing, automobiles, and computers. As with other goods, mental health services must be produced with scarce resources, and distributed to those who want or need the services. The production of mental health services, or other goods, involves an opportunity cost; in other words, resources used to produce mental health services are not available for other purposes, such as caring for cancer patients, educating children, or supporting the local symphony.

As with other goods, consumers are willing to pay for mental health services to obtain benefits (improved health and well-being); and providers are willing to supply those services to obtain profits. Unlike other goods, the connection between demand and supply of health services is disrupted in unusual, or even unique, ways. One source of disruption occurs because the benefits of mental health services are not limited to those who consume the services. When a person with SMI receives treatment, they are less likely to burden their family, annoy their neighbors, or disturb their community. Economists call these benefits to others *positive externalities*. Because of the positive externalities, free markets for mental health services will provide less than the optimal quantity of services. Patients are typically unaware of the way their consumption of services benefits others, and even if aware, they are generally unwilling to pay for benefits that accrue to others. Under these conditions, the government can use tax dollars to pay for services that yield *social benefits above and beyond private willingness to pay.*

A second source of disruption in the market for mental health services is the belief that (at least within reason) everyone should have access to necessary health care, regardless of their insurance status or ability to pay. In other words, we are unwilling to deprive persons with serious mental illness of the health services that they need, even if they do not have the resources to pay for those services themselves. Economists call these kinds of commodities *merit goods*. Free markets tend not to supply the socially optimal quantity of a merit good because, obviously, providing a good without payment is not profitable. Hence, there is a role for government (and charitable organizations) in the provision of mental health services and other merit goods.

Finally, the market for mental health services is disrupted in a way that is virtually unique, namely, that those who need diagnosis and treatment do not necessarily want it. Persons afflicted with SMI often do not believe they are sick.[7] (In the midst of his relapse in Charlotte, David thought his life was just great. He was paranoid and psychotic, but that was clear to everyone except David.) If a person with mental illness lacks insight into their condition and will not seek treatment on their own, and society deems treatment is necessary and appropriate, only government has the coercive power to make an individual consume services involuntarily.

Despite a wide range of opinion on the acceptability of involuntary treatment for persons with SMI, there are good arguments for a government role in the mental health system, solely on efficiency and equity grounds. Free markets will not produce the socially optimal quantity of services that takes account of positive externalities, and free markets will not provide services to persons who are unable to pay. It is, therefore, left to the government to resolve the fundamental questions of resource allocation that are normally decided in a free market:

- What part of society's resources should be allocated to the mental health system?
- What types of services should the system provide?
- How should those services be distributed among the mentally ill?

As the U.S. mental health system has evolved, decisions about services for the mentally ill have been transferred from local to state to federal governments, and finally to a system where decision making is shared. The way government Planners have responded to questions about resource allocation has been heavily influenced by economic circumstances as well as by prevailing social attitudes, legal mandates, advances in medical practice, and politics.

Evolution of the U.S. Mental Health System: 1750–1950

Prior to the late eighteenth century, mental illness was not a major social concern. The U.S. population was small and dispersed, and the number of persons with mental illness was correspondingly small. Virtually every American colony adopted some version of the English Poor Law system, in which local communities assumed fiscal and supervisory responsibility for persons who were unable to care for themselves, including the mentally ill. [8] Persons with mental illness were cared for in their communities, usually by family members. Those without families or private resources became the responsibility of local officials, who boarded them with other families or cared for them in public almshouses.

Local Financing

As the U.S. population expanded and consolidated, and the locus of work moved outside the home, mental illness became a greater problem for communities. Large urban areas like Philadelphia (1752) and New York (1792) established wards in local hospitals for collective care of the mentally ill. [9] In 1773, the first state hospital devoted exclusively to the mentally ill was built in Williamsburg, Virginia. [10] Conditions in these establishments reflected prevailing beliefs that associated mental illness with evil or amoral behavior. Patients were often shackled or isolated in locked cells; treatments were often punitive and abusive. [11]

Toward the end of the eighteenth century, a *moral treatment* movement arose in Europe, in opposition to the harsh institutional treatment of persons with mental illness. Moral treatment reformers believed the mentally ill were sick, not evil, and could be cured if treated with humanity and dignity.

Mental illness was thought to result from living in an adverse environment, hence the "cure" was to treat patients in more desirable surroundings. Reformers advocated for care in small asylums with a family atmosphere. Treatments involved occupational therapy and recreation as well as medical care; there was limited use of restraints, and absolutely no physical violence.[12]

After 1800, the moral treatment movement spread to private and public institutions in the United States. The first private asylums devoted to moral treatment were the Friends Asylum, founded by Pennsylvania Quakers (1817) and the Hartford Retreat (1824). By 1850, thirty private asylums practicing principles of moral treatment for persons with mental illness were operating in the United States.[13]

Simultaneously, Dorothea Dix and other outspoken advocates convinced state legislatures to allocate funds for the construction of public hospitals devoted to more humane care for persons with mental illness. Fifty years after the Williamsburg hospital was built, public mental hospitals were opened in Lexington, Kentucky (1822), Worcester, Massachusetts (1833), and Utica, New York (1833).[14] By the Civil War, almost every state had constructed at least one public mental hospital.[15]

State hospital administrators assumed *supervisory* responsibility for persons referred to them by local authorities, but local authorities retained *fiscal* responsibility for treatment and upkeep. The divided authority eventually created tensions between state and local officials. State officials, who were responsible for the design and administration of patient care, believed the care in local almshouses was "substandard, and fostered chronicity and dependency."[16] Local officials, who paid the bills but had no control over spending, had strong economic incentives to provide custodial care within the community whenever possible. Costs were lower in the local almshouse than in the state hospital, so local officials often exerted pressure on state hospital superintendents to release patients to community care, regardless of the patient's condition.[17]

Around the end of the nineteenth century, states began to pass laws that ended the system of divided responsibility. New York passed the first of these State Care Acts in 1890, transferring full responsibility for the indigent mentally ill to the state, and relieving local authorities of any fiscal obligation to the state hospital.[18] Other states followed New York's lead, and for the next fifty years U.S. mental health policy was centralized at the state level.

State Financing

The State Care Acts had unforeseen consequences for the state hospitals and their capacity to care for the mentally ill. Once the states assumed financial responsibility for patients, local governments had strong incentives to send *all* long-term cases of mental illness, including elderly persons suffering from dementia, to the state hospital. The influx of these patients, together with increasing demand for services from an expanding population, led to overcrowded conditions and a higher proportion of chronic cases in the hospitals.[19] Larger facilities had to be constructed. The moral treatment model, which involved high staff-to-patient ratios and high per-patient costs (and had never demonstrated success in treating long-term and severe cases of mental illness), was impractical in the large custodial institutions which the state hospitals had become. As the hospitals filled to capacity and beyond, living conditions and quality of care deteriorated.

In 1908, Clifford Beers, a former mental patient, published an autobiography recounting his tenure in a state mental hospital. The book describes the harsh treatment he endured, the cruelty exhibited by some of the attendants, and his eventual recovery and release. Motivated by a "consuming desire to effect reforms" of the institution he had observed so intimately,[20] Beers enlisted the help of Adolf Meyer, a prominent psychiatrist, and William James, a Harvard professor of psychology. While Beers's purpose was "to improve the dreadful conditions and eliminate the physical abuse that was so prevalent" in the hospitals, [21] Dr. Meyer had broader goals. Meyer sought to prevent mental illness and preserve mental health, by creating healthy and stable community environments.[22] Hence, when Beers organized a committee to promote his reform objectives,[23] Meyers named the movement[24] the National Committee for Mental Hygiene.

Mental hygiene reformers believed that: (1) mental illness was caused by exposure to unhealthy, unstable environments, and (2) SMI could be effectively treated using the latest scientific advances in psychiatry, including Freudian psychoanalysis. State hospitals were deemed unsuitable environments for treatment, so reformers favored the construction of psychopathic hospitals, connected with large research universities or general hospitals, where patients could be evaluated and receive high-quality care. The nation's first psychopathic hospitals were affiliated with Albany Medical College (1902), the University of Michigan (1906), Harvard University (1912), and Johns Hopkins University (1913).[25]

If, as mental hygiene reformers believed, the root cause of mental illness was exposure to unhealthy environments, it followed that mental illness could be prevented by creating stable and supportive communities that produced mentally healthy children and adults. Dr. Meyer acknowledged that "the art of building a community is an intricate one," but believed that psychiatrists and social workers could play a vital role in helping people achieve well-balanced lives within communities that he called "mental hygiene districts."[26] In 1922, the Committee for Mental Hygiene launched an initiative to develop child guidance clinics in eight major cities. Teams of psychiatric social workers, under the direction of psychiatrists, were assigned to clinics to treat emotionally disturbed children. By the mid-twentieth century, more than six hundred child guidance clinics were operating across the country. [27]

Despite their intimate knowledge of the reality of mental illness (Beers as an ex-mental patient and Meyer as director of the Phipps Psychiatric Clinic at Johns Hopkins University), founders of the mental hygiene movement acted more like Planners than Searchers. Planners are inclined to focus on large and complex problems, for which they develop comprehensive solutions:

> The fondness for the Big Goal and the Big Plan is strikingly widespread. . . .
> The setting of utopian goals means [that Planners] focus efforts on infeasible
> tasks, instead of the feasible tasks that will do some good. . . . Searchers look
> for any opportunity to relieve suffering . . . and don't get stuck on infeasible
> objectives. [28]

Mental hygiene reformers had utopian visions that: new cases of SMI could be prevented by creating mentally healthy communities; existing cases could be cured by applying the latest advances in psychiatry; and the state hospitals would become obsolete once the mental hygiene reforms were implemented. Predictably, the movement failed to achieve its grandiose ambitions. The community clinics, founded with an incomplete understanding of the complexity of the causes of mental illness, and faced with the herculean task of creating mentally healthy communities, could not possibly prevent new cases of severe mental disorders. The psychopathic hospitals, designed as acute care facilities, had insufficient resources to manage patients with SMI who did not respond to "the latest advances in psychiatry." These chronic cases were transferred to the state hospitals for custodial care. [29] Far from becoming obsolete, the census of patients in state and county mental hospitals peaked at 558,922 in 1955. [30]

Evolution of the U.S. Mental Health System: 1950–2015

Between 1930 and 1955, state mental hospitals experienced not only an influx of chronically ill patients, but also a period of financial retrenchment brought about by the Great Depression, and a significant loss of resources diverted to World War II. The combined effects of an expanding patient population and fewer resources, led to further deterioration of conditions in the hospitals. [31]

During the war, more than three thousand conscientious objectors, mostly Quakers and Mennonites, worked in state mental hospitals in lieu of military service. Appalled at the conditions they observed, many of these young men published their stories. [32] As the public became aware of the tragic conditions in the hospitals, the perception grew that the states had failed miserably in caring for the mentally ill. When President Kennedy appointed an interagency task force to make recommendations for a national mental health plan, in December 1961, the time seemed right for a new approach that would move primary responsibility for care of mental patients away from the again-discredited state hospitals.

The approach that emerged was largely the brainchild of Robert Felix, the aggressive and visionary director of the National Institute of Mental Health (NIMH) from 1949 to 1964.[33] In 1941, as part of his master's thesis for Johns Hopkins University, Felix set forth a plan to repair the mental health system by moving the primary locus of care for mental patients from state hospitals to a network of federally supported outpatient clinics.[34]

Felix's plan became the centerpiece of the recommendations the task force forwarded to the president. The idea of federally funded outpatient clinics as substitutes for state mental hospitals was consistent with Kennedy's vision of a larger federal role in mental health policy. At Kennedy's urging, Congress passed the Community Mental Health Centers (CMHC) Act of 1963, which allocated an initial $150 million to construct the centers.[35] Between 1967 and 1980, 789 CMHCs were constructed at a cost of $2.7 billion ($13.3 billion in 2010 dollars).[36] Deliberately bypassing state authorities, none of the federal funds appropriated under the CMHC Act were allocated to state hospitals.

First-Generation Antipsychotic Drugs

Meanwhile, in the decade preceding passage of the CMHC Act, a revolution had taken place in the state hospitals. The change began in 1954, when the Food and Drug Administration approved the first antipsychotic drug, chlorpromazine (trade name, Thorazine) for U.S. markets. By 1956, chlorpromazine and a second antipsychotic, resperine, were being administered to hospital patients in thirty-seven states.[37] The drugs addressed one of the most persistent problems facing hospital administrators, namely, maintaining order among patients whose behavior was so disruptive that they had been "expelled" from their homes and communities. The new drugs were life changing:

> Robert W was admitted to the state hospital in a highly excited homicidal state. . . . This patient was loud, screamed that he would kill someone, and communicated his sincerity in this purpose to attendants and other personnel. [Thorazine] administration was begun soon after admission. . . . In the course of two more weeks of hospitalization, this patient had quieted down, had lost his anxiety almost altogether, and was able to discuss his illness and his future plans in an objective and rational manner. Within two months, Robert W. was discharged.[38]

Entire hospital wards were transformed:

Prior to this study, these wards presented the usual picture . . . namely, 10 to 12 patients in seclusion, some also in camisoles or other types of restraint. In addition, heavy sedation and electroconvulsive therapy, as well as hydrotherapy and wet packs, were necessary and being utilized daily. Owing to the raucous, hyperactive, combative, sarcastic, resistive, uncooperative patients, the ward was in a continual turmoil. . . . Since the advent of therapy with resperine. . . . Patients have undergone a metamorphosis from raging, combative, unsociable persons to cooperative, cheerful, sociable, relatively quiet persons who are amenable to psychotherapy and other rehabilitative measures. [39]

The attitudes of attendants changed dramatically:

They are overjoyed at the prospect of being converted from custodians to rehabilitation therapists. . . . [They] would be alarmed if such therapy were discontinued because they know that their duties would again involve restraining combative patients. [40]

In the years following the introduction of the first-generation antipsychotics, hundreds of thousands of patients were discharged from state and county mental hospitals. From 1956 to 1965, the inpatient population in public mental hospitals decreased by almost 14 percent, reversing a trend of steady increases since passage of the State Care Acts. [41] It is safe to say that this sharp turnabout was the direct result of more effective treatment through antipsychotic drugs. However, the inpatient population decreased by *another 57 percent* in the following decade, primarily for reasons unrelated to the improved treatments for SMI. [42]

Federal Financing

The primary explanation for the exodus from state mental hospitals after 1965 was the introduction of a number of federal social welfare programs. These programs dramatically altered the locus of care for the mentally ill by providing incentives for states to shift fiscal responsibility for mental health services to the federal government. [43] Three federal programs were particularly influential:

- Medicaid, established as part of the Social Security Act Amendments of 1965 to provide health insurance for eligible persons with low income;
- Social Security Disability Insurance (SSDI), established in 1956 to provide income for working-age persons who are unable to support themselves because of a disabling health condition;
- Supplemental Security Income (SSI), established in 1972 to provide subsidies for elderly or disabled persons who have limited income and resources.

Medicaid is funded jointly by state and federal governments. Participation is voluntary (all states have opted to participate), but states must operate their programs within federal guidelines in order to receive federal matching funds. One of those guidelines, known as the IMD exclusion rule, is that Medicaid funds may not be used to pay for care in an Institution for Mental Disease.[44] Funds may be used, however, to pay for long-term nursing home care for elderly patients with dementia. The economic incentives are unambiguous: A state could either pay all the costs of care for elderly dementia patients in the state hospital, or use federal dollars to subsidize 50 to 75 percent of costs in a nursing home. In 1963 (two years before Medicaid), nursing homes cared for 188,000 persons age sixty-five or older with mental disorders. By 1969 (four years after) that number had doubled.[45]

SSDI and SSI are financed entirely by the federal government. Like Medicaid, SSI is unavailable to residents of state mental hospitals. SSI funds may be used, however, to subsidize living expenses of former mental patients who are placed in group homes or boarding facilities. Thus, states could either pay the full costs for patients in the state hospital, or discharge patients to another facility and allow the federal government to subsidize living expenses. In New York, for example, the mental health system could save more than $9,000 per patient transferred out of the state hospital.[46] States responded to the new economic incentives, and the pace of discharge from mental hospitals accelerated after SSI was established.[47]

In addition to deliberate revision of the economic incentives surrounding inpatient psychiatric care, social attitudes changed during the 1960s and 1970s to challenge the concept of involuntary hospitalization. During the 1970s, a series of legislative changes and court decisions established that a person with mental illness has the right to: (1) treatment in the *least restrictive* setting; (2) *due process of law* before being confined to a hospital; (3) *adequate treatment*, if confined; and (4) to *refuse treatment* if they choose. The courts also established that a person with mental illness cannot be committed to a mental hospital involuntarily, unless the person poses "a danger to themselves or others."[48] Each of these changes to the legal structure rendered involuntary commitment more costly and more difficult. It is therefore not surprising that *admission rates* to state hospitals, which had risen steadily since 1955, began a downward trend in 1970.[49]

Community Mental Health Centers

As enrollments in state hospitals declined, community mental health centers were (theoretically) poised to assume primary responsibility for care of the mentally ill. According to the vision of Robert Felix and his followers, Community Mental Health Centers (CMHCs) would both *treat* acute cases of mental illness, without long-term hospital stays, and *prevent* future cases of serious mental illness, through early detection and treatment of less serious cases. If the vision of the CMHC reformers sounds remarkably similar to the vision of the mental hygiene reformers—it was. And if the plan to use community clinics as the mechanism for treatment and prevention of mental illness sounds similar to the plan that failed fifty years earlier—it was. Focused on the Big Goal, Planners of the CMHC movement were not daunted by the failures of others:

> One of the key predictions about Planners . . . is that they keep pouring resources into a fixed objective, despite many previous failures at reaching that objective, despite a track record that suggests the objective is infeasible or the plan unworkable. . . . Planners even escalate the scope of intervention when the previous intervention fails. [50]

Needless to say, the CMHCs failed to achieve the Big Goal of preventing SMI. The centers also failed to achieve the attainable goal of successful treatment for persons with SMI within the community. Part of the problem was that Planners banked their hopes and expectations on *unsupported assumptions*, namely, that: (1) discharged mental patients had homes in the community, (2) a sympathetic family would assume responsibility for their care, (3) the organization of the household would not impede rehabilitation, and (4) the patient's presence would not cause undue hardships for other family members. [51] In 1960, however, more than 60 percent of the patients in mental hospitals were either unmarried, widowed, divorced, or separated. Many discharged patients simply had no home to which to return. Others, who did have a home, had to rely on a family support system that was often ill-prepared to deal with serious mental illness.

Another part of the problem was *bypassing the state authorities* who had responsibility for mental health policy. The legislation establishing CMHCs deliberately eschewed a role for state mental hospitals in its reforms. Robert Felix, and others who were instrumental in the community mental health movement, viewed the state mental hospital as an "inherently repressive institution, on par with the prison." [52] Hence, CMHCs were structured as local/federal partnerships, wholly disconnected from state hospitals and state regulatory authorities, with no formal paths of communication between hospital superintendents and center directors. [53] How could the mental health system possibly provide a continuum of care, when essential components of the system were controlled by different levels of government, operating independently?

A final part of the problem was the *misdirected mission* of the CMHCs. Rather than focusing on treatment of persons with SMI in the community, framers of the 1963 act viewed "prevention of mental illness and promotion of positive mental health" as the primary mission of the CMHCs. [54] In 1968,

Congress expanded the mission to embrace an entirely new set of populations that included substance abusers, at-risk children, and the elderly. Directors of the CMHCs, faced with limited operating budgets and an expanding mission, chose to allocate their resources to treating mild adjustment and behavioral disorders, rather than to providing costly after-care for the severely mentally ill.[55]

Accordingly, most centers treated very few patients with SMI. Between 1968 and 1978, less than 7 percent of patients seen by the CMHCs were discharged mental patients receiving follow-up care. A 1979 report on service utilization in the CMHCs found that only 10 percent of clinic patients were diagnosed with schizophrenia.[56] By 1980, even the strongest advocates of the reforms were forced to admit that the program had not provided coordinated follow-up care for former mental patients. In 1984, Robert Felix publicly expressed doubts about his legacy:

> Many of those patients who left the state hospitals never should have done so. We psychiatrists saw too much of the old snake pit, saw too many people who shouldn't have been there and we overreacted. The result is not what we intended, and perhaps we didn't ask the questions that should have been asked when developing a new concept.[57]

One "unasked question" is simply, where would the patients go? As it turned out, they went to a diverse collection of destinations. A substantial percentage of patients, like Clifford Beers, recovered and were discharged even before the discovery of effective drug treatments.[58] Others found their way to "planned" outcomes, making a successful transition to living in the community or in other institutional settings, supported in part by Medicaid, SSDI, or SSI. Far too many ex-patients ended up in jail or back in a mental hospital after being charged with criminal behavior. (Notably, the rate of involuntary criminal commitments to mental hospitals increased by 81 percent between 1972 and 1980.[59]) Another sizable cohort ended up on the streets. As the problem of the homeless mentally ill became increasingly visible, the failure of the CMHCs to treat or prevent SMI became increasingly obvious.

In 1976, President Carter established a commission on mental health to assess the CMHC program and make recommendations regarding the future of federal mental health policy. Despite the obvious failures of the CMHCs, the commission recommended *continued funding* for the program, and appropriation of *additional* funds for "the prevention of mental illness and the promotion of positive mental health"![60] Here is a spectacular example of Planners responding to failure by proposing more of the same!

Toward the Present-Day Mental Health System

The recommendations of the Carter Commission became the substance of the Mental Health Systems Act, signed into law in October 1980 by President Carter. But the act became moot after Ronald Reagan won the presidential election in November. Reagan favored policies of lower federal taxes and limited federal involvement in social welfare programs. The 1981 Omnibus Budget Reconciliation Act ended federal funding for the CMHC program, and instead appropriated smaller block grants to the states for mental health services.[61] The era of nominal federal "responsibility" for the mentally ill had ended.

The next two decades were a period of rising health care costs and increasing dissatisfaction with the performance of the mental health system. The costs of mental health services did not rise as rapidly as other health care costs in the 1980s and 1990s, but by 1997, the United States spent "almost $71 billion on treating mental illnesses."[62] In terms of inputs, the mental health service system was fragmented and disorganized, and more than half of all persons with SMI were not receiving treatment.[63] In terms of outputs, a disproportionate share of persons with mental illness were either homeless, in prison, or unemployed.

In February 2001, President Bush announced a New Freedom Initiative to improve the lives of persons with disabilities. As part of the initiative, he created a New Freedom Commission on Mental Health "to study the problems and gaps in the mental health system and make concrete recommendations for immediate improvements."[64] The commission released its final report in July 2003. In a cover letter to President Bush, Michael Hogan, president of the commission, wrote that the nation's mental health services were:

> [F]ragmented, disconnected and often inadequate, frustrating the opportunity for recovery. Today's mental health care system is a patchwork relic—the result of disjointed reforms and policies. Instead of ready access to quality care, the system presents barriers that all too often add to the burden of mental illnesses for individuals, their families, and our communities.[65]

The commission's report sets out six broad goals for "fundamentally transforming how mental health care is delivered in America." Accompanying the goals are a set of nineteen recommendations designed to "aid in transforming the mental health system."[66] One has only to peruse the recommendations to know that the commission members were Planners, not Searchers.

Goal 4 states that "Early mental health screening, assessment, and referral to services are common practice." To attain this goal the commission recommends that the government "Promote the health of young children," and "Improve and expand school mental health services."[67] Laudable ideas to be sure, but how are they to be achieved? (*Planners identify a Big Goal, but typically have no concrete ideas how to attain the goal.*)

Where the commission's recommendations are more concrete, the proposed solutions are often costly, naïve, or untested. Goal 2 states that "Mental health care is consumer- and family-driven." One recommendation under this goal is to, "Develop an individualized plan of care for every adult with a serious mental illness and [every] child with a serious emotional disturbance."[68] How can this plan possibly be accomplished when over half of adults with SMI are not receiving treatment? (*Because Planners are disconnected from the problems they are attempting to solve, the ideas that Planners present are often impossible to implement.*)

The report recommends, also under Goal 2, that each state "Create a comprehensive State Mental Health Plan."[69] The plans are intended to hold state authorities accountable for mental health services, and to overcome the problems of fragmentation and lack of coordination in the mental health system. (*One favorite tactic of planners is to recommend more planning.*)

Once it was clear that the CMHCs had failed to achieve the Big Goal, Planners shifted responsibility for results elsewhere, unwilling to hold the federal government accountable for its part in creating the fragmented, uncoordinated system the commission bemoans. Given the kind of roadmap the commission set forth, it is not surprising that their recommendations have had little impact. The fragmented, disconnected, inadequate, and disjointed system described in the report, is what I encountered in Charlotte in 2005, and what we have today.

The Mindset of a Searcher

In 1986, Paul Janssen gave an interview in which he described the steps leading to his discovery of Haloperidol. The following are excerpts from the interview, revealing the mindset and motivations of a Searcher:

Interviewer: What led to the discovery of haloperidol?

Janssen: By varying the structure of some anesthetic drugs, we stumbled upon compounds that antagonized the effects of amphetamines on rat behavior. Since amphetamine poisoning in man produces symptoms which are also observed in paranoid schizophrenics, we did not overlook the idea of trying amphetamine antagonists in psychiatric patients. The lesson is to pay attention to unexpected findings, and to . . . link them to known facts.[70]

Interviewer: What are the responsibilities of an explorer [i.e., Searcher]?

Janssen: The specific responsibility of an explorer is to keep his eyes open and his mind prepared. . . . Somebody once told me that *a human mind is like a parachute. It works better when it's open!*[71]

Interviewer: Who should be involved, financially, in developing new drugs?

Janssen: I don't really care who [is] involved as long as they find a solution. . . . But, there must be a willingness to take needed, calculated risks. . . . Bureaucrats in general hate to take a risk. There is nothing to gain and everything to lose. It's deplorable but it seems to be a fact. . . . Then what is also needed, of course, is the motivation to reach a certain goal. Now for us as a company . . . to succeed in research is a matter of life and death. If we don't succeed we will disappear. It's very simple. The motivation to find something, to do something useful, is very, very, very, great.[72]

Interviewer: What factors are most likely to facilitate the exploratory process for a researcher [i.e., Searcher]?

Janssen: I would say the most important factor there is, is freedom. Freedom of thinking. Freedom of action. Freedom, in a general sense of the word, being the opposite of slavery and bureaucracy. . . . [But] what is most important, I think, is to learn from the past, and try to do better in the future.[73]

As Janssen's comments make clear, Searchers differ from Planners in all phases of the problem-solving process:[74]

- *Approach*—Planners come to a problem with ideology in place and corresponding solutions on the shelf. Searchers come without a preconceived idea of what the solution will be. Searchers find solutions first, ideology later.
- *Implementation*—Planners implement policy at the macro level to achieve the Big Goal. They attempt global, top-down solutions with little understanding of the complexities at the bottom. Searchers look for small opportunities to do something useful, and do not get stuck on unrealistic objectives.
- *Follow-up*—In the aftermath of a policy change, Planners have little interest in objective evaluations of the results. Far-removed from the people who are implementing their ideas, or the people who are supposed to benefit, Planners have little accountability for their actions, and no incentive to obtain feedback from those on the front lines. When Searchers implement a solution, they are accountable for results. Searchers have

incentive to evaluate outcomes because success or failure matters *to them*. In Janssen's words, success "is a matter of life or death."[75]

The NIMH emphasis on prevention activities in the community mental health centers provides a good example of disconnect between Planners at the top and those responsible for implementing plans at the bottom. Administrators of the CMHCs were cognizant of the futility of their efforts to prevent SMI, even as the directors at NIMH continued to press prevention as their primary mission. One clinic administrator declared, "When we in psychiatry wave our preventive banners we must look ridiculous to even the gods on Mount Olympus who once held the keys to all the mysteries of the universe."[76]

In sharp contrast to the glorious visions of Planners, Charles Lindblom calls policy implementation (i.e., problem solving) "the science of muddling through."[77] When I sought Dr. Perkins's advice as David was about to be discharged from his first hospitalization, she told me "trust your instincts." There was no other advice she could give; we had to "muddle through."

Postscript

In a popular educational toy for children, the "problem" is to fit geometric blocks of different shapes into a box with cutouts of corresponding shapes. Solving the puzzle is a metaphor for the cure and prevention of schizophrenia, where the interior of the box represents "mental health" and the blocks represent "persons with mental illness."

The one-year-old (Planner) has a preconceived idea of what *should* work. He finds a cutout and starts pushing blocks into it—one block fits but the rest will not. In frustration, he tries *more of the same*, and continually fails. The two-year-old (Searcher) discovers a solution that *does* work. If a block doesn't fit in one cutout he tries another place, until all the blocks are neatly in the box. The five-year-old (Wise Man) achieves the Big Goal. Just by looking, he knows which block fits which cutout, and he quickly puts the blocks away.

When it comes to treating SMI, we are not Wise Men. Scientists are beginning to unravel the complex causes of schizophrenia, but we do not yet know enough to prevent the disease. Pharmacologists have discovered drug therapies that control the symptoms of illness for many patients, but we do not yet have a cure. In our knowledge of schizophrenia we are at about the two-year-old stage: We've stumbled upon some treatments that work, we're not sure why, and what works for one case won't necessarily work for another. We have to keep trying until we get it right. Until scientists achieve the Big Goal (effective prevention and a cure for schizophrenia), policy makers must do what they can to meet the needs of persons with SMI and the families who are their primary caregivers.

The fact that the CMHCs failed to provide adequate care does not mean that a community care model cannot succeed. Even before the introduction of first-generation antipsychotics, Karl Menninger successfully implemented a model of community care in Kansas, with Topeka State Hospital as the center of an entire mental health system. Large numbers of inpatients, who had improved as much as possible with available treatments, were discharged to their communities with follow-up from hospital staff. Staff members coordinated with local agencies to ensure a successful transition. The state hospital was available if a crisis occurred.[78] Unfortunately, the lessons of Topeka were ignored by Planners of the CMHC movement.

As Menninger demonstrated, a community care model can succeed if it is driven by Searchers who are held accountable for outcomes, and staffed by people who are empowered and motivated to solve the problems that walk through their doors every day. Patients and families in crisis deserve a mental health system that says, "What do you need?" instead of, *"We can't do anything for you."*

There are thousands of Searchers working in today's mental health system. Diana Perkins and her team at UNC Hospital are some of them. But it was Planners who created the dysfunctional mental health system I encountered in Charlotte, where no one had the freedom, or the responsibility, or the motivation, to act. In the end, it took the authority of a judge, and the persistence of a lawyer, to find a solution that worked.

Chapter Five

Default Caregivers

WHAT AM I DOING HERE?

As they were growing up, my two boys had an uncanny ability to alternate periods of problem behavior so as not to overtax their mother's resilience. When Aaron was in fifth grade, David was a well-adjusted kindergartener. Aaron disliked schoolwork and did as little of it as possible. On parents' night, his teacher asked us to sit at our child's desk. All the desks were arranged in neat little groups around the room except one; my desk was next to the teacher's. "I was always a good little girl in school," I thought, "*What am I doing here?*" Fifteen years later, Aaron had a master's degree in computer science from Boston University and a good job working for the Center for Naval Analyses in Virginia. David was having a psychotic breakdown in Charlotte.

Spring 2005

The crisis came on a Saturday morning in April, when David had a fight with his housemate. The young man filed charges for assault, and a warrant was issued for David's arrest. We tried to contact him by cell phone throughout that day and evening, and finally reached him Sunday morning. We advised him to turn himself in to the police, which he did, whereupon he was arrested and incarcerated in the county jail. Through contacts in North Carolina, we found a lawyer who specialized in criminal cases involving persons with disabilities. The lawyer was somewhat reassuring: David had no prior criminal record; his housemate was not seriously injured; David would likely be released on his own recognizance the following day.

My experience with the justice system went no further than jury duty and settling a few traffic tickets. To me, the fact that my son was in jail, and charged with assault, was appalling. To David's lawyer, it was a minor felony. Still, at the arraignment the next day the judge refused to release David without bond, because of his diagnosis of schizophrenia. David, who had been denied admission to the psychiatric hospital because he was "not sick enough," was apparently "too sick" to be released from jail. Once again, we flew to Charlotte.

My first priority was to see my son. We talked by intercom, seated on opposite sides of a glass barricade, David dressed in an orange prison jumpsuit. He looked so pathetic that my eyes filled with tears. He was clearly relieved to see us and agreed to admit himself to the hospital immediately after he was released from jail. He had one pressing concern. "Mom, I parked my car in front of the jail when I turned myself in. Is it still there?" On that awful day, we had one piece of good luck: His car was still there.

Our next task was to post bond. How does one go about bailing someone out of jail? Although the bond office is conveniently located in the same building as the jail, that is the *only* convenient part. Contrary to the advertising slogan ("For everything else there's . . ."), you cannot post bail with MasterCard. We secured a certified check and took our place in line to pay. The scene was surrealistic. The bond office was open; everyone stood obediently in line; but there was no one at the counter. I thought, *"What am I doing here?"*

Eventually, I asked the people ahead of us what was wrong. They obviously had some experience with the system, because they merely sighed and said, "Nothing. It's always like this." I decided it was not prudent to make a fuss about poor service in such close proximity to the jail, so we waited, and waited. Finally, the bond was posted and David was released. He gave me a huge hug.

We proceeded to the hospital, where I was certain David would be admitted now that he was "a danger to himself or others." But no. David had been taking his medications while he was in jail. He was lucid, he was rational, and the physician on call refused to admit him. Instead, she asked me what I wanted to do:

"I want David to come home with us, on certain conditions."

"What conditions?"

"He has to see a psychiatrist regularly and take his medications as prescribed. No drinking. No recreational drugs."

"What about smoking?"

"It's OK—outside the house. I can't take everything away from him."

"That all sounds quite reasonable. What do you say, David?"

David agreed. Our Charlotte nightmare had almost ended—except that David had been living there for nearly three years and we had only two days to pack and store his belongings before flying home. We cleaned and scrubbed the house, assured his roommates we would continue to pay David's share of the rent, loaded a rental truck with his furniture, and left everything with my brother in Wake Forest.

Before departing from Charlotte, we met with David's lawyer. He assured us that David could leave the state, so long as he returned to Charlotte when his case went to court. There was just one glitch in this plan. North Carolina has a jail diversion program designed to redirect persons with SMI out of the criminal justice system and into treatment in the community mental health system. The lawyer wanted David in the program, because once completed, the felony charges against him would be dropped and his criminal record expunged. The glitch was that David would not be living in North Carolina. So the lawyer charged us with finding a similar program in Arizona which the court might be persuaded to allow as a substitute.

With this charge, and our son, we left Charlotte behind. On the flight home to Phoenix, I was physically and emotionally exhausted. I wondered how I could summon the energy to help David put his life back together— one more time.

Summer 2005

Here is the situation we faced when we arrived home: David had nowhere to live, except with his parents. He owned a car, on which he owed monthly payments, and little else. The car was in North Carolina, along with all his other belongings. David had not worked in four months. He had exhausted his savings and charged his credit card to the limits. He was facing assault charges in North Carolina. He had schizophrenia and needed medication and psychiatric care. *If only the system had helped us get him home in February, before the legal problems and the huge debts! Now, where did we begin?*

The first priority was medical care. With the help of friends, I found a wonderful psychiatrist in Phoenix who agreed to treat David until we could enroll him in the state behavioral health system. The state would provide medications and mental health services at no charge. The covered services included physician visits, case management, vocational counseling, even a crisis hotline. Had we found another model system of mental health care such as we had known in Chapel Hill? Not exactly.

The public behavioral health system in Arizona did not have sufficient resources, nor was it structured, to provide the kind of comprehensive, supportive care we received when David was first diagnosed. Staff turnover in the behavioral health offices was so common that I never had regular contact with David's physicians, and even David could not predict who he would see on any given visit. I discovered that the "crisis team," which responded to emergency situations involving a patient with mental illness, could not be activated by family members. The team only responded to calls from a patient, or with a patient's consent. The vocational services were useless. On the plus side, every physician and case manager I encountered while David was a patient in the system was a caring and competent professional, and the system provided psychiatric services and medications for David at no out-of-pocket cost to us.

The second issue was David's finances. We decided that he should declare bankruptcy to eliminate his credit card debt. We salvaged his one valuable possession, his car, by transferring the title to his father's name and assuming the payments. Perhaps I should feel guilty about cheating the system this way, but I don't. I feel the system cheated David, by not allowing anyone to help him until he was penniless and in jail.

The legal issues were some of the most difficult to resolve. I searched in vain for a jail diversion program in Arizona that was comparable to the one in North Carolina. I contacted Arizona Department of Health Services, Division of Behavioral Health Services, Adult Probation Offices, even the Superior Court, with no success. In July, with David's court date approaching, I told his lawyer there was no such program in Arizona, please just settle the case. The lawyer resisted. He requested an extension from the court and told me to keep looking.

Finally, I found the website for the Treatment Assessment Screening Center (TASC). TASC is a private, nonprofit corporation that works collaboratively with the Arizona Department of Corrections to facilitate drug testing and behavioral health programs in the state. In Maricopa County, TASC manages an adult deferred prosecution program for individuals facing felony drug charges, and a misdemeanor deferred prosecution program for first-time offenders whose offense does not involve physical injury to another person. Neither program exactly fit David's situation, but with another court date looming, I was desperate. I called the director of TASC and found—a Searcher. He volunteered to contact David's lawyer and to personally monitor a diversion plan for David. He was confident they could work out a plan the court would accept. He was right.

Fall 2005

David's diversion plan consisted of community service (janitorial work at the local YMCA), regular visits to his psychiatrist, and adherence to his medication. In addition, he had to submit to regular drug and alcohol testing at TASC. Whenever TASC announced a "red" day, David had twelve hours to report for testing. The diversion plan resolved David's legal problems and gave me a few months respite from policing his medications.

We had addressed David's immediate problems, but we were years away from putting his life back together. He was twenty-eight years old, with no job, no money, and no friends. He was living at home, dependent on his parents for everything from food to entertainment. *What was he doing here?*

Most days he amused himself by playing poker online, but as the months wore on, he became more and more depressed.

FAMILY CAREGIVERS

In the wake of massive discharges from state mental hospitals, family members became the default caregivers for persons with serious mental illness. Planners of the community care movement assumed the vast majority of ex-mental patients would return home to live with a sympathetic and supportive family.[1] Quite the contrary, many patients had no home to which to return and nowhere to go. Today, approximately 40 percent of persons with schizophrenia are either homeless (4.5 percent), institutionalized (6 percent in jail; 12 percent in hospitals or nursing homes), or living in other supervised settings (18 percent).[2]

Even so, families shoulder a tremendous share of the caretaking responsibilities for persons with SMI. Approximately 55 percent of persons with schizophrenia either live with their families, or have daily contact with family members.[3] Yet there are few institutional structures in place to educate family caregivers. There is no one to facilitate communication between family members and formal caregivers; no one to provide support in dealing with the challenges of caregiving; and no one to call in a crisis, except the police. In fact, the legal system has erected barriers that often prevent family caregivers from having any input into medical decisions that affect their relatives. Sometimes, as in the case of William Bruce, the results are tragic.

At age twenty-one, William Bruce had a first psychotic episode, but he refused to seek medical care. Two years later, after threatening two men with an assault rifle, William was committed to a psychiatric facility. He was successfully treated with antipsychotic drugs and released, whereupon he stopped taking his medications.

Within one year, William physically attacked both parents. He was committed to an extended care psychiatric facility, but he refused all medical treatment. His psychiatrist described his condition as "hostile, paranoid, and dangerous to others." Nevertheless, patient advocates employed by Disability Rights Maine began working with William to obtain his release. His psychiatrist opposed their efforts, stating that William's paranoid psychosis was unlikely to improve without treatment.

The case became so contentious that a new psychiatrist was assigned. He requested permission to speak with William's parents, but William and his advocates refused. The advocates claimed William's parents were "a negative influence in his life." Given the advocates' position that William was not dangerous, the psychiatrist had no authority to keep him hospitalized beyond his court-ordered confinement. Against his doctors' recommendations,

William was released on April 20, 2006. He returned home to live with his parents. On June 20 of the same year, William killed his mother with an axe to the skull.[4]

Burden of Care

The term *burden of care* (or *family burden*) is used to describe the myriad ways caring for a relative with mental illness affects a family. Fortunately, the story of William Bruce is a rare and extreme example of the price a family pays. It is much more common for the story to end in jail, suicide, or alienation of family members.

Caregiving imposes a combination of physical work, emotional stress, social alienation, and economic pressures, all of which can have a tremendous impact on family members.[5] In the family support group we joined when David first became sick, I was struck by the high proportion of single parents, mostly mothers, in attendance. Many of these families had broken apart under the burden of caring for a son or daughter with SMI.

When caregivers are asked to describe the negative impact of schizophrenia on their family, they talk about *economic* pressures, their own *health* problems, difficulties participating in *social* activities and maintaining social relationships.[6] They also identify *emotions* ranging from depression, embarrassment, and hopelessness to a profound sense of loss. Thus, it is not only the magnitude of the crisis of mental illness that affects family members so deeply, but the sheer breadth of the impact on almost every aspect of their lives.

Economic Burden

The economic burden of caring for a relative with schizophrenia can be a significant drain on family resources. Direct costs borne by family members may include: out-of-pocket expenditures for the *patient's medical care* (psychiatric hospitalizations, outpatient visits, medications, rehabilitation services, etc.); costs associated with the *criminal justice system* (lawyers' fees, damages, fines, etc.); and *travel costs* (if the patient is in a hospital, jail, or living at a distance from their family). Indirect costs include *losses of income* associated with family members' lost work time; and out-of-pocket expenditures for *medical care for family members* whose health is compromised by caregiving responsibilities.

In many cases, the family also provides support for living expenses for the patient (housing, board, clothing, social activities, insurance payments, unpaid bills, etc.). Strictly speaking, these costs represent a transfer of income within the family unit, rather than a net loss of resources. Nonetheless, the costs are a greater burden at the margin to the family than to the patient, if they were well.

There are no current and comprehensive estimates, specific to the United States, of the economic burden on families caring for a relative with schizophrenia. Some studies attempt to parse out the portion of the overall burden of the disease that is borne by family members, but these estimates do not provide micro-measures of the resources expended by individual families. [7] One of the first studies to provide such micro-estimates was conducted by Deborah Franks in the late 1980s. Franks collected data on illness-related expenditures from a sample of 108 Massachusetts families caring for a relative with SMI. Thirty percent of families were caring for their relative at home. Among these families, average annual expenditures associated with the relative's mental illness were $4,458, or 10 percent of median family income in Massachusetts in 1987. [8]

Around the time of the survey, one Massachusetts region was under a consent decree to escalate deinstitutionalization of mental patients and expand community residential facilities for patients who were released. Because of the increased public funding in this region, a smaller proportion of persons with SMI were living with their families, and average family expenditures on SMI were lower than in other regions of the state. Franks exploited this natural experiment to estimate the degree to which family expenditures on mental illness substitute for expenditures by the state. The results showed that for every $1 decrease in state spending, family spending increased by $4. [9] Thus, what is viewed as an economic burden by the family is a major contribution of private resources to the care of the mentally ill. Moreover, shifting the costs onto families increases the total costs of care.

A more recent study of the economic burden of care reports estimates of illness-related expenditures for 150 Belgian families who were primary caregivers for a patient with schizophrenia. The authors conducted face-to-face interviews with family members, asking about various aspects of caregiver burden, including illness-related expenditures. On average, families reported spending 2,623€ (or about US $4,070 in 2013) on patients in the year preceding the interview. Median annual income of respondents was between 14,868€ and 20,820€, so the economic burden represented a significant (13 percent to 18 percent) share of an average family's resources. [10]

Studies such as these suggest that families bear a considerable economic burden when a relative is diagnosed with SMI. We do not have comprehensive, current estimates of the costs to family caregivers in the United States, but the available evidence suggests total annual costs may be 10 to 20 percent of median family income, a nonnegligible sum.

Social Burden

The social burden of care reflects the impact of caregiving on interpersonal relationships and social activities, both within and beyond the immediate family. Within the family, the social impact ranges from small frustrations, such as having difficulty getting away for family outings, to major upheavals, such as alienation of family members, separation, or divorce. Outside the family, the social burden is perceived through experiences of stigma, losses of friendships, and feelings of isolation.

The Belgian survey of families caring for patients with schizophrenia included a number of questions to assess the social burden of care. In response to these questions:

- 46 percent of participants said that their household atmosphere was tense
- 31 percent said that contact with certain friends had diminished or broken off entirely
- 19 percent said that a family member had left home or threatened to leave home [11]

A recent study examined how the social burden of caring for a family member with mental illness changes with duration of illness. [12] The study compared family functioning among 150 Greek families who were either caring for a relative with *first-episode psychosis*, or caring for a relative with *chronic psychotic illness*, or part of a control group that reported no history of psychiatric illness in the family. Family functioning was assessed on measures of cohesion (emotional bonding), flexibility (with respect to leadership and family roles), and communications.

The results showed that *families dealing with chronic illness had significantly higher levels of dysfunction* than families caring for a relative with first-episode psychosis. In other words, family cohesion and flexibility appeared to deteriorate with chronicity. [13] As the woman in my support group (chapter 2) said, "You're new to this dear, wait until you've been dealing with it for years."

In 2002, two nursing professors conducted in-depth interviews with twenty-six families, who were primary caregivers for a relative with schizophrenia, to assess how the family was functioning. The themes that emerged provide poignant evidence of the social upheaval SMI can create within a family:

> It is easier for [other] family members to ignore the problem and offer advice—kick our son out of the house if he wouldn't get help. A parent can't do this to a child. [Our other children] wouldn't visit because of our son's behavior. So we lost all our children and grandchildren. [14]

The social isolation extends beyond the boundaries of the family:

> People are unfriendly. I have not felt that people disliked me, but I do know that mental illness has a strange effect on those not familiar with the illness. [15]

Health Burden

In light of the economic and social stressors associated with caring for a relative with schizophrenia, it is not surprising that caregiving often has a negative impact on the health of family members. Research shows that the health-related burden of care manifests itself in lower self-reported health status, increased utilization of health services, and poorer physical/mental functioning among caregivers, relative to the general population.[16] One study, for example, used 1998 administrative data from Blue Cross/Blue Shield, to compare health care costs for family members living with a relative with SMI, versus control families not dealing with mental illness. Living with a family member who has schizophrenia increased annual expenditures on health care for *others* in the family by $161 (in 2013 dollars) per family member. Surprisingly, health costs were significantly higher for those dealing with bipolar disorder ($312 per family member), despite the fact that patients with schizophrenia were more seriously ill (as measured by the annual health care costs of *patients* in the study).[17]

A more recent study focused on the elevated risk of depression in a sample of eighty-five Latino caregivers of relatives with schizophrenia. Forty percent of participants reported psychiatric symptoms that met or exceeded the criterion for elevated risk of depression, far higher than the norm in general population studies of Latinos (13 percent to 18 percent).[18]

Emotional Burden

The emotional strain of caring for a relative with schizophrenia is intense and, at times, overwhelming. Caregivers express fears about the future, concerns about disruptions in the lives of other family members, feelings of embarrassment or shame, and even a haunting guilt that they somehow caused the illness.[19] The emotional burden is almost universal among family caregivers. In the study of Belgian families caring for relatives with schizophrenia, for example, 98 percent of respondents indicated that they felt emotionally burdened by their role, at least some of the time.[20]

A small Canadian study of parents' reactions to their child's first psychiatric hospitalization reveals some of the emotional turmoil that accompanies a diagnosis of mental illness. Most parents initially responded as I did: with relief, that the problem had been identified; and hope, that the problem could be cured.[21] Once the family realized there was no cure, relief and hope changed to disbelief and shock, "it's like, this is not happening. This is *not* happening."[22]

In the interview study conducted by the nursing professors, participants had, on average, seventeen years of experience caring for their relative. Yet they still reported overwhelming emotions associated with caregiving, ranging from anger and bewilderment, to hopelessness and chronic sorrow.

Watching their relative struggle with schizophrenia, family members said that they felt confused, frightened, and frustrated, because they did not know what to expect, or how to help. One caregiver said, "I felt hopeless. There was nowhere to turn."[23]

Researchers in Italy compared family burden among caregivers dealing with several different types of chronic illnesses, including schizophrenia. Data were collected from more than 1,350 key relatives. The results indicate that the emotional burden of care is significantly more prevalent among families dealing with schizophrenia or brain disease, than among families dealing with other chronic illnesses.[24] Among the families dealing with schizophrenia:

- Eight percent reported that they felt embarrassed by their relative in public places, compared to almost none of the relatives dealing with other diseases.
- Eleven percent said that they "were not able to handle the situation much longer," compared to less than 6 percent of relatives dealing with other diseases.
- Fifty percent reported constant feelings of loss, compared to only 25 percent to 40 percent of relatives dealing with other diseases.[25]

I empathize with these family members. To me, the heaviest burden of having a son with schizophrenia was the grief I felt over the loss of a beloved child. In a very real sense, the person that I watched grow from infant to young adult was gone, along with my hopes for his future. Other parents express similar feelings:

> You've lost the person, the expectations, the athletic guy, the pretty good marks. . . . You're losing your dreams of where he will be, of having a normal life and having a family and of grandchildren . . . and you're grieving for yourself but also grieving for them because you know . . . that their lives will be different.[26]

Determinants of the Burden of Care

As suggested from the various comments here, the nature and intensity of family burden depends on characteristics of both patient and caregiver, and the ways they respond to the near-complete disruption of their lives.

Patient Characteristics

The severity of a patient's symptoms is one of the most important determinants, if not the most important determinant, of family burden. Both positive (e.g., delusions, hallucinations) and negative (e.g., apathy, poverty of speech) symptoms are disruptive to family members. Neither cluster has been established as more troublesome than the other.[27] Simply put, the more severe the symptoms, the greater the burden of care.

Similarly, the greater the functional limitations, the greater the burden of care.[28] If a patient has limited functional capacities (e.g., ability to manage housework, prepare meals, handle money), family caregivers must assume the functions on the patient's behalf, making caregiving more time-consuming and disruptive. On the other hand, if a patient has the capacity to work, the family burden is significantly eased.

A German study of 102 primary caregivers of patients with chronic mental illness evaluated the relative impact of various patient/caregiver characteristics, including the capacity to work, on the family's burden of care. Among the patient characteristics the authors considered (severity of symptoms, duration of illness, problems with everyday living, regular employment), they concluded that a "patients' regular employment appears most important in reducing caregivers' psychological distress and enhancing their well-being."[29] The result makes sense. Regular employment provides income and social connections for the patient, thereby easing some of the family's concerns about the future.

Other research suggests that the younger the patient at onset of illness, the greater the burden of care.[30] Age at onset primarily affects the emotional burden of caregiving. Caregivers express greater emotional concerns about the patient's physical safety, everyday life, financial resources, and prospects for the future, when onset occurs at a young age.[31]

Family burden also increases with patient substance abuse, nonadherence to medications, and suicidal ideation, with the latter being by far the most distressing to caregivers.[32] A study led by a clinical psychologist at Washington State University tested a model of family burden using data from ninety patients with schizophrenia, and their family caregivers.[33] The model included a number of patient behaviors (substance abuse, depression, suicidal ideation) along with other patient characteristics. Caregiver awareness of a patient's suicidal thoughts was found to be a strong and significant predictor of family burden, while substance abuse was only marginally significant.[34]

Unfortunately, thoughts of suicide are common among patients with schizophrenia. Over the course of the study cited previously, 49 percent of patients reported suicidal thoughts, and 13 percent attempted suicide (none were successful). A meta-analysis of more than five dozen studies estimates that the lifetime risk of suicide is 4.9 percent among persons with schizophrenia.[35] The risk of suicide is even higher in the early phases of psychosis, and may be as high as 10 percent in the year following an initial psychiatric hospitalization.[36] The emotional impact on caregivers is unimaginable.

Caregiver Characteristics

On the caregiver side, the burden of care depends largely on an individual's ability to cope with demands that far exceed the demands of everyday life.[37] The capacity to identify and adopt successful coping strategies depends on resources both internal (an individual's innate approach to problem solving) and external (a support network of friends, counselors, spiritual advisors etc.).

With respect to internal resources: A *passive* approach to coping is characterized by strategies such as avoidance, resignation, assigning blame, or wishful thinking. An *active* approach is characterized by problem solving, reaching out to others for support, and thinking positively ("count your blessings").[38] In general, active coping strategies lead to better outcomes for both patient and caregiver. Active and supportive family relationships help patients adapt to their illness, improve their adherence to treatment, and increase their likelihood of recovery.[39] Caregivers with a broad range of active coping skills also experience less burden of care, all else equal, than caregivers who cope in passive ways.[40]

With respect to *external* resources: Support networks ease the burden of care by providing assistance with the practical problems of caregiving (e.g., information, periods of respite) and by helping the caregiver adopt more effective coping strategies. High levels of support are associated with active, problem-solving coping strategies that reduce the burden of care. Low levels of support are associated with passive coping strategies, in part because avoidance and resignation are natural responses to the kind of desperation that external support might alleviate.[41]

Given the many ways that support networks ease the burden of caring for a relative with schizophrenia, it is telling that many family members identify "inadequate economic and social support," and "lack of access to information and support networks" as among the greatest problems they face.[42] In the Italian study of caregivers dealing with various chronic illnesses, schizophrenia differed from all other illnesses in the low levels of professional and social support reported by family members.[43] Similarly, lack of support was frequently mentioned by participants in the study of parents dealing with a child's first psychiatric hospitalization:

> Most of our friends didn't understand it. Lord knows we didn't, so it was hard for them. They stayed away because they didn't know what to say. [So] here we are on this little island and we're all floating and we're going to drown real soon.[44]

I was lucky. When David became ill, I had strong support from family, friends, colleagues at work, and the study team at Chapel Hill.

One encounter in particular stands out. In the first summer after David was diagnosed, I went through a low period of anger and self-pity, wondering "Why did this happen to *my* son?" I sought help from my pastor, who told me the following story:

> My grandchildren and I like to go down to the bay to watch the ducks swimming. They make it look so easy, gliding across the top of the water. But if you look underneath, you'll see their feet are paddling just as hard as they can go. That's how it is with other people. They look like they're gliding easily through life, but underneath they're all paddling just as hard as they can.

After that conversation, instead of wondering, "Why me?" I tried to think, "Why not me?" The story of the ducks pulled me out of many emotional troughs.

The Mental Health System and Family Burden

The American Psychiatric Association (APA) recognizes that the "social circumstances of the patient can have profound effects on adherence and response to treatment."[45] Because the "social circumstances" of so many patients with schizophrenia are confined to their immediate family, the APA practice guideline for schizophrenia includes specific recommendations to involve families in treatment plans. For example:

- *Engagement of family and other significant support persons*, with the patient's permission, is recommended to further strengthen the therapeutic effort.
- *Efforts to engage and collaborate with family members and other natural caregivers* are often successful during the crisis of an acute psychotic episode . . . and are strongly recommended.[46]

The APA guideline recognizes that a family's ability to cope with the demands of caregiving has a significant impact on patient outcomes, and that professional and social support are key determinants of the family's ability to cope. Therefore, the guideline for schizophrenia also recommends,

- *Interventions that educate family members* about schizophrenia . . . to provide support and offer training in effective problem solving and communication,
- It is equally critical to maintain a level of momentum aimed at improving community functioning in order to *instill a sense of hope and progress for the patient and family.*[47]

The support we received from the team in Chapel Hill conformed to every aspect of the guideline. However, this kind of all-encompassing care is not the norm in the U.S. mental health system. Family psychosocial interventions, which have demonstrated efficacy in reducing family burden and improving patient outcomes, are not widely used in practice.[48] Mental health professionals often ignore (and are sometimes even hostile toward) family members.[49] All too often, as we discovered in Charlotte, there is simply no help available when a crisis occurs.

So, why does the mental health system put so much responsibility on family members, yet provide so little support? There are likely many factors involved, but here I will focus on two: the misallocation of resources in the public mental health system, and the still widely held belief that families cause more harm than good.

Resources: An Embarrassment of Riches

In a recent book recounting the evolution of U.S. mental health policy since 1950, economists Richard Frank and Sherry Glied document the tremendous increase in spending for mental health services that occurred over the last half of the twentieth century. "Spending [in current dollars] grew more than seventyfold, from \$1.14 billion in 1956 to \$85.4 billion in 2001."[50] State spending increased more than 440 percent over the period, federal spending increased almost 840 percent.[51]

The tremendous infusion of funds for mental health care, coincident with the movement of patients out of state hospitals, dramatically changed the landscape of mental health services in the United States. The number of inpatient psychiatric beds declined from more than twenty-four per ten thousand persons in 1970, to fewer than seven per ten thousand persons in 2000. The staff-to-patient ratio in state and county mental hospitals increased, and length of stay declined. There was tremendous growth in the size and diversity of the mental health workforce including increases in the number of clinical psychologists, psychiatric nurses, and others providing direct patient care. New institutional arrangements emerged to expand options for community care, including partial hospitalization programs, and specialty managed care programs for behavioral health services.[52] In summing up the expanded supply of mental health services that emerged over this period, the authors say, "The consumer in 2000 had, by historical standards, a vast array of well-trained professionals and institutions from which to receive treatment."[53]

The new psychiatric specialties and institutions that emerged, however, were best equipped to deal with mental illnesses of moderate severity. For persons with serious mental illness, the outlook was not so rosy. The one mental health specialty qualified to prescribe antipsychotic drugs, the psychiatrist, declined in supply relative to other medical specialties between 1965 and 2000. Likewise, the one institution equipped to deal with acute psychosis, the psychiatric hospital, contracted sharply over this period. In many states, the decentralization of mental health services left no one, except families, responsible for persons with SMI. Thus, in describing the overall transformation of mental health services in the last fifty years of the twentieth century, Frank and Glied conclude (emphasis added):

> The consequence has been to exchange a set of bureaucratic failures and tight budgets that took care of all services for a circumscribed population for a vastly richer, decentralized system of care that suffers from market failure, and *allows some people with significant impairments to fall through the cracks.* [54]

The redirection of mental health funds to providers and service organizations best suited to care for the moderately ill is one reason why there are insufficient resources in the public mental health system to provide appropriate care (as outlined in the APA Practice Guideline) for patients with SMI and their family caregivers. Resource constraints help to explain why we could not get David admitted to a psychiatric facility in Charlotte, even when he agreed to voluntary hospitalization.

Between 2001 and 2012, the number of inpatient beds in state psychiatric hospitals in North Carolina declined by nearly 50 percent, from 1,755 to 850. [55] The state hospitals serve a small and well-defined population, namely, persons with chronic and severe mental illness, who are nonresponsive to antipsychotic drugs and lack family or social support. David responded well to antipsychotic medication and had family support, so he clearly did not belong in a state hospital.

Without health insurance, David's only realistic option for inpatient care was Randolph Community Mental Health Center. The center, which serves the city of Charlotte and surrounding Mecklenburg County, maintained forty-four adult inpatient beds in 2005. Between 1998 and 2005, average daily adult occupancy rates at the center increased from 82 to 95 percent of capacity. [56] On the day we tried to admit David in 2005, forty-two inpatient beds were likely occupied. What I understand now, but did not know then, is that David had little chance of being admitted unless he arrived in custody of the police. In fact, among those persons brought to North Carolina hospital emergency rooms with behavioral health crises in 2012, only 28 percent were admitted to a community psychiatric facility. The majority (53 percent) were released to their families or self-care. [57]

Attitudes: Families Are Part of the Problem

Resource constraints can explain, at least in part, why family support services are not common practice in the mental health system, but not why patient advocates for William Bruce expressed such negative attitudes toward his family. Without ever having met Joe and Amy Bruce, the advocates concluded that William's parents were "a negative force" in his life. The attitude is reminiscent of the early twentieth century, when Freudian theories dominated psychiatry, and environmental theorists viewed families as the root cause of mental illness. Today, genetic research has made tremendous strides in identifying the physiological bases for mental illness, but medical models of SMI have not entirely dispelled the view that families are, at least in part, to blame.[58]

A 2003 study reported data from a survey of forty-eight mental health providers and thirty-nine family members that was designed to assess their beliefs about the causes of mental illness. The vast majority of respondents (90 percent of providers and 92 percent of family members) agreed with the statement that "Severe mental illness is biologically based." However,

- Forty-four percent of providers and 23 percent of family members also agreed that, "Behavior of family members can cause the onset of mental illness."
- Twenty-seven percent of providers and 15 percent of family members agreed that "Poor family communication can cause severe mental illness."[59]

It is intriguing that survey respondents expressed beliefs supporting both biological and family causation theories of mental illness. The authors argue that simultaneous support for the two theories is consistent with the prevailing *diathesis-stress* model of mental illness.[60] In this model, the environment is viewed as a contributing risk factor to the onset of mental illness, although not the primary cause. Still, the link to the environment may explain why beliefs in family causation persist, and continue to be a barrier to provider/family interaction.

Providers who believe that a dysfunctional family is partly to blame for mental illness are unlikely to see any point in collaborating with family members.[61] For example, clinicians participating in a Veteran's Administration trial of a family intervention program for patients with psychosis generally perceived patients' families to be "dysfunctional, inconsistent, and usually the problem."[62] These same clinicians expressed skepticism about the benefits of family interventions *even before the study began.*

In the extreme, there are professionals, like the patient advocates for William Bruce, who contend that family engagement is not merely unhelpful, but also harmful for patients with SMI.[63] But where do the patients go, after the advocates obtain their release? To their "dysfunctional" families, *of course*, because there is nowhere else for them to go. And, the families willingly pick up the burden, *of course*, because that is how families become default caregivers in the first place. Amy Bruce paid the ultimate price for the failure of the mental health system to collaborate with family members, but Joe Bruce has not given up on his son.

William Bruce was charged with murder following his mother's death. In March 2007, he was found "not criminally responsible by reason of insanity," and was confined to a psychiatric facility for an indefinite period. Facing the alternatives of taking antipsychotic medication willingly, or being physically restrained and forcibly medicated, William agreed to take the drug as prescribed. Within weeks, his mental status improved.

Joe Bruce is William's court-appointed guardian and talks with his son nearly every day. In May 2013, Joe testified before a Congressional Committee examining the performance of the Substance Abuse and Mental Health Services Administration, the federal agency that supports the patient advocacy program. Mr. Bruce testified that neither he nor his wife had ever met any of the advocates who claimed that William's family was "a negative force in his life." Mr. Bruce further testified that neither the patient advocates, nor Disability Rights Maine, ever admitted any wrongdoing in facilitating William's discharge, or any intention of changing their procedures in the future.[64]

Today, William is doing well. He takes criminal justice classes online and hopes to attend law school someday. Of his mother's death, he says, "I blame the illness and I blame myself. The guilt is—tough." Of his father, "He stood by me the whole time, despite . . . what I did. I am the man I am today because of my dad." Of the patient advocates and the mental health system, "There are times when people should be committed. Institutions can really help. Medications can help. None of this would have happened if I had been medicated."[65]

The U.S. mental health system imposes an enormous burden on families to care for persons with even the most serious mental illnesses. Mental health providers and policy makers must recognize that everyone benefits when the system allocates a share of its resources to ensure that family members are not overwhelmed, or harmed, by the caregiver role. Beyond that, the system has a moral responsibility *to* the families on whom it places such a tremendous responsibility *for* care.

Postscript

The fact that we refer to caregiving as a *burden* gives the role an entirely negative connotation. The word burden derives from an Old English word related to birth, and means "that which is borne." The Oxford English Dictionary (OED) defines burden as "a load of labor, duty, responsibility, blame, sin, sorrow."[66] Caring for a relative with schizophrenia is all these things, and more.

Most of the research on caring for a relative with mental illness focuses on the negative aspects of caregiving, but a few studies investigate positive aspects of the role as well. Caregivers generally are able to identify at least one reward associated with their experience, and most can identify several rewarding aspects. The rewards they mention reflect the growth in character that comes from dealing with adversity: feelings of empowerment and inner strength, increases in self-esteem, and the maturity and life experience that comes with meeting a challenge. [67]

From my own experience I can add two more items to the list, namely, a clear understanding of priorities, and a unique bond with my son. During the summer David was recovering from his first psychotic episode, one of my colleagues told me that he was feeling pressured by the competing demands of teaching, research, and family, and did not know what was more important. I said, "*I always know what is most important.*" He understood. Another wise colleague told me, around the same time, "*You will have a different relationship with your son.*" He was right. David and I walked through hell together. It changes you.

Part II

Working with Schizophrenia

Chapter Six

Work First

HAPPY UN-BIRTHDAY

Fall 2007

David's thirtieth birthday was one of the saddest days of my life. By then, he had been living with us for more than two years and still had no job. We did the usual birthday things: dinner at a nice restaurant, cake and candles, presents. David went through the celebration halfheartedly, but after opening all the presents, his eyes filled with tears. When I asked what was wrong, he said, "I'm thirty years old. I live with my parents. I have no money, no job, and no future. Don't ever celebrate my birthday again. It's just another day." I held my son in my arms and cried with him.

We had tried repeatedly over the previous two years to address David's employment situation. A few months after he arrived in Arizona, in summer 2005, David and I met with his case manager from the state behavioral health services office. I asked about vocational services. "Oh yes, we have a social worker who helps our clients find jobs." I was delighted, and frankly surprised, to have an offer of someone to help. Within a few weeks we met with the social worker, whereupon my delight quickly turned to disappointment. She was a meek little grandmotherly type, whose only suggestion for David was a job collecting coins from vending machines. Was this why he had struggled so hard to complete his degree?

Over the next few months, David made several attempts to find employment on his own. He saw an advertisement online and thought he might try being a model. Of course, I thought he was handsome enough. We paid for a portfolio of photos and David registered with a modeling agency. They

91

called him for one job, a photo shoot for a billboard, but he never heard from the agency again. The possibility of a modeling career fizzled.

Then David interviewed for a job as a cost estimator for a local construction company. During college, he had worked weekends with my brother, Gordon, who was designing and building his own home. It was an enormous project that gave David experience in all aspects of construction, from framing to roofing. He seemed to have an intuitive understanding of the building process. Gordon told me one day, "I love working with David, I only tell him once, and he understands exactly what I want him to do." The experience paid off and David was offered the job with the construction company. I was elated—a real job at last! David completed three half-days of training, but when it came time to work a full day, it was too much. He called me and said, "I couldn't do it, Mom, I was on the highway driving to work, but I just turned around and came home." I was immensely disappointed, but I didn't want to make him feel worse. I simply said, "It's OK. You'll know when the right job comes along."

By fall 2006, David had stopped searching for work. Except for regular visits to his case manager and psychiatrist, he stayed home, where his father and I were his only social contacts. The three of us usually went out to dinner on Friday nights, but otherwise David refused to go to parties or social events. When a close friend invited the three of us to her annual St. Patrick's Day party, I urged him to come along, but he still said "no." "What would I talk about Mom? I don't do anything. I don't have anything to say." In fact, his only regular social interaction was watching *Fear Factor* with me. There's something about watching people leap onto speeding trucks, or eat scorpions, which makes conversation easier—even for someone with mental illness. We laughed together at the crazy stunts, and the *really* crazy people who did them.

During these days, David spent most of his spare time (and *all* of his time was spare) playing poker online. At first he played in no-stakes games, but as he improved he thought he might become good enough to be a professional poker player. Of course, I thought he was smart enough. Eventually, we gave him a $1,000 stake to see what he could win. When it was gone, his poker career fizzled.

By then, I was chair of a dysfunctional department at my university. (Most academic departments are dysfunctional, but ours had more than its share of histrionic personalities.) I was paid well, but working long hours, short on staff, and frustrated that my research was stalled. David had free time, no money, and good computer skills. One day I put the pieces together and told David I would personally pay him to work as my research assistant on an hourly basis. At first he balked; it was easier to simply ask us for what little money he needed. But I told him the free money had stopped. We settled into a work routine, and he was *earning* money again.

Fall 2008

As birthday thirty-one approached, I could not ignore it, but I did not want a repeat of thirty, and David had ordered, "No more birthdays." So I made a card for him saying, "*Happy Un-Birthday!*" I put candles on an *unfrosted* cake and gave him *unwrapped* presents for his *unspecial* day. David smiled. Perhaps there would be better birthdays to come.

It reminded me of an incident that occurred during the first summer he was sick. I had to travel to western North Carolina to visit the worksite of one of our research projects. I invited David to come along, as a break from sitting around home every day. He agreed. We began driving west late one afternoon. As we came over a ridge in the little town of Wilson, North Carolina, the setting sun unexpectedly appeared before us as an enormous, blazing ball of light. "It's a sign," I said, "of better days to come." David smiled.

MENTAL ILLNESS AND WORK

Why work? Work is, first and foremost, a source of income, security, and financial independence. But in modern economies work is much more than a means of support. Work is a source of pride and dignity in a job, any job, well done. Work is a way to connect with others, to make friends, to engage in social interaction. Work is a source of self-esteem, a validation that one is a productive member of society, that one's skills and talents are respected. In a very real sense, work is a source of identity. Meeting a stranger at a party, the first question is, "What is your name?" The second is, "What do you do?"

Work is all this and more to persons with SMI. Gainful employment (i.e., a job in which earnings exceed the threshold for disability benefits) gives workers with SMI both a sense of empowerment (having the resources to achieve one's goals) and inclusion (belonging to a workplace community). Work supports the process of recovery from mental illness by adding structure and purpose to life.[1] Elyn Saks, a professor at the University of Southern California and a patient with schizophrenia, says work is her "best defense" against the symptoms of mental illness she continues to experience. Work "keeps me focused, it keeps the demons at bay."[2]

Work is also an important source of identity for persons recovering from SMI. Rather than assuming the primary identity of a mental health consumer, with all its negative stereotypes, a worker can redefine themselves, as we all do, in terms of a job. "I am a teacher," rather than "I am bipolar." Some workers with SMI say that working in a paid job where no one knows about their mental illness makes them feel, "normal . . . and being normal validates you."[3] Indeed, the ability to support oneself through work may be one of the clearest and most visible signs of recovery from mental illness. Today, it is a realistic goal for many persons with SMI, and ought to be a top priority of the mental health system.

An analogous situation occurs in housing policy. In dealing with the problems of chronic homelessness, many U.S. cities have made safe and permanent housing the top priority. The "Housing First" initiatives provide free and permanent housing (as opposed to temporary shelter) for homeless persons, regardless of income or substance abuse issues. The assumption is that a stable home provides an essential foundation from which other problems, such as substance abuse or psychiatric symptoms, can be addressed.[4] Gainful employment plays a comparable role for persons with SMI who are willing and able to work. A stable job provides a foundation from which other problems, such as damaged self-esteem, financial insecurity, and social isolation, can be addressed. Indeed, employment was one of the primary concerns of the coalition of disability groups that advocated for the civil rights protections embodied in the Americans with Disabilities Act (ADA).

Americans with Disabilities Act of 1990

Title I of the ADA establishes the rights of persons with disabilities with respect to employment. The act declares that persons with mental or physical disabilities have the right to equal treatment in the labor market, with respect to jobs for which they are qualified, and in which their disabilities can be accommodated with relative ease. Supporters of the ADA anticipated dramatic improvements in employment outcomes for the disabled population after the act took effect in 1992, but they were disappointed. Relative employment rates of persons with disabilities actually declined in the immediate post-ADA period.[5] In 2008, Congress passed the ADA Amendments Act of 2008 (ADAAA), in part to strengthen the law's provisions with respect to employment. The story of how the ADA was passed, why it was amended, and why it failed to achieve its employment goals, is instructive for those of us who believe that, with appropriate public policies, many more persons with SMI could be working.

Enacting the ADA

It took twenty-six years from the passage of the Civil Rights Act of 1964, which prohibits employment discrimination against individuals on the basis of "race, color, religion, sex, or national origin,"[6] to extend the same protections to persons with disabilities.[7] One reason for the delay was that passage of the Americans with Disabilities Act presented a number of challenges that did not apply to groups covered under the original Civil Rights Act.

First, "persons with disabilities" is a heterogeneous group, and far more difficult to delineate than persons of a particular race, gender, or ethnic origin. The population with disabilities includes persons with a vast array of health conditions (e.g., blindness, deafness, partial paralysis) who require different aids to ensure their full inclusion in society (e.g., audio signals at crossways; text telephones, wheelchair ramps, and bus lifts). At times, the different subgroups are openly hostile in their competition for scarce resources.

I recall a research conference on disability issues that I attended several years ago, where many of the participants were persons with hearing, mobility, or visual impairments. The conference organizers were diligent in selecting formats and venues for the meetings that were accessible to everyone. The guidelines for presenters, sent in advance, specified that all audience handouts must be available in formats accessible to persons who are blind. Not having access to a Braille printer, I opted not to provide handouts at all. Some presenters, however, overlooked the guidelines and brought handouts in normal typeface. Many of the participants with visual impairments were offended by what they perceived to be exclusion and discrimination, so the conference organizers decided not to allow the handouts to be distributed to anyone. In all fairness, that is exactly what the preconference guidelines established, but participants without visual impairments were disgruntled by what they perceived as spitefulness.

Passage of the ADA occurred only after years of advocacy efforts by a coalition of these diverse disability groups. Organizations such as the American Foundation for the Blind, the Epilepsy Foundation of America, National Association of the Deaf, National Mental Health Association, and many others united to support a broad definition of disability in the act, and strongly opposed any attempts to exclude particular groups from coverage. In reflecting on the meeting I attended, it is amazing that disability groups with such competing needs and agendas were able to maintain unity over two decades to ensure passage of the ADA with a broad and inclusive definition of disability.

Another challenge to extending civil rights protections to persons with disabilities is that, unlike most groups protected by antidiscrimination laws, persons with disabilities may require special accommodations (e.g., ramps or special telecommunications devices) to access their rights. The employment provisions of the ADA require covered employers (all public and private employers with fifteen or more employees) to provide reasonable accommodations to workers with disabilities *at the employer's expense*. Previous antidiscrimination laws, prohibiting race-based discrimination, for example, impose no direct monetary costs on employers. An employer may be discomfited by having to interact with members of a stigmatized group, but these "psychic costs" are the essence of the discrimination that the laws aim to eliminate.

In sharp contrast, the ADA imposes an affirmative obligation to accommodate that may involve direct costs to employers in addition to any psychic distress. Legislators acknowledged the potential costs as they debated the act:

> Some persons may assert that costs should not be a factor in designing a disability civil rights law. In the context of a disability rights law, however, costs may have to be incurred in order to provide nondiscriminatory treatment; e.g., putting in a ramp, providing auxiliary aids and services, and other accommodations. Indeed, the failure to incur reasonable costs in order to provide access is regarded as discriminatory. At some point, however, the undertaking of an accommodation can be so costly or represent such a fundamental alteration in the covered entity's program that the failure to undertake the accommodation is simply not discriminatory.[8]

Some legislators expressed concerns about allocating the entire cost of accommodations to the private sector:

> How will the bill's mandates affect the owners of small businesses who must make reasonable accommodations to handicapped employees? . . . If we are going to ask Americans to bear the costs of this action, we should assure that the real costs are clearly identified and fairly allocated between the public and private sectors. Only then can we vote intelligently on this major civil rights proposal.[9]

Another challenge to enacting the ADA, as with any civil rights law, is the pervasive stigma against some of the persons the law is attempting to protect. Stigmatizing attitudes were quite apparent in the debates that preceded passage of the ADA, in which legislators attempted to restrict the definition of disability. Senator Armstrong, for example, introduced an amendment which explicitly excluded coverage for persons with "certain sexual disorders, impulse control disorders, and drug-related disorders." Even so, he did not think the amendment went far enough in excluding coverage of persons with mental illness:

> [I]f ADA is enacted the private sector will be swamped with mental disability litigation. My amendment excludes some of the mental disorders that would have created the more egregious lawsuits, but my amendment does no more than brush away a handful of the vast numbers of mental disorders and potential mental disorders.[10]

Senator Helms was unflinching in his questions regarding whether the ADA would, or should, cover persons with certain types of mental disorders:

> Does an employer's own moral standards enable him to make a judgment about any or all of the employees identified in our previous question [transvestites, kleptomaniacs, manic-depressives, schizophrenics]? . . . How far does

your covered list of individuals go in denying the small businessman the right to run his company as he sees fit?[11]

Consistent with the theories of stigma (chapter 2), the legislators' objections to coverage under the ADA focused on health conditions for which the individual was believed to be *morally responsible* and/or *unable to control their behavior*. In all the lengthy debates over the definition of disability in the act, the *only* conditions subject to direct attack on the floor of Congress were AIDS, substance use disorders, and various types of mental illness.[12] These conditions top the stigma rankings in almost every social distance study. Nevertheless, the law passed with a broad, albeit ambiguous, definition of disability.

Employment Provisions of the ADA

Title I of the ADA prohibits discrimination against persons with disabilities in: job application procedures and hiring decisions; job training programs; promotion and discharge decisions; wages, and other employee benefits.[13] The law states that (emphasis added):

> The term "disability" means, with respect to an individual—(A) a physical or mental impairment that *substantially limits one or more of the major life activities* of such individual; (B) a record of such an impairment; or (C) being regarded as having such an impairment.[14]

Congress did not specify a list of covered impairments, but the employer guidelines issued by the Equal Employment Opportunity Commission (EEOC) were somewhat more specific. With respect to mental impairments, the guidelines say that persons with a "mental or psychological disorder, such as an intellectual disability (formerly termed "mental retardation"), organic brain syndrome, emotional or mental illness, and specific learning disabilities" are covered by the law.[15] The act itself states that the term disability *shall not include* persons with certain "mental" conditions, namely, current users of illegal drugs, persons with sexual behavior disorders, and persons with certain compulsive disorders (e.g., compulsive gambling).[16]

Prior to extending a job offer, employers are prohibited from asking job applicants about disabling health conditions. Once a job offer is extended, employers are expected to provide *reasonable accommodations* to *otherwise qualified* individuals with a disability, who can perform the *essential functions* of the job. Employers must provide accommodations at their own expense, unless the costs impose *undue hardship* on the firm. The key terms are defined in the ADA, but the definitions are often ambiguous. For example, instead of giving an explicit definition of reasonable accommodation, the act lists a number of actions that may be considered as such:

(A) making existing facilities used by employees readily accessible to and usable by individuals with disabilities, and (B) job restructuring, part-time or modified work schedules, reassignment to a vacant position, acquisition or modification of equipment or devices, appropriate adjustment or modifications of examinations, training materials or policies, the provision of qualified readers or interpreters, and other similar accommodations for individuals with disabilities.[17]

Failure to provide reasonable accommodation is considered discriminatory, but the language of the act provides little guidance to employers regarding what is reasonable. If reassignment to a vacant position violates seniority rules, is that a reasonable accommodation?[18]

The ambiguities in the language of the ADA served a useful political purpose in maintaining the coalition of disability organizations that supported the law. By not identifying specific covered disabilities, or what it means to be substantially limited in a major life activity, supporters of the ADA enlisted the cooperation of the broadest possible spectrum of disability organizations. Nevertheless, once lawsuits were filed alleging disability-related discrimination, the judicial system was obliged to define specifics of the law.

Adjudicating Issues under the ADA

Judges struggled with the meaning of "reasonable" accommodation and other ambiguous terms in the law, but the most contested issue was the definition of a "qualified person with a disability." In deciding whether a claimant was sufficiently limited in major life activities to qualify for the act's protections, courts tended to make narrow rulings that severely restricted eligibility to file claims. As a result of these conservative interpretations of "disability," defendants (employers) won the vast majority of lawsuits filed under Title I in the decade and a half following implementation of the ADA.

In 2001, for example, employers prevailed in more than 95 percent of resolved cases.[19] Plaintiffs with mental disorders fared even worse than others. Employers prevailed in 98 percent of resolved cases involving mental disorders; all of which were summarily dismissed.[20] In other words, the allegations of discrimination were never addressed because a judge determined the plaintiff was not disabled according to the requirements of the ADA, and therefore not entitled to its protections. Similar ambiguities precluded plaintiffs from demonstrating the requirements of an "otherwise qualified person with a disability" that would trigger an employer's duty to provide reasonable accommodation. The following hypothetical scenarios illustrate some of the ways actual cases were lost.

Scenario 1   "Sam" had a first psychotic episode at age nineteen, while he was training to be an auto mechanic. He was admitted to a psychiatric hospital and diagnosed with schizophrenia. Sam's symptoms receded once he started taking antipsychotic medications. He was discharged after three weeks and returned to the training program, which he successfully completed. Sam worked as a mechanic with a large automotive service center for five years. Three years into the job, he weaned himself off medications, with his physician's approval, and has experienced no symptoms since that time. Recently, his employer learned about Sam's diagnosis and psychiatric hospitalization from another employee. When Sam confirmed his medical history, his employer told him, "I don't need any psychos working here." Sam was fired. He filed a lawsuit charging discrimination under the ADA.

In this scenario, the employee neither needed nor requested job accommodations. He was fully capable of performing the tasks required in his job, as evidenced by five years of successful employment. The employer's remark confirms that the worker was fired solely because of his disability. Can we assume that the discrimination claim will be upheld in court?

Not necessarily. In determining whether individuals are entitled to protection under the ADA, judges must determine if the plaintiff has a health impairment that *substantially limits* their activities. In this scenario, the plaintiff is able to function with no apparent limitations, so the lawsuit could be summarily dismissed because the worker does not have a disability within the ADA's definition. There have been cases filed under the ADA in which a worker was fired, demoted, or involuntarily transferred explicitly because of their disability, yet the case was dismissed because the individual was judged not to be "substantially limited."[21]

Scenario 2   "Olivia" had been employed as a registered nurse at a large metropolitan hospital for two years when she suffered an episode of major depression. She attempted to continue working, but was frequently late, forgot important tasks, and had little energy to care for patients. She applied for, and was granted, a medical leave. Olivia's physician prescribed medications, which effectively treated the episode of depression. Olivia also began seeing a therapist regularly. She returned to work, but requested a scheduling accommodation so she could continue her therapist visits. The hospital refused the accommodation, saying it was unfair to other employees. Olivia feared that, without continued therapy, she would become depressed again. She took another medical leave and filed a lawsuit claiming the hospital had a duty to accommodate her under the ADA.

In this scenario, the issue under contention is an employee's request for a job accommodation. Her work performance was satisfactory until she developed a mental condition that limited her ability to function as a nurse. Upon returning from medical leave, her request for a schedule that would accommodate continued psychiatric treatment was denied. Can we expect adjudication of the case to focus on whether the requested accommodation is reasonable?

Not necessarily. Before courts hear arguments on the reasonableness of accommodations, judges must determine if the plaintiff is a "qualified person with a disability," entitled to protection under the ADA. In this case, the plaintiff's mental condition is being treated effectively with medication; thus, when she is on medication she is not substantially limited in her activities and not protected by the ADA. Without medication, her functioning is severely limited, but in this state she is unable to perform the essential functions of her job, and therefore not entitled to reasonable accommodation. Thus, the plaintiff faces an insurmountable burden—to prove that she is both severely limited in activities, *and* able to perform the essential functions of her job. Her case could be summarily dismissed without the issue of reasonable accommodation ever coming before the court.

The U.S. Supreme Court considered an analogous factual scenario in 1999. In *Sutton v. United Airlines*, two sisters sued United Airlines because they were disqualified from employment as commercial airline pilots due to poor but correctible vision. The sisters argued that disqualification on this basis constituted unlawful employment discrimination in violation of Title I of the ADA, because their vision was fully corrected with glasses.[22] The court affirmed dismissal of the sisters' discrimination claim, concluding that the sisters were "not disabled" because their vision could be corrected with glasses. The court's ruling established a precedent that, in determining whether a plaintiff is a "qualified person with a disability," health conditions should be considered in their *ameliorated* state.

Many serious mental illnesses can be treated with medications that restore patients to a near normal level of functioning. According to the Supreme Court ruling, these persons are not "disabled" as defined by the ADA, and therefore are not protected by the ADA, because they are not severely limited when their condition is treated. Without medications, they are severely limited, but then they are excluded from the ADA's protection on the grounds that they are unable to perform essential functions of the job.[23]

Scenario 3   "Alex," a day cashier in a large banking firm, had difficulties interacting with other people. He missed social cues, avoided making eye contact, and often misinterpreted what others said. He had never had a steady girlfriend for longer than a few months. Alex's social problems carried over to the workplace, where he had difficulties getting along with coworkers. He had been reprimanded by his supervisors for making unwanted social advances to a female coworker, and for verbally abusing a male coworker (whom Alex perceived had taken unfair advantage of him). After seeing a psychologist about his problems interacting with others, Alex was diagnosed with an autism-spectrum disorder. He told his supervisors about the diagnosis, assuming that they would be sympathetic. Instead, they demoted him to the position of night clerk, a lower-paying job. Alex filed a lawsuit alleging disability-related discrimination.

In this scenario, the employee performs his cashier responsibilities satisfactorily, but his disability affects the tenor of the workplace. The ADA prohibits discrimination against an "otherwise qualified person with a disability, who can perform the essential functions of the job." Can we expect the court's decision to depend on whether or not interacting with coworkers is an essential function of a cashier's job?

Not necessarily. Before Alex's case can get to trial, the judge must determine whether he has "a physical or mental impairment that substantially limits the performance of one or more *major life activities*." Alex is clearly limited in his ability to get along with others. Is interacting with others a major life activity, like walking, hearing, and seeing? Courts have wrestled with this question, not only with respect to interacting with others, but also regarding other common everyday activities, such as driving.[24] The federal circuit courts are in agreement that driving is *not* a major life activity, but decisions with respect to interacting with others have been mixed.[25]

In a 1995 Compliance Manual issued for employers subject to the ADA, the EEOC included "interacting with others" in a list of examples of major life activities.[26] However, the Court of Appeals for the First Circuit rejected the manual's guidance as "hardly binding," stating that the concept of getting along with others is "remarkably elastic, perhaps so much so as to make it unworkable as a definition," and quite different from the major life activities included in the original EEOC regulations for implementing the act.[27] Paradoxically, the Second and Ninth Circuit Courts have ruled that interacting with others "easily falls within the definition of major life activity."[28] The question of whether or not interacting with others is a major life activity was never fully resolved under the original terms of the ADA.

ADA Amendments Act of 2008

Given the rate at which lawsuits filed under Title I of the ADA were being summarily dismissed, by 2005 it was clear that the law was not working as Congress had intended. In 2008, Congress amended the ADA to resolve some of the ambiguities that were causing plaintiffs to lose their lawsuits even before the cases were argued in court. The clear intent of the ADAAA of 2008 was to reestablish broad coverage of persons with disabilities.

The ADAAA made several key modifications to the original law that were specifically designed to overrule court decisions which had narrowed the ADA's scope of protection. First, Congress clarified its intent that the definition of disability in the ADA should be interpreted broadly:

The definition of disability in this Act shall be construed in favor of broad
coverage of individuals under this Act, to the maximum extent permitted by
the terms of this Act.[29]

Second, Congress clarified its intent that "major life activities" should be
interpreted to include a broad range of normal activities. The ADAAA provides a nonexhaustive list of qualifying activities that includes communicat-
ing, concentrating, and thinking; and adds a new category of "major bodily
functions," that includes functions of the brain.[30]

Third, Congress clarified ambiguities in the interpretation of "substantial
limitations." The ADAAA specifies that, in determining whether a plaintiff is
substantially limited, episodic impairments and impairments in remission
should be evaluated according to their active states. Further, the ADAAA
expressly overrules the Supreme Court's ruling in *Sutton v. United Airlines*
by providing that,

The determination of whether an impairment substantially limits a major life
activity shall be made without regard to the ameliorative effects of mitigating
measures.[31]

The ADAAA also includes a nonexhaustive list of possible mitigating measures, with "medications" first on the list.

Overall, the ADAAA will almost certainly ensure that a larger proportion
of discrimination cases involving persons with mental disorders are heard in
court.[32] The ADAAA makes clear that the main inquiry in a case of disability-related discrimination should not be whether the plaintiff is covered by
the ADA, but whether the covered employer has fulfilled their obligations
under the law.[33] Indeed, in determining who is an "otherwise qualified person with a disability," the ADAAA dramatically expands the reach of "disability."

Some legal analysts, however, argue that the ADAAA may still fail to
protect persons with mental disorders because the ADAAA does not change
the threshold for interpreting what it means to be "qualified." Prior to 2008,
two-thirds of plaintiffs with physical disorders failed to have their cases
heard in court because they were deemed not to be disabled (an issue which
the amendments address), whereas two-thirds of plaintiffs with mental disorders failed because they were deemed not to be qualified individuals with
disabilities (an issue which the amendments do not address).[34]

It is still too soon to draw definitive conclusions regarding the impact of
the ADAAA in the courtroom. The act is not retroactive, so the new standards do not apply to cases in which the alleged discriminatory actions occurred prior to the effective date (July 1, 2009). Between 2009 and 2013, a
substantial proportion of Title I court cases were still decided according to

preamendment standards. That said, there is a small sample of postamendment decisions from which some preliminary findings are available.

In one study, the author examined all summary judgments in cases decided under Title I of the ADA between January 2010 and April 2013, and compared outcomes for cases decided under preamendment and postamendment standards. As expected, the proportion of summary judgments in favor of the employer was significantly lower for cases in which ADAAA standards applied, than for cases in which ADA standards applied (46 percent versus 74 percent).[35] When the standards of the ADAAA applied, there were significantly fewer summary dismissals on the grounds the plaintiff was "not disabled," but significantly more summary dismissals on the grounds the plaintiff was "not qualified." The results suggest that the ADAAA is having an effect on the number of Title I cases that proceed to trial, albeit not to the extent Congress may have expected.

The foregoing describes the current legal landscape under which persons with SMI seek competitive employment: It is clearly unlawful for employers to discriminate against qualified persons with mental disabilities. Any person with a diagnosis of schizophrenia, bipolar disorder, or other psychotic disorder should have little trouble satisfying the disability criterion under the amended ADA. It may be more difficult to convince judges they are qualified for the job, particularly given the negative stereotypes of persons with mental disorders as incompetent, unpredictable, and dangerous. In summarizing the likely impact of the ADAAA, one author states that:

> Although Congress has expressed its disapproval of how "disability" was defined under the pre-Amendments Act ADA and how so few plaintiffs were successful, it is unclear whether such congressional expression will be effective in convincing judges to grant protected class status to the most highly stigmatized sub-group of persons with impairments—those alleging mental disabilities.[36]

The clear intent of the ADAAA is to establish the rights of all persons with disabilities to work in jobs for which they are qualified. Just as persons with mental disorders have the right to live in the least restrictive environment possible, they also have the right to equal employment opportunities in the competitive workplace, wherever they are qualified. Just as a safe and permanent home can be the first step toward normal life for a homeless person, productive work can be the first step toward normalcy for a person with SMI.

The Value of Work

According to the Oxford English Dictionary, the word *work* is derived from an Old English word and has been part of the English vocabulary since at least the tenth century.[37] One of the many meanings of the word is "to accomplish, achieve; to cause, produce." No wonder so many persons with SMI say *work* is their number one recovery goal; those who accomplish, achieve, and produce are valued members of society.[38] In fact, my interest in the *Oxford Dictionary* was piqued by the involvement of one man, Dr. William Chester Minor, whose great achievement in life was his contribution to the making of the dictionary during nearly forty years of confinement in an asylum for the insane.

In April 1872, Dr. Minor was admitted to Broadmoor Asylum for the Criminally Insane in Berkshire, England. Three months earlier, around 2 a.m. on a cold Saturday morning, he had shot and killed George Merrett, a workingman on his way to the morning shift at a local brewery. When the constables arrived, Dr. Minor told them the shooting was a terrible mistake. He was chasing an intruder who had broken into his room and he had accidentally shot the wrong man.[39]

The doctor was charged with murder, but during the trial it became quite clear that he was seriously mentally ill. Dr. Minor told the constables that strangers often came to his room at night, to abuse and violate him in unspeakable ways, so he slept with a loaded revolver to protect himself. The doctor's landlady assured the court his story was unfounded—there were no intruders. Dr. Minor's brother testified that the doctor had a history of persecutory delusions. The jury returned a verdict of not guilty by reason of insanity, and the judge ordered that the doctor be confined to Broadmoor, "until her Majesty's pleasure be known."[40]

Dr. Minor's accommodations at Broadmoor were not uncomfortable. As a well-born, well-educated man with a regular income, he was given two adjoining "cells" in the least secure part of the asylum. The doctor furnished one cell comfortably as a study—with floor to ceiling bookshelves holding a small library of rare volumes. The other cell was for sleeping and painting. These two rooms would likely be the doctor's home for a long time, because the delusions of night visitations and persecution continued. Still, by day, he lacked for nothing except a useful way to employ his mind and energy.

The solution came in the form of an advertisement from the editor of the *Oxford English Dictionary* (OED). The idea for the dictionary was conceived in 1857, almost two decades before George Merrett's murder. The goals were ambitious—to create a dictionary that contained a complete etymology of every word in the English language. The origin and meanings of each word would be illustrated with literary quotations, demonstrating when and how the word was introduced into the English vocabulary. But by the time Dr. Minor was settled in Broadmoor, the project had languished for almost twenty years.

In 1878, James Murray, a schoolmaster and member of the British Philological Society, was hired to edit the dictionary. Murray sent out the advertisement for "a vast fresh corps of volunteers," to read important literary works from the sixteenth through nineteenth centuries and extract quotations for the massive dictionary.[41] Dr. Minor answered the advertisement, offering his services as a volunteer, listing his address only as "Broadmoor, Crawthorne, Berkshire." Murray responded promptly. He sent the doctor an agreement welcoming him as a volunteer reader, along with explicit instructions for reading and citing quotations. From the moment the doctor received the letter, his mental condition seemed to improve.

> The invitation seemed a long-sought badge of renewed membership in a society from which [he] had been so long estranged. By being sent these sheets of rules he was, he felt, being received back into the real world. . . . And with what he saw as this reenlistment in the ranks, so Minor's self-worth began, at least marginally, to reemerge, to begin seeping back. . . . He appears to have started recovering his confidence and even his contentment, both with every moment he spent reading Murray's acceptance letter, and then when he prepared to embark on his self-set task.[42]

Dr. Minor worked on the dictionary project for the next two decades, sending a prodigious number of quotations to Murray and his assistants, as many as one hundred a week. Yet he remained, unquestionably, seriously mentally ill. In letters to the Broadmoor superintendent, he complained that intruders entered his rooms at night and defaced his books, that the attendants were abusing him, that the hospital must install solid wooden floors to prevent fiends from creeping between the floors and ceilings, that the villagers were allowed into his room to abuse him. And yet, his work for the great dictionary continued.

In the preface to the first volume (A–B), completed in 1888, Murray generously acknowledged the "services of Dr. W. C. Minor, which have week by week supplied additional quotations for the words actually preparing for press."[43] The first complete edition of the OED, in twelve volumes, was published in 1928. Dr. Minor's work on the project was his only source of joy, purpose, and accomplishment during the years of his confinement at Broadmoor.

Postscript

Dr. William Minor was fortunate. He had an intelligent mind, well-organized thought processes, and a roomful of rare and old editions. He found a job that required intelligence, organization, and access to old books. As with Elyn Saks, his work "kept the demons away."

The amended ADA guarantees people with mental disorders equal rights in employment, but the legislation cannot guarantee that individuals are able to take advantage of their rights. Have they acquired skills and abilities that are valuable in the competitive labor market; and can they find a job that is a good match for those skills and abilities, considering any residual functional limitations? Are they willing to disclose their diagnosis to an employer, in order to access the job accommodations to which they are entitled; or are they too fearful of the stigma and negative stereotyping that may result? Most important, have they been encouraged to believe it is possible to do valuable work, even after a diagnosis of SMI?

Recall (chapter 2) the young man with schizophrenia who wanted to work as a computer programmer, but was told by his physicians that he "would not be capable of that." In this respect, David was more fortunate. Before he was discharged from his first hospital stay, Dr. Perkins told him, "You *can* recover from this disease." He says, "I held onto those words for my life."

Chapter Seven

The Disclosure Predicament

DON'T ASK. DON'T TELL.

Wilkie Collins, nineteenth-century author and playwright, is best known for his sensation novels in which apparently random forces, outside the control of the characters, propel the plots forward. Often, one or more characters narrates the story, and we discover that a secret from their past threatens to destroy them. Their efforts to evade detection place them in predicaments in which they face no good alternatives and, inevitably, their secret is revealed.

> Nothing in this world is hidden forever. . . . Look where we will, the inevitable law of revelation is one of the laws of nature: the lasting preservation of a secret is a miracle which the world has never yet seen. [1]

Persons with schizophrenia also have a secret that threatens them, and places them in a predicament: to tell, and face the stigma of mental illness; or to conceal, and cope with the stress of keeping a secret.

Summer 2002

The year after David's graduation from Chapel Hill, I accepted a faculty position at Arizona State University, and prepared to move to Phoenix. At the same time, David was preparing to move to Charlotte, where he had accepted a job as a leasing agent for an apartment complex. As his first real job postgraduation (and postschizophrenia), the leasing position had many advantages: David could live onsite for a reduced rent. His commute was trivial—a short walk from his apartment to the front office. If he became tired in the middle of the day (his medications caused fatigue), he could rest at home during his lunch hour. We helped him furnish his apartment, stocked up the cupboards and refrigerator, and, with much trepidation, prepared to leave him on his own.

David's employers knew nothing about his psychiatric history, although their job application asks about chronic physical or mental conditions. When he came to that question, David called to consult with me. "How shall I answer this, Mom?" I had no idea what to say. The question is illegal under the ADA, but if David said "you have no right to ask me this," it was certain that there would be no job offer. If he answered "yes," it was equally certain that there would be no job offer.

My brother Gordon resolved the predicament for us. He argued that the owners of the company *must* know that it is illegal to ask job applicants about their medical history because, by that time, the ADA had been in effect more than ten years. It *is* legal, however, to ask a job applicant if they have a health condition that *prevents them from performing the essential functions of the job.* Therefore, Gordon argued, that must be the intent of the question, and David should answer "no." And that is what he did.

"Say nothing to anyone. Because silence is safe."[2]

David worked in the leasing agent position for two years. None of his supervisors or coworkers ever knew about his history of psychiatric hospitalization. As he gained experience, he helped design marketing materials for the firm and was invited to regional conferences to give training seminars. But he did not particularly like the job or the schedule, which required him to work every Saturday. In 2004, he found a new job with a company that leased commercial security systems.

Fall 2004

At first, David was excited about the new position. It was a small and growing firm, and the earnings potential was good. David would be responsible for managing security contracts, negotiating contract renewals on an annual basis, and developing a long-term marketing plan for the firm. He liked the owner; and the owner liked David's energy and enthusiasm. It appeared that David had made a good career move, but the appearance was short-lived. The energy (restlessness) and enthusiasm (verbosity) that his employer admired were, in reality, the first signs of an acute psychotic episode. Unknown to me, David had been taking a reduced dose of medications ever since his relapse in 2000, and one weekend in December he had forgotten to take any at all.

Within six weeks, David was experiencing delusions and disorganized thinking. With visions of a brilliant new career, he stopped going to work. By February, his condition had deteriorated so badly that his roommates called Gordon, and Aaron and I made the trip to Charlotte to try to get David stabilized and back on his meds.

While in Charlotte, I made an appointment to meet with the owner of the security company. I believed that he deserved an explanation for David's abrupt departure. The meeting was a revelation for both of us: *He* had no idea that he was dealing with SMI. *I* had no idea how David's irrational behavior had upset the workplace.

The owner told me that David's demeanor had changed from outgoing to offensive. He was loud and overbearing in meetings and often had to be told to be quiet. He was reprimanded for making sexually inappropriate remarks to the office receptionist. And then, he just disappeared.

David's employer and coworkers were not aware of his psychiatric history, but once he stopped taking his meds, the symptoms revealed themselves. No one at work could identify the symptoms as *schizophrenia*, but they knew that something was terribly wrong.

> It is the nature of truth to struggle to the light . . . to pierce the overlying darkness, and to reveal itself to view.[3]

Fall 2007

Two years after we brought David home from Charlotte, my marriage was crumbling. It was not that schizophrenia had placed an unbearable strain on our relationship. Rather, the marriage was already stressed, and when schizophrenia came along, it was as if a glacier turned the fissures into chasms. My husband and I separated in December 2007. David chose to live with his father, because, "A guy in his thirties does *not* live with his mother." The two of them moved closer to central Phoenix, near a church that David remembered from an encounter at his psychiatric clinic months before.

On that day, David had gone to a regular appointment with his case manager. In the waiting room, he met a woman with five young children. "You have a beautiful family," he told her. "Thank you, but they're not all mine." After his appointment, David was surprised to find the woman waiting for him outside the clinic door.

"You don't need this," she told him.

"Need what?" he asked.

"The medicine."

"What do you mean?"

"You are a tortured soul."

"Huh?"

"You need to go to a church where they believe in demons."

"Where should I go?"

Pondering for a moment, she finally said, "Right across the street."

"But I can't go there. I live on 114th Street; it's too far away." After he and his father moved, the church was only a few miles from David's new home.

Phoenix First Assembly is a mega-church with a mission: "to reveal Christ to the world by loving people, cultivating community and inspiring hope."[4] The existing church was established in 1980 by Tommy Barnett, author, senior pastor, and chancellor of Southeastern University. By 2011 it was the second-largest Assembly of God church in the United States. Every day, the church aims to carry out Pastor Barnett's vision of compassionate evangelism. "Lost people matter to God, therefore they matter to us. We believe that acts of compassion express the love of God to our community."[5]

Phoenix First welcomes lost people, and I had a son who was lost. David began attending church services there regularly, and soon became involved in the Men's Ministries. One of the projects in which his group participated was the "Great Toy Giveaway." Each December, the church gives away thousands of bicycles and toys to local children who are living in foster homes or in families struggling with poverty. The bicycles are assembled, organized by size and gender, and amassed on the church grounds the day before the Giveaway. David invited me to observe the process. No matter what your religious beliefs, the sight of three thousand new bicycles gleaming in the sunshine, ready to be given away to underprivileged children, is not something you will quickly forget.

I visited Phoenix First Assembly with David in spring 2008. After the service, he introduced me to Pastor Barnett, the man whose vision created the church. The pastor held my hand, looked me in the eye, and said, "We just love your son."

I felt as if someone had pulled me out of a dark place.

"At last," I thought, "there is someone who is willing to help." Tommy Barnett did not know the nature of David's illness at the time. When David eventually told him, *it did not make any difference.*

DISCLOSING MENTAL ILLNESS IN THE WORKPLACE

The decision to disclose a mental illness at work is not simply a question of *whether* or not to disclose, but also a question of *how much* to disclose, *to whom* to disclose, and *when* and *why*. The decision is risky. Sometimes, disclosure is an empowering act that results in necessary job accommodations, as well as greater support from supervisors and coworkers. Then again, disclosure can lead to discrimination, harassment, isolation, negative stereotyping, and even job loss.[6]

Persons with mental illness generally have control over the decision to disclose their diagnosis because, unlike many physical disorders (e.g., vision or hearing impairments, paralysis or disfigurement), mental illness can often be concealed. As with the characters in Collins's novels, however, the "secret" may reveal itself, if the symptoms of mental illness become acute. Alternatively, if a worker participates in a supported employment program, disclosure happens implicitly, if not explicitly. Either a vocational staff member informs the employer about the worker's condition, or the employer knows because particular jobs are set aside for persons with disabilities.[7]

My focus is on workers with SMI in *competitive jobs*. By this I mean, jobs that pay at least the minimum wage, are not restricted to persons with disabilities, and do not involve placement by a vocational or supported employment program. In these jobs, the worker controls the disclosure decision, so long as their symptoms are concealable.

We have very little quantitative evidence pertaining to disclosure of SMI in the competitive workplace. We do not know, for example, what proportion of workers choose to disclose, what their motivations are, or whether the outcome of disclosure is likely to be positive. Most of the evidence that is available comes from descriptive studies with small sample sizes, so it is impossible to draw conclusions that are representative of the population. But the descriptive studies provide a framework from which to model the disclosure decision, by identifying the factors that determine a worker's optimal choice of privacy versus revelation.

Pros and Cons of Disclosure

The word *disclose* has roots in Middle English and Old French, where it originally meant "to unclose, open, free."[8] In modern English, disclose can mean, "to open up to the knowledge of others; to make openly known, reveal, declare," or "to reveal itself, to come to light." A *disclosure* is "a revelation, discovery, or exposure." The nuances of meaning in the words make clear the predicament that one faces in deciding whether or not to disclose a secret. On the one hand, disclosure is "freeing," on the other hand, it is "exposure." Disclosure may be a deliberate act of "revelation," or the secret may "reveal itself."

In the context of telling an employer or coworkers about SMI, disclosure may be *proactive*, a revelation designed to obtain an objective (such as job accommodations), or *reactive*, an explanation of symptoms that have made the illness difficult to conceal.[9] Either way, disclosing a condition like mental illness is a gamble that *might* result in sympathy and support, but could just as easily generate suspicion and rejection. As in the world of fiction, disclosure of private information in the real world fundamentally changes the relationship between the one who tells and the one who hears.[10]

Pros: Disclosure as Revelation

In the best-case scenario, a worker discloses their history of SMI to an enlightened employer and coworkers, who respond with sympathy and support. The worker gains the legal protections of the amended ADA and the right to reasonable accommodations for their disability. The employer is forewarned in case the worker experiences a recurrence of symptoms that affects their job performance. Informed coworkers are in a position to provide practical and emotional support in ways that increase the likelihood of successful employment. As a bonus, the worker is relieved of the stress of trying to keep a secret:

> I feel I would be happier [to disclose] because I could really be myself and not have to work so hard to make sure nobody notices that maybe I'm a little bit stressed or tired. [11]

In the best-case scenario, disclosure can have societal benefits as well as private benefits. Disclosing a diagnosis of SMI provides an opportunity to educate others about the realities of mental illness, as opposed to the negative stereotypes that perpetuate stigma. In fact, research consistently shows that the most powerful antidote to stigma is *personal contact with a stigmatized individual who is occupying a valued role.* [12] Workers who disclose a history of mental illness have a unique opportunity to counteract stereotypes of persons with mental illness as helpless, incompetent, and unable to take care of themselves. For some, this opportunity provides an additional motive to disclose:

> I like to think I've changed people's attitudes. . . . I'd just explain to them what it was like. I said "this is what it was like for me" . . . "everyone's not the same" . . . I said "I'm not dangerous or anything.". . . The only things they hear about [mental illness] are the ones on the news. [13]

Cons: Disclosure as Exposure

In the worst-case scenario, a worker discloses their diagnosis of SMI to an employer and coworkers who respond with negative stereotyping, stigma, and discrimination. Employers with strong tastes for discrimination can react in ways that adversely affect a worker's employment status. Thus, the worker who discloses SMI risks being demoted to a lower-paying job, being passed over for promotion, or even being fired. Disclosure can also trigger changes in performance expectations, with consequences of being assigned to less important tasks, having closer supervision, or being given a heavier workload. [14]

> To a certain extent, I've noticed that normal people, even though they might not work as well, they're tolerated more on a regular job than mentally ill people are. . . . I've also noticed that if you don't watch, the boss will put more on a mentally ill person to do, especially if that mentally ill person doesn't complain.[15]

Coworkers who believe the negative stereotypes may react to disclosure with avoidance, fear, hostility, or condescension (believing the worker with SMI is incompetent). As a result, a worker who discloses their history of mental illness risks becoming socially isolated from their peers. Apprehensions about being ostracized, and being perceived as "different," create powerful motives not to disclose:

> Usually when you start talking about yourself on the job, that tends to make them treat you different. . . . I don't want to tell anybody, because people who aren't ill, they do have a tendency sometimes to treat you different. They'll start teasing you or they'll shy away from you. It's a strange thing about us, the mentally ill, we've got to disguise ourselves a lot, because people who aren't ill, when they know things about you, they tend to treat you different.[16]

Paradoxically, many workers who say they *would not disclose* their diagnosis of SMI at work still believe that *work would be easier for them* if their employer knew about their illness.[17]

Two psychologists have formulated a model of the disclosure decision in which disclosure represents a trade-off between approach and avoidance motivations.[18] In this framework, the decision not to disclose SMI to an employer is primarily an *avoidance* strategy—that is, a worker sacrifices the potential advantages of job accommodations, sympathy and support, in order to avoid potential stigma and discrimination. The decision to disclose SMI is primarily an *approach* strategy. A worker risks being ostracized, demoted, or even being fired, in order to gain the legal protections of the ADAAA, emotional support from supervisors and coworkers, and relief from the stress of keeping their mental illness hidden. Either strategy is a gamble that may turn out badly.[19]

Experiences of Disclosure

It is probably a bad strategy to walk into work one morning and tell a supervisor, "I am psychotic." The outcome of that gamble is almost certain to be negative. Workers with SMI do not, however, have to be so blunt. They typically have some freedom to manage the disclosure event, because mental illness is concealable so long as symptoms are well controlled. Thus, workers with SMI can hedge on the disclosure gamble by strategically controlling how much information they disclose, and when.

Strategies

Under the ADA, a worker may disclose a disability and request employer-provided job accommodations at any time: during the hiring process, after receiving a job offer, immediately after starting a job, or at any time thereafter.[20] However, among workers with SMI who have shared their experiences with disclosure, there is almost universal agreement that revealing a history of psychiatric illness *before* hiring, will likely preclude any job offer:

> I don't think you'd get a foot in through the door that way. You wouldn't get taken on in the first place if you told them you had a big mental history.[21]

After receiving a job offer, workers who need to request job accommodations are forced (by the ADA) to tell their employer something about their illness. Workers whose symptoms of SMI are observable may also be compelled to disclose some information, even if they do not need to request accommodations. In either case, the worker may choose how much detail to provide, and what words to use in describing their diagnosis. Many workers with SMI say they are careful to avoid stigma-laden terms like "schizophrenic" or "psychotic."

> Basically, what I told them at work was that I'd got severe depression and most of them are ok with that. . . . Well, I've only told them an edited version . . . if anybody at work or my professional body knew that I'd got schizo-anything I wouldn't be allowed to practice.[22]

Some workers make up fictional diagnoses, like "metabolic disturbance" or "exhaustion syndrome," to describe their illness.[23] The workers' careful choice of language reflects an awareness of the hierarchy of stigma against different types of mental illness, namely, that depression, anxiety disorders, and other mental illnesses elicit far less stigma than schizophrenia or psychotic disorders (see chapter 2).

> I mean, you can talk about well, perhaps a depression or something but if you say "psychosis"—God forbid! When I recovered from my first episode, I tried to explain [my diagnosis to my previous employer]. . . . They were sort of interested in that they asked whether my wife is still with me, but that was it. "We can't do anything for you anymore," they said, and then they interrupted the conversation. It would have been better not to mention a word.[24]

If a worker does not need to request job accommodations, or does not have obvious symptoms of SMI, their disclosure can be strategically timed. The worker may choose to postpone disclosure until they feel secure in their position, have established themselves with their work group, and are confident about the attitudes of their supervisor and coworkers. Given the intense stigma against mental illness, that may be a long time, or never.

> Believe it or not, I've been on the job for seven months, and they do not know I have schizophrenia. They do not know I have a mental illness. They do know I have diabetes. It's incredible, when you think about it, it being a professional type job, ten and a half hours a day, nine days every two weeks, working closely with these people. I'm doing so well on my new medication that I'm virtually indistinguishable from the normal.[25]

Quantitative Evidence

Most of the evidence we have on disclosure of SMI at work comes from interviews or focus group discussions with small samples of workers with SMI. These types of studies can provide insights into personal experiences of disclosing mental illness in the workplace, but cannot answer questions like,

- What proportion of workers with SMI discloses their illness at work?
- Are they more likely to disclose to their employer or coworkers?
- Is disclosure more often proactive, or reactive?
- Are employers and coworkers more likely to respond with help and support (the best-case scenario) or stigma and discrimination (the worst-case scenario)?

I am aware of only two published studies that have sufficiently large samples to provide this type of quantitative evidence on disclosure of SMI in competitive jobs.[26]

One study reports data on workplace disclosure from a sample of 209 professionals and managers with mental illness.[27] All the respondents were employed in health or social service occupations, or in business, educational, or technical services. About 45 percent of respondents had a diagnosis of bipolar disorder, 10 percent had a diagnosis of schizophrenia, and the remainder had diagnoses of less stigmatized types of mental illness.

Overall, 80 percent of respondents said they had disclosed something about their mental illness at work. On average, they waited six months after beginning the job to disclose. One-third of those who disclosed said the decision was proactive ("when they felt comfortable"); the remainder said that disclosure was a reaction to negative circumstances associated with their illness (e.g., recurrence or escalation of symptoms, psychiatric hospitalization). Respondents who were employed in health or human services were more likely to disclose voluntarily (46 percent) than respondents who were employed in business, educational, or technical services (30 percent).

The second study draws on survey data collected by the National Alliance on Mental Illness (NAMI).[28] It is particularly relevant because the sample was comprised entirely of persons with SMI (schizophrenia, schizoaffective disorder, or another schizophrenia spectrum disorder). The survey included questions about disclosure of mental illness within various relationships (e.g., friends, extended family, employers, coworkers). A total of 258 eligible participants completed the online survey, 178 of whom responded to questions on workplace relationships.

Participants were asked to rate, for each relationship, how open they were about disclosing their diagnosis of schizophrenia. Possible responses were "not at all open" (nondisclosure), "somewhat open" or "quite a bit open" (selective disclosure), and "completely open" (full disclosure). Respondents who indicated that they had disclosed something about their diagnosis within a particular relationship were asked to evaluate whether they were treated "better," "worse," or "about the same" after disclosure.

The average respondent was not particularly open about disclosing SMI at work. Only 40 percent said that they were even "somewhat open" with their employer or coworkers[29] (compared to 80 percent of participants in the study of professionals and managers where half had diagnoses of depression or other less stigmatized mental illness). Respondents to the NAMI survey were most open about their illness in relationships with medical professionals; they were least open with neighbors, telling the neighbors little or nothing about mental illness, on average. ("People have discovered that they can fool the Devil; but they can't fool the neighbors."[30])

Among the respondents who disclosed something about SMI at work, the majority said that they were at least as well accepted by their employer and coworkers after disclosure as before. However, 38 percent of respondents reported being treated "worse" by their employer, and 35 percent reported being treated "worse" by coworkers, after they disclosed something about SMI. Among all the relationships studied, only police and corrections officers were more likely (39 percent) to dole out "worse" treatment after disclosure than employers and coworkers. At the other end of the scale, fewer than 20 percent of respondents said that they were treated "better" at work after disclosure of SMI. Among all the relationships studied (even the neighbors), coworkers were least likely to react to disclosure of SMI with "better" treatment. Only 13 percent of those who disclosed to a coworker reported being treated "better" afterward, compared to 15 percent who disclosed to a neighbor!

For this sample, neither the best-case scenario (sympathy and support) nor the worst-case scenario (stigma, discrimination, and harassment) were the norm following disclosure of mental illness at work. Most respondents, however, said that they were only "somewhat open" about their diagnosis. We can only speculate that the results would have been far more negative if the workers had said "schizo-anything."

Neither the results of the NAMI survey, nor the survey of professionals and managers with psychiatric disorders, can be generalized to describe the experience of disclosing mental illness at work. Respondents to the NAMI survey were a convenience sample contacted through NAMI affiliates nationwide. The sample was not designed to be representative of the overall population of persons with schizophrenia, or those who are employed. Respondents to the professional/manager survey were recruited through advertisement, direct solicitation, and word of mouth, hence also not representative of the population with SMI.

In short, there is no published research that describes the experience of disclosing mental illness in the competitive workplace, using data from a representative sample of workers with SMI. In part, the lack of evidence reflects the almost exclusive focus of research in this area on supported employment programs, where disclosure is almost a nonissue. In part, the lack of evidence reflects the need for a model of disclosure, which yields testable hypotheses to guide the data collection. An economic model of *rational consumer choice* provides a useful starting point for such a model.

A Rational Choice Model of Disclosure

Those who are unfamiliar with modern applications of economics in the social sciences may find it strange to view a person with schizophrenia as a "rational economic agent." Economic theory does not, however, question or pass judgment upon the preferences of the individual. It accepts preferences as they are. Without a pretense of knowing an individual's preferences, economic analysis proceeds from the *fact* that all people (including those with SMI) have preferences, and the *assumption* that people are capable of making choices that they perceive to be in their best interests. This so-called rationality postulate has been fruitfully applied not only in the narrow context of consumer choice, but also to decisions that lie well outside the traditional marketplace, such as decisions regarding marriage, fertility, and drug addiction.

Objectives of the Worker

Following this path, I use consumer choice theory as a framework for analyzing the disclosure decision in the workplace. I will not attempt to justify this approach, but merely point out that persons with SMI who are capable of independent competitive employment are not experiencing flagrant symptoms of mental illness and are capable of thinking clearly. That said, their objectives in seeking employment may differ substantially from the objectives of a "representative employee." Whereas the latter is focused on some combination of desired wages, benefits, hours, and workplace amenities,

these choice dimensions lie well outside this discussion. For both practical
and analytical purposes, I shall ignore them entirely.

Above all, the worker with SMI seeks *acceptance.* Accordingly, acceptance in the workplace becomes a valuable commodity:

> I want to work, and I want to fit in, and I want to be normal. I don't want
> people staring at me like I'm a zombie or something from the zoo. I don't want
> to be stared at like I'm different just because I have bipolar. [31]

Like most economic commodities, greater acceptance is preferred to less, up
to a level of full acceptance, where the worker with SMI is treated just like
any other worker. There is nothing complicated about the objective of maximizing acceptance; the interesting part lies in the trade-offs and constraints
that interact with it.

As noted earlier, *disclosure* is also a valuable commodity in the workplace, particularly for workers who need to request job accommodations, or
want to be "the real person they are," or are burdened by the stress of keeping
a secret. In contrast to preferences for workplace acceptance, however, it is
not always true that more disclosure is preferred to less. Workers with SMI
generally prefer to keep some details of their history of mental illness to
themselves. A simple reason is privacy:

> [If I feel forced to disclose] I'll be angry that I had to reveal the most intimate
> part of myself to people I would not want to do that with. [32]

Another reason is that some memories are painful:

> There are very, very few people that I talk about the [electroconvulsive thera-
> py] to. . . . I don't really want to talk about it because I hate it and it's
> horrible. [33]

A more complex reason not to prefer full disclosure is the likelihood that
disclosing some or all aspects of mental illness will reduce a worker's level
of acceptance. In economic terms, there is a *trade-off* between acceptance
and disclosure.

Formal economic analysis can now proceed from three assumptions: (1)
utility (i.e., happiness or satisfaction) flows from two commodities, acceptance and disclosure; (2) a worker controls the level of disclosure (i.e., symptoms are concealable), subject to a constraint that specifies the relative trade-
off between acceptance and disclosure; (3) the relative trade-off between
acceptance and disclosure varies from one workplace to another.

Trade-off between Acceptance and Disclosure

Just as consumers face trade-offs between desirable goods, because they are constrained by a budget (e.g., I can afford a new car *or* a trip to Hawaii, but not both), workers with SMI face a trade-off between disclosure and acceptance, because they are *constrained by the culture of their workplace*. Workers with SMI may selectively reveal details about their mental illness to their employer or coworkers. Afterward, the extent to which they are accepted at work is determined by the level of disclosure they choose, and the culture of the firm in which they are employed.

For lack of a more useful metric, disclosure may be viewed as a continuum ranging from zero to one. At the lower bound of nondisclosure, the worker is not at all forthcoming, keeping their diagnosis and history of mental illness completely private. At the upper bound of full disclosure, the worker is completely forthcoming, revealing both their diagnosis and entire history of mental illness. Along the disclosure continuum, the worker is somewhat forthcoming, revealing selected pieces of information (laundered diagnoses and limited histories).

Acceptance may also be viewed as a continuum from zero to one. At the lower bound of no acceptance, the worker quits their job, is terminated, or attempts to function in a hostile work environment. At the upper bound of full acceptance, the worker is treated "just like everyone else." Being treated just like everyone else does not necessarily mean an average or normal level of acceptance, because there are social hierarchies of acceptance for all workers in every workplace. The worker with SMI may, for example, exhibit some symptoms of mental illness and therefore be regarded as "odd" or "quirky." In this context, "full acceptance" implies that the worker's behavior is judged impartially (exactly as the behavior of any "quirky" employee is judged) rather than according to the negative stereotypes of mental illness. In Charlotte, David's employer interpreted his symptoms of mental illness as signs of exuberance. Other employers might have thought that he was a little crazy, but none of them could draw inferences from a label of schizophrenia because David *chose* a disclosure of zero.

Workplace cultures vary according to the rate at which the level of acceptance decreases as more details of SMI are revealed. The nature and extent of the trade-off between disclosure and acceptance defines the firm's *culture of discrimination*.[34] Workers with no mental illness are defined as fully accepted because there are no stigmatizing characteristics other than mental illness in this hypothetical workplace. Workers with SMI who choose a disclosure level of zero are also defined as fully accepted because they are sufficiently symptom-free that their illness is not exposed involuntarily.

Under these theoretical conditions, the culture of discrimination in a workplace may be represented as a continuous variable that ranges from zero ("a person with schizophrenia would be fully accepted as a coworker") to one ("a person with schizophrenia should be kept out of this workplace"). In any workplace, the level of acceptance of a worker with SMI is functionally related to the worker's level of disclosure and the culture of that workplace. So long as there is pervasive stigma against SMI, all workplaces are characterized by some level of discrimination greater than zero.

While these conditions are theoretical, the recognition that workplace cultures vary in the tolerance of mental illness is not. In a qualitative study of the impact of bipolar disorder on an individual's quality of life, for example, one worker told researchers that disclosure is not an option for him because, in the corporate environment where he works, having a diagnosis of mental illness is "a sign of weakness" and cause for dismissal.[35]

Every possible combination of disclosure and acceptance available at a firm yields a level of utility (job satisfaction) for the worker with SMI. Utility increases with acceptance up to the level of full acceptance, because workers with SMI want to be treated "just like everyone else." Utility also increases with disclosure, but only up to a *preferred level of disclosure* that is less than complete. In other words, workers with SMI view some aspects of their history of mental illness as private and "nobody's business." They would prefer to keep these details hidden even if there were no threat of stigma or discrimination. Beyond this preferred level, disclosure is perceived as a *bad*, and the worker will only disclose more if they are required to do so. If, for example, the worker needs to request job accommodations, the ADA requires that they tell their employer something about their disability, even if their preferred level of disclosure is zero..

Utility-Maximizing Level of Disclosure

Let us suppose that a worker with SMI has accepted a job and has been employed long enough to appraise the discriminatory culture of the workplace. The worker is now in a position to choose the level of disclosure that will *maximize their utility*, in other words, the level of disclosure that will make them most content, given their preferences for acceptance and privacy, and the culture of the firm in which they are employed.

As a frame of reference, consider a completely nondiscriminatory workplace, where a worker with SMI is fully accepted no matter what level of disclosure they choose. Full disclosure is feasible, with no loss of acceptance, but the rational agent will disclose only up to their *preferred level* of disclosure. Their utility is maximized at this point because they have revealed only those details of SMI that make them most comfortable and, at the same time, they are accepted "just like everyone else."

Now consider a workplace where the worker with SMI faces a trade-off between acceptance and disclosure. Without going into technical detail, I will assume that the worker with SMI has preferences for acceptance and disclosure that are represented by a "well-behaved" utility function, and that acceptance and disclosure are both "normal goods."[36] Within this framework, the worker with SMI chooses a level of disclosure that maximizes their utility subject to the trade-off between acceptance and disclosure imposed by the culture of the firm. The utility-maximizing level of disclosure will be *less than* the preferred level of disclosure because the worker values acceptance, and some acceptance is lost when more is disclosed. The worker's maximum utility is less than it would be in a nondiscriminatory firm, because they must trade off some preferred disclosure for acceptance.

Finally, consider an employment situation where there is a *compulsory level* of disclosure (e.g., because the job is set aside for workers with particular types of disabilities, or because job placement is arranged through a vocational rehabilitation program). The compulsory level of disclosure may be greater than the preferred level of disclosure that the worker would choose, even in the absence of discrimination. In this case, the worker is doubly penalized: Their utility is reduced because they are compelled to reveal details of their illness that they would prefer to keep private, and because the disclosure of these details reduces their level of acceptance. They would be happier (i.e., achieve a higher utility level) in a competitive job, with a similar culture of discrimination, where they could choose their utility-maximizing level of disclosure. In fact, they would be happier in a competitive job, with a slightly *more discriminatory* culture, where they could choose their utility-maximizing level of disclosure.

To summarize the model, it is useful to interpret the firm's culture of discrimination as the *price* that a worker with SMI pays for disclosure. For each "unit" increase in disclosure the worker pays a price in terms of the number of "units" of acceptance lost. In firms with a strong culture of discrimination, the price of disclosure is high. As the price falls, the worker with SMI chooses more disclosure and benefits from the reduced price. Even at a price of zero, however, concerns for privacy ensure that the preferred level of disclosure for most workers with SMI is less than full. For any specific price of disclosure, the worker is worse off when forced to "pay" for a level of disclosure beyond their preferred level.

The predictions of the model can be stated as formal and testable hypotheses:

Hypothesis 1—Even in a completely nondiscriminatory workplace, workers with SMI will not voluntarily disclose their entire psychiatric history, so long as they place any subjective value on privacy.

Hypothesis 2—Workers with SMI will disclose more information about their illness, and attain greater utility, in firms where the culture of discrimination (i.e., price of disclosure) is low.

Hypothesis 3—Workers with SMI who are employed at a firm that compels a level of disclosure beyond the level they would freely choose, could attain greater utility at a more discriminatory firm that does not require a specific level of disclosure.

These hypotheses are not trivial. Beginning with a preferred level of disclosure that is less than full for any individual who values privacy, the hypotheses state that the preferred level of disclosure will apply only in a hypothetical work environment where stigma does not exist. Having to seek acceptance in a discriminatory workplace, the rational worker maximizes utility by disclosing less than the preferred level. The utility-maximizing level of disclosure decreases as the culture of discrimination intensifies. In this context there are two ways to harm an employee with SMI. One is to increase the level of discrimination in the workplace; the other is to force disclosure beyond the level the worker prefers in the absence of discrimination.

Social Model of Disability

Taken together, the hypotheses establish a logical foundation for the social model of disability. According to the social model, workers with health impairments are disabled (unable to participate fully in normal life activities) more by their environment and the attitudes of society than by their functional limitations.[37] Consider, for example, an individual who cannot walk and is unable to use the restroom because their wheelchair is wider than the doorway. The social model of disability says the individual is disabled, not because they cannot walk, but because the doorway is too narrow. Thus, we have laws that public spaces and public transportation must be accessible to persons with disabilities. We have widened doorways, built entry ramps, and installed lifts on buses so people who cannot walk can still function in society. This is good.

Now consider the situation of a worker with SMI whose symptoms are in remission or controlled by medication, so they are able to work, with or without job accommodations. The rational choice model of disclosure implies that the key factor determining employment outcomes for the worker (including their job satisfaction) is the culture of discrimination in their workplace. This prediction is the very foundation of the social construct of disability, which asserts that if the individual is disabled at work it is *not* because of their illness, but because of *the stigmatizing attitudes of others*. Sadly, we have not put the same effort into changing the negative stereotypes of mental illness that foster workplace stigma, as we have put into building wheelchair ramps.

It is a fact that many persons with SMI are working in jobs where they *must disclose* all, or part of, their history of mental illness. These include supported employment jobs set aside for persons with mental disorders, and jobs with mental health agencies providing peer support for other persons with SMI. Presumably, these jobs are found in less discriminatory firms, because the firms have an institutional commitment to hiring persons with mental illness. For some workers, however, the compulsory level of disclosure in these jobs may be greater than their preferred level. Hypothesis 3 says that, given the trade-off between acceptance and disclosure, these workers could be better off at a more discriminatory, competitive firm, where disclosure is not required. To an economist, this hypothesis is obvious. To a social worker or policy wonk, it may be a disturbing "revelation."

Postscript

In his classic book on stigma, Erving Goffman calls the phenomenon of nondisclosure, "passing" (as normal).[38] Passing is possible for persons who have a discreditable stigma, one that is subject to prejudice but not readily apparent to others. Such is the case for persons with SMI, who face a *predicament*: "to tell or not to tell; to let on or not to let on; to lie or not to lie; and in each case, to whom, how, when, and where."[39] The person who passes creates a false identity for themselves, accepting treatment as a "normal" under false pretenses. Nevertheless, the rewards to being perceived as normal are so great, that the temptation to conceal is strong, despite the practical and psychological problems it creates. Many of these problems have been discussed throughout this chapter, but Goffman describes an additional predicament that is worth noting here.

In particular, the individual who passes "will feel torn between two attachments."[40] One is to the stigmatized group that is their real identity; the other is to the normal group from which they seek acceptance. The individual "leaves himself open to learning what others *really* think" of people with SMI, because they do not know that the individual is "one of them." In these situations, the individual faces an additional predicament: to defend their real identity and betray their secret, or to endorse the negative stereotypes that (secretly) apply to themselves.

> [When my co-workers were making disparaging remarks about people with mental illness] . . . for a split second I sort of thought well I could roll my sleeves up and say "You mean someone crazy like me?" Because that always shocks people and they say "Oh well you don't look like one of them." It's like, what am I meant to look like?[41]

Persons with schizophrenia look like just anyone else, and when their symptoms are under control, they are pretty much just like anyone else. They want to be accepted, to be productive, and to keep some parts of their lives private. They can make rational decisions in their own self-interest. *They can work*. They have had experiences of illness unlike other people, but they are disabled, not so much by their illness, as by the negative stereotypes that create an invisible cage around their lives.

Chapter Eight

Finding a Good Job Match

SAVED MY LIFE

On the corner of Grand and Weldon Avenues in central Phoenix is an old Embassy Suites Hotel, which is now home for Anthony, an eighteen-year-old "graduate" of Arizona Child Protective Services. Anthony is part of an outreach program operated by the Phoenix Dream Center, which provides housing, education, emotional and spiritual support for youth who are transitioning from the foster care system to independent living. The foster youth program is only one of the ministries operated by the Dream Center, which provides housing to more than three hundred persons served by its programs in the renovated hotel.[1]

The Phoenix Dream Center was founded by Pastor Tommy Barnett in 2006 to serve as the nucleus for the outreach ministries of his church. Through its faith-based curricula and assistance with basic needs, the Dream Center aims to rescue the vulnerable, rebuild lives, and restore hope. Anthony, who had lived in foster care homes since age four, says he came to the Dream Center,

> looking for how to be independent, how to take care of myself, and be on my own. Before I came, I didn't know God. But God is really not that bad once you get to know Him.[2]

Spring 2009

David had been attending Phoenix First Assembly for nearly a year when he applied to volunteer at the Dream Center. The volunteer application required a personal testimony. David replied guardedly, saying that he had "struggled mentally," and his life "had been off track," before he found the church and felt called to serve. His application was accepted and he was put to work immediately.

I went on a tour of the Dream Center one Tuesday morning. It was something like going to Open House nights when David was in school. Once again, I was "David's mom," only now there were coworkers, instead of teachers, telling me how much they loved my son. David showed me his office and his desk, and he was as proud as any first grader to have his own workspace. I am not sure which one of us was more in need of the validation that this job provided, probably both of us.

Throughout the summer and fall of 2009, David volunteered part time in various capacities at the Dream Center. Working part time gave him the flexibility he needed to reintegrate into employment. In January he began taking courses in Christian Ministry at American Indian College (AIC), a small Christian college in the Phoenix area. I was delighted that he was motivated, and meeting people, and too busy to join me for dinner most Friday nights. Still, I waited and watched for signs of another relapse.

Winter 2010

The primary ministry at the Dream Center is its "Church on the Street" outreach program. Church on the Street is a fifteen-month discipleship program designed to help men and women recover from incarceration, substance use issues, or physical, sexual, or emotional abuse. Participants (called disciples) live on-site at the Dream Center, attend classes and worship services, and conduct more than forty outreach ministries each week on the streets of inner-city Phoenix. The program is designed to reach out to the homeless population and other needy persons in the city, as well as to teach the disciples positive coping skills, and to restore them to healthy relationships with their families. Unfortunately, for some participants there is no supportive family to welcome them home at the end of the program. For others, living with their family would simply encourage a return to the cycle of bad choices and unhealthy behavior that they are trying to escape.

Toward the end of 2009, administrators at the Dream Center decided to start a new ministry, called the "Working Men's Program," which would provide housing for some of the graduates of Church on the Street as they transitioned to paid employment. The plan was to renovate unused space at the Dream Center, to be used as apartments for graduates who had no family support system. Men who participated in the program would pay a small monthly rent from their earnings. In return, they could continue to live in the safe and familiar environment of the Dream Center, even as they began a new job in the "real world."

When the lead pastor asked David to direct the new program, he was amazed. By this time he had disclosed his diagnosis of schizophrenia to

Tommy Barnett and other pastors at the Dream Center. David could not believe that they would entrust the leadership of a new program to someone with a history of mental illness. Over 95 percent of staff members at the Dream Center are volunteers, yet the leadership team had offered David a paid job, and a set of keys. He would be earning a paycheck again, after five years out of work.

Over the next few months, David developed guidelines and eligibility criteria for the Working Men's Program, hired an assistant, created marketing materials, and supervised renovations of the living space. He enrolled the first participants in the program, managed their agreements, and collected their program fees. As the rooms filled and the program began to stabilize, David's responsibilities expanded to other ministries. He took over one of the Saturday morning outreach ministries and began preaching at the Spanish service on Sunday mornings. He helped design and renovate rooms for the foster youth program, which Anthony eventually joined.

In 2012, David invited me back to the Dream Center to see the space prepared for another new program, called the Rescue Project. The Rescue Project aims to restore the lives of women and girls who are victims of human sex trafficking, or who are dealing with crisis pregnancies.[3] The program provides medical and legal services, therapy and counseling, and opportunities to earn a high school diploma or GED, while the women live on-site at the Dream Center. David wanted me to see the new space because each suite was designed by one of the top interior decorators in the Phoenix area. The designers competed to create the dream rooms that these girls never had as children, providing a real and symbolic contrast between their old lives and the new.

If you search Google+ for the Phoenix Dream Center, you will find several reviews. One of them simply says, "Saved my life." I could add, "Saved my son."

JOB MATCHING

David was fortunate to find a perfect job match at the Dream Center, first as a volunteer, then as director of the Working Men's program. The essence of job matching is that workers with disabilities have functional limitations that affect their productivity in some, but not necessarily all, jobs. A worker with SMI whose symptoms include compulsive organizing and checking, for example, might be highly successful as a filing clerk, but virtually useless as a short-order cook. A worker whose symptoms include insomnia or hypersomnia might be perfectly capable of working as a massage therapist, with a flexible schedule, but unable to retain a position as a bank manager, with fixed hours. In general, workers with disabilities who are able to *match* themselves into jobs that minimize the impact of their functional limitations on important job functions can expect better employment outcomes (e.g., higher wages, longer job tenure) than their counterparts who are *mismatched* in jobs where their functional limitations have greater impact.

Finding a good job match can be viewed as the most basic type of job accommodation for workers with disabilities, for at least two reasons. One, the objective of job matching and job accommodation is the same, namely, to minimize the impact of functional limitations on worker productivity. Two, a good job match is the foundation that determines if other accommodations are reasonable and potentially effective. The worker who is a compulsive organizer, for example, may be an effective short-order cook if his employer hires an assistant to keep the kitchen immaculate, but no one is likely to consider such an accommodation to be *reasonable.* The bank manager who experiences insomnia or hypersomnia might be allowed to work flexible hours, but such an accommodation will not enable them to perform the *essential functions* of the job, namely, to supervise bank operations during business hours. These workers are simply mismatched in their jobs.

Job matching has received little attention in the literature on accommodating workers with disabilities. Even when finding a better job match is the most obvious way to increase a worker's productivity, it is typically not suggested. Addison's disease, for example, is a rare hormonal disorder often characterized by weight loss and sensitivity to cold. The Job Accommodation Network (JAN) offers several ways of accommodating Addison's disease, including, wearing specially designed clothing, installing space heaters, and redirecting air conditioning vents. But it neglects the obvious accommodation of transferring to a job out of the cold![4]

Among the population of persons with SMI, there are those with the skills, abilities, and interests to hold almost any job in the economy.[5] The key to their success is finding a good match between their unique skill set, the characteristics of the job, and the functional limitations associated with their illness. My purpose here is to identify the characteristics of firms, and the types of jobs, that make a good match for persons with SMI. To do so, we must first specify the nature of the functional limitations typically associated with a serious mental illness.

Functional Limitations of SMI

Persons with SMI have an *impairment* which may result in *functional limitations.* In other words, their health condition may restrict their ability to perform some of the normal functions of daily living, like concentrating, carrying on a conversation, or managing stress. If the functional limitations interfere with one or more major life activities (e.g., working) the individual is *disabled* according to the criteria of the ADA.

Serious mental illnesses are characterized by a complex array of symptoms that primarily affect an individual's cognitive, emotional, or social capacities, although physical limitations (e.g., maintaining stamina) may be apparent as well.[6] Symptoms are highly variable across patients and, at the same time, the boundaries that define specific disorders (e.g., schizoaffective disorder and bipolar disorder) are indistinct.[7] So, *patients with the same diagnosis may exhibit considerable variation* in the nature and severity of their functional limitations, and *patients with different diagnoses may exhibit similar* functional limitations. Despite the considerable variation in the manifestations of SMI, the following generalizations are useful:

- *Cognitive* limitations are highly prevalent among persons with schizophrenia, albeit to varying degrees. The limitations may be generalized, or affect specific domains of cognitive functioning, such as *working memory, attention span, processing speed, verbal fluency,* and *task flexibility.*[8] Disorganized thinking and behavior are also characteristic of schizophrenia, particularly in the acute phase, and may affect a worker's ability to *stay focused* or *meet deadlines.*
- *Emotional* withdrawal and depression are common in schizophrenia, and extreme fluctuation in emotions is the hallmark symptom of bipolar disorder. Workers with SMI may have emotional limitations that make it difficult to *maintain concentration, to manage stress and emotions,* or *to deal with changes in the workplace.*
- *Social* interactions involving a person with schizophrenia can be strained and tense, given the emotional withdrawal and paucity of language that characterize the disease. In the workplace, social limitations may create *problems working effectively with supervisors,* or *problems interacting with coworkers and customers.*

The problem of job matching is to identify a job where the worker's functional limitations have little or no impact on important job functions. An individual who has difficulty maintaining stamina, for example, may be highly productive as a part-time teacher. An individual who has difficulty interacting with people may be a superb editor, working in a private office. An individual who has difficulty dealing with stress may thrive as a data analyst producing standardized reports. By necessity, the process of job matching is highly individualized, but it *is* possible to define general characteristics of jobs that are a good match for workers with SMI.

Workplace Characteristics that affect Job Matching

Two researchers who study management processes have developed a model of the way persons with disabilities are treated within organizations, which is relevant to the job matching process for workers with SMI. According to the model, the key determinants of how an individual with disabilities is treated-within an organization are individual characteristics (e.g., functional limita-tions), environmental factors outside the control of the organization (e.g., legislation, such as ADA, mandating job accommodations for workers with disabilities), and characteristics of the organization itself (e.g., inclusiveness of the organizational culture).[9] In applying the model to job matching, I am focused particularly on organizational characteristics.

With reference to the workplace, the relevant characteristics can be parsed into three categories: the nature of the *firm* in which the individual is employed, the *relationships* the individual establishes at work, and the nature of the *job* the individual has been hired to do. To be more specific:

- *Firm characteristics* describe the type of firm (e.g., public or private sec-tor, number of employees, industry), the nature of the work environment (e.g., workplace culture, physical characteristics of the workplace, and the policies and procedures established within the firm's management proto-cols).
- *Workplace relationships* describe interactions with supervisors, cowork-ers, or customers. These relationships can be defined by the nature and extent of contact with each group, the frequency and severity of conflict, and experiences of stigma and discrimination.
- *Job characteristics* describe the essential functions of a job, as character-ized by the ADA, as well as a number of ancillary characteristics that define the employment contract (e.g., the number of work hours required; the work pace and schedule; the degree of autonomy the worker has to organize their work).

The literature is largely silent with regard to the combinations of work-place characteristics that are amenable to good job matches for workers with SMI. Some of the best evidence comes from a small focus group study that I conducted with a colleague, Rebecca White. The purpose of the study was to identify workplace characteristics that facilitate, or impede, successful em-ployment outcomes for workers with SMI.

Qualitative Study

In 2003, Professor White conducted three focus group sessions with thirteen mental health professionals working in the southwest. Mental health profes-sionals are the frontline staff in outpatient clinics or private practices, provid-ing direct services to persons with disabling mental illnesses. All of the focus group participants had at least two years of professional experience as a mental health clinician, at least five years of experience in vocational counseling, and had a history of providing services to people with SMI from a wide range of occupations. They were employed as clinical social workers, employee assistance counselors, vocational rehabilitation counselors, or private-practice therapists. All focus group participants were currently serving at least one client with SMI who was working, or seeking to work, in a competitive job.

The research was designed to identify characteristics that help a person with SMI succeed in the competitive workplace, as well as characteristics that make successful employment less likely. Dr. White posed open-ended questions that were intended to encourage discussion among participants. Two questions pertained specifically to workplace characteristics: (1) As a group, can you describe the *ideal work environment* for someone with a serious mental illness? (2) Can you describe the *worst work environment* for somebody with SMI?

The subject of job match (or mismatch) came up repeatedly in the focus group discussions. Participants were keenly aware that the probability of successful employment for workers with SMI depends not only on the skills and abilities of the worker, but also on the extent to which workplace factors accommodate the worker's functional limitations. The comments of Joe and Sarah (names have been changed to protect the participants' anonymity) are instructive:

> *Joe:* To me, it's a match. It's a game of matching the right individual with the right kind of position and the right kind of company, and trying to look at the process . . . six months to a year down the line.

> *Sarah:* The most important is to fit the personalities and the environment and the skills and then the person needs to be allowed to succeed or fail on their own merit and not on the basis of an illness or a diagnosis or what somebody did or didn't do for them.

Below, I draw further on the focus group discussions, as well as the limited research literature, to identify specific workplace factors (firm characteristics, workplace relationships, and job characteristics) that are more (or less) amenable to workers with SMI.

Firm Characteristics

Workplace Culture

One study of the relationship between workplace characteristics and employment outcomes for workers with disabilities used data from a survey conducted through the National Bureau of Economic Research.[10] The survey involved nearly thirty thousand employees of fourteen U.S. companies, at

175 individual worksites. The data did not distinguish among different types of disabilities.

Drawing on this large database, the authors identified workplace characteristics that produced better employment outcomes (e.g., wages, hours worked, job satisfaction) for workers with disabilities relative to their nondisabled counterparts. A key consideration was how employment outcomes for workers with disabilities related to differences in corporate culture across worksites. The results indicated that the worksites that were advantageous for workers with disabilities were those perceived by workers with and without disabilities as "fair" and "responsive to employee concerns." A fair and responsive workplace culture was associated with lower expected job turnover, greater loyalty to the firm, and greater job satisfaction among workers with disabilities.[11]

A smaller study, specific to workers with mental disorders, supports the findings on workplace culture. The authors conducted semi-structured interviews with seventeen mental health service users in Britain, who were participating in employment projects for persons with SMI. The purpose of the study was to identify what types of support, and what types of workplace accommodations, were needed to achieve successful work outcomes in open (competitive) employment settings. The researchers found that the extent to which clients' needs could be met revolved largely around aspects of workplace culture. In particular, "a relaxed informal atmosphere, a culture within which difference was accepted, [and] a concern for employees' welfare" were most conducive to successful work outcomes for clients.[12]

The importance of a *supportive and responsive workplace culture* is echoed in the conversations of our focus groups:

Felicity: I think the culture of the company can make a difference. I noticed with one person where the culture that was very supportive and caring and so forth and an individual worked very well, but then a militaristic-type company bought out the former company and it just made that person go into a number of manic episodes. I think the culture and the management style is critically important.

Brenda: I use the term supportive. I don't mean when other people aren't being . . . nicey-nice and stuff like that, but the protocol within the system supports people being able to do their [best and make mistakes] without having such serious repercussions that they cannot recoup and move on.

Many of the characteristics of a workplace culture that support and encourage workers with SMI are also supportive for workers with physical disabilities, and nondisabled workers. But as "Brenda" suggests, workers with SMI may have less tolerance than other workers for a culture that is bureaucratic, rigid, or insensitive to individual employees.

Physical Environment

Similarly, the physical environment of the workplace matters to workers with and without disabilities, but workers with SMI may be especially sensitive to it because of their functional limitations.[13] Workers whose functional limitations make it difficult to stay focused and meet deadlines will likely struggle in a work environment that is frenzied and hectic, such as the newsroom of a daily newspaper. When we asked our focus group participants to identify specific characteristics of the physical environment that could be challenging for workers with SMI, they said:

> *Angie:* [A workplace that is] very regimented. Loud, chaotic, always changing. . . . It's probably the same work environments that are hard for anybody. It's just the tolerance starts earlier and the ability to adapt to it. Or they just refuse to [adapt].

> *Michael:* Loud, unstructured, high demand and no real supervisory support. It's kind of like if somebody already has a lot going on with their mind, their thoughts, and then the environment is also nonstop, maybe like a cubicle kind of situation where it's that low-level din of busyness and there's noise and that can be very hard on people [with SMI].

All our focus group participants agreed that a noisy, chaotic workplace is likely not a good job match for workers with SMI. They had mixed opinions, however, when asked what size firm tends to be most supportive. Some focused on the friendlier culture of a small firm, while others emphasized the resources of large firms and the mandates of the ADA (that do not affect firms with fewer than fifteen employees):

> *Joe:* In my experience, it's usually been a small company [that is more supportive]. It's like your Mom and Pop pizza shop or a small medical office where a person can manifest their symptoms in a safe environment and people will not be freaked out.

> *Simon:* I think that the larger employers don't want to be sued by ADA and I think it's important. So it helps to have government contracts and be a big employer if you want to be mentally ill and also [it helps if you] have worked there for ten, fifteen, or twenty years!

A study conducted by researchers at Cornell University also reached mixed conclusions regarding the impact of firm size on employment outcomes for workers with disabilities. The authors collected survey data from more than eight hundred human resource professionals to examine how firms of different sizes were complying with the accommodations mandate of the ADA. The results indicated that large (greater than five hundred employees) and small firms were equally likely to provide job accommodations needed by employees with disabilities.[14] Large firms were better prepared and more experienced in providing a wide variety of accommodations, but small firms had less difficulty "changing attitudes of coworkers/supervisors," when accommodations involved workplace relationships.

Workplace Relationships

Workplace relationships are important to the success of any worker, but particularly so for workers with SMI. The relationships that a worker with SMI establishes with supervisors and coworkers can be crucial to their success.

Supervisor

The most important workplace relationship for a worker with SMI is likely to be with their immediate supervisor. This is the person who trains them, oversees their daily tasks, and evaluates their job performance. Perhaps most importantly, this is the person to whom they must disclose their mental illness if they need to request employer-provided job accommodations. Research indicates that supervisors who are a good match for workers with SMI are those who treat workers with respect, provide constructive feedback, and express genuine concern about their employees' welfare.[15]

For workers whose functional limitations include memory deficits and difficulties maintaining concentration, the best match is with a supervisor who establishes clear expectations and boundaries, provides adequate training (including a breakdown of job tasks into manageable units), and provides support when problems arise.[16] Our focus group respondents emphasized the need for supervisors to accommodate the individual needs of employees, but cautioned against supervisors who are hypervigilant in overseeing an employee's every move:

> *Felicity:* I think if the supervisor has an understanding [that], whether it's mental illness or not, different people have different needs to operate to their capacity. Some people need a little bit of attention; other people like to be totally independent.

> *Anne:* Well, to me structure is when there's a set job and protocol by which the job is done. Where expectations about what . . . people should be [doing] in the office, what is the general flow of the day's structure

[are clear] . . . versus supervision which is a . . . manager who is really eyeballing over the shoulder on a continuous basis . . . [asking for] quality assessment reports and time studies . . . and it's like the person has to practically write down when they signed out for the bathroom and when they came back and how many minutes was that.

Coworkers and Customers

Coworker relationships can be critically important to workers with SMI in competitive jobs. Supportive coworkers can increase a worker's confidence, make them feel comfortable in the workplace, help them adjust to the requirements of their job, and provide support through periods of difficulty. [17] In contrast, coworkers who are critical and demanding, or who harass workers whom they perceive to be "different," create conflict in the workplace. Such hostility obviously makes it more difficult for a worker with SMI to succeed.

> *Felicity:* I think the term respect is the best one I can come up with. That within a work situation we all would like to be respected for what we bring to the work situation, to the work that needs to be done. Telling a group of colleagues [to] respect that someone may be having some difficulties with anxiety but that person can still get this job done and [to] focus on that rather than focusing on, "Did you know that she's leaving early every Tuesday afternoon to go see her therapist?"

Ironically, the development of respectful and supportive relationships at work can be hampered by the very functional limitations that characterize SMI. The issue is especially acute when a worker's functional limitations include emotional withdrawal or problems with anger management. So, even though a worker with SMI may need the support and understanding of coworkers, they may not have the social skills to develop a relationship that elicits those responses. One of our focus group respondents expressed the predicament this way:

> *Sandy:* In my experience you have two parts of work. You have the task that you're expected to do every day but almost as big as that is this whole thing that we do every day socially. It's the potlucks; it's who's putting in for so-and-so's baby shower; who's taking their lunch when, with whom. Workers with SMI really lack those skills and it's those skills that could get them into trouble. So if their coworkers could be inclusive and invite them into that environment, or that social aspect of work, but then also respect the fact that they might not want to be doing that. It's a fine line. It says, "Please invite me but then also understand that there may be days where I just can't do it."

Another workplace relationship that can be challenging for workers with SMI is the relationship with customers. Any job that involves dealing with angry, impatient customers will be difficult for most workers with a history of mental illness, because conflict is the nature of the job, and conflict aggravates anxiety and stress.[18] In other words, working in the customer relations department of any large organization will almost certainly be a mismatch for a worker with SMI. Our focus group respondents agreed. When asked about workplace factors that make competitive employment difficult for workers with SMI, several of our focus group respondents immediately said:

Ken: Demanding customers.

Joe: Customer service is not good. That's just my opinion.

Job Characteristics

Occupation

Surprisingly, a worker's occupation is not particularly important in defining a good job match for workers with SMI. The mental health professionals who participated in our focus groups had worked with nurses, engineers, computer programmers, technicians, plumbers, teachers, roofers, telemarketers, construction installers, janitors, phlebotomists, medical assistants, accountants, sales persons, computer repairers, executive directors, program coordinators, nurse's aides, a prep-worker in a fast-food restaurant, a radio disk jockey, in short, a vast array of occupations.

> *Brenda:* We've run the gamut [of occupations]. That's real fun as a rehab counselor because it's then again people achieving their level of potential, utilizing their transferable skills and sometimes along the way the agency helping them with training [and] education, which we do a lot. That's fun. It's really nice.

As Brenda notes, one of the characteristics of a good job match for workers with SMI is that the job allows them *to achieve their potential.* For those whose residual symptoms are severely disabling, a part-time, low-skill job, with or without employment support, may be a sufficient challenge. But many persons who are recovering from mental illness aspire to more than entry-level work.

The desire for more challenging work was a prominent theme emerging from a study of the way persons with SMI navigate employment. Researchers conducted in-depth interviews with thirty-two persons who have significant psychiatric disabilities. Respondents expressed dissatisfaction with vocational rehabilitation counselors who offered low-wage jobs that were neither challenging nor interesting:

> I think the problem that we have with the [VR] program is that we have what is called blue-collar positions, and they probably don't have a means to place you in more difficult things. . . . When people get mentally ill they don't lose their intelligence. So there should be fields for mental illness that could use a higher IQ.[19]

Too often, well-meaning relatives, friends, or mental health providers discourage patients with SMI from seeking anything more than low-level work. The message conveyed to patients is that their future, including the kind of work they can do, is limited by the severity of their illness. Most of the study participants had received these kinds of negative messages regarding their potential work capacity.[20] Some were told by mental health providers that they would never work again. Others were placed by vocational rehabilitation counselors into low-wage, low-skill jobs, and then discouraged from seeking more challenging work because they might experience a relapse, or lose their SSDI benefits. When the focus is on the *illness* rather than the person, "often an individual's talents, abilities, and interests are simply forgotten or unwittingly relegated to the background by the concerned and well intentioned individuals around them."[21]

Work Processes

Provided that the knowledge, skills, and abilities required for a job are a good match for the skills and abilities of the worker, the job characteristics that are most critical for workers with SMI are *autonomy, flexibility*, and *consistent expectations*. These characteristics of the work process facilitate the success of almost any worker, but are particularly important for workers with SMI because of the nature of the functional limitations associated with mental illness. For workers who have difficulty with interpersonal relationships, some degree of autonomy at work is important. For workers who have difficulty dealing with change, consistency of expectations is important. For almost any worker with SMI, flexibility in the way work is accomplished is crucial, because *flexibility allows a worker to adapt their job to their specific functional limitations*. When we asked our focus groups "What characteristics make a job a good match for workers with SMI?" one participant told us:

> *Michael:* Flexibility of schedule. [Flexibility of] work hours. I think that helps folks a lot. Part-time jobs seem to be almost ideal for a lot of folks because full time is a lot, but when there's a flexible kind of schedule and there's that lack of pressure like, "I've got to be here at this time." It helps accommodate, sometimes, a symptom flow.

With respect to other work processes, finding a good job match is a highly individual undertaking. Some workers with SMI find working alone to be intimidating; others thrive on the flexibility that comes from working by themselves. For some workers, the pressure of a job with managerial responsibilities (e.g., overseeing finances, inventories, or other people) is too stressful, but there are many individuals with SMI who are successful accountants, executives, and even kindergarten teachers! Working with computers can be daunting for some workers with SMI; others find that a computer helps them drown out symptoms and focus on job tasks:

> *Simon:* One of the things that is just amazing to me is to take a person who is very, very psychotic, with a lot of symptoms, and put them in front of a computer and it's just great! It's the focus, I think. I have found that if the job has a real focus, then a lot of the symptoms go away while they're focused.

In defining the job requirements that make a good job match for a worker with SMI, there are only a few general rules: The expectations should be consistent; the tasks should be achievable but fulfilling; and the work processes should be flexible. And the greatest of these is flexibility.

Job Matching as a Supply Side Intervention

In the United States, efforts to improve employment outcomes for workers with disabilities have focused almost exclusively on demand-side interventions in the labor market. The ADA and its amendments place the burden of providing job accommodations for workers with disabilities squarely on employers. Although well-intentioned, disability employment policies that focus on employer-provided job accommodations are inherently condescending, such policies emphasize the limitations associated with disability, and implicitly assume that workers with disabilities must be treated differently from others. Many workers with SMI reject these assumptions and choose not to request employer-provided job accommodations at all.[22]

A recurrent theme of this book is to encourage the redirection of disability employment policies to focus on the supply-side of the labor market, for example, by ensuring that persons with SMI acquire human capital that is valued by employers. Job matching is a supply-side policy because it emphasizes placing workers with SMI in jobs that minimize the impact of their functional limitations, hence increasing their value in the labor market. The topic of job matching has received hardly any attention from policy makers, funding agencies, or administrators of the mental health system. Yet the extant literature, combined with excerpts from our focus group participants, demonstrate that the process of job matching should be a critical component of any approach to accommodating workers with mental disabilities.

In fact, job matching can be viewed as the most basic accommodation for workers with disabilities. If a good job match is found, few additional accommodations will be needed. If the job has sufficient flexibility, any additional accommodations can be initiated by the worker, without the need to involve their employer or disclose their diagnosis of SMI. Hence, job matching has the potential to minimize the need for employer-provided accommodations, which impose financial costs on the employer, indirect costs on coworkers, and psychological costs on the employee with SMI.

Employment policies that focus on the supply side of the labor market are inherently empowering because they emphasize the capabilities and autonomy of the worker with SMI. By focusing on accumulation of human capital, and job placements that are a good match for both the talents and functional limitations of the worker, supply-side politics have the potential to reduce dependency on SSDI and SSI.

To promote the concept of job matching, I have identified a number of workplace characteristics that make a good match for the typical worker with SMI. These include: a *workplace* culture that is flexible and supportive; workplace *relationships* that are respectful and reflect genuine concern for individuals; and a *job* with clear and consistent expectations, flexible work processes, and tasks that are appropriate for the worker's skills and abilities. Ultimately, however, the process of finding a good job match is an individual one. Our focus group data suggest that process is happening, for some unknown number of workers with SMI, and it is effective.

> *Brenda:* I'll tell you what, the cool thing is and I don't know if it [is a change] that was conscious or something that was just happening. But [ever] since I've been in this business I know that the trend was to get individuals into entry level positions . . . get them working, get them in a job. What I've seen happen more so lately is that individuals who are getting jobs are more able to sustain themselves financially and get off of benefits and that's just been really cool, the independence and the empowerment and the transformation I've seen in individual's lives because of it.

Postscript

When David first began work at the Dream Center, he had not experienced an acute episode of psychosis for five years. He had also not held a regular job (or any job) for five years. He no longer had delusions about being God, but he was still passionate about his religious beliefs, and religion was his favorite topic of conversation. His medications made him tired, especially in the mornings. He was not accustomed to being around people, other than his parents and the few friends that he had made at church. He was anxious about returning to work and insecure about his capabilities. His cognitive abilities were intact, but he was perhaps more rigid in his opinions and less flexible with changes in routine than he was before schizophrenia. His disease was in remission and he could work, if he could find the right job.

The Dream Center was an almost ideal workplace for David. Its mission is to serve as a resource for needy populations in the City of Phoenix, including the homeless, at-risk youth, families with limited financial resources, persons with alcohol and substance use issues, and persons newly released from prison. By its very nature, the culture of the Dream Center is supportive and tolerant of differences. A person with SMI fits right in!

The Dream Center is a nonprofit organization sponsored by Phoenix First Assembly Church. All its programs are centered on the ideals of the Christian faith, and many of its staff members serve in the ministry. David's deep spiritual convictions and inclination to talk about Christianity were not unusual there. He was accepted, included, and respected by his coworkers and supervisors.

As a volunteer in a newly created position, David had considerable flexibility to set his own work hours (he usually started work after 9 a.m., and worked two to three days a week) and to work at his own pace (there were no deadlines for most of his projects). As his confidence increased, his responsibilities expanded to giving weekly tours of the Dream Center and eventually to running the Working Men's Program. He achieved his goals of launching the new program, completing his associate's degree at AIC, and serving the missionary outreach of the church. The job was full of purpose and challenge (one Christmas his wish list included several books on leadership and management).

The job at the Dream Center was *almost* ideal. The problem was that, even after David started being paid, the income was small and there were no benefits. The job was not on a career path that led to financial security or independence from government support. But it was a perfect job from which to find that path.

Chapter Nine

Job Accommodations for Workers with SMI

A LONG WAY FROM PARIS

I met Chung Choe while he was a graduate student at the University of Arizona, studying for a doctoral degree in economics. He shared my research interests in workplace discrimination and workers with disabilities and hoped that we might collaborate in the future. After graduation, Chung accepted a position at a research institute in Luxembourg. One day I received an email from him, inviting me to spend a month at the institute as part of their Visiting Professor program. "How far is it to Paris?" I wrote back. "Two hours by train," Chung replied.

And so, in June 2010, I was in Luxembourg. On a long weekend I took the train to Paris for four carefree days of art museums, croissants, cathedrals, and *joie de vivre.*

Summer 2010

Chung and I were working at the institute one stifling afternoon (the building had no air conditioning), when I realized that I had not received a single email from David for three weeks. It was odd, because we talked several times a week when I was at home. I confided to Chung that I was worried about my son. He simply smiled and said, "He's met a girl." Impossible, I thought.

Nevertheless, when I returned home in July, David introduced me to Alex. The two had met at the Dream Center that spring and planned to be married on Labor Day weekend! Alex had three young children. I liked her very much; I always liked my sons' girlfriends. (My colleagues once told me it was because my sons were smart enough to introduce me only to the girls I was sure to like.)

We had a short two months to plan a wedding. Alex had no family in the area, so I volunteered to help in any way I could. The two of us shopped for a wedding dress and wedding clothes for her daughters. We addressed and mailed the invitations. We reserved the church for the ceremony and a small reception. One day, David went along with us to order flowers. Alex and I sat down to talk with the florist, but David could not stay still. He kept jumping up, collecting flowers that he liked, experimenting with different color combinations. When he wasn't bouncing out of his chair, he was talking nonstop. I had seen this behavior before.

As we left the store, I asked if he was taking his medicine.

No, he had been off his meds for five months.

Years later, David told me how he had weaned himself off the antipsychotic drugs. In January 2009, he told his psychiatrist that he had been taking a reduced dose of medication and wanted to get off the meds entirely. His doctor agreed to help. Together, they formulated a plan: David saw the psychiatrist every three months; every six months they reduced his dosage of antipsychotics by 30 milligrams. By March 2010, David was off the drugs completely.

I was more than a little distressed by the signs of relapse, certain that David would have another psychotic episode if he did not resume the medications. My distress triggered a firestorm. Alex asked David to go back on the medications "for her sake." He said no. When she then sought my advice, I told her bluntly, "If I were you, I'd run as far away as I could." Alex broke off the engagement. I helped with the process of un-inviting guests and canceling the church and flowers. The wedding dress hung in my closet (where it remained for nearly two years). Meanwhile, I prepared to deal with the relapse that was sure to come. Paris seemed very far away and long ago.

Fall 2010

David did not seem too upset about the canceled wedding plans. He continued working at the Dream Center and attending classes at AIC. As November approached, he asked if he could invite a few friends from the college to share Thanksgiving dinner at my new condominium. I thought it might be fun to show off my new home, so I agreed to do the cooking. A few days before the holiday, I asked David how many friends he expected. "Oh, twenty to twenty-five," he said.

I bought another turkey and doubled my recipes.

What an eclectic group we had for Thanksgiving that year! There was David's favorite professor, who had recently moved to Arizona, but whose family was still back east. There were two Native American women from his classes. There was an African American man and his three teenage daughters. Twenty people in all, crammed into my little home. Before we sat down to eat, David asked everyone to join hands as he said grace.

How much fun it was to listen to the conversation around that Thanksgiving table! The Native Americans told us about their Thanksgiving traditions; the three teenagers challenged the professor with questions about God; like Socrates, he answered their questions with questions of his own. Looking back, that was the night I first had a glimpse of the man my son was becoming. He was not the same person that he would have been without schizophrenia, for he had a compassion and sensitivity that comes only with suffering and pain. He was a gracious host, and exhibited no signs of anxiety or restlessness. Still, part of me waited, and watched, for the relapse that I thought was sure to come.

It never did.

To this day, more than five years after he stopped taking his meds, David has been virtually symptom-free. I do not pretend to understand how his mind was healed, but David has no doubts. The hand of God laid out a divine plan, through the hospitals and jail, to the woman in the psychiatrist's office, to Tommy Barnett and the Dream Center. When God was ready, it was time to let go of the medications; David let go and let God.

There are others with schizophrenia who, like David, have successfully weaned themselves off antipsychotic drugs. In 2012, an article in a leading psychiatry journal asked the question, "Do all schizophrenia patients need antipsychotic treatment throughout their lifetime?" The authors followed seventy patients with schizophrenia, for up to twenty years after being hospitalized with acute psychosis. Beginning with the two-year follow-up, 34 percent of patients were taking antipsychotic medications continuously, 21 percent were not taking medications at all. Those who were not taking medications were a self-selected group, with better prognostic factors at the index hospitalization than the group that was still on antipsychotics. At the twenty-year follow-up, the group not taking medications exhibited a *significantly higher rate of recovery* than the group that was still on antipsychotic drugs. [1]

I am *not* advocating that persons with SMI stop taking their medications. Many persons with mental illness who are working in competitive jobs have told us that they *could not function* without their meds. But in response to the question posed in the article, the answer is no. Not all patients with schizophrenia need to be on antipsychotics for the remainder of their lives.

THE NATURE AND COSTS OF JOB ACCOMMODATIONS

More and more research is discrediting the negative stereotypes of persons with schizophrenia as hopeless and helpless. Not all persons recover from the illness, but many do. Not all persons with schizophrenia are capable of independent, competitive employment, but many are. For those whose symptoms are in remission, with or without medications, success in the labor market depends more on the accommodations that are available, than on the constraints of their illness.

The *Oxford English Dictionary* gives some idea of the scope of what accommodation can mean. The word *accommodate* comes from a Latin root, meaning suited, or suitable. Today, the word means:

1. To fit things to each other; to adjust, reconcile (things or persons that differ), and hence, to compose, settle, their differences; to bring to harmony or agreement . . .
2. To fit (a person with the understood requirements of the occasion); to furnish (a person with something requisite or convenient); to equip, supply, provide . . .
3. To suit, oblige, convenience . . .
4. To adapt oneself to. . . .[2]

Definition 1 captures the very essence of Title I of the ADA, namely, that, "qualified persons with disabilities" have a right to be treated without discrimination (harmoniously) in the workplace. This definition also captures the essence of job matching as an accommodation, namely, *to fit* a worker and a job *to each other.*

Definition 2 applies to the types of employer-provided accommodations that *furnish* or *equip* persons with disabilities with items that they need in order to function in the workplace. Wheelchair ramps for workers who cannot walk, lifting devices for workers with chronic back pain, and telecommunications devices for workers with hearing disabilities, are good examples. Few, if any, of the job accommodations needed by workers with mental illness fall into this category.

Definition 3, which comes directly from the Latin root, meaning *suited*, is the one that best applies to the employer-provided accommodations recommended for workers with SMI. Typically, these accommodations involve changes to the work environment, workplace relationships, or job characteristics that *suit* the functional limitations of workers with mental illness, or make it more *convenient* for them to work. Allowing a worker to take unscheduled breaks to help cope with stress, or to move to a quieter office to minimize distractions, are good examples.

Definition 4 fits a type of accommodation that is not mentioned in the ADA, and has been almost completely overlooked in the literature. Specifically, workers with disabilities often find ways to *adapt themselves or their job* to accommodate their functional limitations. These types of self-initiated accommodations have many advantages relative to the employer-provided accommodations mandated by the ADA.

Self-Initiated Job Accommodations

More formally, *self-initiated accommodations* can be defined as ways in which workers with disabilities adapt themselves or their job to compensate for their functional limitations, on their own initiative, without involving their employer or coworkers. For example, in our qualitative study of workers with SMI, one woman told us:

> When I was working with the developmentally-disabled population and my illness was affecting me at work, I would take them out. We would go to a movie, or go bowling, or something. I kind of just redirected my attention. [3]

As another example, a massage therapist said that he compensates for the side effects of antipsychotic drugs by not scheduling morning appointments, and by canceling appointments when he is symptomatic.

One tremendous advantage of self-initiated accommodations is that there is no need to disclose a diagnosis of SMI to an employer. Thus, contrary to what appears in much of the literature, disclosure of a disability is *not* a prerequisite for accommodation to take place. The worker who can initiate accommodations on their own can avoid a potentially stigmatizing revelation, and continue to feel "just like any other worker."

Relatively simple adaptations (e.g., maintaining a calendar to keep track of deadlines or making organizational charts to help stay focused on job tasks) can be implemented by almost any worker, but most self-initiated accommodations require considerable flexibility in a job. Flexibility might include freedom to change work hours, control over specific job tasks, or mobility around the workspace. The woman working with the developmentally disabled population, for example, could choose the group's daily activities to accommodate her flow of symptoms. The massage therapist was self-employed, so he could adjust his work schedule to accommodate his illness.

In some cases, a job is such a perfect match for a worker's functional limitations that the necessary accommodations are incorporated in the job description. One worker with SMI fortunate enough to be in such a job called these "natural" accommodations:

> Some jobs that I had really had the natural accommodations built into them. One was I was developing x-ray films in the dark room and they'd be sending these films in to me and I would be by myself most of the day, and I felt that was a great job because I didn't have that pressure because I was in that particular spot I felt it was my little world. [4]

No worries about difficult workplace relationships in that job!

All in all, self-initiated accommodations are far easier to implement (because no one else is involved), and have far less potential for negative repercussions (because disclosure is not required), than accommodations that must be requested from an employer. Many workers, however, do not have sufficient autonomy to initiate accommodations on their own. When an employer becomes involved, the accommodations process becomes both more complex and more costly.

Employer-Provided Job Accommodations

Accommodating workers with SMI presents a unique set of challenges for employers, beginning with identifying the particular accommodations that suit an individual worker. There is no well-defined set of functional limitations that characterize mental illness, and no well-defined set of accommodations that apply to all workers with SMI. Workers with schizophrenia, for example, may exhibit cognitive, emotional, or social limitations, or no limitations at all. The wide range of functional limitations gives rise to a correspondingly wide range of suggested job accommodations: from providing headphones to adjusting work shifts, from sensitivity training for coworkers to providing checklists of assigned tasks, from increasing supervision, to being allowed to work from home!

The potential accommodations can be characterized by their nature (*public versus private goods*) and by their impact on coworkers (*positive versus negative externalities*). These distinctions are important because they affect how difficult and how costly it will be to implement an accommodation. In other words, they help to determine if an accommodation is *reasonable*.

Public Goods

An example will help to clarify what economists mean by a *public good*. Many years ago, while traveling in Rome, I visited the church of St. Luigi dei Francesi to view *The Calling of St. Matthew*, a masterpiece by the Italian painter, Caravaggio. All the chapels in the church were brightly lit, except the one that held the famous painting. To illuminate that chapel, visitors had to drop coins into a box on the wall. (The priests were entrepreneurs; they knew they had something of great value, and found a way to profit from it.) Most visitors were eager to contribute, even though the light illuminated the painting for everyone, whether or not they had "paid." The intensity of light did not diminish, whether ten people or one hundred were viewing the painting. The light was a *public good* and those who did not contribute were *free riders*.

Free riders are not always so fortunate: If no one contributes, a public good will not be provided. The entrepreneurial priests did not use the same tactic to illuminate other chapels because, without a famous art work to attract donations, the chapels would remain mostly dark. I mention this because profit-oriented firms provide a number of public goods that benefit their employees and customers (lighting, air conditioning, smoke alarms, etc.), without ever attempting to charge for them directly.

Like the lights in the chapels and the air conditioning in stores and factories, some job accommodations are public goods. Wheelchair ramps, for example, are available to anyone, and the value of the ramps does not diminish with use. Some of the job accommodations that are recommended for workers with SMI, such as sensitivity training for coworkers and supervisors, can be characterized as public goods as well.

Other accommodations are *private goods*, because they are provided only to an individual worker with disabilities. A desk built to exact specifications for a wheelchair user is an example, as is the set of headphones purchased for a worker with SMI.

Externalities

Job accommodations that are public by nature clearly affect other workers, but accommodations that are private goods can impact coworkers as well. If, for example, building a special desk for a wheelchair user means that another worker is displaced, the accommodation has an effect on the coworker. Economists refer to these kinds of effects as externalities, which can be positive (beneficial) or negative (harmful) to others.

The textbook example of a commodity with *positive externalities* is vaccination. Vaccination benefits those who receive the vaccine and *others who have never been vaccinated*, by reducing their likelihood of exposure to disease. Semantically, positive externalities are often attributed to public goods as a matter of emphasis. Sensitivity training may have positive externalities for every worker who has been subject to teasing or harassment, even though the training was offered to accommodate a particular worker with SMI.

The textbook example of *negative externalities* is a manufacturer that dumps waste products in a river, thereby imposing pollution on *others who may never purchase the manufacturer's products*, but happen to be located downstream. With reference to job accommodations, assigning a worker with chronic back pain to light duty (lifting loads of twenty pounds or less) imposes negative externalities on other workers who must then lift a higher proportion of heavy loads. Similarly, allowing a worker with SMI to work only day shifts imposes negative externalities on other workers who must then work the night shift more often.

As noted earlier, the characterization of job accommodations as public versus private goods, with positive versus negative externalities, has important implications for evaluating the costs of employer-provided accommodations. The characterization also provides a convenient way to classify and compare the accommodations recommended for different types of disabilities.

Taxonomies of Job Accommodations

For Serious Mental Illness

I analyzed thirty-five different types of job accommodations for workers with SMI, and classified them as private or public goods, and as goods with positive externalities, negative externalities, or no externalities. The list of accommodations was assembled from recommendations of the Job Accommodation Network[5] and the literature on accommodating persons with mental illness in the workplace.[6] According to this analysis, there are four distinct clusters of accommodations:

1. *Public goods with positive externalities.* For example, promoting a nonhostile work environment, or reducing distractions in the workplace, has benefits available to every worker without diminishing the value to others (20 percent of total).
2. *Private goods with positive externalities.* For example, transferring a worker to another supervisor is an option available only to the worker receiving the accommodation, but the arrangement may benefit coworkers by reducing conflict and tension in the workplace (less than 10 percent of total).
3. *Private goods with few if any externalities* for other workers. For example, a set of headphones provided to a worker to drown out the voices they hear neither benefits nor harms coworkers (approximately 25 percent of total).
4. *Private goods with negative externalities.* For example, allowing one worker to take longer or more frequent breaks imposes costs on coworkers who must cover for them (more than 45 percent of total).

My analysis suggests that nearly half the accommodations recommended for workers with SMI have a negative impact on other workers. These accommodations can be problematic for employers, because the negative externalities increase the real costs of the accommodation.

For Back Pain

To see if this proportion of accommodations with negative externalities is representative of other disabilities, I constructed a similar taxonomy of job accommodations recommended for workers with back pain. Like mental illness, back pain is a chronic disorder that imposes functional limitations ranging from mild to severe, and that is often characterized by periods of remission and relapse. Unlike mental illness, back pain is not stigmatized.

I found a list of twenty-four accommodations recommended for workers with back pain on the JAN,[7] and classified them as public or private goods, with positive, negative, or no externalities. Once again, the recommended accommodations fall into four clusters:

1. Twenty percent of accommodations for back pain are *public goods with positive externalities* (e.g., automatic door openers)
2. Seventeen percent are *private goods with positive externalities* (e.g., a rolling ladder, which might be provided to one worker but shared with others)
3. Forty-six percent are *private goods with no externalities* (e.g., low-task chairs, height-adjustable desks, ergonomic workstations)
4. Seventeen percent are *private goods with negative externalities* (e.g., being allowed to take frequent rest periods, or being assigned to light duty)

Compared to the accommodations recommended for workers with SMI, a greater proportion of accommodations recommended for workers with back pain create *positive* externalities for other workers (37 percent versus 30 percent), and a far smaller proportion create *negative* externalities (17 percent versus 45 percent). As shown next, the difference has important implications for evaluating the relative costs of providing job accommodations for workers with SMI versus workers with back pain.

Real Costs of Job Accommodations

Research on the subject of job accommodations for workers with disabilities indicates that most accommodations can be implemented at minimal, or even zero, cost to employers.[8] This insight would be very encouraging if it were true, or even approximately accurate. Unfortunately, the estimated costs on which the insight is based are almost always lower than the real costs of the accommodations, because some cost categories are not fully counted.

For example, the indirect costs of negative externalities are typically not included in estimates of the costs of job accommodations. These costs involve both the time costs imposed on coworkers or supervisors and the resentment that coworkers naturally feel when one worker receives a benefit for which others bear the costs. Resentment can translate into weakened morale and reduced willingness to work hard; such reactions reduce productivity, which imposes real costs on the employer.[9]

The research on job accommodations also typically ignores the cost implications of accommodations with a public goods nature. It is misleading, for example, to allocate the full cost of constructing a wheelchair ramp to the accommodation of a single worker with a mobility limitation. Other workers who have difficulty climbing stairs benefit from the ramp as well. And, if there were no ramps, there would be more stairways. To make an accurate accounting of costs, the value of the benefits to other workers (positive externalities) must be factored out of the accommodation cost.

The reader should note, however, that making an appropriate adjustment for the indirect costs of positive or negative externalities is extremely difficult. In fact, the adjustment is so difficult that it is almost never attempted. Thus, it is acceptable to count the wheelchair ramp as a cost of accommodating a physical disability, if the external benefits are duly noted: Ramps benefit other workers with mobility limitations, and also reduce the need to construct stairways.

Cost allocation is not much of an accounting problem when the accommodation is a private good. The costs of a specially constructed desk for a worker in a wheelchair, or headphones for a worker with SMI, can be directly allocated to the accommodation of a specific beneficiary.

The nature of job accommodations recommended for workers with SMI is intrinsically different from the nature of accommodations recommended for workers with physical or sensory disabilities. Accommodations for workers with SMI are less likely to involve purchases of equipment, or physical changes to the workplace, and more likely to involve workplace relationships and supervisory time. Hence, accommodations for SMI typically involve lower direct costs, but higher indirect costs, than accommodations for workers with physical or sensory disabilities.[10] The indirect costs reflect the potential loss of morale among coworkers and supervisors are likely to be far greater when an employer is trying to accommodate a worker with SMI.

Cost Categories for Job Accommodations

Suppose we view job accommodations as (nonmarket) transactions between workers with disabilities and employers, who have a legal obligation to provide reasonable accommodations under the ADA. The direct and indirect costs of each transaction can be divided into five general categories: (1) purchases of equipment or alterations to the workspace, for which the firm will have external or internal invoices; (2) negative externalities in the form of supervisory time; (3) negative externalities in the form of coworker time; (4) other negative externalities, including productivity losses associated with coworker anger and resentment; and (5) positive externalities (negative costs) if an accommodation benefits other workers.

Only the first category (equipment purchases/alterations to the work-space) involves observable costs that are relatively easy to measure. The costs of such accommodations (e.g., an ergonomic workstation or an enclosed workspace) will be documented by an accounting trail of paid invoices or service requisitions. In contrast, it is unlikely that any firm keeps an accounting record of the time costs that a job accommodation imposes on supervisors or coworkers.

The fact that a large proportion of accommodations for SMI involve negative externalities in the form of time costs, together with the lack of documentation for time costs, has helped perpetuate the myth that "the majority of job accommodations for workers with mental illness are free, or cost very little."[11] Based on this mistaken perception, one author asserts that an employer's reluctance to accommodate workers with SMI is economically "irrational."[12] In fact, there is no such thing as a free accommodation,[13] and any economically rational employer considers supervisory time as a valid cost of production.

When the accommodations recommended for workers with SMI and workers with back pain are mapped to the five cost categories, the results show that a much larger proportion of accommodations for workers with SMI involve supervisory time (51 percent versus 21 percent), coworker time (34 percent versus 8 percent), or other negative externalities (26 percent versus 17 percent). A far smaller proportion of accommodations for workers with SMI involve direct costs for equipment, or modifications to the workplace (14 percent versus 58 percent). Additionally, a smaller proportion of accommodations for workers with SMI confer positive externalities on other workers (29 percent versus 37 percent).

The preponderance of negative externalities among the job accommodations for SMI suggests that these accommodations may encounter resistance from coworkers, supervisors, and employers who bear the costs. The authors of one study asked 305 employees of a Canadian health-care organization about the appropriateness of various job accommodations for workers with mental illness. Of the seven accommodations considered, "taking time off for counselling" and "banking of overtime hours" were perceived as most appropriate; "taking longer/more frequent breaks," and "working at a slower pace," were perceived as least appropriate.[14] The results suggest that accommodations which involve special privileges *at work* are likely to breed greater coworker resentment than accommodations that involve *time off* work.

The costs associated with coworker anger and resentment tend to be aggravated when a disability is concealable. In this case, coworkers have no way to know that the worker is legally entitled to job accommodations, because the ADA prohibits an employer from disclosing the reason for the apparent special privileges. Other employees wonder why the worker is "getting away with everything" or "being allowed to complain and end up getting a nice work schedule." In our interviews of employers who have supervised workers with SMI, one respondent told us that keeping coworkers "in the dark" exacerbates such feelings of resentment:

> Some people have been wondering about where [he is] and why [he isn't] here. I think their response would have been better if I had been allowed to let them know what the problem was. [15]

Although the real costs of accommodating workers with mental illness are far from negligible, nothing in this discussion implies that the costs are prohibitive, or that the costs outweigh the benefits. In fact, the benefits of providing job accommodations to workers with SMI are numerous: the *employer* benefits through increased productivity from the worker with SMI; the *worker* benefits through improved job performance, increased job security, enhanced self-esteem, and better chances for recovery; *society* benefits through reductions in disability support payments, and increased integration of persons with SMI into the community. The cumulative benefits almost surely outweigh the costs. But it does not follow that the employer should bear *all* the costs.

One economist, who has published numerous studies on disability and work, describes the ADA as an exercise in "morality on the cheap":

> The principal charm of this Act appears to be its ability to provide some help to the disabled at no cost to the federal government. . . . The ADA compels employers to accommodate disabled workers, even [if] the costs to them of doing so exceed the benefits the firm receives. . . . [It is left] to the courts to determine the degree to which firms are required to subsidize work by the disabled. [16]

Reasonable Accommodations in the Courts

It is safe to say that "morality on the cheap" has not fared well in court. Courts have generally taken a narrow view of what is reasonable to impose on employers, acknowledging the potential hidden costs of accommodations and leading to decisions that tend to favor the defendants. The tenor of these decisions is not that the costs of accommodating workers with SMI are prohibitive or unjustified, but that *employers* should not be forced to bear the costs. The following is a review of cases that involved workers with SMI requesting: a job transfer to accommodate work-related stress, a leave of absence for medical care, and negotiated job accommodations after returning from disability-related leave.

Job Transfer

The most common reason for workers with SMI requesting a job transfer is difficulty getting along with a supervisor. [17] So long as the worker is qualified for another position that is available, a transfer can be accomplished at relatively low cost (one-time training costs) and has potential positive externalities for other workers (reduced friction). In our interviews of employers, one respondent tells how easily a request to change supervisors was accomplished for a police detective with mental illness:

> When I came over here to [this department], he was working for a different supervisor. . . . There was constant conflict. The other supervisor was very, I would say, very aggressive, very opinionated, and had a habit of embarrassing this individual. And it just wasn't going to work out. And he . . . asked me if he could come to work for me. And, I said, whatever come on. [18]

Employers are typically more resistant to requests for job transfers than this anecdote implies. Despite the economic conclusion that transfers are relatively low-cost accommodations, courts have almost universally ruled that job transfers requested because of personality conflicts are *not* reasonable. [19] The case of *Gaul vs. Lucent Technologies Inc.* is representative.

Dennis Gaul was employed by AT&T, working on the design of a cordless telephone for international markets. Gaul suffered from depression and anxiety disorders. His condition was serious enough that he had spent time in a psychiatric hospital and taken extended disability leave before returning to work on the telephone project.

Gaul worked without stress for over a year, until he was assigned a new coworker with whom he had conflicts. Gaul complained that the coworker held back information from him, took credit for his ideas, and failed to acknowledge his contributions to the project. Gaul complained to his supervisor that he was under tremendous stress, and requested that he be transferred to a less stressful position:

> *Gaul:* If you don't help me, or if you can't help me at this point, I am going to get very sick, and I'm going to pop. . . . Do you know what I mean by pop?
>
> *Supervisor:* I don't know what you mean by pop.
>
> *Gaul:* Well, I am going to have a nervous breakdown, and I wouldn't be able to come back to work.

The supervisor ignored the transfer request, and Gaul took another disability leave. He then filed suit under the ADA, alleging that AT&T had failed to accommodate his disability. The Third Circuit Court of Appeals affirmed the lower court's decision that Gaul's "request to be transferred away from individuals causing him prolonged and inordinate stress was unreasonable."

The majority opinion held that the proposed accommodation would impose an "extraordinary administrative burden" on the employer, "essentially asking this court to determine the conditions of [plaintiff's] employment, most notably with whom he will work."

In short, an employer cannot be expected to transfer a worker with disabilities whenever the worker becomes "stressed out" by a coworker or supervisor. The court granted summary judgment to the employer, declaring that "nothing in the [ADA] leads us to conclude that . . . Congress intended to interfere with personnel decisions within an organizational hierarchy."[20]

The court explicitly accounted for indirect administrative costs associated with the accommodation request, concluding that the costs placed an undue hardship on the employer. In a similar vein, courts have been hostile toward accommodation requests for a nonhostile work environment. Just as employers cannot be expected to eliminate all sources of stress in the workplace, they cannot be expected to eliminate all sources of conflict. Unfortunately, in closing the door on accommodation requests involving job transfers, the courts may have closed down negotiations that could help some workers with SMI move, relatively easily, into jobs that are a better match for their functional limitations.

Leave of Absence

The most frequently requested accommodations, by workers with any type of disability, are accommodations that involve time off work.[21] Often, the requests are compelled by the need for ongoing medical care. In the case of psychiatric disabilities, such requests range from a few hours for regular therapy visits to long-term leaves of absence for inpatient psychiatric care.

Long-term leaves are disruptive and costly. If the worker is replaced by temporary help, there may be large transaction costs, with additional costs incurred when the worker returns. If the worker is not replaced, substantial negative externalities are imposed on coworkers who must cover the worker's responsibilities. All things considered, leaves of absence tend to be more costly and fraught with substantially more uncertainty (and therefore less reasonable) than internal job transfers. In *Rascon v. U S West Communications*, however, the court ruled differently.

In 1971, after a two-year tour of duty in Vietnam, Robert Rascon began working as a network technician for US West Communications. He received superior job performance ratings, but had anger management problems in the workplace. He was repeatedly suspended, and once fired, for fighting with coworkers.

Rascon attended two posttraumatic stress disorder (PTSD) treatment programs in 1989 and 1991, but his symptoms persisted. Finally, his physician recommended more intensive, inpatient treatment at the National Center for PTSD in Menlo Park, California. Rascon requested long-term disability leave from US West to enroll in the program for an expected period of four months.

His supervisor, Lorrie Sullivan, claimed that she knew nothing about PTSD until Rascon informed her that he had "Vietnam syndrome." Sullivan told him that US West did not have sufficient information to grant him paid disability leave, but that the company would grant unpaid leave in periods of thirty days. Rascon was required to submit documentation of ongoing, beneficial treatment to extend the leave month by month. He signed a waiver allowing the physicians at Menlo Park to communicate with his employer regarding his ongoing treatment, but revoked the waiver before his treatment ended. Rascon told a coworker he "did not wish US West to know every detail regarding his disability and its treatment."

After Rascon revoked the waiver, US West refused to extend further leave and terminated his employment. He filed suit alleging failure to provide reasonable accommodations for his mental condition. US West argued that an extended leave of absence is not a reasonable accommodation because "attendance is an essential function of Mr. Rascon's job." The court sided with Rascon:

> (T)he question of whether attendance is an essential [job] function is equivalent to the question of what kind of leave policy the company has. . . . Although US West characterizes the [requested] leaves as "extraordinary" [they] were less accommodating than company policy required, and the corresponding conditions US West attached to the leaves of absence were more restrictive than company policy allowed. Thus, we conclude that leave to attend the Menlo Park treatment program was a reasonable accommodation.[22]

US West did not hire a replacement for Rascon, so coworkers probably had to cover his job duties. The court opinion did not acknowledge the negative externalities, implicitly declaring that the costs were reasonable because the leave of absence fell within established policies of the firm.

Negotiating Job Accommodations

The EEOC guidelines for administering the ADA impose an affirmative duty on supervisors to negotiate job accommodations with an employee, once the employee has identified themselves as disabled and requested accommodations. The determination of what accommodations are appropriate involves an interactive process to identify the worker's functional limitations and to explore potential accommodations.[23] In *Taylor v. Phoenixville School District*, an employer's motion for summary dismissal was denied because a supervisor failed to engage in the interactive negotiation of reasonable accommodations.

Katherine Taylor was employed as the principal's secretary in Phoenixville School District beginning in 1974. For twenty years, she worked under several different principals, with consistently positive performance evaluations. In August 1993, Ms. Taylor developed symptoms of mental illness and was forced to take a leave of absence. At the time she went on leave, she had been working with the newest principal, Christine Menzel, for one week.

Taylor was hospitalized, diagnosed with bipolar disorder, and treated with antipsychotic medications. Her family kept the school district updated on her health condition during her absence and requested reasonable accommodations when she returned from leave. In October 1993, her psychiatrist said she was able to return to work.

Upon her return, Taylor discovered that Menzel had made a number of changes to the office, including new procedures and forms, a new furniture arrangement, and new computer and filing systems. Taylor also received a new job description, nearly doubling her responsibilities. She was disoriented by the changes and felt that they made her return to work more difficult.

Menzel exacerbated the situation by documenting the secretary's every mistake. Taylor had never been disciplined in twenty years working for the district, but after returning from leave she began receiving disciplinary warnings on a monthly basis. She was eventually placed on probation for unsatisfactory job performance, and finally received a notice of termination in October 1994. Taylor sued the school district, alleging that the principal had failed to negotiate reasonable accommodations when she returned from disability leave.

The court declared that Taylor had established herself as a "qualified individual with a disability"; that the school district had been informed of her disability and associated functional limitations, and received a request for accommodations; and that the school district had failed to fulfill its obligation to engage in an interactive process to negotiate accommodations. The court reversed a prior grant of summary judgment in favor of the employer, and remanded the case for further proceedings.[24]

In this case, the principal appears to have deliberately discriminated against an employee, possibly because Ms. Taylor had been diagnosed with SMI. In contrast, the majority of supervisors that we interviewed for our qualitative study were willing to "go the extra mile" for a worker with mental illness. Their comments made it clear, however, that the demands on supervisory time can be substantial.[25]

According to the supervisors we interviewed, workers with SMI typically require more time to manage than other workers because they need more explanation of what is expected of them, and more frequent reassurance that their job performance is satisfactory. Some supervisors said that they had redone work or taken over job duties for an employee with mental illness. Others talked about dealing with unusual behaviors of a worker with SMI, or with harassment from coworkers. Overall, they indicated that managing a work group that includes a worker with mental illness can be "very stressful" for supervisors. Nevertheless, most of these supervisors expressed empathy for their employee with SMI, and wanted to help them succeed.

Postscript

Title I of the ADA was expected to open the doors to employment for persons with disabilities, with employer-provided job accommodations being the keys to unlock those doors. Instead, there was a significant *decline* in employment rates for persons with disabilities between 1990 and 1995.[26] By 2013, the employment rate for working-age men with disabilities was still less than 40 percent of that for nondisabled men.[27] Clearly, this is not the world the framers of the ADA envisioned.

Numerous pundits have tried to explain why the ADA has failed to achieve its employment goals. Some blame the courts for conservative interpretations of the act that contravened the original intentions of Congress. Others point to work disincentives inherent in public disability programs, noting the steady decline in employment of persons with disabilities as SSDI enrollment expanded after 1989.[28] The economic explanation is more straightforward: The reasonable accommodation mandates of the ADA make it more costly to employ workers with disabilities; therefore employers are less likely to hire them.[29]

Few authors have questioned the fundamental assumption of the ADA, namely, that the way to improve employment outcomes for workers with disabilities is through employer-provided job accommodations. And few authors have challenged the myth that the majority of employer-provided accommodations can be implemented at little or no cost. I have argued that the hidden costs of job accommodations can impose a substantial burden on employers, and even the most accommodating supervisor cannot rescue a worker whose functional limitations and job demands are mismatched. The story of the police detective, for example, did not have a happy ending:

> His behavior was so extreme at times that everybody here knew that something was very much wrong. I tried to help keep him afloat. First I gave him . . . some time to catch up. And he did. And he did pretty darn well at it. . . . But he was always falling behind because he had these [mental health] issues you know. I [told my staff], I want you all to pitch in and help John.

And people volunteered to take cases and help him. But soon, I realized that I
couldn't . . . put this added responsibility and burden and work on everybody
else continually.[30]

The detective was eventually transferred to an administrative position
with regular hours and less time pressure. He worked in that position successfully for two years, but then requested to go back out on patrol. His
former supervisor tried unsuccessfully to dissuade him. She told us, "I'm
afraid this is a disaster waiting to happen."

All things considered, the ADA is fundamentally flawed in its emphasis
on employer-provided job accommodations, and its implicit assumption that
such accommodations can be implemented without undue costs for employers. The law is an exercise not only in "morality on the cheap," but in
"morality without reality." The framers of the ADA did not understand the
multifaceted nature of job accommodations (including job matching and self-
initiated accommodations) or their real costs (including negative externalities). They were *Planners* rather than *Searchers*, and the law has failed to
achieve its goals.

A smarter strategy would be to study the success stories, the stories of
people with serious mental illness who are independently and gainfully employed in competitive jobs. Once we understand how *real* people with SMI
have succeeded in *real* jobs in the competitive labor market, we will be better
equipped to craft policies that recreate the conditions of success for other
workers. The success stories are out there, if we search for them.

Chapter Ten

Beyond Schizophrenia

ALWAYS MORE MIRACLES

In December 2012, David resigned his position at the Dream Center. He had completed his associate's degree in ministry from AIC and told me, "It's time to move on." He planned to search for a job in the Phoenix area, and continue his part-time ministries in the city.

Spring 2013

Over the next few months, I helped David develop several versions of his resume. Each version had one intractable problem: an unexplained employment gap from 2005 to 2009. This would be a red flag for any personnel department, but telling the truth ("Diagnosed with schizophrenia, lived with parents after relapse of psychotic symptoms, now in recovery") was unlikely to produce many job interviews. I feared that David's job search would not go well.

After months with no good leads, my fears were confirmed. By then, however, David had decided to start his own small business providing carpentry, repair, and painting services to homeowners. He had construction experience working with my brother during college and, more recently, he had worked part time for several friends who were licensed contractors. He had acquired a set of *transferable skills* in construction; he had a talent for visualizing the final product of a construction job, and he enjoyed the variety and independence of construction work. Most importantly, he could set his own hours and work at his own pace.

We supported the small business idea enthusiastically and, over the next few months, provided capital to help with start-up costs. The business was officially established in August 2013. David acquired his first paying client in September and by March 2014, he was fully licensed, bonded, and insured.

One of David's first major projects was to re-paint our deck. We expected it to be a small job, but did not fully appreciate the training he had received from Uncle Gordon. David discovered that several support beams were deteriorating and many of the surface boards had been damaged by weather. With our approval, he made the necessary repairs before starting to paint. After four days, my husband asked, "Do you suppose he will ever finish? This deck will be here for the next fifty years!" I smiled and replied, "Yes, dear," recalling that Gordon's deck had withstood a hurricane.

Fall 2014

By the end of year one, David was working steadily and needed more help. He found a ready supply of labor among the men who were living at the Dream Center. David had come full circle: from being out of work, to organizing the Working Men's program for the Dream Center, to being an employer himself. For him, the construction company was more than a business; it was part of his ministry.

David found other ways to minister as well. Every Sunday night, as part of Alongside Ministries, he preaches to men in the Maricopa County Jail. On Wednesday evenings, he preaches at the House of Healing, a nondenominational ministry in central Phoenix, specializing in healing, teaching, and deliverance.

One Wednesday night, I visited the House of Healing to hear David preach. I had a queasy feeling in my stomach, like the butterflies I had when he was six and played goalie for his soccer team. Could my little boy really defend that big goal all by himself? Could my little boy really preach a sermon?

David's topic that evening was "Out of Captivity and Hope for a Future." Preaching from the book of Joshua, his message was to keep moving forward, no matter what the obstacles. God, he said, is bigger than any problem we might encounter.

> God will never take something away from you that he does not return something better. There is always more to God, more revelation, and more miracles to come. [1]

I was amazed—my little boy could really preach. I sat back and watched the miracle unfold.

EXTRAORDINARY LIVES

How many other miracle stories are out there, of people who have recovered from schizophrenia to find gainful competitive employment? The literature does not say. Psychosocial rehabilitation studies have focused mainly on barriers encountered by persons with SMI who are seeking employment, on increasing access to vocational rehabilitation programs, and on identifying best practices among supported employment programs.[2] There is almost nothing in the research literature about the career paths of persons with SMI who support themselves through independent competitive employment.

Such information cannot be gleaned from large-scale, nationally representative surveys designed to measure employment or health outcomes for the U.S. population. Several national databases provide detailed information on employment and earnings (e.g., the Survey of Income and Program Participation), but these data have limited information on health and health conditions. Likewise, databases that provide detailed information on health conditions (e.g., the Medical Expenditure Panel Survey) have limited information on employment and earnings. In short, nationally representative data that describe employment experiences unique to workers with SMI (e.g., stigma, disclosure, and job accommodations) do not exist. Nearly ten years ago, Steven Marcus and I set out to collect the data ourselves.

The Survey

The first challenge was how to obtain a representative sample of persons with SMI, who were gainfully employed in competitive jobs. We called them the "hidden population" because the problem stymied us for several years. Screening for the hidden population by random sampling would be prohibitively expensive because the prevalence of employed persons with schizophrenia (or other SMI) is so low. Asking employers to identify their workers with SMI would be fruitless because an employer would not necessarily know about an employee's history of mental illness and could not reveal the information if they did. The screening problem seemed insurmountable, until a chance encounter at a research conference.

In a casual conversation with a stranger, I mentioned that I was a health economist. She told me that her employer, Truven Health Analytics, conducts an ongoing survey (the PULSE), to collect information on health conditions, health insurance, and utilization of health services. The PULSE gathers data from large, random samples of the U.S. population by conducting telephone interviews with a new set of nine thousand households each month.[3] Most importantly, researchers can contract with Truven to add their own questions to the survey.

Could we add questions to the PULSE to screen for our target population? Could we then call back and ask additional questions specific to their employment experiences? Yes, PULSE interviewers ask all participants if they are willing to be called back for other surveys. Approximately 60 percent give permission to be called again, and follow-up surveys are routine. When I returned home, I called Steven. "I know how to find the hidden population!" I told him.

We contracted with Truven to screen for our target population over an eight-month period in 2012–2013. They identified households where someone had been diagnosed with serious mental illness *and* that person was currently employed in a competitive job or had been employed in a competitive job for at least six months post-onset of SMI.

Over the screening period, Truven identified 677 households in which a resident reportedly met our screening criteria and the survey participant was willing to be called back.[4] We were able to contact and verify eligibility for 377 households. A separate survey firm completed interiews with 230 eligible participants, for a 61 percent response rate.[5]

The survey generated information on *hours and earnings* in the worker's current job or, if not currently employed, their most recent job post-onset of SMI, as well as information about the *work environment, workplace relationships,* and *job characteristics.* The survey also included questions about *disclosure* of SMI, *job accommodations* requested and received, current *symptoms and treatment* history, investments in *human capital* (e.g., education or job training), and *support* from family, friends, or government programs.

The results presented here provide the first-ever information on the experiences of workers with SMI in competitive jobs, from a representative sample of persons with SMI who are capable of mainstream competitive employment. To add context to the survey data presented below, I include several case studies of extraordinary lives—people whose lives have been disrupted by mental illness but who are now gainfully employed in competitive jobs.

Ben's Story

Ben Rinaudo grew up in the Republic of Niger, where his parents were development workers. Ben aspired to a career in international development, and completed the coursework for a degree in development studies from the University of Melbourne. While he was writing his honors thesis on female slavery in West Africa, he developed the first symptoms of mental illness. He became anxious and depressed, his thinking became confused, and he developed feelings of disorientation, even in familiar settings. Within a few months, his symptoms escalated to paranoia, panic attacks, racing thoughts, and hallucinations.

Ben's family took him to a hospital emergency room, where he was transferred to a psychiatric inpatient unit. Like many first-time patients, Ben felt both relief and fear. He was treated with antipsychotics and antidepressants, which controlled the most overt symptoms of mental illness, but the medications left him feeling lethargic, bored, and hopeless. One year after his release from the hospital, with little accomplished since he became ill, Ben felt a tremendous sense of grief and guilt over his lost ambitions. He asked his psychiatrist, "Will I be like this forever?"

During the following year, Ben's mood improved. His energy returned sufficiently to begin a supported education course offered by Mental Illness Fellowship (a coalition of organizations across Australia, working to facilitate recovery from mental illness). Toward year's end, Ben's uncle offered him a part-time job with his piano tuning and restoration business. Ben had been out of work for nearly two years, and the thought of working regular hours was overwhelming to him. The part-time job, with flexible hours and a sympathetic employer, was ideal.

A few months later, Ben took on a second part-time job helping a friend who was a self-employed gardener. When his friend left the area, Ben took over the business. The coursework, piano tuning, and gardening business gave Ben a renewed sense of purpose for his life.

In due course, Ben completed three Graduate Education Certificates with the Mental Illness Fellowship, where he was eventually offered part-time employment. At the time his story was written in 2012, Ben was working full time at the fellowship, managing peer and community education, advocacy efforts, and community outreach. He was completing a fourth graduate certificate in mental health services, with the long-term goal of helping to improve mental health treatment in developing countries. In this way he planned to return to his original ambition of a career in community development.[6]

Survey Results I

There are striking similarities between Ben's story and David's. Both young men became ill while they were in college, returned to school when their acute symptoms were in remission, completed their college degrees, were absent from the workforce for a significant period of time, found an entrée back to work with a flexible employer, and became self-employed in a services occupation. How typical is this story? Is self-employment a common pathway back to work? Is it significant that both young men earned a college degree? Our survey was designed to answer exactly these types of questions.

Employment Status

Among the persons we interviewed, 27 percent said that they were currently working in a competitive job. Three-quarters of current workers were *gain-*

fully employed (i.e., not receiving disability benefits). Among those who were not working, over half (52 percent) had left their most recent job for reasons unrelated to mental illness (e.g., to care for a child or return to school). (That result is strikingly similar to the findings of another, smaller study, in which participants with SMI were asked why they had left each job they held post-onset of mental illness. More than half—53 percent—of the time participants had resigned a job for reasons unrelated to their illness.[7])

We are particularly interested in two comparison groups: those who are currently employed, and those who left their jobs because of their mental illness. We define as successfully employed the sixty-one persons working in a competitive job on the date of interview, and refer to them as *stayers*. The eighty persons who left their most recent competitive job because of their mental illness we define as unsuccessfully employed, and refer to them as *leavers*. In subsequent analyses, we aim to identify characteristics that distinguish the two groups, and that may guide policy makers in developing ways to improve employment outcomes for this population.

Twenty percent of current workers (stayers) were self-employed at the time of our survey. Their jobs ranged from housekeeper to financial planner; one owned a pottery school. The rate of self-employment in this group was almost twice that of the U.S. workforce (20 percent versus 11 percent) at the time.[8] Accordingly, the survey findings are consistent with the hypothesis that *self-employment is a good job match for workers with SMI,* possibly because it offers the ultimate potential for flexibility.

Occupation

We asked all respondents about their occupation in their current or most recent job. Their responses ran the entire gamut of occupations: nurses, teachers, cooks, cleaners, home health-care workers, cashiers, receptionists, salespersons, construction workers, machinists, production workers. The survey is concrete evidence that *among the population of persons with SMI, there are those with the skills, abilities, and interests to hold almost any job in the economy.*

The distribution of our sample across major occupational categories was, however, quite different from that of the general workforce. Compared to all U.S. workers, those in our sample were overrepresented in professional or service occupations (57 percent versus 40 percent) and underrepresented in managerial and sales occupations (26 percent versus 39 percent).[9] The differences in occupational distributions are consistent with the idea that workers with SMI are matching into jobs that minimize the impact of their functional limitations. The workers in our survey appear to avoid managerial and sales occupations, where interpersonal interactions are essential, in favor of professional and service occupations, which offer greater autonomy.

Human Capital

Both David and Ben had education and job training that provided an entrée to the competitive labor market. David acquired construction skills as an "apprentice" to his uncle and returned to school to complete a degree in ministry. Ben acquired piano tuning and gardening skills on-the-job, and completed graduate certificates in mental health services. The survey results provide objective evidence that, on average, investments in human capital improve employment outcomes for persons with SMI.

Our sample had higher average educational attainment than the U.S. population as a whole at the time the data were collected (2012–2013). Over 80 percent of respondents reported at least some postsecondary education, compared to only 58 percent of all U.S. adults. [10] Inasmuch as schizophrenia does not disproportionately affect the intelligent and well-educated, education evidently raises the probability that a person with SMI returns to independent competitive employment (and was eligible for our sample).

Although respondents to our survey were more likely to have *attended* college than U.S. adults overall, they were also more likely to have *dropped out* of college (47 percent versus 27 percent). The reason for the disproportionately high dropout rate is obvious. Onset of SMI often strikes young adults of college age. The symptoms disrupt, and all too often end, progress toward a college degree. Consequently, the proportion of our survey respondents with a college degree was similar to the proportion in the U.S. population overall (roughly one-third), even though many more of the persons in our sample had some postsecondary education.

Comparing the stayers and leavers in our sample, there is a clear education gap, which multiplies during the college years. Stayers were 15 percent more likely to attend college than leavers, but *twice as likely* to complete a four-year college degree, and *five times more likely* to complete a postgraduate degree. Thus, a key distinguishing characteristic between the two groups is that *stayers found a way to complete their education.*

We asked all respondents about investments in job training. We were particularly interested in job coaching, transitional work training, or any other form of supported employment. Only 15 percent of respondents said they had participated in a supported employment program. Stayers were more likely to have participated in supported employment than leavers (20 percent versus 13 percent), suggesting that supported employment helps some workers transition to independent, competitive jobs. That inference is tentative, however, because the number of workers in our sample who had experience with supported employment is so small. Of course, that is a key point: 80 percent of stayers said that they had never participated in supported employment, casting doubt on the claim that "the single best predictor of competitive employment for patients with schizophrenia is enrollment in IPS, or evidence-based supported employment."[11]

Kurt's Story

Kurt Snyder was a good student in high school and doing well in college until he began to experience symptoms of mental illness. The first manifestation was grandiose thinking; Kurt believed he was destined to discover a mathematical principle that would transform our understanding of the universe. He spent so much time focusing on his principle that his grades suffered. He eventually dropped out of college at age twenty-four.

After leaving school, Kurt made several attempts at starting a business (as a computer graphics designer and as a handyman), but each attempt failed. He began to experience feelings of paranoia, to the point that he believed he was under continuous surveillance and being followed whenever he went outside.

With the aid of a friend, Kurt was able to obtain a job as a repairman for a large telecommunications firm. However, the high-security worksite, with ever-present surveillance cameras, intensified Kurt's feelings of paranoia. He began experiencing hallucinations: hearing clicking noises that did not exist and seeing car doors lock and unlock themselves. He wondered if he was living in an alternate universe or had been drugged with hallucinogens.

The paranoia forced Kurt to quit his job. He stayed at home, afraid to go outside. Eventually, the self-isolation relieved his feelings of paranoia and he decided to take a train trip, both as a vacation and a chance to ponder his great mathematical principle. Almost as soon as Kurt boarded the train, however, the paranoid thoughts returned. When the train stopped, he abruptly disembarked, with no luggage and nowhere to go. By now his psychotic symptoms were so blatant that his family was notified and he was hospitalized. A psychiatrist prescribed antipsychotics, which Kurt refused to take.

Three months later, Kurt was hospitalized again. A psychiatrist prescribed an atypical antipsychotic, which Kurt again refused to take. This time the psychiatrist told Kurt he would not continue to treat him, unless he took his medications. Kurt relented and agreed to try the meds. The hallucinations ceased almost immediately. The delusions and paranoia faded over time.

With the acute symptoms of mental illness under control, Kurt returned to school to earn a certificate in database management. Upon completion of the program, he found a job as a database administrator with the state of Maryland. At the time his story was written (2007), he was working full time for the state and performing volunteer work with the local fire department. He was thirty-six years old.[12]

Survey Results II

As Kurt's story shows, a workplace filled with surveillance cameras is a poor job match for someone with paranoid schizophrenia. Kurt finally found a good match as a computer programmer; David and Ben found good matches in self-employment. In chapter 8, I identified a number of work-related characteristics that make a good job match for workers with SMI, based on theory and anecdotal evidence. The survey data are consistent with all these predictions.

Work-Related Characteristics

With respect to firm characteristics, I argued that a *supportive culture* and *calm environment* were important to the success of workers with SMI. In our survey, workers who were successfully employed reported a less hostile and less stressful work environment than those who left their job for reasons related to SMI. Stayers were less likely than leavers to report that, because of their mental illness, they had been teased, bullied, or harassed at work (21 percent versus 29 percent), or had been treated unfairly (26 percent versus 45 percent). Stayers were also less likely to say that their job involved working at high speed (43 percent versus 60 percent), or working to tight deadlines (51 percent versus 58 percent).

With respect to workplace relationships, I argued that *supportive supervisors* and *sympathetic coworkers* were important. Indeed, workers who were successful in their most recent job were more positive about their workplace relationships than those who were unsuccessful. Exactly the same proportion (41 percent) of each group said that their employer did not know about their mental illness, but stayers were less likely than leavers to say that the main reason for not disclosing was "fear of what their supervisor would do" or "fear of how coworkers would react" (8 percent versus 34 percent). Stayers were also less likely than leavers to say that stigma had affected their relationships with coworkers (18 percent versus 38 percent).

Finally, with respect to job characteristics, I argued that the most important features of a good job match were consistency, autonomy, and flexibility. Shift work may be the ultimate inconsistency in job requirements. As expected, stayers were less likely than leavers to say that their job involved working in shifts (44 percent versus 62 percent). Stayers also reported greater autonomy and flexibility across multiple dimensions of their jobs. Relative to leavers, stayers were more likely to say that they could choose/change their order of tasks (70 percent versus 53 percent), choose/change their methods of work (68 percent versus 42 percent), choose/change their speed of work (69 percent versus 58 percent), and take their break when they wished (54 percent versus 34 percent). Stayers were also more likely to have influence over the choice of a working partner (32 percent versus 18 percent).

Some specific results cited previously (e.g., those pertaining to tight dead-lines or speed of work) fall short of accepted criteria for statistical signifi-cance. Nonetheless, the collectivity of results are highly supportive of the job matching hypotheses in that the quantitative measures *all point in the ex-pected direction*. Overall, the survey provides the first quantitative evidence suggesting that a good match between functional limitations and job charac-teristics is important to successful employment outcomes for workers with SMI.

Illness and Treatment

Anecdotal evidence, like the testimony of Elyn Saks, indicates that many persons with SMI who are successfully employed in competitive jobs still experience symptoms of mental illness. In our survey data, some proportion of both stayers and leavers reported current symptoms and corresponding functional limitations associated with their illness. However, the proportion was smaller among stayers.

With respect to negative symptoms, the proportion of workers who re-ported difficulties with interpersonal relationships was twice as high among leavers as among stayers. The limitations related to difficulties "carrying on a conversation," "dealing with strangers," and "making/keeping friendships." One striking example is that nearly three-fourths of leavers said they had "difficulty joining in community activities," compared to only one-third of stayers. This result suggests that the leavers may have had similar difficulties assimilating at work.

Regarding cognitive deficits, the most frequently reported limitation was "difficulty concentrating on a task for more than ten minutes." However, stayers were far less likely than leavers to report difficulty concentrating (57 percent versus 83 percent). Stayers were also less likely to report "difficulty remembering to do important things" (52 percent versus 69 percent), "diffi-culty understanding what is going around them" (26 percent versus 59 per-cent), and "difficulty learning new things" (23 percent versus 47 percent). Clearly, the differences in prevalence of functional limitations distinguishes between stayers and leavers in our sample. Still, substantial numbers of stay-ers reported functional limitations associated with the symptoms of SMI, demonstrating that *it is not necessary to be symptom-free to be successfully employed*.

Nor is it *necessary* to be taking antipsychotic medications to be able to work in a competitive job. Within our survey sample, the majority of both stayers and leavers said they were taking their medications as prescribed, but the proportion following their prescribed medication regimen was *smaller* among stayers (75 percent versus 90 percent). Moreover, 20 percent of stay-ers (compared to only 6 percent of leavers) said that they were not taking antipsychotic medications at all. Surprisingly, stayers had poorer adherence to their medications as a group than leavers, but stayers reported fewer symptoms of SMI—and the stayers were still working.

The results are consistent with at least one prior study that identifies a cohort of persons who recover from SMI in every sense of the word: They do not take antipsychotic drugs; they are virtually symptom-free; and, on average, they function at least as well as others with the same illness who are taking their medications.[13] Brett Hartman is one of these.

Brett's Story

Brett Hartman was a college freshman when he first experienced symptoms of mental illness. As images tumbled through his brain, he thought that he was receiving messages from God, that the moon was transmitting messages from God, and that perhaps the moon was God. Upon admission to a psychiatric unit, he was treated with a first-generation antipsychotic. After a month, he was discharged with a diagnosis of "adjustment reaction to adolescence," a "less pejorative" label than schizophrenia.

At home and experiencing the drowsiness and lethargy that are side effects of the antipsychotic, Brett decided to stop taking it. When the delusions returned, his psychiatrist warned him to get back on the meds. Brett followed the advice, but when he shook the bottle of pills, three tablets fell out. He thought the number three must be symbolic, so he took them all. He tried the "experiment" again and again until he had taken six times his usual daily dose.

Brett was readmitted to a psychiatric unit. This time he expected to be discharged quickly; when he was not, he became belligerent. He was placed in restraints, in seclusion, and his medication was forcibly administered. He was soon submissive enough to move out of seclusion, then to an unlocked unit. There he became friends with an older patient named Arthur. One day on the fitness track, Brett asked Arthur how he managed to deal with the hardships in his life. "Walking, keep on walking. Whatever you do, that'll help." Brett thought, "this is the kind of simplistic nonsense I can do without." Tired of waiting to be discharged, he left the hospital on his own. Police returned him to the locked psychiatric unit. When he finally was discharged, the diagnosis was unequivocal: "acute schizophrenia."

The pattern of delusions, hospitalization, belligerence, restraints, and forcible administration of antipsychotics, continued until Brett had "escaped" from hospitals four times. When he at last realized there was no escape, he became deeply depressed. One sleepless night, he remembered Arthur's advice. The next morning he began to walk, deliberately and purposefully, up and down the halls. The walking had a calming effect. (Is this why the staff member at UNC walked round and round with her patient?)

Brett's outlook improved and he was released from a psychiatric unit for the last time. Now he began the arduous process of rebuilding his life. He returned to college and a full courseload. He soon realized that he couldn't maintain that pace while taking antipsychotics, so he stopped his meds once again. His grades improved, but he worried about a relapse of psychotic symptoms. The relapse never happened, and he graduated with honors.

After graduation, Brett applied to several prestigious univerisities offering doctoral degrees in psychology. He disclosed his history of mental illness on the applications, thinking his firsthand experience would be a plus. It was not—every school rejected his appliction. Two years later, he applied to another university without revealing his history of schizophrenia. This time, he was accepted. When he published his story in 2005, Dr. Hartman was working as a licensed psychologist in upstate New York. [14]

Survey Results III

Disclosure and Accommodations

Brett learned firsthand the risks of disclosing a history of mental illness. Anecdotal evidence suggests that most workers with SMI are reluctant to volunteer information about their illness, for fear of stigma and discrimination. [15] Our survey provides the first-ever representative data on disclosure rates of SMI in the workplace, among individuals who are capable of independent, competitive employment. The results are surprising. More than half (59 percent) of the workers in our survey sample said that their employers knew about their mental illness; in three-quarters of those cases, the workers informed their employer themselves. (The exact circumstances and extent of disclosure were not reported.)

Stayers were far more likely to have informed their employer themselves (83 percent versus 59 percent). This result suggests that *voluntary disclosure* is correlated with more successful work outcomes, but the nature of the causality, and even whether or not there is a causal relationship is unclear. It could be that stayers were more likely to voluntarily disclose because they anticipated a more favorable response from their employer, or stayers may have received a more favorable response because they chose to voluntarily disclose. Alternatively, the mere fact that the workers stayed with the firm implies a comfort level that is conducive to disclosure.

We also asked our survey respondents about sixteen different types of job accommodations that they might have requested for their mental illness. Overall, sixty-five workers (28 percent) asked their employer for some type of accommodation in their current or most recent job. Among those who requested an accommodation, 40 percent requested a change to their work schedule (i.e., a flexible schedule, part-time work, or different work hours).

No other single accommodation was requested by more than 15 percent of workers who asked for an accommodation.

Stayers were somewhat *less likely* to have requested job accommodations than leavers (26 percent versus 35 percent), possibly because they had fewer functional limitations. Alternatively, stayers may have found a better job match, where they either did not need accommodations, or could initiate accommodations themselves. (Recall that stayers had far more flexibility and autonomy in their jobs than leavers.) On the other hand, stayers were *more likely* to have received the accommodations they requested. Here, the differences are startling. Among those who requested schedule changes, *100 percent* of stayers said that their employer granted their request, compared to only 50 percent of leavers. This could be one of the primary reasons that the workers left their jobs.

Overall, the responses on disclosure and job accommodations suggest that stayers were employed in firms where the workplace culture was more supportive, and their supervisor was more accepting, than leavers. These are exactly the results that the theory of job matching would predict.

Support Networks

In each of the foregoing case studies, the support of family and friends played a crucial role in the patient's return to competitive employment. My husband and I provided startup capital for David's business. Ben's uncle gave him a job restoring and tuning pianos; a friend started him in the gardening business. Kurt had a friend who bought him a computer and paid for one of his classes in database management. Brett's father helped him pay for graduate school.

Consistent with the case studies, a majority of our survey participants said that family and friends supported their return to work. Stayers were only *slightly* more likely than leavers to acknowledge support from family members (72 percent versus 66 percent), but *considerably* more likely to report support from friends (81 percent versus 66 percent). (Recall that leavers reported more difficulty making and maintaining friendships than stayers.)

Most of the participants said that they had a social circle of family and friends with whom they maintained contact. Only 35 percent lived alone. When asked if they had frequent ("almost daily" or "a few times a week") contact with others, stayers were less likely than leavers to report frequent contact with family members (43 percent versus 58 percent), but more likely to report frequent contact with friends (45 percent versus 37 percent).

The results reinforce the belief that support from family members and friends plays an important role in recovery from SMI.[16] Most of our survey respondents had supportive relationships, but the social circle of those who were currently employed was more balanced between family and friends.

Could this be another indicator of recovery? I observed the same pattern with David. As he became more involved with work and made friends at the Dream Center, his cell phone started ringing again.

Postscript

Although the inferences drawn from the survey remain in the "preliminary" stage, they collectively form a consistent whole. The story that emerges from both case studies and survey responses is not one of stigma and intimidation, but one of empowerment and success. The first crucial element of success is *control of the acute symptoms of SMI*. Persons who are experiencing acute psychotic symptoms cannot work in any meaningful way. They deserve the best medical care available. Today, that means short-term hospitalization and stabilization on antipsychotic medications.

The second element of success is *education and skills training*. Schizophrenia is a cruel disease in many ways, not the least of which is timing. It strikes most often when a young adult is in college or just entering the labor force, disrupting their acquisition of human capital. The impact upon future earnings and employment is tremendous. Contrary to the stereotype of incompetency, many persons with SMI are capable of completing advanced skills training and college degrees. These investments in human capital help to ameliorate the negative impact of functional limitations on work outcomes.

Third, in the wake of deinstitutionalization, we depend on families to be primary caregivers for persons who are recovering from SMI. In his lowest moments, when Brett Hartman thought everyone else might abandon him, he could still rely on his mother to bring him milkshakes every week.[17] Families can provide crucial support on the path to competitive employment. Policy makers take note: If the emotional and financial burdens of caregiving become overwhelming, so that family members "give up" on their relative with SMI, an important support network for return to work may be lost.

Finally, finding a good job match is crucial to employment outcomes for workers with SMI. In defining a good match, the single most important characteristic appears to be flexibility. David is self-employed; Ben was self-employed and now works in mental health services; Kurt works as a database administrator; Brett travels across New York State conducting disability evaluations. All of these jobs give workers considerable control over their job tasks and their pace of work. In our survey data, measures of job flexibility clearly distinguish workers with SMI who are employed from those who have left their jobs because of their mental illness.

There are many stories of super-extraordinary people who suffered from schizophrenia or other SMI, yet made brilliant contributions to the arts, sciences, and humanities. John Nash, mathematics prodigy and winner of the

Nobel Prize in economics, is one example. Vincent Van Gogh is another. Robert Lowell, U.S. Poet Laureate from 1947 to 1948, and twice winner of the Pulitzer Prize for Poetry, is another. In fact, there are so many names on the list that the concept of the "mad genius" has become a stereotype in fiction and research. But a person need not be a genius to be a productive and contributing member of society after a diagnosis of schizophrenia. In the throes of mental illness, Brett Hartman wrote:

> I could shine before and I remember what it was like to shine. Now I've lost it, and the reality of the loss goes deep. To regress this way, with full awareness of the regression, seems unmatched as far as life's frutsrations go. [18]

We all deserve our chance to shine. With appropriate mental health policies, there can be a full life and productive work after schizophrenia.

Chapter Eleven

Toward a More Rational Mental Health Policy

IT

During the years I struggled to help my son recover from mental illness, I did not think of schizophrenia as merely a disease. To me, it was the enemy. Like the clown-monster in Stephen King's *It*, schizophrenia lurked at the corners of our lives, threatening to snatch my son away at any time:

> What he saw then was terrible enough to make his worst imaginings of the thing in the cellar look like sweet dreams; what he saw destroyed his sanity in one clawing stroke. [1]

With every passing year, I become more confident that David has defeated the enemy. We had some lucky breaks along the way, but there were stumbling blocks as well.

The first obstacle was my complete failure to recognize that David was suffering from SMI. As the symptoms of schizophrenia developed, David's personality and behavior changed radically. I thought he was using drugs, or excited about starting college, or just being insufferable. Looking back, I wonder if I was too uninformed to recognize the signs of mental illness, or if I closed my mind to a possibility that was too frightening to face. "We lie best when we lie to ourselves." [2]

After David was diagnosed, he was fortunate to be enrolled in a research study under the direction of Diana Perkins. It was not, however, blind luck that led us to her. David had health insurance, which allowed him to be admitted to the psychiatric unit at UNC Hospital, rather than the state hospital near Durham. I had contacts in the psychiatric research community, who strongly recommended Dr. Perkins. When it came time to sign the informed consent, I requested that she be David's physician and made that a condition for his participation in the study. *Excellent care for SMI is available within the U.S. health care system, if patients and their families have the knowledge and resources to access it.*

The medical staff at UNC Hospital was incredibly supportive of David during the early years following his diagnosis. In contrast, UNC administrators made the path to completing his college degree more difficult. When I contacted the Disability Services Office about readmission after his first episode of psychosis, the response I received ("when your son got in trouble . . .") made me determined never to contact that office again. Had we been unaware of our son's rights under the ADA, David might not have been readmitted to school. I expect the response to parents of a student with schizophrenia would have been similar at almost any university in the country. This is tragic, because *graduating from college gives persons with SMI options in the labor market that can help them accommodate their mental illness and succeed in gainful employment.*

The disaster in Charlotte was avoidable. David's psychiatrist was either unable or unwilling to refer David for inpatient care, even though David was experiencing acute symptoms of mental illness. Later, the CMHC refused to admit David, even though he was exhibiting psychotic symptoms and willing to be hospitalized. Social services, community mental health services, and the local police could not or would not intervene. As David became increasingly psychotic, quit his job, ran up huge credit card bills, and began intimidating his roommates, there was nothing we could do, except wait and watch as his life crumbled, and bail him out of jail when he finally crashed.

In resolving the felony charges, we had three pieces of good fortune: (1) North Carolina has a jail diversion program for defendants with mental illness. (2) We found an attorney who specialized in disability law and was determined that David should participate in the diversion program, despite the fact that he was living out of state. (3) I found a Searcher at the Treatment Assessment Screening Center in Phoenix, who volunteered to organize and manage a diversion plan for David.

Once again, it was not all blind luck. We had no experience with the criminal justice system, but we had the financial resources to hire a knowledgable attorney, and the connections to find him. We had no knowledge of alternative sentencing rules, but we had the wherewithal to search for a rehabilitation program in Arizona that could substitute for jail diversion, and the imagination to think that a program designed for drug offenders might work for someone with SMI. Completing the diversion program meant that the charges against David were expunged. He was fortunate, because *a criminal record makes it more difficult for persons with SMI to return to the labor force, yet prison has become a de facto substitute for the mental hospital for many persons with SMI.*

Once he was living in Arizona, David became eligible for psychiatric care and medications through the public mental health system, at no out-of-pocket cost. The medical care was more than adequate, but the vocational services were abysmal ("he could collect coins from vending machines"). David spent four long years doing virtually nothing before he found a godsend at the Dream Center. What the church program could do, that the public mental health system could not, was return David to the real world.

Schizophrenia takes a terrible toll on family members. When David returned to live with us in Arizona, I was emotionally exhausted. We had invested years helping him rebuild his life after that first psychotic episode; now we had to begin all over again. All the problems he faced—the legal issues, the credit card bills, the mental illness, the depression—were ours to solve. I remember telling my therapist, "Maybe I can handle him living with us for six months, but absolutely no longer than that." It was three years before he moved out to live with his father. Somehow, I survived:

> [Schizophrenia] was, after all, only a [disease]. Perhaps at the end, when the masks of horror were laid aside, there was nothing with which the human mind could not cope. [3]

MENTAL HEALTH POLICY

Prior to the introduction of antipsychotic medications in the 1950s, the best outcome most patients with SMI (and their families) could hope for was, to *survive*. In fact, E. Fuller Torrey's *Surviving Schizophrenia* was my textbook in the early days of David's illness. Today, many persons with even the most serious mental illnesses can live independently and work in gainful employment. The tragedy is that so many do not. Too many persons with SMI are homeless, in jail, or dependent on government entitlement programs. Our mental health policy has failed to keep up with the possibilities our medical system has created.

The ADA and its amendments are the primary federal policies designed to improve employment outcomes for workers with disabilities. The acts prohibit discrimination against otherwise qualified persons with disabilities in decisions regarding hiring, compensation, promotion, and other employee benefits. To say that the ADA has failed to achieve its promise for workers with SMI is an understatement. The amended act may have a greater impact, but many legal analysts are skeptical. [4]

Why, with improved treatments and tougher laws, have we not observed better employment outcomes for this population? One part of the problem is the persistent stigma against mental illness, which cannot be legislated away.

Another part of the problem is the exclusive focus of disability employment policy on the demand side of the labor market. The ADA imposes a mandate on employers to offer equal employment opportunities to *qualified* workers with mental disorders, but there are no complementary policies to ensure that persons with mental disorders have opportunities to *become qualified* for the jobs that are now open to them.

In particular, current policies do not address the functional limitations and human capital losses that stand between a person with SMI and sustainable employment. Current policies do little to help persons with SMI acquire general human capital, which is *the* entrée to good jobs in the contemporary labor market. Finally, current policies are not geared to support the families, who support the recovery, of persons with SMI. The root cause of these failures is that mental health policy has been driven by Planners committed to an ideology, rather than by Searchers who are close to the problems that need to be solved.

Background

According to the *Oxford English Dictionary*, the word "policy" derives from the Greek "polis," meaning city-state, the unit of government in ancient Greece. Policy was once a verb with a meaning equivalent to "police." Today, the word is a noun, meaning:

> A course of action pursued by a government, party, ruler, statesman, etc.; any course of action adopted as advantageous or expedient. [5]

The definition makes clear that policy should be welfare-enhancing (advantageous). In a democracy, the welfare to be enhanced (at least in theory) is that of the city-state.

Government policy has the potential to increase social welfare in situations where free markets fail to achieve socially desirable outcomes, such as when there are negative externalities (as with untreated mental illness). In theory, government actions can enhance welfare in such situations because government has the authority to coerce socially desirable behavior from its citizens. It does so by enacting *laws*, by establishing *rights*, or by exercising the *authority* of local, state or federal governments. [6]

Laws motivate desirable behavior by creating incentives in the form of rewards (granted for compliance with a policy) or penalties (imposed for noncompliance). [7] The Mental Health Parity and Addiction Equity Act of 2008, for example, requires health insurers to establish equity between coverage for mental/substance use disorders and coverage for medical/surgical disorders. The act carries substantial penalties for noncompliance (up to $100 per covered member, per day). [8]

Declarations of *rights* establish claims to certain privileges on behalf of a designated group. A relevant example is the United Nations Convention on the Rights of Persons with Disabilities. Among many enumerated rights, the convention states that:[9]

- Persons with disabilities have the right to enjoy the highest attainable standard of heath, without discrimination on the basis of disability. [Article 25]
- Health care professionals [shall] provide the same quality of care to persons with and without disabilities, including on the basis of free and informed consent. [Article 25]
- The existence of a disability shall in no case justify a deprivation of liberty. [Article 14]

Finally, the power of government rests on its *authority* to act in the interests of the society. In the United States, authority may be shifted among local, state, and federal governments to achieve particular policy objectives. The State Care Acts, passed at the end of the nineteenth century, are a good example. The acts shifted responsibility for the care of persons with SMI from local authorities to state mental hospitals, where state officials believed patients would receive higher-quality care.

Unfortunately, the shift of authority to state mental hospitals did not evolve as planned, nor did the subsequent shift to federal authority under the Community Mental Health Act of 1963. The result is today's chaotic mental health system, wherein the welfare of patients and their families are too often sacrificed to the ideologies of Planners with Big Goals. Not since the moral treatment model of the 1700s has mental health policy been driven by persons who actually lived with someone suffering from SMI. It makes a difference.

What kinds of policies are needed to ensure that persons with schizophrenia and other SMI have the highest possible quality of life, including the opportunity for gainful, competitive employment if they are capable? In the following, I set forth a package of proposals, designed to remove barriers to successful employment for this population, to the extent that is possible within the bounds of current medical knowledge.

The proposals fit into three broad categories: restoration of health capital, investments in higher education, and training in transferable skills. For each category, there is a conventional wisdom, or ideology, that confines persons with SMI within negative stereotypes of incompetence and hopelessness. The foundation underlying the proposals is that the negative stereotypes can best be combatted, and the objectives of mental health policy can best be achieved, by Searchers who are close to the problems they aim to solve. Hence, wherever possible, authority for developing solutions should be shifted away from the federal government, to the states, communities, and families, who struggle with It every day.

Restoring Health Capital

Anyone who surveys the landscape of U.S. mental health services in 2015 must conclude that our mental health policies do not meet the standards of the UN Convention on Disability Rights. In particular, current policy does not support the rights of persons with SMI to the *highest attainable health.* Many vulnerable patients receive substandard treatment or none at all, because effective systems for treating them in the community never materialized. [10] Today, the mental health system imposes barriers that make it difficult, or even impossible, to get patients the treatment they need. The barriers are legal, economic, and systemic.

Legal Barriers

The central legal issue is how to obtain care for patients who have acute symptoms of SMI, but do not believe they need treatment at all. Legislation in many states prohibits involuntary inpatient treatment of persons with mental illness, unless they pose "an imminent danger to themselves or others," or are "gravely disabled" (i.e., they are in physical danger because they have neglected their basic needs). Only eighteen states allow involuntary hospitalization on the basis of a demonstrable "need for treatment." [11]

These well-intentioned laws are designed to protect vulnerable persons from lengthy and unjustified confinement to a psychiatric institution. In the real world, the laws make it virtually impossible for family caregivers to obtain appropriate care for their relatives until *after* they become dangerous. A recent study reveals the anguish that the "imminent danger" provision imposes on families. The authors interviewed mothers caring for a child with SMI who had exhibited violent or threatening behavior toward their parent. The study describes the period of frustrated waiting until the police could be called:

> While their children decompensated right before their eyes, mothers waited for the inevitable point at which their children would meet criteria to be hospitalized involuntarily. Their living environments were filled with stress and growing tension. Mothers knew that their children needed help, but had no other option than to wait until something dangerous, even life threatening, happened. One woman said, "So what do I have to do? Do I have to sit here and wait and wait and wait and wait until that explosion happens?" [12]

Economic Barriers

In one sense, the "imminent danger" criterion is a crude mechanism for rationing inpatient psychiatric beds that are in short supply. The diversion of funding away from state mental hospitals that accompanied the community mental health movement spurred a drastic reduction in the number of inpatient psychiatric beds. In 1970, there were 525,000 psychiatric beds in the United States, by 2002 there were fewer than 212,000.[13] In a 2006 survey, more than two-thirds of state mental health authorities reported a shortage of inpatient beds for acute psychiatric care.[14] The shortages mean that patients who enter an emergency room with an acute psychiatric crisis may wait days or weeks for a bed, inmates who qualify for psychiatric care may wait in jail for several months before a bed becomes available, and patients who are admitted to a psychiatric hospital are often released too soon, in order to make room for other patients.[15]

Psychiatric inpatient beds are rationed among patients according to a priority status determined largely by forces external to the mental health system. Patients whose treatment is mandated by a court have the highest priority; patients who are referred to the system by a family member or physician have the lowest.[16] Police officers familiar with the mental health system say that they take offenders who are exhibiting signs of mental illness to jail rather than to an emergency room, because jail is the more likely route to the mental health services they need.[17]

Systemic Barriers

In spite of Robert Felix's acknowledgment that his vision of community-based care and prevention of mental illness had failed, federal policy makers continue with *more of the same.* The inefficient allocation of funding in today's mental health system, and ideological biases within the agencies that receive those funds, create systemic barriers to providing the best possible care for persons with SMI. In fiscal year 2014, for example, the Substance Abuse and Mental Health Services Administration (SAMHSA), the agency that directs federal mental health policy, allocated more than $480 million in Mental Health Block Grants to states for *community care and prevention.*[18] The funding increases annually despite the demonstrable failure of Community Mental Health Centers to provide adequate treatment for persons with the most serious mental illnesses, and despite the fact that we do not know how to predict or prevent SMI.

Appallingly, some federal mental health funds are used to support efforts to *withhold* necessary treatment from patients with SMI. In particular, the 2014 SAMHSA operating plan includes $36 million to support the Protection and Advocacy for Individuals with Mental Illness (PAIMI) Program.[19] In fiscal year 2012, the program investigated serious allegations of abuse, neglect, or civil rights violations on behalf of approximately eleven thousand persons, but performed proactive advocacy on behalf of *more than twenty-four million.*[20] In effect, "advocacy efforts" focus on ensuring that no one receives treatment for mental illness without their free and informed consent, even if the individual's decision-making capacity is impaired by acute symptoms of SMI. Such efforts often directly undermine the best interests of the patients, their families, and the community.[21] Can you imagine funding a program that advocates for children who do not want to attend school, or for elderly persons who want to keep driving even though their eyesight is failing? Funding for PAIMI continues, despite the fact that advocacy efforts outnumber protection efforts by more than two thousand to one, and despite the fact that patient advocates express no responsibility, and plan no change in tactics, following tragedies like the murder of Amy Bruce.

Flawed Ideology

If jail is the most direct route to mental health services for persons with SMI, current mental health policy warrants serious reconsideration. Current policy has failed because it has been driven by flawed ideologies, namely, that: (1) treatment for mental illness without a patient's consent is a violation of the patient's civil rights; and (2) community-based care is capable of treating and preventing acute cases of SMI.

The first ideology ignores the simple fact that mental illness attacks the brain. The brain is the center of rational thought, the organ that enables a person to understand stimuli, evaluate options, and make rational decisions. When a person is experiencing acute symptoms of SMI, their brain does not function properly; often they do not understand that they are ill, do not appreciate that treatment can help, and neither seek nor accept the care that they need. Asking a person with acute symptoms of mental illness to make rational decisions about their treatment is like asking a person in a wheelchair to get up and walk. *They cannot.* Society has an obligation to protect persons in acute phases of mental illness from the consequences of refusing treatment that can restore their health. Laws that prohibit involuntary treatment essentially deny treatment to persons with SMI who lack insight into their condition. It is this *failure to treat* that violates their right "to enjoy the highest attainable standard of health."[22]

With respect to the second ideology, fifty years of experience with community-based care has demonstrated that outpatient services cannot substitute for short-term hospitalization when a person is experiencing acute symptoms of SMI. A minimum fourteen-day period of treatment is necessary to stabilize a patient on antipsychotic medications.[23] The best way, sometimes the only way, to ensure that a patient adheres to the medication regimen is by admitting them for a short-term hospital stay. But beds are in such short supply that the only way to guarantee inpatient care is by court order.

A revised mental health policy should focus on solutions that promote both the welfare of the individual and the security of the community. Individuals have a right to be protected from making poor choices when their decision-making capacity is impaired by mental illness, and communities have a right to be protected from the potential dangers posed by persons whose symptoms of SMI are untreated. Contrary to the prevailing ideology, *there is no fundamental right to be mentally ill.*

Solutions

A bill introduced by Representative Tim Murphy (R-PA) in the 114th Congress proposes changes to federal mental health policy designed to improve access to mental health services for patients with SMI and their families. [24] If the bill becomes law, it will be a good beginning, but only a beginning. The U.S. mental health system is in need of fundamental reforms that *focus the system on the problems of persons with the most serious mental illnesses*, and *shift decision-making authority to Searchers who understand those problems.* To those ends:

(1) Congress should revamp the structure, administration, and mission of SAMHSA to focus on promoting the welfare of the agency's core constituencies (persons with SMI or substance use disorders), through activities that increase their access to high-quality mental health services.

    a. To ensure that services reflect the specific needs and research-based best practices for each constituency, SAMSHA should be replaced by two agencies: a Substance Abuse Administration and a Mental Health Services Administration (MHSA). The new organizational structure aligns the service agencies with the structure of the NIH, where research on substance abuse is supported by the National Institutes on Drug and Alcohol Abuse and research on mental disorders by the National Institute of Mental Health (NIMH).

    b. To ensure that leadership is highly qualified, Congress should mandate that the director of the MHSA be a physician with recognized expertise in treating SMI. No one among the current leadership team at SAMHSA has a medical degree. In contrast, the current director of NIMH (Dr. Thomas Insel) is a physician, former professor of psychiatry at Emory University, and respected research scientist.

c. To ensure that programs directed by the MHSA concentrate on the most serious and disabling mental illnesses, the agency's mission statement should reflect that focus. The current SAMHSA mission, "To reduce the impact of mental illness and substance abuse on America's communities"[25] has no focus and no measurable outcomes. One imagines an agency that expects little of itself, and accomplishes little as a result. Here is an alternate suggestion: "To increase and actively promote access to high-quality mental health services for persons with serious mental illness, with the goal of restoring each person to their maximum attainable mental health, and best possible quality of life."

(2) This mission can best be accomplished by supporting Searchers, at the state and community levels, who work closely with the target population and understand the problems they face. Hence, the locus of decision-making authority for public mental health services should be decentralized to reside with state mental health authorities.

a. To ensure that state mental health systems are adequately funded, MHSA should direct a major portion of its budget to State Mental Health Grants in support of its revised mission.

b. To ensure that states have freedom to innovate and develop best practices in the delivery of mental health services, the Mental Health Grants should have minimal restrictions, that define *what* is to be accomplished (improve access to high-quality mental health services) and for *whom* (persons with SMI), but place no restrictions on *how* the goals are to be accomplished.

c. To ensure that best practices in mental health services are disseminated nationwide, MHSA should collect a standard set of objective performance and expenditure measures from all states. Analyses of the data will identify the most cost-effective approaches to the delivery of mental health services, which MHSA should be responsible for disseminating.

(3) The federal government should adopt policies aimed at eliminating economic, legal, and systemic barriers to short-term inpatient care for persons experiencing acute symptoms of SMI.

a. To address economic barriers, the Centers for Medicare and Medicaid Services should eliminate restrictions that prohibit states from covering the costs of inpatient psychiatric care for Medicaid insureds. The policy creates disparities between persons with SMI covered by Medicaid (who may need hospital care for their mental illness but cannot get it) and persons with SMI covered by private insurance (who can).

b. To address legal barriers, the MHSA should draft, and provide incentives for states to adopt, a Model Involuntary Treatment Law. The law should make it possible for caregivers or mental health providers to obtain necessary *short-term* care for persons who have diminished decision-making capacity because of the acute symptoms of mental illness. In particular, the Model Law should expand the criteria for treatment without consent to include, with appropriate safeguards, *any person who is in need of medical treatment who is not mentally capable of understanding that need.*[26]

c. To address systemic barriers, Congress should de-fund the Patient Advocacy Program and replace it with an office empowered only to field complaints of abuse, neglect, or civil rights violations on behalf of persons with mental disorders. There is abundant evidence that the Advocacy Program *reduces* social welfare by depriving persons with SMI of the medical care they need, jeopardizing the welfare and security of family members, and imposing unnecessary costs on the social services and criminal justice systems.[27]

When we left David in Charlotte, after unsuccessful efforts to bring him back to Arizona or have him hospitalized, my greatest fear was that he would hurt himself or someone else. I was not concerned about deliberate acts of violence (David had never been threatening to anyone), but about poor judgment. I imagined a fatal car accident, a fight in a bar, David sleeping on the street, or becoming the victim of violent crime. There was nothing I could do except wait for the inevitable disaster, and pick up the pieces afterward. A functional mental health system would facilitate intervention before the disaster occurred.

Investing in Higher Education

The onset of SMI occurs most often in late adolescence, exactly when many young adults are making significant investments in human capital at a college or university. For the unlucky ones who become afflicted, the shock of SMI can derail their plans for graduation, career, and future. Students with bipolar I disorder, for example, are 70 percent more likely to drop out of college than students with no mental disorder.[28] The loss of human capital is tragic.

Structural Discrimination

Prior to the discovery of antipsychotic medications, it would have been almost unthinkable for a person with mental illness to aspire to a college education. The uncontrolled symptoms of SMI would be too great an obstacle to success. Now that we have treatments that control the acute symptoms for many patients, many college students with a diagnosis of SMI can return to school and complete their degrees. The primary obstacles to their success are the pervasive stigma against mental illness, the diminished self-confidence associated with a diagnosis of SMI, and the lack of necessary resources and support.[29]

At most U.S. colleges and universities, students with SMI are more likely to encounter structural discrimination than structural support. *Structural discrimination* is defined as a set of institutional practices that marginalize a disadvantaged group (e.g., students with mental illness).[30] Colleges and universities are not immune from such practices, even though they exist primarily for the purpose of promoting education and enlightenment. Examples of potential structural discrimination in higher education include: a disability services office that serves students with physical disabilities, but is unable or unwilling to support students with SMI; admission/readmission standards that are more stringent for students with SMI than for other students; campus residency policies that restrict the housing choices of students with SMI, solely on the basis of their illness.

The federal government provides no incentive or mandate to colleges and universities to eliminate structural discrimination against students with mental illness. In contrast, the government expends millions of dollars on higher education programs for other disadvantaged groups.[31] There are programs to support postsecondary education for blacks, Hispanics, migrants, Native Americans, and other minorities. There are programs to support special institutions of higher education for persons who are blind or deaf. But for persons with mental illness, there is vocational rehabilitation, supported employment, and SSDI.

Flawed Ideology

The structural discrimination against students with SMI on college and university campuses is fueled by negative stereotypes of persons with mental illness as dangerous, disruptive, and somehow responsible for their illness. Recall the college administrator who characterized my son's illness as "getting into trouble." Such discrimination would not be tolerated if it were directed at a member of another minority group.

Research shows that gender (male) and ethnicity (Hispanic) are stronger predictors of violent behavior than SMI.[32] Do colleges and universities have more stringent readmissions standards for Hispanic men (with no history of violence) than for other students? Of course not. Violent behavior among persons with SMI is strongly linked to acute psychotic symptoms.[33] There is simply no justification for universities to discriminate against students with mental illness who have no history of violence, who are responsive and adherent to medication, and who are not experiencing acute symptoms.

The failure of the federal government to establish any higher education programs for persons with SMI, one of the most disadvantaged and stigmatized of minority groups, suggests that policy makers are also driven by negative stereotypes. Why create policies or programs to support higher education services for persons with SMI, if you believe that they are incompetent and incapable of taking care of themselves? In fact, the stereotype is false. There are many examples of persons with schizophrenia and other serious mental illnesses who have completed college and postgraduate degrees.

Colleges and universities are in a unique position to help students with SMI acquire the human capital they need, both to qualify for stable jobs in the primary labor market and to find jobs that are a good match for their residual functional limitations. Colleges and universities are also in a position of authority, from which they can provide incentives (i.e., the opportunity to stay in school) for students with SMI to adhere to their prescribed treatment. Thus, public policies that encourage institutions of higher education to support their students with SMI can enhance the welfare of the students, increase equity in the market for higher education, and improve long-term employment outcomes for this population.

Solutions

The NIMH is ideally poised to create incentives for universities to provide supported education services for students with SMI. In fiscal year 2014, NIMH awarded more than $927 million in research grants to U.S. institutions of higher education.[34] In addition to supporting basic and clinical research that will develop better treatments for mental disorders, the funds support interventional research aimed at developing (emphasis added):

> new and better interventions that incorporate the diverse needs and circumstances of persons with mental illness, . . . allowing those who may suffer from these disorders to *live full and productive lives*.[35]

The vast amount of research funds awarded by NIMH give the institute considerable leverage to motivate welfare-enhancing behavior from grant recipients. NIMH already uses its leverage to ensure that research protocols have adequate protections for human and animal subjects, include appropriate representation of women and minorities, and provide training opportunities for undergraduate and graduate students. It is perfectly consistent with the strategic objectives of NIMH to ensure that its partner universities support their students with SMI. In fact, it is ironic that institutions can accept millions of dollars of grant support from NIMH to study mental disorders, but have no reciprocal obligation to provide educational supports for their students with mental illness. Therefore:

(4) The NIMH should use existing grant mechanisms to force U.S. universities to offer supported education programs for students with SMI. Qualifying programs should be designed to attain significant increases in graduation rates for this population.

   a. To ensure that supported education services are widely available, NIMH should require all funding applications from universities to include a detailed statement regarding on-campus services provided for students with SMI. The services should be aimed at encouraging and supporting return to school, academic achievement, graduation, and job placement.

   b. To encourage innovation in supported education services for students with SMI, NIMH should issue a special Request for Applications (RFA) for projects that develop, test, and disseminate best practices in providing educational services to university students with mental illness. The RFA is appropriate under the Child and Adolescent Research Program, which aims to "accelerate the implementation of evidence-based services for youth within and across service sectors" (including schools), and to support the "integration of mental health services across sectors" (including education).[36] Consistent with the idea that solutions will be developed by Searchers, the RFA should allow broad scope for innovation in the nature of services delivered, provided that those services are delivered in integrated settings *on-campus* (so that students with SMI are not marginalized), and that the expected outcome measure is *graduation*.

The proposed MHSA provides another mechanism to promote supported education services for students with SMI. As set forth previously, a primary mission of the agency should be to ensure that persons with SMI have the best possible quality of life. That mission naturally includes the opportunity to complete their education. Hence:

(5) Once established, the MHSA should fund targeted grants to states, public universities, and local community colleges to develop supported education services for students with SMI. Qualifying programs should be designed to attain significant increases in graduation rates for this population.

a. To ensure that grantees have maximum flexibility to develop effective interventions, targeted grants should have few restrictions beyond the basic objectives to eliminate structural discrimination, and provide pro-active, on-campus support, for students with SMI who are enrolled in regular university degree programs.

b. To ensure that best practices are encouraged and disseminated, the MHSA should collect data from grantees on particulars of the programs and outcomes attained (admission/readmission rates, retention rates, graduation rates, employment rates, earnings, etc.). Results should be distributed and posted on the agency's website, both to encourage the spread of on-campus supported education, and to counteract negative stereotypes of persons with SMI as incapable of earning a college degree.

Parents, university administrators, and others may raise concerns that increasing access to higher education for students with SMI will create risks for the campus community. What if a student stops treatment and suffers a relapse of psychotic symptoms? The risk is slight because, even among persons with SMI who are suffering acute symptoms of psychosis, only a small fraction will commit acts of violence. The risk can be minimized even further if NIMH and MHSA require colleges and universities to include strategies for monitoring a student's adherence to their prescribed medications. For students with SMI, the *privilege* of attending college should include the *responsibility* of adhering to treatment.

Training in Transferable Skills

Vocational training for persons with SMI is dominated by models of supported employment, and the current gold standard is the Individual Placement and Support (IPS) model. The consensus in the literature is that IPS out-performs other models of vocational rehabilitation in terms of job placement, hours worked per month, and monthly earnings.[37] Still, IPS, like other models of supported employment, has almost no impact on moving participants off disability benefits and into gainful competitive employment.

Evaluation of IPS

In 2005, the SSA launched a study to determine if a combination of IPS, systematic medication managment, and behavioral health services could succeed in moving persons with SMI off SSDI. The Mental Health Treatment Study (MHTS) enrolled more than 2,200 SSDI recipients, with schizophrenia or affective disorders, at twenty-three sites across the United States.[38] Subjects were randomized to either an intervention group, which received IPS vocational services plus medication management and behavioral health services, or a control group, which received the usual mental health services covered by Medicare.

Vocational services provided to the intervention group adhered to the core principles of IPS:

- *Eligibility based on consumer choice*, with no exclusions for treatment noncompliance, co-occurring substance use disorders, lack of work readiness, etc.
- *Integration of employment service*s with mental health services
- A *focus on competitive employment*, meaning jobs in regular work settings, paying at least the minimum wage
- *Rapid job search* beginning immediately upon admission to the program
- *Individual employment support*, as needed, after job placement
- *Job placement based on client preferences* rather than availability of jobs
- *Benefits counseling* to mitigate the impact of employment on government entitlements such as SSDI and Medicaid[39]

The MHTS tracked employment outcomes for participants over a two-year period. The intervention group attained significantly better outcomes, on average, than the controls.[40] Nevertheless, those among the intervention group who obtained a job typically worked less than half the months in the follow-up period, with mean weekly earnings of $192.[41] Only 8 percent of the intervention group attained earnings above the level for "substantial, gainful activity."

The MHTS is stark evidence of the problems with current vocational services for persons with SMI. IPS is the best model of supported employment we have, but it is not successful in placing persons with SMI in *full and gainful competitive employment.* One analyst summarizes the "take-home messages" as follows (emphasis added):

> People with severe mental illness often want to work and to feel socially included, and the MHTS demonstrated an ability to improve those outcomes. The MHTS also establishes strongly that the best we have will have only a small effect on employment and earnings and essentially *no effect on exit from SSDI into mainstream economic life.* [42]

Many thousands of persons with SMI are capable of full and gainful competitive employment but are disadvantaged by disruptions to schooling and gaps in work experience that leave them with diminished human capital. Participation in IPS-type supported employment programs will not provide the *transferable skills* they need to succeed in today's competitive labor market. The broad eligibility criteria (no exclusions) and rapid job placements characteristic of IPS virtually condemn clients to low-skill, low-wage jobs, where any human capital they acquire is job-specific. Such jobs do not lead to long-term stable employment.

Flawed Ideology

Better models of vocational training are needed for persons with SMI who are capable of independent, competitive work. We are not, however, *searching* for new and different ways to provide vocational services to this population. Research in the area of vocational rehabilitation is dominated by studies of the outcomes of IPS, the relative merits of IPS versus other models of supported employment, and the degree to which IPS programs maintain fidelity to its core principles. In the vocational services literature, the commitment to IPS has become almost an ideology in itself.

Paradoxically, some of the core principles of IPS reinforce negative stereotypes of persons with SMI that create barriers to successful employment. Providing individual employment supports after job placement suggests that persons with SMI are incapable of independent work. Counseling to ensure that disability benefits continue suggests that persons with SMI will always be dependent on government support. Rapid job placement without training suggests that persons with SMI are incapable of holding more than menial jobs. Allowing participation of those who are not work-ready suggests that persons with SMI must be exempted from normal work requirements.

For reasons cited throughout this book, work is an important part of recovery from a serious mental illness. Accordingly, there is a role for IPS in providing employment opportunities for persons who are so severely disabled by mental illness that they are unable to succeed in independent, competitive jobs. But, continuing the *exclusive* focus on IPS is prejudicial and counterproductive, because it creates the mindset that all persons with SMI are so severely work-limited. New models of vocational services need to be developed to ensure that all persons with SMI achieve their maximum potential at work. Policy solutions should aim to increase efficiency in the labor market by enhancing the general human capital (transferable skills) of workers with SMI, and placing those who are capable of gainful employment in stable and well-paying competitive jobs.

Solutions

New models of vocational training for persons with SMI are being piloted in both Canada and Australia. In Ontario, Frontenac County Mental Health Services and St. Lawrence Community College jointly developed a retail skills training program to improve competitive employment outcomes for persons with SMI.[43] The focus of the program was on retail skills because skilled retail workers were in demand (the retail sector was expanding in

Ontario) and because many clients expressed interest in careers in retail sales (and had related work experience). The training program consisted of twelve weeks of classroom instruction, and a three-week community work placement.

> Eleven individuals enrolled in the inaugural program. All expressed great enthusiasm for the program, based on the novelty of being in school, connecting to the world of work, and feeling more a part of the community at large. The group formed friendships and acquired new learning. All completed the rigorous classroom training.[44]

By 2010, the Skills for Retail training program had been offered three times, to a total of twenty-nine participants. Twenty graduates (69 percent) were working in competitive retail sales positions, with job tenure ranging from six to twenty-four months.[45]

In Australia, the Division of Mental Health Services for Liverpool and Fairfield Counties partnered with the Southwestern Sydney Institute of Technical and Further Education to offer trainings in horticulture, hospitality, and computer literacy for clients with SMI. Classes were taught by instructors from the institute, with counseling and support services provided by an occupational therapist from the Division of Mental Health. Sixty-one clients participated in one or more trainings. Most clients (nearly 90 percent) had diagnoses of schizophrenia, schizoaffective disorder, or bipolar disorder. No client who expressed an interest in the training was excluded. The overall course completion rate was 72 percent. Within six to twelve months of completion, two-thirds of graduates were either employed in mainstream "open" employment (18 percent), or had continued on with further education (51 percent).[46]

These programs are too small to provide more than illustrative evidence of what might be accomplished with vocational services targeted at developing the general human capital of persons with SMI. However, they demonstrate that people with even the most serious mental illnesses can aspire to more than menial employment and can acquire skills of value in the labor market. There is no indication in the literature that programs like these are even being pondered in the United States. The almost exclusive focus of research on supported employment models appears to have crowded out other models that can enhance the productive potential of persons with SMI. Hence:

   (6) The federal government should direct grant monies appropriated to the National Institute of Disability and Rehabilitation Research (NIDRR) and NIMH to support research aimed at developing and evaluating new models of vocational skills training for persons with SMI. These vocational services are not intended to supplant the IPS

model, but to serve the "hidden population" of persons with SMI who are capable of supporting themselves in competitive jobs, but have thus far been ignored. To ensure that new training models serve the target population and maximize their productive potential, the following core principles should be applied:

- *Eligibility is based on the capacity for independent and gainful employment,* meaning that the most acute symptoms of SMI are controlled, with or without antipsychotic drugs.
- *The focus is on gainful competitive employment,* in other words, mainstream jobs, not set aside for persons with disabilities, which provide sufficient income for financial independence.
- *Education and/or vocational skills training* is provided to enhance the general human capital of participants before job placement.
- *Job placement is focused on finding a good match* between the client's skills, abilities and functional limitations, and the requirements of a potential job.
- The expectation is that clients will *not need long-term support from government entitlements* such as SSDI or Medicaid.

(7) Once established, the MHSA should provide funding to state mental health authorities to develop vocational services programs consistent with these principles.

(8) The MHSA should also provide funding to states to support ventures in *entrepreneurship and self-employment* for the target population. Self-employment is a good job match for many persons with SMI, because of the flexibility that comes with being in charge. One participant in our qualitative study, for example, told us that:

> One of my major decisions was to get out of real estate and go back to school and become a massage therapist. [Now] if I am not feeling well I don't have to worry about the whole anxiety attack to have to call in and explain to somebody that I am not feeling well and that I can't come to work. So if I am sick, I am sick and I don't have to answer to no one, but me. . . . And so, just knowing that I can have time to do what I need to do for myself with my new career is just worth its weight in gold. [47]

In a recent twenty-year update on the IPS model of supported employment, two of its ardent proponents stated:

> Some professionals in many countries, including the U.S., persist in believing that many people [with SMI] cannot work and need to be protected in sheltered settings. These latter arguments recall paeans for long-term institutional-

ization in the 1970s and, like those cries, are likely to become historical anach-
ronisms.[48]

The authors continue on to say that (emphasis added):

> Current research on IPS supported employment shows that the majority [of
> people disabled by psychiatric disorders] can succeed as *steady part-time
> workers.*[49]

The statement implies that the best a person with SMI can hope for, in the
competitive workplace, is a steady, part-time job. I look forward to the day
when *that belief* becomes an historical anachronism.

Postscript

The history of mental health policy in the United States has been a series of
well-intentioned attempts by Planners to solve problems they did not fully
understand. The policies have been implemented with little accountability, a
general lack of foresight regarding unintended consequences, and sometimes
a callous disregard for the well-being of persons with SMI and their families.
The outcomes have been largely unsuccessful and, in some cases, tragic.

Current mental health policy is rife with irony and inconsistency. Government policy turns family members into default caregivers for persons with
SMI, but denies them decision-making authority or access to medical information in times of crisis. Policy makers fund patient advocates to ensure that
persons with mental illness are not hospitalized against their will, then decry
the fact that the criminal justice system is overrun by persons with mental
illness who ought to be hospitalized. Researchers and policy makers who
insist that persons with SMI can make competent decisions about treatment
when they are ill seem to believe these same persons are incapable of full
employment when they are well.

With the vision of a more rational mental health system in mind, my
policy proposals are designed to improve employment outcomes for persons
with SMI. In the belief that solutions will come from visionary Searchers
rather than ideologically-driven Planners, I have identified policies that shift
decision-making authority for mental health services away from the federal
government and empower Searchers at the state and local levels to develop
creative solutions.

Some readers will criticize these policies as overly paternalistic (e.g.,
involuntary hospitalization based on the "need for treatment," or adherence
to treatment as a condition for attending a college or university). Therefore,
let me reiterate the logic that led to these proposals: Mental illness is a
disease of the *brain*, which compromises a person's *decision-making capacity*. Adherence to prescribed treatment in the first five years after onset of

SMI is critical to prevent relapse, to increase the probability of recovery, and to minimize the subsequent loss of functional capacity. Investments in general human capital can protect individuals from some of the disabling effects of mental illness, and significantly increase the probability of gainful, competitive employment. Thus, policy interventions that optimize the health, functional capacities, and employment prospects of persons with SMI, are both justifiable and humane. *There is no fundamental right to be mentally ill.*

My faith in the creative problem-solving power of Searchers comes from both research and experience. For the past fifteen years, the overriding purpose of my life has been to help my son reclaim his life from schizophrenia. It has been my greatest challenge. I have had family, friends, and colleagues for support; access to the best physicians and lawyers; and a lot of luck. But in the end, the solutions have come, not from others and not from chance, but from intuition, determination, and desperation to save my son. "Once you get into cosmological [muck] like this, you got to throw away the instruction manual."[50]

Chapter Twelve

Life Reclaimed

EPILOGUE

Summer 2012

In June 2012, I was back in Luxembourg working at the Research Institute and enjoying my European lifestyle: commuter train to and from work, daily shopping trips to the village market, and occasional weekend trips to Paris. I didn't hear much from David, but I wasn't particularly worried this time. He was busy too. He had his own friends, and his job at the Dream Center, and classes at American Indian College.

Still, I always worried about David's future. We revised our will, setting up a trust to ensure that he had an income after we were gone. Aaron knew that it would eventually be his responsibility to make sure David was never homeless or alone. Sometimes, I imagined the kind of wife I wished David could find. She would be confident, decisive, and organized, but compassionate and caring. Of course, this was all an impossible dream. I never expected David to marry. I grieved for the life he had lost, and the grandchildren I would never see.

But, when I returned home from Europe that summer, David had a surprise for me. "Let's have lunch," he suggested. "Someplace special, Mom, because there's someone I want you to meet." And so Megan walked into our lives. She was everything I had imagined in my wishful thinking, and more. She loved my son, which is really the only important selection criteria for a daughter-in-law, and he was obviously in love with her. They planned to be married in December.

When I returned home from lunch, I told my fiancé that David was engaged. "You don't seem very excited," he said. "You don't understand," I told him, "I've been down this path before." And I worried that the stress of an impending marriage would trigger a relapse of psychotic symptoms again.

Others were worried as well. When Megan's family learned about David's diagnosis of schizophrenia they were, understandably, concerned. (I have to admit, a man with SMI is not most parents' idea of the perfect son-in-law.) David and Megan scheduled an intervention with her family to discuss their objections to the marriage. David told them, "I'm glad you raised your concerns. I want to have everything out in the open about my illness. Ask me whatever questions you like." Brother Mike, David's pastor at the House of Healing, mediated the session. After David finished answering questions, Mike told Megan's family about David's healing from mental illness. To their great credit, they were able to see past the stereotypes of schizophrenia, and accept David into their family.

It was delightful to watch Megan plan her wedding. She knew exactly where she wanted to be married, but it was outside her budget. So she planned the wedding for a Thursday, when there was less demand, and negotiated a rate she could afford. About two months before the wedding, she went shopping for a dress. Sales clerks at the bridal shop were appalled; "You can't possibly order a dress and have it altered in time." They did not know Megan. She found her perfect dress and took it home that day. In short, Megan had all the details of the wedding under control. The only thing for me to do was choose a song for my dance with David.

Winter 2012

David and Megan were married in December, outdoors, in view of Camelback Mountain in Phoenix. Aaron's children were flower girl and ring bearer. Little Zachary (age four) at first refused to participate. When he tried on his tuxedo, however, he decided he liked his ring-bearer "costume" and agreed to walk down the aisle with sister, Audrey. Pastor Tommy Barnett conducted the ceremony, and Brother Mike was part of the wedding party. One of my favorite moments was when Megan's brother toasted the newlyweds during the reception. He said that, even at a young age, older sister Megan was clearly in charge. "I was more afraid of getting in trouble with Megan than getting in trouble with my mother."

David and Megan planned to honeymoon in Mexico. My husband offered his time-share points to rent a condo for them. When they told Allan where they wanted to stay, he said to me, "Do you know how many points this is costing me?" "Welcome to parenthood," I told him.

Spring 2015

One year ago, with his construction business bringing in a steady income, David wrote to the Social Security Administration to inform them that he no longer needed monthly checks from SSDI. The letter he received in reply said, "You are not eligible to withdraw from SSDI at this time." He waited six months and tried again. This time, SSA agreed. David received his last government check in February 2015—in March, his construction business multiplied four-fold and he had to hire additional workers to keep up with the demand.

Last December, David and Megan celebrated their second wedding anniversary. She works for Phoenix First Assembly as their event planner, where she manages all the weddings. David preaches every Sunday evening at the state prison. Since he met Megan, he is more relaxed, more accepting, and better dressed. Gradually, I am beginning to relax as well, and to believe that David's victory over *It* is real. The song I chose? "The Impossible Dream."

Notes

1. A DISEASE UNLIKE ANY OTHER

1. Rajiv Tandon, Matcheri S. Keshavan, and Henry A. Nasrallah, "Schizophrenia, 'Just the Facts' What We Know in 2008. 2 Epidemiology and Etiology," *Schizophrenia Research* 102 (2008): 3–4.

2. Tandon, Keshavan, and Nasrallah, "Epidemiology and Etiology," 4–5.

3. R. Walter Heinrichs, "Historical Origins of Schizophrenia: Two Early Madmen and Their Illness," *Journal of the History of the Behavioral Sciences* 39 (2003): 357.

4. Heinrichs, "Historical Origins of Schizophrenia."

5. Heinrichs, "Historical Origins of Schizophrenia," 356.

6. Heinrichs, "Historical Origins of Schizophrenia," 354.

7. Heinrichs, "Historical Origins of Schizophrenia," 354.

8. Celeste Silveira, Joao Marques-Teixeira, and Antonio Jose de Bastos-Leite, "More Than One Century of Schizophrenia: An Evolving Perspective," *Journal of Nervous and Mental Disease* 200 (2012): 1054.

9. Rajiv Tandon, Matcheri S. Keshavan, and Henry A. Nasrallah, "Schizophrenia, 'Just the Facts' 4. Clinical Features and Conceptualization," *Schizophrenia Research* 110 (2009): 2.

10. Michael D. Hunter and Peter W. R. Woodruff, "History, Aetiology and Symptomatology of Schizophrenia," *Psychiatry* 4 (2005): 2; Nick Craddock and Michael J. Owen, "The Kraepelinian Dichotomy—Going, Going . . . But Still Not Gone," *British Journal of Psychiatry* 196 (2010): 92.

11. Silveira, Marques-Teixeira, and Bastos-Leite, "One Century of Schizophrenia," 1054; Hunter and Woodruff, "History, Aetiology and Symptomatology," 3.

12. Silveira, Marques-Teixeira, and Bastos-Leite, "One Century of Schizophrenia," 1054.

13. Rajiv Tandon, Henry A. Nasrallah, and Matcheri S. Keshavan, "'Just the Facts': Meandering in Schizophrenia's Many Forests," *Schizophrenia Research* 128 (2011): 5. Pathoplastic factors are factors, like personality, that can affect the way an illness is expressed.

14. Tandon, Keshavan, and Nasrallah, "Clinical Features and Conceptualization," 2.

15. Heinrichs, "Historical Origins," 352.

16. Tandon, Keshavan, and Nasrallah, "Clinical Features and Conceptualization," 4–5.

17. Tandon, Keshavan, and Nasrallah, "Clinical Features and Conceptualization," 6.

18. Matcheri S. Keshavan et al., "Schizophrenia, 'Just the Facts': What We Know in 2008 Part 3: Neurobiology," *Schizophrenia Research* 106 (2008): 90–96.

19. Manfred Bleuler, "A 23-Year Longitudinal Study of 208 Schizophrenics and Impressions in Regard to the Nature of Schizophrenia," *Journal of Psychiatric Research* 6 (1968, Supplement 1): 10.

20. Tandon, Keshavan, and Nasrallah, "Epidemiology and Etiology," 6.

21. John H. Gilmore, "Understanding What Causes Schizophrenia: A Developmental Perspective," *American Journal of Psychiatry* 167 (2010): 8.

22. Tandon, Keshavan, and Nasrallah, "Epidemiology and Etiology," 12.

23. K. H. Nuechterlein et al., "The Vulnerability/Stress Model of Schizophrenic Relapse: A Longitudinal Study," *Acta Psvchiatrica Scandinavica* 89 (1994): 58–60.

24. Elaine F. Walker and Donald Diforio, "Schizophrenia: A Neural-Diathesis Stress Model," *Psychological Review* 104 (1997): 677–79.

25. Keshavan et al., "Schizophrenia, 'Just the Facts' 6. Moving Ahead with the Schizophrenia Concept: From the Elephant to the Mouse," *Schizophrenia Research* 127 (2011): 7.

26. Keshavan et al., 4–7.

27. Keshavan et al.

28. Francisco Lopez-Munoz and Cecilio Alamo, "The Consolidation of Neuroleptic Therapy: Janssen, the Discovery of Haloperidol and Its Introduction into Clinical Practice," *Brain Research Bulletin* 79 (2009): 133.

29. Lopez-Munoz and Alamo, "The Consolidation of Neuroleptic Therapy," 134–35.

30. Rajiv Tandon, Henry A. Nasrallah, and Matcheri S. Keshavan, "Schizophrenia, 'Just the Facts' 5. Treatment and Prevention Past, Present, and Future," *Schizophrenia Research* 122 (2010): 2–6.

31. Tandon, Nasrallah, and Keshavan, "Treatment and Prevention"; George Foussias and Gary Remington, "Antipsychotics and Schizophrenia: From Efficacy and Effectiveness to Clinical Decision-Making," *Canadian Journal of Psychiatry* 55 (2010): 117–23.

32. Foussias and Remington, "Antipsychotics and Schizophrenia," 121–22.

33. Tandon, Nasrallah, and Keshavan, "Treatment and Prevention," 5.

34. Eric Q. Wu et al., "The Economic Burden of Schizophrenia in the United States in 2002," *Journal of Clinical Psychiatry* 66 (2005): 1125–26.

35. Marjorie L. Baldwin and Steven C. Marcus. "Labor Market Outcomes of Persons with Mental Disorders," *Industrial Relations* 46 (2007): 481–96.

2. THE MARK OF SCHIZOPHRENIA

1. Nathaniel Hawthorne, *The Scarlet Letter* (Reprint, New York: Simon & Schuster, 2004), 62.

2. *Oxford English Dictionary*, 1st ed., s.v. "stigma."

3. Emory Bogardus, "A Social Distance Scale," *Sociology and Social Research* 17 (1933): 269.

4. Erving Goffman, *Stigma: Notes on the Management of Spoiled Identity* (Englewood Cliffs, NJ: Prentice-Hall, 1963), 3.

5. Goffman, *Stigma*, 4–18.

6. Mary T. Westbrook, Varoe Legge, and Mark Pennay, "Attitudes towards Disabilities in aMulticultural Society," *Social Science and Medicine* 36 (1993): 617.

7. Westbrook, Legge, and Pennay, "Attitudes towards Disabilities in a Multicultural Society," 619.

8. John. L. Tringo, "The Hierarchy of Preference toward Disability Groups," *Journal of Special Education* 4 (1970): 299; Gary Albrecht, Vivian G. Walker, and Judith A. Levy, "Social Ddistance from the Stigmatized: A Test of Two Theories," *Social Science and Medicine* 16 (1982): 1323.

9. Bruce Link et al., "Public Conceptions of Mental Illness: Labels, Causes, Dangerousness, and Social Distance," *American Journal of Public Health* 89 (1999): 1331–32.

10. Caroline E. Mann and Melissa J. Himelein, "Factors Associated with Stigmatization of Persons with Mental Illness," *Psychiatric Services* 55 (2004): 186–87; Ross Norman, Deborah

Windell, and Rahul Manchanda, "Examining Differences in the Stigma of Depression and Schizophrenia," *International Journal of Social Psychiatry* 58 (2012): 74.

11. Marc Franchot Weiss, "Children's Attitudes toward the Mentally Ill: A Developmental Analysis," *Psychological Reports* 58 (1986): 12.

12. Marc Franchot Weiss, "Children's Attitudes toward the Mentally Ill: An Eight-Year Longitudinal Follow-Up," *Psychological Reports* 74 (1994): 52.

13. Weiss, "Children's Attitudes toward the Mentally Ill," 55.

14. Weiss, "Developmental Analysis," 16.

15. Matthias C. Angermeyer and Herbert Matschinger, "Public Beliefs about Schizophrenia and Depression: Similarities and Differences," *Social Psychiatry and Psychiatric Epidemiology* 38 (2003): 529.

16. Patrick W. Corrigan, "Mental Health Stigma as Social Attribution: Implications for Research Methods and Attitude Change," *Clinical Psychology: Science and Practice* 7 (2000): 51–54; Bernard Weiner, Raymond P. Perry, and Jamie Magnusson, "An Attributional Analysis of Reactions to Stigmas," *Journal of Personality and Social Psychology* 55 (1988): 738–39.

17. Bernard Weiner, "On Sin versus Sickness: A Theory of Perceived Responsibility and Social Motivation," *American Psychologist* 48 (1993): 959–61.

18. Corrigan, "Stigma as Social Attribution," 52.

19. Corrigan, "Stigma as Social Attribution," 50–57.

20. Craig Hemmens et al., "The Consequences of Official Labels: An Examination of the Rights Lost by the Mentally Ill and Mentally Incompetent Ten Years Later," *Community Mental Health Journal* 38 (2002): 132–34.

21. Patrick Corrigan et al., "An Attribution Model of Public Discrimination towards Persons with Mental Illness," *Journal of Health and Social Behavior* 44 (2003): 166; Angermeyer and Matschinger, "Public Beliefs," 529.

22. Nava R. Silton et al., "Stigma in America: Has Anything Changed? Impact of Perceptions of Mental Illness and Dangerousness on the Desire for Social Distance: 1996 and 2006," *Journal of Nervous and Mental Disease* 199 (2011): 363; Bernice A. Pescosolido et al., "'A Disease Like Any Other?' A Decade of Change in Public Reactions to Schizophrenia, Depression, and Alcohol Dependence," *American Journal of Psychiatry* 167 (2010): 1324.

23. Ross Norman et al., "The Role of Perceived Norms in the Stigmatization of Mental Illness," *Social Psychiatry and Psychiatric Epidemiology* 43 (2008): 855.

24. Matthias C. Angermeyer and Herbert Matschinger, "Labeling—Stereotype—Discrimination: An Investigation of the Stigma Process," *Social Psychiatry and Psychiatric Epidemiology* 40 (2005): 393.

25. Norman et al., "Perceived Norms," 855.

26. Angermeyer and Matschinger, "Labeling—Stereotype—Discrimination," 393.

27. David B. Feldman and Christian S. Crandall, "Dimensions of Mental Illness Stigma: What about Mental Illness Causes Social Rejection?" *Journal of Social and Clinical Psychology* 26 (2007): 145–46; Matthias C. Angermeyer, Michael Beck, and Herbert Matschinger, "Determinants of the Public's Preference for Social Distance from People with Schizophrenia," *Canadian Journal of Psychiatry* 48 (2003): 666.

28. Corrigan et al., "An Attribution Model," 165.

29. John Read, "Why Promoting Biological Ideology Increases Prejudice against People Labelled 'Schizophrenic.'" *Australian Psychologist* 42 (2007): 118.

30. Pescosolido et al., "A Disease Like Any Other?" 1322–24.

31. Lisa Wood et al., "Public Perceptions of Stigma towards People with Schizophrenia, Depression, and Anxiety," *Psychiatry Research* 220 (2014): 605–6.

32. Pescosolido et al., "A Disease Like Any Other?" 1324; G. Schomerus et al., "Evolution of Public Attitudes about Mental Illness: A Systematic Review and Meta-Analysis," *Acta Psychiatrica Scandinavica* 125 (2012): 446.

33. Wood et al., "Public Perceptions of Stigma," 606.

34. Read, "Promoting Biological Ideology," 121–23.

35. Matthias C. Angermeyer et al., "Biogenetic Explanations and Emotional Reactions to People with Schizophrenia and Major Depressive Disorder," *Psychiatry Research* 220 (2014): 702–3.

36. Wood et al., "Public Perceptions of Stigma," 606.

37. Silton et al., "Stigma in America," 363.

38. Pescosolido et al., "A Disease Like Any Other?" 1324.

39. Corrigan et al., "Newspaper Stories as Measures of Structural Stigma," *Psychiatric Services* 56 (2005): 552–53.

40. Corrigan et al., "Newspaper Stories," 554.

41. Pamela J. Taylor, "Psychosis and Violence: Stories, Fears and Reality," *Canadian Journal of Psychiatry* 53 (2008): 647.

42. Patrick W. Corrigan and Amy C. Watson, "Findings from the National Comorbidity Survey on the Frequency of Violent Behavior in Individuals with Psychiatric Disorders," *Psychiatry Research* 136 (2005): 156–57.

43. Linda A. Teplin et al., "Crime Victimization in Adults with Severe Mental Illness," *Archives of General Psychiatry* 62 (2005): 914.

44. Gary S. Becker, *Economics of Discrimination*, 2nd ed. (Chicago: University of Chicago Press, 1971), 39–40, 55–56, 75–77.

45. Marjorie L. Baldwin and William G. Johnson, "Labor Market Discrimination against Men with Disabilities in the Year of the A.D.A.," *Southern Economic Journal* 66 (2000): 558.

46. Marjorie L. Baldwin, "The Effects of Impairments on Employment and Wages: Estimates from the 1984 and 1990 SIPP," *Behavioral Sciences and the Law* 17 (1999): 20–23; Melanie K. Jones, Paul L. Latreille, and Peter J. Sloane, "Disability, Gender, and the British Labour Market," *Oxford Economics Papers* 58 (2006): 434; Baldwin and Marcus, "Labor Market Outcomes," 496–502.

47. Baldwin and Marcus, "Labor Market Outcomes."

48. Marjorie L. Baldwin and Steven C. Marcus. "Perceived versus Measured Stigma among Workers with Serious Mental Disorders," *Psychiatric Services* 57 (2006): 390.

49. Janice Hunter Jenkins and Elizabeth A. Carpenter-Song, "Awareness of Stigma among Persons with Schizophrenia," *Journal of Nervous and Mental Disease* 197 (2009): 522.

50. Jenkins and Carpenter-Song, "Awareness of Stigma among Persons with Schizophrenia," 524.

51. Patrick W. Corrigan and Amy C. Watson, "The Paradox of Self-Stigma and Mental Illness," *Clinical Psychology: Science and Practice* 9 (2002): 35–36.

52. Beate Schulze and Matthias C. Angermeyer, "Subjective Experiences of Stigma: A Focus Group Study of Schizophrenic Patients, Their Relatives and Mental Health Professionals," *Social Science and Medicine* 56 (2003): 303–4.

53. Marjorie L. Baldwin and Rebecca M. B. White. "Workplace Accommodations That Work for Persons with Mental Illness." In *Perspectives on Disability and Accommodation*, edited by Kelly Williams-Whitt and Daphne G. Taras (Victoria, BC: National Institute of Disability Management and Research, 2010), 123.

54. Corrigan and Watson, "Paradox of Self-Stigma," 40.

55. Goffman, *Stigma*, 7–9.

56. Amy C. Watson, Frederick E. Miller, and John S. Lyons, "Adolescent Attitudes toward Serious Mental Illness," *Journal of Nervous and Mental Disease* 193 (2005): 771–72.

57. Corrigan and Watson, "Paradox of Self-Stigma," 44.

58. Schulze and Angermeyer, "Subjective Experiences of Stigma," 303–304.

59. Corrigan and Watson, "Paradox of Self-Stigma," 40.

60. Kristin Viana. "People That Have Won," *Soundings East* 17 (1993): 11.

61. Schulze and Angermeyer, "Subjective Experiences of Stigma," 303.

62. Sara Kvrgic et al., "Therapeutic Alliance in Schizophrenia: The Role of Recovery Orientation, Self-Stigma, and Insight," *Psychiatry Research* 209 (2013): 15–16.

3. LIFE INTERRUPTED

1. Edward L. Glaeser et al., "An Economic Approach to Social Capital," *Economic Journal* 112 (2002): F438.

2. Rafael Gomez and Eric Santor, "Membership Has Its Privileges: The Effect of Social Capital and Neighbourhood Characteristics on the Earnings of Microfinance Borrowers," *Canadian Journal of Economics* 34 (2001): 960–61; Michael Bernabé Aguilera, "The Impact of Social Capital on Labor Force Participation: Evidence from the 2000 Social Capital Benchmark Survey," *Social Science Quarterly* 83 (2002): 864–68.

3. Richard C. Baron and Mark S. Salzer, "Accounting for Unemployment among People with Mental Illness," *Behavioral Sciences and the Law* 20 (2002): 588.

4. Christopher J. L. Murray et al., "Disability-Adjusted Life Years (DALYs) for 291 Diseases and Injuries in 21 Regions, 1990–2010: A Systematic Analysis for the Global Burden of Disease Study 2010," *Lancet* 380 (2012): 2197.

5. Joshua Salomon et al., "Common Values in Assessing Health Outcomes from Disease and Injury: Disability Weights Measurement Study for the Global Burden of Disease Study 2010," *Lancet* 380 (2012): 2131–37.

6. Salomon et al., "Common Values in Assessing Health Outcomes."

7. Harvey A. Whiteford et al., "Global Burden of Disease Attributable to Mental and Substance Use Disorders: Findings from the Global Burden of Disease Study 2010," *Lancet* 382 (2013): 1578.

8. Christopher J. L. Murray et al., "DALYs for 291 Diseases and Injuries," 2216.

9. Harvey A. Whiteford et al., "Burden of Disease Attributable to Mental Disorders," 1578.

10. Theo Vos et al., "Years Lived with Disability (YLDs) for the 1160 Sequelae of 289 Diseases and Injuries 1990–2010 . . . ," *Lancet* 380 (2012): 2184.

11. Christopher J. L. Murray et al., "DALYs for 291 Diseases and Injuries," 2204–209.

12. Murray et al., "DALYs for 291 Diseases and Injuries," 2207.

13. Harvey A. Whiteford et al., "Burden of Disease Attributable to Mental Disorders," 1582.

14. Christopher J. L. Murray and Alan D. Lopez, eds., *Global Burden of Disease: A Comprehensive Assessment of Mortality and Disability from Diseases, Injuries and Risk Factors* (Cambridge, MA: Harvard School of Public Health, 1996), 415.

15. Joshua Salomon et al., "Disability Weights Measurement Study," *Lancet* 380 (2012): 2136.

16. "Where Next with Psychiatric Illness?" *Nature* 336 (1988): 95.

17. Baron and Salzer, "Accounting for Unemployment," 589.

18. Robert Rosensheck et al., "Barriers to Employment for People with Schizophrenia," *American Journal of Psychiatry* 163 (2006): 414; David Salkever et al., "Measures and Predictors of Community-Based Employment and Earnings of Persons with Schizophrenia in a Multisite Study," *Psychiatric Services* 58 (2007): 318–19.

19. Hector W. H. Tsang et al., "Review on Vocational Predictors: A Systematic Review of Predictors of Vocational Outcomes among Individuals with Schizophrenia," *Australian and New Zealand Journal of Psychiatry* 44 (2010): 499.

20. Kevin Hollenbeck and Jean Kimmel, "Differences in the Returns to Education for Males by Disability Status and Age of Disability Onset," *Southern Economic Journal* 74 (2008): 719–20.

21. Michael Spence, "Job Market Signaling," *Quarterly Journal of Economics* 87 (1973): 356–58.

22. Goffman, *Stigma*, 10.

23. Chung Choe and Marjorie L. Baldwin, "Onset of Disability, Job Matching, and Employment Outcomes," MPRA Paper No. 63805 (January 2015): 12-14, http://mpra.ub.uni-muenchen.de /63805/.

24. Lachlan J. Best, Megan Still, and Grant Cameron, "Supported Education: Enabling Course Completion for People Experiencing Mental Illness," *Australian Occupational Therapy Journal* 55 (2008): 65–66.

25. Best, Still, and Cameron, "Supported Education," 65.

26. Carol T. Mowbray et al., "Supported Education for Adults with Psychiatric Disabilities: An Innovation for Social Work and Psychosocial Rehabilitation Practice," *Social Work* 50 (2005): 12.

27. Gary R. Bond et al., "A Randomized Controlled Trial Comparing Two Vocational Models for Persons with Severe Mental Illness," *Journal of Consulting and Clinical Psychology* 75 (2007): 969.

28. Cathaleene Macias et al., "What Is a Clubhouse? Report on the ICCD 1996 Survey of USA Clubhouses," *Community Mental Health Journal* 35 (1999): 181.

29. Macias et al., "What Is a Clubhouse?" 186–88.

30. Bond et al., "A Randomized Controlled Trial," 969.

31. Gary R. Bond and Robert E. Drake, "Predictors of Competitive Employment among Patients with Schizophrenia," *Current Opinion in Psychiatry* 21 (2008): 362.

32. Bond and Drake, "Predictors of Competitive Employment," 365.

33. Bond and Drake, "Predictors of Competitive Employment"; Gary R. Bond, Robert E. Drake, and Deborah R. Becker, "An Update on Randomized Controlled Trials of Evidence-Based Supported Employment," *Psychiatric Rehabilitation Journal* 21 (2008): 284–86.

34. Kikuko Campbell, Gary R. Bond, and Robert E. Drake, "Who Benefits from Supported Employment: A Meta-Analytic Study," *Schizophrenia Bulletin* 37 (2011): 374.

35. Bond and Drake, "Predictors of Competitive Employment," 365.

36. Anna M. Lucca et al., "Evaluation of an Individual Placement and Support Model (IPS) Program," *Psychiatric Rehabilitation Journal* 27 (2004): 253–54.

37. Anthony F. Lehman et al., "Improving Employment Outcomes for Persons with Severe Mental Illnesses," *Archives of General Psychiatry* 59 (2002): 170.

38. Morris D. Bell et al., "Neurocognitive Enhancement Therapy with Vocational Services: Work Outcomes at Two-Year Follow-up," *Schizophrenia Research* 105 (2008): 19.

39. Bell et al., "Neurocognitive Enhancement Therapy with Vocational Services," 26.

40. Abraham Rudnick and Maya Gover, "Combining Supported Education with Supported Employment," *Psychiatric Services* 60 (2009): 1690.

41. Rudnick and Gover, "Combining Supported Education with Supported Employment."

4. THE SUPPLY OF MENTAL HEALTH SERVICES

1. E. Fuller Torrey, *American Psychosis* (Oxford: Oxford University Press, 2014), 124.

2. Henry J. Steadman et al., "Prevalence of Serious Mental Illness among Jail Inmates," *Psychiatric Services* 60 (2009): 764.

3. William Easterly, *The White Man's Burden* (New York: Penguin Books, 2006), 5–6.

4. Sijo J. Parekattil and Michael E. Moran, "Robotic Instrumentation: Evolution and Microsurgical Applications," *Indian Journal of Urology* 26 (2010): 398.

5. Paul Janssen, "The Social Chemistry of Pharmacological Discovery: The Haloperidol Story," *International Journal of the Addictions* 27 (1992): 331.

6. Hiroko Beck et al., "50th Anniversary of the First Successful Permanent Pacemaker Implantation in the United States," *American Journal of Cardiology* 106 (2010): 810.

7. R. Shennach et al., "Insight in Schizophrenia—Course and Predictors during the Acute Treatment Phase of Patients from a Schizophrenia Spectrum Disorder," *European Psychiatry* 27 (2012): 626.

8. Gerald N. Grob, "Mad, Homeless and Unwanted: A History of the Care of the Chronically Mentally Ill in America," *Psychiatric Clinics of North America* 17 (1994): 542.

9. "Diseases of the Mind: Highlights of American Psychiatry through 1900, Early Psychiatric Hospitals and Asylums," *U.S. National Library of Medicine*, last modified September 13, 2013, http://www.nlm.nih.gov/hmd/diseases/early.html.

10. Albert R. Roberts and Linda Farris Kurtz, "Historical Perspectives on the Care and Treatment of the Mentally Ill," *Journal of Sociology and Social Welfare* 75 (1987): 79.

11. Shomer S. Zwelling, *Quest for a Cure: The Public Hospital in Williamsburg: 1773–1885* (Williamsburg, VA: Colonial Williamsburg Foundation, 1985): 13–18.

12. Joseph P. Morrissey and Howard H. Goldman, "Care and Treatment of the Mentally Ill in the United States: Historical Developments and Reforms," *Annals of the American Academy*

of Political and Social Science 484 (1986): 14–17; Clifford Farr, "Benjamin Rush and American Psychiatry," *American Journal of Psychiatry* 151 (1994): 72.

13. Roberts and Kurtz, "Historical Perspectives," 79.

14. Roberts and Kurtz, "Historical Perspectives."

15. Gerald N. Grob, "Mental Health Policy in the Liberal State: The Example of the United States," *International Journal of Law and Psychiatry* 31 (2008): 90.

16. Grob, "Mad, Homeless and Unwanted," 548.

17. Grob, "Mad, Homeless and Unwanted," 545–46, 90.

18. Howard Goldman and Gerald N. Grob, "Defining 'Mental Illness' in Mental Health Policy," *Health Affairs* 25 (2006): 739.

19. Roberts and Kurtz, "Historical Perspectives," 80.

20. Clifford Whittingham Beers, *A Mind That Found Itself: An Autobiography* (Garden City, NY: Doubleday, 1965), 228.

21. Roberts and Kurtz, "Historical Perspectives," 81.

22. Barbara A. Dreyer, "Adolf Meyer and Mental Hygiene: An Ideal for Public Health," *American Journal of Public Health* 66 (1976): 998–1000.

23. Morrissey and Goldman, "Care and Treatment of the Mentally Ill," 18.

24. Beers, "Mind That Found Itself," 263.

25. Morrissey and Goldman, "Care and Treatment of the Mentally Ill," 18.

26. Dreyer, "Adolf Meyer," 1000.

27. Roberts and Kurtz, "Historical Perspectives," 82.

28. Easterly, *White Man's Burden*, 12–20.

29. Zigmond M. Lebensohn, "General Hospital Psychiatry U.S.A.: Retrospect and Prospect," *Comprehensive Psychiatry* 21 (1980): 500.

30. Morrissey and Goldman, "Care and Treatment of the Mentally Ill," 22.

31. Grob, "Mad, Homeless and Unwanted," 550.

32. Torrey, *American Psychosis*, 22–23.

33. Grob, "Mental Health Policy," 92–93.

34. Torrey, *American Psychosis*, 17.

35. Grob, "Mental Health Policy," 93.

36. Torrey, *American Psychosis*, 62.

37. William Gronfein, "Psychotropic Drugs and the Origins of Deinstitutionalization," *Social Problems* 32 (1985): 441.

38. Gronfein, "Psychotropic Drugs," 443.

39. Robert H. Noce, David B. Williams, and Walter Rapaport, "Reserprine (Serpasil) in the Management of the Mentally Ill and Mentally Retarded," *Senate Interim Committee Report on the Treatment of Mental Illness* 20 (1956): 30–31.

40. Noce, Williams, and Rapaport, "Reserprine (Serpasil) in the Management of the Mentally Ill and Mentally Retarded."

41. Gronfein, "Psychotropic Drugs," 440.

42. Gronfein, "Psychotropic Drugs."

43. Grob, "Mental Health Policy," 94–95.

44. Joe Parks and Alan Q. Radke, eds., *The Vital Role of State Psychiatric Hospitals* (Alexandria, VA: National Association of State Mental Health Program Directors, 2014), 9.

45. Grob, "Mental Health Policy," 94.

46. Stephen M. Rose, "Deciphering Deinstitutionalization: Complexities in Policy and Program Analysis," *Milbank Memorial Fund Quarterly* 57 (1979): 447.

47. Gronfein, "Psychotropic Drugs," 440.

48. Saleem A. Shah, "Legal and Mental Health System Interactions: Major Developments and Research Needs," *International Journal of Law and Psychiatry* 4 (1981): 224; Grob, "Mental Health Policy," 94.

49. Morrissey and Goldman, "Care and Treatment of the Mentally Ill," 22.

50. Easterly, *White Man's Burden*, 12.

51. Grob, "Mental Health Policy," 93.

52. Bernard E. Harcourt, "From the Asylum to the Prison: Rethinking the Incarceration Revolution," *Texas Law Review* 84 (2006): 1759.

53. Harcourt, "From the Asylum to the Prison."

54. Grob, "Mental Health Policy," 92.

55. Richard G. Frank and Sherry A. Glied, *Better but Not Well: Mental Health Policy in the United States since 1950* (Baltimore: Johns Hopkins University Press, 2006): 60.

56. Torrey, *American Psychosis*, 77.

57. Richard D. Lyons, "How Release of Mental Patients Began," *New York Times*, October 30, 1984, C1.

58. Grob, "Mental Health Policy," 92.

59. Morrissey and Goldman, "Care and Treatment of the Mentally Ill," 26.

60. Torrey, *American Psychosis*, 87.

61. Grob, "Mental Health Policy," 96.

62. New Freedom Commission on Mental Health, *Achieving the Promise: Transforming Mental Health Care in America.* DHHS Pub. No. SMA-03-3832 (Rockville, MD: 2003), 3.

63. Ronald C. Kessler, "The Prevalence and Correlates of Untreated Serious Mental Illness," *Health Services Research* 36 (2001): 993.

64. New Freedom Commission, *Achieving the Promise*, 1.

65. New Freedom Commission, *Achieving the Promise*, Letter to President Bush from Michael F. Hogan, Chairman.

66. New Freedom Commission, *Achieving the Promise*, 4–7.

67. New Freedom Commission, *Achieving the Promise*, 57.

68. New Freedom Commission, *Achieving the Promise*, 35.

69. New Freedom Commission, *Achieving the Promise*, 44.

70. Janssen, "The Haloperidol Story," 331.

71. Janssen, "The Haloperidol Story," 339.

72. Janssen, "The Haloperidol Story," 335–36.

73. Janssen, "The Haloperidol Story," 341–45.

74. Easterly, *White Man's Burden*, 5–18, 100–116.

75. Janssen, "The Haloperidol Story," 335.

76. Fuller, *American Psychosis*, 66.

77. Fuller, *American Psychosis*, 15.

78. John C. Burnham, "A Clinical Alternative to the Public Health Approach to Mental Illness: A Forgotten Social Experiment," *Perspectives in Biology and Medicine* 49 (2006): 222–29.

5. DEFAULT CAREGIVERS

1. Grob, "Mental Health Policy," 93.

2. E. Fuller Torrey, *Surviving Schizophrenia: A Manual for Families, Patients, and Providers.* 5th ed. (New York: HarperCollins, 2006), 409.

3. Helen J. Stain et al., "Understanding the Social Costs of Psychosis: The Experience of Adults Affected by Psychosis Identified within the Second Australian National Survey of Psychosis," *Australian and New Zealand Journal of Psychiatry* 46 (2012): 884; Joshua E. Wilk et al., "Family Contact and the Management of Medication Non-adherence in Schizophrenia," *Community Mental Health Journal* 44 (2008): 378.

4. Elizabeth Bernstein and Nathan Koppel, "A Death in the Family: Aided by Advocates for the Mentally Ill, William Bruce Left the Hospital—Only to Kill His Mother," *Wall Street Journal*, August 16, 2008, A1.

5. George A. Awad and Lakshimi Voruganti, "The Burden of Schizophrenia on Caregivers," *PharmacoEconomics* 26 (2008): 152.

6. Susana Ochoa et al., "Do Needs, Symptoms or Disability of Outpatients with Schizophrenia Influence Family Burden?" *Social Psychiatry and Psychiatric Epidemiology* 43 (2008): 613; L. Magliano et al., "Family Burden in Long-Term Diseases: A Comparative Study in Schizophrenia vs. Physical Disorders," *Social Science and Medicine* 61 (2005): 314.

7. Awad and Voruganti, "Burden of Schizophrenia," 156–57.

8. Deborah D. Franks, "Economic Contribution of Families Caring for Persons with Severe and Persistent Mental Illness," *Administration and Policy in Mental Health* 18 (1990): 12; "Median Income for Four-person Families, by State," *U.S. Bureau of the Census*, last modified, April 3. 2015, http://www.census.gov/hhes/www/income/data/statistics/4person.html.

9. Franks, "Economic Contributions of Families," 14–16.

10. B. Lowyck et al., "A Study of the Family Burden of 150 Family Members of Schizophrenic Patients," *European Psychiatry* 19 (2004): 398.

11. Lowyck et al., "A Study of the Family Burden."

12. Katerina Koutra, "Family Functioning in Families of First-Episode Psychosis Patients as Compared to Chronic Mentally Ill Patients and Healthy Controls," *Psychiatry Research* 45 (2014): 486–87.

13. Koutra, "Family Functioning in Families of First-episode Psychosis Patients," 492–93.

14. Jana C. Saunders and Michelle M. Byrne, "A Thematic Analysis of Families Living with Schizophrenia," *Archives of Psychiatric Nursing* 16 (2002): 222.

15. Saunders and Michelle M. Byrne, "A Thematic Analysis of Families Living with Schizophrenia."

16. Anniqa Foldemo et al., "Quality of Life and Burden in Parents of Outpatients with Schizophrenia," *Social Psychiatry and Psychiatric Epidemiology* 40 (2005): 136; Sally K. Gallagher and David Mechanic, "Living with the Mentally Ill: Effects on the Health and Function of Other Household Members," *Social Science and Medicine* 42 (1996): 1695–96; Frank D. Gianfrancesco, Ruey-hua Wang, and Elaine Yu, "Effects of Patients with Bipolar, Schizophrenic, and Major Depressive Disorders on the Mental and Other Healthcare Expenses of Family Members," *Social Science and Medicine* 61 (2005): 307–8.

17. Gianfrancesco, Wang, and Yu, "Effects of Patients with Bipolar, Schizophrenic, and Major Depressive Disorders," 307–10.

18. Sandy M. Magaña et al., "Psychological Distress among Latino Family Caregivers of Adults with Schizophrenia: The Roles of Burden and Stigma," *Psychiatric Services* 58 (2007): 382.

19. Awad and Voruganti, "Burden of Schizophrenia," 155; Lowyck, "Study of Family Burden," 398; Foldemo et al., "Quality of Life," 135.

20. Lowyck, "Study of Family Burden," 398.

21. Diana Clarke and Joanne Winsor, "Perceptions and Needs of Parents during a Young Adult's First Psychiatric Hospitalization: 'We're All on This Little Island and We're Going to Drown Real Soon,'" *Issues in Mental Health Nursing* 31 (2010): 244.

22. Clarke and Winsor, "First Psychiatric Hospitalization," 244.

23. Saunders and Byrne, "Families Living with Schizophrenia," 220.

24. Magliano et al., "Family Burden in Long-Term Diseases," 316–18. The physical disorders were diabetes, brain disease, heart disease, lung disease, and renal disease.

25. Magliano et al., "Family Burden in Long-Term Diseases."

26. Clarke and Winsor, "First Psychiatric Hospitalization," 245.

27. Awad and Voruganti, "Burden of Schizophrenia," 154; Magaña et al., "Distress among Latino Caregivers," 380; Ochoa et al., "Needs, Symptoms, or Disability," 616 .

28. Ochoa et al., "Needs, Symptoms, or Disability," 615.

29. Anne Maria Möller-Leimkühler and Andreas Wiesheu, "Caregiver Burden in Chronic Mental Illness: The Role of Patient and Caregiver Characteristics," *European Archives of Psychiatry and Clinical Neuroscience* 262 (2012): 158–61.

30. Ochoa et al., "Needs, Symptoms, or Disability," 613–17; Michael G. McDonell et al., "Burden in Schizophrenia Caregivers: Impact of Family Psychoeducation and Awareness of Patient Suicidality," *Family Process Journal* 42 (2003): 98; Magaña et al., "Distress among Latino Caregivers," 381.

31. Ochoa et al., "Needs, Symptoms, or Disability," 613–17.

32. Awad and Voruganti, "Burden of Schizophrenia," 155; Ochoa et al., "Needs, Symptoms, or Disability," 615; Saunders and Byrne, "Families Living with Schizophrenia," 220–21.

33. McDonnell et al., "Burden in Schizophrenia Caregivers," 93–94.

34. McDonnell et al., "Burden in Schizophrenia Caregivers," 98.

35. Brian A. Palmer, V. Shane Pankratz, and John Michael Bostwick, "The Lifetime Risk of Suicide in Schizophrenia: A Reexamination," *Archives of General Psychiatry* 62 (2005): 249.

36. Merete Nordentoft, Trine Madsen and Izabela Fedyszyn, "Suicidal Behavior and Mortality in First-Episode Psychosis," *Journal of Nervous and Mental Disease* 203 (2015): 387–88.

37. L. Magliano et al., "Social and Clinical Factors Influencing the Choice of Coping Strategies in Relatives of Patients with Schizophrenia: Results of the BIOMED I Study," *Social Psychiatry and Psychiatric Epidemiology* 33 (1998): 413.

38. McDonnell et al., "Burden in Schizophrenia Caregivers," 96.

39. Magliano et al., "Family Burden in Long-Term Diseases," 313–14; Anthony F. Lehman et al., *Practice Guideline for the Treatment of Patients with Schizophrenia*, 2nd ed. (Arlington, VA: American Psychiatric Association, 2010): 10.

40. L. Magliano et al., "Burden on the Families of Patients with Schizophrenia: Results of the BIOMED I Study," *Social Psychiatry and Psychiatric Epidemiology* 33 (1998): 409–11.

41. Magliano, et al., "Choice of Coping Strategies," 418.

42. Awad and Voruganti, "Burden of Schizophrenia," 155.

43. Magliano et al., "Family Burden in Long-Term Diseases," 317–19.

44. Clarke and Winsor, "First Psychiatric Hospitalization," 244.

45. Lehman et al., *Practice Guideline for Schizophrenia*, 10.

46. Lehman et al., *Practice Guideline for Schizophrenia*.

47. Lehman et al., *Practice Guideline for Schizophrenia*, 12–15.

48. Elizabeth Kuipers, "Family Interventions in Schizophrenia: Evidence for Efficacy and Proposed Mechanisms of Change," *Journal of Family Therapy* 28 (2006): 76–77; M. Giron et al., "Efficacy and Effectiveness of Individual Family Intervention on Social and Clinical Functioning and Family Burden in Severe Schizophrenia," *Psychological Medicine* (2009): 9; Jacqueline Sin and Ian Norman, "Psychoeducational Interventions for Family Members of People with Schizophrenia: A Mixed-Method Systematic Review," *Journal of Clinical Psychiatry* 74 (2013): 1159; Phyllis E. Smerud and Irwin S. Rosenfarb, "The Therapeutic Alliance and Family Psychoeducation in the Treatment of Schizophrenia," *Journal of Consulting and Clinical Psychology* 76 (2008): 505; Amy N. Cohen et al., "Implementation of a Family Intervention for Individuals with Schizophrenia," *Journal of General Internal Medicine* 25 (2009): S32.

49. Merrie J. Kaas, Suzanne Lee, and Carol Peitzman, "Barriers to Collaboration between Mental Health Professionals and Families in the Care of Persons with Serious Mental Illness," *Issues in Mental Health Nursing* 24 (2003): 744–45; Clarke and Winsor, "First Psychiatric Hospitalization," 244–45.

50. Frank and Glied, *Better but Not Well*, 49.

51. Frank and Glied, *Better but Not Well*, 49–51.

52. Frank and Glied, *Better but Not Well*, 72–89.

53. Frank and Glied, *Better but Not Well*, 90.

54. Frank and Glied, *Better but Not Well*, 69.

55. NC Division of Mental Health, Developmental Disabilities and Substance Abuse Services, "Exploring the Costs and Feasibility of a New Psychiatric Facility" (Raleigh: North Carolina Department of Health and Human Services, 2013), 2.

56. Behavioral Health Centers, "CMC Randolph: Annual Mental Health Report Mecklenburg County" (Charlotte, NC: Carolinas HealthCare System, 2005), 15.

57. NC Division of Mental Health, *Feasibility of a New Psychiatric Facility*, 2.

58. Tina Marshall et al., "Provider and Family Beliefs Regarding the Causes of Severe Mental Illness," *Psychiatric Quarterly* 74 (2003): 232.

59. Marshall et al., "Provider and Family Beliefs," 230.

60. Marshall et al., "Provider and Family Beliefs," 232.

61. Marshall et al., "Family and Provider Beliefs," 232.

62. Cohen et al., "Family Intervention for Schizophrenia," S35.

63. Kaas, Lee, and Peitzman, "Barriers to Collaboration," 747–49.

64. U.S. Congress, House Committee on Energy and Commerce, *Examining SAMHSA's Role in Delivering Services to the Severely Mentally Ill: Hearings before the Subcommittee on Oversight and Investigations*, 113th Cong., 1st sess., May 22, 2013 (statement of Robert "Joe" Bruce and exhibits): 2–3.

65. Bernstein and Koppel, "A Death in the Family," A1.

66. *Oxford English Dictionary.* 1st ed., s.v. "burden."

67. Möller-Leimkühler and Wiesheu, "Caregiver Burden," 161; Rita Bauer et al., "Burden, Rewards and Coping—The Ups and Downs of Caregivers of People with Mental Illness," *Journal of Nervous and Mental Disease* 200 (2012): 932–33; Sandeep Grover, "Comparative Study of the Experience of Caregiving in Bipolar Affective Disorder and Schizophrenia," *International Journal of Social Psychiatry* 58 (2011): 619–20.

6. WORK FIRST

1. Miles Rinaldi et al., "First Episode Psychosis and Employment: A Review," *International Review of Psychiatry* 22 (2010): 148.

2. Elyn R. Saks, "Successful and Schizophrenic," *New York Times*, January 27, 2013, SR5.

3. Baldwin and White, "Workplace Accommodations That Work," 122.

4. Ronni Michelle Greenwood, Ana Stefancic, and Sam Tsemberis, "Pathways Housing First for Homeless Persons with Psychiatric Disabilities: Program Innovation, Research, and Advocacy," *Journal of Social Issues* 69 (2013): 648.

5. Thomas DeLeire, "The Wage and Employment Effects of the Americans with Disabilities Act," *Journal of Human Resources* 35 (2000): 701; Daron Acemoglu and Joshua D. Angrist, "Consequences of Employment Protection? The Case of the Americans with Disabilities Act," *Journal of Political Economy* 109 (2001): 917.

6. Civil Rights Act of 1964, U.S. Code 42 (1964) § 2000 e-2.

7. Americans with Disabilities Act of 1990, U.S. Code 42 (1990), § 12101–12117.

8. 135 Cong. Rec. S10617 (1989), statement by Senator Hatch.

9. 135 Cong. Rec. E3644 (1989), statement by Representative Bereuter.

10. 135 Cong. Rec. S11173 (1989), statement by Senator Armstrong.

11. 135 Cong. Rec. S10734 (1989), statement by Senator Helms.

12. James Concannon, "Mind Matters: Mental Disability and the History and Future of the Americans with Disabilities Act," *Law and Psychology Review* 36 (2012): 91.

13. Americans with Disabilities Act, § 12112.

14. Americans with Disabilities Act, § 12102.

15. Equal Employment Opportunity Commission, Regulations to Implement the Equal Employment Provisions of the Americans With Disabilities Act, as Amended, 29 C.F.R. 1630 (March 25, 2011): 17000.

16. Americans with Disabilities Act, § 12211.

17. Americans with Disabilities Act, § 12211.

18. Concannon, "Mind Matters," 96.

19. Amy L. Allbright, "2001 Employment Decisions under the ADA Title I—Survey Update," *Mental and Physical Disability Law Reporter* 26 (2002): 394–95.

20. Allbright, "2001 Employment Decisions under the ADA," 398.

21. Susan Stefan, *Hollow Promises: Employment Discrimination against People with Mental Disabilities* (Washington, D.C.: American Psychological Association, 2002), 76; *Schwartz v. the Comex and New York Mercantile Exchange*, DC SNY, No. 96, Civ. 3386.

22. *Sutton v. United Airlines*, 527 U.S. 471 (1999).

23. Allbright, "2001 Employment Decisions under the ADA," 395.

24. *Jacques v. DiMarzio, Inc.*, 386 F.3d 192, 203–04 (2d Cir. 2004); *Carlson v. Liberty Mut. Ins. Co.*, 237 F. App'x 446 (11th Cir. 2007); *Littleton v. Wal-Mart Stores, Inc.*, 231 F. App'x 874, 877 (11th Cir. 2007).

25. Stefan, *Hollow Promises*, 74–75.

26. Patrick A. Hartman, "'Interacting with Others' as a Major Life Activity under the Americans with Disabilities Act," *Seton Hall Circuit Review* 2 (2005): 157–58.

27. *Soileau v. Guilford of Me., Inc.*, 105 F.3d 12, 15 (1st Cir. 1997).

28. *McAlindin v. County of San Diego*, 192 F.3d 1226 (9th Cir. 1999); *Jacques v. DiMarzio, Inc.*, 386 F.3d 192 (2d Cir. 2004).

29. ADA Amendments Act of 2008, Public Law 110-325, *U.S. Statutes at Large* 122 (2008): 3555.

30. ADA Amendments Act, 3555.

31. ADA Amendments Act, 3556.

32. John Petrila, "Congress Restores the Americans with Disabilities Act to Its Original Intent," *Psychiatric Services* 60 (2009): 879; Concannon, "Mind Matters," 105.

33. ADA Amendments Act, 3554.

34. Concannon, "Mind Matters," 107.

35. Stephen F. Befort, "An Empirical Examination of Case Outcomes under the ADA Amendments Act," *Washington and Lee Law Review* 70 (2013): 2046–55.

36. Concannon, "Mind Matters," 113–14.

37. *Oxford English Dictionary.* 1st ed., s.v. "work."

38. Rinaldi et al., "First Episode Psychosis," 148.

39. Simon Winchester, *The Professor and the Madman: A Tale of Murder, Insanity, and the Making of the Oxford English Dictionary* (New York: HarperCollins, 1998): 2–21.

40. Winchester, *The Professor and the Madman.*

41. Winchester, *The Professor and the Madman*, 113.

42. Winchester, *The Professor and the Madman*, 133.

43. Winchester, *The Professor and the Madman*, 167.

7. THE DISCLOSURE PREDICAMENT

1. Wilkie Collins, *No Name*, Penguin Classics (London: Penguin Group, 1995), 34.

2. Wilkie Collins, *Woman in White*, Penguin Classics (London: Penguin Group, 1994), 235.

3. Wilkie Collins, *Man and Wife*, Oxford World's Classics (New York: Oxford University Press, 1995), 312.

4. "Our Mission," Phoenix First, accessed April 14, 2014, http://www.phoenixfirst.org/about-us/mission-values.

5. "Our Mission."

6. Amanda M. Jones, "Disclosure of Mental Illness in the Workplace: A Literature Review," *American Journal of Psychiatric Rehabilitation* 14 (2011): 223–25.

7. Susan G. Goldberg, Mary B. Killeen, and Bonnie O'Day, "The Disclosure Conundrum: How People with Psychiatric Disabilities Navigate Employment," *Psychology, Public Policy and Law* 11 (2005): 467; Jones, "Disclosure of Mental Illness," 217.

8. *Oxford English Dictionary.* 1st ed., s.v. "disclose."

9. Jones, "Disclosure of Mental Illness," 220; Gerald O'Brien and Melinda S. Brown, "Persons with Mental Illness and the Americans with Disabilities Act: Implications for the Social Work Profession," *Social Work in Mental Health* 7 (2009): 446–47.

10. Stephenie R. Chaudoir and Jeffrey D. Fisher, "The Disclosure Process Model: Understanding Disclosure Decision Making and Post-disclosure Outcomes among People Living with a Concealable Stigmatized Identity," *Psychological Bulletin* 136 (2010): 239.

11. Melanie Boyce et al., "Mental Health Service Users' Experiences of Returning to Paid Employment," *Disability and Society* 23 (2008): 80.

12. Patrick W. Corrigan and John R. O'Shaughnessy. "Changing Mental Illness Stigma as It Exists in the Real World," *Australian Psychologist* 42 (2007): 92.

13. Vicky Nithsdale, Jason Davies, and Paul Croucher, "Psychosis and the Experience of Employment," *Journal of Occupational Rehabilitation* 18 (2008): 178.

14. Rebecca Spirito Dalgin and Dennis Gilbride, "Perspectives of People with Psychiatric Disabilities on Employment Disclosure," *Psychiatric Rehabilitation Journal* 26 (2003): 308.

15. Goldberg, Killeen, and O'Day, "Disclosure Conundrum," 477.

16. Goldberg, Killeen, and O'Day, "Disclosure Conundrum," 463.

17. Steven Marwaha and Sonia Johnson, "Views and Experiences of Employment among People with Psychosis: A Qualitative Descriptive Study," *International Journal of Social Psychiatry* 51 (2005): 309.

18. Chaudoir and Fisher, "Disclosure Process Model," 237–42. The model is developed for any type of concealable stigmatized identity, but easily applies to persons with serious mental illness.

19. For a more detailed discussion of the pros and cons of disclosing SMI at work, refer to Chaudoir and Fisher, "Disclosure Process Model," 244–49, or John E. Pachankis, "The Psychological Implications of Concealing a Stigma: A Cognitive-Affective-Behavioral Model," *Psychological Bulletin* 133 (2007): 331–37.

20. Marsha Langer Ellison et al., "Patterns and Correlates of Workplace Disclosure among Professionals and Managers with Psychiatric Conditions," *Journal of Vocational Rehabilitation* 18 (2003): 4.

21. Marwaha and Johnson, "Views and Experiences," 309.

22. Sokratis Dinos et al., "Stigma: The Feelings and Experiences of 46 People with Mental Illness: Qualitative Study," *British Journal of Psychiatry* 184 (2004): 178.

23. Schulze and Angermeyer, "Subjective Experiences of Stigma," 307.

24. Schulze and Angermeyer, "Subjective Experiences of Stigma," 307–8.

25. Mary B. Killeen and Bonnie L. O'Day, "Challenging Expectations: How Individuals with Psychiatric Disabilities Find and Keep Work," *Psychiatric Rehabilitation Journal* 28 (2004): 161.

26. Several studies provide quantitative evidence on disclosure of mental illness in supported employment settings in the United States. In particular, see Becky R. Banks et al., "Disclosure of a Psychiatric Disability in Supported Employment: An Exploratory Study," *International Journal of Psychosocial Rehabilitation* 11 (2007): 78–83; and Angela L. Rollins et al., "Social Relationships at Work: Does the Employment Model Make a Difference?" *Psychiatric Rehabilitation Journal* 26 (2002): 53–59.

27. Ellison et al., "Patterns of Disclosure," 7–9.

28. Anand Pandya et al., "Perceived Impact of the Disclosure of a Schizophrenia Diagnosis," *Community Mental Health Journal* 47 (2011): 614.

29. Pandya et al., "Perceived Impact," 616.

30. E. W. Howe, *Ventures in Common Sense* (New York: Alfred A. Knopf, 1919), 80.

31. Goldberg, Killeen, and O'Day, "Disclosure Conundrum," 485.

32. Goldberg, Killeen, and O'Day, "Disclosure Conundrum," 479.

33. Dinos et al., "Stigma: Feelings and Experiences," 177.

34. Gary Becker (chapter 3) refers to these stigmatizing preferences as "tastes for discrimination."

35. Erin E. Michalak et al., "The Impact of Bipolar Disorder upon Work Functioning: A Qualitative Analysis," *Bipolar Disorders* 9 (2007): 136.

36. In the language of economics, the utility function yields convex, two-dimensional indifference curves, and the quantity demanded of each good is negatively correlated with its price.

37. Sophie Mitra, "The Capability Approach and Disability," *Journal of Disability Policy Studies* 16 (2006): 237.

38. Goffman, *Stigma*, 73–91.

39. Goffman, *Stigma*, 42.

40. Goffman, *Stigma*, 87.

41. Debbie Peterson, Nandika Currey, and Sunny Collings, "'You Don't Look Like One of Them': Disclosure of Mental Illness in the Workplace as an Ongoing Dilemma," *Psychiatric Rehabilitation Journal* 35 (2011): 146.

8. FINDING A GOOD JOB MATCH

1. "About Us," Phoenix Dream Center, accessed June 3, 2014, http://www.phxdreamcenter.org /about_us.

2. John W. Kennedy, "Phoenix Dream Center Opens Program for Foster Youth," *Pentecostal Evangel*, December 12, 2013, http://ag.org/top/news/.

3. The Rescue Project has since been renamed "Where Hope Lives." "Rescuing Victims of Human Trafficking," Where Hope Lives, accessed May 20, 2015, http://www.rescueprojectphx.org/index.php.

4. "Accommodation Ideas for Addison's Disease," Job Accommodations Network, accessed June 3, 2014, https://askjan.org/soar/Other/addisons.html.

5. Sheila K. Akabas, "Workplace Responsiveness: Key Employer Characteristics in Support of Job Maintenance for People with Mental Illness," *Psychosocial Rehabilitation Journal* 17 (1994): 95.

6. Kendra M. Duckworth, "Employees with Psychiatric Impairments," Accommodation and Compliance Series: The ADA Amendments Act of 2008, U.S. Department of Labor, last modified, December 17, 2008, https://askjan.org/bulletins/adaaa1.htm.

7. Tandon, Keshavan, and Nasrallah, "Clinical Features and Conceptualization," 2.

8. Tandon, Keshavan, and Nasrallah, "Clinical Features and Conceptualization," 5–6.

9. Dianna L. Stone and Adrienne Colella, "A Model of Factors Affecting the Treatment of Disabled Individuals in Organizations," *Academy of Management Review* 21 (1996): 354–57.

10. Lisa Schur et al., "Is Disability Disabling in All Workplaces? Workplace Disparities and Corporate Culture," *Industrial Relations* 48 (2009): 387–403.

11. Schur et al., "Is Disability Disabling in All Workplaces?"

12. Jenny Secker and Helen Membrey, "Promoting Mental Health through Employment and Developing Healthy Workplaces: The Potential of Natural Supports at Work," *Health Education Research* 18 (2003): 212.

13. Akabas, "Workplace Responsiveness," 95.

14. Suzanne Bruyère, William A. Erikson, and Sara A. VanLooy, "The Impact of Business Size on Employer ADA Response," *Rehabilitation Counseling Bulletin* 49 (2006): 199.

15. Secker and Membrey, "Promoting Mental Health," 213–14; Schur et al., "Workplace Disparities and Corporate Culture," 399.

16. Akabas, "Workplace Responsiveness," 94.

17. Secker and Membrey, "Promoting Mental Health," 211.

18. Secker and Membrey, "Promoting Mental Health," 209.

19. Goldberg, Killeen, and O'Day, "Disclosure Conundrum," 475.

20. Mary B. Killeen and Bonnie L. O'Day, "Challenging Expectations: How Individuals with Psychiatric Disabilities Find and Keep Work," *Psychiatric Rehabilitation Journal* 28 (2004): 158–59.

21. Killeen and O'Day, "Challenging Expectations," 159.

22. Baldwin and White, "Workplace Accommodations That Work," 126.

9. JOB ACCOMMODATIONS FOR WORKERS WITH SMI

1. M. Harrow, T. H. Jobe, and R. N. Faull, "Do All Schizophrenia Patients Need Antipsychotic Treatment Continuously Throughout Their Lifetime? A 20-Year Longitudinal Study," *Psychological Medicine* 42 (2012): 2146–48.

2. *Oxford English Dictionary.* 1st ed., s.v. "accommodate."

3. Baldwin and White, "Workplace Accommodations that Work," 123.

4. Dalgin and Gilbride, "Perspectives of People with Psychiatric Disabilities," 307–8.

5. Duckworth, "Employees with Psychiatric Impairments," https://askjan.org/bulletins/adaaa1.htm.

6. Stefan, *Hollow Promises*, 169–70; Heather Peters and Travor C. Brown, "Mental Illness at Work: An Assessment of Co-worker Reactions," *Canadian Journal of Administrative Sciences* 26 (2009): 41; Gerald V. O'Brien, and Melinda S. Brown. "Persons with Mental Illness and the Americans with Disabilities Act: Implications for the Social Work Profession," *Social*

Work in Mental Health 7 (2009): 450; Samantha Fairclough et al., "In Sickness and in Health: Implications for Employers When Bipolar Disorders Are Protected Disabilities," *Employee Responsibilities and Rights Journal* 25 (2013): 285.

7. Beth Loy, "Employees with Back Impairments," U.S. Department of Labor, last modified, March 4, 2013, https://askjan.org/bulletins/adaaa1.htm.

8. Stefan, *Hollow Promises*, 169.

9. Fairclough et al., "In Sickness and in Health," 284.

10. Helen A. Schartz, D. J. Hendricks, and Peter Blanck, "Workplace Accommodations: Evidence Based Outcomes," *Work* 27 (2006): 346.

11. Peters and Brown, "Mental Illness at Work," 41; Rebecca Spirito Dalgin, "Impact of Title I of the Americans with Disabilities Act on People with Psychiatric Disabilities," *Journal of Applied Rehabilitation Counseling* 32 (2001): 47.

12. Stefan, *Hollow Promises*, 168–69.

13. Fairclough et al., "In Sickness and in Health," 284.

14. Peters and Brown, "Mental Illness at Work," 45.

15. Baldwin and White, "Workplace Accommodations That Work," 125.

16. Richard V. Burkhauser, "Morality on the Cheap: The Americans with Disabilities Act," *Regulation* 13 (1990): 48–49, 53.

17. Stefan, *Hollow Promises*, 177–78.

18. Interview with supervisor, June 29, 2004. All interviews were conducted in confidentiality and the names of interviewees are withheld per the informed consent agreements with participants.

19. Stefan, *Hollow Promises*, 178.

20. *Gaul v. Lucent Technologies*, 134 F.3d 576 (3rd Cir. 1998).

21. Stefan, *Hollow Promises*, 182.

22. *Rascon v. US West Communications Inc.* 143 F.3d 1324 (10th Cir. 1998).

23. Equal Employment Opportunity Commission, Interpretive Guidance on Title I of the Americans with Disabilities Act, 29 C.F.R. 1630 App. (July 1, 2012): 403–4.

24. *Taylor v. Phoenixville School District*. 184 F.3d 296 (3rd Cir. 1999).

25. Baldwin and White, "Workplace Accommodations That Work," 126.

26. DeLeire, "Wage and Employment Effects of the ADA," 701.

27. "Labor Force Statistics (CPS)," Bureau of Labor Force Statistics, accessed July 12, 2014, http://www.bls.gov/webapps/legacy/cpsatab6.htm.

28. Nicole Maestas, Kathleen J. Mullen, and Alexander Strand, "Does Disability Insurance Receipt Discourage Work? Using Examiner Assignment to Estimate Causal Effects of SSDI Receipt," *American Economic Review* 103 (2013): 1798, 1818–23.

29. DeLeire, "Wage and Employment Effects of the ADA," 708.

30. Interview with supervisor, June 29, 2004.

10. BEYOND SCHIZOPHRENIA

1. David Baldwin, preaching at the House of Healing, October 8, 2014.

2. Richard C. Baron and Mark S. Salzer, "The Career Patterns of Persons with Serious Mental Illness: Generating a New Vision of Lifetime Careers for Those in Recovery," *Psychiatric Rehabilitation Skills* 4 (2000): 139.

3. "Pulse Healthcare Survey," Truven Health Analytics, accessed January 19, 2015. http://truven   health.com/portals/0/assets/ HOSP_12463_0313_PULSEHealthcareSurvey_WEB_032913.pdf.

4. The screening sample represented 1.6 percent of households that agreed to participate in follow-up interviews.

5. The survey was conducted by the Behavior Research Center in Phoenix, Arizona. http://www.brc-research.com/.

6. Ben Rinaudo and Priscilla Ennals, "Mental Illness, Supported Education, Employment and Recovery: Ben's Story," *Work* 43 (2012): 100–102.

7. Baron and Salzer, "Career Patterns of Persons with SMI," 142.

8. "Employed Persons by Occupation, Sex, and Age—2013," Bureau of Labor Statistics, accessed January 19, 2015, http://www.bls.gov/cps/tables.htm#empstat.

9. Calculations by the author. Text descriptions of respondents' occupations were matched to 2010 Standard Occupational Classification (SOC) codes (http://www.bls.gov/ soc/2010/ soc_alph.htm#N). The occupational distribution of the survey sample was compared to the occupational distribution of the U.S. workforce in April–June 2013, using data from the Bureau of Labor Statistics (http://www.bls.gov/cps/cpsaat09.pdf).

10. "Educational Attainment in the United States—2013 Detailed Tables," U.S. Census Bureau, accessed January 19, 2015, http://www.census.gov/hhes/socdemo/education/ data/ cps/ 2013/ tables.html.

11. Bond and Drake, "Predictors of Competitive Employment," 364.

12. Kurt Snyder, *Me, Myself, and Them* (Oxford: Oxford University Press, 2007), 1–4, 19–40, 53–67, 79–84, 103–8.

13. Harrow, Jobe, and Faull, "Do All Schizophrenia Patients Need Antipsychotic Treatment," 2146–50.

14. Brett Hartman, *Hammerhead 84* (Niskayuna, NY: Graphite Press, 2004), 44–50, 81–95, 117–23, 190–91, 226–47, 272–74, 321.

15. Goldberg, Killeen, and O'Day, "Disclosure Conundrum," 476–79.

16. Magliano et al., "Family Burden in Long-Term Diseases," 313; Lehman et al., *Practice Guideline for Schizophrenia*, 105–6.

17. Hartman, *Hammerhead 84*, 188.

18. Hartman, *Hammerhead 84*, 213.

11. TOWARD A MORE RATIONAL MENTAL HEALTH POLICY

1. Stephen King, *It* (New York: Viking Penguin, 1986), 14.

2. King, *It*, 439.

3. King, *It*, 1075.

4. Concannon, "Mind Matters," 112–14.

5. *Oxford English Dictionary*. 1st ed., s.v. "policy."

6. Deborah Stone, *Policy Paradox* (New York: W.W. Norton, 2012), 289–90, 331–56.

7. Anna D. Sinaiko and Thomas McGuire, "Patient Inducement, Provider Priorities and Resource Allocation in Public Mental Health Systems," *Journal of Health Politics, Policy and Law* 31 (2006): 1087.

8. Steve Melek, Clare Miller, and Irvin L. Muszynski, "Employer Guide for Compliance with the Mental Health Parity and Equity Addiction Act." Partnership for Workplace Mental Health. December 2012, 3. http://www.workplacementalhealth.org/erguide.

9. George Szmukler, Rowena Daw, and Felicity Callard, "Mental Health Law and the UN Convention on the Rights of Persons with Disabilities," *International Journal of Law and Psychiatry* 37 (2014): 246–50. The Convention passed the U.N. General Assembly in 2006, and has since been signed by 155 countries, including the United States in 2009. United Nations Enable, accessed September 30, 2014, http://www.un.org/disabilities /countries.asp?id=166.

10. Torrey, *American Psychosis*, 113–28.

11. Brian Stettin et al., "Mental Health Commitment Laws: A Survey of the States" (Treatment Advocacy Center, 2014): 4–7. http://www.tacreports.org/storage/documents/2014-state-survey-abridged.pdf.

12. Darcy Ann Copeland and Mary Sue V. Heilemann, "Getting *to the Point*: The Experience of Mothers Getting Assistance for Their Adult Children Who Are Violent and Mentally Ill," *Nursing Research* 57 (2008): 139.

13. Steven S. Sharfstein and Faith B. Dickerson, "Hospital Psychiatry for the Twenty-first Century," *Health Affairs* 28 (2009): 685–86.

14. Sharfstein and Dickerson, "Hospital Psychiatry," 686.

15. Stettin et al., "Mental Health Commitment Laws," 19–20.

16. Sinaiko and McGuire, "Patient Inducement," 1084–85.

17. Testa and West, "Civil Commitment," 34.

18. "Operating Plan for FY 2014," Substance Abuse and Mental Health Services Administration, accessed September 23, 2014, http://beta.samhsa.gov/budget/fy-2014-budget.

19. "Operating Plan for FY 2014."

20. "Protection and Advocacy for Individuals with Mental Illness Program (PAIMI)," National Disability Rights Network, accessed October 21, 2014, http://www.ncmhr.org/ downloads/ PAIMI-fact-sheet-2013.pdf.

21. Amanda Peters, "Lawyers Who Break the Law: What Congress Can Do to Prevent Mental Health Patient Advocates from Violating Federal Legislation," *Oregon Law Review* 89 (2010): 135.

22. Szmukler, Daw, and Callard, "Mental Health Law," 250.

23. Stettin et al., "Mental Health Commitment Laws," 9.

24. Helping Families in Mental Health Crisis Act of 2013, H.R. 3717, 113th Cong. (2013).

25. "About Us," Substance Abuse and Mental Health Services Administration, accessed September 26, 2014. http://www.samhsa.gov/about-us.

26. Szmukler, Daw, and Callard, "Mental Health Law," 247–50.

27. Peters, "Lawyers Who Break the Law," 164–72; Bernstein and Koppel, "A Death in the Family," A1; "Provisions in HR 3717 that Improve Protection and Advocacy for Individuals with Mental Illness (PAIMI) Program," Mental Health Policy Organization, accessed June 7, 2015, http://www.mentalillnesspolicy.org/hr3717/paimiexplanationhr3717.html.

28. Justin Hunt, Daniel Eisenberg, and Amy M. Kilbourne, "Consequences of Receipt of a Psychiatric Diagnosis for Completion of College," *Psychiatric Services* 61 (2010): 402.

29. Jackie Stoneman and Rosemary Lysaght, "Supported Education: A Means for Enhancing Employability for Adults with Mental Illness," *Work* 36 (2010): 257.

30. Patrick W. Corrigan, Fred E. Markowitz, and Amy C. Watson, "Structural Levels of Mental Illness Stigma and Discrimination," *Schizophrenia Bulletin* 30 (2004): 481.

31. "Fiscal Year 2014 Budget: Summary and Background Information," Department of Education, accessed October 27, 2014, 56–65. http://www2.ed.gov/about/overview/budget/ budget14/ summary/14summary.pdf.

32. Corrigan and Watson, "Frequency of Violent Behavior," 160.

33. Taylor, "Psychosis and Violence," 651.

34. "NIMH Awards to Domestic Higher Education," National Institutes of Health, accessed June 7, 2015, http://report.nih.gov/award/index.cfm.

35. *National Institute of Mental Health Strategic Plan*, NIH Publication No. 08-6368 (Washington, D.C.: U.S. Department of Health and Human Services, 2008), 18.

36. "Child and Adolescent Services Research Program," National Institute of Mental Health, accessed October 26, 2014. http://www.nimh.nih.gov/about/organization/dsir/services-research-and-epidemiology-branch/child-and-adolescent-services-research-program.shtml.

37. Bond, Drake, and Becker, "Update on Randomized Controlled Trials," 284–86; Lehman et al., "Improving Employment Outcomes," 168.

38. Robert E. Drake et al., "Assisting Social Security Disability Insurance Beneficiaries with Schizophrenia, Bipolar Disorder, or Major Depression in Returning to Work," *American Journal of Psychiatry* 170 (2013): 1434.

39. William D. Frey et al., *Mental Health Treatment Study: Final Report* (Rockville, MD: Westat, 2011), chap. 1; 2.

40. Frey et al., *Mental Health Treatment Study*, chap. 4: 3; Richard G. Frank, "Helping (Some) SSDI Beneficiaries with Severe Mental Illness Return to Work," *American Journal of Psychiatry* 170 (2013): 1380.

41. Frey et al., *Mental Health Treatment Study*, chap. 4: 7, 29.

42. Frank, "Helping (Some) SSDI Beneficiaries," 1380.

43. Stoneman and Lysaght, "Supported Education," 257–58.

44. Stoneman and Lysaght, "Supported Education."

45. Stoneman and Lysaght, "Supported Education," 259.

46. Best, Still, and Cameron, "Supported Education," 66–67.

47. Interview with patient, October 25, 2003.

48. Robert E. Drake and Gary R. Bond, "IPS Support Employment: A 20-Year Update," *American Journal of Psychiatric Rehabilitation* 14 (2011): 156.

49. Drake and Gary R. Bond, "IPS Support Employment," 160.

50. King, *It*, 1054.

Bibliography

Acemoglu, Daron, and Joshua D. Angrist. "Consequences of Employment Protection? The Case of the Americans with Disabilities Act." *Journal of Political Economy* 109 (2001): 915–57.

Aguilera, Michael Bernabé. "The Impact of Social Capital on Labor Force Participation: Evidence from the 2000 Social Capital Benchmark Survey." *Social Science Quarterly* 83 (2002): 853–74.

Akabas, Sheila K. "Workplace Responsiveness: Key Employer Characteristics in Support of Job Maintenance for People with Mental Illness." *Psychosocial Rehabilitation Journal* 17 (1994): 91–101.

Albrecht, Gary, Vivian G. Walker, and Judith A. Levy. "Social Distance from the Stigmatized: A Test of Two Theories." *Social Science and Medicine* 16 (1982): 1319–27.

Allbright, Amy L. "2001 Employment Decisions under the ADA Title I—Survey Update." *Mental and Physical Disability Law Reporter* 26 (2002): 394–98.

Andreasen, Nancy C., William T. Carpenter, Jr., John M. Kane, Robert A. Lasser, Stephen R. Marder, and Daniel R. Weinberger. "Remission in Schizophrenia: Proposed Criteria and Rationale for Consensus." *American Journal of Psychiatry* 162 (2005): 441–49.

Angermeyer, Matthias C., and Herbert Matschinger. "Labeling—Stereotype—Discrimination: An Investigation of the Stigma Process." *Social Psychiatry and Psychiatric Epidemiology* 40 (2005): 391–95.

Angermeyer, Matthias C., and Herbert Matschinger. "Public Beliefs about Schizophrenia and Depression: Similarities and Differences." *Social Psychiatry and Psychiatric Epidemiology* 38 (2003): 526–34.

Angermeyer, Matthias C., Aurélie Millier, Mokhtar Kouki, Tarek Refaï, Georg Schomerus, and Mondher Toumi. "Biogenetic Explanations and Emotional Reactions to People with Schizophrenia and Major Depressive Disorder." *Psychiatry Research* 220 (2014): 702–4.

Angermeyer, Matthias C., Michael Beck, and Herbert Matschinger. "Determinants of the Public's Preference for Social Distance from People with Schizophrenia." *Canadian Journal of Psychiatry* 48 (2003): 663–68.

Awad, A. George, and Lakshimi Voruganti. "The Burden of Schizophrenia on Caregivers." *PharmacoEconomics* 26 (2008): 149–59.

Baldwin, Marjorie L. "The Effects of Impairments on Employment and Wages: Estimates from the 1984 and 1990 SIPP." *Behavioral Sciences and the Law* 17 (1999): 7–27.

Baldwin, Marjorie L., and Rebecca M. B. White. "Workplace Accommodations That Work for Persons with Mental Illness." In *Perspectives on Disability and Accommodation*, edited by Kelly Williams-Whitt and Daphne G. Taras, 115–31. Victoria, BC: National Institute of Disability Management and Research, 2010.

Baldwin, Marjorie L., and Steven C. Marcus. "Labor Market Outcomes of Persons with Mental Disorders." *Industrial Relations* 46 (2007): 481–510.

———. "Perceived vs. Measured Stigma among Workers with Serious Mental Disorders." *Psychiatric Services* 57 (2006): 388–92.

Baldwin, Marjorie L., and William G. Johnson. "Labor Market Discrimination against Men with Disabilities in the Year of the A.D.A." *Southern Economic Journal* 66 (2000): 548–66.

Banks, Becky R., Jeanne Novak, David M. Mank, and Teresa Grossi. "Disclosure of a Psychiatric Disability in Supported Employment: An Exploratory Study." *International Journal of Psychosocial Rehabilitation* 11 (2007): 69–84.

Baron, Richard C., and Mark S. Salzer. "Accounting for Unemployment among People with Mental Illness." *Behavioral Sciences and the Law* 20 (2002): 585–99.

Bauer, Rita, Franziska Koepke, Linda Sterzinger, and Herman Spiessl. "Burden, Rewards and Coping—The Ups and Downs of Caregivers of People with Mental Illness." *Journal of Nervous and Mental Disease* 200 (2012): 928–33.

Beck, Hiroko, William E. Boden, Sushmitha Patibandla, Dmitriy Kireyev, Vipul Gupta, Franklin Campagna, Michael E. Cain, and Joseph E. Marine. "50th Anniversary of the First Successful Permanent Pacemaker Implantation in the United States: Historical Review and Future Directions." *American Journal of Cardiology* 106 (2010): 810–18.

Becker, Gary S. *The Economics of Discrimination.* 2nd ed. Chicago: University of Chicago Press, 1971.

Beers, Clifford Whittingham. *A Mind That Found Itself: An Autobiography.* Garden City, NY: Doubleday, 1965 (1st ed., 1908).

Befort, Stephen F. "An Empirical Examination of Case Outcomes under the ADA Amendments Act." *Washington and Lee Law Review* 70 (2013): 2027–71.

Behavioral Health Centers. "CMC Randolph: Annual Mental Health Report Mecklenburg County." Charlotte, NC: Carolinas HealthCare System, 2005.

Bell, Morris D., Wayne Zito, Tamasine Greig, and Bruce Wexler. "Neurocognitive Enhancement Therapy with Vocational Services: Work Outcomes at Two-Year Follow-up." *Schizophrenia Research* 105 (2008): 18–29.

Bernstein, Elizabeth, and Nathan Koppel. "A Death in the Family: Aided by Advocates for the Mentally Ill, William Bruce Left the Hospital—Only to Kill His Mother." *Wall Street Journal*, August 16, 2008.

Best, Lachlan J., Megan Still, and Grant Cameron. "Supported Education: Enabling Course Completion for People Experiencing Mental Illness." *Australian Occupational Therapy Journal* 55 (2008): 65–68.

Bleuler, Manfred. "A 23-Year Longitudinal Study of 208 Schizophrenics and Impressions in Regard to the Nature of Schizophrenia." *Journal of Psychiatric Research* 6 (1968, Supplement 1): 3–12.

Bogardus, Emory. "A Social Distance Scale." *Sociology and Social Research* 17 (1933): 265–71.

Bond, Gary R., and Robert E. Drake. "Predictors of Competitive Employment among Patients with Schizophrenia." *Current Opinion in Psychiatry* 21 (2008): 362–69.

Bond, Gary R., Michelle P. Salyers, Jerry Dincin, Robert E. Drake, Deborah R. Becker, Virginia V. Fraser, and Michael Haines. "A Randomized Controlled Trial Comparing Two Vocational Models for Persons with Severe Mental Illness." *Journal of Consulting and Clinical Psychology* 75 (2007): 968–82.

Bond, Gary R., Robert E. Drake, and Deborah R. Becker. "An Update on Randomized Controlled Trials of Evidence-Based Supported Employment." *Psychiatric Rehabilitation Journal* 21 (2008): 280–90.

Boyce, Melanie, Jenny Secker, Robyn Johnson, Mike Floyd, Bob Gove, Justine Schneider, and Jan Slade. "Mental Health Service Users' Experiences of Returning to Paid Employment." *Disability and Society* 23 (2008): 77–88.

Bruyère, Suzanne, William A. Erikson, and Sara A. VanLooy. "The Impact of Business Size on Employer ADA Response." *Rehabilitation Counseling Bulletin* 49 (2006): 194–206.

Burnham, John C. "A Clinical Alternative to the Public Health Approach to Mental Illness: A Forgotten Social Experiment." *Perspectives in Biology and Medicine* 49 (2006): 220–37.

Campbell, Kikuko, Gary R. Bond, and Robert E. Drake. "Who Benefits from Supported Employment: A Meta-Analytic Study." *Schizophrenia Bulletin* 37 (2011): 370–80.

Carpenter, William T. "The Facts of Schizophrenia: A Personal Commentary." *Schizophrenia Research* 128 (2011): 2–4.

Chaudoir, Stephenie R., and Jeffrey D. Fisher. "The Disclosure Process Model: Understanding Disclosure Decision Making and Post-Disclosure Outcomes among People Living with a Concealable Stigmatized Identity." *Psychological Bulletin* 136 (2010): 236–56.

Choe, Chung, and Marjorie L. Baldwin. "Onset of Disability, Job Matching, and Employment Outcomes." MPRA Paper No. 63805 (January 2015). http://mpra.ub.uni-muenchen.de/63805/.

Civil Rights Act of 1964, U.S. Code 42 (1964), §§ 1971 et seq.

Clarke, Diana, and Joanne Winsor. "Perceptions and Needs of Parents during a Young Adult's First Psychiatric Hospitalization: 'We're All on This Little Island and We're Going to Drown Real Soon.'" *Issues in Mental Health Nursing* 31 (2010): 242–47.

Cohen, Amy N., Shirley M. Glynn, Alison B. Hamilton, and Alexander S. Young. "Implementation of a Family Intervention for Individuals with Schizophrenia." *Journal of General Internal Medicine* 25 (2009): 32–37.

Collins, Wilkie. *Man and Wife*. Oxford World's Classics. New York: Oxford University Press, 1995 (1st ed., 1870).

———. *No Name*. London: Penguin Group, 1995 (1st ed., 1862).

———. *The Woman in White*. London: Penguin Group, 1994 (1st ed., 1868).

Concannon, James. "Mind Matters: Mental Disability and the History and Future of the Americans with Disabilities Act." *Law and Psychology Review* 36 (2012): 89–114.

Corrigan, Patrick W. "Mental Health Stigma as Social Attribution: Implications for Research Methods and Attitude Change." *Clinical Psychology: Science and Practice* 7 (2000): 48–67.

Corrigan, Patrick W., Amy C. Watson, Gabriela Gracia, Natalie Slopen, Kenneth Rasinski, and Laura L. Hall. "Newspaper Stories as Measures of Structural Stigma." *Psychiatric Services* 56 (2005): 551–56.

Corrigan, Patrick W., and Amy C. Watson. "Findings from the National Comorbidity Survey on the Frequency of Violent Behavior in Individuals with Psychiatric Disorders." *Psychiatry Research* 136 (2005): 153–62.

Corrigan, Patrick W., and Amy C. Watson. "The Paradox of Self-Stigma and Mental Illness." *Clinical Psychology: Science and Practice* 9 (2002): 35–43.

Corrigan, Patrick W., and John R. O'Shaughnessy. "Changing Mental Illness Stigma as It Exists in the Real World." *Australian Psychologist* 42 (2007): 90–97.

Corrigan, Patrick, Fred E. Markowitz, Amy Watson, David Rowan, and Mary Ann Kubiak. "An Attribution Model of Public Discrimination towards Persons with Mental Illness." *Journal of Health and Social Behavior* 44 (2003): 162–79.

Craddock, Nick, and Michael J. Owen. "The Kraepelinian Dichotomy—Going, Going . . . But Still Not Gone." *British Journal of Psychiatry* 196 (2010): 92–95.

Dalgin, Rebecca Spirito, and Dennis Gilbride. "Perspectives of People with Psychiatric Disabilities on Employment Disclosure." *Psychiatric Rehabilitation Journal* 26 (2003): 306–10.

DeLeire, Thomas. "The Wage and Employment Effects of the Americans with Disabilities Act." *Journal of Human Resources* 35 (2000): 693–715.

Dinos, Sokratis, Scott Stevens, Marc Serfaty, Scott Weich, and Michael King. "Stigma: The Feelings and Experiences of 46 People with Mental Illness; Qualitative Study." *British Journal of Psychiatry* 184 (2004): 176–81.

Dreyer, Barbara A. "Adolf Meyer and Mental Hygiene: An Ideal for Public Health." *American Journal of Public Health* 66 (1976): 998–1003.

Duckworth, Kendra M. "Employees with Psychiatric Impairments." Accommodation and Compliance Series: The ADA Amendments Act of 2008. *U.S. Department of Labor*. Last modified, December 17, 2008. https://askjan.org/bulletins/adaaa1.htm.

Easterly, William. *The White Man's Burden*. New York: Penguin Books, 2006.

Ellison, Marsha Langer, Zlatka Russinova, Kim MacDonald-Wilson, and Asya Lyass. "Patterns and Correlates of Workplace Disclosure among Professionals and Managers with Psychiatric Conditions." *Journal of Vocational Rehabilitation* 18 (2003): 3–13.

Fairclough, Samantha, Robert K. Robinson, Dave L. Nichols, and Sam Cousley. "In Sickness and in Health: Implications for Employers When Bipolar Disorders Are Protected Disabilities." *Employee Responsibilities and Rights Journal* 25 (2013): 277–92.

Farr, Clifford. "Benjamin Rush and American Psychiatry." *American Journal of Psychiatry* 151 (1994): 65–73.

Feldman, David B., and Christian S. Crandall. "Dimensions of Mental Illness Stigma: What about Mental Illness Causes Social Rejection?" *Journal of Social and Clinical Psychology* 26 (2007): 137–54.

Foldemo, Anniqa, Maths Gullberg, Anna-Christina Ek, and Lennart Bogren. "Quality of Life and Burden in Parents of Outpatients with Schizophrenia." *Social Psychiatry and Psychiatric Epidemiology* 40 (2005): 133–38.

Foussias, George, and Gary Remington. "Antipsychotics and Schizophrenia: From Efficacy and Effectiveness to Clinical Decision-Making." *Canadian Journal of Psychiatry* 55 (2010): 117–25.

Frank, Richard G., and Sherry A. Glied. *Better but Not Well: Mental Health Policy in the United States since 1950.* Baltimore: Johns Hopkins University Press, 2006.

Franks, Deborah D. "Economic Contribution of Families Caring for Persons with Severe and Persistent Mental Illness." *Administration and Policy in Mental Health* 18 (1990): 9–18.

Freuh, B. Christopher, Anouk L. Grubaugh, Anthony T. Lo Sasso, Walter J. Jones, John M. Oldham, and Richard C. Lindrooth. "Key Stakeholder Perceptions Regarding Acute Care Psychiatry in Distressed Publicly Funded Mental Health Care Markets." *Bulletin of the Menninger Clinic* 76 (2012): 1–20.

Gaebel, Wolfgang, Mathias Riesbeck, Wolfgang Wölwer, Ansgar Klimke, Matthias Eickhoff, Martina von Wilmsdorff, and Isabella Heuser. "Rates and Predictors of Remission in First-Episode Schizophrenia within 1 Year of Antipsychotic Maintenance Treatment." *Schizophrenia Research* 152 (2014): 478–86.

Gallagher, Sally K., and David Mechanic. "Living with the Mentally Ill: Effects on the Health and Function of Other Household Members." *Social Science and Medicine* 42 (1996): 1691–701.

Gianfrancesco, Frank D., Ruey-hua Wang, and Elaine Yu. "Effects of Patients with Bipolar, Schizophrenic, and Major Depressive Disorders on the Mental and Other Healthcare Expenses of Family Members." *Social Science and Medicine* 61 (2005): 305–11.

Gilmore, John H. "Understanding What Causes Schizophrenia: A Developmental Perspective." *American Journal of Psychiatry* 167 (2010): 8–10.

Giron, M., A. Fernandez-Yanez, S. Mana-Alverenga, A. Molina-Habas, A. Nolasco, and M. Gomez-Beneyto. "Efficacy and Effectiveness of Individual Family Intervention on Social and Clinical Functioning and Family Burden in Severe Schizophrenia." *Psychological Medicine* (2009): 1–12.

Glaeser, Edward L., David Laibson, and Bruce Sacerdote. "An Economic Approach to Social Capital." *Economic Journal* 112 (2002): F437–58.

Goffman, Erving. *Stigma: Notes on the Management of Spoiled Identity.* Englewood Cliffs, NJ: Prentice-Hall, 1963.

Goldberg, Susan G., Mary B. Killeen, and Bonnie O'Day. "The Disclosure Conundrum: How People with Psychiatric Disabilities Navigate Employment." *Psychology, Public Policy and Law* 11 (2005): 463–500.

Goldman, Howard, and Gerald N. Grob. "Defining 'Mental Illness' in Mental Health Policy." *Health Affairs* 25 (2006): 737–49.

Gomez, Rafael, and Eric Santor. "Membership Has Its Privileges: The Effect of Social Capital and Neighbourhood Characteristics on the Earnings of Microfinance Borrowers." *Canadian Journal of Economics* 34 (2001): 943–66.

Greenwood, Ronni Michelle, Ana Stefancic and Sam Tsemberis. "Pathways Housing First for Homeless Persons with Psychiatric Disabilities: Program Innovation, Research, and Advocacy." *Journal of Social Issues* 69 (2013): 645–63.

Grob, Gerald N. "Mad, Homeless and Unwanted: A History of the Care of the Chronically Mentally Ill in America." *Psychiatric Clinics of North America* 17 (1994): 541–56.

———. "Mental Health Policy in the Liberal State: The Example of the United States." *International Journal of Law and Psychiatry* 31 (2008): 89–100.

Gronfein, William. "Psychotropic Drugs and the Origins of Deinstitutionalization." *Social Problems* 32 (1985): 437–54.

Grover, Sandeep, Subho Chakrabarti, Munish Aggarwal, Ajit Avasthi, Parmanand Kulhara, Sunil Sharma, and Nitacha Khehra. "Comparative Study of the Experience of Caregiving in Bipolar Affective Disorder and Schizophrenia." *International Journal of Social Psychiatry* 58 (2011): 614–22.

Harcourt, Bernard E. "From the Asylum to the Prison: Rethinking the Incarceration Revolution." *Texas Law Review* 84 (2006): 1751–86.

Hartman, Patrick A. "'Interacting with Others' as a Major Life Activity under the Americans with Disabilities Act." *Seton Hall Circuit Review* 2 (2005): 138–73.

Hawthorne, Nathaniel. *The Scarlet Letter*. New York: Simon & Schuster, 2004 (1st ed., 1850).

Heinrichs, R. Walter. "Historical Origins of Schizophrenia: Two Early Madmen and Their Illness." *Journal of the History of the Behavioral Sciences* 39 (2003): 349–463.

Hemmens, Craig, Milo Miller, Velmer S. Burton, and Susan Milner. "The Consequences of Official Labels: An Examination of the Rights Lost by the Mentally Ill and Mentally Incompetent Ten Years Later." *Community Mental Health Journal* 38 (2002): 129–40.

Hollenbeck, Kevin, and Jean Kimmel. "Differences in the Returns to Education for Males by Disability Status and Age of Disability Onset." *Southern Economic Journal* 74 (2008): 707–24.

Howe, E. W. *Ventures in Common Sense*. New York: Alfred A. Knopf, 1919.

Hunter, Michael D., and Peter W. R. Woodruff. "History, Aetiology and Symptomatology of Schizophrenia." *Psychiatry* 4 (2005): 3–6.

Janssen, Paul. "The Social Chemistry of Pharmacological Discovery: The Haloperidol Story." *International Journal of the Addictions* 27 (1992): 331–46.

Jenkins, Janice Hunter, and Elizabeth A. Carpenter-Song. "Awareness of Stigma among Persons with Schizophrenia." *Journal of Nervous and Mental Disease* 197 (2009): 520–29.

Job Accommodations Network. "Accommodation Ideas for Addison's Disease." Accessed June 3, 2014. https://askjan.org/soar/Other/addisons.html.

Jones, Amanda M. "Disclosure of Mental Illness in the Workplace: A Literature Review." *American Journal of Psychiatric Rehabilitation* 14 (2011): 212–29.

Jones, Melanie K., Paul L. Latreille, and Peter J. Sloane. "Disability, Gender, and the British Labour Market." *Oxford Economics Papers* 58 (2006): 407–49.

Kaas, Merrie J., Suzanne Lee, and Carol Peitzman. "Barriers to Collaboration between Mental Health Professionals and Families in the Care of Persons with Serious Mental Illness." *Issues in Mental Health Nursing* 24 (2003): 741–56.

Kennedy, John W. "Phoenix Dream Center Opens Program for Foster Youth." *Pentecostal Evangel*, December 12, 2013. http://ag.org/top/news/.

Keshavan, Matcheri S., Henry A. Nasrallah, and Rajiv Tandon. "Schizophrenia, 'Just the Facts' 6. Moving Ahead with the Schizophrenia Concept: From the Elephant to the Mouse." *Schizophrenia Research* 127 (2011): 3–13.

Keshavan, Matcheri S., Rajiv Tandon, Nash N. Boutros, and Henry A. Nasrallah. "Schizophrenia, 'Just the Facts': What We Know in 2008 Part 3: Neurobiology." *Schizophrenia Research* 106 (2008): 89–107.

Kessler, Ronald C. "The Prevalence and Correlates of Untreated Serious Mental Illness." *Health Services Research* 36 (2001): 987–1007.

Killeen, Mary B., and Bonnie L. O'Day. "Challenging Expectations: How Individuals with Psychiatric Disabilities Find and Keep Work." *Psychiatric Rehabilitation Journal* 28 (2004): 157–63.

Koutra, Katerina, Sofia Triliva, Theano Roumeliotaki, Zacharias Stefanakis, Maria Basta, Chritos Lionis, and Alexandros N. Vgontzas. "Family Functioning in Families of First-episode Psychosis Patients as Compared to Chronic Mentally Ill Patients and Healthy Controls." *Psychiatry Research* 45 (2014): 486–96.

Kuipers, Elizabeth. "Family Interventions in Schizophrenia: Evidence for Efficacy and Proposed Mechanisms of Change." *Journal of Family Therapy* 28 (2006): 73–80.

Kvrgic, Sara, Marialuisa Cavelti, Eva-Marina Beck, Nicolas Rusch, and Roland Vauth. "Therapeutic Alliance in Schizophrenia: The Role of Recovery Orientation, Self-Stigma, and Insight." *Psychiatry Research* 209 (2013): 15–20.

Lebensohn, Zigmond M. "General Hospital Psychiatry U.S.A.: Retrospect and Prospect." *Comprehensive Psychiatry* 21 (1980): 500–503.

Lehman, Anthony F., Jeffrey Lieberman, Lisa B. Dixon, Thomas H. McGlashan, Alexander L. Miller, Diana O. Perkins, and Julie Kreyenbuhl. *Practice Guideline for the Treatment of Patients with Schizophrenia.* 2nd ed. Arlington, VA: American Psychiatric Association, 2010.

Lehman, Anthony F., Richard Goldberg, Lisa B. Dixon, Scot McNary, Leticia Postrado, Ann Hackman, and Karen McDonnell. "Improving Employment Outcomes for Persons with Severe Mental Illnesses." *Archives of General Psychiatry* 59 (2002): 165–72.

Link, Bruce, Jo C. Phelan, Michaeline Bresnahan, Ann Stueve, and Bernice A. Pescosolido. "Public Conceptions of Mental Illness: Labels, Causes, Dangerousness, and Social Distance." *American Journal of Public Health* 89 (1999): 1328–33.

Lopez-Munoz, Francisco, and Cecilio Alamo. "The Consolidation of Neuroleptic Therapy: Janssen, the Discovery of Haloperidol and Its Introduction into Clinical Practice." *Brain Research Bulletin* 79 (2009): 120–41.

Lowyck, B., M. De Hert, E. Peeters, M. Wampers, P. Gilis, and J. Peukens. "A Study of the Family Burden of 150 Family Members of Schizophrenic Patients." *European Psychiatry* 19 (2004): 395–401.

Lucca, Anna M., Alexis D. Henry, Steven Banks, Lorna Simon, and Stephanie Page. "Evaluation of an Individual Placement and Support Model (IPS) Program." *Psychiatric Rehabilitation Journal* 27 (2004): 251–57.

Lyons, Richard D. "How Release of Mental Patients Began." *New York Times*, October 30, 1984.

Macias, Cathaleen, Robert Jackson, Carolyn Schroeder, and Qi Wang. "What Is a Clubhouse? Report on the ICCD 1996 Survey of USA Clubhouses." *Community Mental Health Journal* 35 (1999): 181–90.

Magaña, Sandy M., Jorge I. Ramirez Garcia, Maria G. Hernandez, and Raymond Cortez. "Psychological Distress among Latino Family Caregivers of Adults with Schizophrenia: The Roles of Burden and Stigma." *Psychiatric Services* 58 (2007): 378–84.

Magliano, L., Andrea Fiorillo, Corrado De Rose, Claudio Malagone, Mario Maj, and the National Mental Health Project Working Group. "Family Burden in Long-Term Diseases: A Comparative Study in Schizophrenia vs. Physical Disorders." *Social Science and Medicine* 61 (2005): 313–22.

Magliano, L., G. Fadden, M. Economou, M. Xavier, T. Held, M. Guarneri, C. Marasco, P. Tosini, and M. Maj. "Social and Clinical Factors Influencing the Choice of Coping Strategies in Relatives of Patients with Schizophrenia: Results of the BIOMED I Study." *Social Psychiatry and Psychiatric Epidemiology* 33 (1998): 413–19.

Magliano, L., G. Fadden, M. Madianos, J. M. Caldas de Almeida, T. Held, M. Guarneri, C. Marasco, et al. "Burden on the Families of Patients with Schizophrenia: Results of the BIOMED I Study." *Social Psychiatry and Psychiatric Epidemiology* 33 (1998): 405–12.

Mann, Caroline E., and Melissa J. Himelein. "Factors Associated with Stigmatization of Persons with Mental Illness." *Psychiatric Services* 55 (2004): 185–87.

Marshall, Tina, Phyllis Solomon, Sara-Ann Steber, and Eddie Mannion. "Provider and Family Beliefs Regarding the Causes of Severe Mental Illness." *Psychiatric Quarterly* 74 (2003): 223–36.

Marwaha, Steven, and Sonia Johnson. "Views and Experiences of Employment among People with Psychosis: A Qualitative Descriptive Study." *International Journal of Social Psychiatry* 51 (2005): 302–16.

McDonell, Michael G., Robert Short, Christopher M. Berry, and Dennis G. Dyck. "Burden in Schizophrenia Caregivers: Impact of Family Psychoeducation and Awareness of Patient Suicidality." *Family Process Journal* 42 (2003): 91–103.

Michalak, Erin E., Lakshmi N. Yatham, Victoria Maxwell, Sandra Hale, and Raymond W. Lam. "The Impact of Bipolar Disorder upon Work Functioning: A Qualitative Analysis." *Bipolar Disorders* 9 (2007): 126–43.

Mitra, Sophie. "The Capability Approach and Disability." *Journal of Disability Policy Studies* 16 (2006): 236–47.

Möller-Leimkühler, Anne Maria, and Andreas Wiesheu. "Caregiver Burden in Chronic Mental Illness: The Role of Patient and Caregiver Characteristics." *European Archives of Psychiatry and Clinical Neuroscience* 262 (2012): 157–66.

Morrissey, Joseph P., and Howard H. Goldman. "Care and Treatment of the Mentally Ill in the United States: Historical Developments and Reforms." *Annals of the American Academy of Political and Social Science* 484 (1986): 12–27.

Mowbray, Carol T., Mary E. Collins, Chyrell D. Bellamy, Deborah A. Megivern, Deborah Bybee, and Steve Szilvagyi. "Supported Education for Adults with Psychiatric Disabilities: An Innovation for Social Work and Psychosocial Rehabilitation Practice." *Social Work* 50 (2005): 7–20.

Murray, Christopher J. L., and Alan D. Lopez, eds. *The Global Burden of Disease: A Comprehensive Assessment of Mortality and Disability from Diseases, Injuries and Risk Factors in 1990 and Projected to 2020.* Cambridge, MA: Harvard School of Public Health, 1996.

Murray, Christopher J. L., Theo Vos, Rafael Lozano, Mohsen Naghavi, Abraham D. Flaxman, Catherine Michaud, and Majid Ezzati. "Disability-Adjusted Life Years (DALYs) for 291 Diseases and Injuries in 21 Regions, 1990–2010." *Lancet* 380 (2012): 2197–223.

NC Division of Mental Health, Developmental Disabilities and Substance Abuse Services. "Exploring the Costs and Feasibility of a New Psychiatric Facility." Raleigh: North Carolina Department of Health and Human Services, 2013.

New Freedom Commission on Mental Health. *Achieving the Promise: Transforming Mental Health Care in America.* DHHS Pub. No. SMA-03-3832. Rockville, MD: 2003.

Nithsdale, Vicky, Jason Davies, and Paul Croucher. "Psychosis and the Experience of Employment." *Journal of Occupational Rehabilitation* 18 (2008): 175–82.

Noce, Robert H., David B. Williams, and Walter Rapaport. "Reserprine (Serpasil) in the Management of the Mentally Ill and Mentally Retarded." *Senate Interim Committee Report on the Treatment of Mental Illness* 20 (1956): 29–35.

Nordentoft, Merete, Trine Madsen, and Izabela Fedyszyn. "Suicidal Behavior and Mortality in First-Episode Psychosis." *Journal of Nervous and Mental Disease* 203 (2015): 387–92.

Norman, Ross, Deborah Windell, and Rahul Manchanda. "Examining Differences in the Stigma of Depression and Schizophrenia." *International Journal of Social Psychiatry* 58 (2012): 69–78.

Norman, Ross, Richard M. Sorrentino, Deborah Windell, and Rahul Manchada. "The Role of Perceived Norms in the Stigmatization of Mental Illness." *Social Psychiatry and Psychiatric Epidemiology* 43 (2008): 851–59.

Nuechterlein, K. H., Dawson, M. E., Ventura, J., Gitlin, M., Subotnik, K. L., Snyder, K. S., Mintz, J., & Bartzokis, G. "The Vulnerability/Stress Model of Schizophrenic Relapse: A Longitudinal Study." *Acta Psychiatrica Scandinavica* 89 (1994): 58–64.

O'Brien, Gerald, and Melinda S. Brown. "Persons with Mental Illness and the Americans with Disabilities Act: Implications for the Social Work Profession." *Social Work in Mental Health* 7 (2009): 442–57.

Ochoa, Susana, Miriam Vilplana, Josep Maria Haro, Victoria Villalta-Gil, Franciso Martinez, Mari Cruz Negredo, and Pilar Casacuberta. "Do Needs, Symptoms or Disability of Outpatients with Schizophrenia Influence Family Burden?" *Social Psychiatry and Psychiatric Epidemiology* 43 (2008): 612–18.

Oxford English Dictionary. Oxford: Oxford University Press, 1970 (1st ed., 1884–1928).

Pachankis, John E. "The Psychological Implications of Concealing a Stigma: A Cognitive-Affective-Behavioral Model." *Psychological Bulletin* 133 (2007): 328–45.

Palmer, Brian A., V. Shane Pankratz, and John Michael Bostwick. "The Lifetime Risk of Suicide in Schizophrenia: A Reexamination." *Archives of General Psychiatry* 62 (2005): 247–53.

Pandya, Anand, Catherine Bresee, Ken Duckworth, Katrina Gay, and Michael Fitzpatrick. "Perceived Impact of the Disclosure of a Schizophrenia Diagnosis." *Community Mental Health Journal* 47 (2011): 613–21.

Parekattil, Sijo J., and Michael E. Moran. "Robotic Instrumentation: Evolution and Microsurgical Applications." *Indian Journal of Urology 26* (2010): 395–403.

Parks, Joe, and Alan Q. Radke, eds. *The Vital Role of State Psychiatric Hospitals*. Alexandria, VA: National Association of State Mental Health Program Directors, 2014.

Pescosolido, Bernice A., Jack K. Martin, J. Scott Long, Tait R. Medina, Jo C. Phelan, and Bruce G. Link. "'A Disease Like Any Other?' A Decade of Change in Public Reactions to Schizophrenia, Depression, and Alcohol Dependence." *American Journal of Psychiatry* 167 (2010): 1321–30.

Peterson, Debbie, Nandika Currey, and Sunny Collings. "'You Don't Look Like One of Them': Disclosure of Mental Illness in the Workplace as an Ongoing Dilemma." *Psychiatric Rehabilitation Journal* 35 (2011): 145–47.

Petrila, John. "Congress Restores the Americans with Disabilities Act to Its Original Intent." *Psychiatric Services* 60 (2009): 878–79.

Phoenix Dream Center. "About Us." Accessed June 3, 2014.http://www.phxdreamcenter.org/about_us.

Phoenix First Assembly of God. "Our Mission." Accessed April 14, 2014. http://www.phoenixfirst.org/about-us/mission-values.

Read, John. "Why Promoting Biological Ideology Increases Prejudice against People Labelled 'Schizophrenic.'" *Australian Psychologist* 42 (2007): 118–28.

Rinaldi, Miles, Eoin Killackey, Jo Smith, Geoff Shepherd, Swaran P. Singh, and Tom Craig. "First Episode Psychosis and Employment: A Review." *International Review of Psychiatry* 22 (2010): 148–62.

Roberts, Albert R., and Linda Farris Kurtz. "Historical Perspectives on the Care and Treatment of the Mentally Ill." *Journal of Sociology and Social Welfare* 75 (1987): 75–91.

Rollins, Angela L., Kim T. Mueser, Gary R. Bond, and Deborah R. Becker. "Social Relationships at Work: Does the Employment Model Make a Difference?" *Psychiatric Rehabilitation Journal* 26 (2002): 51–61.

Rose, Stephen M. "Deciphering Deinstitutionalization: Complexities in Policy and Program Analysis." *Milbank Memorial Fund Quarterly* 57 (1979): 429–58.

Rosensheck, Robert, Douglas Leslie, Richard Keefe, Joseph McEvoy, Marvin Swartz, Diana Perkins, Scott Stroup, John K. Hsiao, and Jeffrey Lieberman. "Barriers to Employment for People with Schizophrenia." *American Journal of Psychiatry* 163 (2006): 411–17.

Rudnick, Abraham, and Maya Gover. "Combining Supported Education with Supported Employment." *Psychiatric Services* 60 (2009): 1690.

Saks, Elyn R. "Successful and Schizophrenic." *New York Times*, January 27, 2013.

Salkever, David, Mustafa C. Karakus, Eric P. Slade, Courtenay M. Harding, Richard L. Hough, Robert A. Rosenheck, Marvin S. Swartz, Concepcion Barrio, and Anne Marie Yamada. "Measures and Predictors of Community-Based Employment and Earnings of Persons with Schizophrenia in a Multisite Study." *Psychiatric Services* 58 (2007): 315–24.

Salomon, Joshua, Theo Vos, Daniel R. Hogan, Mohsen Naghavi, Nazma Begum, Razibuzzaman Shah, and Muhammad Karyana. "Common Values in Assessing Health Outcomes from Disease and Injury: Disability Weights Measurement Study for the Global Burden of Disease Study 2010." *Lancet* 380 (2012): 2129–43.

Salomon, Joshua, Theo Vos, Daniel R. Hogan, Mohsen Naghavi, Nazma Begum, Razibuzzaman Shah, and Muhammad Karyana. "Supplement to Common Values in Assessing Health Outcomes from Disease and Injury." *Lancet* 380 (2012): 1–25.

Saunders, Jana C., and Michelle M. Byrne. "A Thematic Analysis of Families Living with Schizophrenia." *Archives of Psychiatric Nursing* 16 (2002): 217–23.

Schennach, R., S. Meyer, F. Seemüller, M. Jäger, M. Schmauss, G. Laux, H. Pfeiffer, D. Naber, L.G. Schmidt, W. Gaebel, et al. "Insight in Schizophrenia—Course and Predictors during the Acute Treatment Phase of Patients Suffering from a Schizophrenia Spectrum Disorder." *European Psychiatry* 27 (2012): 625–33.

Schomerus G., C. Schwahn, A. Holzinger, P. W. Corrigan, H. J. Grabe, M. G. Carta, M. C. Angermeyer. "Evolution of Public Attitudes about Mental Illness: A Systematic Review and Meta-Analysis." *Acta Psychiatrica Scandinavica* 125 (2012): 440–52.

Schulze, Beate, and Matthias C. Angermeyer. "Subjective Experiences of Stigma: A Focus Group Study of Schizophrenic Patients, Their Relatives and Mental Health Professionals." *Social Science and Medicine* 56 (2003): 299–312.

Schur, Lisa, Douglas Kruse, Joseph Blasi, and Peter Blanck. "Is Disability Disabling in All Workplaces? Workplace Disparities and Corporate Culture." *Industrial Relations* 48 (2009): 381–410.

Secker, Jenny, and Helen Membrey. "Promoting Mental Health through Employment and Developing Healthy Workplaces: The Potential of Natural Supports at Work." *Health Education Research* 18 (2003): 207–15.

Shah, Saleem A. "Legal and Mental Health System Interactions: Major Developments and Research Needs." *International Journal of Law and Psychiatry* 4 (1981): 219–70.

Silton, Nava R., Kevin J. Flannelly, Glen Milstein, and Margaret L. Vaaler. "Stigma in America: Has Anything Changed? Impact of Perceptions of Mental Illness and Dangerousness on the Desire for Social Distance; 1996 and 2006." *Journal of Nervous and Mental Disease* 199 (2011): 361–66.

Silveira, Celeste, Joao Marques-Teixeira, and Antonio Jose de Bastos-Leite. "More Than One Century of Schizophrenia: An Evolving Perspective." *Journal of Nervous and Mental Disease* 200 (2012): 1054–57.

Sin, Jacqueline, and Ian Norman. "Psychoeducational Interventions for Family Members of People with Schizophrenia: A Mixed-Method Systematic Review." *Journal of Clinical Psychiatry* 74 (2013): 1145–62.

Smerud, Phyllis E., and Irwin S. Rosenfarb. "The Therapeutic Alliance and Family Psychoeducation in the Treatment of Schizophrenia: An Exploratory Prospective Change Process Study." *Journal of Consulting and Clinical Psychology* 76 (2008): 505–10.

Spence, Michael. "Job Market Signaling." *Quarterly Journal of Economics* 87 (1973): 355–74.

Stain, Helen J., Cherrie A. Galletly, Scott Clark, Jacqueline Wilson, Emily A. Killen, Lauren Anthes, Linda E. Campbell, Mary-Claire Hanlon, and Carol Harvey. "Understanding the Social Costs of Psychosis: The Experience of Adults Affected by Psychosis Identified within the Second Australian National Survey of Psychosis." *Australian and New Zealand Journal of Psychiatry* 46 (2012): 879–89.

Steadman, Henry J., Fred C. Osher, Pamela Clark Robbins, Brian Case, and Steven Samuels. "Prevalence of Serious Mental Illness among Jail Inmates." *Psychiatric Services* 60 (2009): 761–65.

Stefan, Susan. *Hollow Promises: Employment Discrimination against People with Mental Disabilities.* Washington, D.C.: American Psychological Association, 2002.

Stone, Danielle, and Adrienne Colella. "A Model of Factors Affecting the Treatment of Disabled Individuals in Organizations." *Academy of Management Review* 21 (1996): 352–401.

Tandon, Rajiv, Henry A. Nasrallah, and Matcheri S. Keshavan. "'Just the Facts:' Meandering in Schizophrenia's Many Forests." *Schizophrenia Research* 128 (2011): 5–6.

Tandon, Rajiv, Henry A. Nasrallah, and Matcheri S. Keshavan. "Schizophrenia, 'Just the Facts' 4. Clinical Features and Conceptualization." *Schizophrenia Research* 110 (2009): 1–23.

Tandon, Rajiv, Henry A. Nasrallah, and Matcheri S. Keshavan. "Schizophrenia, 'Just the Facts' 5. Treatment and Prevention Past, Present, and Future." *Schizophrenia Research* 122 (2010): 1–23.

Tandon, Rajiv, Matcheri S. Keshavan, and Henry A. Nasrallah. "Schizophrenia, 'Just the Facts' What We Know in 2008. 2 Epidemiology and Etiology." *Schizophrenia Research* 102 (2008): 1–18.

Taylor, Pamela J. "Psychosis and Violence: Stories, Fears and Reality." *Canadian Journal of Psychiatry* 53 (2008): 647–59.

Teplin, Linda A., Gary M. McClelland, Karen M. Abram, and Dana A. Weiner. "Crime Victimization in Adults with Severe Mental Illness." *Archives of General Psychiatry* 62 (2005): 911–21.

Torrey, E. Fuller. *American Psychosis.* Oxford: Oxford University Press, 2014.

————. *Surviving Schizophrenia: A Manual for Families, Patients, and Providers*, 5th ed. New York: HarperCollins, 2006.

Tringo, J. L. "The Hierarchy of Preference toward Disability Groups." *Journal of Special Education* 4 (1970): 295–306.

Tsang, Hector W. H., Ada Y. Leung, Raymond C.K. Chung, Morris Bell, and Wai-Ming Cheung. "Review on Vocational Predictors: A Systematic Review of Predictors of Vocational Outcomes among Individuals with Schizophrenia; An Update since 1998." *Australian and New Zealand Journal of Psychiatry* 44 (2010): 495–504.

Tsemberis, Sam. *Housing First: The Pathways Model to End Homelessness for People with Mental Illness and Addiction.* Center City: Hazelden, 2010.

U.S. National Library of Medicine. "Diseases of the Mind: Highlights of American Psychiatry through 1900, Early Psychiatric Hospitals and Asylums." Last modified September 13, 2013. http://www.nlm.nih.gov/hmd/diseases/early.html.

Viana, Kristin. "People That Have Won." *Soundings East* 17 (1993): 9–12.

Vos, Theo, Abraham D. Flaxman, Mohsen Naghavi, Rafael Lozano, Catherin Michaud, Majid Ezzati, and Kenji Shibuya. "Years Lived with Disability (YLDs) for the 1160 Sequelae of 289 Diseased and Injuries 1990–2010: A Systematic Analysis for the Global Burden of Disease Study 2010." *Lancet* 380 (2012): 2163–96.

Walker, Elaine F., and Donald Diforio. "Schizophrenia: A Neural-Diathesis Stress Model." *Psychological Review* 104 (1997): 667–85.

Watson, Amy C., Frederick E. Miller, and John S. Lyons. "Adolescent Attitudes toward Serious Mental Illness." *Journal of Nervous and Mental Disease* 193 (2005): 769–72.

Weiner, Bernard, Raymond P. Perry, and Jamie Magnusson. "An Attributional Analysis of Reactions to Stigmas." *Journal of Personality and Social Psychology* 55 (1988): 738–48.

Weiner, Bernard. "On Sin versus Sickness: A Theory of Perceived Responsibility and Social Motivation." *American Psychologist* 48 (1993): 957–65.

Weiss, Marc Franchot. "Children's Attitudes toward the Mentally Ill: A Developmental Analysis." *Psychological Reports* 58 (1986): 11–20.

————. "Children's Attitudes toward the Mentally Ill: An Eight-Year Longitudinal Follow-Up." *Psychological Reports* 74 (1994): 51–56.

Westbrook, Mary T., Varoe Legge, and Mark Pennay. "Attitudes towards Disabilities in a Multicultural Society." *Social Science and Medicine* 36 (1993): 615–23.

Where Hope Lives. "Rescuing Victims of Human Trafficking." Accessed May 20, 2015. http://www.rescueprojectphx.org/index.php.

Whiteford, Harvey A., Louisa Degenhardt, Jurgen Rehm, Amanda J. Baxter, Alize J. Ferrari, Holly E. Erskine, and Fiona J. Charlson. "Global Burden of Disease Attributable to Mental and Substance Use Disorders: Findings from the Global Burden of Disease Study 2010." *Lancet* 382 (2013): 1575–86.

Wilk, Joshua E., Joyce C. West, Steven C. Marcus, Lisa Countis, Darrel A. Regier, and Mark Olfson. "Family Contact and the Management of Medication Non-Adherence in Schizophrenia." *Community Mental Health Journal* 44 (2008): 377–80.

Winchester, Simon. *The Professor and the Madman: A Tale of Murder, Insanity, and the Making of the Oxford English Dictionary.* New York: HarperCollins, 1998.

Wing, Victoria C., Ingrid Bacher, Kristi A. Sacco, and Tony P. George. "Neuropsychological Performance in Patients with Schizophrenia and Controls as a Function of Cigarette Smoking Status." *Psychiatry Research* 188 (2011): 320–26.

Wood, Lisa, Michele Birtel, Sarah Alsawyc, Melissa Pyle, and Anthony Morrison. "Public Perceptions of Stigma towards People with Schizophrenia, Depression, and Anxiety." *Psychiatry Research* 220 (2014): 604–8.

Wu, Eric Q., Howard G. Birnbaum, Lizheng Shi, Daniel E. Ball, Ronald C. Kessler, Matthew Moulis, and Jyoti Aggarwal. "The Economic Burden of Schizophrenia in the United States in 2002." *Journal of Clinical Psychiatry* 66 (2005): 1122–29.

Zwelling, Shomer S. *Quest for a Cure: The Public Hospital in Williamsburg: 1773–1885.* Williamsburg, VA: Colonial Williamsburg Foundation, 1985.

Index

acceptance of SMI, 18, 118, 118–121, 122, 123

accommodations, employer-provided, 112, 134, 144, 146–149, 157; adjudication, 152–157; externalities, 147–149, 151–152, 153, 155; costs of, 96, 149–152, 157, 158; public goods, 146–147, 148–149. *See also* Americans with Disabilities Act, employment provisions

accommodations, impact of,: on coworkers, 149, 150, 151–152, 155; on supervisor, 151, 153, 156–157; on worker with SMI, 150, 152

accommodations, self-initiated, 139, 144–146, 158, 171

accommodations, types of,: job transfer, 153–154; leave of absence, 154–155; time off work, 151, 154; unscheduled breaks, 144, 148, 151. *See also* job matching, nature of; stayers vs. leavers, employment

advocacy. *See* patient advocates

Alongside Ministries, 160

American Indian College, 126, 142, 197

American Psychiatric Association, 83

Americans with Disabilities Act, adjudication of, 98, 102, 103, 152–153; "major life activity", 100–101; "qualified person with a disability", 98, 99–100; "substantial limitations",

98–99; *See also Gaul v. Lucent Technologies; Rascon v. U S West Communications; Taylor v. Phoenixville School District*

Americans with Disabilities Act, employment provisions, 94, 97–98, 133, 144, 177; definition of disability, 97, 128; disclosure of disability, 106, 108, 114, 120, 151; reasonable accommodation, 95–96, 97–98

Americans with Disabilities Act, enactment of, 94–97

Americans with Disabilities Act Amendments Act, 94, 101–103

anxiety disorders, 23, 26–27, 114, 153

asylums, 58, 103–104

atypical antipsychotics. *See* second generation antipsychotics

Barnett, Tommy, 110, 125, 127, 143, 198

Becker, Gary, 25–26, 26

Beers, Clifford, 59, 60, 65

barriers to accessing care for SMI: in the legal system, 75, 180, 182, 183; in the mental health system, 54, 181, 182; resource constraints, 84–85, 181, 182

bipolar disorder, 7, 16, 79, 93, 103, 115, 118, 120, 129, 156, 185, 192

Bleuler, Eugen, 7, 9

Bleuler, Manfred, 9, 10

Bogardus, Emory, 17

brain disease, schizophrenia as, 9, 10, 23, 24, 182, 194
Broadmoor Asylum for the Criminally Insane, 104, 104–105
Bruce, Joe, 86, 87
Bruce, William, 75–76, 85, 86–87
burden of care, determinants of, 80–83; caregiver characteristics, 82–83; mental health system, x, 66, 83–87; patient characteristics, 80–81. *See also* barriers to accessing care for SMI; support networks
burden of care, nature of, 73–74, 76–80, 87–88, 177; economic, 76–77; emotional, 76, 79–80, 83; health-related, 79; social, 77–78
burden of disease: definition of, 38; mental illness, 39–40, 40; schizophrenia, 40, 40–41. *See also* Global Burden of Disease project
Bush, George W., 66

Carter, Jimmy, 65–66
causes of SMI, 9–10; environmental factors, 9, 86; genetic factors, 9, 85–86; public perceptions of, 23. *See also* diathesis stress model
clozapine, 11, 12
Collins, Wilkie, 107, 111
community mental health: centers, 61, 63–66, 69, 181; services, 70, 85, 176, 180, 181, 182
Community Mental Health Act, 179
Community Mental Health Centers Act, 61
competitive employment, 49, 103, 106, 117, 132, 135, 143, 144, 158, 161; definitions of, 46, 111; and disclosure of SMI, 111, 115–117; qualitative study of SMI and, 130–131, 132–133, 134, 135–136, 215n18; survey of workers with SMI in, 161–162, 163–165, 167–169, 170–171. *See also* mental health policy; vocational training
concealment of SMI, 16, 28, 107, 170; at work, 27, 111, 151–152; "passing", 123. *See also* disclosure of SMI at work, levels of
Corrigan, Patrick, 24, 28

costs of SMI, 12, 58, 61, 63, 65, 66; to families, 76–77
coworkers. *See* workplace relationships
criminal justice system, 71–73, 176, 194. *See also* jail

delusions, 8, 34; of grandeur, 6, 6–7, 108, 166; of paranoia/persecution, 6–7, 104, 162, 166; of religious nature, 4, 5, 8, 139, 169
deferred prosecution. *See* jail, diversion programs
deinstitutionalization, 62, 63, 65, 75, 77, 172
dementia praecox, 7
depression, 18, 23, 40, 79, 114, 116, 153. *See also* burden of care, emotional; symptoms of SMI, depression
diathesis-stress model of SMI, 10, 86
disability: and education, 34, 42, 176, 186; employment policy, 138–139, 152, 157, 177–178; rights, 179, 180; social model of, 122. *See also* Americans with Disabilities Act, provisions of
disability-adjusted life-years. *See* Global Burden of Disease project
disability-related discrimination, 18; in higher education, 34–35, 186–187; in the law, 21, 63; in the workplace, 25–26, 26–27
Disability Rights Maine, 75, 87
disclosure of SMI at work, impact of, 107, 110, 111, 115–117, 213n19, 213n26; benefits, 112; costs, 112–113, 118
disclosure of SMI at work, involuntary: because of acute symptoms, 109, 111, 114, 115; as a job qualification, 111; to request job accommodations, 106, 114, 134, 145
disclosure of SMI at work, voluntary, 110–111; approach-avoidance model, 113, 213n18; full disclosure, 116, 119, 126; strategies for disclosure, 114–115; non-disclosure, 108, 114–115, 116, 119, 145. *See also* rational choice model of disclosure; stayers vs. leavers
discrimination. *See* disability-related discrimination
Dix, Dorothea, 58

dopamine, 11

Easterley, William, 55
education, ix, 33–36, 49, 176, 185; and job
 matching, 43–44; as human capital, 36,
 37, 41–42, 165, 172; as a signal of
 worker quality, 42–43. *See also*
 supported education; mental health
 policy
employment outcomes, 12, 26, 128, 157;
 survey of, for persons with SMI,
 161–162, 163–164, 167–168, 170–171;
 and symptoms of SMI, 37, 38, 41, 47,
 93, 127, 172. *See also* accommodations,
 self-initiated, disclosure; job matching
employment policy, 94, 97–98, 138–139,
 157–158. *See also* mental health policy
Equal Employment Opportunities
 Commission, 97, 101, 155
etiology of schizophrenia. *See* causes of
 schizophrenia
externalities, 146, 147–148, 149; negative,
 147, 148, 149, 150, 151, 154, 155, 158,
 178; positive, 56, 147, 148, 149, 150,
 151, 153

family caregivers, 37, 57, 64, 163, 177,
 194; coping strategies, 82; "giving up",
 20, 172; positive aspects for, 88;
 provider attitudes toward, 84, 85–87;
 safety of, 75, 87, 180, 185. *See also*
 burden of care
family interventions, 83, 84, 86, 198
Felix, Robert, 61, 63, 64, 65, 181
firm characteristics and employment of
 persons with SMI, 130, 131–133, 139;
 work environment, 133–134; workplace
 culture, 131–132, 140. *See also* stayers
 vs. leavers; disclosure of SMI at work
first-generation antipsychotics, 11, 61–62,
 169; impact on chronic patients, 61–62;
 side effects of, 11, 169. *See also*
 haloperidol
Fountain House, 46
Frank, Richard, 84
Franks, Deborah, 77
free riders, 146
Fuller, E Torrey, 177

functional limitations of SMI, 44, 81, 102,
 127–129, 146; cognitive, 48, 129, 133,
 134, 144; emotional, 129, 137; social,
 129, 135, 137, 145. *See also* job
 matching; job mismatch; stayers vs.
 leavers

gainful employment, 94, 139, 161, 162,
 163, 176, 189, 190; definition of, 93,
 163; as a policy goal, 158, 177, 179,
 191, 193, 195
Gaul v. Lucent Technologies , 153–154
general human capital: definition of, 37
Glied, Sherry, 84
Global Burden of Disease project, 38–41;
 disability-adjusted life-years, 39, 40;
 measures of disease burden, 39. *See*
 also burden of disease
Goffman, Erving, 17–18, 19, 28, 123
"gravely disabled", 180

Haldol. *See* haloperidol.
hallucinations, 5, 6–7, 8, 162, 166; hearing
 voices, 8, 148
haloperidol, 11, 12, 51, 55, 67
Hartman, Brett, 169–170, 171, 172,
 172–173
health capital, 38–41, 41, 49. *See also*
 mental health policy
"hidden population", 161, 162, 192
historical evidence of schizophrenia, 5–6
homelessness, ix, 17, 54, 65, 66, 75, 94,
 103, 126, 140, 177, 197
hospitals. *See* psychiatric hospitals
House of Healing, 160, 198
human capital, 138, 139, 172, 178, 185,
 187, 190; general, 37, 37–38, 45, 49,
 178, 191, 192, 193; investments in,
 36–37, 41–42, 45, 47, 49; job-specific,
 37, 38, 45, 47, 49, 190; nature of,
 37–38. *See also* health capital; social
 capital; stayers vs. leavers

IMD exclusion rule, 63
"imminent danger", 180, 181
impairment, 44, 95, 122, 128; in the ADA,
 97, 99, 101; in the ADA Amendments
 Act, 102, 103
incarceration. *See* criminal justice system

Individual Placement and Support, 46–47,
    166, 191, 193–194; core principles of,
    190, 191; evaluations of, 47, 189–190
insight, lack of, 8, 56, 180, 182, 185, 194
involuntary hospitalization, 63, 65, 169,
    180, 194
involuntary treatment, 56, 169, 182, 185
It, 175, 177, 195

jail, ix, 54, 65, 71–72, 74, 75, 76, 143, 160,
    176, 177, 181, 182; diversion programs,
    73, 74, 176
James, William, 59
Janssen, Paul, 11, 55, 67–68
Job Accommodation Network, 128, 148,
    149
job accommodations. *See* accommodations
job characteristics and employment of
    persons with SMI, 130, 136–138, 144;
    flexible schedule, 126, 127–128, 137,
    140, 145, 163, 172; occupation,
    136–137; work processes, 137–138,
    139. *See also* employment outcomes for
    SMI; stayers vs. leavers
job matching, nature of, 127–128, 129; as a
    job accommodation, 128, 131, 139,
    144, 158; as a supply-side intervention,
    138–139
job matching, workplace characteristics,
    129–130, 131, 145–146; firm
    characteristics, 131–133, 139; job
    characteristics, 136–138, 139;
    workplace relationships, 134–136, 139.
    See also education; stayers vs. leavers
job mismatch, 44, 128, 131, 136, 157, 167

Kennedy, John F., 61
Kraeplin, Emil, 7

leavers. *See* stayers versus leavers
Lindblom, Charles, 69
Lowell, Robert, 172

manic depressive disorder. *See* bipolar dis-
    order.
Marcus, Steven, 161, 162
marginal value product, 42
Medicaid, 62, 63, 65, 184, 190, 193
Medical Expenditure Panel Study, 26, 161

Medications: adherence to, 12, 52, 53, 142,
    143, 166, 169–170, 182, 189. *See also*
    first-generation antipsychotics; second-
    generation antipsychotics
Menninger, Karl, 70
Mental Health Association, 16, 95
Mental Health Block Grants, 66, 181
Mental Health Parity and Addiction Equity
    Act, 178
mental health policy, x, 172, 177–179,
    194–195; history of, 58, 61, 64, 65–66,
    66, 84, 87; proposals to invest in higher
    education, 185–189; proposals for
    training in transferable skills, 189–194;
    proposals to restore health capital,
    180–185. *See also* employment policy
mental health services: for families in
    crisis, 55, 70, 73, 84, 217n24; market
    for, 55–57; vocational, ix, 46, 73, 91,
    136–137, 177. *See also* mental health
    policy; psychiatric hospitals; vocational
    training
mental health system, history of, 54–55,
    66–67; Federal authority, 62–66; local
    authority, 57–58; state authority, 58–62
mental health system, present-day, 51–54,
    55, 67, 70, 176, 179, 180; collaboration
    with family members ix, 83–87;
    resource allocation, 77, 84–85, 181,
    183–185. *See also* mental health policy
Mental Health Systems Act, 66
Mental Health Treatment Study, 189–190
mental hygiene, 59–60, 64
Mental Illness Fellowship, 163
merit good, 56
Meyer, Adolf, 59, 59–60
Minor, William Chester, 103–105
moral treatment, 57–58, 59, 179
Murphy, Tim, 183
Murray, James, 104–105

Nash, John, 172
National Alliance on Mental Illness, 115,
    116, 117
National Committee for Mental Hygiene,
    59
National Health Interview Survey, 27
National Institute of Disability and
    Rehabilitation Research, 192

National Institute of Mental Health, 61, 69, 183, 187–188, 189, 192
National Mental Health Association, 95
natural accommodations, 145
New Freedom Commission on Mental Health, 66–67
normal good, 121

olanzapine, 11, 15, 51
onset: of disability, 42; of schizophrenia, 3–4, 7, 10, 12, 36, 49, 175; of SMI, 49, 81, 86, 165, 185, 194
opportunity cost, 55
Oxford English Dictionary , 103–105; "accommodate", 144; "burden", 87; "disclose", 111; "policy", 178; "stigma", 17; "work", 103
"passing.". *See* concealment of SMI

pathoplastic factors, 7, 201n13
patient advocates, 75, 85, 86, 87, 181, 194
patient rights, ix, 21, 35, 75, 87, 176, 179; to adequate treatment, 63, 179, 180, 182–183, 194; to refuse treatment, 63, 179; to treatment in the least restrictive setting, 63, 103, 179. *See also* Americans with Disabilities Act, employment provisions
Perkins, Diana, 51, 52, 69, 70, 106, 175
Phipps Psychiatric Clinic, 60
Phoenix Dream Center, 125–127, 139–140, 141, 142, 143, 159, 160, 171, 177, 197, Church on the Street, 126; Foster Care Relief, 125; Rescue Project, 127; Working Men's Program, 126, 127, 140, 160
Phoenix First Assembly, 110, 125, 140, 199
Planners vs. Searchers, 54–55, 60, 68–69, 70, 158, 178, 194; nature of Planners, 56, 57, 63–64, 65, 66–67, 75, 179, 194; nature of Searchers, 67–68, 74, 176, 179, 183, 184, 188, 195
post-traumatic stress disorder, 155
practice guideline for schizophrenia, 83–84, 85
prevalence of schizophrenia, 5, 40
private goods, 146, 147, 148, 149, 150

prognosis for schizophrenia, 7, 21, 22, 41, 52, 106, 143, 169, 172–173
Protection and Advocacy for Individuals with Mental Illness Program, 181, 185
psychiatric hospitals, 4, 52–53, 84–85, 169, 181. *See also* state hospitals
psychopathic hospitals, 59, 60. *See also* Phipps Psychiatric Clinic
psychosis, in, 9, 10, 16, 25, 35, 75, 78, 81, 85, 86, 114, 143, 176; symptoms of, 8, 53, 75, 108, 139, 142, 162, 166, 169
public goods, 146–147, 147, 148, 149, 150
Pulse survey, 161–162

Rascon v. U S West Communications , 154–155
rational choice model of disclosure, 117–122; objectives of the worker, 117–118; trade-off between acceptance and disclosure, 119–120; utility-maximizing level of disclosure, 120–121
Read, John, 23
Reagan, Ronald, 66
reasonable accommodations. *See* Americans with Disabilities Act, employment provisions
recovery, 30, 52, 59, 65, 143, 162–163, 166, 169–170, 171, 194; attitudes of providers toward, 29, 30, 106; attitudes of public toward, 20, 23; effect of employment on, 93, 105, 152, 191
relapse, 10, 30, 126, 137, 142, 143, 149, 159, 198; after stopping medications, 35, 52, 53, 56, 108, 142, 143, 170, 189, 194
restraints, 57, 58, 62, 87, 169
Rinaudo, Ben, 162–163, 165, 167, 171, 172
risk of schizophrenia, 5, 9–10, 86

Saks, Elyn, 93, 105, 168
The Scarlet Letter , 15, 16
schizoaffective disorder, 27, 116, 129, 192
second-generation antipsychotics, 11, 37, 51, 166; side effects of, 12, 145, 163. *See also* clozapine; olanzapine; stayers vs. leavers

self-employment, 145, 159–160, 163, 164, 167, 172, 193
self-stigma, 28–30, 30
Snyder, Kurt, 166–167, 171, 172
social capital, 38, 48
social distance, 17–19, 97; and discrimination against persons with SMI, 25–26; and negative stereotypes of SMI, 22. *See also* stigma of SMI
social model of disability, 122
Social Security Disability Insurance, 62, 63, 65, 186, 199; and employment of workers with SMI, 137, 157, 189, 190, 193
social welfare, 55, 62, 66, 178, 185
Spence, Michael, 42–43
Standard Occupational Classification codes, 216n9
State Care Acts, 58, 62, 179
state mental hospitals: history of, 57, 58–59, 60–62, 63–64, 179; present-day, 84–85, 175, 181. *See also* deinstitutionalization; Topeka State Hospital; Williamsburg public hospital
stayers versus leavers, 163–164; employment, differences in, 164, 167–168, 170–171, 172, 216n9; human capital, differences in, 165, 168; illness and treatment, differences in, 168–169, 171; support networks, differences in, 171
stereotypes of SMI, 19–21, 43, 113, 143, 172, 179, 186–187, 191; in the media, 24–25; patient endorsement of, 28–30; public endorsement of, 23–24, 25, 29. *See also* social distance
stigma of SMI, ix, 17, 19–20; compared to physical illness, 18, 20; passage of the ADA and, 96–97, 103; strategies to combat, 23, 43; workplace, 25–28. *See also* self-stigma; social distance; stereotypes of SMI
stigma of schizophrenia, x, 15–17, 30; compared to other mental illness, 18, 22, 114
structural discrimination, 186, 189
Substance Abuse and Mental Health Services Administration, 87, 181. *See also* mental health policy

substance use disorders, 65, 81, 94, 126, 140, 178, 183, 190; burden of disease, 39, 40; stigma of, 18, 20, 22, 96, 97
suicide, 4, 24, 40, 76, 81
supervisors. *See* workplace relationships; accommodations, employer-provided
Supplemental Security Income, 62, 63
support networks: for family, 51–52, 75, 82, 83–84; for patient, 76, 83, 112, 135, 171, 172
supported education, 44–45, 163, 187–189; with supported employment, 48
supported employment, 110–111, 117, 122; clubhouses, 44, 46; Diversified Placement Approach, 46–47; employment outcomes of participants, 47, 49, 165; with neurocognitive enhancement therapy, 48. *See also* Individual Placement and Support; mental health policy
Survey of Income and Program Participation, 42, 44, 161
Surviving Schizophrenia, 177
Sutton v. United Airlines, 100, 102
symptoms of schizophrenia, nature of, 7–9, 129; anger, 3, 5, 30, 54, 169; anxiety, 8, 30, 61, 135, 136, 162, 193; confusion, 6, 129, 162; depression/emotional withdrawal, 8, 129, 162, 177; disorganized/racing thoughts, 8, 108, 129, 162; incoherent speech/writing, 3, 6, 17. *See also* delusions; hallucinations; insight, lack of; stayers vs. leavers
symptoms of schizophrenia, positive vs. negative, 8, 11, 15, 80

tastes for discrimination, 25, 112, 213n34. *See also* social distance; stigma of SMI
Taylor v. Phoenixville School District, 155–156
Topeka State Hospital, 70
training. *See* vocational training
transferable skills, 37, 45, 49, 136, 159, 179, 189–194
Treatment Assessment Screening Center, 74, 176
treatment of SMI, ix, 69, 84–85, 155, 180; failure to treat, 181, 182; schizophrenia,

11–12, 51–52. *See also* barriers to accessing care for SMI; first-generation antipsychotics; second-generation antipsychotics; mental health system, history of

Truven Health Analytics, 161–162

UN Convention on the Rights of Persons with Disabilities, 179, 180, 216n9

utility, 118, 120–121, 121–122, 213n36

Van Gogh, Vincent, 16, 172

victimization of persons with SMI, 25

violence and mental illness, 25, 41, 75–76, 180, 185, 186, 189; against persons with SMI, 25, 57–58, 59; media portrayals of, 24, 25. *See also* stereotypes of mental illness

vocational rehabilitation. *See* vocational training

vocational training, 45–49, 189–194; and disclosure of SMI, 121; as an investment in human capital, 36, 37, 45, 172; outcomes of, x, 47, 136–137, 165;

Skills for Retail training program, 191–192. *See also* Individual Placement and Support; mental health policy; supported employment; transferable skills

Watson, Amy, 28

Weiner, Bernard, 20

Weiss, Marc, 19

White, Rebecca, 130–131

Williamsburg public hospital, 57, 58

work, value of: to family members, 81, 126; to patient, 93–94, 103, 104–105, 126, 139, 140, 152, 163

workplace culture. *See* firm characteristics and employment of persons with SMI

workplace relationships and employment of persons with SMI, 38, 130, 139, 150; coworkers, 135, 153–154; customers, 136; supervisor, 37, 134, 155–156. *See also* disclosure of SMI at work, impact of; stayers vs. leavers

workplace stigma. *See* stigma of SMI

About the Author

Marjorie L. Baldwin is a professor in the Department of Economics at the W. P. Carey School of Business, Arizona State University, and academic director for Public Health Programs in the College of Health Solutions at ASU. Professor Baldwin is a health economist who has devoted a major part of her career to studying work disability and disability-related discrimination, with a particular focus on persons with serious mental illness. She is the author or coauthor of more than fifth articles and book chapters and has been a principal investigator for major studies of labor market discrimination against persons with mental disorders sponsored by the National Institutes of Health. She is a member of the National Academy of Social Insurance, the American Society of Health Economists, the National Alliance on Mental Illness, and holds an adjunct faculty positon with the University of Minnesota School of Public Health.